THE COMPLETE PHILOSOPHY PRIMER

An Undergraduate Study Companion

THE COMPLETE PHILOSOPHY PRIMER

An Undergraduate Study Companion

First Edition

J. Frankle
Editor In Chief

Alan Axelrod, PhD
Mia Wood, PhD
Paul Dicken, PhD
Editors

Aristotle Publishing Group, New York

Published 2021
First Edition 2021

ISBN: 978-0-578-79134-0 (paperback)

For questions, comments or corrections,
please email us at: info@aristotlepublishing.com

Visit AristotlePublishing.com for more resources and information

For a wealth of information on anything philosophy, visit The Stanford Encyclopedia of Philosophy at: Plato.Stanford.edu

Table of Contents

PREFACE

Ever since I started my formal education in philosophy, I dreamed of a book that would open the door for novice philosophy students who are starting out with a deep curiosity and an unyielding desire, yet without knowing how best to grow, learn, and succeed in their studies. Thus, the telos of this book is for this student to have a primer offering under one roof everything a novice philosophy student needs to know in order to succeed.

Philosophy sets itself apart from other disciplines by its promise to offer far more questions than answers. This takes some getting used to. These questions typically concern things most people take for granted. They are questions about existence, knowledge, mind, reason, language, and values, among other matters. Big topics.

If philosophy courses stand out from the crowded college catalog by reason of an abundance of questions, this book stands out from philosophy books by offering more answers than questions. No, they are not the answers to those big philosophical questions. Instead, they are answers to questions you may have—should have—about what to do now that you are taking a class in philosophy. These answers will inform and enrich your academic study of philosophy. They will help you perform optimally in some of the most challenging and exciting coursework you will ever do, as well as guide and improve your academic performance, your test results, and the grades you receive on the papers you write.

My ambition and my hope is that what you find here will lead you to a rewarding lifetime study of philosophy. Philosophy has the great benefit of informing and even driving everything else you study in college. As mathematics is a necessary foundation for the science student, philosophy is an essential foundation for virtually any field of study, whether undertaken at the university or on your own.

Philosophy opens your mind and imagination, but insists on doing so in a disciplined manner. It is about learning more productive ways to think and to write and to argue, and in writing well and arguing effectively, to think with even more originality and greater clarity. Although this "companion" makes no claim to being exhaustive, it is a comprehensive and inclusive start. Accordingly, we begin with an introduction to the study of philosophy. We ask and answer: What is philosophy? What are the branches of philosophy? What is logic and where does logic fit into philosophy? What is the history of philosophy?

And then we answer the questions most germane to what you, as a student, will do in a philosophy course: How do you do philosophy? How do you create effective philosophical writing? What processes and skills are needed to write a philosophy paper? What are the forms of philosophical writing? What strategic writing choices will best serve you in your class assignments?

Philosophy is less about facts than about methods, processes, and procedures. Yet a discipline as venerable and ambitious as philosophy does generate many mountains of facts, and the final part of this book delivers the most essential, helpful, and useful of them. You will find a concise but comprehensive reference section, containing the key philosophical terms and concepts, biographical essays on philosophers whom most philosophy professors consider most important, and a list of resources, including the books, websites, blogs, films, TV programs, and institutions you need to know about.

Above all else, what you will find in this book is what I, when I was an undergraduate, always felt I needed: a book to introduce me to the many new concepts, approaches, and terms in philosophy. I discovered what many, perhaps most, philosophy students discover: Starting out can be elating and yet bewildering. Where do I start, and what is *my* best path? This is what I want to offer the novice philosophy student—a way to avoid aimless wandering.

Another goal of mine is to encourage—no, to recruit—more students to study and love philosophy. But if just one student ends up pursuing a life of philosophy because of something in this book, my work will have been worth the effort. For it surely will have made the world a better place!

This book is dedicated to my dear friend Juda. In *The Four Loves*, C.S. Lewis writes: "Friendship is born at the moment when one man says to another 'What! You too? I thought that no one but myself . . .'" And that: "Friendship is unnecessary, like philosophy, like art, it has no survival value; rather it is one of those things which give value to survival."

I thank Alan Axelrod, PhD; Mia Wood, PhD; and Paul Dicken, PhD, my three editors, for their tremendous work in editing this book.

I thank my wonderful and brilliant professors at Brooklyn College for opening the doors of philosophical wisdom to me. And deepest thanks to my professors at The Graduate Center, all giants in their respective fields, for so graciously bestowing on me the best philosophy has to offer.

And finally, I thank my wife and kids, who are endless sources of hope, strength, and happiness. Without you, I could never have imagined how sweet life can be. You are all a most cherished gift, for which I am grateful every single day.

—J. Frankle
Student at The Graduate Center (CUNY)

Part I

Introduction to the Study of Philosophy

1

What Is Philosophy?

Philosophers ask questions and think about things that most people take for granted. So, philosophy is the study of general and fundamental questions about existence, knowledge, mind, reason, language, and values. Strange but true, it is the general and fundamental things that most people take for granted and therefore do not question. Why is this so? That is precisely the kind of question a philosopher would ask. Maybe you should consider asking—and answering—it in an essay for your philosophy class.

Another way to express the business of philosophy and philosophers is *Thinking about Ordinary Things,* which is the title of an excellent "short invitation to philosophy" by the Czech philosopher Jan Sokol.[1] It is a provocative title in that it *provokes* a question: What's the use of thinking about ordinary things? If that question crossed your mind when you read the title of Sokol's book, you are already *starting* to think like a philosopher. If you decide next to pursue an answer to that question, you *are* in fact thinking like one.

That puts you in ancient and distinguished company. When Democritus, a Greek philosopher who was born about 460 BC in Thrace, looked around him at ordinary things, the things most people never thought about, he saw great diversity, of course, but asked what all these *diverse* physical things had *in common.* His answer was the "atomic hypothesis," the idea that everything is composed of atoms. *Atomos* is the ancient Greek word for "indivisible," and Democritus hypothesized that matter (every physical thing) is composed of tiny indestructible atoms, between which is empty space. The atoms are in continuous motion, he said, and they are of infinite number and kind, differing in size and shape.

Brilliant and incredible! Democritus described atoms some 2,200 years before the British scientist John Dalton (1766-1844) introduced atomic theory into chemistry in 1805 as part of his explanation of an "ordinary thing" called the absorption of gases by water and other liquids.

Dalton, by the way, probably did not call himself a scientist. From the era of another Greek philosopher, Aristotle (364-322 BC), to at least the mid-nineteenth century, people we today call scientists called themselves "natural philosophers"—essentially, curious individuals who asked questions about the ordinary things around them (in other words, nature). You should know, then, that philosophy and science share not only a common root but a common trunk, which began growing distinct *philosophy* and *science* branches less than 200 years ago.

To this day, both philosophers and scientists can still be accurately described as people who think about things that most people take for granted. No wonder the "natural philosophers" did not stop thinking about matter and atoms. In the late nineteenth century, an Irish physicist, George Johnstone Stoney (1826-1911), theorized that atoms were not, in fact, indivisible, but contained subatomic particles. In 1897, another physicist, J. J. Thomson (1856-1940), discovered one of those particles, the electron. Ever since, even more natural philosophers/scientists asked questions about this most fundamental aspect of matter, the atom, and not only were numerous subatomic particles identified, but nuclear fission—"splitting" the supposedly indivisible atom—was discovered and even induced artificially both to generate power in peace and, in war, to destroy entire populations.

What is the use of thinking about ordinary things? Well, doing so has a way of producing extraordinary new insights. If you are the kind of student who believes that "learning" should be about something more than acquiring existing knowledge, that it should also create new knowledge, new perspectives, new ideas and insights, then you have within you the makings of a successful philosophy student.

As the history of atomic theory proves, new insights can be pried out of knowledge that has been around even for thousands of years. Here's a tip: Question everything—especially the most ordinary, and fundamental things, the things you think you know, the most familiar things practically everybody thinks they know. Go ahead, be annoying.

What Is the "Subject Matter" of Philosophy

"There is a common misunderstanding that philosophy—like chemistry or history—has a content to offer, a content that a teacher is to teach and a student is to learn," writes Professor James L. Christian. "This is not the case. There are no facts, no theories, certainly no final truths that go by the name of philosophy."[2]

So, what are you doing in a philosophy course? What is the professor professing? What are you supposed to be learning?

The best answer, I believe, is that you are learning a way of intellectual life or, put a little differently, a way of intellectually being in the world. Philosophy is a method, not a set of content. It is a form of intellectual discipline, which is both facilitated by and expressed in what Professor Mark Andrew Holowchak calls "philosophical argument."[3]

Then is the answer to *What are you doing here?* "I'm learning how to argue"?

In part, yes. But, in philosophy—as in the practice of law, for example—"argument" is not about shouting, swearing, trading insults, and quite possibly coming to blows. It is about formulating and expressing a reason or set of reasons aimed at persuading others that your idea, stance, interpretation, or hypothesis concerning some topic is desirable or correct. Now, more specifically, *philosophical argument* attempts to persuade by identifying and clarifying everything relevant to the issue at hand and, in interpreting it, rendering an opinion on it, holding for or against it, "ridding everyday language of ambiguity and vagueness." The objective is to allow you and others to attain "a better grasp of the issues and perhaps even a solution to some mulish problem."[4]

Philosophical argument is to discourse or debate what a surgeon's kit of fine, shiny instruments is to an ailing patient's body. It is a set of honed and polished tools designed for close examination and accurate dissection, capable of opening up and probing a system for critical examination. This rigorous analytical approach allows a philosopher who is skilled in the discipline to take "our most fundamental principles and beliefs and [ask] us for a justification of them."[5]

All of this said, as a philosophy student, you may well be expected to learn many facts. In an introductory course, you will likely dip into intellectual history, which is the history not of events or acts of Congress or wars and battles, but of ideas, thinkers, and the world views that emerged and contended with one another at various times in the development of civilization. Such "content" forms a crucial context for understanding various aspects of philosophy through the ages. Indeed, the focus of a course in the *history* of philosophy is the historical evolution—the evolution through time—of thought, with respect to place and culture. This kind of historical study is fascinating and illuminating. Just don't make the mistake of confusing it with philosophy itself, which is a set of skills, a toolkit, a suite of intellectual approaches, and, in general, a way being and thinking in the world.

Philosophy as Method

Our digital age suggests a useful analogy to further explain the role of philosophy in intellectual life. Philosophy is analogous to an operating system (OS), a software platform that enables specialized applications (apps)—other academic and professional disciplines—to operate. The philosophical method, philosophical argument, enables orderly, persuasive discourse in any academic or professional discipline that relies primarily on language.

The OS loaded on your computer can support everything from a sober spreadsheet program to a virtual-reality first-person shooter. The same is true of philosophy. While, in and of itself, philosophy is merely a method, it is a method that has launched revolutions—revolutions in thought, in morality, in science and technology, in religion, and in social organization. It is a method, though orderly and persuasive, that has also helped to launch wars. Philosophy is a powerful method, and, like a digital operating system, an indispensable one.

As philosophy disciplines and organizes thinking, facilitating or even enabling operations in many other fields of intellectual endeavor, so those who decide to make use of it have, in essence, chosen to prepare, condition, and discipline their minds, so that they can apply them more effectively to whatever questions and intellectual tasks are put before them. This is a choice every successful philosophy student makes. It is both a basic requirement of a philosophy course and the greatest benefit such a course offers.

As we will see in a moment, one of the branches of traditional philosophy, epistemology, is expressly devoted to mind, thought, perception, and the definition of truth or, put another way, the theory of knowledge. Nevertheless, always remember that philosophy is first and last a method—an interface, an operating system—for systematic thought. It is not *about* mind in the way that psychology and neurobiology are. Rather, it is about *how to use* mind to understand the mind itself and every other "ordinary" thing most of us take for granted.

For a philosopher, and even for a beginning philosophy student, it is not enough to master the philosophical method. Nor is it enough to amass a store of knowledge drawn from the course syllabus. In fact, it is not even a sufficient achievement to know—in philosophical terms—what you are thinking. No. Your objective is to equip yourself to *apply* thought to knowledge and the real world—consciously, rationally, and accountably. If this helps you to decide to vote for candidate A rather than candidate B in the next presidential election, or if it enables you to rationally justify your position on the legalization of marijuana, or if it gives you the moral ground you need to practice civil disobedience in protest of an unjust law, you can call yourself a philosopher.

We are about to discuss the branches of philosophy, which are tremendously varied in their scope. Nevertheless, they all share certain methods, including:

- Use of the analytic method to examine, understand, and challenge even our most basic ("ordinary") assumptions
- Use of the critical method to specifically challenge received wisdom and traditional beliefs
- Use of the synthetic method to bring together ("synthesize") views into a coherent vision
- Use of the rational method, which demands that reasons be given for whatever we assert as true or false, and that these reasons be presented simply, consistently, and coherently
- Use of the imagination, which drives us to search for fresh and novel ways of examining philosophical problems
- Reliance on resourcefulness, which "requires us to consider what is logically possible but asks only that we act as circumstances allow."[6]

2

The Branches of Philosophy

Philosophy embraces the most ambitious field of inquiry—the universe, including the self and everything both physical and metaphysical. It is impossible to list all the branches of philosophy, which are not only numerous but, since the realms of the mind defy taxonomy, so does philosophy.

We can divide the major branches into two categories, the traditional and the modern.

Traditional Branches of Philosophy

Aesthetics

Aesthetics is concerned with the nature of art (whether visual, literary, dramatic, or in some other medium) and the way in which art is experienced. Two principal related issues, therefore, are whether there is a distinctive form of aesthetic experience—to be contrasted with other forms of perceptual experience—and how our aesthetic judgments are to be distinguished from other forms of evaluation. An influential line of thought from Immanuel Kant (1724-1804) is that aesthetic appreciation is entirely divorced from any practical concerns—the object is judged "on its own terms"—but it has proved difficult to fully articulate this idea. Other philosophers have followed David Hume (1711-1776) in attempting to reduce aesthetic appreciation to simply a subjective matter of taste.

Closely related to these concerns are questions about the nature of art. These include whether different media or genres (for instance, found art, graffiti) can legitimately count as art; if we can draw a meaningful distinction between "high" and "low" forms of art; and how one piece of art can be judged as "better" than another. Some of the issues raised in aesthetics naturally overlap with topics in the **philosophy of mind** and the **philosophy**

of language. This includes questions as to how a work of art can be said to represent a particular object or idea, or express a particular attitude or emotion; as in the philosophy of language, debate here often involves assessing the relative importance of the artist's original intentions, the specific properties or arrangement of the object itself, and the social context of the work's reception.

Epistemology

Epistemology is the study of knowledge, including its nature and its extent, and of justification (that is, whether a belief is formed in a valid way to justify its being deemed "knowledge"). Epistemology attempts to distinguish knowledge from merely true belief. The philosophically skeptical ask whether we possess knowledge in general or only with respect to a specific domain. These two issues, knowledge vs. belief and the of issue of skepticism, are closely related, as many proposed definitions of knowledge are simultaneously intended to answer various skeptical challenges.

The so-called standard analysis of knowledge maintains that to know that a "proposition" or "statement," traditionally represented by the letter *p* (or P), one must have a justified true belief that *p*. There is considerable debate over how to articulate the requirement of justification. "Internalists" maintain that justification must be accessible to the subject (so that if one knows that *p*, one knows that one knows that *p*), while "externalists" argue that it is sufficient for the belief to be formed by reliable methods, regardless of whether or not this fact is accessible to the subject.

Other issues concern whether the concept of knowledge is closed under logical entailment, and if the standards of knowledge are fixed or if they vary with context. There is also the question of whether the justification for a belief must ultimately rest on unassailable foundations, or if a web of beliefs can be justified together on grounds of coherence or overall utility. A related issue is whether there are different types of knowledge, and whether one type is more important than the others. It is common to distinguish between knowledge *a priori*—that which can be known without appeal to experience—and knowledge *a posteriori*—knowledge acquired through experience. The relative importance of *a priori* and *a posteriori* knowledge is the primary issue that separates rationalists from empiricists.

Finally, while most examples of knowledge considered in the literature are propositional knowledge (knowledge that *p*), this is sometimes contrasted with practical knowledge (knowledge-how) and theories of direct acquaintance (knowledge-of). Recent work has increasingly attempted to approach these issues by studying the way in which the concept of knowledge is used in our everyday discourse.

Ethics

Ethics is the study of morality and can be divided into three main areas of inquiry. *Descriptive ethics* concerns the actual moral beliefs held by specific individuals or societies and is perhaps better thought of as a branch of sociology or anthropology than of philosophy.

By contrast, *normative ethics* is concerned with what moral beliefs we should hold and what actions can be considered as right and wrong. One important question here concerns the overall goal of our moral actions—whether ethics is about the pursuit of certain intrinsically valuable objects (such as pleasure), or the broader notion of the "good life" (that is, overall human flourishing). The answer to this question has immediate consequences for how we understand the justification of our moral rules: either as self-evident or as derived from fundamental principles of reason, or merely reflecting the *de facto* best way of ensuring social cooperation or the maximization of some other end. Other questions concern the relative importance of an agent's motive or the consequences of his actions in making moral judgments and whether these judgments are held to be objectively true or merely relative to a particular context. Thus, *deontologists* maintain that moral behavior consists in following particular rules, whereas *consequentialists* consider the overall outcome of any particular action. Recent work has, however, reawakened an interest in individual virtue as the locus of moral evaluation.

Finally, *metaethics* is concerned with what it means to make a moral judgment and with the meaning of our moral terms. This includes whether moral judgments seek to describe an independent moral reality or are merely the expression of our own preferences and inclinations (and the respective epistemological or semantic difficulties these positions raise) and whether there is a principled philosophical distinction between facts and values.

Philosophy of Law

The philosophy of law is concerned with all aspects of theoretical reflection on laws and legal systems and therefore encompasses historical and sociological studies in addition to the philosophical questions posed by general jurisprudence (a word that usually connotes the theory or system of law, but is sometimes used synonymously with *philosophy of law*). The philosophical questions are largely concerned with problems internal to law, such as the nature and scope of legal rules, the individuation of different legal systems, and the sort of reasoning employed in legal decisions.

One major line of debate concerns the relationship between our legal obligations and other sources of normativity. According to natural law theorists, there is a close relationship between law and morality either because legal systems are themselves necessarily morally good or because obeying the law is always morally desirable. By contrast, legal positivists argue that the conditions for being a legal system are purely formal, such as the *de facto* existence of a recognized source of legal authority or a coherent set of legal obligations. The positivists therefore argue that there could be a legitimate legal system that was nevertheless morally iniquitous. Similarly, while some philosophers maintain that legal adjudication is ultimately a formal matter of conceptual analysis (that is, applying the law as it stands), others maintain that there is an ineliminable element of interpretation and assert that legal rules are better thought of as general predictions of future court behavior. Answers to these questions, however, are not purely theoretical, and such issues often come to the fore at the highest level of legal adjudication, or in debate regarding the legitimacy of international law.

Logic

Logic is concerned with studying the inferences we make, and the formal languages developed to systematize those inferences. This includes both the proof-theories and semantics for these languages, as well as their various metalogical properties, such as soundness, completeness, and decidability. Much of this work is purely technical, but it raises a number of philosophical issues with regard to application: whether these formal languages are intended to be descriptive or prescriptive regarding our everyday inferential practices, how we are supposed to choose among different logics, and if our choices entail any further philosophical consequences.

It is widely held that logic must be completely neutral with respect to its subject matter and that, therefore, certain metalogical properties are sufficient to disqualify some formal language. Similarly, some philosophers have argued that technical features of a proof theory or semantics of a given logic motivate either a wholesale revision of our inferential practices or the drawing of substantive metaphysical conclusions.

Other important issues in logic concern the philosophical concepts employed in studying these formal languages, such as whether the concept of truth is metaphysically substantive or merely a semantic property, and how to understand the necessity involved in logical inference.

Finally, logic is also concerned with understanding the philosophical consequences of technical results in the foundations of mathematics, such as the set-theoretic paradoxes and the iterative hierarchy of contemporary set theory, and the implications of Gödel's incompleteness theorems for both the notion of computability and the philosophy of mind.

Metaphysics

Metaphysics is the philosophical investigation of reality, including the nature of the world and the entities it contains. While such an investigation inevitably overlaps with **natural philosophy**—the sciences, especially physics and the natural sciences—it can be contrasted in two important respects.

First, the topics of metaphysics are, in a sense, more fundamental than those of the sciences because they are concerned with the presuppositions made within these topics. For example, our scientific theories are often held to discover the laws of nature, but they do not say what it means to be a law of nature—whether a particularly robust regularity that just happens to hold between different entities, a special kind of relationship that holds between certain properties, or ultimately a claim about what happens in other possible worlds. Similarly, while the natural sciences study and manipulate various causal relationships, it is a task of metaphysics to investigate the nature of causation itself, to question (for instance) whether an alleged cause is an objective feature of reality or, rather, a function of the way in which we perceive reality.

Second, the scope of metaphysics is broader than that of the natural sciences in that it is also concerned with the existence of nonphysical entities. This, in fact, is the origin of the name *metaphysics*—it is literally beyond, after, or outside of (*meta-*) physics and the physical. The nonphysical objects of metaphysical contemplation may include (among other things) irreducibly mental entities, abstract objects (such as mathematical objects), and even the existence of other possible worlds.

Metaphysics is also concerned with whether certain properties are essential to an entity (as opposed to merely accidental) and if properties can be multiply instantiated among different entities (or if everything in the world is an individual). In the early half of the twentieth century, various philosophical schools of thought maintained that metaphysics should be abandoned as a philosophical discipline, either on the grounds that it is just bad science or that its statements are unverifiable (and thus meaningless); traditional metaphysical questions were, therefore, reduced to logical questions about the use of language. In the 1970s, however, Saul Kripke's (1940-) work on reference in the **philosophy of language** sparked renewed interest in substantive metaphysics and has produced ongoing research into questions concerning the nature of necessity, essential properties, and the identity conditions of objects across different possible worlds.

Natural Philosophy

An important historical branch designation rather than a current one, natural philosophy was the study of nature and the physical universe by philosophical (that is, largely empirical reason-based) methods. Natural philosophy is considered a precursor of all that is today encompassed by "science," especially physics and the natural sciences. Aristotle (384-322 BC) was the first philosopher to define natural philosophy, and the term was in use through much of the nineteenth century until it was displaced and replaced by "science."

In the eighteenth- and nineteenth-century German philosophical traditions, natural philosophy (*Naturphilosophie*) specifically denoted a philosophical approach that set the goal of demonstrating the unity of nature and spirit.

Political Philosophy

Political philosophy is at least as old as Plato (428/227 or 424/423-348/347 BC) and is concerned with the nature of the state and, more broadly, with coercive institutions, and their justification. One central question, therefore, is whether political rights and obligations can exist independently of state membership, and what rights and obligations may be lost or gained by becoming a member (subject or citizen) of a state. This question immediately leads into how we might justify the existence of a state—such as a natural consequence of enlightened self-interest, or a contractual exchange of individual liberties for social benefits—and the nature of our political and moral obligations to that state.

Provided that some form of state system is deemed desirable, a second set of questions concerns how it is to be organized. This includes issues about the size and scope of the state—independent city-states, national states, or more global spheres of political influence—as well as the distribution of political power and representation. It is widely accepted that some form democracy is desirable, but this in turn raises difficult questions, not least because every democratic institution excludes some individuals from its franchise. A related question is whether democracy is an intrinsically valuable form of political organization or must be justified on more pragmatic grounds, such as the reliability of its decision-making.

Finally, more specific questions concern specific functions of the state. While any state necessarily entails certain constraints on individual liberty, there is arguably a distinction to be made between positive and negative constraints—that is, whether a failure to offer help constitutes a restriction on an individual's liberty. Another important function of the state may be to ensure that the distribution of goods within the society is just, but different political philosophies defend different accounts of justice. On the one hand, we might judge a particular distribution as just if it meets certain criteria at a particular moment of time (such as the standard that everybody has the same). On the other hand, we might judge a given distribution as just if it arose from an ongoing process that meets certain criteria (such as the standard that everybody keeps what they have earned).

Philosophy of Religion

Many religions distinguish between truths accessible through reason (natural theology), and truths accessible through faith (revealed theology). Both natural and revealed theology raise interesting philosophical questions about these two sources of knowledge and the relationship between the two. The philosophy of religion is primarily concerned with natural theology and, therefore, with the four traditional arguments for the existence of God.

The ontological argument proceeds via definition. Early articulations maintained that the perfection of God entails his existence, while recent versions proceed on the (controversial) modal principal that the possibility of a necessary being entails its actual existence. The cosmological argument maintains that since every event must have a cause, the existence of God is required to explain the existence of the universe. Critics counter that such explanatory requests are either unnecessary or constitute a **category mistake**—that is, an error of reasoning based on placing an entity in the wrong ontological or semantic category.

The teleological argument proceeds on the grounds that the best explanation for the design of the universe is that it was created by God. There are, however, other explanations available for apparent design and concerns about how far such analogical reasoning can be pushed.

Finally, the moral argument attempts to establish the existence of God as the ultimate explanation for our moral beliefs, but such arguments are clearly dependent on specific ethical theories. Conversely, the problem of evil maintains that the (Judeo-Christian) conception of God as omnipotent, omniscient, and benevolent is inconsistent with the existence of evil. In response, most theodicies (arguments in vindication of divine goodness) maintain either that such evil is nevertheless part of an overall best possible world or that it is an inevitable consequence of free will.

Other work in the philosophy of religion involves applying results from the **philosophy of language** to the vexed question of divine attribution; and, in the Continental tradition, applying phenomenological and existentialist analyses to the understanding of religious experience.

Modern Branches of Philosophy

Bioethics

A branch of **ethics** concerned with the moral and political issues raised by medical science, and with advances in medical technology, bioethics has now become a largely autonomous area of study, which intersects with topics in philosophy, legal theory, sociology, and other disciplines. Along with such traditional moral issues as abortion and euthanasia, which arguably depend in part on the level of medical technology available, bioethics is concerned with the ethical relationship between medical practitioners and their patients, and, more generally, with social justice in healthcare. At the individual level, medical decision-making has traditionally prioritized the expertise of practitioners but is increasingly shifting to a model of informed consent, which raises questions about both individual autonomy and how to provide patients with the necessary information to make informed decisions. At the community level, there is the question of whether a natural (human) right to healthcare exists and, if so, how it should be rationed.

As medical technology advances, bioethics becomes increasingly concerned with existential questions about balancing quality of life against medical expediency, the limits of medical intervention, and how our capacity to (for example) alter our genetic makeup and other aspects of biology affects our understanding of what it means to be human.

Hermeneutics

Originally applied to scriptural exegesis (interpretation), hermeneutics is more generally the theory and method of all "textual" interpretation. In the modern context, this refers to both verbal and non-verbal "texts" or communications. It encompasses semiotics (the study of semiosis, or sign process—a "sign" being anything that communicates a meaning) and pragmatics (presupposition, the role of implicit assumptions about the world in creating meaning).

Although exegesis has existed in many cultures since antiquity, the self-reflexive use and study of interpretation and meaning-creation began in the eighteenth and nineteenth centuries with such philosophers as Friedrich Schleiermacher (1768-1834) and Wilhelm Dilthey (1833-1911) and transitioned into the twentieth century with Hans-Georg Gadamer (1900-2002).

Philosophy of Language

The study of natural languages is conventionally divided among questions of syntax, semantics, and pragmatics, all of which raise significant issues for the philosophy of language. In terms of syntax for example, it is clear that speakers of a language are able to construct a potentially infinite number of sentences on the basis of (presumably) a finite grasp of its rules; and this places considerable philosophical constraints on any satisfactory grammatical theory. In terms of semantics, the primary focus of the philosophy of language has been on how an utterance (or linguistic inscription) can be meaningful.

One approach to this question focuses upon the speaker, arguing that since different words can mean different things in different contexts, it is the intentions of the speaker that primarily govern communication; difficulties with this view are that it threatens to make language use private and inaccessible.

A second approach focuses upon the actual words used. In this view, singular terms are meaningful because they refer to individual objects, and sentences are meaningful because they refer to complete states of affairs. Such an approach, however, would only apply to a limited range of simple (declarative) utterance, and thus more complex theories associate the meaning of an utterance with its overall truth conditions or with the evidence that would verify its truth. A related approach maintains that the meaning of an utterance is simply the way it is used within a linguistic community.

A third approach dispenses with the notion of meaning altogether in favor of analyzing patterns of behavior (for example, assent and dissent) or the construction of empirically adequate translation manuals between different speakers. An important subtopic here is how linguistic terms can refer to external objects. According to descriptivist accounts, singular terms refer in virtue of an associated set of descriptions, while causal accounts maintain that singular terms refer by virtue of the causal chain of competent language use to the original referent.

Finally, pragmatics is concerned with the different ways we use meaningful language, any associated conversational implication, and how certain speech acts (such as promises) can constitute social arrangements.

Philosophy of Mathematics

The philosophy of mathematics is traditionally concerned with the ontological and epistemological foundations of mathematics. The two questions, of ontology and epistemology, are intimately related, as a satisfactory account of our mathematical knowledge often entails a more controversial metaphysics, and *vice versa*. On the one hand, it would appear that our mathematical knowledge cannot be understood in terms of our empirical knowledge, as mathematics is both more reliable (mathematical truths are necessary truths) and can be grasped independently of experience (mathematical knowledge is *a priori* knowledge). This has led some philosophers to argue that mathematics is concerned with *sui generis* mathematical objects, which exist independently of the physical world. On the other hand, it is difficult to see how we could have epistemic access to causally isolated mathematical objects. This has led some philosophers to argue that mathematics is concerned with mental operations or the manipulation of arbitrary formal systems. But, contemplating this view, it is hard to see how such finite bases could ground either the reliability of our mathematical knowledge or its scope.

Many of these debates have their origin in the early twentieth century and the foundational crisis in set theory. The proposals offered in response to the various paradoxes of impredicative definition (for example, "the set of all sets that are not members of themselves") have established the pattern for the major philosophical positions still debated in the literature. These positions include adopting the further regimentation of our mathematical practice (such as a hierarchy of constructions that prevent the paradoxes being stated); showing that certain "problematic" branches of mathematics can, at least in principle, be eliminated as mere conversation extensions over the more secure branches; or recognizing that the legitimate scope of our mathematical practices are constrained by the existence of actual mental constructions.

All three of these positions face significant technical challenges but nevertheless remain open projects. By contrast, more recent work in the philosophy of mathematics has attempted to reconsider the relationship between mathematics and the natural sciences, maintaining that since mathematics plays an indispensable role in our scientific theories, the same arguments deployed for ontological commitment to sub-atomic particles, for instance, apply similarly to numbers and sets.

Philosophy of Science

Many of the topics within the philosophy of science overlap with topics in **metaphysics**, **epistemology,** and the **philosophy of language** insofar as they apply within our scientific practice. Metaphysical issues, for instance, concern the existence of natural kinds and laws of nature, which appear to underlie the regularities investigated by our scientific theories, and whether these are objective features of the world or merely conventional features of our scientific models. Epistemological issues include how evidence confirms (or falsifies) a scientific theory and the structure of a scientific explanation. There also remains ongoing interest in the structure of a scientific theory and the reference of our central theoretical terms, especially through periods of radical theory change. These latter topics overlap with the philosophy of language.

More specific topics in the philosophy of science involve scientific methodology and how it might be contrasted with other ways of acquiring knowledge of the external world. This includes the role of inductive and deductive forms of inference, the extent to which scientific theories are to be rejected in the face of falsifying evidence or amended to accommodate anomalous data, and the role of broader sociopolitical considerations in the eventual adoption of a new scientific paradigm. The scientific realism debate concerns whether the predictive success of a scientific theory gives us grounds to believe its theoretical content, or if the history of science calls for a more skeptical attitude. The debate also asks if there is a principled distinction between those parts of a theory that do the important work and those parts that are dispensable. A central issue here is whether it is possible to distinguish between the predictive success of a scientific theory and its explanatory power.

Finally, the philosophy of science is also concerned with interpretative issues that arise in specific scientific theories, such as the interpretation of measurement events in quantum mechanics and the so-called collapse of the wave-function, or the structure of explanations in evolutionary biology, as well as the difference between the natural sciences and the social sciences.

3

Logic

Logic is the systematic study of patterns of inference and is intended to clarify the underlying structure of "good" arguments. When we call an argument *valid*, we are not judging the truth or falsity of its premises or conclusion. We are evaluating its structure. An argument is said to be *sound* if it is both valid in argumentative structure and its premises are in fact true. This principle was articulated by Aristotle (384-322 BC) as the syllogism, which may be seen as an early and durable basis for logic but is more accurately considered a structure for argument and rhetoric (see "What Philosophy Professors Want from Student Writers" in Chapter 5) because it falls far short of creating a fully descriptive system of logic. That is, syllogistic logic does not address such areas as propositional calculus (also called propositional logic), predicate calculus (also called predicate logic), modal logic, and other, newer logics. Thus, logic is a discrete branch of philosophy of great importance and (often) technical complexity.

Note

Most introductory philosophy courses and many traditional or classical philosophy courses do not touch upon modern logics. Indeed, the technical nature of these logical disciplines may be outside the course curriculum for the general philosophy student. Some of the content in this chapter, therefore, may be advanced significantly beyond both the interests and (at this point) competence of novice philosophy students. Nevertheless, even such students may encounter advanced material and the terms associated with it. For this reason, we include a compact yet comprehensive introductory treatment of major modern logics.

A key issue in logic is whether the various formal languages developed to study patterns of inference are primarily *descriptive* or *prescriptive*—that is, whether they are to be thought of as merely making explicit the underlying logical structure of natural language arguments that we already make, or as constructing alternatives to our natural language arguments to which we should aspire. For example, there is a range of different conversational and conventional implications associated with the English connectives "and" and "but," although both are formalized in terms of the same truth tables. Similarly, a conditional statement of the form "if P, then Q" is usually rendered in terms of the material conditional ($P \supset Q$), which is evaluated as true whenever the antecedent P is false, or the conclusion Q is true. It is not clear, however, that this captures what we mean when we use such a construction. There is a question, then, as to whether these differences are something that a logical language will inevitably fail to capture or superfluous idiosyncrasies of natural language that a logical language manages to avoid.

A second issue concerns the competing desiderata involved in constructing our formal languages. On the one hand, we want our logical languages to be *exhaustive* insofar as they can capture as many of our (valid) patterns of inference as possible. On the other hand, however, we want these languages to be *conservative* in the sense that they do not add anything or introduce arbitrary new patterns of inference merely as a consequence of their technical construction. These desiderata can pull apart, and there are now a range of fully developed nonclassical logics that are argued to provide a better compromise between these competing demands. Some of these languages, in turn, involve further philosophical commitments. Thus, in the same way that we might take the theoretical virtues of a scientific theory (such as simplicity and predictive power) as an argument for accepting its ontological commitments, so some philosophers argue that the technical virtues of a logical language (such qualities as completeness and harmonious proof system) provide arguments for different metaphysical conclusions.

The existence of different logical languages also raises questions about the universality of logic: whether there is one "correct" logic that somehow captures the underlying structure of reality, or whether different logics can be thought of as merely useful tools for describing different domains of inquiry.

Propositional Calculus (Propositional Logic)

The simplest formal (logical) language is the propositional calculus. This considers the logical relationships that hold between complete propositions. The language of the propositional calculus consists of an infinite number of atomic propositional variables P, Q, R, ... and a set of logical connectives ¬ ("not"), & ("and"), ∨ ("or"), ⊃ (the material conditional "if ... then ..."), and ≡ (the bi-conditional "... if and only if ..."). The set of logical connectives {¬, &, ∨, ⊃, ≡} is expressively complete for the propositional calculus, although some of the connectives are inter-definable, and smaller sets of logical connectives can also be shown to be expressively complete. A well-formed formula (wff) of the propositional calculus is any atomic propositional variable or a molecular formula built up recursively via the following formation rules:

If P is a wff, then ¬P is a wff;
If P is a wff and Q is a wff, then (P & Q) is a wff;
If P is a wff and Q is a wff, then (P ∨ Q) is a wff;
If P is a wff and Q is a wff, then (P ⊃ Q) is a wff;
If P is a wff and Q is a wff, then (P ≡ Q) is a wff;
Nothing else is a wff.

Semantics

An *interpretation* for the propositional calculus is a function that assigns to every propositional variable a truth value (either true or false). The truth values for complex, molecular formulas can then be built up compositionally via the truth tables for the logical connectives:

P	Q	¬P	P & Q	P ∨ Q	P ⊃ Q	P ≡ Q
T	T	F	T	T	T	T
T	F	F	F	T	F	F
F	T	T	F	T	T	F
F	F	T	F	F	T	T

By inspection of the truth tables, it can be seen how many of the logical connectives are inter-definable; for example, (P ⊃ Q) is equivalent to (¬P ∨ Q).

Proof Theory

In simple terms, a proof for a formula φ is nothing more than a list of well-formed formulas (in the relevant formal language) containing φ as the last step. To be convincing, however, each step in the proof must either consist of an initial premise whose truth is taken for granted or derived from a previous step by a transformation rule shown to be truth-preserving. The most straightforward proof theory for the propositional calculus, therefore, proceeds via the truth tables. It can be established by inspection whether there is any possible interpretation (that is, assignment of truth values) whereby one step of the proof is true but the next step is false, and thus whether the proposed transformation is necessarily truth-preserving. This method is purely mechanical and can be performed by a machine (the propositional calculus is therefore said to be *decidable*) but is unwieldy for longer proofs and provides little philosophical insight into the derivation.

A *natural deduction* system is a set of inference rules intended to produce a more intuitive proof sequence. Any proposition φ can be introduced as an assumption at any stage of the proof and will remain an assumption of the proof unless it is later discharged. The other rules of the natural deduction system essentially provide the conditions for introducing or eliminating the logical connectives; in each case, any new formula will depend upon the same assumptions as the premises from which it is derived. Here is a concise set of natural deduction rules for the propositional calculus:

Rule of Assumption: Any proposition φ can be introduced at any stage of the proof.

Modus Ponens/Modus Tollens: Given φ and (φ ⊃ ψ), we can derive ψ; given (φ ⊃ ψ) and ¬ψ, we can derive ¬φ.

Conditional Proof: Given a proof of ψ from φ, we can derive (φ ⊃ ψ).

Double Negation Introduction and Elimination: Given φ, we can derive ¬¬φ; given ¬¬φ, we can derive φ.

&-Introduction and &-Elimination: Given φ and ψ, we can derive (φ & ψ); given (φ & ψ), we can derive both φ or ψ individually.

∨-Introduction and ∨-Elimination: Given either φ or ψ separately, we can derive (φ ∨ ψ); given (φ ∨ ψ), along with a proof of θ from φ, and a proof of θ from ψ, we can derive θ.

Reductio ad Absurdum: Given a proof of (ψ & ¬ψ) from φ, we can derive ¬φ.

In addition to capturing the intuitive meaning of the logical connectives, these rules can also be shown via the truth tables to be necessarily truth-preserving. In addition, any tautology (a logically true wff that, therefore, does not depend upon any assumptions) can also be introduced at any time, usually as a way to shorten the proof.

Meta-Logical Results

The propositional calculus is both *sound* and *complete*. Informally, a logical language is said to be sound if it is only possible to prove a formula that is true; that is to say, if a set of well-formed formulas X syntactically entails a formula φ, then X semantically entails φ (if $X \vdash \varphi$, then $X \vDash \varphi$). Similarly, a logical language is said to be complete only if every true formula also has a proof; that is to say, if a set of well-formed formulas X semantically entails a formula φ, then X syntactically entails φ (if $X \vDash \varphi$, then $X \vdash \varphi$). Formal proofs can be provided for both results, but the idea should be intuitive: informally, given that an interpretation of the propositional calculus assigns truth values to complex formulas compositionally via the truth tables for the logical connectives, and given that the steps for any proof theory for the propositional calculus involves (truth-preserving) introduction and elimination rules for the logical connectives, it is easy to see why the propositional calculus should be both sound and complete.

Predicate Calculus (Predicate Logic)

The next development of the propositional calculus is the predicate calculus. This considers the logical relationships that hold between predicate expressions, along with the quantifiers ∃x ("there is at least one x, such that ...") and ∀x ("for all x, it is the case that ..."). The language of the predicate calculus consists of proper names of the form n, m, o, ...; arbitrary names of the form a, b, c, ...; variables of the form x, y, z, ...; and predicates of the form F^n, G^n, H^n, ... where n is the number of terms the predicate takes. An atomic predicate sentence consists of an n-place predicate followed by n-terms; complex, molecular formulas are then built-up compositionally via the usual logical connectives ¬, &, ∨, ⊃, ≡, along with the quantifiers ∃ and ∀. In addition to the formation rules of the propositional calculus, the predicate calculus therefore also has the following rules for the quantifiers:

> If P is a wff, then ∀xP is a wff;
> If P is a wff, then ∃xP is a wff.

An atomic predicate sentence is said to be *closed* if every variable is bound by a quantifier (otherwise the sentence is said to be *open*); truth for atomic predicate sentences is only defined for closed sentences.

Semantics

In the propositional calculus, truth values can be assigned directly to atomic propositions. By contrast, in the predicate calculus, an atomic sentence consists of an n-place predicate followed by the appropriate number of terms. The most basic semantic concept in the predicate calculus is therefore one of *satisfaction*: in the simplest case, an object a is said to satisfy an atomic sentence Fa just in case the predicate F applies to a. More formally, a model M for the predicate calculus is of the form <D, val>, where D is the domain of quantification, and val is a function that maps names onto single elements of D and n-place predicates onto ordered n-tuples of D. A model M is then said to satisfy an atomic predicate sentence φ just in case it is mapped to an ordered n-tuple within the domain for which the predicate in φ holds; that is, if φ is an atomic predicate sentence of the form $P(t_1, t_2, \ldots t_n)$, then $M \vDash \varphi$ iff $(t_1, t_2, \ldots t_n) \in val[P]$. Satisfaction for complex, molecular sentences can then be built up recursively via the truth tables for the logical connectives in the usual way—for example, $M \vDash (\varphi \ \& \ \psi)$ iff $M \vDash \varphi$ and $M \vDash \psi$. A model M satisfies an existential quantifier expression of the form $\forall x\varphi$ provided there is *some* n-tuple within the domain for which φ holds; a model M satisfies a universal quantifier expression of the form $\exists x\varphi$ just in case φ holds for *every* n-tuple within the domain. The two quantifiers can therefore be seen to be inter-definable: $\forall x\varphi$ is equivalent to $\neg\exists x\neg\varphi$.

Proof Theory

The predicate calculus does not admit of proof by inspection in the way allowed by the propositional calculus; however, the system of natural deduction introduced for the propositional calculus can be easily extended with introduction and elimination rules for the two quantifiers:

> *Existential Quantifier Introduction and Elimination:* Given φm, we can derive $\exists x\varphi x$; given $\exists x\varphi x$, we can derive φm (but only provided that m is a new name).

> *Universal Quantifier Introduction and Elimination:* Given φm for every $m \in D$, we can derive $\exists x\varphi x$; given $\exists x\varphi x$, we can derive φm (but only provided that m is an old name).

The restrictions on existential quantifier elimination follow from the fact that while we know that there is *some* object in the domain that is φ, we don't know which one. The restrictions on universal quantifier elimination follow from the fact that the domain of quantification might be empty.

Meta-Logical Results

As with the propositional calculus, the predicate calculus is both sound and complete. In the case of soundness, this can again be intuitively seen by the way in which the rules of derivation are constructed to fit the possible models of the language. The completeness of the predicate calculus is, however, technically demanding and was first proved in 1929 by Kurt Gödel (1906-1978).

Higher-Order Logics

The language sketched above is better referred to as *first-order* predicate calculus, as the language only quantifies over (first-order) individuals. A stronger language, second-order predicate calculus, can therefore be constructed by allowing quantification over predicates—that is, second-order sets of individuals. The language is the same as first-order predicate calculus, with the addition of the second-order quantifiers $\exists X$ ("there is at least one predicate X, such that ...") and $\exists X$ ("for all predicates X, it is the case that ..."). Even higher-order logics can similarly be constructed by allowing quantification over predicates of predicates, predicates of predicates of predicates, and so forth.

There are several examples of natural language expressions that are better expressed in a second-order language. The claim that there is something which a and b have in common would require a possibly infinite disjunction in a first-order language of the form $(Fa \& Fb) \vee (Ga \& Gb) \vee (Ha \& Hb) \vee \ldots$, but can be succinctly rendered in a second-order language e.g. $\exists X(Xa \& Xb)$. There are also examples that cannot be expressed in a first-order language—for example, the statement "there are some critics who only admire each other" asserts the existence of a set of individuals with a certain property, but does not entail how many such individuals this includes.

The second-order predicate calculus is therefore more expressively powerful than first-order predicate calculus. If it is a desideratum of our logical languages that they adequately capture our natural language arguments, then this motivates the adoption of higher-order logics. However, this expressive power comes at a cost; in particular, the standard semantics for second-order predicate calculus are *incomplete*. Thus, if it is a desideratum of our logical languages that they be both sound and complete (roughly that all theorems are provable and *vice versa*), then this is an argument against adopting higher-order logics. Finally, given that the extension of a predicate is a set of individuals, it has been argued that second-order predicate calculus is better considered as a branch of set-theory rather than logic, with the possible ontological commitments that entails.

Modal Logic

A common extension to the standard formal languages outlined above is to introduce the technical machinery required to evaluate natural language arguments containing modal terminology (that is, talk of possibility and necessity). A simple modal language is formed by expanding the language of the propositional calculus with the two one-place logical connectives □ ("it is necessary that ...") and ◇ ("it is possible that ..."), along with the corresponding formation rules:

> If P is a wff, then □P is a wff;
> If P is a wff, then ◇P is a wff.

Semantics

The semantics for modal propositional calculus is not straightforward, as modal locutions are not transparently truth-functional; that a proposition P is false does not logically entail whether it is possibly true or necessarily false. It follows therefore that the modal operators cannot simply be introduced along the same lines as the other logical connectives. Instead, the semantics for a modal language is usually given in terms of *possible worlds*. Informally, each possible world can be thought of as a distinct interpretation (that is, assignment of truth values) for the language, with the modal operators □ and ◇ making a claim about the truth values that hold at every interpretation, or at another interpretation, respectively. A model M for the modal propositional calculus is therefore of the form <W, R, val>, where W is a set of possible worlds, R is the accessibility relationship holding between members of W, and val is a function that assigns to every propositional variable a truth value (either true or false) at each possible world w Î W.

The truth values for complex, molecular sentences at each possible world w are then built up compositionally via the truth tables for the logical connectives: that is, $M \models (\varphi \,\&\, \psi)$ at a world w iff $M \models \varphi$ at a world w, and $M \models \psi$ at a world w.

The truth values for complex molecular sentences formed with the modal operators are given in terms of the truth values that hold at other accessible possible worlds as specified by the accessibility relationship R—that is, M $\vDash$ ($\Diamond\varphi$) at a world w iff M $\vDash$ φ at some world w' Î W such that R(w, w'); and M $\vDash$ ($\Box\varphi$) at a world w iff M $\vDash$ φ at all worlds w' Î W such that R(w, w'). It follows from these definitions that the two modal connectives are interdefinable—that is, $\Box$P is equivalent to $\neg\Diamond\neg$P. Similarly, other modal claims can be defined in terms of these basic connectives. To say that P is impossible is to say that P is necessarily false—that is, $\Box\neg$P; to say that P is contingent is to say that both it and its negation are possible—that is, ($\Diamond$P & $\Diamond\neg$P).

Proof Theory

A natural deduction system for modal propositional calculus is formed by extending the system introduced for the propositional calculus with the following rules that allow for the introduction and manipulation of the modal operators:

Rule of Necessitation: if φ is a theorem (i.e. $\vdash \varphi$) then we can derive $\Box\varphi$.

Rule of Distribution: given $\Box(\varphi \supset \psi)$, we can derive $(\Box\varphi \supset \Box\psi)$.

Different modal logics are then constructed by the addition of different axioms determining the behavior of the modal operators. The two most common modal axioms are the following:

(D): $\Box\varphi \supset \Diamond\varphi$
(T): $\Box\varphi \supset \varphi$

The combination of (D) and (T) provides the basis for most of the "interesting" (that is, expressively powerful) modal logics. Three further well-known modal logics can be constructed by adding each of the following axioms respectively:

(B): $\varphi \supset \Box\Diamond\varphi$
(S4): $\Box\varphi \supset \Box\Box\varphi$
(S5): $\Diamond\varphi \supset \Box\Diamond\varphi$

These axioms are presented in descending order of strength: a modal logic containing (S5) can derive all the previous axioms; a modal logic containing (S4) or (B) can derive the axioms (T) and (D); and a modal logic containing (T) can derive the axiom (D). Some of these axioms are associated with particular interpretations of the modal operators; the axiom (D) is usually taken as a base for *deontic logic*—that is, the logic of obligation, where $\Box\varphi$ is read as "it ought to be that φ," and $\Diamond\varphi$ is read as "it is permissible that φ."

Meta-Logical Results

The accessibility relationship R introduced in the semantics for modal propositional logic helps to illuminate the different modal axioms discussed above. In particular, it can be shown that (T) is valid on every frame <W, R> where R is a *reflexive* relation (that is, where every possible world is accessible to itself); it can, therefore, be shown that the modal propositional calculus with (T) as its only additional axiom is sound and complete with respect to the class of all reflexive models. Similarly, (B) is valid on every frame <W, R> where R is *symmetrical* (that is, if w_1 is accessible from w_2, then w_2 is accessible from w_1; (S4) is valid on every frame that is *transitive* (that is, if w_2 is accessible from w_1, and w_3 is accessible from w_2, then w_3 is accessible from $w_{1)}$; and (S5) is valid on every frame that is reflexive, symmetrical, and transitive (that is, where the set of possible worlds form an *equivalence class*). While the concepts of possibility and necessity obviously play an important role in metaphysics (such as the analysis of counterfactuals), there is no philosophical consensus on the logical form of this relationship.

Non-Classical Logic

While both the predicate calculus and the modal propositional calculus may be seen as extensions of the basic propositional calculus, there are also a variety of formal languages intended as genuine alternatives. These non-classical logics typically argue that the logical connectives are governed by different truth tables (often with more than two truth values), or they impose additional constraints on what counts as a valid inference. Given that the meaning of the logical connectives is largely exhausted by their truth tables, this immediately raises the question as to whether these non-classical logics are proposing a *revision* of how we understand our fundamental logical concepts or merely proposing new formal systems of only technical interest to sit alongside classical logic.

If genuinely alternative logics do exist, then a second question concerns how we might decide among them. Some philosophers maintain that our formal languages are intended to capture our various pretheoretical—and presumably self-evident—logical understanding, and that there are, therefore, philosophical reasons for favoring one logical language over another. Other philosophers argue that just as we might revise even our most fundamental scientific concepts on the grounds of, for instance, overall simplicity and strength, so, too, might a change in our logic be part of an overall improvement in our conceptual worldview.

Many-Value Logics

In the classical logics already discussed, the logical connectives are taken to be bivalent—that is, they allow of only two different truth values: true and false. One natural extension to classical logic, therefore, is to introduce additional truth values into our semantics, leading to many-valued logics with corresponding many-valued truth tables.

One of the earliest such proposals concerned the valuation of *future contingents*, statements about the future concerning events or states that have not yet happened. We may for instance be unwilling to say that a future contingent statement P ("it will rain tomorrow") is true, on the grounds that it has yet to happen and, indeed, might not happen at all; however, just because P is not true, it does not follow that we would be willing to say that ¬P is true (since it might rain after all). It has been proposed, therefore, to assign such future contingents a third truth value *i* to indicate that they are *indeterminate*. One of the earliest examples of this is Ignacy Łukasiewicz's (1822-1882) three-valued logic, which has the following truth-tables:

P	Q	¬P	P & Q	P v Q	P ⊃ Q	P ≡ Q
T	T	F	T	T	T	T
T	F	F	F	T	F	F
T	*i*	F	*i*	T	*i*	*i*
i	T	*i*	*i*	T	T	*i*
i	F	*i*	F	*i*	*i*	*i*
i	*i*	*i*	*i*	*i*	T	T
F	T	T	F	T	T	F
F	*i*	T	F	*i*	T	*i*
F	F	T	F	F	T	T

Łukasiewicz's system, however, is controversial for future contingents, as it evaluates (P ∨ ¬P) as indeterminate, even though, intuitively, it is true that it will either rain tomorrow or not rain tomorrow.

Similar proposals have been made in the case of *vagueness*. A vague predicate is one for which there are undecidable or borderline cases as to whether it is satisfied by a particular object. The typical examples follow the **Sorites Paradox**, insofar as while we would be unwilling to say that a single grain of sand "is a heap," and unwilling to say that adding one more grain of sand will make something a heap that was not so already, at some (vaguely specified) point we will have enough grains of sand whereby it is appropriate to say that it "is a heap." If this vagueness cannot be explained away in epistemological terms, then the alternative is to concede that some predicate expressions are neither true nor false, but rather indeterminate.

Intuitionism

One of the most familiar non-classical logics is intuitionism, which, in simple terms, is based upon the rejection of the law of excluded middle: (P ∨ ¬P). There are both philosophical and technical arguments that can be offered in favor of this restriction upon classical logic. Intuitionism was originally developed as a view about the **philosophy of mathematics**, which maintained that mathematical objects are mental constructions, and that therefore certain branches of traditional mathematics—those involving non-constructible objects, such as a completed infinity—are illegitimate. It similarly followed that some mathematical statements involving objects that had not yet been constructed were neither true nor false, and thus the law of excluded middle was invalid. A related line of argument has also been advanced within the philosophy of language. If we suppose that meaning is in part determined by use, then some statements (for example, inaccessible statements about the past) must be understood in terms of their *assertibility* conditions rather than their truth conditions; the fact that there will be circumstances in which it is not appropriate to assert a statement does not entail that it is appropriate to assert its negation.

Both lines of thought are philosophically controversial.

Another argument for restricting classical logic with respect to the law of excluded middle is based on a consideration of the nature of the logical connectives themselves. It seems reasonable to suppose that any formal language must be entirely neutral with respect to its subject matter; that is, it does not add anything to a proof not already present. One way to make this requirement explicit is for the introduction and elimination rules for the logical connectives to balance each other out, in which case they are said to be *harmonious*. The introduction and elimination rules for "&" are clearly harmonious in this sense, since we can only introduce (P & Q) if we have already assumed P and Q separately (&-Introduction), and the elimination of (P & Q) only allows us to derive P and Q (&-Elimination). By contrast, however, the introduction and elimination rules for double negation are not harmonious. If we can derive a contradiction on the assumption of ¬P, then we can derive ¬¬P (Reductio ad Absurdum), and from ¬¬P we can derive P (Double Negation Elimination). The elimination rules, therefore, leave us with something that was not previously assumed in the proof (that is, P). Intuitionists therefore conclude that the introduction and elimination rules for double negation must be abandoned, and since this rule is necessary to derive the law of excluded middle, we reach the intended result.

There are several different ways to formalize intuitionist logic. In terms of semantics, it is important to note that while intuitionists reject the law of excluded middle, they do not posit a third (that is, indeterminate) truth value. It is, therefore, not possible to provide a finite truth-table interpretation for intuitionist logic. It is, however, possible to provide an interpretation of the language within a possible-worlds framework, with structural similarities to S4. By contrast, in terms of a natural deduction proof theory, it is sufficient to remove the introduction and elimination rules for double negation, along with the Reductio ad Absurdum rule, but it is also necessary to replace them with a more restrictive rule:

> *Ex Contradictione Quodlibet:* "From contradiction, anything [follows]"; given a contradiction (ψ & $\neg\psi$), we can derive any proposition φ.

This allows a similar range of derivations but without the problematic consequences of unrestricted double negation elimination.

Relevance Logics

A relevance logic is motivated by the idea that the premises of a valid argument must be somehow "relevant" to its conclusion. The idea is motivated by the fact that the formal notion of implication based upon the truth tables of the logical connectives does not always match our pretheoretical understanding of implication; this includes, for instance, the so-called paradoxes of material implication—for instance, $\neg\varphi \supset (\varphi \supset \psi)$—and the principle of explosion—$(\varphi \,\&\, \neg\varphi) \supset \psi$. (A logic that denies the principle of explosion is called *paraconsistent.*) The precise definition of *relevance*, however, remains vague, although a necessary condition is usually understood to be that the premises and conclusions of an argument must share a propositional variable. In terms of a natural deduction system, this requirement can be met by indexing the assumptions in a proof and ensuring that these are persevered in any derivation—for instance:

Relevant &-Introduction: Given $\varphi_{[i]}$ and $\psi_{[i]}$, we can derive $(\varphi \,\&\, \psi)_{[i]}$

This ensures that we cannot introduce a conjunction on the basis of a relevant and irrelevant assumption and then eliminate the conjunction and derive a conclusion on the basis of the irrelevant assumption alone.

The semantics for a relevance logic is often extremely complex. One semantic option is to introduce four-valued truth tables, in which atomic propositions can be evaluated as true, false, both (a *truth-value glut*), or neither (a *truth-value gap*), and the truth value for complex molecular formulas built up from the corresponding four-valued truth tables. Another option is to provide a possible-worlds semantics for such logics, in which the domain is understood to include both *normal worlds*, governed by classical logic, and *non-normal worlds*, where these laws can vary. A more straightforward option, however, is to maintain only two truth values but to understand an interpretation as a *relationship* between propositional variables and truth values, in which relationship is more liberal than a function insofar as a proposition may be related to the value true, related to the value false, related to neither truth value, or related to both. We write Pr1 to say that P is true, Pr0 to say that P is false, and we place no restrictions upon an interpretation that asserts neither or both of these clauses. Complex formulas are again built up truth-functionally, just as in the classical case, and indeed with the same recursive clauses. For instance:

$(\varphi \,\&\, \psi)\rho 1$ iff $\varphi\rho 1$ and $\psi\rho 1$
$(\varphi \,\&\, \psi)\rho 0$ iff $\varphi\rho 1$ or $\psi\rho 1$

But we include the exception that just because a propositional variable is true, it does not automatically follow that it is also not false. For example, suppose that $v(\mathrm{P}) = 1$ and $v(\mathrm{Q}) = b$: since P is true and Q is true, (P & Q) is true; but since Q is also false, (P & Q) is also false; hence $v(\mathrm{P} \,\&\, \mathrm{Q}) = b$.

Quantum Logic

Most non-classical logics are motivated by either philosophical considerations, such as the metaphysical status of the future, or technical concerns about the neutrality of the logical connectives or the notion of implication. One notable exception to this are the proposals to revise classical logic in the face of empirical results in quantum mechanics.

It is a consequence of quantum mechanics that some properties are *complementary*. For example, a particle measured to have a determinate momentum cannot simultaneously be measured to have a determinate position, and *vice versa*. It has been proposed, therefore, that any satisfactory logic for quantum mechanics must reject the laws of distribution:

$$((\varphi \vee \psi) \,\&\, (\varphi \vee \theta)) \supset (\varphi \vee (\psi \,\&\, \theta))$$
$$((\varphi \vee \psi) \,\&\, \theta) \supset ((\varphi \,\&\, \theta) \vee (\psi \,\&\, \theta))$$

Thus, just because a particle is measured to have a determinate momentum (M_1), and a probabilistic range of positions (P_1 or P_2 or P_3 or ...), it does not logically follow that the particle has any one combination of determinate momentum and position (M_1 and P_1) or (M_1 and P_2) or ..., any one of which quantum mechanics tells us is impossible.

Such restrictions do not require a great deal of revision in either the semantics or natural deduction systems for the classical propositional calculus, although there have also been proposals to introduce three-valued truth tables, in which problematic conjunctions are evaluated as indeterminate. The main difficulty with quantum logic is that the proposed restrictions seem only to apply to a limited range of cases, as the laws of distribution will continue to hold for non-quantum phenomena. Quantum logic may therefore be better seen as merely a technical framework for accommodating quantum phenomena, rather than a global non-classical logic.

List of Basic Logical Symbols

- ¬ one-place logical connective read as "not" or as "is not the case"
- ~ alternative notation for "not"
- & two-place logical connective read as "and"
- ∧ and
- • and, both, yet, still
- ∨ two-place logical connective read as "or"

- ⊃ two-place logical connective read as the material conditional "if ... then ..."
- → alternative notation for if ... then
- ≡ two-place logical connective read as material equivalence "...if and only ..."
- ↔ ... if and only if, both or neither ...
- ∀ the universal quantifier read as "for all"
- ∃ the existential quantifier read as "there is some"
- □ one-place modal operator read as "necessarily"
- ◇ one-place modal operator read as "possibly"
- ∈ set-theoretic relationship read as "...is a member of ..."
- ⊤ logical constant for a tautology
- ⊥ logical constant for a contradiction
- ⊢ meta-logical constant for syntactic entailment (there is a proof that ...)
- ⊨ meta-logical constant for semantic entailment (there is a model such that ...)
- ∴ therefore

4

A Brief History of Philosophy

Because Western philosophy has proved most globally pervasive and has created a remarkably contiguous record—a genuine dialogue among philosophers over the centuries—our concise historical overview focuses on the Western tradition and reviews Middle Eastern, Indian, East Asian, and African philosophies only briefly. This is not intended as a cultural or intellectual value judgment but, rather, reflects the focus of philosophy as it is most frequently created, studied, and taught in universities worldwide. Since this book is intended chiefly for the undergraduate-level philosophy student, the Western focus is a pragmatic choice.

It is recommended that this brief history be read in conjunction with consulting the frequently used philosophical terms and concepts in Chapter 11 and the philosopher biographies in Chapter 12, both of which include many entries concerning non-Western philosophies.

The Pre-Socratics

The origins of Western philosophy are usually attributed to Thales of Miletus (fl. sixth century BC), who taught that "everything was made of water" and thus that the universe, all creation, was essentially one. In philosophical terms, however, the innovation Thales introduced was primarily methodological. In contrast to contemporary historical or religious modes of thought, which were broadly teleological in nature, he attempted to provide explanations in terms of the internal composition of objects and the mechanical principles they obey. The subsequent development of Western philosophy, therefore, involved a combination of this novel proto-scientific attitude with its emphasis upon investigating the underlying structure of the external world (as exemplified by the Atomists), together with a traditional mysticism that nevertheless took abstract mathematical speculation as its principal source of inspiration (thanks mainly to Pythagoras). The contrast between the ideal and empirical approaches became most prominent in the contrast between Plato and Aristotle in the so-called Classical Period of philosophy.

Pythagoreanism

Based on the teachings of Pythagoras (c. 570–495 BC) and the school he established in Croton in southern Italy, we may conclude that, in many ways, Pythagoreanism was more of a mystery religion than a philosophical school. It taught the immortality and transmigration of the soul and imposed various strictures and observances upon the behavior of its followers. Unlike other such movements, however, Pythagoreanism attached mystical significance to mathematics and has been credited with several important mathematical discoveries, including harmonic progressions in music and the eponymous results in trigonometry (flowing from the Pythagorean theorem).

Philosophically, the Pythagoreans were impressed with the certainty and exactness of mathematical knowledge, in contrast to what we can know about the physical world; they therefore concluded that the physical world was merely a poor shadow of some superior form of existence, that all knowledge should be based on the mathematical (that is, the axiomatic) example, and that the contemplative existence was the highest ideal to which man can aspire. These conclusions had a major influence on the metaphysical, epistemological, and ethical theories of many subsequent philosophers in the Western tradition, especially as transmitted through the work of Plato and his later adoption by the Scholastics in the Middle Ages.

The Eleatic School

Based in the Ionian colony of Elea (modern-day Velia) in southern Italy, and primarily associated with Parmenides (early fifth century BC) and Melissus of Samos (mid fifth century BC), the Eleatic school shared the Pythagorean disregard for the changeable world of everyday appearances and argued that true being was neither created, changed, nor destroyed. Parmenides is credited here with offering an early example of a deductive argument for his claims, based on considerations of thought and language: We cannot have knowledge of something that does not exist (nor can we speak intelligently of it). Change implies the creation or destruction of something that either did not previously exist or that no longer exists; therefore, we cannot know (or even speak about) anything that changes. A similar line of thought also establishes that everything that exists is one and the same, presumably on the grounds that a plenum of unchangeable entities would be redundant. While there are clearly problems with this argument, the importance of the Eleatic school lies in its methodological approach, and the attempt to reason from first principles rather than transmit mystical inspiration.

Atomism

Atomism was founded by Leucippus (who flourished around 440 BC) but was primarily elaborated by Democritus (c. 460-370 BC) as a way of reconciling the Eleatic doctrine of the impossibility of change with our observational evidence for the reality of change. According to Democritus, the world consists of an infinite number of indivisible atoms moving within a void, and while the atoms themselves neither come into being nor perish, we can accommodate our observation of (macroscopic) change in terms of the continuous (microscopic) variation in the position and configuration of these atoms. While any specific similarity to contemporary subatomic physics is quite limited, Atomism represents a methodological shift toward a more recognizably scientific attitude in two important respects: the importance given to reconciling abstract theory with observational evidence, and the attempt to provide a mechanistic explanation for phenomena, in contrast to the genealogical or teleological attempts favored at the time. Democritus further held that since the only real properties are the properties of atoms (namely, weight and mass), and since atoms are invisible, we have no direct knowledge of the world. Much as the Empiricists of the seventeenth century concluded, such properties as taste, color, and sound are primarily due to our sense organs rather than to the inherent reality of the physical world.

The Sophists

The Sophists were not a single school but a professional grouping of largely itinerant teachers of rhetoric, philosophy, and legal argumentation. Their importance lies not in any specific doctrines but in their general shift of emphasis toward philosophical questions of politics and ethics in contrast to the predominantly metaphysical speculations of the period and in the gradual professionalization of the philosophic discipline.

Some of the most important Sophists have become associated with skeptical and/or relativist positions, although this may simply reflect their overriding interest in philosophical technique rather than in its conclusions. Protagoras (c. 490–420 BC), for example, stated that "man is the measure of all things," which has been taken as the thoroughgoing rejection of objective truth. He also maintained, however, that some opinions can be better than others in terms of their practical consequences—an idea taken up by the American Pragmatists in the nineteenth and twentieth centuries. Similarly, Protagoras argued that laws and customs are merely the result of human agreement rather than natural principle or divine command, and they are justified in terms of their overall utility, a view that finds echoes in the political Liberalism of the Enlightenment.

Classical Philosophy

The Classical Period in philosophy was dominated by the teachings of Plato (427–347 BC) and Aristotle (384–322 BC) but gradually fell into a decline following the conquest of the independent Greek city-states by Alexander the Great and, later, by the Roman Republic. While Plato and Aristotle constructed grand systems of metaphysics, epistemology, political philosophy, and ethics, all of which were to have a profound influence on the development of Western thought, the subsequent Hellenistic Schools—Skepticism, Epicureanism, and Stoicism—largely reflected the political uncertainty of the time. They either rejected the possibility or desirability of objective knowledge and advocated a retreat from the public sphere to cultivate instead an inward-looking sense of personal virtue and equanimity. Both elements—the theoretical speculation of Plato and Aristotle, as well as the ascetic individualism of the Hellenistic Schools—were nevertheless to shape future developments and influence the Christian tradition in Europe.

Plato

Plato (427–347 BC) was born into a powerful family in Athens but abandoned politics after the execution of his teacher, Socrates; he subsequently traveled, became influenced by the Pythagoreans, and eventually established his own school—the famed Academy—in Athens. Almost all of Plato's surviving work takes the form of a dialogue between Socrates and other interlocutors, and while the earlier dialogues merely demonstrate that many of our (primarily ethical) concepts are poorly understood, later dialogues increasingly present a positive philosophical doctrine. The centerpiece of Plato's system is the claim that the physical world is a pale imitation of an ideal world consisting of the "Forms," unchangeable and incorporeal objects accessible only through theoretical reflection. Physical objects are held to be similar in virtue of instantiating the same Form ("universal"), and it is through direct contact with the Forms that objective knowledge is ultimately possible.

This metaphysical picture also underpins Plato's ethics. Just as the best life must be one devoted to the appreciation of the Form of Beauty (rather than particular instances of beauty), so, too, must the virtuous life be understood as the harmonious balance of the different parts of the soul focused on the appreciation of the Form of the Good.

In his most famous dialogue, the *Republic*, Plato theorized the structure, constituency, and conduct of the ideal state. The work has stood the test of time as one of the benchmarks of good government and governance.

Aristotle

Aristotle (384–322 BC) was born in Stagira but moved to Athens as a young man to study at Plato's Academy. Following Plato's death, Aristotle traveled, became tutor to Alexander the Great, and eventually returned to Athens to establish his own school, the Lyceum. He produced an extraordinary wealth of material on almost every topic, although much that remains and has come down to us are lecture notes and drafts rather than finished books.

Aristotle developed an early logical system based on four general categorical statements (roughly, simple quantifier statements) and the fourteen syllogistic inferences that they can form. This formal structure subsequently provides the framework for the natural sciences, which are considered deductively ordered bodies of knowledge, differentiated only in terms of their starting premises. Aristotle's logic was accepted with only minor improvements until the twentieth century, and his model of scientific explanation as the deduction of particular phenomena from general principles continues to shape contemporary philosophy of science. Also influential was Aristotle's reliance on teleology as an explanatory principle, both in terms of the overall behavior of physical phenomena and in understanding the development of biological systems. This framework was not challenged until the nineteenth century.

It was Aristotle's explicit disagreement with Plato that had the most immediate impact on all subsequent philosophy. Given his empirical orientation, Aristotle argued that the Forms did not exist independently of the physical world and that virtuous behavior was to be understood in (teleological) terms of human flourishing rather than by the abstract appreciation of ideal entities.

Cynicism

Founded by Antisthenes (c. 445–360 BC), who taught the importance of individual virtue over material luxury, Cynicism was contemptuous of political institutions and organized religion. It rejected refined philosophical speculation and sought instead conversation with the "common man."

These ideas were developed and taken to an extreme by Diogenes of Sinope (c. 400–325 BC), who is said to have lived in a barrel and begged for scraps. Indeed, the term *Cynic* derives from the Greek word for dog and referred to the almost feral lifestyle deliberately adopted by Diogenes and his followers. While lacking any detailed philosophical doctrine, Cynicism advocated an indifference to the variable fortunes of the everyday world in favor of the pursuit of individual virtue, a creed that reflected both the sense of political instability at the time and that has continued to influence the more introspective schools of philosophy seeking to retreat from their own political anxieties.

Skepticism (Pyrrhonism)

Pyrrhonian Skepticism was founded by Pyrrho of Elis (c. 360–275 BC), who argued that knowledge is impossible. The Skeptics proposed various arguments for their conclusions, including Platonic doubts about the world of our senses, and through offering opposing arguments for any position. Timon of Philius (c. 315–225 BC) further introduced the dilemma that, in the absence of self-evident principles, any argument will either be circular or face an infinite regress of justification. In consequence, the Skeptics proposed that we should suspend judgment on all matters of life and thereby attain a state of *ataraxia*, or peace of mind. This was regarded as both a practical response to a philosophical problem and a healthy corrective to the excesses of dogmatism.

After the Pyrrhonian Skeptics, the school flourished in Athens (as the so-called Academic Skeptics), where Arcesilaus (c. 268–241 BC) taught the Socratic Dialogues not as advocating a positive doctrine but as the methodical refutation of any unwarranted position. In both its Pyrrhonian and post-Pyrrhonian iterations, Skepticism offered an alternative approach to the political uncertainties of the time. Rather than withdrawing from the world (the Cynical course), the Skeptics proposed attaining an untroubled equanimity based on accepting our epistemic limitations.

Epicureanism

Founded by Epicurus (341–271 BC), this eponymous philosophy is best known through the Roman poet Lucretius (mid first century BC). Like the Atomists, the Epicureans maintained that everything is made up of indivisible atoms in a constant state of flux. They rejected any form of determinism, however, by arguing that these atoms were capable of random motion ("swerve") in addition to their natural impetus. The resulting metaphysics was of a world governed by mechanical (if occasionally indeterministic) forces, yet which nevertheless allowed for the operation of free will. This in turn allowed the Epicureans to overcome two significant fears. First, since the world is governed by mechanical forces, we have nothing to fear from the gods. Second, since there is no continued existence following the dissolution of our bodies, there is no experience of death that we might dread. The pursuit of happiness similarly governs the other main tenets of Epicureanism. Our senses are taken to be reliable, since the alternative is a self-defeating (and therefore unpleasant) form of Skepticism; and while our ethical goal is the pursuit of pleasure, this should be moderate in form, based on simple living, immune to the instabilities associated with great wealth and power.

Stoicism

Founded by Zeno of Citium (334–262 BC), early Stoicism shared many similarities with Epicureanism, including the belief that the world was largely deterministic and that the overall goal of the ethical life consisted in the resigned acceptance of this fact. Unlike the Epicureans however, the Stoics maintained that the evolution of the world was predetermined by the divine will (rather than purely mechanical) and that virtue consists in acting according to this plan (rather than avoiding unnecessary risk). Such a view naturally leads to an indifference toward everyday concerns. Pleasure and pain are irrelevant. Only virtue matters, and the truly wise man who acts according to the divine plan is thus one who is free from his passions and concerned only with being virtuous. By contrast, such a metaphysical position encourages a degree of epistemological optimism, and the Stoics anticipated later views that reliable knowledge could be either built up from self-evident acts of perception (Empiricism) or would be deduced from indubitable innate principles (Rationalism).

Stoicism became extremely influential in both the Roman Republic and the Roman Empire, particularly in the work of Cicero (106–43 BC) and Marcus Aurelius (121–180), but primarily as an ethical doctrine largely stripped of its metaphysical and epistemological elements.

Medieval Philosophy

The Medieval Period is usually dated between the fall of the Western Roman Empire (476) and the beginning of the Renaissance (c. 1300). In terms of philosophy, the period begins in the attempt to reconcile Plato's writings with orthodox Christian doctrine. The Neoplatonism of Plotinus

(204–270), for instance, extended the Platonic distinction between the physical and the ideal into a three-part distinction that roughly mirrored the Christian Trinity. The approach reached its culmination with Saint Augustine (354–430), whose work was to dominate philosophical and theological investigation for much of the Medieval Period. By the twelfth century, however, wider access to classical texts became available through Arabic sources, and Aristotle emerged as the dominant influence. His work on logic and disputation influenced a range of disparate thinkers broadly classified as the Scholastics, while the theological implications where developed most notably by Saint Thomas Aquinas (1225–1274).

Saint Augustine

Like his contemporaries, Saint Augustine (354–430) was primarily influenced by Neoplatonism, and, indeed, credited Plotinus with helping him to understand Christian theology. Some of these elements are explicit—including the trinitarian elaboration of Plato's metaphysics—but difficulties in accommodating specific theological doctrines, such as the incarnation, ultimately led to increasing divergence philosophy and theology. Nevertheless, Augustine's attempted reconciliation of the two produced a wealth of philosophical innovation. In his refutation of Academic Skepticism, Augustine anticipated Descartes, arguing that certain propositions, self-referential propositions about our own existence, provide an indubitable epistemological foundation.

Augustine also identified the will as a distinct source of motivation and the locus of moral responsibility, even if handicapped by original sin and requiring divine assistance in the form of grace. Augustine introduced a semiotic distinction between object and sign as the basis of a philosophy of language, and he sketched a phenomenological account of our experience of time that has directly influenced later Existentialists. Probably Augustine's most important contribution, however, was his *On the City of God* (1470). While putatively a plea for the adoption of Christian virtue, the book also argues for the political separation of Church and State and introduces an eschatological view of history that underpins contemporary historicism, such as that of Karl Marx.

Scholasticism

A general term for those philosophers influenced by the medieval rediscovery of classic texts, Scholasticism is broadly characterized by an interest in logic and disputation and is motivated to resolve the metaphysical disagreements between Aristotle and Plato, especially on the subject of universals. These two topics were closely related. Peter Abelard (1079–1144), for instance, argued that universality is a feature of our language, not a metaphysical distinction between types of entity. He subsequently drew several important distinctions between the signification of an expression—what it names—and the ideas of the speaker.

Abelard is also credited with developing an early form of propositional logic. William of Ockham (c. 1285–1347) similarly argued that only particulars exist and that universality is a property pertaining to names. From this, he concluded that the causal properties of objects must operate in and of themselves. That is, no *sine qua non* causation operates behind the scenes, and not even God could make (for example) the property of heat to cause things to cool. The conflict between Plato and Aristotle was therefore intellectually liberating, and early examples of an experimental approach, such as in the work of Roger Bacon (c. 1214–1293), can also be found in Scholasticism.

Thomism

A school of thought based on the work of Saint Thomas Aquinas (1225–1274), Thomism is, like Scholasticism, principally concerned with metaphysics and understanding the attributes of God. Aquinas expanded Aristotle's investigation into the nature of being by distinguishing between the empirical and quantitative studies of being, with the distinctive negative judgments required for studying being *qua* being. He also developed a theory of analogy to explain how we can speak intelligently about God.

One of the most distinctive contributions of Thomism is a clear distinction between theological investigation, which presupposes faith, and philosophical investigation, which depends solely on the light of natural reason. He argued that, while some truths are only available through faith, philosophy is consistent with theology and can even help illuminate it. Thus, Aquinas presented his "Five Ways" for proving the existence of God based on reason alone by starting from the Aristotelean proposition that the causal order of the universe must originate in a First Cause. This approach helped lead to the development of Natural Theology in the seventeenth century. Similarly, the Neo-Thomist revival in the late nineteenth century was an important contribution to a renewed interest in virtue ethics.

The Early Modern Period

Philosophical thought during the Enlightenment was characterized by a rejection of existing sources of authority. The broadly Aristotelean scientific worldview was undermined by a period of scientific revolution—conventionally beginning with Copernicus' *De revolutionibus orbium coelestium* (1543) and culminating with Newton's *Philosophia Naturalis Principia Mathematica* (1687)—which raised important questions about our epistemological practices. Simultaneously, the rise of an increasingly powerful mercantile middle class challenged the traditional political order and the legitimacy of government. As a result, philosophical emphasis turned toward the individual, giving rise to the idea that our knowledge of the world is to be built up from either personal observation or deduction from self-evident principles, rather than from reading ancient authors. Citizenship came to be understood as a voluntary contract between individuals and the state, rather than decreed by God. These two strands of thought received their most sophisticated articulation in Immanuel Kant (1724-1804), whose legacy has profoundly influenced all subsequent philosophy.

Rationalism

Rationalism designates a variety of philosophical schools maintaining that reason, as opposed to empirical investigation, is the most important method of acquiring knowledge. There are several ways in which this epistemological conviction can be articulated, depending upon what is understood by "reason." Plato's view that genuine knowledge can only come through reflecting upon the unchangeable realm of the Forms can be classified as a branch of Rationalism, but the Rationalist view is most prominently associated with the so-called Continental Rationalists of the seventeenth-century, who were inspired by developments in the mathematical sciences. René Descartes (1596–1650), for instance, argued that all knowledge must be based on indubitable first principles (such as *cogito ergo sum,* "I think; therefore, I am"). Baruch Spinoza (1632–1677), in contrast, maintained that the logical connection between our ideas will mirror the actual (causal) connections between objects; thus, a complete axiomatization of our *a priori* knowledge could yield empirical results. Gottfried Wilhelm Leibniz (1646–1716) argued that even scientific laws could be derived from purely intellectual considerations, although he did so on the assumption that God never does anything without sufficient reason. Rationalism is usually contrasted with Empiricism, which maintains that our physical senses are the most important vehicles for acquiring knowledge.

Empiricism

Empiricism covers a range of views prioritizing experience as the primary source of knowledge. During the Early Modern Period, this view was expounded by the so-called British Empiricists—Locke, Berkeley, and Hume—who sought to replace the appeal to authority with an alternative epistemological foundation, articulated in conjunction with a particular view about mental content.

According to John Locke (1632–1704), we only have knowledge through direct awareness, and the only direct awareness are our ideas, which are mental representations of external reality. More complex knowledge can be constructed from simpler ideas, and instances of apparently non-empirical knowledge (such as mathematics) were dismissed as the purely formal relationships that exist between our ideas. One central problem with the view, however, concerns how mental ideas can accurately represent non-mental objects. As a result, George Berkeley (1685–1753) concluded that we could only have reliable knowledge if the external world were also composed of mental ideas, and David Hume (1711–1776) concluded that we cannot have reliable knowledge at all.

Empiricism is usually contrasted with Rationalism, which posits a more extensive role for non-empirical knowledge. It was the attempt to find a compromise between the Rationalism and Empiricism that motivated Kant's Transcendental Idealism.

Liberalism

A political philosophy whose central claim is that a government's authority is justified only insofar as it secures the liberty of its subjects, Liberalism is generally traced to John Locke (1632–1704), who argued that man has a natural right to both self-preservation and private property, but that individuals might choose to submit to political authority as a way of best protecting these rights. This account of the justification of political power also entails constraints on how it can be exercised, since, to preserve the liberty of all of citizens, a government must remain neutral regarding their individual pursuits. This idea was developed by Immanuel Kant (1724–1804) as a principle of autonomy, whereby citizens have liberty only when living under rules they would choose for themselves—an idea that continues to influence contemporary political philosophy, most notably John Rawls's *A Theory of Justice* (1971).

Given its original motivation and its almost exclusive emphasis on the individual, it is unsurprising that Liberalism has been criticized for downplaying the importance of tradition and community as part of a stable political system. The position also raises issues regarding the legitimacy of coercive government intervention as a means of preserving liberty.

Transcendental Idealism

The philosophical system developed by Immanuel Kant (1724–1804), Transcendental Idealism sought to overcome the epistemological problems of Empiricism while providing a rational justification for Liberalism.

Kant argued that we cannot have knowledge of things-in-themselves (the noumena), but only how they appear (the phenomena). We can, however, understand the conditions for any possible experience by investigating how our cognitive faculties systematize these phenomena. Thus, mathematics can be derived from our spatial-temporal ordering of phenomena (via the faculty of sensibility), while the principles of Newtonian Mechanics follow from our judgments regarding, for instance, the identity and continuity of phenomena (via the faculty of understanding). Since any experience must be systematized in these ways, our mathematical and scientific knowledge is guaranteed to be reliable, not because our representations necessarily conform to the external world but because our experience of the external world necessarily conforms to our representations. This solves the problem of how our mental ideas can accurately represent non-mental objects. The political ideals of tolerance and autonomy are also shown to follow as universal principles of pure reason. Finally, by sharply delineating the boundaries of theoretical reason, Kant also sought to leave room for free will and religious duty in an otherwise mechanistic universe.

Post-Kantian Philosophy in the Nineteenth Century

Kant's philosophy continued to dominate throughout the nineteenth century, although there were increasing concerns about the overall coherence of his system; in particular, there was doubt as to whether the notion of things-in-themselves was intelligible and about the interaction among the different faculties of the mind. In extremely broad terms, there thus began a schism between those philosophers who prioritized the faculty of sensibility and those who prioritized the faculty of understanding. In the twentieth century, this led to an often bitter division between Continental Philosophy (via Phenomenology) and Analytic Philosophy (via Logical Atomism).

At the same time, the nineteenth century saw the fallout of the French Revolution and its consequences for political philosophy. In the United

States, the end of the Civil War similarly influenced philosophical thought, nudging it toward an increased orientation toward practical consequences.

Hegelianism

One common theme in post-Kantian philosophy was an attempt to overcome the remaining divisions between noumena and phenomena, and to reconcile the distinct faculties of sensibility and understanding into a unified whole. According to Georg Wilhelm Friedrich Hegel (1770–1831), this was an ongoing and dynamic process, which recognized the fundamental interconnectedness of all things. Thus, human history itself is to be understood as the collective subject—the *Geist*—coming to a state of self-understanding through the dialectic process of overcoming opposition until it reaches Absolute Truth, in which lingering divisions are finally dissolved. It follows that the job of the Hegelian philosopher is to provide an encyclopedic assimilation of almost every branch of human knowledge as part of a rational reconstruction of human development toward the ultimate goal of achieving synthesis through the contention of thesis and antithesis.

These themes are perhaps best illustrated in Hegel's political philosophy. Whereas Kant maintained that human freedom consists in a constant opposition between duty and inclination, Hegel argued that this is overcome in obedience to the state, a collective entity that is therefore better placed to realize our individual will. Nevertheless, while the metaphysical prioritization of the state over the individual followed from Hegel's post-Kantian methodology, it was also symbiotic with the rise of German Nationalism and the increasing power of the Prussian State under Frederick II the Great.

Hegel remains one of the most influential post-Kantian philosophers. Perhaps most consequentially, his underlying dialectical metaphysics was recast in terms of economic processes and class consciousness in the philosophy of Marxism.

Utilitarianism

The French Revolution sparked legal and political reforms across Europe, which brought with them their accompanying philosophical frameworks. In England, Jeremy Bentham (1748–1832) advocated for a variety of democratic reforms in terms of parliamentary representation and prison sentencing, all of which were articulated within his philosophy, later dubbed "Utilitarianism" by John Stuart Mill (1806-1873). Bentham's leading idea was that, since happiness is the only good, our ethical obligations are simply to maximize the overall happiness of society, the "greatest good for the greatest number."

Such a philosophical view provided a straightforward justification for Bentham's political views, including his advocacy of women's (at least partial) equality. It also led him to reject any notion of individual rights or the idea of a contract between individuals and the state. One obeys the law simply because it maximizes the overall happiness.

Utilitarianism was further developed and refined by Mill, who attempted to put the principles on more empirical grounds. He agreed with Bentham that man is primarily motivated by the pursuit of pleasure (psychological hedonism) but argued that this can take on associative meanings, and that such pursuits need not be entirely egoistic. Problems remained, however, as to how overall happiness was to be calculated and in the notion that no amount of individual injustice was prohibited provided it added to the "greater good."

Pragmatism

Pragmatism was a philosophical movement in the United States concerned with the relationship between abstract theory and practical activity, and with the value of philosophical reflection. Beginning with Charles Sanders Peirce (1839-1914) and William James (1842-1910), the Pragmatists stressed that the meaning of our concepts was determined principally by their practical consequences and that our epistemological practices were determined as much by personal value judgments (regarding, for example, our desire to maximize truth at the expense of cautiously avoiding error) as they are by objective standards of evidence. This consequently led to various Pragmatist theories of truth, arguing that a statement is true if it is useful to believe (James) or if it would be the stable result of a suitably conducted inquiry (Peirce). Both positions were intended more as an explication of the role "truth" plays in our lives rather than as strict logical definitions.

Pragmatism has had an enormous influence on subsequent American philosophy, as well as producing theories of jurisprudence, education, and the development of psychology as an autonomous discipline, while Peirce's work on language and meaning forms the basis for contemporary semiotics.

Continental Philosophy in the Twentieth Century

While the focus of western philosophy has primarily been on the analysis and understanding of our most basic concepts, another important theme has been the preparation and education of man to live a more authentic form of life. One way in which to understand the divergence of philosophical thought in the early twentieth century is in terms of this contrast, with the so-called Continental tradition in France and Germany increasingly concerned with authenticity. In part this can be explained by the relative influence of Edmund Husserl (1859-1938) on continental philosophers, as opposed to the influence of Gottlob Frege (1848-1925) on the so-called Analytic tradition. At least as important is the European political and historical context of the twentieth century, which saw the rise of fascism and Nazism and the impact of the devastation of World War II. These prompted a renewed focus on the human condition and the structure of society.

Phenomenology

As originally developed by Edmund Husserl (1859–1938), phenomenology seeks to provide a detailed description of the way in which things are presented to us—that is to say, phenomena—in an attempt to uncover the fundamental structure of consciousness and our relationship to the world. This involves both a phenomenological description of the object as it is presented (the *noematic analysis*) and a phenomenological description of the cognitive activity performed to allow the object to be presented (the *noetic analysis*). By seeing which features of these descriptions are necessary to the phenomena, we can thereby uncover its essence (or *eidos*). Crucial to the phenomenological method is a suspension (or *epoché*) of our natural attitudes and presuppositions about the origin or causal explanation of our experiences, which in turn allows them to become the subject of phenomenological analysis.

Modeled on René Descartes' (1596-1650) method of doubt, the modern phenomenological analysis shows how our fundamental scientific concepts are based on, and thus presuppose, the phenomenological structure of a pre-scientific form of existence (the *Lebenswelt*). While the motivation of Husserl's work was predominately epistemological, the phenomenological method has been extended to broadly ontological issues by the Existentialists and provides the basis for Martin Heidegger's (1889-1976) early work.

Existentialism

A broad philosophical and literary movement that flourished during the first half of the twentieth century, Existentialism emphasized the uniqueness of human experience over the generalizations of traditional scientific or philosophical analysis ("existence precedes essence"). In the early work of Martin Heidegger (1889–1976), these generalizations are argued to depend upon a more phenomenologically immediate "being-in-the-world," one shaped by our individual and open-ended projects and rooted in a specific historical context.

For Jean-Paul Sartre (1905–1980), with whom Existentialism is most closely identified, the focus is more individualistic, and the reality of the radical freedom lying at the heart of the human condition is illustrated by strategies we undertake to delude ourselves into avoiding this fact ("bad faith"). Heidegger was later to distance himself from the Existentialist movement, whereas Sartre struggled to integrate his existential analysis with Marxist political theory. The lasting influence of Existentialism has therefore been in specific applications: Simone de Beauvoir (1908–1986), Sartre's long-time partner, famously articulated her feminist philosophy in terms of the existential condition of women forced to identify with (unchosen) societal roles.

As an important precursor to Existentialism in the **philosophy of religion**, Søren Kierkegaard (1813–1855) argued that the paradoxical nature of religious experience and its inability to be situated within a systematic philosophy are collectively the justification of faith.

The Frankfurt School

A group of philosophers, cultural critics, and social scientists based around the Frankfurt (Germany) Institute for Social Research were primarily concerned with integrating philosophical analysis with then-recent results in the social sciences as part of a political critique of society. Early work in the Frankfurt School, exemplified by Max Horkheimer (1895–1973), sought to interpret the social sciences within a Marxist framework, whereby norms of evaluation were to be understood as determined by historical context. Such Marxist restrictions were later relaxed, but the Frankfurt School remained committed to the idea that philosophical interpretation of the social sciences could be used as a tool for political emancipation. Following World War II, this emphasis turned to an increasingly pessimistic "critique of instrumental reason," a term for the dehumanization of man caused by a bureaucratic society that treats nature as nothing more than a resource. In response, Theodor W. Adorno (1903–1969) argued that only aesthetic experience allowed the possibility of a genuine (that is, non-instrumental) relationship with the world. The second generation of the Frankfurt School has been more optimistic. Jürgen Habermas (b. 1929) developed theories of communication, arguing that the possibility of political emancipation lies not in Marxist dialectic, but the discursive practices of liberal democracy.

Structuralism

Structuralism refers to research undertaken in the social sciences, predominantly in France, between the 1950s and 1970s, which sought to understand various social phenomena as a "closed system" of elements. This approach derives from the structural linguistics of Ferdinand de Saussure (1857–1913) in the early twentieth century, which argued that a language is to be understood in terms of its internal (phonetic, grammatical) rules of organization rather than its arbitrary semantic relationships to the external world. In the 1940s and 1950s, Structuralism was applied to anthropology by the anthropologist Claude Lévi-Strauss (1908–2009), who argued that society itself is organized according to forms of communication and exchange.

Later work by the so-called Post-Structuralists extended the Structural approach to psychoanalysis, literary theory, and philosophy. Michel Foucault (1926–1984) offered a structuralist analysis of political power, arguing that the social sciences seek to define—and thereby control—the individual in terms of their own internally ordered structure of knowledge, whereby the internal (political, epistemological) rules governing the use of concepts like "madness" or "criminality" similarly constrain the individual's actual existence.

Structuralism's relative neglect of the individual's subjective experience, and its limited range of applications, stood in marked contrast to traditional phenomenological and existential analyses, and this criticism still shapes contemporary Continental philosophy.

Analytic Philosophy in the Twentieth Century

The analytic tradition arose partly as a rejection of Hegelian idealism in favor of what George Edward Moore (1873–1958) called a "common sense" view of the world, alongside developments in mathematical logic due to Gottlob Frege (1848–1925) and Bertrand Russell (1872–1970). This initially led to an increasingly sharp focus on the logical structure of language as a guide to resolving philosophical problems and, later, to a renewed interest in the structure of our scientific theories. Eventually, the everyday usage of natural language became the focus of attention, a change of direction most notably associated with the later work of Ludwig Wittgenstein (1889–1951).

From the 1960s onward, the analytic tradition began to fragment into various subfields, and while certain broad similarities remain—the logical analysis of concepts and a methodological reliance upon the natural sciences—it is no longer helpful to speak of specific schools of thought within this tradition.

Logical Atomism

Although mostly associated with the logical analysis of language, analytic philosophy began in the philosophy of mathematics. Working independently, both Gottlob Frege and Bertrand Russell pursued programs of reducing mathematics to logic, and the philosophical motivations behind these projects were to find broader application. The most important was the rejection of psychologism—the idea that logical objects are reducible to mental activity—and hence the careful distinction between the (objective) semantic content of a proposition and the (subjective) activity of, for example, believing that proposition. Thus, Frege was to distinguish between the sense and reference of a denoting concept—the former being the way in which the latter was "presented" to a competent speaker of the language—which explained how identifying statements ("Hesperus is Phosphorus") could nevertheless be surprising. Russell proposed that denoting concepts was ultimately reducible to definite descriptions that contained only logical proper names, which explained how statements about non-existing entities ("the present King of France") could nevertheless be meaningful. This approach culminated in Wittgenstein's *Tractatus Logico-Philosophicus* (1921), which argued that every meaningful proposition must have a precise logical structure, and that this structure mirrors the logical structure of the world.

Logical Positivism

Originally founded by Auguste Comte (1798–1857), Positivism was primarily a view about science. Influenced by Immanuel Kant's (1724-1804) assertion that knowledge of things-in-themselves was impossible, Comte argued that our scientific theories should be understood as mere tools for systematizing and predicting observation, and that further (metaphysical) speculation must be rejected as unfounded.

Comte was also important for the foundation of sociology as a science and introduced the idea that there are laws of social development that can be studied and manipulated. Comte's ideas were refined and extended in the early twentieth century by developments in logical analysis and the prospects of reducing complex theoretical concepts into an observational language. The so-called Logical Positivists thus pursued a foundationalist epistemology based on the immediacy of self-evident "sense data." They argued that any statement that was not (at least in principle) verifiable by observation was to be rejected as meaningless. Such epistemological restrictions were deemed impractical and gradually relaxed, but many Logical Positivists maintained a focus on applying logical analysis to the understanding of science. Logical reduction was thus no longer a tool to ensure epistemological reliability but, rather, a political project for constructing a universal language of science that could maximize democratic participation.

Ordinary Language Philosophy

Between the 1940s and the 1960s, analytic philosophy shifted away from investigating the (supposed) underlying logical structure of language. While it was still primarily concerned with conceptual analysis, this was increasingly pursued through studying everyday linguistic practice. One consequence of this was a greater appreciation of how natural language works, and John Langshaw Austin (1911–1960) laid the groundwork for contemporary speech-act theory.

A second consequence was the attempt to dissolve philosophical problems as issues that arose from linguistic confusion. In connection with this, Gilbert Ryle (1900–1976) argued that grammatical similarities between the words "body" and "mind" lead us to suppose that minds must be some (unusual) kind of entity, but closer attention to our mental discourse reveals that these similarities actually function to make (dispositional) claims about physical activity.

Ludwig Wittgenstein's later work can also be considered a form of Ordinary Language Philosophy. In his posthumously published *Philosophical Investigations* (1953), he argued that language learning requires initiation into a broader "form of life," in which linguistic rules presuppose regular social practice. For Wittgenstein, such investigations are intended to be "therapeutic." Skepticism, for instance, is defeated not because some propositions cannot be doubted, but because these propositions constitute the very framework in which skeptical doubts can be raised.

Non-Western Philosophical Traditions

As explained at the beginning of this chapter, this book is intended primarily for philosophy students, especially new philosophy students, whose focus is mainly or even exclusively on Western philosophical traditions. For this reason, the discussion of non-Western philosophical traditions, which ends this chapter, is no more than a cursory review. Those interested in studying non-Western philosophies in depth may refer to "Resources" in Chapter 14.

Middle Eastern Traditions

As the Middle East is often called the cradle of civilization, it is also the source of some of the earliest philosophical literature. Much of it is devoted to what the Western tradition calls **Ethics**, although the philosophies of Ancient Egypt and Babylonia are also rich with astronomical writings (classifiable as **Natural Philosophy**) and cosmogony and cosmology, the origin of the universe and the nature of creation. It is likely that this earliest body of work influenced the Ancient Greeks.

Jewish philosophy and Christian philosophy developed in this region and, only later, in Europe as well. The thinkers of the Babylonian Talmudic academies drew on both Greek and Islamic philosophy, and later Jewish philosophy was strongly influenced by Western philosophy, especially the works of Aristotle, rediscovered during the European Middle Ages and transmitted far and wide. In an instance of cultural and intellectual reciprocity, Middle Eastern philosophers who wrote commentaries on Aristotle and other ancient Greek thinkers enriched the medieval European understanding of this classical tradition.

Prior to the emergence of the Abrahamic religions (Judaism, Christianity, and Islam) in the Middle East, the Iranian spiritual leader Zoroaster (who lived probably during the second millennium BC) evolved a theology and philosophy of religion and cosmogony that combined monotheism with a dualist opposition of good and evil. Zoroastrianism shaped such Iranian religious philosophies as Manichaeism, Mazdakism, and Zurvanism, and it went on to inspire and influence the nineteenth-century German philosopher Friedrich Nietzsche (1844-1900).

After the Muslim conquests, beginning in the seventh century AD, Islamic philosophy displaced Zoroastrianism and built upon Greek philosophical traditions, especially Aristotelianism and Neoplatonism, to create what has been called the Islamic Golden Age (eighth to fourteenth centuries AD), which featured many innovations in philosophical, scientific, and mathematical thought as well as in medicine. The Aristotelian tradition was elaborated into such Islamic intellectual and spiritual movements as Illuminism, Sufism, and Transcendent theosophy, which, in various ways, carried even into the late nineteenth and early twentieth centuries during the so-called Arab Renaissance, also known as the Nahda. During the early Middle Ages, in addition to harmonizing and even synthesizing Aristotle and other classical Greek philosophers with Islam, the Middle East became the keeper of the classical Western intellectual flame, not only preserving but interpreting the work of Plato, Aristotle, and others, which was then transmitted to Europe.

Indian Philosophy

Philosophy on the Indian subcontinent between 1000 BC and the early centuries of the first millennium was comprised of six major schools of Hindu philosophy (Nyaya, Vaisheshika, Samkhya, Yoga, Mimamsa, and Vedanta) and Jain, Buddhist, Ajivika, Ajñana, and Charvka philosophical traditions. While these are diverse, they share eleven essential religious and philosophical concepts and virtues:

- *Dharma*: Behaviors considered harmonious with *Rta*, the natural order that enables the universe and life
- *Karma*: Relating to action, work, deed, and cause and effect
- *Artha*: Relating to the aims, means, and purpose of life
- *Kama*: Aspiration, longing, and sexual desire
- *Duhkha*: The existential role of suffering and pain
- *Anitya*: The existential role of change and impermanence
- *Dhyana* (*Jhana*): The epistemological and existential roles of meditation and contemplation
- *Samnyasa*: The existential and spiritual role of renunciation
- *Samsara*: The cycles of death and rebirth
- *Kaivalya*: The role of solitude in Raja yoga and in the concept of *nirvana*; the release from the cycle of eternal rebirth
- *Ahimsa*: The virtue of nonviolence, a key value in Buddhist and other Indian religions

The most widely known philosophical texts from the Indian subcontinent are the Upanishads (a collection of religious and philosophical teachings) and the scriptures known as the Vedas. Ancient Indian philosophical schools were organized chiefly around the Upanishads and Vedas, investigating metaphysics, ethics, psychology, and hermeneutics, as well salvation (soteriology). Four prominent philosophical traditions, however, rejected the authority of the Vedas: Carvaka was a school of materialist belief, which accepted free will; Ajivika was also materialist but rejected the notion of free will; Buddhism, denying the existence of *atman*—the self, based on the concept of an unchanging soul—followed the teachings of Gautama Buddha; and Jainism, a philosophy that embraced *atman* but, rejecting the Vedas, followed the twenty-four ascetic teachers known collectively as the *tirthankaras*.

Philosophies of East Asia

The dominant philosophical traditions in this part of the world began in Ancient China from the sixth century to 221 BC, which saw the development of China's great philosophical movements during the Hundred Schools of Thought era. The primary movements during this long epoch were Confucianism, Legalism, and Taoism. These spread out to influence Korean, Vietnamese, and Japanese philosophy, although the latter developed its own strong Shinto and State Shinto traditions, which were very much native to the country and, ultimately, nationalist in their effect.

Buddhism exerted a powerful influence in China beginning during the Han Dynasty (206–220 BC), but the Chinese made significant adaptions, especially with respect to Zen, a transformation of Buddhism that spread throughout East Asia.

Confucianism, which developed from the teachings of Confucius (551–489 BC) during the Hundred Schools of Thought epoch emerged as a hybrid of religion and philosophy that made a profound and enduring impact on theology, ethics, and political philosophy. Primarily, Confucianism emphasized morality and governance built on the "correctness" of social relationships as well as the doctrine of justice and the virtues of kindness and honesty. It was embraced as a guide for living legitimated largely through a cult of ancestor worship, which elevated precedent and tradition in all things.

Legalism (*Fajia*) emerged during the fourth century BC as a philosophy of government and administration, which has been compared to the political philosophy of Niccolò Machiavelli (1469–1527) in Renaissance Italy. A philosophy of Realpolitik, it has exerted a major influence on Chinese bureaucratic administration.

Legalism drew on Confucianism and influenced Taoism, mostly with respect to these as political philosophies. Taoism is the philosophy of living in harmony with the Tao, which may be interpreted as the source, pattern, and substance of all that exists. All three major schools of ancient Chinese thought were ultimately aimed at aligning politics and government with natural or enduing order. The connection to Taoism tended to provide a basis for linking to eternal and universal values both Confucian and Legalist approaches to governance. Of the three schools, Confucianism had the greatest practical impact during the later Chinese dynasties, especially the Ming Dynasty (1368–1644) in China and the Joseon Dynasty (1392–1897) in Korea. The philosopher Wang Yangming (1472–1529) reinvigorated Confucianism as so-called Neo-Confucianism. As a result, the Confucian philosophical tradition was embraced by the imperial Chinese throne.

Confucianism continued to influence the structure of bureaucratic and institutional government in China through the nineteenth century. As late as the twentieth century, elements of Confucianism began to be combined with Western philosophies, most notably Marxism, and figured importantly in Chinese Marxist doctrine as developed by Mao Zedong. As a counterpoint to this, Hu Shih (1891–1962), who had studied in the United States under John Dewey, introduced to China what came to be called the New Pragmatism along with a form of Skepticism. Both politically and philosophically, Hu opposed Mao Zedong, and his work fell into disrepute by the time he died, of a heart attack, in 1962. Its rehabilitation, however, began in the 1980s, and Hu Shih is once again studied in China.

Japanese philosophy became increasingly influenced by the West in the nineteenth century until State Shinto emerged during the Meiji era (1868–1912). Even during this period, strong Western influences continued in Japan, including the study of Western Sciences (Rangaku) and the modernist Meirokusha intellectual society, which drew from European enlightenment thought.

State Shinto outlived the Meiji era and became philosophical and religious basis of the political doctrine of the Japanese emperor as a divine being. This came to its apex in Emperor Hirohito (reigned 1926–1989), during whose reign Japan entered into a period of imperial expansion, which led to its involvement in World War II.

Even as State Shinto assumed the sanction of the imperial state, the Kyoto School, a philosophical movement founded by Kitaro Nishida (1870-1945) about 1913 (although not given its name until 1932) was beginning a synthesis of Western phenomenology with Medieval Japanese Buddhism, including the Zen teachings of Dogen Zenji (1200–1253). It was not widely perceived as what it, in fact, was: a philosophical rival to State Shinto.

African Philosophy

The earliest indigenous African philosophy to produce written documents emerged during the seventeenth century, especially in Ethiopia. Zera Yacob

(1599–1692), whose *Hatata* (1667) has been compared to René Descartes' *Discourse on the Method of Rightly Conducting One's Reason and of Seeking Truth in the Sciences* (1637) as a manifesto on reason as a method for investigating the key questions of philosophy.

In the modern era, African philosophical thought has focused on ethnophilosophy, essentially an effort to define a specifically African philosophy that embodies unique characteristics of being African. Existentialism has played an important role in African philosophy of the twentieth century and has influenced a Black existentialist movement among some African-American philosophers. Marxism rose to prominence in Africa during the early post-colonial period, beginning after World War II, and, more recently, structuralism and post-structuralism have been gaining importance as African philosophers investigate the institutional and semiotic underpinnings of post-colonial government and culture.

Part II

Writing Philosophy

5

Doing and Writing

How Do You Do Philosophy?

How do you do *philosophy?* Unlike many of the questions asked in the name of philosophy, this one has a straightforward answer. You *do* philosophy primarily through writing. Now, if you are already behaving like a philosophy student, you should be challenging this answer. One highly plausible challenge is, *No. You* do *philosophy by thinking.*

It is a fair point. I suggest, however, that you consider the following quotation, which has been attributed to everybody from the great British novelist E. M. Forster and the great American storyteller Flannery O'Connor to "an Anonymous Little Girl." Whoever said it or said it first, it is brilliant and brilliantly provocative: "How can I know what I think till I see what I say?"[7]

Epistemologists as well as neuroscientists, linguists, and semioticians (students of signs, symbols, and their interpretation) dispute the primacy of language, especially written language, in thinking. Rather than take up such disputes here, we can instead stake out an area about which most academics and others agree. Whatever role writing plays in the process of thought, writing at the very least facilitates and systematizes thinking. Writing gives it clear, symbolic form, and the symbols it creates—words, sentences, paragraphs, and so on—can be readily modified, arranged, and rearranged, thereby aiding thought. Let's concede that some folks can play entire chess games, even multiple games, simultaneously and entirely in their heads. But let's also admit that these are very exceptional people. The great majority of chess players, even good ones, *need* to see and move pieces on a physical board. The physical form of chess facilitates and systematizes play. For most players, it *enables* play.

So, let's repeat. You *do* philosophy by *writing* philosophy.

For the student taking a philosophy course, this significantly ups the ante of writing and writing well. For writing is not only the skill needed to take a course exam or to simply prove to the instructor that you have assimilated the course material, it *is* the course "material"—the substance of the course, the be all and end all of the course—in the same way that sitting down and playing the piano is the raison d'etre of Piano 101.

As instrumental as writing is to philosophy, it is for philosophers only the first of two indispensable processes. The second is publishing what has been written. Writing your thoughts in a private journal or diary may be deemed a philosophical process, but it is not practicing philosophy. Sharing what you have written is essential to philosophy because philosophical discourse is not a monologue but a dialogue, a global exchange and interchange with the community of philosophers. In this, philosophy resembles modern science, which requires researchers to publish their hypotheses and experimental results so that they can be reviewed by others in the field, who can also set out to replicate results and thereby support or question or even refute the published results. While the work of philosophers is rarely supported by experiment, it still must be subject to critical discussion, suggested correction or elaboration, and even outright refutation.

Writing Is Central to Philosophy

For the great majority of us, writing is instrumental to thinking. Since it is reasonable to describe philosophy as the application of disciplined thought to a variety of topics, issues, and problems, it follows that writing is instrumental to philosophy. Therefore, we can also describe any philosophy course as a specialized course in writing.

For philosophy students, this truth has a downside and an upside. The downside is that most philosophy professors do not see themselves as writing teachers. That is a job for personnel in the English Department. Perhaps you have already taken a composition or "rhetoric" course in that department. Good. You have a leg up on your fellow philosophy students. If you have not had such instruction, however, you are not alone. This book will help.

As for the upside of a philosophy course being by default a writing course, if you can learn to write a persuasive philosophy paper, you have gained a skill that can be applied to any college course or, indeed, virtually any field of endeavor. The writing chops you develop in doing philosophy carry over to all manner of disciplined presentation and argument. The discipline acquired in studying philosophy is portable. You can apply it to anything to which you turn your mind. The same is true of the writing skills you develop in a philosophy class. They travel well because they do not belong to any one subject area. Master these skills of thought and expression—rational analysis and orderly argument—and they belong to you, to be applied wherever and whenever you need them.

What Philosophy Professors Want from Student Writers

Some 2,300 years ago, Aristotle introduced the syllogism into the intellectual world. A three-element formula, it is the elementary building block of syllogistic logic and deductive reasoning. The syllogism combines a general statement (called the major premise) and a specific statement (the minor premise) to reach a conclusion. Below is the classic pedagogical (instructional) example of a syllogism, which contains two premises and a conclusion; in practice, however, a syllogism may contain any number of premises:

Major premise: *All men are mortal.*
Minor premise: *Socrates is a man.*
Conclusion: *Socrates is mortal.*

In contrast to inductive reasoning, which looks out into the world and searches for probable evidence to create the premises that support a conclusion, deductive reasoning assumes the factual truth of the premises. So, you may believe that we are taking a bit of a risk in the formulation of the major premise of the syllogism that follows—

All philosophers are human.
My philosophy professor is a philosopher.
Therefore, my philosophy professor is human.

But we know the syllogism is valid, and we can draw on experience to evaluate the truth of its premises.

That brings us to one more syllogism:

Most literate humans prefer good writing to bad writing.
My philosophy professor is a literate human.
My philosophy professor likely prefers good writing to bad writing.

You can reasonably assume that what your philosophy professor wants to see in your writing is the same thing most literate human beings want to see: good writing. Since philosophers are radically different from most people in that the business of a philosopher is to ask questions about ordinary things, the very things the majority takes for granted, it should be reassuring that, when it comes to writing, your philosophy professor shares certain basic expectations, preferences, and standards with most other literate people, including you. In short, come to the philosophy class with the same intention you bring to your other classes, which is to produce good work, including good writing.

What Is Good Writing?

What is good music? What is good art? What is good writing? Such questions unleash many opinions. The branch of traditional philosophy called Aesthetics is devoted to answering such questions with thoughtful discipline. But let's apply the approach of a philosophical school or tradition that emerged in America late in the nineteenth century. It is called Pragmatism, and it endeavors to make philosophy more practical by setting aside the notion that thought serves to somehow represent or reflect reality. Instead, Pragmatism embraces both thought and words as instruments to be used for solving problems, making predictions, and determining courses of action.

What, then, is good writing?

From the perspective of Pragmatism, the answer goes something like this: *Good writing is an instrument for solving problems, making predictions, and determining courses of action.*

This prompts a question: What does this instrument called good writing look like?

Good writing is clear writing

Clarity requires fluency in the language in which you are writing. This means understanding and appreciating the vocabulary of the language in its range of meaning, connotation, and nuance. It means being practiced and skilled in the syntax of the language and in its grammar. We will discuss these and other basics shortly, but, expressed in a simple sentence: *Clarity requires literacy.*

Literacy is the table stakes of clarity. This means that literacy is *necessary* to achieving clarity in writing, but it is not *sufficient* to creating this result—much as knowing the rules of baseball is *necessary* but hardly *sufficient* to playing baseball, especially if your goal is to win the game.

Beyond competence and fluency in the language, clarity requires the writer to accomplish three things:

1. State the subject of the writing. In the case of an essay written for a philosophy class, the subject is often a question that is to be answered or a problem that is to be solved.
2. Supply the key content the subject demands. Again, for most philosophical writing, this means stating the answer to the question or the solution to the problem.
3. Supply the relevant data and analysis to support the key content. If you have answered a question or solved a problem, supply the data and the reasons that support your answer or your solution. As a rule, this constitutes the body, the major portion, of a clearly written paper.

Not all writing needs to be or even should be structured strictly in this way. But unless you have a good reason to depart from this basic blueprint, it is hard to go wrong if you accept this as the default structure of a clearly written paper. Structure implies disciplined thought, and disciplined thought is both a prerequisite for and evidence of clarity in expression. Even if you do depart from these three pillars, beginning with a paragraph that states what you intend to accomplish in the paper and ending with a paragraph that clearly states your conclusion and reviews your argument go a long way toward creating clarity of understanding.

Clarity creates satisfaction in a reader's mind, which greatly inclines that reader to judge the writing as "good." The opposite of clarity—which ranges from obscurity to chaos—creates dissatisfaction, which, naturally, will incline the reader to judge the work as "bad."

Good writing is no more complex than it needs to be

Good writing enlightens readers concerning its subject. Bad writing obscures its subject, leaving readers in darkness greater than what prevailed before they read the writing.

We don't always write about simple subjects. This is especially true in writing about many of the topics encountered in the study of philosophy. An essay that dumbs down its subject, simplifying it to the point of distortion, misstatement, and omission, is bad writing. But writing that creates its own obscurity by unnecessarily complicating already challenging material is likewise bad writing.

So, good writing is as simple as it can be without compromising any necessary complexity inherent in the subject. If you are asked to write a description of the philosophy of Jean-Paul Sartre, and you write a paper boiling down his philosophy to atheism, you are clearly oversimplifying the subject. While Sartre was a so-called existential atheist and his philosophy certainly included atheism, his version of existential thought encompassed far more.

As a virtue of good writing, simplicity consists of trying to identify and express the essence of concepts and putting the emphasis on these. It also requires focusing on discussion relevant to your subject, your argument, your solution to a problem, or your answer to a question while avoiding superfluous material, long detours, and irrelevant background information. Finally, simplicity is also achieved through careful writing:

- Find the right word and use it.
- Do not use two, three, or more words if there is one word that expresses your point completely.
- Use correct syntax and grammar. (We will have more to say on this shortly.)
- Complex sentences are often necessary to express complex, sophisticated, and nuanced thought, but avoid excessively complicated and overly long sentences. When a sentence grows substantially in length, even if it is grammatically and syntactically correct, consider breaking it into two or more sentences. How do you know a sentence is too long? Read it as if somebody else wrote it and you are reading it for the first time. Is it easy to follow? Do you have to reread it several times to understand it? If your answer to the first question is no and your answer to the second is yes, break the sentence up.
- Let nouns and verbs do your heavy lifting. Be stingy with adjectives and adverbs.
- Wherever possible, use the active voice.

This last piece of advice merits some discussion.

Writing a sentence in the "active voice" puts the subject at the beginning of the sentence and makes clear that the subject performs the action the verb expresses. "Kant wrote *Critique of Pure Reason*" is a sentence in the active voice. The subject, Kant, performed the action of writing the object, *Critique of Pure Reason.* It is also possible to write the sentence in the passive voice, a sentence construction that makes the object the subject of the sentence: "*Critique of Pure Reason* was written by Kant." Both sentences are grammatically and syntactically correct, but the active voice is usually preferable because it is simpler (and therefore easier to understand) and almost always more natural. The doer of the action is given logical precedence over the object of the action: subject (doer), verb (what is done), object (that to which something is done). This order is both simpler and more lifelike. In a word, it is *active.* Moreover, it usually puts the emphasis on a person, and human readers are naturally more interested in human beings than in things.

To use the passive voice is not to commit a grammatical error, but its use can make it difficult for the reader to determine who is taking the action of the verb. Additionally, the passive voice usually requires more words. In the two Kant examples, for instance, the active voice requires six words; the passive voice version requires eight. Moreover, the construction of a sentence in the passive voice is more complicated and can be awkward.

To complexity and awkwardness, we can add two more sins of the passive voice.

The passive voice sometimes suppresses useful information. Compare "I wrote a recent study of Kant's *Critique of Pure Reason*" with "A study of Kant's *Critique of Pure Reason* was recently written." Who wrote it? We don't know. If we add the information and retain the passive voice, it comes out like this: "A study of Kant's *Critique of Pure Reason* was recently written by me." The grammar is fine, but the sentence sounds as if it had been written by a visitor from another planet.

But the worst offense of all is that the passive voice makes for boring writing. It takes the spotlight off the person—the actor, the doer—and puts it on the object. In the case of the Kant example, the object is a book, but could just as easily be a block of wood. Neither is more interesting than a person.

No wonder, then, that teachers have been trying to pound the passive voice out of their students for a long time. And yet even the passive voice, pompous and dreary as it can be, has its proper uses. Sometimes a writer purposefully wants to reduce the emphasis or importance of the subject in the sentence. For instance, the professor may prefer to post the warning that follows in the passive voice rather than the active voice to put the emphasis on the object ("Students failing to complete ...") instead of on the subject (the professor, "I"). In fact, by using the passive voice, the professor removes himself or herself from the sentence entirely:

Passive voice: "Students failing to complete their 1000-word Kant assignment on time will be required to write 2000 words on Sartre next week."

Active voice: "I will require students who fail to complete their 1000-word Kant assignment on time to write 2000 words on Sartre next week."

The point of this warning is not that the *professor* has the power to penalize students (implied by the active voice), but that the *students* have responsibility to do their assigned homework (conveyed by the passive voice).

Good writing is economical

Related to simplicity is economy of expression. Strive to make every word count. Fight the temptation to string together two or three or more synonyms or near-synonyms. In a first draft, it is usually a good idea to let the words flow as they will. But when you return to the essay to create a second draft, cut away the excess. "He struggled to overcome his fear, his trepidation, his dread, his terror, his anxiety" should become in a second draft, "He struggled to overcome his fear" unless your point is that this man was more than simply afraid, in which case you may decide to settle on "He struggled to overcome his terror."

On Thursday, November 19, 1863, Edward Everett, now largely forgotten but famed at the time as America's foremost orator, delivered a two-hour, 13,607-word speech called "The Battles of Gettysburg." It was the featured speech accompanying the dedication of the new military cemetery on the site of the momentous Civil War battle. After Everett concluded, Abraham Lincoln delivered his own untitled Gettysburg Address, which, at 271 words, clocked in at just under two minutes. Which speech is remembered today?

"Standing beneath this serene sky, overlooking these broad fields now reposing from the labors of the waning year, the mighty Alleghenies dimly towering before us, the graves of our brethren beneath our feet, it is with hesitation that I raise my poor voice to break the eloquent silence of God and Nature" runs Everett's first sentence.[8] You may be among the many of us able to recite Lincoln's first sentence from memory: "Four score and seven years ago our fathers brought forth on this continent, a new nation, conceived in Liberty, and dedicated to the proposition that all men are created equal." The point of Everett's first 52 words? He is afraid he might not be eloquent enough for the commemorative job assigned to him. The point of Lincoln's 19 words? Nothing less than what the United States—the Union—stands for. Both Everett and Lincoln speak the language of eminently literate men, but by comparison with what Lincoln accomplished in 19 words, Everett comes off as having squandered his 52. (And his audience could look forward to sitting through 13,555 more!)

Economy of expression does not skimp. It does not neglect writing about what is worth writing about. But it avoids what professional writers and editors call "overwriting." Symptoms of overwriting include:

- *Padding.* Some writers (especially those who are paid by the word) pad their work with extra words that deliver nothing meaningful. For instance, we often encounter the phrase *close proximity.* It sounds right because it's so familiar. The problem is that *proximity* means closeness. No matter how eager you were to pad your essay, you wouldn't write "close closeness." Yet that is precisely what *close proximity* means. Consider:

  actual experience = experience
  advance planning = planning
  armed gunman = gunman
  twelve midnight = midnight
  twelve noon = noon
  autobiography of my life = autobiography
  basic fundamentals = fundamentals (or basics)
  cease and desist = cease
  cold temperature = cold
  consensus of opinion = consensus
  each and every = each
  empty space = space
  end result = result
  estimated roughly at = estimated at
  filled to capacity = filled
  free gift = gift
  frozen ice = ice
  general public = public
  join together = join
  natural instinct = instinct
  null and void = void

pair of twins = twins
past experience = experience
prerecorded = recorded
regular routine = routine
tiny speck = speck
suddenly exploded = exploded
surrounded on all sides = surrounded
unexpected surprise = surprise

Finding padding in an essay is like encountering oatmeal in a hamburger. You paid for meat, and, finding yourself eating oatmeal, you feel cheated. Such is the reader's feeling. Discerning readers—and this includes professors of philosophy—see in padded writing a deficiency of disciplined thought, and they feel cheated.

- *Pretentiousness.* A specialized form of padding is the use of pretentious words in place of simpler, more direct words. A common example is the use of *utilize* in place of *use.* This is not incorrect, but it is pompous and officious. Who wants to spend valuable time reading the words of a pompous and officious writer? To come across as honest and earnest, use words that sound honest and earnest. Consider the following pretentious words and their honest and earnest equivalents:

ascertain = find out
optimal = best
commence = begin
purchase = buy
deceased = dead
reside = live
endeavor = try
terminate = end
finalize = finish, or complete
ergo = therefore
plethora = too much

Foreign words and phrases are often pretentious and best avoided when a perfectly good English equivalent is available. For instance:

oeuvre = body of (artistic, literary, philosophical) work
corpus = body of (artistic, literary, philosophical) work
coiffure = hairdo
haute couture = high fashion
milieu = environment or setting
sans = without
faux pas = blunder
soi-disant = self-proclaimed, self-styled, or so-called

What Is Good *Philosophical* Writing?

Writing effectively for a philosophy course does not merely start with the general principles of good writing just outlined, it sets out to show mastery of these principles. It embodies them thoroughly, especially with respect to achieving—

- Clarity
- Simplicity without distortion by oversimplification
- Economy of expression or, to put it negatively, the absence of padding

The writing assignments you will be given in philosophy class are of course varied, but they almost always fall into two broad categories:

1. Expository assignments
2. Argumentative assignments

Expository writing describes and explains. "Concisely characterize the philosophy of Jean-Paul Sartre" is an example of an expository assignment. Argumentative writing, as the adjective implies, does not merely describe but argues for a position, interpretation, or conclusion. "Support or refute Sartre's assertion that the existence of a person precedes their essence."

We need to note that argumentative writing always requires some exposition, and expository writing typically calls for some argument. So, the two categories are not pure. Moreover, as members of the Department of Philosophy at Oregon State University observe in their excellent *Writing Philosophy Papers: A Student Guide,* "Philosophy is a problem-solving enterprise."[9] This being the case, most philosophical writing requires elements of sound argumentation. Following the Oregon State philosophers, we can add to the principles of good philosophical writing eight philosophy-focused skills:

1. The ability to identify a philosophical problem
2. The ability to organize ideas effectively
3. The ability to define concepts clearly
4. The ability to analyze arguments clearly and effectively
5. The ability to compare and contrast clearly and effectively
6. The ability to give relevant examples
7. The ability to convincingly apply theory to practice
8. The ability to test hypotheses

Grading Criteria for Philosophy Essays

The eight skills just listed are so central to philosophical writing that we may count them among the criteria most instructors use in grading essay assignments. Keep these eight skills in mind as you read the rest of this book, and we will dig into each more deeply in just a moment. But first, let us review the more general criteria that guides instructors in evaluating your written work.

Understand the assignment[10]

Some students regard the classroom instructor as their boss. I won't debate the merits of this analogy, but I do suggest that, where assigned work is concerned, the better comparison is to a customer or client. Given an assignment, your first task is to understand what your customer wants, so that you can deliver it and create customer satisfaction.

Sometimes, a professor will explain assignments orally. Sometimes these instructions will be delivered when the assignment is made. Sometimes they will be given as part of general introductory remarks at the start of the semester. Sometimes instruction will be a combination of both general and specific remarks. In other cases, the professor will create written instructions.

In whatever form the assignment is given, understand all instructions and guidelines. If you were absent on the day that the assignment was discussed, visit the professor after class or during office hours. You might also ask a classmate for his or her notes. Read your own notes. Read any handouts or online messages. Be certain you understand what is being asked for. If you have questions, ask them—and do so as early in the process as possible. Do not hesitate to ask for an explanation or clarification of anything you do not understand. Asking questions is at the heart of philosophy. Your instructor knows this and appreciates it.

Understand the criteria for evaluation of the assignment[11]

Your instructor may deliver, orally or in writing, specific or general criteria by which your work will be evaluated. Take the requirements seriously. If the criteria are not clear to you, ask questions. If you are uncertain of the scope of the assignment—what you should/may include or consider and what you should/may exclude—ask questions about this.

Beyond any specific criteria your professor may stipulate, you can generally count on being judged by the following:

- *Originality (and absence of plagiarism).* Nothing will kill your grade—and your reputation with it—faster than plagiarism. If you borrow, steal, rip off another author's words or ideas without attributing their source and/or with the purpose of passing them off as your own, you are committing plagiarism. This has nothing to do with copyright infringement, which is a violation of federal civil law. If you try to pass off the words of John Locke (1632-1704) as your own, you won't be sued for copyright infringement, because his works are in the public domain, but you will still be guilty of plagiarism, an offense against ethics, which is not tolerated in academia. Giving credit where credit is due by citing anything you borrow from another writer will save you from an accusation of plagiarism, but it may not save you from a disappointing grade. Unless your assignment asks you to collect writings on a certain philosophical issue or subject and present quotations from them, your professor expects a significant degree of originality from you, not just a collection of quotations.

- *Clarity.* Review what has already been said about clarity and follow the advice given. Failing to create clarity will sabotage even the most brilliant writing. Imagine your favorite movie. What kind of review would you give it if the only version available was dark and blurry?

- *Structure (organization).* We have already touched on structure and will have more to say about it as we explore specific approaches and subjects. The basics are simple. Devote your opening paragraph to an announcement of the tasks or objectives you are undertaking in the essay and then provide an overview or preview of the principal parts of the paper. Sometimes the nature of the assignment will dictate a specific type of organization. Sometimes the professor will even specify the basic parts of the paper. In these cases, follow instructions. Deliver what your "customer" orders.

- *Language and tone.* Correct grammar, syntax, and even spelling count. Literacy is a baseline requirement of any assignment. We will have more to say about this shortly but know that you can intercept a great many errors on rereading your paper for a second draft. Never plan on turning in your first draft. Some of the most creative steps in writing take place in a second or third draft. Leave plenty of time between your first and second draft—at least overnight and preferably a full twenty-four hours. In reviewing your own work, look for more than grammatical and other errors. Rewrite anything that is obscure—that makes *you* read it over again. Transform passive voice into active voice where you can and break up unusually long or complicated sentences into smaller units. Check your vocabulary. If a word does not seem quite right, find another. Achieve precision.

  Let's add a word on tone. "Tone" describes how a written work conveys the writer's attitude. Word choice can convey seriousness or flippancy. It can convey sarcasm or sincerity. Word choice may create a tone appropriate or inappropriate to the subject. If you are writing on a serious issue in ethics, for instance, you want to ensure that your choice of words reinforces rather than undercuts your argument. If you are writing on a complex issue of aesthetics or epistemology, you should use vocabulary appropriate the subject, including technical terms that have specific meaning in these areas of philosophy. Where special terminology is essential to the discussion, you will be evaluated in part on how you use these terms. It is up to you to acquire the understanding required to establish a knowledgeable tone.

  Tone is also important when you are making an argument for one point of view or another in the case of a controversial subject. You can express a strong point of view, but it is always counterproductive to use language that conveys a closed mind.

- *Topic or thesis.* Often, the choice of topic will be left to you. Even when a subject area or topic is specified, it may well be up to you to fashion a thesis or a hypothesis concerning it. Your choice of topic or thesis is one of the first features of your essay the reader will evaluate.

A topic has a Goldilocks zone. It should be neither too narrow nor too broad, but just right. If it is too broad, it will be impossible to cover adequately in the space of a typical essay exam, paper, or even term paper. If it is too narrow, the subject is likely to be too limited or too trivial to be worth writing about. Similarly, if you are formulating a thesis, hypothesis, or argument, it should not be so general or non-contentious that agreement will be virtually universal. ("Child molestation is immoral.") On the other hand, if you take a point of view that is bizarre, outlandish, or far-fetched, it will be virtually impossible to make a viable or even plausible argument in its defense. ("Sometimes, child molestation is justifiable.") Philosophy professors have little interest in affirmation of the bland and the easy, but neither are they typically impressed by an attempt to shock.

- *Argument and consistency.* Because argument is so central to most philosophical writing, we will have a good deal more to say about it. For now, understand that your instructor is looking for a strong argument, which means an argument supported by evidence and reasoning that any intelligent and unbiased (open-minded) reader would find compelling. Moreover, your argument should be clearly and effectively organized, exhibiting an understanding of both inductive and deductive reasoning. It should also exhibit consistency, with terms defined and then used in accordance with the definition and without shifts in the definition (equivocation). No statement or conclusion should conflict with another. If an apparent conflict emerges in your discourse, it must be explained and resolved. It cannot be left standing.

- *Argumentative balance and accuracy.* An argument for one point of view cannot simply ignore other points of view. If, for instance, you present and advocate for an ethical argument against abortion, you must also present relevant ethical arguments in favor of abortion and persuasively argue how and why they are flawed. As you cannot simply ignore the alternatives to your point of view, you must not misrepresent or distort them but must take care to present them accurately. A common flaw in arguing against a position is to create a so-called **strawman** to represent the opposing position and then knock that down. For instance, some who support stringent voter ID laws defend them by arguing that they are needed to combat "rampant" voter fraud. Statistics, however, do not support the contention that voter fraud is rampant. In fact, by the numbers, it is quite rare. The voter fraud argument in favor of voter ID laws is therefore a strawman.

- *Research.* In many introductory philosophy courses, writing assignments do not call for research. In fact, one prominent philosophy professor advises students that they are "unlikely" to find most library research helpful in writing a paper for an introductory philosophy course. "Professional philosophers usually write for one another, not for the general public, and what they write for one another is often technical and obscure for the beginner."[12] There is some truth to this, but research is not limited to reading the work of professional philosophers. For instance, if you are asked to argue for or against abortion rights, you will probably want to find legal opinions and decisions, medical opinions, ethical opinions, statistics, and so on to support your argument. Your research should be relevant and never one-sided, and it should come from informed, unbiased, and credible sources. Philosophy professors are accustomed to evaluating the quality of data sources, and they will evaluate those you use.

- *Housekeeping.* How you present your paper communicates how seriously you take your work. It should be thoughtfully formatted, and if your instructor prescribes certain formatting rules, follow them. If you believe that your approach cannot follow the prescribed format, discuss the matter with your professor before proceeding. Follow any instructions you are given concerning citation of sources and footnoting. Professional philosophers often use documentation (citation and footnoting) styles prescribed by the Modern Language Association (MLA), the American Psychological Association (APA), or the *Chicago Manual of Style* (CMS). If your instructor does not specify one of these models to follow, ask. CMS is often the default choice.[13]

6

Philosophical Writing

Basics of Good Philosophical Writing: A Deeper Dive

Having surveyed the elements of good writing from 30,000 feet, let's swoop in on some of the most important specifics. This means starting not with writing but with reading.[14]

Practice Reading Effectively and Deeply

Good writers are invariably good readers. They read thoughtfully and analytically rather than hoping to absorb the material by a sort of passive osmosis. Analytical reading is essential not just to reading philosophical works but any material you intend to use as research or background for your own writing.

When you enroll in a biology class, an economics class, a political science class, you recognize and accept that you are going to have to learn many new concepts and analytical approaches as well as the specialized vocabulary that goes with them. The same is true of philosophy. It has a range of specialized vocabularies, which might seem off-putting at first, but, as with the vocabularies in other disciplines, these have evolved to suit the field more effectively and efficiently than the language available in general usage. Learning and using the appropriate intellectual and technical terms will make the study of philosophy both easier and more rewarding.

Analytical reading demands that you acquire the necessary vocabulary. As you read, look up any terms you *know* you don't know or you even *suspect* you don't know. Looking things up requires an active approach rather than the passive attitude of the couch-potato reader.

Looking things up is necessary to analytical reading, but you must do even more.

Read with a pencil in hand. If you are working with a printed book—and you own it!—mark it up. Underline key passages, but don't assume that underlining and making checkmarks in the margin constitutes analytical reading. Use your pencil to engage in a dialogue with the author. Jot down any ideas that the reading inspires. Challenge the author. Like a good philosopher, question everything. If, by the way, you are reading an e-book or reading online, use any highlighting and comment features your computer, tablet, Kindle, or other e-reader may offer, or keep your notes separately, either handwritten or in a digital notebook that you leave open next to the e-text you are reading.

Analytical reading typically begins by identifying the author's slant, angle, or point-of-view. Put more aggressively, you are looking for the writer's bias or biases. These don't necessarily invalidate the author's thesis, analysis, or opinions, but your understanding of point-of-view should influence *your* interpretation of these things.

Read interactively. As I have suggested, take notes. Question. Dispute. Jot down any thoughts that occur to you as you read. You will find it especially helpful to *clarify* the author's discussion by putting important points in your own words. Doing this will also aid understanding and memory. Respond in real time to what you read.

Be patient

Much of the media we take in these days assumes a very brief attention span. On television, in film, and online, pacing is important. Ideas come fast, and subjects change even faster. Reading—especially reading *in* the field of philosophy or *for* a philosophical paper—demands patience and a slower pace.

Plan your time and give yourself plenty of it. The all-nighter approach to assignments that have been put off day after day is rarely successful when the material demands close attention. If you wait until the day before the due date, you will be driven by panic, which will cause you to overlook or even misinterpret important material. Find some peace, quiet, and time.

You don't have to start digging right away. Survey the material first. Some instructors call this "pre-reading." It is probably more useful to think of it as surveying or skimming. Examine chapter titles and subheads. If there is an abstract or "executive summary" at the beginning of the work you are reading, read it. If there are charts, graphs, and other illustrations, study them. Get a picture of the intellectual landscape into which you are about to venture. For one thing, if you are doing preliminary research for paper, this surveying approach will allow you to narrow your reading. Skimming a prospective source may be sufficient to let you know whether it is valuable for your purposes. This will allow you to manage your time more effectively. On the other hand, skimming makes it possible to survey more works than fewer, so that there is less of a chance of missing a valuable resource.

The one thing you should not skim, even in a preliminary survey, are the opening paragraphs or page. This is where good authors tell you what they are about, what they hope to accomplish in their work. By understanding the writer's objectives, you will be able to follow the text more fluently.

Take notes

Your note taking should begin in the survey phase. Jot down first impressions. Make a quick assessment of the work's potential usefulness to you for the subject you are contemplating writing about. Effective note-taking tactics include:

1. *Making the author's thinking your own.* Restate the author's big ideas to make them easier for you to evaluate.
2. *Thinking of the notes as a dialogue with the writer—and with yourself, through time.* When you review a source prior to incorporating it into your own writing, you will find it helpful to have a record of your first impressions.
3. *Rephrasing and restating key points does not mean merely copying them.* By engaging with the author's language through your own language, you make the author's thoughts your own. They become more malleable and more meaningful, which is a big help when you sit down to write.

Steal from the best

Even the most inventive and original writers readily admit to being intellectual thieves. The do not plagiarize, but they do seize, borrow, and emulate what they most admire in other writers. As you read, look for what you can steal—especially with respect to structure, use of analogy and metaphor, and mastery of research and facts. Don't just reduce the author's work to a dull summary or lifeless outline. Acquire the tools of effective expression and presentation. Just as watching a skilled carpenter wield a saw will help you to become a better woodworker, appreciating the architecture of an essay will enable you to become a more persuasive writer. Unlike the chemist who may jealously guard a cache of secret formulas, the writer's tricks of the trade are on public display, waiting to be appropriated by anyone with the wit to appreciate them.

Be or Become Fully Literate

In the interest of good manners, fair warning: some material in this section will offend some readers, who may feel that they are being talked down to. Others may well feel they are being talked down to but will be secretly grateful for it. The point is that most of us can use a refresher in the rules of basic English. A lot of us chronically or habitually make a handful of grammatical and usage errors. Why not choose to fix these now?

If this section persuades you that you could use more help, we suggest Strunk and White, *The Elements of Style.*[15] It has been the classic *brief* (weighs in at a mere 105 pages) handbook of essential English usage since its first publication in 1920—and it has been repeatedly revised and updated to keep up with the times.

Use correct grammar and syntax

"Grammar" refers to the *entire* structure and system of a language. "Syntax" is the subset of grammar that concerns *sentence* structure. For practical purposes, however, grammar and syntax can be discussed together and constitute the most basic rules of English. The discussion that follows puts the emphasis on common errors and how to avoid them.

Sentence Structure

The basic units of a simple sentence are the subject (dominated by a noun or nouns) and the predicate (dominated by a verb or verbs and an object—a noun or nouns on which the subject acts). A sentence that lacks either a subject or a predicate is a sentence fragment. The only exceptions are imperative sentences, such as "Run!"

The subject is the person, organism, thing, place, entity, or idea that is being described in the sentence or that is preforming the action described in the sentence.

The predicate expresses action and includes a verb (the action word) and generally says something more about the subject or is directly acted upon by the subject.

The basic structure is **subject + predicate**, and the predicate can be subdivided into **verb + direct object**. In the sentence "I lost a red wallet," *I* is the subject, and the rest of the sentence is the predicate, consisting of the verb *lost* and the direct object *a red wallet.* The direct object, in this case, consists of three parts of speech, an article (*a*), and adjective (*red*), and a noun (*wallet*).

Structurally, every complete sentence has a subject and verb, or predicate (except imperative sentences, in which the subject is implied but not present). The number of the subject and verb must agree. The sentence *"Joe and I are good friends."* illustrates correct number agreement. "Joe and I" is a compound or plural subject, so the plural verb "are" is required. *"We are good friends."* is a plural subject but not a compound one. *"I am a philosopher."* has a singular subject, so takes a singular verb ("am"). But even though *"Neither Joe nor I is a philosopher."* has a compound subject, it does not have a plural subject. "Neither/nor," like "either/or," makes the subject singular. The verb must agree with each singular noun. Contrast *"Both Joe and I are philosophers."* The "and" creates a plural subject, with which the verb (and the entire predicate) must agree. What if you have a compound subject like this: *"Neither I nor they"*? The common usage rule is that the noun closest to the verb determines the number of the verb: *"Neither I nor they are philosophers."* But: *"Neither they nor I am a philosopher."*

As subjects and verbs must agree in number, so must pronouns and antecedents (the word or phrase to which the pronoun refers). This presents two problems, one traditional and one rather new.

Everyone should bring their own lunch. By the rules of traditional grammar, this sentence is incorrect because *everyone* is a singular—not a plural—pronoun, so the pronoun in the predicate should be *his, hers,* or *his or hers*, or *hers or his.*

More recently, people have become increasingly aware of the gender bias toward males that is ingrained in the English language. The plural third-person pronouns *they* and *we* are and have always been gender-neutral, but the singular third-person pronouns (*he*, *she*, and *it,* along with their possessive forms, *his, hers,* and *its*) are gender-specific: male, female, neuter (not "neutral," but sexless).

A note on gender-neutral language. How do we accommodate traditional English grammar without reinforcing male gender bias? As a philosophy student, perhaps you will question whether this is an important issue. We will not offer an opinion except to point out that the staff and students in most colleges and universities are sensitive to gender issues, and you can expect that the instructors who evaluate your work will likely be. Indeed, some instructors may articulate a policy on this issue. If so, you are best served by following it.

Let us assume that you want to avoid even the appearance of gender bias in your writing. One increasingly popular solution is to violate traditional grammar rules by simply substituting the gender-neutral plural pronouns (they, them, theirs) for the gender-specific singular pronouns. This is a simple solution that is gaining some traction, but many readers are likely to be put off by a sentence such as this: *"A doctor should use their best judgment."* So, here are other alternatives for addressing gender bias in pronouns, adapted from recommendations in *The Chicago Manual of Style,* which is widely accepted by academic philosophers:

1. *Just don't use the pronoun.* Change "the philosopher should revise the study when new information is made available to him" to "the philosopher should revise the study when new information is made available."
2. *Repeat the noun.* Change "a philosopher should avoid gender bias because it will damage her reputation for objectivity" to "a philosopher should avoid gender bias because it will damage a philosopher's reputation for objectivity."
3. *Substitute a plural antecedent.* Change "a philosopher must conduct himself with professional decorum" to "philosophers must conduct themselves with professional decorum."
4. *Substitute an article for the personal pronoun.* Change "a philosopher accused of plagiarism should not renounce her right to present exonerating evidence" to "a philosopher accused of plagiarism should not renounce the right to present exonerating evidence."
5. *Substitute the singular pronoun "one."* Change "a philosopher in Paris can expect to be more respected than he would be in Pine Bluff" to "a philosopher in Paris can expect to be more respected than one in Pine Bluff."
6. *Substitute the relative pronoun "who."* Change "philosophy professors expect that if a student writes well, she will be successful in philosophy class" to "philosophy professors expect that a student who writes well will be successful in philosophy class."
7. *Write an imperative sentence.* Change "a philosopher must write clearly if he expects to be understood" to "write clearly to be understood."

8. *Rewrite the clause.* Change "a philosopher who claims to have read Plato in the original Greek will be considered highly learned until he is exposed as a liar" to "a philosopher who claims to have read Plato in the original Greek will be considered highly learned until the fraud is revealed."
9. *Use the inclusive phrase "he or she."* Change "if a philosopher wants to get rich, he should become a plumber" to "if a philosopher wants to get rich, he or she should become a plumber." (Unfortunately, this common alternative is wordy and awkward.)

The Role of Punctuation in Sentence Structure

Perhaps the most practical way to achieve correct and effective sentence structure is through understanding the proper use of punctuation.

Sentences begin with a capital letter and end with a period (declarative sentence), a question mark (an interrogatory sentence), or an exclamation point (an exclamatory sentence). The use of the first two pieces of punctuation is obvious—the period punctuates a statement, the question mark a question—but the exclamation point requires more finesse. Indeed, in *most* academic writing, the exclamation point has no place or, at most, must be used sparingly. Like typing texts or tweets in all caps, the exclamation point makes the sentence the equivalent of shouting. The exclamation point does have an important role in punctuating interjections—those emotional outbursts that do not require a full sentence to express their content: *Wow! Holy cow! Amazing! Astounding!* These, too, are rarely used in serious academic writing.

Generally, the period, question mark, and exclamation point (except when used with an interjection) come at the end of a complete sentence and thus usually indicate the completion of a thought or an action.

Sentences often include commas. By the numbers, the comma is the most commonly used punctuation mark, and yet it is also the most commonly misused.

Many writers make the mistake of using a comma where a period should go: "Kant is one of the most important figures in modern philosophy, he brought together the rational and empiricist traditions." This error in structure is called a comma splice and results when a comma is the only thing used to join two complete sentences. "Kant is one of the most important figures in modern philosophy" is one complete sentence and should be ended with a period. "He brought together the rational and empiricist traditions" is another complete sentence, which should begin with a capital H and end with a period.

The problem with a comma splice is not the presence of the comma but the misguided attempt to use it in place of a period.

Consider: "Kant is one of the most important figures in modern philosophy, and he brought together the rational and empiricist traditions." This is not a comma splice because the conjunction *and* following the comma makes the rest of the sentence an independent clause. It has a subject and a verb, which means that it would be a sentence if it were not preceded by the conjunction.

Consider: "Kant is one of the most important figures in modern philosophy because he brought together the rational and empiricist traditions." The use of *because*, which is often classified as a subordinating conjunction, forms the beginning of a dependent clause, a clause that cannot stand on its own as a sentence but relates to (in this case, elaborates upon) the first part of the sentence, which could stand alone as a complete sentence but is made more richly meaningful by the addition of the dependent clause.

Both sentences are grammatically correct, but most critical readers (such as philosophy professors) would find the second sentence significantly better than the first. The conjunction *and* does not subordinate anything. It merely joins two things. As such, it performs a simple act of addition: *this thought* and *that thought*. The subordinating conjunction *because* does more than simply add. It explains. The product of analytical thought, it shows the relationship between the two parts of the sentence, which, together, explain why Kant is so important. We could justly venture to say that the second sentence delivers greater value than the first. The first is merely expository. It lays out two facts. The second is analytic or even argumentative. It offers a reason for Kant's importance.

Consider: "Kant is one of the most important figures in modern philosophy; he brought together the rational and empiricist traditions." If the comma is the most common of punctuation marks, the semicolon is comparatively little used and not always correctly understood. As it is used here—correctly, by the way—it both joins and separates two independent clauses, which can stand on their own as sentences. The semicolon is used in place of a period when you want to imply a close relationship between two independent clauses. A better example might be this: "The Danish philosopher Kierkegaard was plagued lifelong by self-doubt and regret; yielding to second thoughts, he had broken off his engagement to Regine Olsen, with whom he was deeply in love." Here, the writer feels that the two independent clauses stand on their own but are too closely related to be expressed as two entirely separate sentences. Would the writer have been better served by using the subordinating conjunction *because*? "The Danish philosopher Kierkegaard was plagued lifelong by self-doubt and regret because, yielding to second thoughts, he had broken off his engagement to Regine Olsen, with whom he was deeply in love." Maybe. But maybe not. The use of *because* reveals analytical thought, but it also says something that the writer may not intend, namely that Kierkegaard's self-doubt and regret were directly and exclusively caused by his decision to break off his engagement with Regine Olsen. While we know that the decision to break the engagement haunted Kierkegaard—his journals and letters tell us this—it is not possible to attribute his chronic self-doubt and regret exclusively to this decision, fateful as it seems to have been. In fact, it is likely that his habit of self-doubt motivated the breakup, not the other way around. This being the case, the use of the semicolon juxtaposes two facts, implying a connection but ultimately leaving it to readers to draw their own conclusions.

The semicolon serves another purpose in the structure of some sentences. To get to it, we must return briefly to the comma.

Commas are used to punctuate items in a series within a sentence: "The three earliest books of William James are *The Principles of Psychology, Psychology (Briefer Course),* and *Is Life Worth Living?*"

There are two schools of thought about whether to include a comma before the *and*. Some authorities think this so-called "Oxford comma" or "series comma" is superfluous, but most writers use it because it avoids certain misunderstandings, as the Grammarly blog points out[16]:

> Without the series comma—"I love my parents, Lady Gaga and Humpty Dumpty."
>
> With the series comma—"I love my parents, Lady Gaga, and Humpty Dumpty."

Sometimes, series do get complicated. In these situations, the semicolon comes to the rescue: "I have lived in Chicago, New York, and Atlanta" is perfectly clear. But consider this: "I have lived in Chicago, Illinois, New York, New York, and Atlanta, Georgia." When such internal commas create confusion, use semicolons to separate the units: "I have lived in Chicago, Illinois; New York, New York; and Atlanta, Georgia."

Semicolons versus colons. The name *semicolon* might lead you to think of this punctuation as a sort of weak form of the colon. In fact, its function is more complex than that of the colon, and the two are decidedly not interchangeable.

A colon is used to introduce distinctive material either within a sentence or following one. "According to *ancienthistorylists.com,* the following are the top four ancient Greek philosophers: Thales of Miletus, Aristotle, Plato, and Socrates." The colon may be used as well to introduce a more formal list. "According to *ancienthistorylists.com,* the following are the top four ancient Greek philosophers:

1. Thales of Miletus
2. Aristotle
3. Plato
4. Socrates."

A colon can also be used to introduce a quotation. "Emerson took up his pen and wrote: 'To be great is to be misunderstood.'"

It can introduce a description or restatement. "After you finally begin a task, there is only one thing left to do: you must complete it."

The Comma as the Skeleton Key to Complex Sentence Structure

Commas are essential to building compound and complex sentences. A compound sentence is composed of two or more independent clauses. To be used correctly, the comma must come before a coordinating conjunction (such as *and, or, neither, nor*).

"The professor said he would hold extra office hours and work with any students who need help and then he hurriedly left the classroom." This is an example of an utterance aspiring to be a compound sentence but getting only as far as being a run-on sentence. All we need is a single comma in the right place: "The professor said he would hold extra office hours and work with any students who need help, and then he hurriedly left the classroom." Notice that the two independent clauses (one before, the other after the comma) could stand on their own as separate sentences.

"Philosophers neither make laws nor enforce them nor do they wield political power." This is another run-on sentence in need of a comma: "Philosophers neither make laws nor enforce them, nor do they wield political power." Some people might look at this sentence and conclude that the function of the comma is like a rest in a musical score. It indicates a pause.

There is an element of truth in this conclusion. If you read the sentence aloud, you will indeed tend to pause at the comma, as you should. However, the more important function of the comma here is grammatical. It separates the independent clauses, thereby preserving their independence.

Commas are essential to differentiating between restrictive and nonrestrictive clauses in a complex sentence.

> Consider: "The professor congratulated the student, who had passed the test."
> Compare: "The professor congratulated the student who had passed the test."

In the first sentence, the presence of the comma signals that what follows it is a non-restrictive clause. That is, the clause adds information about the student, but it does not restrict the meaning of the first part of the sentence. The takeaway from this sentence is simply "The professor congratulated the student," and the material after the comma just fills in some additional information. If we deleted the clause, the sentence would retain its most central and important meaning: "The professor congratulated the student." In the second sentence, the absence of the comma signals that what follows is a restrictive clause. That is, it restricts the meaning of the sentence to the condition the second clause states. The takeaway is *not* "The professor congratulated *the student*," but "The professor congratulated *the student who had passed the test.*"

The presence or absence of the comma, this modest speck of punctuation, speaks volumes about the professor's character. In the non-restrictive version, in which the comma separates the non-restrictive clause from the rest of the sentence, the professor appears as a jovial soul who takes pleasure in congratulating (presumably) all his students. In the restrictive version, without a comma, in which the final clause is integral to the meaning of the sentence, the professor appears far more selective in dispensing congratulations, reserving this cordial sentiment for those students diligent enough to pass the exam he administered to them.

It is on such details that meaning and logic in expression depend. In complex sentences, commas are vital to evaluating the very sense of the sentence.

> Consider: "Walking down the garden path, the butterfly was the object of contemplation." Upon the comma, the two clauses balance, but something went wrong. Are we supposed to imagine the butterfly

strolling down the garden path? Seems unlikely. And who is hanging around to do the contemplating?
Compare: "Walking down the garden path, the philosopher made the butterfly the object of contemplation."

The first sentence is an example of a common but destructive grammatical catastrophe called the misplaced modifier or dangling modifier. Grammatically, we expect that the phrase "Walking down the garden path" *modifies* (acts upon, refers to) the phrase that follows it. Hence our impression of a strolling butterfly. We need to make sure that the opening clause modifies what we intend it to modify. In this case, we need to supply the missing subject, the philosopher, who does the walking and who focuses contemplatively on the butterfly.

The first sentence is absurd, so it is relatively easy to see that something is very wrong. Unfortunately, not all instances of dangling modifiers are sufficiently odd to present so bright a red flag.

Consider: "To create a convincing logical argument, a great deal of effort went into the research."

This seems to make sense. But missing in action is the true subject of the sentence, the doer of the action.

Compare: "Philosophers make a great effort to research the data needed to create a convincing logical argument."

Commas are instrumental in executing a syntactical technique called parallelism or parallel structure. This is a powerful rhetorical tool, which infuses sentences with balance and a strong argumentative direction. The authors of *The Philosophy Student Writer's Manual and Reader's Guide* cite a familiar example of parallelism from no less than the Preamble to the Constitution of the United States:

We the People of the United States, in Order to **form a more perfect Union, establish Justice, insure domestic Tranquility, provide for the common defence, promote the general Welfare,** and **secure the Blessings of Liberty to ourselves and our Posterity**, do **ordain** and **establish** this Constitution for the United States of America.

Boldface marks the parallel structures in this sentence. The sentence contains two parallel sets. The first completes the infinitive phrase (a verb phrase beginning with *to*). The *to* in "to form" applies to all the verbs in the long phrase and thereby ties them together into a strong, powerfully balanced, rhetorically rhythmical series. The second parallel structure balances the verbs *ordain* and *establish*[17]

What does parallelism accomplish? The simple answer is that it lends eloquence to a statement. But, more importantly, it engages our natural craving for balance, pattern, and order. It promises relief from chaos and confusion, and it conveys a tone of authority, which helps to drive any argument to persuasive success. What is more, like balanced musical phrases—think Mozart—parallelism makes what you write more memorable and gives your words greater weight. Finally, those capable of creating parallel structure reveal themselves as accomplished writers who know what they want to say and how to say it. This makes a favorable impression on any reader, especially a philosopher who appreciates clear, confident argument.

If parallelism is a mark of good writing, faulty parallelism is not just indicative of bad writing, it tends to stick out like the proverbial sore thumb.

> *Consider:* "The cost of taking an unethical shortcut is greater than the labor necessary to do the right thing." The statement is not incorrect, but it falls flat.
> *Compare:* "The **cost of taking** an unethical shortcut is greater than the **cost of doing** the right thing." The two balanced phrases, each beginning with "the cost of" and each concluding with a gerund (a verb ending in *-ing* and used as a noun), give the sentence memorable rhetorical force. It makes the writing quotable.

Two Matters of Agreement

Parallelism is all about creating balance in a sentence. A quality related to balance is agreement. For instance, a sentence should not shift among first person ("I" and "we"), second person ("you"), and third person ("he," "she," "it," "one," and "they") or between singular and plural.

> *Consider:* "Most philosophers (third person plural) believe that if you (second person singular or plural) argue persuasively, they (third person plural) will make your point." The shift in person and number is confusing.

Compare: "Most philosophers (third person plural) believe that if they (third person plural) argue persuasively, they (third person plural) will make their point." Agreement preempts a possible cause of confusion.

Shifting number not only makes for an awkward sentence, it can also cause confusion in meaning.

Consider: "One is so confused (third person singular), they (third person plural) don't know left from right."
Compare: "One is so confused (third person singular), one (third person singular) doesn't know left from right."

Pronouns, words that take the place of nouns or other pronouns, must agree with their antecedent in both gender and number.

Consider: "Each of us must stand up for what they think is right." *Each* is singular. In this sentence, however, it is the antecedent of the plural pronoun *they*. This is an error in number agreement.
Compare: "Each of us must stand up for what he or she thinks is right." This is correct, but the "he or she" is one of those awkward efforts to avoid gender bias. So, try this instead: "We must all stand up for what we think is right."

Sometimes it is difficult to determine the antecedent of a pronoun. This creates a sentence so vague that its meaning may evaporate completely.

Consider: "We rather loudly tried to persuade the professor to extend the deadline for turning in our papers. This became a sore point for the class." What is the antecedent of the pronoun *this*? Is it the loud attempt to persuade the professor? Or is it the matter of extending the deadline? The sentence does not make it clear.
Compare: "We rather loudly tried to persuade the professor to extend the deadline for turning in our papers. His refusal became a sore point for the class." When you have more than one candidate for the office of antecedent, don't use a pronoun (*this*), use the noun itself ("His *refusal*"). Sometimes there's just no good substitute for the real thing.

Use correct spelling

Since you are a good philosophy student, you may ask, "What's so important about spelling?" The short answer is that correct spelling is widely perceived as an element and indicator of basic literacy. Misspelling undercuts your intellectual authority. It makes it difficult for a reader to take you seriously. At the very least, misspelling conveys a careless attitude toward your work. Either way, spelling errors sabotage your success.

Fortunately, thanks to the spell check feature of all popular word processors, it has never been easier to correct misspelling. Use that feature. Additionally, if you are aware of words that often trip you up, look them up, and practice spelling them.

Let's not waste space here on a list of commonly misspelled words, but let's take time to go back to a pronoun that is often misspelled. Here is a blunt question: Do you know the difference between *its* and *it's*? If your answer is no, read on.

Its is the possessive form of the pronoun *it*. "I dropped my smartphone and shattered *its* screen." Of course, most English possessives use an apostrophe: "I dropped *Joe's* smartphone and shattered *its* screen. It ruined the poor *guy's* day." So, force of habit may prompt you to mistakenly use *it's* when you should use *its*. But *it's* is not even a pronoun. It is (it's) a contraction for *it is,* which is a pronoun followed by a verb.

Use appropriate tone or diction

"Diction" refers to the choice of words in your writing. For all practical purposes, it is closely related to the concept of "tone," which is the way writers choose their words to convey a distinctive *voice,* a sense of the kind of person who is "talking" to the reader through the words on the page (or on the screen).

We speak and write in multiple voices. To a friend to whom you want to convey your enthusiasm about philosophy, you might remark, "I think Kant is cool." To your philosophy professor, it would be something more like, "I am impressed by Kant's ambition in his project of synthesizing rationalism and empiricism without sacrificing the one to the other."

In everyday encounters, as with friends, the emphasis is often on how we feel. "I think Kant is cool" is an expression of how you feel about Kant. It is valid—for a brief, informal exchange. It is not suited, however, to an academic discussion. The diction and tone of an academic discussion—the kind of discussion you want to create in an essay for philosophy class—should embody the following:

- Absence of bias
- Clarity of argument
- Strong use of data and facts (evidence) to support the argument
- Respect for others; the word choice should be non-combative
- Emphasis on intellectual substance rather than emotion; compare "I think Kant is cool," an emotional statement with no intellectual content, with "I am impressed by Kant's ambition in his project of synthesizing rationalism and empiricism without sacrificing the one to the other," which justifies the emotion ("I am impressed") with substantive intellectual content.

The diction and tone of an academic paper should be formal in the sense of eschewing the clipped style of a text message, tweet, or slang. This does not mean that you should interpret the adjective "academic" as an implied call for dull, tedious, pedantic language and an ostentatious display of jargon. Use straightforward, literal language that is precise and that explains meaning rather than obscures it. "In light of recent academic commentary on Kant's intellectual journey ..." may be some people's idea of academic writing, but that does not make it good writing or, for that matter, good *academic* writing. This is far preferable: "Based on recent analysis of Kant's intellectual development ..." Getting more specific would be even better: "Based on Professor X's analysis of Kant's mature view of empiricism ..." Focus on substance rather than opinion. Use the fewest but most precise words possible.

Striking the right note in effective academic diction and tone is as much about what to avoid as it is about what to include. Avoid:

- Broad generalizations, such as *always* and *never*
- Hyped adjectives, such as *greatest, obvious, spectacular*
- Adverbs—wherever possible—such as *clearly, truly, really*
- Weasel-word qualifiers, such as *more or less, all things being equal, sort of*
- Emotional or inflammatory language, such as *breathtaking, heartbreaking, disgusting*

Use Structural Logic

Writing a philosophical paper typically has certain specialized requirements, which, be assured, we will discuss. But the structure of good philosophical writing is best built on a foundation of good general writing. So, let's enumerate the essentials of writing with sound logical structure.

1. ***Formulate a thesis.*** Inside or outside the philosophy classroom, good non-fiction writing usually begins with a strong, clear thesis statement. A thesis is nothing more than the idea or point of view you intend to explain or prove in your paper. It is not just your subject, but your interpretation of it, your unique angle on it.

2. ***Let your thesis be your guide.*** If your thesis is well-written, it will pack enough information to point you the right way toward organizing your paper. Suppose you are assigned to briefly explain Marxism. That is a big subject, but it will be made manageable by formulating a straightforward thesis statement:

   Marxism holds that societies come into being through class struggle. In capitalist societies, the struggle is a conflict between the ruling classes (the "bourgeoisie") and the working classes (the "proletariat"). The bourgeoisie control the means of production, while the proletariat sell their labor to the bourgeoisie, enabling that class to use the means of production for profit. Based on history, Marxism predicts that the internal social tensions created in a capitalist society will lead to its destruction and replacement by socialism.

3. ***Using the thesis, sketch an outline.*** It might look something like this:
   - Marxism holds that societies come into being through class struggle.
   - Define the struggle in capitalist societies
     Describe capitalism
     Define the two classes in capitalism
     Discuss the nature of the conflict between the two classes
   - How Marx used history to predict the self-destruction of capitalism
     Define "historical materialism"
     Summarize Marx's reasoning for why socialism will inevitably replace capitalism
   - End by describing the nature of a socialist revolution
     National allegiance replaced by allegiance to class: "Workers of the world, unite"
     The more numerous global class (proletariat) will necessarily prevail over the minority class (bourgeoisie)

4. For some writers—and depending on the length of the essay—a simple sketch like this will be all that is needed to guide writing the whole essay. Others may want to create a more elaborate and formal outline. The "outlining" feature of such popular word-processing programs as MS Word can facilitate such an outline. But unless your instructor requires a formal outline as part of the writing process, do not feel obliged to create one if you feel ready to write the essay.

Embody structural logic in every paragraph

Structuring a paper logically requires each of its building blocks, each paragraph, to be logically structured as well. Just as a single weak pillar can cause a building to collapse, a single poorly structured or less than coherent paragraph can undermine an entire essay. Each paragraph should contribute to developing your thesis or supporting your argument.

Unlike sentences, which are governed by grammatical and syntactical rules, paragraphs are intellectual/argumentative units rather than grammatical ones. Begin with a strong topic sentence, which tells your reader what to expect the paragraph to accomplish. Orienting your reader in this way makes your writing more effective because it makes it more logically coherent.

Think of the topic sentence as a mini thesis that states and controls the main idea of that paragraph. Fail to provide a strong topic sentence, and you risk casting your reader adrift. When you write a topic sentence, consider the following specifications:

1. The topic sentence should state a single key point in support of the thesis of your paper. Don't bite off more in the topic sentence than the paragraph can chew. If you find that your topic sentence points to two or three big ideas, construct the paragraph as an introduction to at least two or three additional paragraphs, which develop *each* idea one at a time. Don't cram too much into a single paragraph.
2. A topic sentence should support and advance your thesis. When you draft a topic sentence, ask yourself if it truly drives your paper forward.
3. Ensure that the topic sentence is relevant to the paper's thesis. As we discussed earlier, writing and thinking have a mutual or reciprocal relationship. Thought drives writing even as writing enables thought. If you find yourself writing a topic sentence that breaks

new ground not contemplated in your thesis, you have three choices. One is to modify the topic sentence to refocus it. Another is to skip the paragraph or cut it from your final draft. A third option is to reconsider your paper's thesis. There is nothing wrong with this. Remember, writing is not just the expression of ideas, it is also the discovery of ideas.

4. The topic sentence of paragraph #2 should relate not only to that paragraph, but also to paragraph #1. That is, paragraph #2 should develop from paragraph #1. If it fails to do so, you have probably omitted some necessary steps in your exposition or argument. Topic sentences for paragraphs in the body of your essay must often include useful transitional phrases, which serve the reader as directional signposts: *As we saw earlier; In contrast to; In consequence of; In some cases, we need to consider ...*
5. Each topic sentence should control its paragraph. Often, a paragraph that seems loose or rambling when you reread it is the result of a weak topic sentence. Start by rewriting that sentence, and then edit the paragraph it begins.
6. A topic sentence should be positioned at the start of the paragraph unless you have a good reason to put it elsewhere. Some subjects require filling in background or contextual information before presenting your thesis. If you are confronted with this situation, consider deploying the background information first and then placing your topic sentence somewhere in the middle of the paragraph. You may even find it most effective to put the topic sentence at the end of a paragraph if you feel that it is necessary to lay out your complete line of reasoning first.

Aim to achieve stylistic success

Creating a successful style—a style that enhances the clarity and persuasiveness of your writing—begins with the issues of tone and diction discussed earlier as well as the use of direct language, language that presents your ideas precisely, without superfluous words and without jargon. In direct language, every word contributes to your intended meaning, revealing rather than obscuring.

A good way of achieving direct language is to put your emphasis on nouns and verbs—words that express things and actions—rather than adjectives and adverbs, words that elaborate on things and actions. Use these sparingly. It is always better to show than to tell, to present things and actions through nouns and verbs rather than layer on a lot of adjectives and adverbs.

Skilled writers have long used analogy and metaphor to "show" ideas and concepts rather than merely "tell" them. When the Scots poet Robert Burns wanted to write about what love felt like to him, he did not write a long explanatory paragraph but declared, "O my Love is like a red, red rose / That's newly sprung in June." Or take Plato. He believed that "knowledge" gained exclusively through the senses was actually no more than subjective opinion and that true knowledge required philosophical reasoning. To get this point across, he included in his masterpiece, *The Republic* (VII, 514-517), the so-called Allegory of the Cave, an elaborate metaphor in which he pictures a group of prisoners who have lived chained to the wall of a cave since birth. They face a blank wall, on which they observe shadows projected from objects that pass to and fro before a fire burning behind them. Looking at these shadows, the prisoners give them names. For these shadows are their "reality," much as our version of reality—unassisted by philosophy—is built on the mere shadows our senses convey to us.

Use analogy and metaphor to help explain complex ideas but, in so doing, always favor directness and simplicity of expression over flights of flowery eloquence.

Be Aware of Your Audience

Finally, all good writers, whatever their subject or intention, write with a keen awareness of their readers. If you know that your best friend hates kale, you will make it your business not to feature kale in the dinner you prepare for her. Just as you make a meal to satisfy what you have reason to believe are the preferences of your dinner guest, so you should write on the basis of what you have reason to believe are the preferences of your reader. An essay on baseball written for an audience of baseball coaches will be markedly different from an essay on the same subject intended to be read by people seeking a general introduction to the game. In writing, one size does not fit all. The most successful writers aim to create the one size that fits *their* target readers.

7

Philosophical Writing: Process

Writing is work, and for many of us, writing is hard work. Writing philosophy adds to this labor an element of intimidation. Whether you are writing an expository—explanatory and descriptive—essay or an argumentative essay, writing for a philosophy class has a higher bar than writing in most other academic contexts. You are expected to be precise in word usage, economical in expression, and logical in structure. Since philosophers take nothing for granted, you can expect that your philosophy professor will be unlikely to overlook anything in your work. By the same token, most good instructors do not set out to penalize you for mistakes and missteps. They may not readily overlook them, and they will likely point them out. But they are also unlikely to overlook the positive aspects of your work, the instances of sound argument and precise expression and, especially, the appearance of original thought. So, while philosophical writing assignments may appear to be sown with landmines and boobytraps, they are also rich with opportunities to excel.

First: Just Get Started

In common usage, *inertia* refers to a tendency to do nothing and, even more commonly, the difficulty many of us feel to get a project under way. Writers often call this "writer's block." Because philosophical writing promises to be more demanding than general writing, it is quite possible that your inertia will be formidable. I have a few suggestions for overcoming it.

Overcoming Inertia (Writer's Block)

First, go to the physical source of the word *inertia,* Sir Isaac Newton's First Law of Motion. In summary, it states that an object either remains at rest *or continues to move at a constant velocity* unless acted upon by a force.

For a writer worried about writer's block, the metaphorical implication of this is twofold. First, the inertial state of rest is not permanent. It can be overcome by the action of a force—that is, a push. Second, "inertia" is *not* a synonym for motionlessness. If an object is in motion, inertia is the quality that keeps it in motion. For a writer, this means, once you get going, you tend to keep going.

What forces can "force" you to get into motion?

1. Finding a topic that interests or even excites you, a topic you *feel* like writing about
2. Finding an intellectually or morally important topic
3. A competitive need to do well on an essential class assignment
4. A dread of failing an essential class assignment

Whichever of these forces you feel (from one to all four), harness them. Let them get you off the dime and into the writing assignment.

Know where you are going to go

Another "force" that will help you move and remain in motion is ensuring that you thoroughly understand the assignment you have been given. If the instructor has given you written directions, follow them. If anything is unclear, ask questions. If instructions are given verbally, take thorough notes. Compare notes with a classmate or two. Again, ask questions about anything that is unclear.

Inventio

The ancient Romans worked hard to refine the art of persuasive expression (both oratorical and written) into the discipline called rhetoric. The first step in composition they termed *Inventio,* which combined the meanings of the modern English words *discovery* and *invention.* The great Roman orators recognized that good composition begins with a process that requires both discovering an appropriate topic and inventing approaches to it. That is, a "topic" is both a given subject and the ideas the writer brings to it and extracts from it.

For some assignments, research will constitute the ground on which you search out and discover a topic. For others, even when the instructor gives you a general topic or poses a specific question or problem, you will simply have to generate your own ideas.

Some writers sit and stare at a blank page or a white screen (on which the relentless cursor pulsates), waiting for an idea to hit them. This passive approach can, in fact, invite ideas to come. But under the pressure of a class assignment, with time limited and an assignment due, you may want to try something more proactive.[18]

Freewriting

Freewriting takes literally the notion that thinking *is* writing and writing, thinking. Instead of just letting ideas come to you, write them as they enter your head. Don't self-censor. Don't worry about grammar or spelling. Make sentences if you wish or just spit out phrases or even single words. Put down whatever comes to mind. Some writers find it easier to do this with a pencil or pen on a sheet of paper, but, these days, as more of us have become wedded and welded to keyboards and screens, most writers tap out their thoughts. Whatever technology you use, analog or digital, put the emphasis on *free*. This material is for your eyes only. Let it flow. And keep writing for as long as the writing comes. When it peters out, stop, make sure you save your work (if you are using a computer), and put it away for an hour or a day. Then come back to it and start mining. Look for the ore from which you will refine a paper.

Looping

A variation on freewriting is sometimes called looping. This imposes a degree of discipline on the freewriting. You free-write for a set amount of time—say five minutes or ten—at the end of which you pause to read what you have written. From this material, you pull out the core of a concept or whatever strikes you as most interesting. You take the time to refine this core into a good sentence that summarizes the theme. This completed, you dive into another five or ten minutes of freewriting, stop, and repeat the extraction and refining process. Keep going, repeating the alternating freewriting and extraction process, as long as it is productive.

Brainstorming

Brainstorming can be done alone or (more often) with others. This differs from freewriting in that it is a deliberate attempt to generate ideas. As with freewriting, don't censor yourself. The goal is to push out as many ideas as possible. If you are working with others, do not comment on the ideas generated. Just record them.

Class notes and learning journals

There are four kinds of note takers in any class. The first kind are what you might call "the stenographers," who endeavor to write down every word that comes out of the professor's mouth. The second kind are "the highlighters," who try to summarize the most important things that are discussed in class. The third type of note takers are "the thinkers." These students note the key points raised in class—whether by the instructor or others—but also write down their own thoughts as they occur. In effect, they conduct a kind of dialogue with the others in the class. Sometimes it is a counterpoint.

And the fourth category? It is those who take no notes at all. Good luck with that.

The first three notetaking styles are all useful, but by far the most effective in a class where essays will be written is "the thinker." What good reason is there *not* to use each class session as an opportunity to generate writing ideas?

The learning or class journal

Some professors encourage students to take "the thinker" style a step further by keeping a "learning journal" or "class journal." This is a collection of notes, observations, and thoughts you compile not during class but after class or maybe even at the end of each week of classes. It is a kind of learning log intended to provide *you* with a picture of your growing understanding of the subject at hand—in this case, philosophy. It is an opportunity to record ideas that occur to you close to the time that they are formed. The document becomes a record of your evolving understanding and ideas. In addition to providing grist for later writing, the learning journal also helps you to identify your strengths and weaknesses, areas you can exploit in an essay, and areas in which you need more work.

The Writing Process

Up to this point in this section, we have been discussing what might be called "prewriting," the steps taken prior to formally beginning a writing project. The transition from prewriting to writing comes when you have selected your topic.

Selecting a Topic

Assuming that you are not assigned a topic, the first criterion for selecting one is to try to discover a topic that interests you or, even better, excites you. It is far easier to write *well* about something that engages you mind, your imagination, and your feelings than it is to try to gin up interest in a topic to which, in fact, you are indifferent.

But before you pounce on this labor of love, ensure that it is a topic sufficiently narrow to cover adequately in the space you have. Nothing kills a good topic faster than having to broadly generalize. On the other hand, topics that are too narrow may be insufficiently ambitious to engage your interest—and if you are not engaged, how do you expect to enthrall your reader? Generally, far more novice philosophical writers make the mistake of selecting a topic too broad or general or vague than one that is too narrow.

Another criterion for topic selection is the presence of controversy. If you choose a topic on which everyone generally agrees—say, sexual assault is morally wrong—you will have a very difficult time finding something novel, original, or even interesting to say about it. In short, the reader will ask, *Why am I reading this?* On the other hand, if you choose such a topic and perversely decide to write a paper opposed to it, you may be putting yourself in a difficult, even impossible, situation. *Sexual assault is justified* ... when, how, and why?

Good topics are often those that naturally have two major opposed points of view, pro and con. These may be in the political, legal, or moral/ethical realms, or you may choose to dive into philosophy itself by identifying a controversial philosophical question: *Are mind and body dual or one?* Or: *Does existence precede essence?*

The Thesis Statement

Deciding on a topic is a necessary first step to writing a paper, but it isn't a sufficient first step. The topic must be followed by a thesis statement, which clearly identifies the main point you want to make about the topic or an argument related to the topic. An effective thesis statement will not only guide your reader through your paper, it will guide you in writing the paper.

Here are some examples of thesis statements capable of launching an effective essay:

- René Descartes' model of a mind separate from the body is successfully refuted by William James's 1884 essay "What Is an Emotion?"
- The dramatic rise in American populism seen during the 2016 presidential election was overwhelmingly a response to increasing globalization.

- Assisted suicide is both moral and ethical and, therefore, should be protected as a human right.
- Public libraries "promote the general welfare" and should therefore be subsidized by the federal government.

To Outline or Not to Outline?

Some writers create a thorough outline before beginning to draft an essay. Others just dive in. And still others sketch out a basic, rough outline with points that serve as prompts and reminders more than make up a detailed blueprint.

There is no single right answer to the question posed by the subhead above. As you write more papers, you will learn which of the three options works best for you. This said, however, in writing for philosophy class, it is best to *try* beginning with an outline. Then, after you have finished the whole project—outline and essay—decide whether the outline was worth the effort. The fact is that most philosophical assignments are sufficiently complex that the demands of logical structure require proceeding step by step while also ensuring that you do not forget to include everything important. Ideally, an outline serves as a structural blueprint or a map to get you from Point A to Point F via Points B, C, D, and E. At the very least, however, an outline can serve as a checklist to ensure that you are covering what must be covered and that you don't omit anything vital.

Outlines can be invaluable in helping you put your thoughts or main points in order before you begin to write. Let's say you have decided to write on the mind/body dualism. You jot down the main points you want to cover:

- Embodied cognition (mind-body unity)
- Descartes' idea of the mind's relationship to the body as being like that of a "pilot" to the ship he guides
- William James's idea about the origin of emotion (we do not run because we are afraid; we are afraid because we run)
- Plato's cave analogy

A rough outline might simply consist of putting these things in logical order:

- Plato's cave analogy
- Descartes' idea of the mind's relationship to the body as being like that of a "pilot" to the ship he guides

- William James's idea about the origin of emotion (we do not run because we are afraid; we are afraid because we run)
- Embodied cognition (mind-body unity)

This might be enough to get you started on your rough draft. Or you might decide you need to use the more formal traditional outline format, which works like this:

I. First Major Topic
   A. First supporting or subordinate point
   B. Second supporting or subordinate point
      1. First subordinate point to point B
      2. Second subordinate point to point B
         a. First subordinate point to point B2
         b. Second subordinate point to point B2

II. Second Major Topic

And so on. The utility of the formal outline is that it can prompt or even compel you to work out the logical arrangement of your various points. You decide on your major topics (numbered with roman numerals). Under *I. Major Topic* go the subpoints that directly support this Major Topic. Under subpoint *I.A* go the subpoints that directly support *I.A.* and so on, down the line. In this way, you make your most comprehensive points and support them logically. Here is an example of a formal outline summarizing Descartes' argument that the mind is more certainly known than the body:

I. The mind is more certainly known than the body

   A. Perhaps all I know of external objects, including my own body, is false because of the maleficent acts of some demon.
   B. But it is not possible that I could be deceived about my existence as a thinking being.
   C. Even physical objects, including my body, are known more distinctly through the mind than through the body itself.
      1. Consider the example of wax
         a. All properties of a chunk of wax that I can perceive with my senses change as the wax melts.

b. This is also the case with the chunk's primary properties, such as shape, extension, and size, which exist apart from my own perception of them.
c. Nevertheless, the wax remains the same piece of wax even as it melts.

2. Therefore, what I know of the wax, I know through my mind (the faculty of judgment) and not through my senses or my imagination, which is fed by my senses.
3. Therefore also, every instance of distinct knowledge of physical matter provides certain evidence that I am a thinking being.

D. In conclusion, I know my mind more clearly and distinctly than I know my body.

When you are faced with having to summarize an orderly argument like this one, it is almost always best to begin with a full formal outline, which shows the relationship between each point and subpoint and sub-subpoint of the argument.

Rough Draft

Once you have your thesis statement and whatever form of outline—if any—you have chosen to create, you are ready to write the first draft, which is called a rough draft because it is still very much a work in progress. Some writers create more polished first drafts than others. This does not matter. It is your final draft that counts. In fact, the best strategy is simply to get the writing done. You don't have to rush through it, but you should not let yourself get bogged down agonizing over each word. Nor should you worry too much about length. Right now, you want to get your thoughts into the form of words, sentences, and paragraphs. If you have been given a strict word count to meet, you can add or cut as part of the work of preparing the final draft. You are not Michelangelo carving in marble. Language is far more malleable than stone, and you can lengthen, shorten, and reshape readily.

Think of the rough draft as your opportunity to see what you are thinking. Allow not only ample time to self-edit and polish your work into a final draft, but make sure you can set the first draft aside at least overnight—preferably for a full twenty-four hours—so that you can come back to the work cooled off from the heat of original composition, with a fresh perspective, and ready to view with a cold eye all that you have written.

This cooling-off period between completing the rough draft and starting the final draft is valuable for gaining objectivity on your work. Do not cheat yourself out of it. It will improve your writing.

Self-edit, better known as revision

Once you are "cold" from the rough draft, it is time for self-editing. Some writers call this *revising,* and that is a good word for it. It is all too easy to become wedded to your rough draft and therefore opposed to looking at it objectively. You may be nervous about what you will think on reading your own work. You may be asking yourself, *Oh, God! What if this needs revision?*

The good news is that you can set your fear aside. The bad news is that your first draft will almost certainly require revision because virtually *all* first drafts require revision. In fact, most professional writers will tell you that the "real" writing comes in revising the rough draft. Revision is a vital part of the writing process.

Think about the word *revision.* You don't need a dictionary. The prefix *re-*means to "do again," and *vision*—well, you know what that means. So, to *revise* is to re-see or to see again.

1. Don't rush the revision. Give yourself plenty of time reread your draft carefully. Many writers read their own first drafts aloud to themselves. This helps them "hear" their work as others will.
2. Correct any typos, spelling, or grammatical errors you find. Fix each as soon as you find it. Some experts advise writers to focus first only on the big stuff and save the details for the proofreading stage. Bad idea. When you find a mistake, just fix it. Now.
3. This said, do focus on the big picture. Reread your thesis statement carefully. As you go through the rest of your paper, keep asking yourself: *Does what I have written in* this *sentence and in* this *paragraph relate to and support my thesis?* If you cannot answer yes, you have now identified something requiring revision.
4. The big picture also includes structure. Is the progression from section to section (if your paper has sub-headed sections), paragraph to paragraph, and (within each paragraph) sentence to sentence logical? It should be like a set of directions to get from point A to the endpoint—let's call it point G. Does the paper progress A to B to C to D to E to F to G? Or is something out of order? Do you detect A to C to B? Or is a necessary point missing?

5. Check for overall unity. Each part of the essay should relate logically to every other part, to the essay as a whole, and to the thesis. This is not some mystical sense of wholeness. Just ask yourself if anything you say at point D (for instance) contradicts something in A or G. Your essay will likely include counterarguments to your thesis. As long as you deal effectively with these, they are *not* contradictions. What you must avoid, however, is contradicting yourself and your own thesis.
6. Check your transitions. The coherence of your essay, especially when detailing a philosophical argument or concept, requires a seamless progression from point to point. These transitions are aided by verbal signposts, such as *however, therefore, fortunately, in any case, nevertheless,* and so on. Major transitions require more, often an entire sentence or even a whole paragraph: "To understand the impact of Sartre on existentialism, we must briefly survey existential thought as far back as Kierkegaard." A sentence like this will explain why everything from, say, point A to point D deals with the twentieth century, but point E is about to take us back to the nineteenth. Such an explanation will prevent the reader from getting lost in time en route to your conclusion. Transitions keep you and your reader on course.
7. Look for repetition. In our anxiety to get our main points across, most of us tend to become repetitive. A certain amount of repetition of key points can be quite useful, and your conclusion will likely reprise the highlights of your essay. But relentless repetition is counterproductive. Look for the same points repeatedly made. Jettison some of these.

   We don't just repeat our major ideas. We also often repeat certain words and phrases as well as monotonous sentence constructions. If you are writing in the first person, you are almost certainly overusing the pronoun *I*. Vary your expressive palette.

   All of this said, repetition, used thoughtfully, can be both intellectually and stylistically powerful. Don't arbitrarily banish it all. Just be certain that when you repeat, you do so for a good reason.

Most word-processing programs include a means of "tracking" changes that you make—edits, additions, deletions, and movement of words, sentences, paragraphs, and sections from one place in the essay to another. Turn on "track changes" and keep it on.

Final Draft

How do you know when your "final" draft is final? When you have passed through the seven steps of revision enumerated above and can answer yes to every question about whether each sentence, paragraph, and section relates to and supports your thesis and creates overall unity free of self-contradiction.

Once you have reached this point, you have what can be called a final *draft*, with the emphasis, however, on the word "draft." You have one more crucial step, so do *not* turn off your word processor's change-tracking feature yet.

Proofread

Set your final draft aside overnight or for at least twenty-four hours. Reread it—yes, again. You are looking for the same errors and wrong turns you were searching for when you read through the rough draft, but, this time, you are also paying close attention to the details of punctuation and spelling. Make use of the tools just about every word processing program provides, both spell-check and grammar check. They are not 100% reliable, but whatever potential problems these checking programs highlight is always worth doublechecking.

As you proofread, pay close attention to words you used in the essay but have rarely or never used elsewhere, including the specialized vocabulary of philosophy. Don't assume or guess that you understand these words unless you are certain that you do. Resolve any doubt by looking them up. The same goes for any items of research. Doublecheck references to dates, people, places, book titles, and the like.

Before you turn off "track changes" in your word processor and irrevocably "accept" all the edits you have made, examine the deletions you have made. Are all of them intentional? Or was something deleted by accident? Now is the time to doublecheck. This said, storage space on personal computers is cheap and plentiful—and the cloud offers virtually boundless digital real estate. Before you accept all your edits and finalize them, save under a distinctive file name a copy of your essay with all edits fully tracked and preserved. After you have done this, accept all your changes and turn off the tracking feature. It is, however, a good idea to scroll or click through each full page of your work to make certain that paragraphing, paragraph indents, and spacing all look correct. These often get out of whack when you work with the change-tracking feature turned on.

Publish

The final step is the same for you as it is for professional philosophers: publish. Philosophical writing is intended to be shared with others. Practicing philosophers seek publication in the professional journals read by other philosophers, just as scientists seek publication in the scientific journals that are important to colleagues in their discipline. As a student in a philosophy course, "publication" may consist of nothing more than handing in your work, on paper or online. In some courses, essays are posted online for everyone in the class to access and even comment on. Either way, recognize this last step as much more than a course requirement. It is the way of a philosopher.

8

Philosophical Writing: Essential Skills

Having just walked through the basic process of writing a philosophy paper, we turn now to the essential skillset you should develop and apply not only to the writing of papers for philosophy class but to the disciplined study of philosophy itself.[19]

Defining Concepts

An important skill in philosophical writing is defining key concepts. You can look up words in the dictionary, and that is an essential start and a good one, as far as it goes. But, in philosophy class, the professor is usually looking for analytical definitions of key terms. Such definitions are intended to show how a term is used in philosophy, not in general discourse. If a key term can be understood as philosophers or as a specific philosopher uses it, the underlying thought can be explored more meaningfully.

Analytical definition is a common writing exercise in philosophy classes. Typically, the focus is on creating a definition that accomplishes two objectives. It tells what features are common to all things of a certain class, and it tells what features are unique to the class in question. A definition that can accomplish both objectives is the kind of precise definition philosophers find most useful.

If you are asked to analytically define *automobile,* for instance, you will probably want to define the word within its class (the class of vehicles? the class of things that move under their own power?) in terms of what automobiles have in common with all members of the class and what makes them unique within the class. If you define *automobile* too broadly, you may end up including trucks, tanks, SUVs, and motorcycles in your definition, which is almost certainly too diffuse a definition. On the other hand, if you define *automobile* too narrowly, you may end up excluding certain types of cars.

The method by which philosophers define a term so that it is neither too broad nor too narrow with respect to its class is one that ensures the definition satisfies both *necessary* and *sufficient* conditions. A necessary condition is one without which a given thing cannot be what it is. You may decide, for instance, that self-powered movement is a necessary condition for a thing to be called an automobile. But there are many things, including animals, that are capable of self-powered movement. For this reason, this aspect of the definition may be necessary, but it is not sufficient. A sufficient condition specifies *one way* of being a given thing. A sufficient definition of an automobile *might* extend the necessary definition into something like this: *An automobile is a self-powered motor-driven vehicle with four tires, used mainly to transport one to eight people (not cargo) primarily on roads.*

Doubtless, any competent philosophy student would find fault with this definition and offer something even more rigorous in terms of the two dimensions, necessity and sufficiency. What this tells us is that writing an analytical definition is a challenging project. Indeed, many philosophers insist that only formal logic and mathematics or perhaps physics and chemistry have reliably developed fully satisfactory analytical definitions. So, why should mere philosophers, laboring in language, even try? The answer is that the act of definition gets to the very heart of philosophy, which is about questioning ordinary things, the nature of the world around us and ourselves within the world, experiencing that world, perceiving it, thinking about it, and generally processing it.

Formulating a Philosophical Problem

Writing assignments generally fall into two categories, argumentative and expository. Argumentative assignments require taking a position on some controversial question, problem, or issue in anything from politics to ethics to aesthetics or within the discipline of philosophy itself. Such assignments are common in philosophy courses at every level.

Expository assignments are explanatory and descriptive. For instance, the assignment "Identify and discuss three of G. W. F. Hegel's key concepts in the creation of German idealism" can be completed chiefly by doing the relevant research on Hegel, German idealism, and absolute idealism. Yet, in the discipline of philosophy, even such expository assignments typically require an element of argument. For instance: Why did you choose A, B, and C as more "key" than D, E, and F? Defend and justify. And presumably you will want to rate Hegel's contribution to German idealism, so there is another judgment you will need to justify. Finally, while you can rely heavily on your research in the history of philosophy to define "German idealism," you may exercise some of your own judgment in writing about how it differs from idealism (such as that of Plato) prior to Hegel. Again, this will require sound argument.

In short, whatever your writing assignment, you can usually count on argument or problem-solving as being central to it if for no other reason than that problem solving is the essence of philosophy.

To create your essay's argument, its approach to its topic, you must first identify a philosophical problem. Sometimes your instructor will make this easy by asking a specific question you must answer. The question is thus the philosophical problem at the core of your paper. But it is also quite possible that you will be turned loose to identify a problem.

In general, a philosophical problem worth writing about may be defined as a question that is not easily answered. Classic questions abound: "Is there a God?" "What is reality?" "Do people have free will?" "Are mind and body separate?" "Is moral relativism truly moral?" And so on. They are all fascinating questions. The trouble is that questions such as these take at least a lifetime to answer persuasively, and you have a semester or less.

You will need to identify a problem narrow enough to be adequately discussed in a paper that may be 500, 1000, 2500, 5000, words or, if it is a term paper, perhaps somewhat longer. You have limited time and space to treat the problem. Yet if you choose a problem too narrow, you will have a difficult time writing *anything* significant about it.

You can productively narrow down philosophical problems in at least four ways:

1. Take a question, such as *Is there free will?*, discuss the views of two contrasting philosophers on the question (say, the eighteenth-century American theologian Jonathan Edwards and the nineteenth-century American philosopher Ralph Waldo Emerson), and present an argument supporting one position over the other. In such a paper, you would briefly lay out the problem, present Edwards's and Emerson's solutions to the problem (with relevant examples), and then present an argument for which philosopher's solution is stronger.
2. Find a relatively narrow, focused aspect of a larger problem. For instance, instead of tackling the great question of subject versus object—How do I know that what I perceive is real?—you might argue

that Hegel succeeded in supplying a workable answer by resolving the subject/object dualism with his concept of absolute idealism.

3. Apply a philosophical solution to a practical problem. Instead of tackling the massive yet amorphous question *Is it ever ethical to lie?* ask, *Can diplomacy be practiced without secrecy?*
4. Slice that question—*Is it ever ethical to lie?*—even thinner: How would Kant, as the author of *Critique of Pure Reason*, respond to the question, *Can diplomacy be practiced without secrecy?*

However you approach identifying a problem for philosophical discussion, avoid the extremes: problems that are simply too large to discuss in a half-dozen pages; problems that are by any reasonable measure unimportant ("Why is the water always colder from the bathroom faucet?"); problems that are too broad to be treated meaningfully in a paper of modest length; problems that are too narrow to generate interest in most readers; problems that are easily solved and therefore not worth writing about; and problems that are intractable and cannot be reasonably answered. Instead, work the fertile middle ground with a problem that is both interesting and important *to you*—because, chances are, if you find the problem genuinely interesting, others will as well. Focus narrowly enough to create a thorough discussion that gets beneath the surface. Find something with demonstrable difficulties that require thought and skill to solve. Writing about easy problems with obvious answers is like playing tennis without a net.

One last point about identifying a problem. Robert Browning famously agued in his poem "Andrea del Sarto": "A man's reach should exceed his grasp, / Or what's a heaven for?" Suppose you set out in a paper to solve some problem that simply eludes a persuasive answer. Should you throw the paper away and look for something more manageable? Perhaps. But perhaps there is a better way. Consider making the subject of your paper the difficulties of solving the problem you have posed for yourself. You may even argue that the problem is unsolvable and provide persuasive reasons for that conclusion.

Anatomy of an Argument

Knowing how to analyze an argument will help you in two ways. First, early assignments in many philosophy courses ask you to analyze arguments that are presented in textbooks or in class. Second, analyzing arguments—reverse-engineering them, as it were—is one of the best ways to learn how to construct a persuasive argument.

Argument Form

We know that reasoning comes in two flavors, deductive and inductive. Arguments derive from these forms of reasoning.

A *deductive argument* assumes that the major and minor premises offered are true and therefore support the conclusion: *All men are mortal* (major premise); *Socrates is a man* (minor premise); Therefore, *Socrates is mortal* (conclusion). Since the premises are assumed to be true, the only dimension of the deductive argument that is subject to analysis is its mechanics. *All men are mortal*; *Socrates is an aardvark*; Therefore, *Socrates is not mortal.* Factually, the minor premise is clearly false, but if we are only analyzing the mechanism of the argument, we don't comment on this. For the question at issue is not whether the conclusion of the argument is *true* or *false*, but whether it is *valid* or *invalid*. In this case, the conclusion, Socrates is not mortal, happens to be false. But that is rather beside the point in a deductive argument. The point is that the conclusion is invalid because the two premises, All men are mortal and Socrates is an aardvark, do not *logically* support the conclusion that Socrates is not mortal. Neither do they refute that conclusion. They are simply logically irrelevant to the conclusion. Indeed, from the two premises, it is impossible to reach a logically valid conclusion.

In some imaginary universe, it might be possible to do all reasoning in arguments that proceed from premises absolutely known to be true. Thus, all conclusions would be drawn deductively. Get the logical mechanics right, and you would infallibly have your answer. However, we do not live in such a universe, and, usually, each premise requires a data-based or experientially based argument on its behalf. So, while the ability to identify flawed deductive reasoning is essential, inductive argument is found far more often than deductive argument, not just in philosophy but in everyday life.

In our world, the premises of an argument are rarely so self-evident that they can be assumed true. *Frank has white hair. Frank is older than sixty. Therefore, everyone over sixty has white hair.* Let us say that both the major and minor premises are factually true. Nevertheless, the conclusion is both invalid and false. It does not follow deductively from the premises, nor can it be supported by diligent inductive methods based on experience and observation.

In a two-premise deductive argument, validity or invalidity is independent of the factual truth of the premises. Thus[20]:

PREMISES	CONCLUSION	ARGUMENT
True	True	Valid
True	True	Invalid
False	False	Valid
False	False	Invalid
False	True	Valid
False	False	Invalid
True	False	Invalid

Refutation

To refute a deductive argument, you have two choices. You can refute it deductively, showing that its mechanics are wrong: *Frank has white hair. Frank is older than seventy. Therefore, everyone over sixty has white hair.* The conclusion does not follow logically from the two premises. You can also refute it inductively by showing that one or both premises are factually false or that the conclusion is not supported by statistics or observation. An inductive refutation can succeed even if the two premises happen to be true: *Frank has white hair. Frank is older than sixty.* Observation and statistics—the facts—do not, however, support the conclusion, *Everyone over sixty has white hair.* After all, not everyone older than sixty has white hair.

Inductive argument is empirical. It is based on observation, knowledge, and research. It is also, to an extent, speculative. Whereas the standard of deductive argument is validity, which is binary—the conclusion is either valid or invalid—the standard of inductive argument is the preponderance of fact, experience, and observation, truth as far as truth can be ascertained. In U.S. law, the verdict of a jury is governed by a well-articulated inductive standard. Jurors are to return a verdict of guilty only if they conclude that the prosecution has proved its case "beyond a reasonable doubt." If reasonable doubt exists, the defendant must be found not guilty.

Both building and refuting inductive arguments therefore require knowledge, experience, observation, and research to collect evidence and ascertain fact. To this is added hypothesis, the interpretation of the facts that the philosopher proposes and endeavors to prove or at least persuasively support with a sound argument.

The Fallacies

As we learn from deductive argument, it is quite possible to have logic without necessity; that is, a deductive argument may have one or more factually false premises yet still yield a valid conclusion, which would nevertheless be factually false. Arguing from factually false premises is not, however, the only cause of a false conclusion, whether that conclusion is logically valid or invalid. Many of the reasoning errors people make are not errors of fact but errors of irrelevance. That is, one or more of the premises is irrelevant to the conclusion. There is yet another category of error in reasoning, which, unlike error of fact or relevance, takes identifiable forms. These are called "fallacies."

Should you choose to study classical rhetoric, you will find a long list of formal fallacies, usually with Latin names.[21] Here (in English) are the most commonly encountered fallacies to look for in the arguments of others and to avoid in your own:[22]

Denying the Antecedent
Example: If I get paid, I will eat. I did not get paid; therefore, I will not eat.
Error: Maybe someone will buy my dinner.

Affirming the Consequent
Example: If I get paid, I will eat. I ate; therefore, I was paid.
Error: Maybe someone treated me to dinner.

The Exclusive Fallacy
Example: I will buy a car or a boat. I will buy a car; therefore, I will not buy a boat.
Error: I might buy a car and a boat.

Invalid Appeal to Authority
Example: William James is a great psychologist; therefore, he will be a great philosopher.
Error: One type of authority does not necessarily ensure the presence of another type of authority.

Strawman (or Straw Man, or Strawperson, or Straw Person)
Example: "Welfare Queens" use federal entitlements to feather their nests and, therefore, entitlements should be abolished.
Error: That some individuals may abuse federal entitlement programs does not disprove the utility or necessity of these programs for the many in genuine need.

False Dilemma

Example: If you order beans, you cannot order rice.

Error: These are nonexclusive alternatives presented arbitrarily as exclusive.

Note: "You can't have your cake and eat it too" presents genuinely exclusive alternatives. You can either save your cake ("have" it in the sense of preserve it) or consume it. You cannot do both. The alternatives are mutually exclusive, so the dilemma, in this case, is genuine.

Complex Question

Example: "When will you act reasonably?"

Error: Assumes, without presenting evidence, that you are not reasonable. You may, in fact, be quite reasonable.

Begging the Question

Example: "Should you quit smoking? Well, do you want to avoid dying from cancer?"

Error: The question assumes there are absolute methods of avoiding cancer or curing it; that is, the conclusion is assumed in the premises.

Suppressed Evidence

Example: "Nothing the dentist can do will kill you."

Error: The dentist can do any number of things that may prove fatal. Not mentioning them does not prove the conclusion.

Note: An inductively reasonable statement would be, "Very little the dentist can do will kill you."

Appeal to Unknowable Statistics

Example: "Prayer has reduced the incidence of cancer by at least 50 percent."

Error: The factual truth here is unknowable.

Guilt by Association

Example: "Your brother is a thief; so, clearly, you stole my wallet."

Error: The behavior of one sibling proves nothing about the other.

Appeal to Ignorance
Example: "You can't prove that smoking cigarettes will kill me."
Error: Evidence exists that cigarette smoking may cause cancer and heart disease. Failure to *prove* that smoking is invariably lethal does not disprove its harmful effects.

Composition
Example: "All Asians are hard workers."
Error: Maybe some work no harder than non-Asians.

Division
Example: "All Democrats favor healthcare reform."
Error: Some may not.

Hasty Conclusion
Example: "My lawyer overcharged me. All lawyers are swindlers."
Error: The action of a single lawyer is an inadequate sample on which to base a conclusion about lawyers in general.

Questionable Cause
Example: "Violent video games encourage violent behavior."
Error: Unsupported by research.

Questionable Analogy
Example: "Communism is a cancer on society."
Error: Cancer, unlike communism, cannot be refuted by argument and political example.

Appeal to Pity
Example: "If I don't get at least a B in philosophy, I will kill myself."
Error: Argument irrelevant to evaluation of academic achievement; however, the instructor may advise the student to seek professional counseling.

Intimidation
Example: "You'd better agree to these conditions if you don't want things to turn very ugly for you."
Error: Might does not make right.

Appeal to Loyalty

Example: "The president may well be making the wrong decision, but we owe him our agreement with his policies."

Error: Loyalty is not a universal guide to making the best decisions.

Appeal to Stereotype

Example: "All Jews are rich."

Error: Both vague and demonstrably untrue.

Double Standard

Example: "Do as I say, not as I do."

Error: Hypocrisy is not a compelling argument.

Ad Hominem

Example: "You are temperamentally unfit to manage a business."

Error: This attack on personal character (*ad hominem* = "to the person") is both irrelevant and unprovable.

Note: This fallacy is commonly known by its Latin description.

Post Hoc Ergo Propter Hoc

Example: "I forgot to say my morning prayer, so I fell down the stairs this afternoon."

Error: The correlation or coincidence of failing to pray and later suffering an accident is groundlessly assumed to be proof of cause and effect.

Note: This fallacy is commonly known by its Latin description, which may be translated as "after this, therefore because of this."

Cum Hoc Ergo Propter Hoc

Example: "I won the bet because I was carrying my lucky rabbit's foot."

Error: The correlation or coincidence of simultaneous events or facts (possessing a rabbit's foot while winning a bet) is groundlessly assumed to be proof of cause and effect.

Note: This fallacy is commonly known by its Latin description, which may be translated as "with this, therefore because of this." It is a variation on the more commonly used "Post hoc ergo propter hoc" fallacy, which is founded on temporal sequence rather than simultaneity.

Organizing Your Thoughts

Recall that writing assignments in philosophy class typically fall into two broad categories, the expository essay and the argumentative essay.

Here is the overall pattern of an expository essay:

A. State your topic
B. State your thesis. In an expository paper, this can consist simply of defining the scope of your exposition or it may be a position you take on the topic.
C. Provide an overview or roadmap of your exposition of the topic.
D. Write the exposition so that it supports your thesis and follows your roadmap.
E. Reach a conclusion that supports your thesis.

The overall pattern of an argumentative essay that addresses a problem or controversy may look something like this:

A. State the problem/controversy
B. Present your thesis, which may consist of two parts.
   1. Analysis of the problem/controversy, including its crux
   2. Statement of your solution
C. Discuss your solution, including:
   1. Criteria of adequacy for a solution
   2. Proposed solutions alternative to yours and why each is inadequate
D. Write the exposition of your solution
E. Anticipate criticisms and respond to them
F. Write a conclusion summarizing the benefits/virtues of your solution

A subset of the argumentative essay is sometimes called the adjudicatory essay.[23] Your role is to resolve a dispute between two parties/points of view on a philosophical issue, problem, or controversy:

A. Explain the dispute, including any necessary background
B. Explain position 1 in the dispute
C. Evaluate position 1 in the dispute
D. Explain position 2 in the dispute
E. Evaluate position 2 in the dispute
F. Present your resolution
G. Anticipate objections to your resolution and defend against them.

Comparing and Contrasting

Because philosophical thought typically entails comparison and contrast, writing assignments often pivot on this operation. You may be assigned to compare and contrast philosophical traditions, or the ideas of one philosopher with another, or philosophic positions on a given concept, such as the criteria for beauty in art.

A compare and contrast assignment requires a thorough understanding of what you are comparing and contrasting, whether ideas or philosophers. You need to decide whether you want to focus primarily on similarities or differences. If you believe that most readers will appreciate the similarities before distinguishing the differences, it is a good idea to begin with the similarities and then move to the differences. If you believe that, in the minds of most readers, differences will predominate, begin instead with these. Either way, start with the general areas of similarity or dissimilarity and proceed to greater levels of specificity and detail. You will find that the more obvious view—either that A and B are more similar than different or that A and B are more different than similar—will recede, and your readers will be exposed more fully to the less obvious point of view. For instance, the superficial similarities between Plato's and Kant's views of the role of the senses in communicating reality to an observer will recede into the background as you explore in depth the philosophers' differences on this topic.

Using Examples

We often think of philosophy as abstract and general, but the point of philosophical discourse is to apply general principles and abstract concepts to the specifics of the real world. So, an essential skill in writing philosophically is knowing how to use examples to clarify a principle or concept. This requires understanding the principle or concept and an ability to identify an example that is truly an instance of the principle or concept at issue. Moreover, the purpose of an example is to help you and your reader understand the principle or concept. Take care, therefore, to choose an example that genuinely enlightens.

For instance, suppose you are discussing Kant's *categorical imperative.* You may first want to define what Kant meant by an *imperative.* It is something a person must do. An example? Lost in the desert, George has gone without water for three days. At last, he discovers in the dry sand the trickle of a stream. His intense thirst has made taking a drink imperative. Kant called this kind of imperative "hypothetical," meaning that the imperative is driven by a certain situation. George drinks because of the situation of his great thirst. If he were not thirsty, he would have no imperative to drink. In contrast to the hypothetical imperative, Kant's categorical comparative is a moral imperative, meaning (as Kant saw it) that it applies always and in all situations. If thirsty George saw thirsty Tom drinking from a precious canteen of water in the desert, he would feel a hypothetical imperative to seize the canteen and drink; however, he might also be aware of a categorical imperative to act in accordance with morality and refrain from grabbing the canteen. George might resolve the conflict by asking Tom for permission to take just a sip from his canteen. For Tom, the categorical imperative would be to share the life-giving drink with George.

Formulating and Testing Hypotheses

Applying philosophical theory to the real world calls for more than merely finding examples. Philosophers create theories or models to analyze and explain aspects of the real world. The theory is expressed in the form of a hypothesis, which is a proposed explanation for some problem, event, or phenomenon.

A viable hypothesis—that is, one with a reasonable probability of being true—includes an accurate and persuasive identification and description of the problem, event, or phenomenon being addressed. The hypothesis reveals its author's understanding of the theory that is being applied and requires asking the key questions about relevant facts that are as yet unknown. The hypothesis reaches a conclusion about what to believe or do about the problem, event, or phenomenon in question. Moreover, the conclusion is clearly supported by the theory. To be considered valid, the hypothesis must also be capable of being implemented.

A hypothesis is valuable only insofar as it explains something we do not understand or successfully predicts what will happen if certain actions are taken. Here is an example: James Q. Wilson and George L. Kelling, social scientists in the early 1980s, wanted to test the greater implications of a common observation among cops on the beat that "if a window in a building is broken *and is left unrepaired,* all the rest of the windows will soon be broken."[24] Now, the existence of a broken window is not a crime. To leave a broken window unrepaired is not a crime. But, Wilson and Kelling theorized, unrepaired broken windows signal that the community cares little for law and order. From this theory, they hypothesized that the presence of broken windows—or some equivalent visible sign of local disorder—will tend to generate crime.

Wilson and Kelling pointed to the work of another researcher, a Stanford University psychology professor named Philip Zimbardo, who tested the so-called Broken Windows Theory by parking an automobile, without license plates and with its hood up, on a street in a tough section of the Bronx. He did the same in an upscale neighborhood in Palo Alto, California. Within ten minutes of the automobile's abandonment in the Bronx, the car was attacked by scavengers and vandals. In Palo Alto, the car was not merely attacked, but turned upside down and destroyed.[25]

When you are proposing a hypothesis in a philosophy paper, it is usually sufficient merely to describe an experiment to test the truth of the hypothesis rather than actually conduct it. In some cases, however, you may be able to find historical evidence to back up your theory and any hypothesis emerging from it.

In the case of the Broken Windows Theory, the formulation and testing sequence may be summarized this way:

1. Observation: Neighborhoods in which broken windows are left unrepaired often have high crime rates.
2. Theory: The presence of broken windows in a neighborhood signals an environment of disorder, in which enforcement of law is unlikely.
3. Hypothesis: Deliberately creating the equivalent of broken windows as a sign of local disorder will generate criminal activity such as vandalism.
4. Test of the theory and hypothesis: Experimentation and observation of results.

9

Forms of Philosophical Writing

The word *essay* comes from the French infinitive verb *essayer,* meaning "to try" or "to attempt." In fact, when the word was first borrowed into the English language, as *essay,* it served as a verb, with the same meaning as the French original, and as a noun, meaning "an attempt" or "a trial." The great French philosopher Michel de Montaigne (1533-1592) titled his voluminous collection of observations on himself and the world around him *Essais* because he considered them attempts or trials at understanding. So, the "essay" is the perfect vehicle for doing philosophy. It is a trial or attempt to understand.

The kinds of essay assignments with which you are likely to be tasked in a philosophy class include personal essays, and essays of assertion, affirmation, or refutation.[26]

The Personal Essay

The personal essay is a self-reflective search for meaning. Unlike most philosophical writing, it is not argumentative. Instead, it is exploratory and speculative, often even somewhat confessional. It is typically written in the first person and is broadly autobiographical. When writing a personal essay for philosophy class, the usual approach is to tell a personal story or present a memory. That is part 1 of the essay. In part 2, find meaning in the experience, recollection, or reflection. What meaning does it have for you? What might it communicate to others? Montaigne was an early master of the personal philosophical essay. The great American moralist, naturalist, and philosopher Henry David Thoreau (1817-1862) took the personal essay to memorable artistic and philosophical heights.

The Essay of Assertion

The essay of assertion takes the position *I believe.* It is an argumentative essay in which you convey to the reader some belief or beliefs that you hold. If you are assigned to write an essay of assertion—or if you decide to write one—you should write about a belief that is genuinely important to you. It should be a product of your identity, of who you are, of your values. From a philosophical standpoint, it is an attempt to show how your belief extends from who you are.

An assertion is not necessarily right (factually true) or wrong (factually false). But neither is it a mere opinion. In a philosophical essay, you are expected to convey your belief persuasively, making a genuine effort to be understood. You need to choose your descriptive words carefully and with an eye toward precision. You should show how your belief operates in the real world. An autobiographical example or anecdote is the ideal vehicle for describing and illustrating what you believe.

It is not enough to state your belief. You must present the reasoning behind it. Remember, you are presenting your belief as an expression of who you are, so you need to show how it is consistent with your personality, your personal history, and your values. You should make an effort to describe and explain the consequences of your belief. Indeed, you can envision the general structure of the assertion as consisting of four parts: the title, the exposition of your belief, the reasoning behind the belief, and some significant consequences of the belief.

The Essay of Affirmation

The essay of affirmation takes the position *I agree.* If you want to write an essay agreeing with—affirming—the ideas of another, such as a philosopher, a simple statement of agreement ("Works for me!") will not cut it in a philosophy class. You will need to present an exposition of the philosopher's point of view, identify your areas of agreement, and then present these along with reasoning that supports your agreement. An especially strong development to include in an essay of affirmation is available to you if a philosopher's insight inspires in you not mere affirmation but a significant change in your own thinking and belief system.

Remember, you are writing an essay, not a book. You may certainly express admiration for a philosopher's body of work (to the extent that you know it), but your essay should focus on some specific insight, concept, or relatively brief published work of your chosen philosopher. A workable format for an essay of affirmation might adhere to this outline:

1. State your purpose and define your focus: "Ralph Waldo Emerson's metaphor of the 'transparent eyeball' in his 1836 essay *Nature* showed me a way in which philosophy can explain how one may feel the presence of God in nature."
2. Explain the "transparent eyeball" metaphor.
3. Present Emerson's reasoning behind the metaphor.
4. Present your support for this metaphor, including your argument for that support.
5. Present the broader significance of the metaphor—not just its implications for your beliefs, but for those others as well.

The essay of affirmation needs to exhibit three skills:

1. Expository skill adequate to explain the expressed thought of another person.
2. Expository and argumentative skill adequate to explain and justify your support for that thought.
3. Argumentative skill adequate to persuade others that your position of support is relevant to them.

The Essay of Refutation

The essay of refutation takes the position "I disagree." Its objective is to persuade the reader that the argument of another is false, flawed, unlikely, implausible, or in some other way objectionable (for instance, unethical).

There are three intellectually and philosophically legitimate ways to refute an argument:

1. You may attack the content of the argument.
2. You may attack the form of the argument.
3. You may attack both content and form.

It is usually easier to attack the content of an argument than it is to attack its form. A premise can be factually refuted through research that finds contrary facts, facts that appear either more persuasive, or facts that otherwise show one or more of the premises of the argument under discussion to be false. Arguments that rely on statistics or extensively studied historical facts are most readily refuted by the presentation of research. Where the facts are subject to a range of interpretation, the task of refutation becomes an endeavor to persuade readers of the superiority of your interpretation over the position you are refuting.

To refute an argument based on form requires you to show that, even if the premises are true, the conclusion reached does not necessarily follow from them. Look especially for internal contradictions or the fallacy of equivocation, the bending of language by using a key word or expression in multiple senses throughout the argument. For instance, the word *man* means an adult male human being and, for most of history, has also been synonymous with a human being or humankind in general, regardless of gneder. So, the following syllogism is equivocal:

Man alone is rational.
No woman is a man.
Therefore, no woman is rational.

In the major premise, "man" is used as a synonym for humankind. In the minor premise, however, the usage stealthily shifts to "man," in the restrictive sense of male, to "prove" that no woman is rational because no woman is a man (male).

If you were setting out to refute an argument against legal abortion based on the assertion that an embryo is a person, you could attack either the content of the argument, its form, or both. You could marshal facts (based on research) that counter the concept of embryonic personhood by showing that a collection of cells does not exhibit the properties and characteristics of personhood that have historically constituted the definition of a person. You could also argue that merely applying the word "person" to an "embryo" is an instance of equivocation, the arbitrary application of multiple meanings to the same word used in an argument. (This is not to say that a skilled and well-informed opponent of abortion would be unable to more successfully argue, on some other basis, against abortion or even argue on a moral basis for revising the meaning of "person.")

Refutation can be difficult, and, like most issues in philosophy, it is rarely absolute. This said, a good refutation must satisfy at least three requirements and, ideally, a fourth as well:

1. It must clearly state the question or issue under dispute.
2. It must fully and fairly present the point of view you intend to refute. You must be careful to avoid setting up a strawman to knock down.
3. It must present your refutation and an argument to support it.

4. It should anticipate and refute objections to your position (in #3) based on the point of view you have fairly represented (in #2).

Other Categorizations of Philosophical Writing

There are other ways of classifying the forms of philosophic writing you may be asked to produce. The most prominent of these are:

1. The expository paper
2. The argumentative paper
3. The position paper
4. The case study
5. The "Socratic" dialogue
6. The research paper

The Expository Paper

We have already touched on the expository paper, but let's discuss it briefly here. Look at the adjective *expository.* It is derived from the noun *exposition,* which is the noun form of the verb *expose.* An expository essay exposes a subject, explaining it and illustrating it. It may be descriptive, describing something, someplace, some person, some experience, or it may be a process essay, explaining the process of making or doing something. It differs from both an argumentative paper and a position paper by its intellectual neutrality. It strives to be objective, favoring neither one position nor another.

The Argumentative Paper

Essays of assertion, affirmation, and refutation are all examples of the argumentative paper. An effective argument relies on factually true premises or premises for which you have strong support.

Any argument worth making in a philosophy class will not be simple in the sense of *A is true because B is true.* It will consist of intermediate arguments clearly linked together and ultimately supporting your principal point. The philosophical argument is an intellectual journey, and the effective writer of such an argument provides directional signposts to guide the reader through the argument to its conclusion. The most effective argumentative essays end with the author in effect telling readers that they have reached their destination and expanding on the significance of their arrival.

Most arguments share this characteristic: they are intended to win an argument. Arguments have a variety of stakes. They may aspire to sell a product, promote a political candidate, promote a governmental policy, promote an intellectual or moral or political point of view, persuade a jury to acquit or convict a defendant, and so on. A minority of arguments, especially in a philosophical context, are not about winning. Instead, they pit against one another points of view on a question or problem for the purpose of discovering the truth about something of importance.

Philosophical arguments do not rely on shouted threats and curses. Their authors try hard to avoid these kinds of things, along with other tactics often used in arguments outside of the philosophy class, including appeals to received wisdom, tradition, arbitrary authority, and popularity. They avoid attacking an opponent's personality or character. They do not attempt such tricks as equivocation.

A philosophical argument is not a shouting match between child and parent, customer and store owner, husband and wife. A philosophical argument describes a sequence of statements, which include at least one premise, a conclusion, and logical links between the premise or premises and the conclusion. In philosophy, "argument" describes a mode of expression intended to reach the truth in a dispute.

As we have seen, a premise is a statement offered as evidence for a conclusion. The premise is sometimes assumed to be true, at least in the context of the argument. Often, however, each premise must be supported by observed fact or a fact derived from researching reliable sources.

Getting from premise(s) to conclusion requires the proper use of the connective words English offers. Among these are *and*, *or*, and *if... then* as well as the phrase, *it's not the case that*, which negates a statement or a group of statements connected by the other connective words.

And joins two or more statements.

Or joins two or more statements with the logical meaning of "at least one."

If ... then, when used in a conditional statement, connects two statements. The statement that comes after *If* but before *then* is called the antecedent, and the statement that comes after *then* is the consequent. The use of *if ... then* is not restricted to simple sentences. Compound sentences that are formed by *if ... then* are called conditionals. These are often the premises of arguments.

If ... then also functions as the connective in any argument that connects the premise(s) to the conclusion. Indeed, you could express any logical argument in a single long conditional sentence in which the conjunction of all the premises is the antecedent, and the conclusion is the consequent.

The resulting sentence would likely be extremely difficult to follow, but it would still be logical.

As for the conclusion, it is a statement that results from the premise(s). The linking words and phrases that signal the approach of a conclusion include: *therefore, if ... then, hence, I conclude that, consequently, so, it follows that, it is true that,* and *it is the case that.* Some of these lend themselves to modification. For instance, if the conclusion is less than certain, the appropriate link to that conclusion might be *it is probably the case that* or *it is likely true that.* Philosophical argument recognizes probability and the absence of certainty. A conclusion need not be absolute. Indeed, few are.

The Position Paper

A position paper may be viewed as a type of argumentative paper in that it states a claim—your position—concerning a topic, issue, or question and presents a justification for that claim. The position paper should be limited to a single, well-defined issue or point. It is often used to define the writer's position on a question of policy. A good letter to the editor is an example of a position paper. This is the general format to follow:

1. Clearly state the question or issue under dispute.
2. State your claim. Ideally, this should be a single sentence that defines your position on #1. It is this position that the rest of the paper will justify.
3. Develop your claim as necessary, defining key terms as *you* intend to use them
4. State the opposition to your claim (the "counterclaim"). As in any argumentative paper, be fair in this statement. It is important to state at least two reasons that some people support the counterclaim.
5. Argue *your* position. Restate your claim, refute the counterclaim, and present at least two strong reasons in support of your claim.
6. Summarize your supporting argument.

10

Strategic Writing Choices for Philosophy Class

Writing philosophy should not be easy, but you cannot allow it to become impossible. Here are five strategic rules of thumb for embarking on a successful writing project for philosophy class:

1. Choose a manageable philosophical topic. It should be neither too obvious to be worth writing about nor too obscure to interest anyone; neither too broad in scope nor too limited.
2. Know when to narrow and when to enlarge your scope. If you are in doubt, sketch a high-level outline. If you cannot get beyond the first two roman numerals (major topics) in that outline, you need to go bigger. If, however, your major topics go on and on, you should narrow and sharpen your focus. Take into account any page limits or word count ranges your instructor may have specified.
3. Define novel approaches to familiar topics. Remember, the essence of philosophy is in ordinary things that few people think about. Look for new and interesting angles on the subjects that most folks take for granted.
4. Be a contrarian. Philosophers heed the original corporate motto of Apple Computer: "Think different." Take a common assumption and formulate its contrary. For instance: *Low prices sell more products.* Consider arguing instead: *Higher prices sell more of certain products.*
5. Question everything: Dig to the root of any philosophical discussion and you will eventually reach a question. Questions are the seeds of philosophical thought and, therefore, philosophical writing. Question everything.

Writing as "Doing" Philosophy

Any subject or field philosophy touches can be written about—although it is true that some philosophical disciplines, such as mathematical and symbolic logic and semiotics (the study of semiosis, or sign process) often venture beyond conventional ("ordinary") language. Conversely, with the exceptions noted, writing can "do" all categories of philosophy. Writing is the primary instrument of philosophy.

Depending on your interests and the demands of your philosophy class or classes, you may choose to do philosophy by writing a paper in the areas of—

- Ethics

  Personal ethics. What should guide the behavior of the individual?

  Public and political ethics. What should guide public policy and those who create and implement it?

- Government and politics

  Nature of government. This is the subject of Plato's *Republic,* history's first great philosophical treatise on the proper basis, aims, and form of government and society.

  Public policy issues. What principles should guide the creation and execution of public policy (with a focus on specific issues of importance)?

- Legal philosophy

  Applying ethics to a law or legal problem. How can philosophical principles be used to guide the writing of laws and the enforcement of law as well as the just resolution of legal issues?

  The ethics of breaking the law. Under what circumstances is it permissible or even imperative to break the law?

- Mind and epistemology

  Historical essay. Write about one or more of the philosophers who explored the nature of mind, knowing, and knowledge.

Critical essay on a particular philosopher of mind. Investigate the thought of a specific philosopher on some aspect of mind through an expository or argumentative essay.

Compare and contrast epistemological theories.

Problems posed by artificial intelligence. The digital world has opened up a whole new aspect of mind science and epistemology. How are philosophers responding?

- Art and popular culture

  Historical essay on aesthetics. Tastes change. Why? Good question. Write about it.

  Critical essay on a work of art, literature, or film based on a specific theory of aesthetics. Ground your aesthetic opinion in philosophical principles.

  Problems in aesthetic criticism. What is beauty? What is sublimity? What is tragedy? What is comedy?

- Science

  Philosophical approach to a specific science. Ask philosophical questions about aspects of scientific insight and method.

  Relationship between philosophy and science. Science was once a subordinate branch of philosophy. The modern relationship between philosophy and science remains fertile ground for a writer.

Some Topics for Philosophy Essays

Should people always obey the law?
Is speeding immoral?
What is loneliness?
What is the most difficult ethical decision you have ever made? Why?
What is the perfect life?
Truth is relative. Support or refute.
Democracy is the best form of government. Support or refute.

Utopia is possible. Support or refute.
Should organized religion be involved in politics?
Is euthanasia ethical?
Is morality objective or subjective?
Freedom of speech should be without limit. Support or refute.
Can murder be justified?
Abortion is a human right. Support or refute.
Is torture ever ethical?
Can science and religion coexist in terms of epistemology?
Animal experimentation is unethical. Support or refute.
Is artificial intelligence really intelligence?
Is human cloning ethical?
Is honesty necessary?
Is lying ever justified?
Is patriotism a virtue?
Is marriage obsolete?
Law *x* does more harm than good. Support or refute.
George Orwell's *Animal Farm* is useless as political criticism. Support or refute.
George Orwell's *Animal Farm* is valuable as political criticism. Support or refute.
"I think, therefore I am" is obviously true. Support or refute.
"I think, therefore I am" is obviously untrue. Support or refute.
"I think, therefore I am" proves nothing. Support or refute.
Mind and body are separate. Support or refute.
"It is better to have loved and lost than never to have loved at all" is true. Support or refute.
"It is better to have loved and lost than never to have loved at all" is false. Support or refute.

Part III

Reference

11

Frequently Used Philosophical Terms and Concepts

A

a posteriori (always with lowercase a)
Literally, "after experience." It is often intended in that way or as generally meaning that which is empirical, or with experience. (See **Empirical**.)

a priori (always with lowercase a)
Literally, "prior to experience." Commonly in philosophical thought, this priority is considered a logical one. Even more commonly, it is used to mean that which is independent of all experience.

A-proposition
A universal affirmative categorical claim that asserts the subject class is entirely included in the predicate class. (See also **Categorical Proposition**.)

Absolute idealism
An ontologically monistic philosophy, associated mainly with G. W. F. Hegel and Friedrich Schelling, that dominated philosophical thought in Britain and Germany until the twentieth century.

Absolute space
The view that space exists independently of (that is, not relative to) objects and events said to be in them. (See also **Absolute time**.)

Absolute time
The view that time exists independently of (that is, not relative to) objects and events said to be in them. (See also **Absolute space**.)

Absolutism
The view that there is a single, knowable truth. Moral absolutism is typically contrasted with moral relativism.

Abstract
General, as opposed to concrete, and thus independent of any particular.

Absurdity
The sense, typically associated with existentialism, that existence in general (and life in particular) is meaningless and the universe indifferent, and therefore irrational. This sense arises from the conflict between meaninglessness and indifference on the one hand and the human need to find meaning and purpose on the other.

Act utilitarianism
The view that the rightness of actions is entirely dependent upon the overall happiness individual acts produce.

Ad-hoc hypothesis
A hypothesis added to avoid falsification; more specifically, a hypothesis that does not increase the overall content, hence falsifiability, of the theory. An example is the hypothesis of the cosmological constant, which Albert Einstein added to his theory of general relativity to allow a static universe.

Ad hominem argument
Literally, "to the man," an ad hominem is an attack on the person, rather than a critical engagement with their position. Versions of the ad hominem are 1) ad hominem circumstantial, where a person's circumstances—for example, political or religious affiliations—are used as grounds to dismiss a claim rather than critically engaging with the claim itself; and 2) "Tu quoque," or "you're one, too," in which a person accuses someone of hypocrisy, rather than addressing that person's position.

Agnosticism
The belief that it is impossible to know whether God exists; therefore, the agnostic suspends judgment.

Ahimsa
The Hindu, Buddhist, and Jainist principle of not harming living beings; often referred to as the "non-harm" or "nonviolence" principle.

Akrasia
Weakness of the will as exhibited in intentional behavior that conflicts with an agent's values (such as overindulgence). The possibility of akrasia is seen as paradoxical for certain philosophical theories regarding the motivation of our actions, the basis of decision theory, and the connection generally between rationality and behavior.

Alienation
A psychological or social ill, in which a self and other, which properly belong together, are separated. Alienation is a concept central to Marxism and denotes the result of separating a person from their labor, identity with the products of that labor, from others, and from themselves. Such separation, Marxism holds, is the unnatural, exploited condition of workers in a capitalist economy.

Altruism
The belief in, or practice of, selfless concern for others' well-being; typically contrasted with selfishness.

Ambiguity
A property of a sentence in natural (or "ordinary") language that has two or more meanings. The multiple meanings are the result either of using a word in more than one sense (see **Equivocation**) or because of imprecise sentence structure.

Amoral
Neither moral nor immoral.

Analects
Literally, "selected sayings" attributed to Confucius, this text constitutes the founding philosophical document of Confucianism.

Analytic philosophy
The twentieth-century philosophical movement (active predominantly in the United States and Britain) that focuses primarily on language and linguistic analysis; opposed to Absolute Idealism.

Analytic statement
A logically true statement, the denial of which results in a contradiction.

Analytic-synthetic distinction
An analytic statement is true in virtue of the meaning of its terms (for instance, "all bachelors are men") while a synthetic statement is true based on how its meaning relates to the world. The analytic-synthetic distinction has been challenged as imprecise, circular, and because no statements are immune from empirical revision.

Analytic truth
Both demonstrably and necessarily true, owing to the logical form of the sentence or the meanings of its component words.

Analytical consequence
In formal logic, a statement (or sentence) is an analytical consequence of another because of one or more logical features. These logical features are truth-functional connectives, identity, predicate symbol, and quantifier.

Anarchism
The view that individual rights and the public interest cannot be served by a state because no government has the legitimate authority to coerce people.

Anatta
The Buddhist doctrine of the impermanence of the self; also describes the not-self or no-soul view.

Ancient atomism
The theory, typically associated with the Pre-Socratic thinkers Leucippus and Democritus, that reality consists of an infinite number of "uncuttables"—atoms—indivisible bits that move randomly in an infinite void.

Anicca
The Buddhist doctrine of impermanence. Together with **anatta** and **dukkha**, anicca is one of the fundamental characteristics of things.

Animism
1) The view that the universe is an organism. 2) The view that all things are imbued with sentient life.

Antecedent
In a conditional claim, the "if" clause is called the antecedent. More generally, that which is logically prior.

Antecedent conditions
Those happenings that precede and are said to cause another or other happening. Antecedent conditions are said to be sufficient for a happening. In a conditional claim, the antecedent is the "if" clause.

Appeal to force or fear (ad baculum)
An informal fallacy constituted by using a threat, rather than relevant reasons, to get someone to accept a claim.

Appeal to pity (ad misericordiam)
An informal fallacy constituted by imploring someone to accept a claim on the basis of pity, rather than relevant reasons.

Appeal to unqualified authority
An informal fallacy constituted by relying on an unqualified authority as evidence for the truth of a claim.

Apeiron
Literally, "the unlimited," or "boundless." The Pre-Socratic philosopher Anaximander held that aperion is the basic stuff of the universe.

Aphorism
A short sentence or two that expresses a novel, insightful, or startling observation.

Appearance
That which seems to be; that which appears to the senses. Thinkers such as Plato and Kant distinguish between appearance and reality.

Applied ethics
The field of ethics concerned with controversial moral issues—for example, abortion, environmental ethics, and so on.

Archē
From the Greek for "source," or "beginning," it is a term used by Pre-Socratic philosophers to describe the first principle of existing things.

Areté
From the Greek for "excellence" or "moral virtue," it is used in ancient Greek philosophy to denote fulfilment of purpose or achieving one's potential in life.

Argument
The reasoning process constituted by a series of statements, one of which (the conclusion) is inferred from the other statement(s). In formal logic, the word has two senses: 1) A series of statements, one of which (the conclusion) is claimed to follow from another or others (the premise or premises). 2) The number of individual constants or variables a predicate takes in a **well-formed formula (wff)**.

Argument from design
An argument that attempts to prove God's existence from the uniformity, or apparent design, of nature. Since the universe looks as if it has been designed, and that which is designed has a designer, it follows that the universe has a designer, which must be God. The argument involves an analogy between human-made things and the natural world. (See also **Teleological argument**.)

Aristocracy
A society ruled by the best citizens. Plato is among those thinkers who favored an aristocracy over a democracy.

Aristotelian forms
The four claim types in Aristotelian logic, which are the universal

affirmative (All S are P; **A-proposition**), universal negative (No S are P; **E-proposition**) particular affirmative (Some S are P; **I-proposition**); and particular negative (Some S are not P; **O-proposition**).

Arity
In formal logic, the number of arguments (see **Argument**) a predicate takes.

Asceticism
The belief in and practice of self-denial and material simplicity as a means to achieve philosophical or spiritual goals.

Assertion
A stated position or declaration. Without reasons to support it, an assertion is merely an opinion. Any claim that is either true or false. (See also **Statement.**)

Association of ideas
In empiricist thought, ideas are associated through experience; a theory of how mental representations are connected.

Assumption
1) In an argument, that which is taken for granted so that the argument may proceed. 2) An unproven assertion taken as true.

Assumptive proof
A nested proof—that is, a proof that occurs within a larger proof sequence. (See also **Subproof.**)

Atheism
The belief that there is no God.

Atman
The Hindu term for one's essence, soul, or true self.

Atomic sentence
In formal logic, the most basic sentence corresponding to the simplest sentence in ordinary language. An atomic sentence consists of a predicate and the relevant **arity**.

Attribute
A property, either essential or inessential.

Authority
That which, typically by right, controls.

Autonomy
From the Greek words for "self" and "law," self-legislation, or the ability to freely determine one's life.

Axiology
The branch of philosophy concerned with the study of value, both aesthetic value and moral value.

Axiom
A proposition (or claim) that is accepted as true about some domain and used to establish other truths about that domain; a principle, generally accepted at the outset as an argument's starting point.

B

Bad faith
The refusal to accept responsibility for one's freedom and, therefore, also for one's choices. The term comes from the twentieth-century existentialist Jean-Paul Sartre.

Bayes's Theorem
Named after Thomas Bayes (1701?-1761), Bayes's Theorem describes how to update belief in the likelihood of an event, given the occurrence of evidence relevant to that event. While Bayes's Theorem thus states minimal conditions of probabilistic consistency among our beliefs, Bayesians disagree regarding the extent to which other epistemological problems can be similarly resolved.

Becoming
In Plato, the world of appearance is the world of becoming—coming to be and passing away—that characterizes our daily experience.

Begging the question
An informal fallacy, begging the question occurs when the arguer assumes the very claim they intend to prove. For instance: "God exists because the Bible, which comes from God, says He exists." Question begging is related to circular reasoning, where the conclusion is simply a restatement of a premise, as in: Shakespeare's *Hamlet* is a great play because Shakespeare is a great playwright.

Behaviorism
A theory of mind in which features of an individual's mental states are inferred from what is publicly observable.

Being
Plato's realm of reality, contrasted with the realms of appearance and becoming, is *being*, the realm of eternal and immutable Forms. More generally, the term "being" is used by philosophers for what there is—that is, fundamental reality. (See also **Ontology**.)

Belief
A psychological state usually characterized as a disposition to assent to a certain proposition (the intentional object of the belief) or otherwise act as though that proposition were true. In more formal models, a belief is characterized by a probabilistic degree of certainty in the truth of the proposition.

Best of all possible worlds
Gottfried Wilhelm Leibniz's (1646-1716) view that this world is the best of the possible worlds God could have created. The claim was advanced as the argument of Leibniz's theodicy, his vindication of the goodness of God despite the problem of evil in the world.

Bhagavadgītā ("Gītā")
The sixth book of the Hindu epic poem, *Mahabharata*.

Biconditional
A two-way conditional claim, typically expressed by the phrase, "if and only if." In symbolic logic, the phrase is often notated by a two-way arrow (↔) or a triple bar (≡). In a truth table, the biconditional is true whenever the sentences on either side of the operator have the same value on a given row.

Biconditional elimination
In symbolic logic, a valid inference in a system of truth-functional rules. The affirmation of one side of the biconditional yields the other.

Biconditional introduction
In symbolic logic, a valid inference in a system of truth-functional rules. A biconditional sentence is inferred from deriving one side of the sentence (Q) from the assumption of the other (P) in a subproof sequence, followed by a parallel sequence for deriving P from the assumption, Q.

Boolean connectives (Boolean operators)
Named after mathematician and logician George Boole, these are the three fundamental truth-functional building blocks of compound sentences. They are *negation*, *conjunction*, and *disjunction*. The ordinary language words for each are "not," "and," and "or." The logical symbols for each are commonly as follows:

Negation: ¬ and ~
Conjunction: ^, •, and &
Disjunction: ∨

Bound variable
A variable (such as x, y, and z) is bound by a quantifier that is used with the same variable—for example, $\forall x\ (Px \rightarrow Qx)$.

Brahman
The Hindu conception of the impersonal, universal all-pervading spirit; it is both the universe and transcends space and time. The word also signifies a member of the highest caste in Hinduism, the priestly caste.

Brentano's Thesis
Named for Franz Brentano (1838-1917), this is the claim that since all and only mental phenomena are intentional (that is, they are *about* other things), the mental cannot be reduced to the physical.

C

Cartesian
1) A follower of René Descartes. 2) Descartes' method, which is deductive and, like geometry, begins with self-evident axioms.

Categorical Imperative
Kant's name for the expression of reason's supreme moral principle; it commands under all circumstances to either do, or not do, something. It is an ethical directive based on the perspective of pure reason alone (rather than contingent on personal circumstances). According to Kant, to act in accordance with a categorical imperative is to act only according to maxims that can be consistently willed as universal laws—for instance, Do unto others as you would have them do unto you.

Categorical Logic
A deductive system of logic first established by Aristotle, which studies the relations between categories of things.

Categorical proposition
An assertion relating two classes of object: universal affirmative (All S are P), universal negative (No S are P), particular affirmative (Some S are P), and particular negative (Some S are not P).

Categorical syllogism
A syllogism consisting entirely of categorical claims; three terms (categories) each appear twice.

Categories
1) Aristotle's four-fold classification system of language and ontology. 2) Kant's term, which he took from Aristotle, for the basic and a priori concepts that structure human knowledge.

Category mistake
An error of reasoning based on placing an entity in the wrong ontological or semantic category; Gilbert Ryle (1900-1976) famously argued that the metaphysical distinction between the mind and body was based on the category mistake of treating mental discourse as about particular entities, rather than as dispositions toward certain behavior.

Causal interactionism
The theory of mind that mind and body causally interact: mental events cause bodily events, and vice versa.

Causal theory of perception
The theory that sensations and ideas are caused by physical things acting upon our organs of sense.

Causation (or causality)
One event (cause) brings about another event (effect). Causes and effects are considered law-like natural events.

Cause
That which brings something about. That which explains a happening.

Cause-of-itself (*causa sui*)
That which is self-caused, or whose essence includes existence—that is, necessary existence. Often said of God.

Certainty
That which is beyond doubt, but not merely psychologically. Philosophical certainty involves finding no reasons for doubt.

Change of Quantifier (Quantifier Exchange) Rule
In quantifier logic, one quantified statement can be substituted for another that is logically equivalent to the original. A universally quantified statement is equivalent to an existentially quantified statement (and vice versa), provided the relevant negations are added or removed:

$\forall x\, P(x) :: \neg \exists x\, \neg P(x)$
$\neg \forall x\, P(x) :: \exists x\, \neg P(x)$
$\exists x\, P(x) :: \neg \forall x\, \neg P(x)$
$\neg \exists x\, P(x) :: \forall x\, \neg P(x)$

The statements in each pair can be substituted for each other in a proof. The ordinary language version of the equivalences is as follows:

> "Everything is P" is equivalent to "It's not the case that something is not P."

"It's not the case that everything is P" is equivalent to "Something is not P."
"Something is P" is equivalent to "It's not the case that everything is not P."
"It's not the case that there is P" is equivalent to "Everything is not P" or "Nothing is P."

Church-Turing Thesis
The Church-Turing Thesis states the extensional equivalence of several different methods of formalizing the notion of computability (for example, any general recursive function can be computed by a Turing Machine) and thus conjectures that the informal notion of computability captures a well-defined set of functions.

Civil rights
Rights determined by laws—such as constitutional rights.

Claim
A statement in an argument, typically the one to be proved. (See also **Proposition and Statement**.)

Cogent argument
An evaluation concept of inductive logic. An argument is cogent when it is strong and the premises are true.

Cogito, ergo sum
Literally, "I think, therefore I am." This is the certainty René Descartes establishes as the foundation of his system of philosophy and as the certain foundation for knowledge even in the face of radical doubt.

Coherence
Fitting together in a logical, orderly fashion.

Coherence theory of truth
The theory that a statement or a belief is true if and only if it coheres with a specified system of statements or beliefs.

Communism
The political theory derived from Marx's argument in favor of a class war

that would result in publicly owned property and "each works and is supported according to his abilities and needs."

Communitarian ethic
An ethical theory that values community and communal relationships, which form individuals.

Compatibilism
The view that free will (in some sense) and determinism are compatible.

Compensatory justice
A theory of justice that requires the restoration of any loss to the person wronged.

Complement
The set of objects not included in a class; expressed by "non-."

Completeness
A formal deductive system is complete if each valid inference can be proved by means of the rules in that system—that is, when no invalid arguments are provable within it. (See also **Soundness**.)

Conceptual truth
1) A statement whose truth is determined by its concepts; understanding the meaning of the concepts shows their relation. 2) For Aristotle, a conceptual truth describes a thing's essence.

Conclusion
The statement in an argument claimed to follow from the premise(s). An argument's supported statement. In ordinary language, the conclusion is indicated by words and phrases such as: "Therefore," "It follows that," "Consequently," and "So."

Conditional
A claim having a form such as "If...then," "X...then," "If...X," and "X only if..." The conditional is symbolized in formal logic by the arrow (→) and horseshoe (⊃). In truth-functional (sentential or propositional) logic, the conditional is false when the antecedent is true and the consequent is false. (See also **Material Conditional** and **Truth-Functional**.)

Conditional elimination
In symbolic logic, a valid inference in a system of truth-functional rules. The consequent of a conditional claim is inferred when the antecedent of that claim is affirmed. (See also **Modus ponens**.)

Conditional introduction (Conditional proof)
In symbolic logic, a valid inference in a system of truth-functional rules. Conditional introduction is the method of proof whereby a conditional claim is proved by deriving a statement Q from the assumption of P in a subproof.

Conjunct
A component of a sentence governed by the Boolean connective, **conjunction**.

Conjunction
The ordinary language name for the Boolean connective that corresponds to, for example, "and," "both...and," and "but." On a truth table, the conjunction of sentences is true if, and only if, each of the conjuncts is true.

Conjunction elimination
In symbolic logic, a valid inference in a system of truth-functional rules. Because a statement governed by a conjunction is true if, and only if, each of the conjuncts is true, it follows that one of the conjuncts may be inferred from the statement.

Conjunction introduction
In symbolic logic, a valid inference in a system of truth-functional rules. In a derivation, two statements can be inferred using the conjunction symbol, since a statement governed by the conjunction is true if, and only if, each of the conjuncts is true.

Connective
In symbolic logic, a connective (negation, conjunction, disjunction, conditional, and biconditional) is used to make new statements out of simpler ones.

Conscience
One's internal moral compass, as in the view that God instills in us a moral sense. Conscience is a sort of moral intuition—that is, an undefended or unexamined moral sense.

Consequent
The "then" clause in an "if…then" (conditional) claim is the consequent.

Consequentialism
The ethical view that the rightness or wrongness of an action is determined by its consequences.

Consistent
Non-contradictory principles or statements.

Constitute
First used in a technical way by Immanuel Kant (1724-1804), and later by Edmund Husserl (1859-1938), to synthesize experience through a priori categories.

Contingent truth
A truth dependent on facts. As such, it is neither logically necessary nor logically impossible. In propositional logic, a contingently true statement is true on at least one row of the truth table, in the column under the (main) operator.

Contradiction
That which is logically incompatible. A statement is self-contradictory when it is necessarily false; a contradiction obtains between two sentences when they cannot be simultaneously true or simultaneously false.

Contradiction introduction
In symbolic logic, a valid inference in a system of truth-functional rules. The rule whereby a contradiction (P and ¬ P) is proved on separate lines in a proof or subproof.

Contradiction elimination
In symbolic logic, a valid inference in a system of truth-functional rules. From a contradiction, anything follows. So, once a contradiction has been established in a proof, any statement is permitted immediately after.

Contradictories
Two statements that cannot be simultaneously true or simultaneously false. In categorical logic, the A-proposition and O-proposition are contradictories,

and the E- and I-propositions are contradictories. (See also **A-proposition**, **O-proposition**, **E-proposition**, and **I-proposition**.)

Contraposition
An immediate inference made by exchanging the subject and predicate terms of a categorical proposition, and then adding the complement to the subject and predicate terms. Contraposition is a valid inference when the resulting proposition is equivalent to the original. As such, it is valid only for A- and O-propositions.

Contraposition by limitation
A two-step inference involving the subalternation from the E-proposition to its corresponding O-proposition and then contraposing the result. Contraposition by limitation is a valid inference only for the E-proposition on the Aristotelian, or traditional, interpretation of the universal—that is, on the assumption of existential import.

Contraries
A pair of propositions that cannot both be simultaneously true but can be simultaneously false. In categorical logic, A- and E-propositions are contraries. If one is true, the other must be false. If one is false, however, the other is undetermined. (See **Categorical proposition**, **A-proposition**, and **E-proposition**.)

Conversion
An immediate inference made by exchanging the subject and predicate terms of a categorical proposition. Conversion is a valid inference when the resulting proposition is equivalent to the original. As such it is valid only for E- and I-propositions.

Conversion by limitation
A two-step inference involving the subalternation from the A-proposition to its corresponding I-proposition and then converting the result. Conversion by limitation is a valid inference only for the A-proposition on the Aristotelian, or traditional, interpretation of the universal—that is, on the assumption of existential import.

Correspondence theory of truth
The theory that the truth of a statement is its correspondence to facts or states of affairs.

Cosmogony
The study of the origins of the universe.

Cosmological argument
An argument that God exists because there must have been a first cause—that is, an ultimate reason for the universe.

Cosmology
The study of the origins and development of the universe.

Cosmopolitanism
The view that human beings belong to a single community.

Counterexample
An argument that shares the same form as the original but consists of true premises and a false conclusion. A counterexample shows an argument is invalid, since there is at least one possible scenario in which the premises are true and the conclusion is false or not necessarily true. (See also **Demonstration of Non-Consequence**.)

Counterfactual
A contrary-to-fact conditional—for example, "if P were true, then Q would be true." A counterfactual is true if the antecedent, in conjunction with the laws of nature, logically entails the consequent, or if the closest possible world where P is true also one where Q is true.

Criterion
A standard of judgment.

Critical thinking
1) The systematic process of open-minded, objective, and thorough reasoning to a conclusion. 2) The systematic process of analyzing concepts, theories, and arguments.

Cultural relativism
In anthropology, the descriptive theory that different societies have fundamentally different moralities. It is taken up in ethical relativism. (See also **Relativism.**)

D

Dao
See *Tao.*

Data
Latin for the plural of "what is given."

Datum
Latin (singular) for "what is given."

Declarative sentence
A sentence asserting a fact, position, or proposition.

Deconstruction
A philosophical school of thought begun by twentieth-century philosopher Jacques Derrida (1930-2004). Often contrasted with the Anglo-American analytic tradition, deconstruction involves a specifically critical reading of a text that upends the traditional value hierarchy and is an internal critique of a philosophical position, using its own assumptions to show the position to be incoherent. Derrida argued that this was the only legitimate form of philosophical critique, on the grounds that there is no objective standpoint (or philosophically uncontaminated language) from which we can otherwise proceed.

Deductive argument
An argument that attempts to show the conclusion must be true if the premises are true. (See also **Indictive argument.**)

Deductive system
A formal system of rules and instructions for use in the construction of formal proofs.

Deism
The belief, popular in the eighteenth century, that God exists in order for the universe to have been created, but we are not justified in believing that God is concerned about us.

Democracy
A system of government by the members of the society, typically through elected representatives.

Demonstration of non-consequence
An argument that shares the same form as the original but consists of true premises and a false conclusion. A counterexample shows an argument is invalid, since there is at least one possible scenario in which the premises are true and the conclusion is false or is not necessarily true. (See also **Counterexample**.)

DeMorgan's Laws
Named after the British mathematician and logician Augustus deMorgan (2806-1871), two sets of statements are truth-functionally equivalent:

$\neg (P \wedge Q) :: \neg P \vee \neg Q$

and

$\neg (P \vee Q) :: \neg P \wedge \neg Q$

The statements in each pair can be substituted for each other in a proof. The ordinary language version of the rules is as follows:

"Not both P and Q," is equivalent to "Either not P or not Q."

and

"Neither P nor Q," is equivalent to "It is not the case that P and it is not the case that Q."

There are also two DeMorgan laws for quantifiers:

$\neg \forall x Px :: \exists x \neg Px$

and

$\neg \exists x\, Px :: \forall x\, \neg Px$

In ordinary language, DeMorgan's laws for quantifiers can be read as follows:

"Not everything is P" is equivalent to "Something is not P."

and

"It's not the case that there is a P" is equivalent to "Everything is not P."

Deontological
A duty-based ethical theory; an action is moral if it is done from duty, irrespective of the consequences. (Typically opposed to consequentialist ethical theories.)

Deontology
From the Greek, the study of duty.

Derivation
A formal proof enlisting logical rules.

Determinism
The view that all events are determined, which means there is no free will and that there is only one possible history of the world, either because every event in the universe is sufficiently caused by prior events (causal determinism, natural determinism, or hard determinism), divine providence (theological determinism), or on the semantic grounds that propositions about the future must already have fixed truth values (logical determinism). A variant of causal determinism, termed "soft determinism" or "compatibilism," holds that human behavior and actions are determined by causal events but free will exists when defined as acting according to one's nature.

Dharma
In Hinduism, the moral law that governs individual conduct and is one of the four ends of life. In Buddhism, dharma is the universal truth.

Dialectic

From Plato through Hegel and Marx, a form of progressive reasoning. In ancient Greek philosophy, methods of reasoning for discovering truth. Dialectic is an argumentative exchange in the form of questions and answers, in which an initial thesis coming into opposition to its antithesis results in a synthesis. According to Hegel, this logical structure forms the metaphysical basis of historical evolution; and, in Marx, dialectic is the inevitable development of politico-economic systems (so-called Dialectical Materialism).

Dialetheism

The view that some contradictions are actually true, this is a metaphysical thesis usually based upon the technical advantages of a paraconsistent logic for some domain.

Difference principle

A principle of distributive justice associated with John Rawls, the difference principle states that inequalities in society are only justified if they nevertheless ensure the maximum benefit to the least advantaged members of that society. It can thus be thought of an example of a maxi-min strategy.

Disjunct

One of the components in a sentence governed by the connective **disjunction**.

Disjunction

One of the basic Boolean connectives that corresponds to the following English words and phrases: "Or," "Either…or." A statement governed by a disjunction is true if at least one of the disjuncts is true.

Disjunction elimination

In symbolic logic, a valid inference in a system of truth-functional rules. This rule relies on the truth definition of the disjunction: Since a disjunction can be true in three ways, the desired statement must be derived from the assumption of each side of a disjunction. The rule involves successive subproof sequences for the desired statement, after which the second subproof is discharged and the desired statement is inferred. (See also **Disjunctive Syllogism** and **Proof by Cases**.)

Disjunction introduction
In symbolic logic, a valid inference in a system of truth-functional rules. This rule relies on the truth definition of the disjunction: Since a disjunction is true when at least one of the disjuncts is true, a disjunction can be inferred from any proven statement in a derivation.

Disjunctive syllogism
In symbolic logic, a valid inference in a system of truth-functional rules. This rule relies on the truth definition of the disjunction: Since a disjunction is true when at least one of the disjuncts is true, the denial of one side of a disjunction yields the other.

Disposition
A property of an object that only manifests under certain conditions—for example, fragility. Some philosophers argue that dispositional properties are ultimately reducible to non-dispositional (categorical) properties such as non-dispositional facts about underlying molecular structure; whereas other philosophers maintain that irreducible dispositional properties can support laws of nature.

Distributive justice
The theory that provides the conceptual framework for distributing burdens and benefits across members of society.

Domain of discourse
That set of objects over which a quantifier "ranges." The scope of a quantifier "covers" the set of objects in the universe or more restricted universal classes, such as all X in a country, all X in a state.

Divine preordination
The view that God, being omniscient, knows our future actions.

Divine command theory
The view that what is moral is what God commands.

Double effect, doctrine of
The view that there is a morally relevant distinction between the intended consequences of an action and their unintended (even if foreseeable)

consequences. This allows greater scope for ethical action for those who posit exceptionless moral principles, but it is rejected by those who judge actions entirely on their consequences. It is a view that it is never acceptable to perform a bad action, even if it produces a good effect. It may, however, sometimes be acceptable to perform a good action, even if it produces a bad effect.

Dolor
A utilitarian ethical theory's name for a unit of pain or displeasure. (See also **Hedon**.)

Doubt
A demonstrable lack of certainty, rather than a mere psychological state.

Dual aspect theory
The theory that mind and body are not two ontologically distinct kinds of thing, but instead are two aspects of the same substance.

Dualism
1) The view that mind and body are two ontologically distinct kinds of thing.
2) Mental states and bodily states are distinct kinds of thing with radically different properties.

Duhem-Quine Thesis
The claim that since physical theories are never tested in isolation and any experimental failure can always be accommodated by making adjustments among the auxiliary theories involved. It follows from the thesis, therefore, that experimental evidence alone can never conclusively falsify a hypothesis.

Dutch Book Theorem
A Dutch Book is a combination of bets for which an individual is guaranteed to lose money regardless of the outcome. The Dutch Book Theorem states that such a combination of bets can always be constructed for an agent whose degrees of belief do not conform to the probability calculus.

Duty
A moral obligation.

Dukkha
The Buddhist concept that expresses the "suffering" and "pain" of existence.

E

E-proposition
A universal negative categorical claim that asserts the subject and predicate classes are mutually exclusive of each other—that is, the subject class is excluded from the predicate class and vice versa. (See also **Categorical proposition**.)

Efficient cause
The primary source of change. In Aristotle, one of four explanations of coming to be.

Egalitarianism
The view that all people have equal rights and deserve equal respect.

Egoism (or psychological egoism)
The descriptive theory that people act in their own interests. (See also **Ethical egoism**.)

Eliminative materialism
The theory that the terminology of mental states will be abandoned as more is known about the brain.

Emotivism
The theory that moral judgments are nothing other than expressions of positive or negative feelings.

Empirical
That which is experiential or derived from experience.

Empirical ego
Those features of a (specific) person discoverable through experience. Compare with **Transcendental ego**.

Empirical idealism
The view, most prominently represented by George Berkeley (1685-1753), that only ideas and minds exist; there are no material objects.

Empiricism
The philosophical view that knowledge is derived from sense experience.

Empiricist
One who holds that knowledge of the empirical world is derived solely from sense experience.

Enlightenment
(1) The period of intense intellectual development, from roughly the end of the sixteenth century through the end of the eighteenth, on the Continent and Britain. Enlightenment thought is characterized by optimism about human reason's capacity to achieve knowledge. (2) In Buddhism, nirvana (enlightenment) is the goal of human existence.

Entitlement
The having of a right.

Epicureanism
Epicurus's view that a life of moderate pleasures and the avoidance of pain (mental disturbance) is the goal of happy human existence.

Epiphenomenalism
The theory that bodily states cause mental states but mental states do not affect the body. These mental states are the effects of physical processes (brain and nervous system). An epiphenomenon is a phenomenon that lacks causal efficacy. In the philosophy of mind, this would be the claim that while mental states are caused by physical states, they do not have any causal influence on the physical world since mental-physical interaction only operates in one direction).

Epistemic closure
Knowledge is closed (under entailment) if we know every proposition entailed by a known proposition. Epistemic closure is central to skepticism, since the truth of everyday facts entail that skepticism is false. Various

definitions of knowledge (for example, counterfactual accounts) thus violate epistemic closure as a response to skepticism.

Epistemology
The branch of philosophy concerned with the nature, limits, sources, and justifications of human knowledge.

Equality
A social, political, governing, and philosophical principal that bars religion, race, sex, physical or mental abilities, wealth, social status, and so forth from being used as bases for discrimination.

Equivocation
An informal fallacy constituted by a shift in the meaning of a term from one instance to another, which prompts an erroneous inference. (See also **Ambiguity**.)

Essence (or an essential property)
That without which something would not be what it is; a thing's defining property, or that which makes something what it is, rather than something else.

Ethical absolutism
The view that there is one, and only one, morality.

Ethical egoism
The view that one should act in one's self-interest. (See also **Egoism**.)

Ethical relativism
The view that moral rightness and wrongness are relative to 1) the individual, 2) a given culture, or 3) a historical period.

Ethics
1) The branch of philosophy that studies moral theories, beliefs, and practices. 2) From the Greek *ethos*, a custom or habit. 3) A set of rules, policies, or principles that govern behavior.

Ethics of care
A theory that emphasizes the moral significance of relationships and the virtue of care.

Eudaimonia
Ancient Greek concept of "happiness" or "flourishing" as the ultimate justification of ethical activity; usually explicated in terms of the exercise of (public) virtue as part of the overall fulfilment of one's proper function or purpose, rather than the mere pursuit of personal pleasure.

Evidentialism
The view that a belief is justified only if it is supported by sufficient evidence.

Ex contradictione quodlibet
The logical principle that from a contradiction everything follows. Non-classical logics designed to invalidate this principle are known as paraconsistent logics.

Exclusive disjunction
In formal logic, a disjunction is inclusive, so the expression, "One or the other" includes "...or both." Exclusivity must be explicitly noted, as in, "One or the other, but not both."

Existential elimination
In symbolic logic, a valid inference in a system of quantifier rules. An existential claim is "eliminated" by way of a subproof that assumes a name for the claim in question, provided that the name is not already in use. For example, if the claim is "Some dogs are playful," ∃x (Dog(x) ^ Playful(x)), the assumptive name could be "Walter," with the resulting assumptive sentence, Dog(walter) ^ Playful(walter). The ensuing subproof involves the derivation of the statement S, which closes the subproof. The statement S has then been proved from that existential quantifier *elimination.*

Existential import
The assumption that at least one member of the subject class of a universal proposition exists. Aristotelian, or traditional, logic assumes existential import. The modern interpretation does not. (See also **Categorical proposition**.)

Existential introduction
In symbolic logic, a valid inference in a system of quantifier rules. From a singular sentence, the inference to an existentially quantified claim is valid. The inference is to a restricted generalization, such as, in ordinary language, the inference from "Roberta is in the room" to "Someone is in the room."

Existential quantifier
The symbolic logic notation used to make claims about the existence of at least one object in a domain of discourse. The notation ∃ followed by a variable is used to symbolize ordinary language expressions such as, "There is something," "There is at least one thing," and "Something is."

Existentialism
The twentieth-century philosophical movement popularized by atheistic existentialist Jean-Paul Sartre; but some core elements were developed by nineteenth-century Christian thinker Søren Kierkegaard.

Explanation
In contrast to a justification for a claim, whereby one attempts to prove the claim is true, an explanation provides an account, usually causal, of a claim already accepted as reflecting a fact.

Extended
That which occupies space; used by, such philosophers as Descartes, Spinoza, and Leibniz to define physical bodies.

Extension
The set of things to which an expression applies; to be contrasted with the **intension** of an expression (roughly, its meaning). Extension is also not the same as reference—for instance, the term "red" refers to the property of redness, while its extension are those objects that are red.

External meaning
Meaning or purpose originating outside humanity.

F

Fact-value distinction
The apparently fundamental contrast between descriptive statements and their evaluation, as exemplified by David Hume's contention that one cannot logically derive an "ought" (such as an ethical proscription against murder) from an "is" (for instance, a purely physical description of the act).

Facticity
First employed by Johann Gottlieb Fichte (1762-1814), the word can be used to refer to facts and factuality, but as used by Wilhelm Dilthey (1833-1911) and Neo-Kantian philosophers, has come to mean that which resists explanation and interpretation. Martin Heidegger (1889-1976) used the term to describe the "thrownness" of individual existence—that is, factuality of certain facts of a person or a historical situation that are unalterably part of existence, even if unnoticed or unattended. Jean-Paul Sartre (1905-1980) and Simone de Beauvoir (1908-1986) used *facticity* to signify all concrete facts that form the background against which human freedom both exits and is limited at a particular point in history. For instance, before medicine advanced to the point of making highly advanced artificial limbs, a person born without legs was not free to stroll on the beach.

Faith
A belief (most commonly in God) absent rational reasons or even in direct opposition to rationality. (Note that some have defended faith in God as rational.)

Fallacy
An error in reasoning. While fallacious reasoning can be apparently persuasive argument, there is a flaw either in the structure of the reasoning (a formal fallacy) or because the arguer has committed an informal fallacy. (See **Formal fallacy** and **Informal fallacy**.)

False cause
An informal fallacy constituted by arguing that two events are causally related when, in fact, a more plausible explanation is available.

False dichotomy
The informal fallacy in which two options are presented as exclusive and exhaustive when, in fact, they are not and others exist.

False dilemma
The informal fallacy in which two choices, one of which is more unpalatable than the other, are presented as the only options when, in fact, other options exist.

Fascism
The political view that an authoritarian government is best. More particularly, a form of far-right authoritarian ultranationalism characterized by dictatorship, forcible suppression of opposition, and economic and social regimentation. Leading exemplars in the twentieth century are Benito Mussolini and Adolf Hitler (whose from of fascism was called National Socialism or Nazism).

Fatalism
The view that specific events are pre-determined; historically associated with the ancient Greek view embodied by the Fates, three goddesses who control human birth and life, and more generally associated with the life view of "what will be will be."

Feminist ethics
The moral theories that explain and reject patriarchy.

Fideism
The view that faith is independent of, or even opposed to, reason.

Final cause
In Aristotle's teleology, the cause that defines the end, purpose, or (proper) function of a thing. It is one of Aristotle's four causes.

First-order consequence
A statement that follows from premises exclusively by way of truth-functional connective definitions, identity, and quantifiers.

First-order contradiction
A sentence that is false by way of the truth-functional connective definitions, identity, and quantifiers.

First-order logic
A system of logic that includes propositions (sentences), truth-functional connectives, predicates, and quantifiers.

First-order validity
An argument is valid when a sentence is logically true by way of truth-functional connective definitions, identity, and quantifiers.

First principles
The initial and firm rules, or axioms, with which a philosophy begins, either as assumptions or as believed truths.

Folk psychology
A set of commonsense principles regarding human cognition, including the distinction between beliefs and desires, and the link between such propositional attitudes and behavior. This framework is challenged by eliminativists (see **Eliminative materialism**), who maintain, for example, that these concepts have no corresponding neurological basis and therefore mislead philosophical reflection.

Formal cause
The essence, structural features, or attributes of a thing; one of Aristotle's four explanations for a thing's coming to be.

Formal fallacy
An error in the structure or form of reasoning. The most common formal fallacies include Affirming the Consequent and Denying the Antecedent. A formally fallacious argument is an invalid one.

Formal logic
The study of systems of reasoning, the principles of reasoning as such, and the relationships between the symbols that express that reasoning. Also: logic based on deductive argument using syllogisms and quasi-mathematical symbols (symbolic language).

Formal proof
In a formal deductive system, a step-by-step demonstration of the truth of a claim following from a set of premises. (See also **Proof**.)

Forms
In Plato's metaphysics, the immaterial, immutable, eternal entities that make individual things possible and are the pure objects of knowledge. Usually capitalized.

Four Noble Truths
One of Buddha's most significant teachings, namely the truth that there is suffering; the truth that suffering has a cause; the truth that suffering has an end; and the truth that there is a cause to its end.

Free-Rider Problem
A "free rider" benefits from a social arrangement without bearing the costs; for example, he rides the bus without buying a ticket. Without some mechanism to disincentivize free riders (such as punishment), any co-operative arrangement will be unstable because potentially everyone is similarly motivated to be a free rider.

Free variable (unbound variable)
A free variable is an instance of a variable that is not bound by some condition—for instance, *x* is a free variable, whereas in "for some *x*," it is a bound variable. (See **Bound variable**.)

Free will
The idea that humans are capable of behaving and acting without external compulsion or constraint. Free will is often viewed as a necessary condition of moral responsibility (See also **Liberty**.)

Functionalism
The view that mental states can be explained in terms of activities and functions.

G

Game theory
The use and study of mathematical models of strategic interaction among rational decision makers.

General conditional proof
In symbolic logic, a valid inference in a system of quantifier rules. From the assumption that an individually named thing has a specific property, an inference is drawn that that same thing has another property. The sub-proof is exited (discharged) in the same was as is a **Conditional proof** or **Conditional introduction** but to the universally quantified statement.

Generalization
1) A statement about a group or set. 2) An inference from empirical observation(s).

Generalization from experience (or Inductive generalization)
An inference from experience; more specifically, an inference from observation and experimentation to a generalization about the class of the thing investigated.

Gettier problem
A series of examples constructed by Edmund Gettier (1927-) in which justified true belief intuitively falls short of knowledge. These cases involve drawing a true conclusion based on a false (although justified) premise; as a result, it is argued that justification must be appropriately "sensitive" to the epistemological context.

Ghost in the Machine
Rejection of the Cartesian notion of a non-physical mind as based on linguistic confusion; according to Gilbert Ryle, mental statements (for instance, "he is intelligent") do not refer to properties of a non-physical entity but describe dispositions to perform physical activity in a certain way; that is, Ghost in the Machine rejects the Cartesian proposition that mental and physical activity occur simultaneously but separately.

Gödel's Incompleteness Theorems
For any axiomatic theory (including axiomatizations of arithmetic), there

will be a sentence in the language of the theory that cannot be proved. Such a sentence may be either a true sentence of the theory (the First Incompleteness Theorem) or a sentence expressing the consistency of the theory (the Second Incompleteness Theorem).

Golden Rule
"Do unto others as you would have them do unto you"—the principle of treating others as you want to be treated. This principle is found in most major religions.

Government
That authoritative body that legislates and enforces laws.

Grue Paradox
Nelson Goodman's (1906-1998) argument that every inductive basis supports an infinite number of incompatible predictions: for instance, "all emeralds are green" versus "all emeralds are grue," where *grue* means green now, but blue later. Any justification of induction must, therefore, also specify which properties are "projectable" to avoid such problems.

H

Happiness calculus (felicity calculus or hedonic calculus)
Utilitarian thinker Jeremy Bentham's (1748-1832) quantitative method of determining an action's total yield of pleasures and pains, and, thus, its moral value.

Hasty generalization
An informal fallacy constituted by inferring a generalization from too few instances.

Hedon
The Utilitarian term (from the Greek "hedon") for a quantifiable unit of pleasure; the opposite of **dolor**, which is a unit of pain (displeasure).

Hedonism
The conception of the good life that takes pleasure to be the ultimate good. Hedonism is the premise of most forms of **Utilitarianism**. It is

often the premise—although sometimes a consequence—of **ethical egoism**.

Hedonistic
Pleasure-seeking, or related to pleasure, typically associated with Epicurus, Jeremy Bentham (1748-1832), and John Stuart Mill (1806-1873).

Hermeneutics
Theory of interpretation (originally applied to incomplete texts) that acknowledges how interpretation of individual words depends upon the interpretation of the whole text, and *vice versa* (the so-called Hermeneutic Circle); this provides a model for the human sciences in general, where interpretation can itself influence what is being studied.

Heteronomy
For Kant, heteronomy is the opposite of **autonomy**. Whereas an autonomous person is one whose will is self-determined, a heteronomous person is one whose will is determined by something outside of him or her, such as overwhelming emotions. Etymologically, heteronomy is derived from the Greek words for "other' and "law."

Historicism
Originally the view that all human knowledge is irreducibly historical, and thus to some extent relativistic, historicism increasingly came to mean the (largely unfalsifiable) view that historical development is subject to its own invariable laws and processes, which can in turn be identified and studied by the social sciences.

Human rights
Those entitlements humans are thought to have by virtue of their humanity. (See also **Rights**.)

Hume's fork
How philosophers characterize David Hume's (1711-1776) claim that a belief is justified either as a "relation between ideas" or as a "matter of fact."

Hypothesis
A provisional conclusion accepted as most probable in the light of the known facts or tentatively adopted as a basis for analysis.

Hypothetical imperative
That which commands hypothetically, asserted in the form of a conditional claim, as in, "If you want X, you should do Y." (See also **Categorical imperative**.)

Hypothetico-Deductive Method
Method of testing scientific theories whereby an observable prediction is logically deduced from the hypothesis in question (in conjunction with relevant auxiliary hypotheses and initial conditions). Repeated occurrences of the prediction provide increasing confirmation for the hypothesis, while the non-occurrence of the prediction falsifies the hypothesis.

I

I-proposition
A particular affirmative categorical proposition that asserts at least one member of the subject is included in the predicate class. (See also **Categorical proposition**.)

Idea
The mental object immediately presented to the mind; according to representational theories of perception, we are only ever directly acquainted with ideas which represent external objects. In Plato, another term for Form.

Idealism
The view that only mental entities are real.

Identity of indiscernibles
Gottfried Wilhelm Leibniz's (1646-1716) principle that it is impossible for two numerically distinct things to be absolutely identical in all respects.

Identity theory
The thesis that the mind and brain are ontologically one and the same or, more accurately, that mental states and events are in fact certain brain and nervous system processes. The theory is usually presented as a form of **materialism**, but it is important to emphasize that unlike many materialistic theories, it does not deny the existence of mental events. It denies only that

they have independent existence. Mental events are nothing other than certain bodily events.

Immanent
Inherent or operating within nature or physical reality. (See also **Transcendent**.)

Immaterialism
The view that non-material entities are real. (See also **Materialism**.)

Immediate inference
An inference from one statement to another. In categorical logic, immediate inferences are made "around" the square of opposition. Other immediate inferences in categorical logic are conversion, obversion, and contraposition.

Immoralist
One who rejects ultimate or absolute moral claims, even if they do not violate moral rules.

Immortality
The idea that one continues to live, in some way, indefinitely.

Impartiality
A standpoint from which everyone is viewed equally, from a perspective without a vested interest.

Imperative
A command that prescribes how we should, or ought, to act.

Implication
In formal logic, "implication" is the name commonly given to the substitution of one of the statements for another, where the two are truth-functionally equivalent: $\neg P \vee Q :: P \rightarrow Q$. More generally, what the premises in an argument imply—that is, the conclusion.

Impression
David Hume's term for sensations or sense data.

Inclusive disjunction
In formal logic, a disjunction is inclusive, so the expression, "One or the other" includes "...or both." Exclusivity must be explicitly noted, as in, "One or the other, but not both." (See also **Exclusive disjunction**.)

Incoherent
That which does not fit together; that is, that which is not coherent.

Incommensurability
Two scientific theories are incommensurable if there is no shared body of data or standards of evaluation by which to compare them—either because of non-overlapping domains of application, disagreement on the meaning of terms (see **Semantic holism**), or theory-relative judgments about the importance of different results.

Inconsistent
1) In formal logic, two sentences are inconsistent when they are not true on even one row of the truth table in the column under the (main) operator. 2) Incompatible, as in incompatible beliefs or positions.

Incorrigibility
Attribute of that which cannot be mistaken.

Indeterminacy of translation
Thesis of Willard Van Orman Quine (1908-2000) stating that, in the context of radical translation (that is, translation based purely on observable behavior), it is possible to construct multiple translation manuals that are empirically adequate but mutually inconsistent and, moreover, that there is no fact of the matter which is correct.

Indeterminism
The view that some events are not caused; often associated with positive accounts of **free will**.

Indirect proof
A proof whereby a statement's negation is proved by assuming the statement is true. That assumption leads to a contradiction, which proves the assumption is false. (See also **Proof by contradiction** or **Negation introduction**.)

Individual constant
In first-order logic, symbols stand for individually named things (object, person, place, time, and so on). An individual constant is assumed to denote one, and only one, thing.

Induction
Reasoning from experience to a conclusion that is claimed likely to be true.

Inductive argument
An argument from experience; experiential inferences; contrasted with **Deductive argument**. Inductive arguments do not reflect the guaranteed truth of the conclusion claimed in deductive arguments. Instead, the conclusion is probably true.

Inference
Also known as a conclusion, an inference is the result of an evidence-based reasoning process.

Inference rule
In a formal system of logic, a principle whereby one statement is inferred from another or others; the logical rules by which validity is defined.

Inference to the best explanation
Ampliative method of inference concluding that the explanation that best explains the available evidence is likely to be true.

Infinite regress (or regression)
An endless sequence.

Informal fallacy
An error in reasoning that is not the result of a formal, or structural, flaw. There are myriad informal fallacies, many of which involve distraction techniques and exploiting psychological vulnerabilities.

Informal proof
An ordinary language demonstration of a claim.

Innate idea
An idea inherent in the mind; or an inborn idea. More generally, inborn knowledge; not to be confused with instinct.

Instrumental goods
Things that are considered valuable because they lead to other good things.

Intension
The meaning of an expression, as opposed to its **extension** (the set of things to which it applies). The intension of a declarative sentence is usually taken to be a **proposition**. Expressions with different intensions can nevertheless have the same extension—for instance, "things with hearts" and "things with kidneys."

Intention/intentionality
The "aboutness" exhibited by our mental states, or their directness toward other states of affairs. The orientation or directness of mental states; what a mental state is about. It is an important feature of intentional contexts that co-extensive terms cannot be substituted *salva veritate* ("with unharmed truth") since, for example, I may not believe that I am encountering the same object in different ways.

Internal meaning
That meaning or purpose originating in, or given to, oneself.

Intrinsic good
That which is inherently good, good for its own sake, and/or good in itself.

Intuition
Knowledge unaided by reason or experience; in this sense, immediate knowledge.

Invalid
An evaluation term for a formally fallacious argument. An argument is invalid when the premises are true, but the conclusion is false.

J

Justice
In a general sense, the equitable distribution of societal goods, rewards, benefits, and burdens; the principle that people receive what they deserve.

Justification
The formal or informal defense of a **claim**.

K

Karma
Literally, "action": the Hindu view of causation.

KK Thesis
Epistemological principle holding if one knows that p, then one knows that one knows that p. This is based on the internalist claim that knowledge requires an element of justification that must be accessible to the knower in question; the KK Thesis is therefore rejected by epistemological externalists.

Krishna
The Hindu avatar, or God incarnate.

L

Language game
That linguistic activity in which meaning and use are understood by those who use the activity.

Law (in society)
That which objectively binds or obligates individuals, regardless of their acceptance of it.

Law of contradiction
The formal logic principle that a statement and its negation cannot be simultaneously true.

Law of nature
A conditional statement expressing a general regularity (for example, all Fs are Gs) that is considered necessarily true—although philosophers disagree as to whether this is because it captures a metaphysically robust feature of reality, or because it plays an epistemologically central role in our scientific practice.

Law of the Excluded Middle
The logical principle that a statement or its negation must be true: $P \vee \neg P$.

Legitimate
Properly authoritative; legal.

Leibniz's Law
Two principles regarding identity and indiscernibility; namely, if two objects are identical, then every property of one is a property of the other (the indiscernibility of identicals); and, conversely, if two objects have all and only the same properties in common, they are identical (the identity of indiscernibles).

Li
The Confucian term for conscientious behavior and right action.

Libertarianism
1) The view that human freedom is a good, such that political institutions should be severely limited, so that they do not interfere with an individual's pursuit of their own interests. 2) A free will theory holding that human freedom is real and determinism, therefore, false.

Liberty
In political philosophy, one's ability to act without constraint or coercion, or without fear of punishment from others, especially the state.

Literal
An atomic sentence or the negation of an atomic sentence.

Logic
The systematic study of correct reasoning, including the valid rules of inference.

Logical consequence
A statement is a logical consequence of another or others when it is impossible for that statement to be false and if the other(s) is (are) true. (See also **validity**.)

Logical contradiction
A statement that is false in every possible circumstance.

Logical equivalence (logically equivalent statements)
Two statements are logically equivalent if they have the same truth values in all possible circumstances. It is never the case that one of the statements is true while the other is false, and vice versa.

Logical necessity
A sentence that is true in all possible circumstances. A sentence that is never false—that is, a sentence true by its logical form and, therefore, a logical consequence of any set of premises. (See also **Logical truth**.)

Logical operator
A logical symbol that operates on a statement, the result of which, in combination with the statement's truth value, makes the statement true or false.

Logical possibility (Logically possible statement)
A statement that can be true in at least one circumstance. There is no logical reason the statement cannot be true.

Logical truth
A sentence that is true in all possible circumstances. A sentence that is never false—that is, true by its logical form. So, it is a logical consequence of any set of premises. (See also **Logical necessity**.)

Logical validity
A conclusion that is true by virtue of the logical structure of the argument.

Logos
From the Greek, meaning, among other things, "account," "reason," and "word." According to Heraclitus, logos is the fundamental organizing principle or law of the cosmos.

M

Major premise
In a standard-form categorical syllogism, the premise that contains the major term. It is the premise that appears first. (See also **Categorical syllogism** and **Standard form.**)

Major term
The predicate of the conclusion in a categorical syllogism. (See also **Categorical syllogism** and **Standard form.**)

Master morality
Friedrich Nietzsche's (1844-1900) concept of the morality of self-realization, associated with the ethos of masters in ancient slave states. (See also **Slave morality.**)

Material cause
A thing's material composition.

Material conditional
The truth-functional conditional in which the statement is false when the antecedent is true and the consequent is false—that is, on the second row of the truth table. (See also **Conditional.**)

Materialism
The view that reality consists entirely and exclusively of material or physical things and their properties.

Matter of fact
David Hume's term for an empirical claim, which is the result of empirical observation and experience. Also: reasoning experientially, versus via relations of ideas.

Maxim
Kant's term for the subjective rule an individual uses in making a decision, which is a universalizable rule that an individual could expect everyone else to follow.

Metaethics
The study of the nature and meaning of ethical concepts—for instance, good.

Metaphysics
1) The branch of philosophy that studies reality and first principles. 2) Literally, "after (or beyond) physics," where "physics" is the transliteration of the Greek for "nature." (See also **Ontology**.)

Method
An approach to addressing or solving a problem.

Method of doubt (Methodological doubt)
Descartes's procedure for uncovering certainty; or those principles that cannot be doubted or refuted.

Mimesis
In aesthetics, the modeling or representation of an object by a work of art. The mimetic theory of art dominated aesthetics from Plato and Aristotle, but was eventually challenged by the increased importance attached to the artist's intentions (rather than the artwork itself) and, further, by contemporary developments in abstract and non-representational art, such abstract expressionism.

Minor premise
In a standard-form categorical syllogism, the premise that contains the minor term. It is the premise that appears second in the syllogism. (See also **Categorical syllogism** and **Standard form**.)

Minor term
The subject of the conclusion in a categorical syllogism. (See also **Categorical syllogism** and **Standard form**.)

Mixed quantifiers
A first-order logic sentence that consists of at least one universal quantifier and at least one existential quantifier.

Modal logic
A body of formal systems used to represent statements about necessity and possibility.

Modus ponens
"Mode of affirmation," the Latin name for the formal logic rule that allows the inference of the consequent of a conditional claim from the affirmation of the antecedent. Argument of the form that if A is true, and the conditional (if A then B) is true, then you can infer B. (See also **Conditional elimination**.)

Modus tollens
"Mode of Denial," the Latin name for the formal logic rule that allows the negation of the antecedent of a conditional claim from the denial of the consequent. Argument of the form that if the conditional (if A then B) is true, and ¬B is true, then you can infer ¬A.

Monad
Gottfried Wilhelm Leibniz's (1646-1726) term for the simplest immaterial substances that ultimately constitute reality.

Monadic predicate
A single-place predicate. (See also **Argument** and **Arity**.)

Monotheism
The belief in a single God.

Moral calculus
The procedure of determining the morality of a particular case, typically in connection with deliberations about what to do.

Moral evil
A way of appraising human choices, actions, and outcomes.

Moral luck
The idea that at least some actions depend in part on luck or chance.

Moral reasoning
Reasoning about right and wrong, or that which is praiseworthy or blameworthy.

Moral theory
A theory about right and wrong, or that which is praiseworthy or blameworthy.

Morality
The set of beliefs about right and wrong, or that which is praiseworthy or blameworthy.

Myth of the given
Argument due to John Sellars against the traditional empiricist view that knowledge of the external world is inferred from immediately given sense data, on the grounds that any such sense data must already be conceptualized to allow inferential relationships with the rest of our knowledge.

N

Natural kind
Those entities that reflect the underlying structure of reality and therefore provide the modal basis for laws of nature.

Necessary condition
A condition without which another statement does not obtain. Q is a necessary condition for P in the claim, "If P then Q." If Q does not obtain, P does not obtain. It is not the case, however, that if Q obtains, P does, as well.

Natural law theory
The ethical theory that there are natural laws and a natural order that ought not to be violated.

Natural right
An entitlement with which one is born.

Naturalism
The theory that everything can be explained in terms of causal claims and facts.

Naturalistic fallacy
Argument advanced by G. E. Moore (1873-1958) that any attempt to define

"good" in terms of some other property (such as pleasure) will either conflate ethical propositions with psychological propositions about our use of language (if the proposed definition is a natural property) or merely result in an empty tautology.

Necessary and sufficient condition
That which both guarantees and is required. It is typically expressed by the phrase, "if, and only if."

Necessary truth
A statement that cannot be otherwise than true.

Necessity
That without which cannot be otherwise. Also: A statement that must be true. A statement is necessarily true (or false) if it could not have been otherwise; it has the same truth value in every (relevantly accessible) possible world. A statement is contingently true (or false) if it could have been otherwise; it has different truth-values at different possible worlds.

Negation
In symbolic logic, the operator that denies a claim. When a statement is negated, its truth value is the opposite of the original: When P is true, ¬ P is false. When ¬ P is true, P is false.

Negation elimination
In symbolic logic, a valid inference in a system of truth-functional rules. This rule relies on the truth definition of the negation, where a doubly negated statement (¬¬P) is truth-functionally equivalent to the statement (P) without the negations. (See also **Double negation**.)

Negation introduction
In symbolic logic, a valid inference in a system of truth-functional rules. This rule relies on the concept of noncontradiction: A valid argument's conclusion cannot be false if the premise(s) is (are) true. The negation introduction rule proceeds by assuming a statement at the start of a subproof, from which a contradiction is derived. That contradiction shows the assumption is false. The subproof ends with the introduction of a negation of that assumption.

Negative right
An entitlement not to be interfered with in the pursuit of one's interests.

Neoplatonism
Literally, "new Platonism," Neoplatonism is a form of principle-monism that comprehends all on the basis of a single cause, considered divine, and called "the First," "the Good," or "the One."

Nihilism
From *nihil*, or "nothing," the view that there are no truths or values.

Nirvana
The goal of all Buddhist practice, the highest state of enlightenment, which brings perfect peace and happiness in which desire and suffering disappear.

Nominalism
The metaphysical position that the only things that exist are particulars (as opposed to universals). Similarities shared by objects apparently instantiating the same properties are therefore to be understood as the individual instantiation of (particular) members of a class or dismissed as a mere similarity in linguistic description.

Noncognitivism
The view that the assertions of a certain domain (usually ethics) do not express propositions but, rather, indicate the speaker's approval or disapproval. Such assertions are neither true nor false and therefore entail no problematic ontological commitments; noncognitivism, however, struggles to capture the inferential (that is, truth-functional) role of these assertions.

Normative ethics
That area of ethics concerned with developing theories of right and wrong actions.

Noumenal
Kant's term for the "thing in itself" (*Ding an sich*)—that is, that which is beyond the bounds of possible experience.

O

O-proposition
A negative categorical claim that asserts at least one member of the subject class is excluded from the predicate class. (See also **Categorical proposition**.)

Obligation
That which is binding, as in a duty.

Obversion
An immediate inference in which the proposition's quality is changed and the predicate is replaced with its complement. (See also **Categorical proposition**, **Complement**, and **Quality**.) Obversion is valid for all four claim types (A-, E-, I-, and O-propositions), because the obverted claim is equivalent to the original.

Ockham's (Occam's) Razor
A methodological principle of parsimony, which states that the simplest theory is probably best. There is, however, no philosophical consensus on what constitutes simplicity (for example, number of posited entities versus number of different types of posited entities) or if a better theory is more likely to be true, even if it is not the simplest. Applied with less philosophical rigor as a rule of thumb, Ockham's Razor is "the simplest explanation is usually the most likely to be true."

Omnipotent
Literally, "all-powerful."

Ontology
The study of being; that part of metaphysics addressing such questions as What is there? and What it is to be?

Ordinary language
The meaning of expression (words) in everyday use (as opposed to words coined or defined for technical philosophical purposes).

Original position
A hypothetical situation from which individuals are best positioned to make

decisions about the principles of justice that will constitute a fair society. According to John Rawls (1921-2002), this will be characterized as involving a "**veil of ignorance**," whereby each individual does not know their actual position within that society.

Ought
A moral term, often contrasted with "should." As such, it is obligatory, rather than suggestive.

P

Pantheism
The belief that God is one and the same with the universe and is, therefore, "in" everything.

Paradigm
In the philosophy of science, a set of scientific and philosophical assumptions, often based around "exemplary" results, that guides scientific research. According to Thomas Kuhn (1922-1996), on this model falsified theories are maintained until a paradigm can no longer maintain cohesion and the paradigm "shifts," at which point a "scientific revolution" occurs.

Paradox
A self-contradictory (and therefore absurd) conclusion drawn from seemingly true premises.

Parallelism
In the philosophy of mind, the view that mental events and bodily events occur in parallel but do not interact.

Participation
One of Plato's terms for how particulars relate to Forms.

Perception
Awareness via sensation.

Phenomenal
That which is experiential or appears.

Phenomenology
1) The philosophical study of the structures of experience and consciousness, and an important philosophical movement based on Immanuel Kant (1724-1804) but originating with Edmund Husserl (1859-1938). It dominated much of twentieth-century European philosophy. 3) The study of human consciousness in terms of orientation.

Philosophical method
1) The study of doing philosophy. 2) The systematic employment of philosophy to answer questions about reality, knowledge, morality, logic, and so on.

Phronesis
Practical wisdom; prudence.

Physicalism
Usually with reference to the philosophy of mind, physicalism is the view that everything that exists is adequately accommodated by our best theories of physics. One weakness of the position is that it depends upon philosophically ungrounded assumptions about the development of physics and its future ontological commitments.

Picture theory of meaning
Ludwig Wittgenstein's (1889-1951) early theory of meaning, in which the logical structures of language mirror the structures of the world.

Pluralism
The position that there is a plurality (multiplicity) of (legitimate) views on an issue.

Polytheism
The belief in multiple gods.

Positive right
An entitlement to something. That which obligates another to do or provide something for the holder of a positive right, so that this individual may pursue their interests.

Possible world
A semantic device for evaluating modal discourse, whereby claims of possibility are made true by what happens at other (accessible) possible worlds. The utility of the semantics leads some philosophers to posit the existence of possible worlds, either as abstract objects or as distinct (although causally isolated) spatiotemporal objects.

Pragmatic theory of truth
A statement is true if it works—that is, if it yields a result satisfactory in practice. (See also **Pragmatism**.)

Pragmatism
A philosophy, originating with Charles Sanders Peirce (1839-1914), and developed by William James (1842-1910) and John Dewey (1859-1952), holding that epistemological and metaphysical claims are best evaluated in terms of practical considerations, especially the outcomes they produce.

Predestination
The view that God preordains every event.

Predicate
A property of an object or a relation between objects; that which is asserted or denied of a thing.

Preestablished harmony
Gottfried Wilhelm Leibniz's (1646-1716) view of the universe as ordered by God.

Premise
The statement that supports or provides a reason to believe the conclusion of an argument. The premises begin the argument.

Pre-Socratics
Ancient Greek thinkers living and working before, and/or contemporaneously with, Socrates (died 399 BC).

Presupposition
The requirement for a statement to have a truth value; that is, to be a claim. Also: that which is presupposed.

Prima facie
"On the face of it," or that which is ostensibly the case at first glance.

Primary qualities
Those qualities that inhere in, or are inextricable from, their object.

Prime Mover
Also known as the Unmoved Mover or First Mover, Aristotle's (385-323 BC) term for that which is responsible for all change in the universe but which does not itself change.

Principle of charity
The principle whereby the utterances of a speaker (usually of an unknown language) are interpreted so as to maximize the overall truth of what they say; contrasted with the more demanding **Principle of humanity**, whereby such utterances are interpreted so as to accommodate assumptions about the speaker's erroneous beliefs.

Principle of equal liberty
The principle that each person's freedom is equal to every other person's freedom.

Principle of equality
The principle that each person is equal to every other person and, as such, should be treated equally.

Principle of humanity
The principle whereby the utterances of a speaker (usually of an unknown language) are interpreted so as to accommodate assumptions about the speaker's erroneous beliefs; contrasted with the more demanding **Principle of charity,** whereby the utterances of a speaker (usually of an unknown language) are interpreted so as to maximize the overall truth of what they say.

Principle of induction
The rule that nature is uniform—that is, that the future will resemble the past.

Principle of sufficient reason
The principle that every event has an explanation.

Principle of universal causation
The view that all events are caused.

Principle of utility
In Utilitarian philosophies of Jeremy Bentham (1748-1832) and John Stuart Mill (1806-1873), the principle that morally right actions are those that produce the least pain and greatest pleasure or happiness for the greatest number.

Prisoner's Dilemma
A co-ordination problem in game theory, where each player is individually motivated to cheat the others, but suffers if every other player reasons the same way; it provides a formal model for problems in social choice theory or political philosophy where mutual cooperation is difficult to secure. (Also see **Game theory**.)

Private language argument
An argument, identified by Ludwig Wittgenstein (1889-1951), that no fixed meaning can be given to a language in the absence of a wider social context because there are no constraints on how an individual speaker can choose to interpret any previous rules they have stipulated for their future linguistic behavior.

Probable
That which is likely but not certain or guaranteed.

Problem of evil
The term for attempts to address or reconcile the reality of evil (moral badness) in a world created by an omnipotent and omnibenevolent God.

Proof
A proof is a step-by-step demonstration that one statement (the conclusion) follows logically from some others (the premises). A **formal proof** is a proof given in a formal system of deduction; an **informal proof** is generally given in **ordinary language**, without the benefit of a formal system.

Proof by cases
A **proof** strategy whereby a conclusion is proved from a disjunction. (See also **Disjunction elimination**.)

Proof by contradiction
A **proof** strategy whereby a statement's negation is proved by assuming the statement is true. This assumption leads to a contradiction, which proves the assumption is false. (See also **Negation introduction** and **Indirect proof**.)

Proof without premises
A necessarily true statement is typically proved with an assumptive **proof** sequence that is discharged, or closed, to yield that statement.

Propensity
An irregular (usually probabilistic) disposition of an object or system to produce some result; for example, a tossed coin has a propensity of 0.5 to land heads.

Property
A feature that inheres in a substance.

Proposition
An abstract object that provides the shared meaning of different utterances of the same sentence, and its synonymous expressions in different languages. Also: A declarative sentence that is either true or false. (See also **Claim** and **Statement**.)

Propositional knowledge
Knowledge that some **proposition** is true.

Psychologism egoism
The descriptive theory that human beings are ultimately motived by self-interest.

Q

Qualia

The qualitative (and non-intentional) properties of mental states that determine "what it is like" to, for example, experience pain. Proponents of qualia maintain that such facts are irreducible to physical facts and therefore reject **physicalist** theories of the mind. Opponents, in contrast, frequently dismiss the existence of qualia altogether.

Qualities

Properties or characteristics of objects, usually divided into three types: primary qualities are physical properties of objects (such as shape or mass); secondary qualities are dispositions to produce sensory experiences (for example, color or smell); tertiary qualities are dispositions that are not dependent on being experienced (such as fragility or solubility).

Quality

1) A property of an object or a mode of being. 2) A categorical claim's status as affirmative or negative. (See also **Categorical proposition**.)

Quantified statement

An assertion about an unspecified class of thing, a quantified statement consists of a quantifier, at least one class, and a variable.

Quantifier

In symbolic logic, there are two quantifier symbols, which refer to quantified expressions: ∀ (universal), x (universal), and ∃ (existential). In categorical logic, there are two types of quantified claim: universal (affirmative and negative) and particular (affirmative and negative).

Quantity

A categorical claim's status as universal or particular. (See also **Categorical proposition**.)

R

Rational

That which accords with rules of reason.

Rationalism
The view that knowledge is achieved through reason unaided by experience.

Rationalist
One who believes knowledge is achieved through reason unaided by experience.

Rationality
Acting in accordance with reason or one's rational capacity.

Raven Paradox
A paradox of confirmation based on the fact that if a hypothesis is confirmed by its instances, then any hypothesis will also be confirmed by evidence for its contrapositive; thus, both black ravens and non-black non-ravens (for example, red herrings) confirm the hypothesis that all ravens are black. (See also **Red herring**.)

Realism
The view that reality is objective.

Reason
1) Justification for a claim. 2) The capacity, faculty, or ability to think abstractly, such as drawing an inference or contemplating general concepts.

Red herring
An informal fallacy constituted by shifting someone's argument from one direction to another by changing the subject.

Reductio ad absurdum
An argument that concludes the negation of a proposition, on the grounds that a contradiction can be derived from that proposition. "Reductio ad absurdum" is literally "reduction to absurdity." Here, "absurdity" is a contradiction. A reduction argument involves demonstrating that a certain assumption yields a contradiction. (See also **Contradiction introduction**, **Modus tollens**, **Negation introduction**, **Indirect proof**, and **Proof by contradiction**.)

Reflective equilibrium
A method for justifying a set of beliefs by the simultaneous adjustment of initial principles and resulting theories. For instance, Nelson Goodman

(1906-1998) argued that we can justify a particular deductive inference by its conforming to accepted deductive principles, while these principles are in turn justified by their conformity to accepted deductive practice.

Reflexive property
The expression of a self-identity—that is, that a thing is identical to itself. (See also **Identity of indiscernibles.**)

Relational predicate
A multi-place predicate that expresses a relation between things.

Relations of ideas
David Hume's (1711-1776) term for those beliefs formed entirely by the mind, as in beliefs demonstrable exclusively by rational processes, such as deduction.

Relativism
The view that reality, knowledge, truth, or morality is relative to an individual, culture, or historical period.

Reliabilism
Epistemological theory that knowledge must be acquired via a reliable mechanism, such as a counterfactually sensitive causal connection to the fact in question. It is not, however, necessary for the subject to know which mechanism was used or to assess its reliability. Reliabilism is thus a form of epistemological externalism.

Ren
Confucian virtues, such as benevolence, sympathy, and respect for others.

Retributive justice
The view that justice is proportionate punishment for wrongdoing.

Rhetoric
The study and practice of verbal persuasion.

Rights
Entitlements, natural or conventional, to do or have something without either interference or compulsion from an external source.

Rule utilitarianism
The utilitarian view that right actions are those that, if everyone performed them, would produce good consequences.

S

Samsara
In Buddhism, one's cycle of repeated deaths and rebirths.

Secondary quality
A feature or "power" of an object to produce sensations—for instance, sweet, cold, and so on; most commonly associated with John Locke (1632-1704).

Self-consciousness
Awareness of oneself as oneself.

Self-contradictory
Said of a statement that conflicts with itself and is, therefore, always false.

Self-evident
That which is obvious and not subject to doubt.

Semantic holism
The claim that the meaning of a symbol (for instance, individual terms of a scientific theory) is relative to the entire system (such as the scientific theory as a whole). As a consequence, a change of theory entails a change of meaning, making successive theories empirically incommensurable.

Semantic theory of truth
1) A formal mathematical theory that defines truth in terms of set theory and satisfaction, with truth taken to be a property of sentences; commonly associated with the work of Alfred Tarski (1901-1983). 2) A version of the correspondence theory of truth.

Semiotics
The theory of signs and signification, including symbols (conventional signs such as language), indexes (natural signs with a causal correspondence to their referent), and icons (signs whose form resembles their referent).

Semiotics, therefore, encompasses a more anthropological/sociological approach than traditional linguistics and suggest a general framework for philosophical investigation.

Sensation
The conscious awareness of the experience of an external world through organs of sense.

Sense data
Immediate objects of sense, prior to any conceptual organization. According to representational realists, we do not have direct perception of external objects but, rather, of their effects upon our senses. External objects are inferred from these intermediary sense data, which similarly help to explain how our perceptions of an object can change while the object does not.

Sense-reference distinction
According to Gottlob Frege (1848-1925), terms of natural language are to be understood both with respect to the objects they denote (their reference) and their mode of presentation (their sense); thus, an identity statement like "Hesperus is Phosphorus" can be surprising, since "Hesperus" and "Phosphorus" have different senses.

Skepticism
1) The ancient Greek practice of investigating experience and being suspicious of those theories that obscure what experience teaches. 2) In modern philosophy, doubt about the veracity and reliability of sensation and experience generally.

Slave morality
Friedrich Nietzsche's (1844-1900) view of a morality of obligation, where one is a slave to imperatives rather than exerting one's self-driven **will to power**.

Slippery slope argument
An informal fallacy constituted by arguing that a series of increasingly unpalatable events will follow from an initial course of action, resulting in a circumstance no one would want. This result is then used as a reason not to take the first "step." The error occurs when at least one of the events in the series is unlikely to occur. A version of the slippery slope fallacy occurs

when arguing by degrees, rather than events, as when one argues that increasing the speed limit from 55 mph to 65 mph will result in a legal speed limit of 100 mph.

Scope of the quantifier
The range of a quantifier over a domain of discourse; in symbolic logic notation, the quantifier's scope is expressed by parentheses.

Singular statement
An assertion about a specific object, person, place, or time.

Social contract
A political philosophy concept or theory, originating in the Age of Enlightenment, which concerns the legitimacy of state authority over the individual. The term takes its name from *The Social Contract* (1762), by Jean-Jacques Rousseau (1712-1778).

Society
A civilization whose members are tied together by a government, historical bonds, culture, or a set of practices.

Socialism
The political view that members of society should own or control their means of production—that is, property, factories, businesses, and so on.

Socratic method
Socrates' (c. 470-399 BC) method of creating a critical question-answer dialogue to arrive at the truth of the meanings of ethical and other concepts. The "Socratic" method is known exclusively through Socrates' student, Plato (428/427-348/347 BC), all but one of whose *Dialogues* feature Socrates as a character/interlocutor.

Soft determinism
The view that human freedom (in some sense) is compatible with **determinism**. (See also **Compatibilism.**)

Sophists
Ancient Greek philosophers and teachers, living before and during the era of Socrates (c. 470-399 BC), who taught logic and rhetoric for money; Plato

(428/427-348/347 BC) accused them of obscuring rather than facilitating the truth; hence the modern English word, *sophistry*.

Sorites Paradox
Sometimes called the Paradox of the Heap, this is a paradox resulting from vague predicates. We all know what a heap of sand is. We all assume that removing a single grain does not convert a heap into a non-heap. Yet if we remove all but a single grain, is that single grain still a heap?

Sound
The evaluation term in deductive logic for an argument that is valid and whose premises are true.

Sovereign
Not subject or answerable to another (individual or state).

Square of opposition
1) In Aristotelian or traditional categorical logic, immediate inferences are made "around" the square of opposition: Contraries, Subcontraries, Contradictories, Subalternation, and Superalternation. 2) In modern categorical logic, immediate inferences are restricted to contradictories. (See also **Immediate inference**, **Contraries**, **Subcontraries**, **Contradictories**, **Subalternation**, and **Superalternation**.)

Standard form
1) The organization of a categorical proposition: Quantifier, subject term, copula, and predicate term. (See also **Categorical proposition**.) 2) The organization of an argument, where the premises are listed, one on top of the other, with a line drawn below the last to demarcate the inference to the conclusion. 3) The organization of the elements of a categorical syllogism: Major premise, minor premise, and conclusion.

State of nature
A hypothetical situation prior to the creation of any political organization, it is used as a framework to discuss the existence of natural rights, the benefits of political organization, and the grounds on which individuals might choose to give up the former in favor of the latter.

Statement
A sentence that is true or false; that is, a sentence that has a truth value. In **formal logic**, an **atomic statement** is constituted by a predicate and at least one name (individual constant). In **propositional logic**, a simple statement is symbolized by a capital letter. Compound statements are constituted by at least one atomic (or simple) statement and at least one logical operator.

Stoicism
A philosophical system developed by ancient Greek thinkers that integrates metaphysics, epistemology, logic, and ethics. The basic Stoic view is that nature is (providentially) deterministic but that we can achieve happiness by controlling what is up to us (namely, emotions and attitudes).

Strawman (or Straw Man; gender neutral alternatives: strawperson or straw person)
An informal fallacy constituted by distorting someone's position in such a way as to render it unrecognizable and easy to dismiss; analogous to substituting a strawman for the real person and attacking the strawman.

Strong argument
An evaluation term in inductive logic, a strong argument is one in which the premises make the conclusion probably, or likely, true.

Soundness
1) An evaluation term in deductive logic, a sound argument is valid, and the premises are true. 2) A formal system is sound when no invalid arguments are provable within it. (See also **Completeness**.)

Subaltern
On the Aristotelian or traditional square of opposition, the relation between a particular claim and its corresponding universal (**superaltern**).

Subcontraries
A pair of propositions that cannot both be simultaneously false but can be simultaneously true. In categorical logic, I- and O-propositions are subcontraries. If one is false, the other must be true. If one is true, however, the other is undetermined. (See **Categorical proposition**, **I-proposition**, and **O-proposition**.)

Subject Term
In **categorical logic**, the term that comes first in a standard-form proposition. (See also **Categorical proposition** and **Standard form**.)

Subjective truth (subjectivity)
Søren Kierkegaard's (1813-1855) view that "truth is subjectivity" is not to be confused with **relativism**, which is the view that something is true because one believes it. Instead, subjective truth is the view that only the subject, in "passionate inwardness," can commit to the truth; that is, one can only relate to truth subjectively.

Subjectivism
The view that knowledge and morality are relative to the subject; there are no objective truths.

Sublime
Aesthetic experience associated with being overwhelmed—for example, in terms of size (the mathematically sublime) or in terms of power (the dynamically sublime). For Immanuel Kant (1724-1804), this involved the sensation that our powers of reason surpass our sensory perceptions. In his *A Philosophical Inquiry into the Origin of Our Ideas of the Sublime and the Beautiful* (1756), Edmund Burke (1729-1797) argued that beauty and sublimity are mutually exclusive, but, in a work of art, can both nevertheless be pleasurable. In modern art, the sublime is associated with the limits of traditional artistic expression.

Subproof
A nested proof; that is, a proof that occurs within a larger proof sequence. (See also **Assumptive proof**.)

Substance
What a thing is; that which has independent existence and persists through time.

Sufficient condition
That which ensures an outcome. A condition is sufficient when its appearance guarantees an event.

Sufism
A form of Islamic mysticism.

Superaltern
On the Aristotelian or traditional square of opposition, the relation between a universal claim and its corresponding particular (**subaltern**).

Supererogatory
That which is above and beyond the call of duty.

Supervenience
A set of properties of one type (such as mental properties) are said to be supervenient on a set of properties of another type (such as brain states) if and only if an object cannot change with respect to the former without a corresponding change in the latter.

Syllogism
A three-line argument consisting of two premises and a conclusion. The **Categorical syllogism**, **Modus ponens**, **Modus tollens**, and **Disjunctive syllogisms** are all examples of this style of argument.

Sympathy
Fellow feeling; a felt concern for other people's welfare. In the ethics of David Hume (1711-1776) and Jean-Jacques Rousseau (1712-1778), sympathy is the necessary and universal sentiment without which morals—and society—would be impossible.

Synthetic
Kant's term for a judgment whose predicate concept is not contained within the subject concept. As such, the predicate extends what is said in the subject.

Synthetic a priori
Kant's term for a judgment whose truth is not derived from the logical structure or meaning of the sentence (synthetic) but is also necessary and independent of experience (a priori).

T

Tabula Rasa

The epistemological claim that prior to experience, the mind is a "blank slate," with no innate ideas or pre-existing concepts. The concept is at least as old as Avicenna (eleventh century), but the modern theory is found in John Locke's (1632-1704) *Essay Concerning Human Understanding* (1689)

Tao (Dao)

In Confucianism, literally, the "Way." In Taoism (Daoism), it is the underlying and ineffable "way" of nature or reality.

Tarski's T-Schema

An adequacy condition for any definition of truth is that it implies conditionals of the form "'p' is true if and only if p" for every sentence of the language; some philosophers maintain that the T-Schema is also sufficient for any definition of truth.

Tautological consequence

A statement that follows from another statement (or statements) by means of the truth-functional connectives; there is no truth table row on which the statement in question is false, while the other(s) is (are) true, in the columns under the (main) operator(s). Tautological consequence is determined by a truth table. (See also **Validity**.)

Tautological equivalence

Two statements are logically equivalent if they have the same truth values in all possible circumstances. It is never the case that one of the statements is true, while the other is false, and vice versa, in the column under the (main) operator(s). Tautological equivalence is determined by a truth table.

Tautology

A statement that is true in every possible circumstance; that is, it is true on every row of the truth table in the column under the (main) operator.

Teleological argument

An argument that attempts to prove God's existence from the uniformity, or apparent design, of nature. Since the universe looks like it has been designed, and that which is designed has a designer, it follows that the universe was designed. Therefore, God exists. The argument involves an analogy between human-made or human-designed things, and the natural world. From the Greek, *telos*, which means goal, end, or purpose. (See also **Argument from design**.)

Teleology
From the Greek *telos*, meaning "purpose," the view that everything has an end, goal, function, or purpose. The explanation of phenomena in terms of their overall purpose—for example, animals have certain traits because they help them survive. While mechanistic explanations are now generally preferred, teleology remains important in explaining social (that is, intentional) activity. In **virtue ethics**, the good life is intimately connected with fulfilling one's purpose.

Term
A word naming a category or class of things in a proposition or deductive argument.

Theism
The belief in God.

Theory-ladenness of observation
In the philosophy of science, the claim that there is no neutral observational language against which we can test our theories. As all observation is dependent upon theoretical interpretation, scientific theories are therefore incommensurable, and choice of theory depends upon non-empirical (for example, social or political) grounds.

Thick concept
A concept with both substantially descriptive and evaluative content (as opposed to a **thin concept**). Paradigmatic examples are found in **virtue ethics**, and **aesthetics**. Some philosophers maintain that thick concepts cannot be separated into their constituent parts and, therefore, the fact value distinction is not valid.

Thin concept
Evaluative concept without a substantial descriptive quality (as opposed to a **thick concept**, which is both substantially descriptive and evaluative). Examples include "good" and "permissible."

Thing-in-Itself (from German, *Ding an sich*)
Kantian terminology for the unknowable objects of the external world (noumena), which presumably lie behind our perceptions of the external world (phenomena).

Third Man argument
The argument that any theory of universals will entail an **infinite regress** because if a universal is required to explain the similarity between two individual objects, then another universal is required to explain the similarity between the first universal and its instances, and so on ad infinitum.

Transcendent
That which is independent of empirical, finite existence; contrasted with **immanent**.

Transcendental
Relating to the spiritual or nonphysical realm. In Kantian philosophy, something a priori, presupposed and necessary to experience. In some views, applied to the fundamental set of rules of human knowledge or human consciousness.

Transcendental argument
An argument in support of a conclusion on the grounds that it provides a necessary prerequisite for some other (uncontroversial) state of affairs.

Transcendental deduction
Immanuel Kant's (1724-1804) argument for basic a priori concepts or categories that contribute to the constitution of knowledge.

Transcendental ego
Kant's term for the basic logical fact of one's own self-consciousness. Also: That which is necessary for a unified, empirical self-consciousness, and which synthesizes sensations in concert with the categories of the understanding. The transcendental ego is not, however, an object of knowledge but, rather, the condition of knowledge itself. The concept was taken up by such post-Kantian existentialists and phenomenologists as Jean-Paul Sartre (1905-1980) and Edmund Husserl (1859-1938).

Truth of reason
In traditional rationalism, a belief that can be justified solely by appeal to intuition or deduction from premises based upon intuition. Arithmetic and geometry were, for the rationalists as for the empiricists, paradigmatic cases of such truths. The rationalists and empiricists disagreed mainly on the scope of such truths and the restrictions to be placed on the problematic appeal to intuition.

Truth table
A method of demonstrating how a statement's truth value is built up from an atomic or simple sentence and the operation of the (main) connective.

Truth value
The truth or falsity of an atomic, simple, or compound statement.

Truth-functional connective
A logical connective whose truth value is determined by the truth value of the constituent statement(s) and the meaning of the connective itself.

Turing Test
A computer is said to pass the Turing Test if a human subject is unable to distinguish its output from that of another human subject on the basis of conversational interaction alone. It has been proposed that the ability to pass the Turing Test provides grounds for the attribution of consciousness.

Type-token distinction
A *token* is an individual instance of a *type*. For example, two speakers make distinct utterances (*tokens*) of the same sentence (*type*).

U

Unalienable rights
Those rights with which we were born; rights that cannot be taken away by another person, group, or government.

Uncogent argument
An evaluation term in inductive logic for an argument that is either weak or is strong but has at least one false premise. (See also **Inductive argument**, **Strong argument**, and **Weak argument**.)

Underdetermination
A theory is said to be underdetermined by evidence if that evidence would provide the same degree of confirmation for a rival theory; in particular, a scientific theory that posits unobservable entities will always be underdetermined with respect to the observable evidence (although it may possess other theoretical advantages).

Unextended
That which does not take up space; immaterial things. (See also **Extended**.)

Universal
A property or relation that is multiply instantiated in more than one spatial location. If two objects are exactly alike—for example, are both red—this is either because they each possess distinct (particular) properties that are exactly alike or each possess an instantiation of the same (universal) property.

Universal elimination
In symbolic logic, a valid inference in a system of quantifier rules. In a proof sequence, a universal quantifier is removed, and the variables bound by it are replaced with an individual constant. (In some systems, the quantifier is removed, and the variables are left unbound.)

Universal introduction
In symbolic logic, a valid inference in a system of quantifier rules. A universal claim is derived from the assumption of a hypothetical or arbitrarily chosen name (object) at the outset of a subproof. From this assumption, an instance is derived, at which point the subproof is closed and the universal claim is proved. (See also **General conditional proof**.)

Universal quantifier
The symbol that expresses a universal claim. (See also **Quantifiers**.)

Universalizability
Kant's term for testing a maxim; that is, a subjective rule of action that guides our actions or that ensures that everyone is equally obligated, morally, under morally similar conditions.

Unsound
The evaluation term for an argument that is either invalid or valid with at least one false premise.

Upanishads
Vedic texts in Hindu thought and religion. (See also **Vedas**.)

Utilitarianism
A moral theory that evaluates the rightness of an action in proportion to the overall pleasure or happiness produced by it; conversely, the wrongness of an action is determined in proportion to the overall pain produced by it.

Valid argument
An evaluation term for an argument whose conclusion cannot be false if the premises are true. A valid argument's evaluation derives from its form, rather than its content. Hence, a valid argument can have a combination of truth values, except for true premises and a false conclusion. (See also **Logical consequence**.)

Variable
A placeholder that functions like an individual constant, in that it is an argument for a predicate. It does not, however, denote a specific object, but is instead bound by a quantifier; as such, it loosely expresses "entity," as in, for instance, "All dog[things] are animal[things]."

Vedas
Early Hindu scriptures, written c. 1500 – 600, BC.

Veil of ignorance
An element of John Rawls's (1921-2002) hypothetical situation in which members of society in the original position deliberate and choose principles of justice. As they deliberate, the "veil" prevents individuals from knowing the particulars about themselves that might bias their choices, such as their sex, race, religion, income, social status, and so on. etc.

Venn diagram
Named after the British mathematician John Venn (1834-1923), Venn diagrams are overlapping circles representing the subject and predicate classes of a categorical proposition.

Verificationism
The claim that the meaning of a statement consists in its method of verification rather than its truth conditions. For the Logical Positivists, this entailed the semantic reduction of, for example, (unobservable) theoretical terms to (observable) experimental results. Others merely propose verificationism as an additional constraint on the semantics of particular domains.

Verisimilitude
The degree of truth likeness, or how much closer one theory is to the truth than another. Early measures of verisimilitude compared the number of true and false sentences; contemporary measures are based on the similarity (or distance) between admissible sets of possible worlds and the actual world.

Vicious circle (circular reasoning)
Fallacious reasoning that involves merely asserting as proof the very claim at issue, and then asserting the claim at issue to support the proof: A is true because B is true; B is true because A is true.

Virtue
Excellence—character that either is essential to happiness or wills what is morally obligated (not because it brings happiness). (See also **Arête**.)

Virtue theory
A theory of human value in which developing and living out various excellences is an essential component of a good life.

Void
That which is empty. In ancient Greek Atomist thought, that through which atoms move.

W

Weak argument
An evaluation term in inductive logic for an argument whose premises do not make the conclusion probably or likely true. (See also **Inductive argument**.)

Well-Formed Formula (wff)
In symbolic logic, a "logically grammatical" statement.

Will
The faculty, or power, of choosing, deciding, and acting.

Will to power
Friedrich Nietzsche's (1844-1900) view of the aim of every human action. Also, fundamental human striving.

Z

Zend-Avesta
Zoroastrian scripture.

Zoroastrianism
The religion founded in ancient Persia by Zoroaster ("Zarathustra").

12

Biographies

Abd al-Latif al-Baghdadi

Born in Baghdad in 1162, Abd al-Latif al-Baghdadi spent some four decades journeying throughout Iraq, Syria, and Egypt in search of a teacher who could satisfy his thirst for philosophy. He was born into a prosperous family and was extensively educated in medicine, grammar, law, alchemy, and philosophy. He read the works of Avicenna, Abu Hamid al-Ghazali, and Shahab al-Din Yahya ibn Habash al-Suhrawardi. His genius was widely recognized by prominent patrons, including Saladin, the sultan of Egypt. It was in Cairo that Abd al-Latif met Maimonides, the great Sephardic philosopher and became thoroughly acquainted with the works of Aristotle and his major Arabic commentator, Abu Nasr al-Farabi.

Abd al-Latif was a polymath, the product of what some call the "golden age" of Arabic philosophy. He wrote on subjects in archaeology, Egyptology, medicine, and alchemy. His philosophical works include a highly original commentary on Aristotle's *Metaphysics*, which is considered a milestone in the Arabic assimilation of classical Greek philosophy. His *Kitāb al-Naṣīḥatayn* (*Book of the Two Pieces of Advice*) includes a defense of philosophy, always a critical target of conservative Islam.

Abd al-Latif returned from Cairo to Baghdad in 1229 and died in his native city on November 9, 1231.

Abelard, Peter

Remembered in history and literature for his love affair with Héloïse d'Argenteuil (ca. 1090-1164), in part memorialized in a classic collection of letters between the couple, Peter Abelard was the most prominent European philosopher and theologian of the twelfth century as well as a celebrated pedagogue, poet, and musician.

Abelard was born Pierre le Pallet about 1079 in Le Pallet, Brittany. Although his father was a military man, Abelard pursued academics, traveling widely throughout France, learning, debating, and teaching. In or about 1100, he studied with William of Champeaux, a so-called Realist—that is, a Neoplatonist philosopher who held that universals are in all things but are individuated in particular things by accident or, conceptually, by the mind. Abelard soon fell out with his teacher, who found him arrogant, and Abelard then established his own school at Melun. He moved his school to Corbeil between 1102 and 1104.

After an absence in Brittany, Abelard returned to his Corbeil school, and a new rivalry developed with William. When the two debated William's Realism, Abelard prevailed and, as a result, was appointed master at Notre Dame (the precursor of the present Parisian cathedral of that name). In 1113, he traveled to Laon to embark on the study of theology and became master of the cathedral school of Notre Dame in 1115.

His prominence and wealth grew as he attracted wealthy students, including Héloïse d'Argenteuil, a brilliant young woman who lived within Notre Dame under the guardianship of her uncle Fulbert, a secular canon. Abelard secured a position in Fulbert's house, became Héloïse's tutor, and sometime in 1115 or 1116, began a romantic affair with her. Fulbert intervened, but the two continued secret trysts. When Héloïse became pregnant, Abelard sent her to live with his family in Brittany. There she gave birth to a son, named Astrolabe, and Abelard and she secretly wed. Ultimately, to protect her from Fulbert, Abelard arranged for Héloïse to live in the convent at Argenteuil, where she dressed like a nun but did not take religious orders. Ever vengeful, Fulbert hired thugs to castrate Abelard. After this assault, Abelard took orders and become a monk at the monastery of St. Denis, near Paris. The celebrated exchange of letters between him and his former paramour conveyed his lyrically philosophical attempts to persuade Héloïse to take vows as a nun. Her replies, included in the collection, were arguments against submitting to a religious life without feeling a calling.

As a monk, Abelard eventually resumed both study and teaching. His controversial theological lectures brought charges of heresy, but he was able to return to his monastery, where he passed his time casually antagonizing his fellow monks. At length, by mutual agreement with them, he left the monastery of St. Denis and took up a secluded existence in a rustic cabin near Nogent-sur-Seine in Champagne.

Although he intended to live as a hermit, students soon discovered his whereabouts and flocked to him. Beside his hermitage, they built an oratory called the Paraclete, where Abelard resumed writing and teaching until about 1126, when he was named abbot of the monastery of Saint Gildas de Rhuys in Brittany. He gifted the Paraclete to Héloïse (with whom he had reestablished correspondence) and the nuns among whom she lived, and he wrote the *Historia calamitatum,* a confessional, poignantly searching, self-analytical memoir.

Abelard returned to Paris in the mid-1130s to teach. His religious superiors objected to his radical views on theology, and he stood trial for heresy. The Church ultimately silenced him as a theologian, he grew ill, and on April 21, 1142, died. Originally interred at the Paraclete, he was later reburied, with Héloïse beside him, in Père Lachaise Cemetery, Paris.

Peter Abelard's pedagogical legacy was a generation of students who included poets, philosophers, kings, and popes. His philosophical legacy consisted essentially in his having created the scholastic method of philosophy, which aimed to give rational philosophical expression to accepted theological doctrine. This melding of theology and philosophy was highly influential throughout the Middle Ages, as was Abelard's role in laying the foundation of Aristotle's preeminence among medieval philosophers. In no small measure thanks to him, Aristotelian empiricism began to make inroads into Platonic authority among medieval scholars and theologians. Toward the end of his life, Abelard grew in prominence as an ethical philosopher when he developed the principle of evaluating the virtue of acts not in terms of their moral *character* but their moral *value*. The result was a turning from Platonic moral philosophy to a rational morality grounded more fully in Aristotelian empiricism.

Abrabanel, Judah Leon

Judah Leon Abrabanel, also known as Leone Ebreo (Leo the Hebrew), was born in Lisbon, Portugal, between 1460 and 1470. His only surviving major work is *Dialoghi d'amore* ("Dialogues of Love"), consisting of three dialogues between Philo (meaning "love" or "appetite") and Sophia ("wisdom" or "science"). The book seeks to define love in philosophical terms and, in effect, defines philosophy as a dialectic between love/appetite and wisdom/science—that is, *philosophia*. The synthesis of the two is developed in the third and longest of the dialogues, in which God's love is shown to encompass all of existence and is responsible for the cohesion of the universe.

Judah Abrabanel was the firstborn of the philosopher Isaac Abrabanel (1437–1508). His father saw to it that Judah received a thorough education in Jewish wisdom and other subjects in the medieval Arabo-Judaic tradition of Maimonides and Averroes. He also benefitted from knowledge of Italian Renaissance humanism.

Judah became a physician and served in the royal court until 1483, when his father, Isaac, was caught up in a political conspiracy against King John (Joao) II. Judah fled with his father and the rest of his family to Seville. There, Isaac found employment in the court of Ferdinand and Isabella as a financial advisor, but he ultimately chose expulsion from Spain in 1492 rather than convert to Catholicism. Naples offered asylum to many of Spain's Jewish exiles, including Judah and his father. In 1495, however, when France took possession of Naples, Judah was again forced into flight, settling first in Genoa, then Barletta, and finally Venice.

In 1501, the French lost control of Naples, whose viceroy, Fernandez de Córdoba, invited Judah back to the court as his personal physician. He likely died here sometime after 1521, perhaps in the 1530s.

Albo, Joseph

A Jewish philosopher active in Christian Spain during the first half of the fifteenth century, Joseph Albo wrote *Sefer ha-'Ikkarim* (*Book of Principles*), which was completed in 1425. Although he discusses a range of theological and philosophical issues, employing a disciplined hermeneutical approach that combines logic and exegesis, it is his theory of principles that constitutes his major contribution to philosophy. Albo presents the necessary and fundamental beliefs that must be upheld for principles of faith to rightly belong to a system of "divine law."

The fundamental principles are belief in the existence of God, belief in the revelation of God, and belief in divine justice. From these three fundamentals, Albo postulates that a true religion must encompass eight *derivative* principles, or roots. From the existence of God, belief in God's unity, incorporeality, timelessness, and perfection are derived. From the revelation of God, there follow belief in God's prophecy and God's authentication as a prophet. Finally, from divine justice come derivative belief in God's omniscience and in the concept of divinely ordained reward and punishment.

Six secondary principles also relate to, but are not derived from, the fundamental and the derivative principles. These are likened to branches of a tree and consist of the following beliefs: creation from nothing, the unique greatness of Mosaic prophecy, the eternity of the Torah, the doctrine that the performance of even a single mitzvah (righteous act) entitles one to enter the World to Come, resurrection, and the Messiah.

As widely recognized and influential as *Sefer ha-'Ikkarim* was in its time, little is known of Albo's life. He was born in Aragon about 1380 and died in Castile about 1444. He studied in the school of Hasdai Crescas in Saragossa and, during 1413–1414, was instrumental in the "Disputation at Tortosa," a forced debate between Christians and Jews ordered by the crown of Aragon. Albo represented the Jewish community of Daroca, Aragon. The so-called disputation was, in fact, a ploy to force the conversion of the Jews, and the unconverted Jews in Daroca were expelled in 1415. Albo moved to Soria in Castile. There he earned some renown as a preacher and a physician and was fluent in Spanish, Latin, and Hebrew, in which he composed *Sefer ha-'Ikkarim.*

Al-Farabi, Abu Nasr

Born about 872 either in Farab (in present-day Kazakhstan) or Faryab (in modern Afghanistan), Abu Nasr al-Farabi was a jurist and one of the earliest of Islamic philosophers. He wrote on language, music, political philosophy, metaphysics, ethics, and logic. In addition, he was a mathematician, scientist, and alchemist. As a philosopher, he was (and remains) revered in the Islamic world as the "Second Teacher" (Aristotle being known throughout the medieval realms of Islam as the First Teacher).

His original contributions in metaphysics, epistemology, ethics, and politics influenced the likes of Avicenna and Maimonides, but, arguably, his greatest contribution to philosophy in the Middle East was his collecting and preserving original Greek philosophical texts.

Little is known about Al-Farabi's life. It is believed, however, that he lived longest in Baghdad, sojourning in Damascus and in Egypt before returning to Damascus, where he died about 950 or 951.

One of Al-Farabi's most influential works, *Enumeration of the Sciences,* contains his analysis of language, including grammar and metrics. His *Great Book of Music* discusses the relationship of music to language, arguing that music serves to enhance the meaning of speech. Indeed, Al-Farabi recommended that rulers should learn to exploit the power of music to enhance the spoken word and thereby amplify the influence of their eloquence upon the people.

From language, Al-Farabi proceeded to an analysis of logic, which he built mainly on an Aristotelian foundation, with an emphasis on the application of logic in metaphysics and ethics. He showed himself especially interested in how language enables logic to treat the future through "contingents." Al-Farabi navigated a narrow course between predetermination and freewill. As an Aristotelian, he advocated the demonstration of theoretical assumptions based on empirical observation.

Al-Farabi studied mathematics and, from it, derived his view of physics and the other natural sciences. He rejected the idea of a vacuum, and he expanded upon Aristotle's views of the function of human organs to argue that the hierarchical structure of those organs reflects a cosmological hierarchy that should be emulated in any plan for creating an ideal state.

From physics, Al-Farabi leapt to metaphysics, which he provocatively defined not as a quasi-theological enterprise but as an investigation into precisely what all living beings have in common. Al-Farabi also sought to outline the relation of logic to metaphysics and, in so doing, to apply both logic and metaphysics to political philosophy as it relates to the hierarchical structure of the state. Indeed, it is characteristic of Al-Farabi that he almost always sought to apply philosophy, metaphysics included, to politics, government, and society. In this, he was influenced both by Aristotle and Plato, emphasizing (in emulation of *The Republic*) that philosophy must be both theoretical and practical. Those thinkers who remained in strictly theoretical realms Al-Farabi dismissed as "futile philosophers."

He saw the role of philosophy as guiding the creation of an ideal state, whose objective was the realization of "happiness," by which he principally meant rational enlightenment. The philosopher, Al-Farabi argued, has a responsibility to minister to the health of society much as a physician ministers to the health of his patient. Comparing an immoral society to a human being suffering from an imbalance of humors, Al-Farabi wrote that the duty of the philosopher is to heal the unbalanced souls of society's members to establish balance and justice, thereby leading the society to "true happiness." Al-Farabi died in Damascus about 950. His great popularity in his own time resulted in a degree of preservation of his works that is rare in the early Middle Ages. In the West, philosophers are just beginning to translate and study many of Abu Nasr al-Farabi's surviving writings.

Al-Ghazali

Abû Hâmid Muhammad ibn Muhammad al-Ghazâlî was born in 1055, 1056, 1058, or 1059 in Tabarân-Tûs, near Meshed, Iran. Educated in Tus and at the Nizâmiyya Madrasa in Nishapur, he became known to Sultan Malikshâh and his grand-vizier, Nizâm al-Mulk, and was thus soon brought within the circle of the caliphal court in Baghdad. By early adulthood, he was the most influential intellectual in the Islamic world. In 1095, under the influence of Sufi texts, he decided to relinquish his distinguished posts in Baghdad and devote himself instead to Sunni theology and mysticism as well as the Arabic tradition of Aristotelian philosophy.

Some seventy works are attributed to al-Ghazali, the most important of which are discussed below.

The Incoherence of the Philosophers is a work of epistemological skepticism devoted to theological occasionalism—the idea that causal events are not products of material actions but the immediate will of God. Al-Ghazali offered as an example the ignition of cotton when it comes into contact with fire. This seems a clear instance of a natural law, but, al-Ghazali argued, it happened only because God willed it. The event was "a direct product of divine intervention." This was a contradiction of the Aristotelian Averroes, who argued that God created natural law, including that which caused cotton to burn.

Al-Ghazali's autobiography, *Deliverance from Error*, recounts how the philosopher's crisis of epistemological skepticism was resolved by "a light" that God Himself "cast into my breast," providing "the key to most knowledge." The *Deliverance* speaks of how he found much to admire in Islamic philosophy but came to the conclusion that only the Sufi mystical experience, which induces prophecy (*nubuwwa*), produces genuine knowledge ("insight").

In *The Revival of Religious Sciences,* al-Ghazali addressed most fields of Islamic science, including jurisprudence, theology, and Sufism. The work is credited with synthesizing orthodox Sunni theology with Sufi mysticism in a guide to Muslim life and belief.

The Alchemy of Happiness is a revision of *The Revival of the Religious Sciences* that emphasizes al-Ghazali's belief that embracing God is essential to the joy of living. The book begins with Knowledge of Self and progresses to Knowledge of God, Knowledge of the World, and Knowledge of the Future World—the afterlife.

Al-Ghazali died, in Tus, on December 19, 1111, leaving several daughters but no sons.

Al-Kindi, Abu Yusuf Ya'qub ibn Ihaq

Born about 801 in Basra (then a city of the Abbasid Caliphate; now in Iraq), Abu Yusuf Ya'qub ibn Ishaq Al-Kindi is considered the first Arabic philosopher. He translated Aristotle, the Neoplatonists, and Greek mathematicians into Arabic and wrote original treatises (drawing on Aristotle), including *Theology of Aristotle* and *Book of Causes.* His *On First Philosophy* argues against the idea of an eternal earth and argues for a divine simplicity, defining God, simply, as "One."

Al-Kindi was a member of the Arab Kinda tribe, which was instrumental in the early development of Islam. Educated in Baghdad, al-Kindi was employed by caliph al-Ma'mun as a court scholar and also served al-Ma'mun's successor, al-Mu'tasim. While in service to the latter, he wrote *On First Philosophy*, which remains his best-known work.

Al-Kindi's most important contribution to Arab philosophy was as the leader of efforts to translate Aristotle and other Greek philosophers into Arabic. This put the Arab intellectual world in advance of medieval Europe in rediscovering the classical thinkers of the Western world. Beyond leading and coordinating this great scholarly effort, al-Kindi worked assiduously to popularize the tradition of Greek thought in the Arab world.

Although much of al-Kindi's work has been lost, we know that he was extremely prolific, especially in the fields of science and mathematics. His major work of original philosophy, *On First Philosophy*, exists only in its first part, beginning with an injunction to the reader to honor Greek philosophical wisdom. The second section of Part One encompasses a refutation of the idea of the eternity of the world, and the final two extant portions of the third and fourth sections of Part One present the philosophical argument for the existence of a "true One," God, who is the source of unity in all things.

Other surviving works include *On the Intellect*, the first Arabic treatise to provide a taxonomy of types of intellect; *Discourse on the Soul,* an anthology of quotations from Greek philosophers; *That There are Separate Substances*, an Aristotelian effort to prove the immateriality of the soul; and *On Sleep,* a discourse on prophetic dreams framed by Aristotle's theory of the imagination.

Al-Kindi was a cosmologist (*On the Proximate Agent Cause of Generation and Corruption* and *On the Prostration of the Outermost Sphere*) and, in a more practical vein, wrote on weather forecasting.

It is certain that al-Kindi died after 866, and most scholars believe his death, in Baghdad, occurred around 873.

Anaxagoras

Anaxagoras was born about 510 BC in Clazomenae, Ionia, at the time part of the Persian Empire and today located on what is the west coast of Turkey. He was the scion of aristocratic landowners but renounced his patrimony to study philosophy—with whom, however, is not known. By the middle of the fifth century, he arrived in Athens, where he became a protégé of Pericles, the great statesman and general. He lived in Athens for at least two decades before he was banished (perhaps in 437/436) on a charge of "impiety" and perhaps for harboring political sympathy with the Persians. He settled in Lampsacus, where he died about 428 BC.

Despite his prominence among the Pre-Socratic philosophers, the works of Anaxagoras have suffered the same fate as those of his fellow Pre-Socratics. What we know of it comes from fragments cited by later philosophers and commentators.

Anaxagoras is best described as a cosmologist. His theory of the origin of the universe is that all things existing today existed from the beginning, but in infinitesimally small fragments of themselves combined into an amorphous, chaotic mixture. Although infinite in number, the fragments existed in parts that were either homogeneous or heterogeneous. The arrangement of this infinitude of things, beginning with the segregation of like from unlike, was achieved by the *Nous,* or Cosmic Mind. As described by the sixth century AD Neoplatonist Simplicius of Cilicia (c. 490-c.560), the *Nous* set the particle mixture into rotary motion, the action of which effected shifts in the proportions of the ingredients in various portions of the mixture. The rotation expanded the mixture, thereby producing the still-evolving world (or universe), including what we currently perceive.

The concept of a Cosmic Mind is the most familiar philosophical artifact that has come down to us from Anaxagoras. As the philosopher imagined it, it was no less infinite than the material on which it operated, yet it existed independently of and apart from that material, a pure and finer substance, perfectly uniform, encompassing all knowledge and all power. Evidence of the existence of this *Nous* is the life around us, which it both animates and rules.

Through time, the still-rotating universe changes, producing new aggregations and new disruptions. Yet the original mixture of things is neither destroyed nor entirely converted from chaos to order. For this reason, everything that exists contains within its structure fragments of other things. All material reality is heterogeneous in composition. Only the preponderance of some homogeneous components gives each thing what we perceive as its distinctive character.

Anaximander

Born about 610 BC in the Ionic city of Miletus in what is today Turkey, Anaximander is not only an important Pre-Socratic philosopher but is believed to be the first philosopher who wrote down his studies and ideas. His principal mentor was Thales of the Milesian school of philosophy, and Anaximander succeeded him as that school's master. His most illustrious student, quite likely, was Pythagoras.

Anaximander was an empiricist who undertook the close observation of the natural world around him and the heavens above. Like so many other philosophers, he was intensely interested in the origins of things and was an early cosmologist. His leading theory of the natural world held that it was governed in a manner analogous to human society—that is, by law, the violation of which was an assault on the natural balance and would not long escape correction.

In the field of astronomy, Anaximander endeavored to observe and explain the mechanics of celestial bodies. These observations led him to theorize that the origin of the universe was driven by what he termed *apeiron,* meaning the infinite or the limitless. Thus, infinitude not only characterized the universe, it was the original principle of the universe, what Anaximander called the *arche,* the "beginning" or, more accurately, the "source of action." Using the concepts of *apeiron* and *arche,* Anaximander explained how the traditional Four Elements—air, earth, water, and fire—were formed. Through the action of these original creations, in turn, everything in the universe as it exists in the present was created.

Anaximander did not limit his vision of creation to the world that is known to humanity. He spoke of "all the worlds," thereby implying a universe in which many worlds exist, though they are as yet unknown. *Apeiron* endures eternally. In dying, beings and inanimate things alike return to the *apeiron.*

Anaximander is sometimes called the Father of Cosmology, not just because of his *apeiron* concept but because of his widely disseminated map of the universe, which was based not on the prevailing mythological concepts but on his own observations and conclusions. Although he conceived of the existence of other worlds, he regarded earth as the center of the universe, floating unsupported and motionless in the infinite. He conceived the earth as a cylinder, one third the height of its diameter. The flat top is the inhabited world, which is surrounded by the ocean. The idea that the earth required no support in space was revolutionary and would linger to shape many future theories of the universe.

Anaximander created a narrative of the earth's formation in the separation of hot from cold, a process that caused a ball of flame to engulf the earth, partially breaking it apart. The fragments formed the rest of the universe, which took the shape of a series of concentric wheels, each filled with fire. The wheels were pierced with holes, through which the fire was visible as the stars (the first concentric ring out from the earth), the moon (the next ring), and the sun (the third ring).

Anaximander also theorized on the origin of animal and human life. His view was an adumbration of the concept of evolution. Animals, he argued, were created out of the sea, originally born encased within a bark. The bark dried up, allowing the maturing animal to break free of it. In the course of evolution, the oceans retreated in partial evaporation, and animals, freed from their casing, occupied the land, learned to adapt to its conditions, and, in the fulness of time, gave rise to humanity.

Like most early philosophers, Anaximander was eager to give his theories practical application and adapted his cosmology to create a map of the world, with (it is believed) three continents—Libya, Asia, and Europe—separated by the Nile River, the Phasis River, the Mediterranean Sea, and the Black Sea, and the whole encircled by one vast ocean. The philosopher is also widely credited with having invented the gnomon or, more accurately, having adapted the gnomon for use in the invention of a practical sundial.

In addition to philosophy, Anaximander apparently was interested in the politics of Miletus and was sent to Apollonia, a Milesian colony established on the coast of the Black Sea, possibly to draw up a constitution for the colony or in some other way to ensure the maintenance of its allegiance to Miletus. It is believed he died in Apollonia about 546 BC.

Anaximenes of Miletus

Born about 586 BC, presumably in Miletus, Anaximenes was a Pre-Socratic, taught by Anaximander, who had been the student of Thales. It was this trio who made up the so-called Milesian school. Material monists, they shared the belief that everything was composed of a single element. Anaximenes believed that this *arche*—the underlying element of the world—was *aer,* that is air, vapor, or mist. Unlike Thales, Anaximenes theorized that things retained properties of the *apeiron* (the ambiguous substance of infinity) but could assume a tangible state capable of creating other things through two processes, condensation and rarefaction. Like the *apeiron, aer* was infinite. He also brought material monism to a more empirical level by associating hot and dry and cold and wet states with the density of a material. Anaximenes' emphasis on changing forms rather than new acts of creation simultaneously brought cosmology a step closer to the modern view even as it may have influenced Plato.

As a cosmologist, Anaximenes held that air "coagulated" or "felted" to create the earth, a flat disk, which behaved like a leaf floating in the wind. While the earth and sun were bodies, stars were the ignited product of air, exhaled from the earth. The sun, although also aflame, was composed of earth, as was the moon. The motion of the sun and other heavenly bodies was likened to a cap turning around upon the head that wears it.

Unfortunately, nothing of Anaximenes' writing survives, but his fundamental contribution to philosophy and science, conveyed by others, is his emphasis on the changing forms of underlying matter. This contributed to a movement away from mythological explanations of genesis and cosmology and toward a view more closely resembling that of natural philosophy or science. Anaximenes is believed to have died about 526 BC.

Anselm of Canterbury

Born in Aosta, Italy, in 1033 or 1034, Anselm was a Benedictine monk and theologian who was Archbishop of Canterbury from 1093 until his death on April 21, 1109. He was canonized by Pope Alexander III in 1163.

When he was twenty-three, Anselm left his family's home and wandered in Burgundy and France for three years, entering the Benedictine abbey of Bec when he was twenty-seven. Early in his career as a monk, he wrote *De Gramatico,* a dialogue that is considered his first work of philosophy because it uses Latin syllogisms to resolve paradoxes that arise from the grammar of Latin nouns and adjectives.

He went on to write more dialogues, *De Veritate* ("On Truth"), *De Libertate Arbitrii* ("On the Freedom of Choice"), and *De Casu Diaboli* ("On the Devil's Fall"), between 1080 and 1086. The first of these extends the conception of truth from fact to "correctness" of will, action, and what he refers to as essence. Using Aristotelian logic, Anselm proves the existence of an absolute truth, of which all other truths are formed. Absolute truth is directly attributed to God, and it affirms God as the fundamental principle of things and ideas. "On the Freedom of Choice" elaborates upon Anselm's conception of absolute truth by discussing its relation to free will. The third dialogue, "On the Devil's Fall," argues that human beings are incapable of willing justly except through the divine Grace of God, the source of absolute truth.

Cur Deus Homo ("Why God Was a Man"), composed between 1095 and 1098, is a philosophical dialogue that argues for the necessity of the mystery of atonement, the doctrine that Christ's crucifixion was necessary to atone for humankind's sins. Although this dialogue is widely considered Anselm's greatest work of theology, its argument is based on a philosophical view of justice and is divorced from grace.

Antiphon

Known as Antiphon the Sophist and associated with a collection of Sophistic writings, this philosopher was probably active in Athens at the end of the fifth century BC. Nothing specific is known of his life—though there is a long-standing controversy over whether Antiphon the Sophist was the same person as Antiphon of Rhamnus, an Attic orator.

The fragmentary *On Truth* is the most important work attributed to Antiphon the Sophist. It is a work of political philosophy, which adumbrates a theory of natural rights. The most intriguing concept is the idea that nature *requires* liberty. All forms of repression, Antiphon argues, are painful, and nature abhors pain. Many institutional conceptions of justice are at their core repressive and, therefore, unnatural. Some regard Antiphon as the philosophical ancestor of John Locke and his conception of natural rights.

Antiphon was not only a political philosopher but also a mathematician and was, with Bryson of Heraclea, among the first who provided an upper and lower bound for *pi* using geometry.

Aquinas, Thomas

Thomas Aquinas (1225–1274) was an intellectual very much of his age. Only recently had Aristotle been translated from Greek (read by few theologians) into medieval Latin (read by many of them), igniting a debate between those who advocated the supremacy of Christian faith and those who elevated the status of reason. Both a theologian and a philosopher, Aquinas, who was recognized as a great interpreter of Aristotle, struggled to reconcile theology with philosophy.

Thomas Aquinas was born in 1225 at Roccasecca, a hilltop village midway between Rome and Naples. He began his studies at the tender age of five in the monastery at Montecasino and later studied at the University of Naples. He became a Dominican monk and continued his studies at the University of Paris, where he met the great Dominican scholar Albertus Magnus, whom he subsequently followed to the University of Cologne. In 1252, he returned to Paris, where he earned a master's degree in theology and taught through 1259. He then served in Italy in various offices at the behest of the Pope. He died on March 7, 1274, at Fossanova, Italy, from an illness following a head injury.

Aquinas wrote voluminously on the works of Aristotle (*On the Soul, On Interpretation, Nichomachean Ethics,* and *Metaphysics*), in which connection he evolved a view of epistemology that sought to reconcile *divine* revelation with the *natural* human faculties of perception and understanding. Ultimately, however, Aquinas subordinated the Aristotelian elevation of rationality (the human capacity for understanding via the senses) to divine revelation in those instances in which the two apparently conflict. Despite his elevating theology over philosophy, Aquinas's epistemological outlook has been described as a "double-truth theory," in which religion and philosophy might arrive at mutually exclusive conclusions yet without detriment to either religion or philosophy.

Aquinas was also an ethical, legal, economic, and political philosopher. His ethics were based on "first principles of action," by which acts are virtuous insofar as they are prescribed by "natural law." Nature does not always appear virtuous, but acts conforming to natural law are seen to be virtuous by "inquiry of reason." For Aquinas, four cardinal virtues, prudence, temperance, justice, and fortitude, flow from natural law. These exist alongside three theological virtues, faith, hope, and charity. Human law, Aquinas argued in his *Treatise on Law,* coexists with both natural law and eternal law, natural law defined as human participation in God's eternal law. Economic acts are both ethical and just, provided sellers sell at a "just price," defined as a price that covers the costs of production.

Politically, Aquinas recognized division of labor as a cornerstone of society but made a sharp distinction between being a "good man" and a "good citizen," defining an aspect of individual autonomy with which the state might not interfere. Libertarians thus point to Aquinas as a source of their political philosophy.

Thomas Aquinas's best-known epistemological work is *Disputed Questions of Truth* (1256-1259), which essentially explores the extent to which people can teach one another. His magnum opus is the unfinished *Summa Theologica* (1265-1274), a great compendium of all the theological teachings of the Catholic Church, which, however, veers profoundly into philosophy by presenting five arguments for the existence of God.

At the spiritual heart of Aquinas's thought is theology, the interpretation of divinely revealed truth. At the intellectual heart of his philosophy is epistemology, as evidenced by the five arguments for the existence of God presented in the *Summa.* While both theologians and philosophers lay claim to the legacy of Thomas Aquinas, and while Christians regard his as the most important founding voice of Christian philosophy, Aquinas considered himself, first and last, a theologian rather than a philosopher.

Arendt, Hannah

A writer of great eloquence, Hannah Arendt was one of the seminal political and ethical philosophers of the twentieth century. A German Jew, she was born Johanna Cohn Arendt on October 14, 1906, into a cultured commercial family in Linden, Prussia, where she was educated through high school before enrolling at Marburg University for study with Martin Heidegger, who made major contributions in the fields of phenomenology, hermeneutics, and existentialism. Arendt had a brief love affair with Heidegger, who remained a great influence on her philosophical thought. Heidegger subsequently became a controversial figure among intellectuals because of his membership in the Nazi Party (joined on May 1, 1933). Irony may be found, perhaps, in the fact that Arendt, author of *The Origins of Totalitarianism* (1951), achieved her broadest renown among the general public for her intellectual reportage (*Eichmann in Jerusalem: A Report on the Banality of Evil*, 1963) on the 1961 trial of Adolf Eichmann, one of the architects of the Holocaust.

In addition to Marburg, Arendt studied at the University of Freiburg (attending lectures by Edmund Husserl) and the University of Heidelberg, where in 1929, she completed her Ph.D. dissertation under Karl Jaspers on the subject of the concept of love in the thought of Saint Augustine. Within five years, in 1933, she fled Germany as Adolf Hitler rose to power. She stayed briefly in Prague and Geneva before settling in Paris, where she worked for several Jewish refugee organizations. She fled German-occupied France in 1941 and moved to New York with her mother and second husband, the Marxist philosopher and poet Heinrich Blücher.

Arendt's reputation as an intellectual grew through work she published in the New York-based *Partisan Review,* and, after World War II, she became a sought-after lecturer at Princeton, Berkeley, Chicago, and other universities. She was on the faculty of the New School for Social Research in New York, where she served as professor of political philosophy. In 1951, she published *The Origins of Totalitarianism*, a magisterial study of Nazism and Stalinism, which established her as the premier philosophical commentator on anti-democratic regimes. She located the root of modern tyranny in Immanuel Kant's concept of "Radical Evil," through which the regime's victims were identified as "Superfluous People."

The Human Condition, published in 1958, is widely considered Arendt's most influential work of political philosophy. In it, she developed her important theory of "political action," focusing on two beneficial acts she considered essential to society: forgiving past wrong and promising future benefit. The former "unfixes the fixed past," while the latter "fixes the unfixed future." For Arendt, the concept of action brings rationally justified hope. Although human beings must die, she argued, they are born not to die but "to begin"—that is, to act.

In 1963, the same year she published her book on Eichmann, she published *On Revolution*, comparing the French and the American revolutions, arguing that the French Revolution brought disaster by abandoning the goal of liberty to instead embrace compassion for the masses, whereas the American Revolution succeeded by never abandoning the concept of liberty within constitutional law.

Arendt's 1968 *Men in Dark Times* presents intellectual biographies of exemplary moral figures of the twentieth century, whereas *Crises of the Republic* (1972) is a rather darker view of then-recent shortcomings in American democracy. "On Violence," one of four essays in the book, presents the provocative theory that power is not derived from violence (as is commonly assumed) but that violence is a property of groups that perceive themselves as powerful.

Arendt, a heavy smoker lifelong and grief-stricken by the sudden death of Blücher, succumbed to a heart attack on December 4, 1975. She left unfinished or incomplete a trove of works, many of which have been edited and posthumously published. The most important of these, *The Life of the Mind* (published in 1978), turns from political to moral philosophy and explores the relationship between the "active life" (life based on moral actions) and what Arendt believed to be the essentially solitary self-dialogue that is thought. The interaction between these two, she concluded, is what we call "conscience."

Aristotle

Aristotle is second only to Plato as a towering figure in philosophy and Western civilization. His influence on the course of philosophy from his own time and through the Renaissance is foundational. The range of his surviving works—some thirty-two treatises out of a corpus conjectured to number close to two hundred—is staggering. He wrote in the philosophical fields of logic, mind, epistemology, metaphysics, ethics, political theory, aesthetics, and rhetoric as well as in science, including physics, astronomy, geology, biology, and psychology. Aristotle was a virtuosic theorist but also an intensely observant empiricist. So compelling is Aristotle's work that scholars of the Medieval and even early Renaissance periods often heeded his opinions slavishly. Yet, even today, his empirical methodology exerts a profound influence, as does his approach to literary criticism.

All that we know of Aristotle's life comes from the largely conjectural work of ancient historians and biographers. It is generally agreed that he was born in 384 BC in the Macedonian city of Stagira, from which he was sent when he was about seventeen to Athens for study at Plato's Academy. He remained associated with the Academy until Plato's death in 347. In that year, he moved to Assos, on the northwest coast of modern Turkey, as the guest of his fellow Academic, Hermias. When his host died some three years later, Aristotle moved to Lesbos. Both in Assos and Lesbos, Aristotle continued to pursue philosophy as well as what today is called marine biology. He found time as well to meet and marry Pythias, the niece of Hermias. The couple had a daughter, named for her mother. Aristotle earned sufficient renown to merit a summons, in 343, from King Philip of Macedon, to serve as tutor to the king's thirteen-year-old son Alexander. He took up residence in the Macedonian capital, Pella, and tutored the future Alexander the Great for anywhere from two to eight years. Historical opinion varies on the span, largely because almost nothing is known of the philosopher's life between 341 and 335, when he returned to Athens to establish his own school, dedicated to the god Apollo Lykeios and thus known as the Lyceum (or Lycaeum).

The early generations of philosophers associated with Aristotle became known as the Peripatetics, perhaps because they conversed along the *peripatos*, or walking area, on the Lyceum grounds. Lyceum students and teachers both studied and researched in virtually every field of philosophical, scientific, and aesthetic endeavor. Under Aristotle's guidance, the Lyceum compiled a large library, which some describe as the first notable library of antiquity.

During his Lyceum years, 335-323 BC, Aristotle wrote his chief works, *Physics*, *Metaphysics*, *Nicomachean Ethics*, *Politics*, *On the Soul,* and *Poetics*. Pythias died during this time, and Aristotle became involved with Herpyllis, who may have become his wife or was merely his slave. Among the children of Aristotle and Herpyllis was a son, Nicomachus, named after the philosopher's father and presumably the namesake of the *Nicomachean Ethics*.

Aristotle felt compelled to leave both the Lyceum and Athens in 323 due to an upsurge in anti-Macedonian sentiment in that city. He settled on Euboea, an Aegean island off the central Greek coast. There, in 322, he died, presumably of natural causes.

Vast as Aristotle's contributions are, they fall into three broad areas: philosophy, practical or applied philosophy, and natural philosophy (or "science"). Within the first area, he wrote foundational works on logic, metaphysics, and epistemology. In practical or applied philosophy, he wrote on ethics (from a practical rather than theoretical perspective), war, politics, and economics. We can also include his extremely influential practical works on rhetoric (oratorical persuasion) and aesthetics. In the field of natural philosophy, Aristotle contributed to physics, astronomy, geology, biology, and psychology.

Philosophy

Logic

Prior Analytics (ca. 350 BC) contains Aristotle's earliest contribution to deductive (or syllogistic) reasoning and is history's first known work on formal logic. It is the first of six extant Aristotelian works on logic and the scientific method, which were compiled by Andronicus of Rhodes (or his followers) into *Organon* about 40 BC. This work is the essence of "Aristotelian logic," including the concept of the syllogism.

Metaphysics

This work, its date of composition unknown, is a collection of Aristotelian treatises that were first compiled and arranged by Alexandrian scholars in the first century AD. It was they who gave the work its title, meaning roughly "beyond the physical." It is the founding work in the major traditional branch of philosophy called metaphysics, which is dedicated to the examination of the nature of reality itself, including the relationship between mind and matter, substance and attribute, and the potential versus the actual.

Metaphysics questions the "theory of Forms," posited by Aristotle's teacher Plato. The theory holds that the *things* of the physical world, available to us through our senses, is less real (less true) than *ideas* ("Forms"), which are absolute, timeless, and changeless. Aristotle interrogated this theory with three essential questions: What is existence? How can things continue to exist yet undergo the changes that are part of the natural world? How can this natural world be understood? By way of answer, he explored language and its roots, common sense, and the natural world itself (based on his close, empirical observations). He concluded that reality inheres in things (not separate ideas, or "Forms"), which he defined as substances composed of matter and form. Using Socrates as an example, Aristotle asked how he came to be—since he obviously did not exist before he was born—and concluded that matter has its form (in this case, the form of Socrates) imposed on it to become what it is (in this case, Socrates).

Epistemology

Aristotle's metaphysics—the idea that reality inheres in things—is often called "immanent realism," and immanent realism dominates the philosopher's epistemology. Whereas Plato's epistemology begins with ideas ("Forms"), Aristotle's begins with things and rises to ideas—the knowledge of the universal. Thus, syllogistic reasoning, argument from both induction and deduction, achieves access to truth, whereas, for Plato, truth is generated exclusively through deduction from ideas, or Forms, which are effectively *a priori* principles.

Practical Philosophy

Ethics

The essence of Aristotelian ethics is as expressed most thoroughly in the *Nicomachean Ethics.* The basis of ethics is action in accordance with virtue, which is defined as acting according to one's proper function. For a human being, a virtuous action is action of the soul in accordance with reason to achieve "eudaimonia," or happiness. All ethical considerations flow from this concept of virtue.

Politics

In his treatise *Politics,* Aristotle argued that the city is a "natural" form of government and that "man is by nature a political animal." His political philosophy flowed from a contrast between "true" government—defined as government conducted for the good of all—versus "perverted" government, defined as government conducted for the good of one or one section. Ultimately, tyranny is the most perverted because it exists solely for the good of the tyrant. Conversely, constitutional government is the truest because it is of the *many.* Importantly, Aristotelian political philosophy holds that no true government can be of all. A democracy, though less perverted than either tyranny or oligarchy (government of the rich), is nevertheless a perversion because it is government of the poor.

Economics

Also in his *Politics,* Aristotle developed an economic philosophy, addressing the nature of property and trade. He defended both private property and the use of money as practical enablers of the utility of social arrangements. Nevertheless, he objected to profiting from retail trade because it used goods as a means to an end rather as ends in themselves. This, Aristotle reasoned, was contrary to nature, as was profiting through interest.

Rhetoric and *Poetics*

In his *Rhetoric,* Aristotle laid out "rules" for persuasion, describing three basic forms of "appeal": the appeal to ethos (arguing on the basis of one's own good character), to pathos (the emotions of the audience), and to logos (an appeal to logical reasoning). Within these broad categories, his *Rhetoric* is a veritable catalog and handbook of persuasive techniques.

In his *Poetics,* Aristotle essentially created the profession of aesthetic criticism—chiefly literary criticism, although many of the aesthetic principles are also applicable to other art forms. The *Poetics* may be regarded as a founding document of aesthetics as a branch of philosophy.

Natural Philosophy

For Aristotle, "natural philosophy" is the equivalent of what is encompassed today by science. It is philosophy devoted to examining and accounting for the phenomena of the natural world.

Many of Aristotle's most specific concepts are factually incorrect. Nevertheless, they were all very influential through antiquity and into the Middle Age. Chief among these is his concept of the five elements: earth, water, air, fire, and aether (divine substance), from which all matter is made. Also highly influential was the concept of the "four causes," to the interaction of which (he argued) the reason for the happening of anything can be attributed. The four causes are material, formal, efficient, and final. In Aristotle's analysis, dining (for example) is the final cause produced by wood (material cause), design (formal cause—in this case the design of a wooden table), and carpentry (efficient cause—the skilled working of wood in accordance with a design). The result is dining (around a table).

As an empiricist, Aristotle made various significant observations concerning astronomy, geology, and biology. Most extensively, in *On the Soul,* he formulated a theory of mind and psychology, arguing that human beings possess a rational soul (seat of thought and reflection) in addition to a sensitive soul (seat of mobility and sensation) and a vegetative soul (seat of reproduction and growth). Plants possess only the vegetative soul, and animals possess both vegetative and sensitive souls, whereas human beings possess all three.

Aristotle's most enduring contribution to natural philosophy as well as philosophy itself is his elevation of the empirical over Plato's conception of the ideal. This vision of the natural world and humanity's place within it is one in which people are seen as competent not only in mind but in body and sense. In this respect, the philosophy of Aristotle may be said to give humanity a place in the world.

Augustine of Hippo

Aurelius Augustinus, canonized in 1298 as St. Augustine, was born in Thagaste, Roman Africa (Souk Ahras, Algeria), on November 13, 354. An early theologian instrumental in the evolution of the Western Church, Augustine was a profound Christian philosopher but was also a philosopher in a much broader sense, as a student of epistemology and free will and with a deep interest in language and psychology. Without question, he was theologian committed to the revealed word of holy scripture, and yet his mindset was not dogmatic but driven by the spirit of inquiry.

He was the child of Romanized Berber parents. His mother, Monica (or Monnica), was a Christian. Patricius, his father, was a Pagan who did not convert to Christianity until he lay on his deathbed. Augustine had a brother, Navigius, and a sister, on whom history has conferred the name Perpetua.

Augustine began his schooling when he was eleven years old, attending a school at Madaurus (M'Daourouch), some twenty miles south of Thagaste. Here he was exposed to Latin literature, and here he first experienced sin. In his celebrated memoir, *Confessions* (397-400), he recounts an incident in which he and his friends stole fruit from a neighborhood garden. His insight is telling. He stole not because he was hungry but because theft "was not permitted." He recognized the wrong, calling it foul, but confessed that he "loved it," loved his own "error." Reflecting on this incident and insight, the mature Augustine concluded that humanity is inclined to sin and could therefore be saved only through the grace of Jesus. What is significant is that while the insight is consonant with Christian doctrine, it flows not from dogma but self-reflection. The budding theologian thought like a philosopher.

At seventeen, Augustine journeyed to Carthage to further his education in rhetoric. There he lived a life of the flesh in the company of hedonistic companions. At the same time, however, a reading of Cicero inspired in him a love of knowledge and an interest in philosophy. He veered from Christianity and, against his mother's wishes, became a Manichaean. He also began (at age seventeen) a fifteen-year relationship with a Carthaginian woman, with whom he fathered a son.

In 384, Augustine used a political contact to wrangle the prestigious post of rhetoric professor at the University of Milan. Here he met Ambrose of

Milan (later, St. Ambrose), who inspired his conversion from Manicheanism to Christianity and his entrance into the priesthood. In the meantime, his mother, Monica, had arranged a marriage with an heiress. Augustine renounced his longtime lover, but because his betrothed was underage, marriage was delayed. In the interim, he made the decision to become a celibate priest.

Ambrose baptized both Augustine and his natural son, Adeodatus, in 387. The following year, Monica died, and he and Adeodatus returned to Africa, where they embarked on a comfortable residence at the family estate. But Adeodatus soon died, and Augustine sold his inheritance, giving the money to the poor. He retained only the large family house, which he converted into a monastery.

In 391, Augustine was ordained a priest in Hippo Regius (now Annaba, Algeria), earned renown as a preacher, and, in 395, was made coadjutor bishop and then full bishop of Hippo, serving as such until his death on August 28, 430.

His celebrated *Confessions* is considered an important documentation of religious conversion, but it is also a work of personal philosophy and, as such, is precocious in its modernity. Augustine argued that the true philosopher sets out to "know God and the soul" and therefore he saw no conflict between philosophy and theology. From a more modern philosophical perspective, Augustine is looked on as a Neoplatonist, the dominant philosophical tradition from the middle of the third century to the middle of the seventh. Within this framework, he explored the epistemology of skepticism versus divine illumination, arguing that God created the human mind to be receptive to illumination, which is available to all rational persons. While illumination makes use of the senses, it differs from all other forms of sense perception and is a means by which human beings can apprehend what God presents to them.

While exploring illumination, Augustine also addressed the philosophical problem of "other minds." The extreme skeptic, noting that he can do no more than observe the behavior of others, asks how it is possible to know that any other person has a mind. Augustine argued that testimony (such as his own *Confessions*) is essential to the growth of knowledge; therefore, it is apparent that what others tell us does provide knowledge, even without independent evidence of the existence of minds in others. Similarly, divine illumination is knowledge of God, even without corroborating evidence.

Augustine also made philosophically sound arguments in support of freedom of will and the possibility of just war, arguing that, while Christians should be essentially pacifists, the pursuit of peace may have to be defended by war.

As an ethical philosopher, Augustine argued against slavery and in favor of tolerance toward Jews. He deserves to be considered a philosopher in the field of education, advocating the dialectic and dialogue—mainstays of philosophical discourse since Plato's Socrates—as powerful pedagogical vehicles.

Augustine has remained of more than theological or antiquarian interest to philosophers. Arthur Schopenhauer (1788-1860), Søren Kierkegaard (1813-1855), and Friedrich Nietzsche (1844-1900) were all devoted readers of Augustine, focusing primarily on his exploration of free will. Bertrand Russell (1872-1970) and Edmund Husserl (1859-1938) were intrigued by his meditations on the nature of time, and Hannah Arendt (1906-1975) wrote her doctoral dissertation of Augustine's conception of love as the basis of a philosophy of social life.

Averroes (Ibn Rushd)

Among the most important philosophers in the Islamic world, Ibn Rushd—better known in the West by his Romanized name, Averroes—brought the works of Aristotle before an Islamic audience. In the process, his commentaries on Aristotle, in Latin translation, revived European interest in the Greek philosophers. Thus, Averroes was instrumental in establishing Aristotle as a leading source of Medieval European thought.

Averroes was born on April 14, 1126, in Córdoba, Spain—at the time part of the Almoravid emirate. His was a family of eminent judges, and in 1169 the caliph Abu Yaqub Yusuf became his patron, commissioning several of Averroes's works. Yet Averroes never became a fulltime philosopher. He served from 1182 to 1195 as court physician and chief judge of Córdoba. After his patron's death in 1184, he continued to serve the royal court of the caliphate until 1195, when he fell out of favor and was forced into exile to Lucena, not far from Córdoba but sufficiently removed from the royal court. He was reinstated to royal patronage shortly before he died on December 11, 1198.

Averroes was opposed to Neoplatonism, which figured prominently in the work of Avicenna (980-1037), the most prominent philosopher in the Islamic world of the generation preceding Averroes. Instead, he sought to bring to light the more empirically based work of Aristotle. Not only did he defend Aristotelian thought against Neoplatonism, he had to defend philosophy itself against the leading Sunni theologians, who held that it was inherently incompatible with Islam. Averroes countered that philosophy was not only permitted in Islam but was required knowledge among the educated and powerful. In a work known as *Decisive Treatise,* he defined philosophy as a body of conclusions arrived at through the methodical application of reason. He asserted that conclusions thus reached could not possibly contradict the revealed truths of Islam because "truth cannot contradict truth," and philosophy and Islam were simply two methods of reaching the truth. He did not deny that philosophical conclusions may appear to contradict revelation. In these cases, however, Averroes asserted that the sacred text must be interpreted with the proper allegorical understanding until the apparent contradiction was resolved.

Averroes composed commentaries on almost all the extant works of Aristotle, save *Politics,* to which he did not have access. He knew of the existence of *Politics,* however, and by way of compensation wrote a commentary on Plato's *Republic.* Averroes wrote three styles of commentary, which he called short, middle, and long. The short commentaries simply summarize the texts. The middle commentaries contain more extensive paraphrases and aim to clarify difficulties in the original. The long commentaries proceed line by line and reproduce the complete original texts. They are highly analytical, and Averroes made clear his intention to rescue Aristotle from the attempts of others to interpret the work in a Neoplatonic framework or even to synthesize and merge Plato with Aristotle.

In addition to his commentaries on Aristotle, Averroes wrote numerous original treatises, including *On the Intellect, On the Syllogism, On Conjunction with the Active Intellect, On Time, On the Heavenly Sphere*, and *On the Motion of the Sphere.*

Avicenna

Ibn Sina, known in the West as Avicenna, was born on August 23, 980, in Afshona, Persia, in what is today Uzbekistan. He rose to become the most celebrated physician and philosopher of the Islamic world, bringing together the Greek philosophic thought of late antiquity and that of early Islam into a scientific system that addressed essentially every aspect of reality, including religion. Not only did Avicenna's work dominate thought in the Islamic world for centuries, after its translation into Latin in the twelfth century, it exerted a great influence on medieval and early Renaissance philosophy. The Latin translation of Avicenna's medical treatises had a similarly powerful influence on European medicine as late as the seventeenth century.

Avicenna composed an autobiography, in which he reported having committed the Quran to memory by the time he was ten years old. An Indian grocer in his village taught him Indian arithmetic, and he took lessons from an itinerant scholar, who also practiced medicine. From another scholar, he learned the fundamentals of Islamic jurisprudence. He struggled with the *Metaphysics* of Aristotle until its secrets were unlocked for him by a reading of Abu Nasr al-Farabi's commentary. At sixteen, he studied medicine and was deemed a fully qualified physician by his eighteenth year. He excelled in medicine and earned widespread fame, eventually earning appointment as physician to Emir Nuh II, who, in gratitude for helping him to recover from a serious illness, rewarded him with access to the royal library of the Samanids.

When he was twenty-two, Avicenna lost his father and traveled to Urgench in what is now Turkmenistan, where the local vizier subsidized his study. In search of a more remunerative patron, Avicenna wandered as far as Tabaristan in today's northern Iran. There he hoped that the local ruler, Qabus, renowned as a patron of the learned, would give him a place. But he discovered that Qabus had been starved to death by mutinous troops. Avicenna himself fell ill, but finally found shelter and a patron at Hyrcania, near the Caspian Sea. Here he lectured on logic and astronomy and wrote his great *Canon of Medicine.*

Avicenna moved on to Rayy, near modern Tehran, and was highly productive there under the sponsorship of Majd al-Damla, Rayy's young emir. But he soon became embroiled in internecine disputes and was caught in a war between the cities of Hamadan and Isfahan. He had to hide, flee, and hide some more. He was even imprisoned for a time. Nevertheless, he continued to study and write and served several local rulers as physician, political counselor, and philosopher-scientist. He settled about 1025 in Isfahan, where he spent the remainder of his life once again in service to Ala al-Dawla as physician, adviser, and philosopher-in-residence. He died in June 1037.

Fairly late in his life, Avicenna wrote an *Autobiography*, in which he accounted for his development as a philosopher. He set out, he says, to comprehend the structure of all knowledge. He began devouring the works of previous philosophers, whom he read with a critical eye and with the intention of correcting their shortcomings. His readings convinced him that philosophy—by which he meant the state of all knowledge—needed to be revised and elevated. Finally, he explained his belief that the individual could acquire the highest knowledge by comprehensive study of epistemology and eschatology, a project he did not merely intend to accomplish but claimed to have mastered by the time he was eighteen. Reportedly, he wrote his mature masterwork (composed 1014-1020), *The Cure,* without consulting any books.

Monumental in scope, *The Cure* (*al-Shifa,* sometimes translated as *The Book of Healing*) runs to some 22 volumes in the twentieth-century "Cairo edition." It encompasses logic, theoretical philosophy, and practical philosophy.

The logical material is a series of commentaries, beginning with the *Isagoge,* an introduction to Aristotle's "Categories" (the things that can be the subject or predicate of a logical proposition) written by the Neoplatonic philosopher Porphyry. Avicenna went on to comment on, criticize, and extend all of Aristotle's major works of logic, dialectic, rhetoric, and poetics.

Under the category of theoretical philosophy, Avicenna wrote on Aristotelian concepts of physics, on mathematics (based on works by Euclid, Ptolemy, and others), and on metaphysics. In this category, Avicenna explored the varied phenomena of religious life and what we might call the paranormal as functions of the "rational soul." Thus, Avicenna's metaphysics served as the core of his moral and ethical philosophy.

In the area of practical philosophy, *The Cure* treats the role of prophetic legislation in guiding politics. Here Avicenna elaborated on the political works of both Plato and Aristotle to describe the ideal legislator for public administration and for "family law." The section ends with a work on ethics, drawing heavily on Aristotle's *Nicomachean Ethics.* Avicenna envisioned ethics as a field to be legislated by a caliph.

Avicenna's achievement was to synthesize all the philosophical thought he had absorbed, both Hellenic and Islamic, into a coherent rational system capable of explaining reality and ultimately driving a rational and just system of ethics. In this, he sought to harmonize Aristotelian physics and metaphysics with Neoplatonism set within the context of a cosmology as imagined by Ptolemy. In sum, Avicenna can be said to have charted the intellectual civilization of the medieval world, both in its Islamic and Christian aspects.

Bacon, Francis

Francis Bacon was a giant of natural philosophy and is often called the father of science—or, at least, of scientific methodology. He was also prominent in England's Jacobean court as a lawyer and member of Parliament, who wrote extensively on legal and political issues.

Bacon was born on January 22, 1561, to Sir Nicholas Bacon (Lord Keeper of the Seal) and his second wife, Lady Anne Cooke Bacon, whose father was tutor to Edward VI and a leading humanist. Lady Anne was learned, with a fine command of Greek, Latin, Italian, and French.

After attending Trinity College, Cambridge and—for legal training—Gray's Inn, London, Bacon tried unsuccessfully to enter politics during the reign of Queen Elizabeth I. He failed here but rose, under James I, to the office of Lord Chancellor. It was in his later years, after he left politics, that Bacon devoted himself exclusively to philosophy and achieved rare renown.

As a natural philosopher, Bacon brought about nothing less than a paradigm shift in Western thought. He found contemporary philosophy to be dogmatic and tradition-bound, slavishly adhering to both Plato and Aristotle. Although Bacon conceded the value of Aristotle's empirical impulses, he pointed out that the philosopher had failed to create an overarching theory for the conduct of science. More specifically, Bacon criticized Aristotle's cosmology as obsolete, but he reserved his sharper criticism for those contemporary philosophers who endorsed Aristotle's metaphysical approach to natural philosophy at the expense of the empirical. Bacon championed a focus on natural, not ideal, forms and on the effects of natural processes on things.

His master project with respect to knowledge he called the *Great Instauration* (*Instauratio Magna*), an act of renewal, which he laid out as a work consisting of six parts:

1. *The Divisions of the Sciences*
2. *The New Organon; or Directions concerning the Interpretation of Nature*
3. *The Phenomena of the Universe; or a Natural and Experimental History for the foundation of Philosophy*
4. *The Ladder of Intellect*
5. *The Forerunners; or Anticipations of the New Philosophy*
6. *The New Philosophy; or Active Science*

The first part was essentially covered in two earlier works, *The Advancement of Learning* (1605) and a revised edition of *De Dignitate et Augmentis Scientiarum* (1623). These works described all the sciences and their subdivisions as they existed in Bacon's own time. His objective was to present the state of science and contrast it to what science should be or become—that is, what was missing and ought to be present.

Part 2 became Bacon's best-known work, the *Novum Organum* ("New Organon"), which is devoted to radically reforming the methods of creating knowledge. As a basis for this, Bacon presented both a new epistemology and ontology, *Interpretatio Naturae* ("Natural Interpretation"). The new logic of research Bacon set forth here was designed to foster understanding of nature, not merely to defeat an opponent in argument. The *Novum Organum* is the only part of the "Great Instauration" Bacon completed—or, at least, nearly completed.

Part 3, *The Phenomena of the Universe,* was planned as a natural and experimental history of the "phenomena" of the universe. Bacon's concept of natural history was narrative as well as inductive. Narratives, based on close observation, were intended to provide the inductive material for empirical research. Bacon appreciated the complexity of nature and believed natural philosophy should explain nature's complexity rather than create complex philosophical systems. His objective was to use philosophical process to create physical and metaphysical knowledge.

The fourth part, *The Ladder of Intellect* (*Scala Intellectus*) was planned to link the method of creating natural history, laid out in Part 3, to Part 6, *The New Philosophy; or Active Science.* Bacon completed a portion of this work, identifying what he believed was missing in current scientific knowledge and addressing ways of filling the gaps. Even more important, he looked toward a future in which new sciences would be discovered or called for. Bacon aimed science at the new—the newly revealed—and not backward, toward resolving old controversies. Furthermore, he regarded each new empirical discovery as further testament to the glory of God. In this sense, to do the *new* science was to do God's work.

In Part 5, *The Forerunners*, Bacon intended to review the historical adumbrations of the New Science for the purpose of demonstrating that the reformation—the paradigm shift—he hoped to begin would build on aspects of the past and also require time. In the meantime, however, he advanced work on his holistic vision of a natural philosophy system in *De Fluxu et Refluxu Maris* and *Thema Coeli*, which are the complete portions of *The Forerunners.*

The knowledge created by the method outlined in Part 3 was intended to prepare the way for *The New Philosophy; or Active Science,* Part 6 of the projected *Great Instauration.* His intention was to write six prototype natural histories but partially completed just three.

Possibly the most important aspect of Bacon's concept of the New Science was that its aim was not to further what today is called Pure Science but, rather, to foster the creation of Applied Science. Natural science, for him, was applied science, the great importance of which was to improve the lot of humankind. Indeed, he described the inventions he expected empirical science to produce as imitations of divine works. Bacon's vision of both philosophy and science may, then, be described as startlingly modern, even futuristic.

Roger Bacon

Roger Bacon was a major medieval commentator on Aristotle and, as a professor at the universities of Paris and Oxford, he taught Aristotle's works concerning both natural philosophy and metaphysics. In an era dominated by Neoplatonism, with its emphasis on *a priori* deductive reasoning from received theories, Bacon emphasized *a posteriori* inductive reasoning based on the empirical study of nature. His contributions to natural philosophy look ahead to the elevation of science and the scientific method some five hundred years in the future.

Bacon was born at Ilchester, Somerset, England, about 1219 or 1220, the child of a family of some wealth. He studied at Oxford and became a master there, lecturing on Aristotle. In 1237 or sometime thereafter, he taught at the University of Paris, lecturing chiefly on Latin grammar, Aristotelian logic, arithmetic, geometry, and the mathematics of astronomy and music. He left Paris about 1247 and became an independent scholar, although he may have lived mostly in or near Oxford.

He took holy orders, becoming a Franciscan friar in 1256 or 1257, either in Paris or Oxford. He struggled under the yoke of Franciscan discipline until he was able to obtain a commission from Pope Clement IV in 1266 to produced "writings and remedies for current conditions." As Bacon interpreted it, this amounted to an invitation to depart from engaging in disputes over the texts of Aristotle and to instead survey the state of current learning and apply Aristotelian logic and science to it with the objective of creating a new theology.

Clement's commission resulted in Bacon's masterwork, the *Opus Majus,* completed in 1267, and consisting of seven parts:

Part One: "The Four General Causes of Human Ignorance" ponders the impediments to truth and wisdom. Bacon discerns four causes of error: following an unreliable authority; slavishly adhering to custom; heeding the ignorance of others; and attempting to conceal one's own ignorance with specious knowledge.

Part Two: "The Affinity of Philosophy with Theology" explores the relationship between philosophy and theology, reaching the conclusion that scripturally grounded theology is the foundation of philosophy and all its branches.

Part Three: "On the Usefulness of Grammar" follows from the elevation of holy scripture in Part Two, concluding that language and grammar are essential to understanding scriptural truth and are therefore foundational to all manner of knowledge. Bacon's earlier work on grammar hints at the possibility of creating a universal grammar applicable across many languages.

Part Four: "The Usefulness of Mathematics in Physics" is most notable for its application to the reformation of the Julian Calendar then in use.

Part Five: "On the Science of Perspective" is a treatise on optics and visual perception, based largely on Arab writers.

Part Six: "On Experimental Knowledge" is a study of empirically based natural philosophy (science) with an emphasis on alchemy (including its occult aspects), astronomy, and the manufacture of gunpowder.

Part Seven "A Philosophy of Morality" is a study of moral philosophy and ethics.

The *Opus Majus* was followed by the *Opus Minus,* an abstract of the larger work, and the *Opus Tertium,* which was intended to introduce both the *Minus* and the *Majus.* Together, the works were meant to serve both as a justification for and outline of a reformed approach to theology and the education of theologians, which, Bacon argued, should include a thorough indoctrination into natural philosophy.

The death of Pope Clement in 1268 left Bacon without a sponsor and, more important, without a protector. When the Church handed down the *Condemnations* of 1277, which banned the teaching of several philosophical doctrines, Bacon was arrested and either held under house detention or cast into prison. Released sometime after 1278, he returned to Oxford and the Franciscan House there, where he continued to study and write. The *Compendium Studii Theologiae*, his final known work, was completed in 1292. He may have died later that year or as much as two years later and was presumably interred at Oxford.

Beauvoir, Simone de

Simone de Beauvoir always considered herself a writer. She disdained calling herself a philosopher, although she did take credit for acting the role of "midwife" (her term) to the existentialism of her longtime companion Jean-Paul Sartre. Only late in her life and after her death, were her contributions to philosophy fully recognized, especially in politics, ethics, existentialism, and feminist theory. Indeed, she artfully synthesized existentialism and feminism, lending greater urgency and immediacy to both. Moreover, she also elevated feminism to the level of political philosophy with *The Second Sex,* her breakthrough 1949 two-volume answer to the question "What is a woman?"

Simone de Beauvoir was born on January 9, 1908, into a middle-class Parisian family that suffered a financial crisis following World War I and thereafter struggled to maintain its bourgeois status. Profoundly religious as a child, Beauvoir considered becoming a nun but abandoned her religion in her early teens and lived from then on as an atheist.

Thanks to her family's straitened circumstances, Beauvoir realized she would have no dowry and thus decided to prepare to make her own way in the world. She passed baccalaureate exams in mathematics and philosophy in 1925, studied mathematics at the Institut Catholique de Paris and literature and languages at the Institut Sainte-Marie before entering the Sorbonne, from which, in 1928, she received the equivalent of a master's degree in philosophy, writing a thesis on Leibniz.

She prepared for a career as a secondary-school teacher—in company with Maurice Merleau-Ponty and Claude Lévi-Strauss—and unofficially attended courses at the École Normale Supérieure to prepare for the prestigious *agrégation* post-graduate examination in philosophy. There she met Jean-Paul Sartre, to whom first place in the *agrégation* was awarded, with Beauvoir placing second. At twenty-one, she was the youngest candidate ever to pass the examination.

Beauvoir taught in a lycée from 1929 to 1943, at which time she became sufficiently established as a writer to support herself with her pen. The year 1929 also marked the beginning of her lifelong relationship with Sartre, which the couple described as a partnership of the soul. A sexual relationship, it was non-exclusive, and the couple did not live together. They did, however, faithfully read one another's work, a circumstance that triggered an unending debate over who influenced whom in what.

Beauvoir's formal entrée into philosophy came in 1944, when she published *Pyrrhus et Cinéas,* an essay on existentialist ethics. This was followed in 1947 by *The Ethics of Ambiguity* (1947), which three generations of philosophy professors have recommended as the most comprehensive introduction to French existentialism.

With Sartre, she edited *Les Temps modernes* (*Modern Times*), a political periodical Sartre, Merleau-Ponty, and others founded at the end of World War II. She used the journal to publish some of her shorter works and continued as its editor until her death in 1986. In 1949, *The Second Sex* (*Le Deuxième Sexe*) was published. The central theme, building on Sartre's classic existentialist formulation "existence precedes essence," is that "One is not born but becomes a woman," thereby distinguishing between sex and gender and arguing that biological sex did not necessarily coincide with the social construction of gender. This, Beauvoir argued, has resulted in the social oppression of women because of the socio-historical female identity imposed upon them. The essential oppression is that women are defined exclusively in relation to men, thereby becoming relegated to the status of the "second sex." Beauvoir used the lessons of existential thought to reveal women as the equal of men in terms of choice in life.

With *The Second Sex,* Simone de Beauvoir effectively popularized existentialism among women and, conversely, introduced existentialists—male and female—to feminism. In *The Second Sex,* existentialism and feminism are inextricably bound. As provocative as the 1947 book was, her 1954 roman à clef, *The Mandarins*, revealed in frank, albeit novelistic, detail the personal lives of the philosophers and others who made up Sartre's and Beauvoir's circle, thereby providing a unique view of the makers of philosophy in the mid-twentieth century. Recognizable are intimate portraits of herself, Sartre, Albert Camus, Arthur Koestler, and the American novelist and short-story writer Nelson Algren. Beauvoir wrote in especially intimate detail of her extended affair with Algren, who was outraged by her appropriation of their intimacy for public consumption.

Beauvoir succumbed to pneumonia on April 14, 1986 and was buried beside Sartre (who had died six years earlier) in Montparnasse Cemetery, Paris.

Benjamin, Walter

Professors of literature claim Walter Benjamin as one of their own, a student of literature and a critic. Philosophers see him as a great modern aesthetician but also as a political philosopher or, more precisely, as a politically oriented philosopher of aesthetics. For his great contribution was to develop a historically and politically grounded materialist aesthetic theory.

Walter Benjamin was born on July 15, 1892 to a prosperous Jewish family living in Berlin. He received his pre-college education at a progressive boarding school in Haubinda, Thuringia, and there formed a relationship with the liberal educational reformer Gustav Wyneken. As a youngster, Benjamin contributed articles to *Der Anfang* ("The Beginning"), a journal of education inspired by Wyneken.

Benjamin studied at the universities of Freiburg im Breisgau and Berlin. In this second institution, he met Gerhard (later Gershom) Scholem, who introduced him to Kabbalism, which influenced Benjamin's literary interpretations, especially of Franz Kafka. Benjamin earned a Ph.D. from the University of Bern, Switzerland, in 1919, with a dissertation titled *The Concept of Art Criticism in German Romanticism*.

Benjamin wrote *Ursprung des deutschen Trauerspiels* (literally, *Origin of the German Mourning-Play*, but usually translated as *Origin of German Tragic Drama*) as his *Habilitationsschrift*, a post-doctoral thesis necessary to secure a qualification for teaching at the university level. The thesis was not accepted, however, disqualifying him from an appointment to the University of Frankfurt am Main. Nevertheless, he published a version of the work in 1928 and received considerable acclaim.

He had written *Origin of German Tragic Drama* in 1924 on Capri, where he also met the Bolshevik Latvian theatrical director Asja Lacis, with whom he commenced a romantic affair and collaborated on some experimental theater works. His association with Lacis and a reading of Georg Lukács brought about his engagement with Marx's historical materialism, so that, by the opening of the 1930s, he was an intellectual Marxist with a circle of like-minded young men, among them the playwright Bertolt Brecht. With Brecht, Benjamin formed a warm friendship and collaboration.

Benjamin fled Germany after the ascension of Adolf Hitler to the Chancellorship in 1933 and lived in Paris, Ibiza, San Remo, and, as Brecht's guest, in a house near Svendborg, Denmark. He became associated during the decade of the thirties with the Institute for Social Research, which provided a publishing platform and a living.

When World War II broke out in 1939, Benjamin was briefly interned in a French camp, was soon released, and, after a brief stay in Paris, fled as the German army swept into France in 1940. Unable to escape Vichy France in the early autumn of 1940 and turned back by Spanish customs officers after crossing the Pyrenees, Benjamin committed suicide on September 27, 1940. He was forty-eight.

Benjamin's final work, "Theses on the Philosophy of History," published posthumously in 1942, is a critique of historicism, the significance of historical period, geographical place, and local culture as first developed by the German Romantic philosopher Karl Wilhelm Friedrich Schlegel. The work is brief and cryptic, an amalgamation of the Jewish Kabbalistic tradition and Marxist materialism, but is peculiarly suited to the catastrophic time in which it was written, when history had come to seem meaningless, a desperate attempt at holding onto a memory in what Benjamin called a "moment of danger." "Theses" was, in effect, a philosophical statement on the end of history.

Besides the *Origin of German Tragic Drama,* Benjamin's best-known writing is "The Work of Art in the Age of Mechanical Reproduction," which explores the impact of speed and infinite reproducibility on the perception of art, time, place, permanence, and decay for those living in a technological civilization. The essay synthesizes aesthetics, politics, phenomenology, and semiotics, as well as psychology.

Benjamin's longest work is *The Arcades Project,* an incomplete collection of writings, from 1927 to the end of the author's life in 1940, about the life of Paris, especially as manifested in the city's shopping arcades (*passages couverts*). In terms of philosophical reflection, *Arcades* is a thousand-page contemplation of modern urban culture in Europe.

Bentham, Jeremy

Few philosophers, save Karl Marx, have had more practical impact on government and social policy than Jeremy Bentham. The core of his social philosophy, what he himself identified as its "fundamental axiom," has driven innumerable policy decisions and criticisms: "it is the greatest happiness of the greatest number that is the measure of right and wrong."

Jeremy Bentham was born on February 15, 1748 in London, the son of a wealthy Tory family. He was a genius, who read English as an infant, Latin by the age of three, and played Handel on the fiddle by seven. He was educated at Westminster School and, in 1760, when he was twelve, enrolled in Queen's College, Oxford, earning his bachelor's degree in 1763 and his master's in 1766. Trained as a lawyer, he was called to the bar in 1769 but never practiced, having become disgusted with what he considered the unnecessary and fundamentally dishonest complexity of English law.

Despite his Tory ancestry, Bentham early on became a reformer. During 1786-1787, he visited his brother Samuel in White Russia (modern Belarus), where he served Prince Potemkin as manager of several large projects. Samuel's idea of designing a factory as a circular building surrounding a hub, where managers could efficiently oversee workmen, inspired Jeremy to design prisons for similar efficiency, hygiene, and safety.

This led to broader ideas on prison reform, although his design for the "panopticon" prison was never built.

Although the prison project proved abortive, it laid the foundation for Bentham's career as a reformer. He started by attempting a wholesale reform of English law, which he planned to replace with the "Pannomion," a code of law based on his core principle of promoting the greatest good for the greatest number. This philosophy would eventually command global attention and was universally known as Benthamism but is today labeled utilitarianism, which is the name that his most famous student, John Stuart Mill, gave to it.

As the entire "Pannomion" was to flow from what students of utilitarianism call the "greatest happiness principle," so did Bentham's whole philosophy, which encompassed law, economics, society, and ethics. The key to understanding Bentham's utilitarianism is to appreciate how *he* understood the word *happiness,* which was as a state of being in which pleasure was allowed to predominate over pain. These—pleasure and pain—were for Bentham humankind's two "sovereign masters."

Bentham believed that the morality—or moral value—of any action could be quantified and calculated in terms of the degree of happiness it created or destroyed. He called this the hedonistic or felicific calculus. Bentham classified 12 categories of pain and 14 of pleasure, offering these as the counters ("dolors" and "hedons") with which the "happiness factor" of any action could be calculated. The idea was that an action's moral and ethical value could be numerically expressed and compared with the value of a competing action. Ideally, the more felicific action would prevail. What must be borne in mind is that the felicific calculus was not intended to be applied to individuals but to society. The calculation that finally matters is that which reveals the greatest good for the greatest number.

Bentham applied his principle of utility in *An Introduction to the Principles of Morals and Legislation* (1789) as a means of reforming legislative policy such that laws would be crafted to produce the greatest amount of pleasure and the minimum amount of pain. He applied utility as well to economics, arguing for monetary expansion to create full employment and thereby evolved the basis of welfare economics, including a system of "Pauper Management" through a large system of workhouses.

While, in the view of some, Bentham's reduction of morality to a calculus of pleasure and pain denied the existence of natural human rights, Bentham was an early advocate—perhaps the first of any significance—of animal rights. This was no mere whim but, on the contrary, revealed much about Bentham's ethical philosophy. Arguing against the notion that the ability to reason—exclusive province of humans—is the only viable ethical benchmark, Bentham countered with the ability to suffer, something all sentient beings possessed. Animals, then, like humans, had the right to avoid suffering, and, conversely, society and socially sanctioned authority did not have the right to willfully inflict suffering on humans or animals. Importantly, Bentham applied this same reasoning to the mistreatment of the mentally ill, of disabled people, and of slaves or others deemed to be of "inferior" races.

Bentham did not argue that killing animals for food, killing them in self-defense, or even performing medical experiments on them was immoral. In all three instances, an argument could be made that killing the animal was for the greater good. He did, however, proscribe making the animal suffer needlessly or gratuitously.

Bentham advocated total equality of the sexes, including enfranchisement, property ownership, the right to get a divorce, and eligibility for political office. Women were human beings and were part of the greatest number to whom the greatest good should be made available. He also argued against punishing homosexuality, acts which he did not consider unnatural but merely "irregularities" in sexual appetite.

Bentham died, at eighty-four, on June 6, 1832. He was closely associated with University College London, in the establishment of which he played a role. This institution became a center of research into Bentham's philosophy and, in 1850, the home to the "Auto-icon," a cabinet containing Bentham's skeleton stuffed with hay and dressed in Bentham's clothes. Bentham had willed his body for dissection by the physician George Fordyce. Even in death, Bentham wished to be of some utility.

Bergson, Henri

Henri Bergson sought to free philosophy from mechanistic views of causality and argued for the role of free will in creating new things and ideas in a gloriously unpredictable fashion. In contrast to Immanuel Kant, for whom free will was a concept wholly apart from the world of time and space, a matter of spiritual faith, Bergson endeavored to redefine time, space, and causality as duration (*la durée*), the inner experience (or perception) of time, which may speed up or slow down and is, in essence, immeasurable. For Bergson, duration is the mental or imaginative space in which freewill causality can coexist. This inner realm is at once apart from time and space and yet very much encompassed within it. Reality, therefore, can best be described as a continuous stream of movement and change, whose essence Bergson called *élan vital* (vital impulse), a force apprehended not by the intellect but by intuition. The former isolates the moment, attempts to fix and measure it, and thereby kills it, whereas the latter experiences the moment as duration, without compromising its movement or presence within the stream.

Henri Bergson was born in Paris on October 18, 1859 and was trained as a mathematician but went on to the École Normale Supérieure, from which he graduated in 1881 and became a professor, working simultaneously in the fields of psychology and philosophy. He wrote and published prodigiously, but his four principal works are *Time and Free Will* (1889), *Matter and Memory* (1896), *Creative Evolution* (1907), and *The Two Sources of Morality and Religion* (1932).

Time and Free Will developed the concept of duration, in which free will and causality are reconciled as what Bergson called the "immediate data of consciousness."

Matter and Memory explored the mind-body problem, which has proved durable in both philosophy and psychology. The book was a direct response to Théodule Ribot's *Maladies of Memory* (1881), an early work of physiological psychology, which argued that memory is wholly contained within a structure of the brain. Bergson countered that memory is inherently metaphysical—beyond the physical—and is thus of a spiritual nature yet is also built of perceptions of an immediate nature, through embodied cognition and not just within the physiology of the brain.

Creative Evolution proposed replacing Charles Darwin's mechanistic vision of evolution with the idea of an evolution driven by élan vital, the vital impulse that is linked to creativity in the narrower human sense. Published in 1907, the book revisited the duration concept and memory, evoking a picture of an inner reality that served to inspire the likes of Marcel Proust (who, in the multivolume *Á la recherche de temps perdu* [*Remembrance of Things Past*], endeavored to reconstruct decades of memory without destroying its immediacy) and other modernist authors and artists.

The Two Sources of Morality and Religion was an attempt to develop his philosophical theories in the context of religion, morality, and art, but was not successful. By this time, Bergson was no longer regarded as a radical but as a "respectable" professor. He lived to see the Nazi invasion and occupation of France and, as a Jew, would most likely have been deported to a concentration camp had he not succumbed to bronchitis on January 3, 1941. He was eighty-one.

Berkeley, George

Born on March 12, 1685, in County Kilkenny, Ireland, George Berkeley, Bishop of Cloyne, formulated a philosophical theory he called "immaterialism" but that is better known today as subjective idealism. It holds that material things do not exist and that reality is entirely ideal, existing as mental content.

At fifteen, Berkeley left Kilkenny College to enter Trinity College, Dublin, of which he was made a fellow in 1707, three years after graduating. He was ordained in the Anglican Church shortly after this.

Trinity was, at the time, a very modern university, and Berkeley imbibed anti-Aristotelianism, which fed into his early philosophical evolution toward immaterialism. His first published work, *An Essay Towards a New Theory of Vision* (1709), examined the phenomena of visual perception, concluding that the real "objects of sight" do not lie outside of the mind. This adumbration of subjective idealism was elaborated in the 1710 *Treatise Concerning the Principles of Human Knowledge.* It was in this work that Berkeley sought to refute John Locke's empiricism by arguing that material "reality" is an illusion and that the experience of the outside world is the creation of internal ideas by experience of external ideas. Berkeley's theory was that ideas can be produced only by other ideas, and, therefore, the external world is not physical but ideational. It has been given its logic, its ideational form, by God.

In 1720, during a four-year European tour as a tutor, Berkeley wrote *De Motu*, a philosophical approach to physics, which argued that the forces of which Newton wrote were not physical but "occult" and existed not in the world of phenomena but within an occult realm analogous to the soul. The great twentieth-century Austro-British philosopher Karl Popper saw in *De Motu* a more powerful version of Ockham's Razor, the principle that "entities should not be multiplied without necessity," often paraphrased as the simplest solution is most likely the correct one. Popper dubbed this modification "Berkeley's razor" and described it as the thesis that the empirical scientific method yields no true picture of the nature of the world, whose truth may be approached only through metaphysical reasoning. As Popper saw it, Berkeley's analysis of physics yielded an extremely empirical view of scientific observation as beginning and ending empirically, without the possibility of deeper insight.

On his return to Ireland, Berkeley resumed teaching at Trinity until 1724, when he became Dean of Derry. Having decided that Europe was in irreversible spiritual decay, Berkeley began planning to found a college across the Atlantic, in Bermuda. He sailed in 1728 with his young wife, Anne Forster, and landed in Newport, Rhode Island, where he awaited promised funding for the next three years. When it failed to materialize, Berkeley returned to Britain in 1731.

He continued to write, defending his *Essay Towards a New Theory of Vision* with *Theory of Vision, Vindicated and Explained* and following it with the *Analyst*, a critique of Newton's calculus—in part intended to counter a religious interpretation of Newton that was producing deism, a doctrine Berkeley regarded as heretical.

Berkeley became Bishop of Cloyne in 1734. A decade later, his *Siris* appeared, which is a peculiar treatise on the medicinal value of tar-water (made by letting pine tar stand in water). The work supplies ample scientific material bolstering the medical claims for tar-water and ends by inviting the reader to a contemplation of God.

Berkeley died in Oxford, on January 14, 1753.

Bhartrhari

Bharthari lived in the fifth century AD and is known through two texts, *Satakatraya,* a Sanskrit poetic work, and *Vakyapadiya,* a work of linguistic philosophy concerning Sanskrit grammar. It is the grammatical work that elevates Bhartrhari to an important place in the history of philosophy.

Bhartrihari was not merely a grammarian but a linguistic philosopher, who is associated with the term *sphota* ("bursting," or "opening"). As the philosopher used it, the word refers to how the mind transforms linguistic units into coherent speech. He conceptualized *sphota* as the act of meaningful speech consisting of three elements, conceptualization by the speaker, the performative act of speaking, and comprehension by the interpreter of the speech. Bhartrihari theorized that language and cognition are essentially one. He argued that the meaning of any utterance is known only after the complete sentence is spoken or read. Individual words take on their meaning only in the context of each sentence in which they occur. Bhartrihari derived this understanding from observing speech acquisition in children. The young child watches and listens as one person asks another to perform an action. That utterance is followed by the performance of the action, which thus teaches the child the "meaning" of the spoken words.

Bhartrihari also pondered the capacity of language for expressing self-referential paradox. He cited the example of the phrases "this is unnameable" and "this is unsignifiable," pointing out that the very act of writing these statements makes the statements both nameable and signifiable.

Bhartrihari concluded from this that the act of verbal communication has the potential of transforming a mundane, non-problematic statement into a paradox. He attempted to resolve this paradox by arguing that even what cannot be named or signified can be "indicated," so that the receiver of the communication understands that, signifiable or not, the thing does exist.

Boethius (Anicius Manlius Severinus Boëthius)

Boethius is believed to have been born the year after the "barbarian" Odoacer overthrew the last emperor of the Western Roman Empire and proclaimed himself King of Italy. Thus, this philosopher, whose *Consolation of Philosophy* (*De consolation philosophiae*) would become enormously popular throughout the Middle Ages, came into the world at the end of a world.

He was born, in Rome, into the patrician Anicii family about AD 477. His father, Manlius Boethius, served as consul in 487 but died early in his son's life. Boethius was adopted by Quintus Aurelius Memmius Symmachus, who acquainted the boy with both literature and philosophy. Little is known of his formal education; however, given his fluency in Greek, some speculate that he was educated in Athens. Others argue that he studied with the Neoplatonist philosopher Ammonius Hermiae at Alexandria.

Wherever he acquired his erudition, it was sufficient to prompt Theodoric the Great to engage him in his court. By twenty-five, Boethius became a senator. He was also consul for the year 510, and both of his sons became co-consuls for 522. That was the year in which Boethius was appointed *magister officiorum*, head of all government and court services

In 523, Boethius defended an ex-consul, Albinus, against charges of treasonous correspondence with Justin I, the Eastern Roman Emperor. In doing this, he incurred a charge of treason himself and was imprisoned in Pavia before suffering execution in 524. While imprisoned, Boethius wrote his most famous work, *The Consolation of Philosophy*. The book is a colloquy between the author and Lady Philosophy, who consoles him by asserting the transitory nature of wealth and fame while elevating the work of the mind, which she defines as the "one true good."

In the course of the conversation, Boethius epitomizes his philosophical views on determinism and free will, good and evil (Why do the evil seem to prosper?), and the omniscience of God. He develops a view of the essential goodness of humanity but concedes that people can become depraved if they allow themselves to sink to the level of beasts. Boethius discusses many aspects of religion, arguing finally that Christianity will arrive at the same truths as philosophy.

While *The Consolation* became one the most widely read books of the European Middle Ages, Boethius' most important philosophical works were his translations of and commentaries on the logical writings of Aristotle, which served Europe until the twelfth century as the only significant portions of Aristotle available in Latin. The commentaries have been lost, but two books, *In Ciceronis Topica* and *De Topicis Differentiis,* contain virtually all that survives of Boethius' logic outside of parts of *The Consolation. In Ciceronis Topica* and *De Topicis Differentiis* develop a logic based on Plato and Aristotle and apply it to questions of morality and conduct. *De Topicis Differentiis* served many medieval students and scholars as a handbook on dialectic and rhetoric, which gave special emphasis to the topics of arguments.

Boethius wrote treatises on mathematics and on music. To some extent, his *De arithmetica* was a manual of instruction, but he went beyond this in his commentary on Porphyry's *Isagoge,* tackling the problem of universals, asking whether universal concepts exist only as ideas or are "subsistent entities" in themselves.

Closely related to *De arithmetica* is *De institutione musica,* a pedagogical text and theoretical treatise that explains the relationship of mathematics to music. In this work, he classifies music into three categories: *Musica mundane,* the music of the spheres, which could be understood but not heard; *Musica humana,* the harmony of body and of spirit; and *Musica instrumentalis,* instrumental music.

In addition to his philosophical work, Boethius wrote theological treatises, which are important in the history of the early Roman church.

Bonhoeffer, Dietrich

Born on February 4, 1906, in Breslau, one of eight children of psychiatrist and neurologist Karl Bonhoeffer, Dietrich Bonhoeffer earned both an undergraduate degree and the equivalent of a master's at the Protestant Faculty of Theology of the University of Tübingen and went on to a doctorate in theology from the University of Berlin in 1927. He traveled to the United States in 1930 for postgraduate work and to teach at the Union Theological Seminary in New York City, where he also studied under Reinhold Niebuhr. He attended services at the Abyssinian Baptist Church in Harlem, where he was impressed with the preaching of Adam Clayton Powell Sr. and became attuned to the relation of religion to social justice.

Back in Germany, Bonhoeffer lectured in theology at the University of Berlin and, having reached the age of twenty-five, was ordained a minister.

When Adolf Hitler rose to the chancellorship in the German government of Paul von Hindenburg, he became an outspoken opponent of Nazism and enlisted the faithful to fight alongside him. After the Protestant establishment declared its allegiance to Hitler and National Socialism, Bonhoeffer and another minister, Hermann Sasse, drafted the Bethel Confession, which opposed the Nazi "German Christian" movement. Nevertheless, the national synod approved the so-called Aryan paragraph, which barred non-Aryans from the Protestant churches and led to a demand for the removal of the Old Testament from the churches as well.

In this climate, Bonhoeffer declined the offer of a parish in Berlin in fall 1933 and accepted a two-year appointment as pastor of two German-speaking churches in London. His plan was to garner support for a breakaway German Protestant movement called the Confessing Church. After his English appointment ended, in 1935, Bonhoeffer turned down an offer to study under Gandhi in his Indian ashram and returned to Germany to head a covert seminary to train Confessing Church pastors. This was the beginning of an underground spiritual movement, in which he trained anti-Nazi pastors across Germany. He returned to the Union Theological Seminary in New York in 1939 but almost immediately sailed back to Germany. Forbidden to speak or to publish, he joined the Abwehr, German military intelligence, using it as cover for his work as a resistance movement courier. He also began writing *Ethics* but was arrested and imprisoned on April 5, 1943. After the Abwehr was discredited as a haven for double-agents, Bonhoeffer was tried and condemned on April 8, 1945 at Flossenbürg concentration camp. He was hanged the next day. Flossenbürg was liberated just two weeks later by American troops.

Bonhoeffer was a pioneer in the modern theology of protest, resistance, and social justice. For him, theology, philosophy, and social activism intersected at the question of truth. "No man in the whole world can change the truth," he wrote. "One can only look for the truth, find it and serve it. Truth is in all places." The idea that truth is supreme and can be found everywhere has led some to see Bonhoeffer as the unwitting founder of the so-called Death of God movement, the rise of secularism—what Bonhoeffer himself called "religionless Christianity"—in the postwar world.

Boole, George

George Boole was born on November 2, 1815 in Lincoln, England, into the family of a shoemaker, who had an avocational interest in technology and science. His family's modest means kept young Boole from receiving formal education beyond primary school. Yet he would go on to create the algebraic tradition in logic, applying symbolic algebra—at the time, an emerging field—to logic. This turned Aristotelian logic on its head. Instead of learning and applying Aristotelian syllogisms to solve problems, Boole generated general algorithms using algebraic language and applied these to virtually any argument. He presented his work in two books, *The Mathematical Analysis of Logic* (1847) and *The Laws of Thought* (1854).

At sixteen, Boole began working as a teacher in local private schools, earning a small salary to support a family for which his father could no longer provide. Three years later, at the age of nineteen, he started his own small school in Lincoln, where he taught for fifteen years. In 1849, on the strength of mathematical papers he was publishing and his first book, *Mathematical Analysis of Logic*, the newly established Queen's University in Cork, Ireland, appointed him to a professorship. Although his teaching responsibilities were heavy, he continued his own original research, working mostly on differential equations and the calculus of variations. In 1851, the University of Dublin awarded him an honorary LL.D. degree, and he received an honorary DCL from Oxford eight years later.

His 1847 *Mathematical Analysis of Logic* was not intended to replace Aristotelian syllogistic logic but to systematize it and extend its applicability. The work introduced the concept of holistic reference, the principle that every proposition of number theory refers not only to the numbers it happens to mention but to the whole universe of numbers. This laid the foundation for much of modern logic. Boolean algebra, or Boolean logic, which was developed in the 1847 volume, was brought to intellectual maturity in *The Laws of Thought* (*An Investigation of the Laws of Thought on Which are Founded the Mathematical Theories of Logic and Probabilities*). Boolean algebra injected mathematics into logic by introducing variables that are the truth values *true* or *false,* which Boole represented as 1 and 0, respectively. Whereas basic algebra deals with numerical values and operates on them primarily with addition and multiplication, Boolean algebra operates with the conjunction (*and,* ∧), the disjunction (*or,* ∨), and the negation (*not,*¬).

Boolean algebra would become the foundation of computing and computer programming using the binary base, with values of 0 (to denote false) and 1 (to denote true). Thus, it is fair to say that this philosopher was a founder of computer science.

Boole was caught in a rainstorm while on his way to give a lecture. Soaked by the time he arrived, he did not change into dry clothes. He fell ill shortly after this and, on December 8, 1864, in Ballintemple, County Cork, succumbed to pneumonia. He was forty-nine.

Buber, Martin

Martin Buber was a polymath, whose interests encompassed literary translation, political activism, Zionism, Jewish mysticism, biblical study, art, politics, and philosophy, including social philosophy, religious phenomenology, and philosophical anthropology. Yet the crux of his philosophical thought is found in one brief book, published in German in 1923 and translated into English in 1937: *Ich und Du* (*I and Thou*).

Buber believed that people may look at existence in two ways: As the *I* with respect to an *It,* an object separate from us, which we use or experience; or as the *I* with respect to *Thou,* a relationship in which the other is not separated from the *I* by discrete boundaries. Indeed, Buber contended that human beings are defined by these two dyads: *I-It* and *I-Thou,* and that life is meaningful to the extent that each of us develops *I-Thou* relationships. From a theological and philosophical perspective, each *I-Thou* relationship brings us into a relationship with God, the Eternal Thou. From a more purely philosophical perspective, the *I-Thou* relationship transcends Descartes's sharp division between subject and object and thus serves to interconnect humanity at the deepest of levels, through God.

The *I-Thou* paradigm has proved influential in religion—both in terms of its theology and its phenomenology—in the philosophy of education, in philosophical anthropology, and philosophical psychology.

Buber was born in Vienna on February 8, 1878, the child of Orthodox Jews and the descendant of prominent rabbis. As he came into young adulthood, Buber began a break with Orthodox traditions. Inspired by reading Kant, Kierkegaard, and Nietzsche, he turned away from a rabbinical career to study philosophy, art history, and philology in 1896. He became a Zionist in 1898, and married Paula Winkler, a Catholic woman he met while studying in Zurich. She left the Church in 1901 and converted to Judaism in 1907.

Buber was appointed to an honorary professorship at the University of Frankfurt am Main in 1930 but resigned in 1933 in protest of Adolf Hitler's ascension to the German chancellorship. He quickly founded the Central Office for Jewish Adult Education, which provided alternative education as universities and secondary schools closed to Jews. At last, in 1938, he immigrated to Jerusalem as a professor of anthropology and sociology at Hebrew University. He lived the rest of his life in Jerusalem, where he died on June 13, 1965, aged eighty-seven.

Camus, Albert

With Jean-Paul Sartre, Albert Camus is perhaps the most famous, even iconic, exponent of existentialist philosophy. And yet, he always rejected the label "existentialism" and preferred "absurdism."

His absurdism was, in any case, like Sartre's existentialism, a response to living in a world without God. Camus vigorously rejected the all too obvious alternative of nihilism and despair and instead embraced a voluntary acceptance of the value of humanity and a duty to be active in its service. His 1938 play *Caligula* portrays the monstrous Roman emperor as a sensitive young man who discovers in life not meaning but absurdity. "The world has no importance," he declares. "Once he realizes that, a man wins his freedom." The "freedom" Caligula finds unleashes his scorn and vengeance. Before the play ends, however, he realizes he has "taken the wrong path," that his "freedom is not the right one." Camus argued that respect for human life and love for the limitations of human endeavor engender an attitude of moderation (*la mesure*). On these values, one can live a life with shape, purpose, and integrity. Camus was an atheist endowed with a religious spirit, and this drove his philosophy, which he expressed in essays, drama, and fiction, as well as resistance against the German occupiers of Paris in World War II.

Albert Camus was born on November 7, 1913 in Mondovi (today, Dréan), in French Algeria. His father, an agricultural worker, died in the World War I Battle of the Marne in 1914, before his son was a year old. Camus and his mother lived in semi-poverty with other relatives in Algiers. An early teacher, Louis Germain, recognized young Camus's intelligence and helped him win a scholarship to a fine lyceum near Algiers. Tuberculosis in 1930 forced him to move in with his uncle, however, and he began reading philosophy under the mentorship of his philosophy teacher, Jean Grenier.

While continuing to study, he worked as a tutor, a store clerk, and a functionary in the Meteorological Institute but was able in 1933 to enroll at the University of Algiers, where he completed the equivalent of a bachelor's degree in philosophy. Although he was drawn to the early Christian philosophers, he was compelled by study of Nietzsche and Schopenhauer toward atheism. As he read these philosophers, he also discovered the work of such fiction writers as Stendhal, Dostoyevsky, Melville, and Kafka.

In 1934, the twenty-year-old Camus fell in love with Simone Hié, a morphine addict. Over his uncle's objections, Camus married her, largely out of a sense of duty to help her overcome her addiction. When he discovered she was having an affair with her physician, he became estranged from her (they later divorced), and he soon earned a reputation as a womanizer.

For a time, Camus was a communist and, in 1938, began writing for a leftist newspaper, *Alger républicain*. He became an anticolonialist, but when the government shut down *Alger républicain* in 1940, Camus moved to Paris to become editor-in-chief of *Paris-Soir*.

In the French capital, he wrote the novel *L'Étranger* (*The Stranger*), the philosophical essay *Le Mythe de Sisyphe* (*The Myth of Sisyphus*), and the play *Caligula*. His history of tuberculosis disqualified Camus from military service, and he fled Paris as the Germans advanced into it, settling for a time in Lyon. He married the pianist and mathematician Francine Faure. The couple moved back to Algeria, where Camus taught school. Hoping to keep his tuberculosis at bay, he moved to the French Alps, where he wrote *La Peste* (*The Plague*) and a play titled *Le Malentendu* (*The Misunderstanding*).

Camus returned to Paris, was befriended by Sartre and became an intimate of the existentialist circle. He also became a member of the resistance and edited the resistance newspaper *Combat*. After the war, he enjoyed financial and critical success as a philosophical novelist and completed a new novel, *L'Homme révolté* (*The Rebel*).

He was awarded the Nobel Prize for Literature in 1957 and began writing an autobiography, *Le Premier Homme* (*The First Man*). He also adapted Dostoyevsky's novel *Demons* for the stage. It debuted in Paris in January 1959 to critical acclaim. A year later, on January 4, 1960, he was killed in a car accident near Sens, France.

Carnap, Rudolf

For a time, Rudolf Carnap was among the most famous philosophers of the twentieth century. He was a member of the so-called Vienna Circle of the 1920s and 1930s, instrumental in formulating logical positivism, which was also known as logical empiricism, or neopositivism, and was associated with the creation of the field of philosophy of science.

The cornerstone of logical positivism is the verification principle (or verifiability criterion of meaning), which holds that only statements verifiable through direct observation or logical proof are meaningful. The ambition of this proscriptive principle was to preempt confusion that produced unclear language expressing unverifiable claims. This preemption, it was hoped, would "raise" philosophy to the level of science; indeed, the term "scientific philosophy" was coined to describe philosophical work conducted according to strict empirical principles. The logical positivists held up as exemplary

Albert Einstein's general theory of relativity (1915), which uses mathematical expressions (Einstein field equations) to revise Newtonian gravity as a geometric property of spacetime. The Einstein theory, advocates of logical positivism argue, describes a basic aspect of reality without any of the ambiguity of language and in a way that is mathematically verifiable.

By the 1960s, logical positivism was under heavy attack and claimed fewer and fewer advocates. The objection was to the reduction of philosophy to a mimicry of science. Diehard proponents of the approach countered that it was actually a means of applying stricter philosophical standards to science. In the end, what survived of logical positivism was a concern for scientific methodology and a belief that a philosophy of science could be instrumental in guiding the role of science in reshaping society.

Rudolf Carnap was born in Düsseldorf, Germany, on May 18, 1891, the son of an impecunious laborer in a ribbon factory who rose to become the proprietor of such an enterprise. His mother, however, was highly educated, the sister of the archaeologist Wilhelm Dörpfeld, whom the ten-year-old Carnap accompanied on a dig in Greece.

After graduating from the Barmen Gymnasium, Carnap enrolled in 1910 at University of Jena. His intention was to write a thesis in physics and become a scientist, but he became more interested in philosophy after reading Kant's *Critique of Pure Reason*. A young man of pacifist tendencies, he nevertheless believed it his patriotic duty to serve in the German army in World War I, and did so for three years when, in 1917, he was granted permission to study physics at the University of Berlin, where he met Albert Einstein.

Carnap later returned to the University of Jena, where the physics department rejected his doctoral thesis on an axiomatic theory of space and time as "too philosophical" even as Professor Bruno Bauch of the philosophy department rejected it as physics, not philosophy. Bauch supervised a revision of the thesis in 1921, along Kantian lines, which was published in 1922 as *Der Raum* ("Space"). It was no longer subtitled as a space and time theory but as "A Contribution to the Theory of Science." Nevertheless, it was an attempt to inject philosophy into physics and vice versa, as Carnap developed a logical theory of space and time. This involved defining space as three different things, physical space, intuitive space, and formal (mathematical) space. The definition thus implied that space had to be approached through the acquisition of three very different kinds of knowledge, and the first step was to remove the ambiguity and imprecision of the language used to describe space.

Der Raum thus adumbrated the foundation of logical positivism, which was elaborated in his next book, *The Logical Structure of the World* (1928). This articulated the epistemological foundation of logical positivism, namely that the prevailing epistemology, based on symbolic logic, is applied to the analysis of scientific propositions, but science itself is not based on symbolic logic. Rather, it deems empirical experience as the only valid source of knowledge of the external world. Philosophy makes statements about the language of science and are thus neither true nor false but merely descriptive. The propositions of science, in contrast, are factual statements about experienced reality. Their truth or falsity can be tested by further observation.

Carnap was appointed a professor at the German University of Prague in 1931, but he left this position and, amid the rise of Nazism, immigrated to the United States in 1935, becoming a naturalized citizen in 1941. He taught at the University of Chicago from 1936 to 1952 and then at the Institute for Advanced Study at Princeton before joining the philosophy faculty of UCLA in 1954. He died, in California, on September 14, 1970.

Cassirer, Ernst

Ernst Cassirer began as a philosophical idealist in the tradition of Kant and aimed to create an idealistic philosophy of science. As his thought evolved, however, his philosophy came to embrace the epistemology of both mathematics and natural the sciences in addition to aesthetics, history, and culture. In its way, this project was still rooted in Kant, who sought to build bridges between mathematics and science on the one hand and humanistic study on the other. In terms of twentieth century, Cassirer looked for ways to bridge the so-called analytic approaches to philosophy (popular in American and British university philosophy departments) and the "continental" approaches (which held sway in European institutions). The analytic approach relies on logical analysis, making use of mathematical logic and symbolic logic, whereas the continental approach is more subjective, emphasizing idealism and hermeneutics (interpretation). A *New York Times* article by Gary Gutting (February 19, 2012) cited a famous—or infamous—"debate between Jacques Derrida (continental) and John Searle (analytic)," which "ended with Searle denouncing Derrida's 'obscurantism' and Derrida mocking Searle's 'superficiality.'" Cassirer endeavored to drink from both wells.

Ernst Cassirer was born in Breslau, Silesia (today, Poland), on July 28, 1874, the son of a Jewish family. He studied literature and philosophy at the University of Marburg, earning a doctorate in philosophy with a dissertation on René Descartes's attempt to analytically reconcile mathematical and natural scientific knowledge. A similar project would absorb Cassirer's mature career. He went on for further work at the University of Berlin, completing his *habilitation* (a university teaching qualification) on *The Problem of Knowledge in Philosophy and Knowledge in the Modern Age,* another step toward his enduring philosophical concerns.

Cassirer taught at the Friedrich Wilhelm University in Berlin and subsequently chaired the philosophy department at the University of Hamburg. Like so many other Jewish intellectuals, he left Germany in 1933, with the elevation of Adolf Hitler to the chancellorship. He found an academic home at Oxford, then moved to Gothenburg University in Sweden before he decided that Europe was simply too dangerous everywhere. He secured a position at Yale University and then moved to Columbia University, where he was a lecturer from 1943 until a fatal heart attack on April 13, 1945.

From early in his career, Cassirer wrote on the history of science, emphasizing the intellectual and cultural effects of the scientific revolution of the early modern period. His *Substance and Function* (1910) explores the impact of physics, including relativity theory, on philosophy and culture. In 1921, Cassirer argued in *Einstein's Theory of Relativity* that contemporary physics supports a neo-Kantian conception of knowledge.

Philosophy of Symbolic Forms (1923-1929) is Cassirer's most widely read book and argues that human beings are "symbolic animals, creating a universe through symbolic meanings." His next major work, *Philosophy of the Enlightenment* (1932), argues for the liberating power of self-realization, which is born of ideas irrespective of their social context. Ten years later, in *The Logic of the Cultural Sciences* (1942), Cassirer argues against logical positivism by asserting that objective, universal validity is possible in all spheres of thought, not just science and mathematics.

Church, Alonzo

Born in Washington, DC, June 14, 1903, Alonzo Church was a mathematical logician, who applied formal logic to mathematics. He was instrumental in creating theoretical computer science, including contributing to the basic theory of computation.

Church was the son of a DC Municipal Court judge, and, thanks to help from his uncle, was able to enroll at Ridgefield School for Boys (Ridgefield, Connecticut), which prepared him for Princeton University, where he earned both his undergraduate degree and Ph.D. in mathematics. After teaching briefly at the University of Chicago, he was awarded a National Research Fellowship, which sent him to Harvard, University of Göttingen, and University of Amsterdam during 1927-1929, when he joined the faculty of Princeton. For nearly the next forty years, he taught in both the philosophy and mathematics departments before moving to Los Angeles in 1967 and to teach at UCLA until his retirement in 1990. He died on August 11, 1995, having lived long enough to witness the computing revolution in which he had played a foundational role.

Most of his published work was in mathematical logic. He is celebrated for four groundbreaking achievements in the field. He provided the formal mathematical proof that the *Entscheidungsproblem* (which asks for an algorithm that considers a statement and answers yes or no according to whether the statement is universally valid) is undecidable. Alan Turing had provided a thought experiment that reached the same conclusion as Church's mathematical proof. From their work, the Church-Turing (computability) thesis emerged, which formalized the concept of computability and thus provided a foundation for computer theory. In a broader philosophical context, the Church-Turing thesis has led to advances in the philosophy of mind, especially with respect to the notion of the mind as a computer and the equivalency of the universe with a Turing machine.

From his work on the *Entscheidungsproblem* and the Church-Turing thesis, Church created the lambda calculus, which is a formal system in mathematical logic that serves as a universal computation model and can be used to simulate any Turing machine. It has applications not only in computer science but in linguistics, logic, and in various areas of philosophy. Church also proved that the axioms of Peano arithmetic are undecidable.

Beyond the applicability of his mathematical insights to philosophy, Church contributed more directly to philosophy through his work on logical methodology, criticism of nominalism (the view that mathematical objects, relations, and structures do not exist), and his conclusions regarding the theory of meaning. The American philosopher C. Anthony Anderson has called Church one of the most important philosophers of the twentieth century.

Cicero, Marcus Tullius

Although best known as a Roman orator, lawyer, and statesman, renowned as a champion of the Roman republic in opposition to the establishment of an empire, Cicero was a rhetorician and an Academic Skeptic philosopher. The skeptical period of Platonic philosophy spanned approximately 266 to

90 BC in the Academy Plato had founded in Athens about 387 BC. In contrast to the established school of skepticism, the so-called Pyrrhonists, the Academic Skeptics did not deny the possibility of the knowledge of things. Rather, they held that ideas are never true but are instead subject to degrees of probability, which enable degrees of belief and, therefore, enable decision-making and action.

Marcus Tullius Cicero was born in Arpinum (Latium, Italy) into a middle-class family. He received an excellent education in law, oratory, Greek literature, and philosophy. He served in the Roman military under Strabo and then under Sulla and was appointed quaestor in Sicily in 75 BC. He earned renown for his prosecution of Sicily's corrupt governor Gaius Verres for maladministration in 70 and became curule aedile in 69, praetor in 66, and consul for the year 63. In this office, he crushed the conspiracy of Senator Lucius Sergius Catiline to overthrow the republic. Subsequently, the First Triumvirate (Julius Caesar, Pompey, and Marcus Licinius Crassus) accused Cicero of executing Catiline without trial. Cicero went into voluntary exile during 58-57.

Cicero returned from exile as a determined champion of the preservation of republican government in opposition to Caesar's proposal of a popularly supported dictatorship. Cicero, however, compromised his position with the oligarchic senators because he advocated compromise on the then-current form of the republic to create "*concordia ordinum*," harmony among the classes.

After Caesar's military victory at Pharsalus, the decisive battle of 48 BC in Caesar's Civil War, which elevated Caesar to political preeminence and effectively ended the Roman Republic, Cicero retired from politics and pursued literature, producing some of his great oratorical works. After the assassination of Caesar in 44, however, Cicero reentered the fray and delivered his fourteen Philippics, orations in opposition to Mark Antony. The Second Triumvirate, consisting of Octavian (the future Emperor Augustus), Lepidus, and Antony, proscribed Cicero, who was hunted down and murdered on December 7, 43, before he was able to take ship for Macedonia.

Cicero's achievements as an orator and rhetorician have overshadowed his modern reputation as a philosopher. Indeed, he is largely dismissed as derivative in his Academic Skepticism and denounced as superficial for his view of Stoicism and Peripateticism (that they were largely one and the same) and his disdain for Epicureanism. Historically, however, from the ancient era through most of the nineteenth century, he was esteemed as one of the great Roman philosophers. No less a figure than St. Augustine wrote that Cicero's *Hortensius* (a praise or exhortation of philosophy, which survives today only in a few fragments) persuaded him away from the sinful life he was leading and guided him first toward philosophy and then to God. Indeed, Augustine appropriated Cicero's definition of a commonwealth to bolster his argument that the barbarians, not Christianity, precipitated the fall of Rome.

His philosophical writings include *On Invention, On the Orator, On the Republic, On the Laws, Brutus, Stoic Paradoxes, The Orator, Consolation, Hortensius, Academics, On Ends, Tusculan Disputations, On the Nature of the Gods, On Divination, On Fate, On Old Age, On Friendship, Topics, On Glory*, and *On Duties*. The texts of several of these are either fragmentary or lost entirely.

Comte, Auguste

Auguste Comte established positivism, a pervasive philosophical movement from the mid-nineteenth century into the early twentieth, when it was dethroned by the advent of logical positivism, or neopositivism. In Comte's positivism, certain knowledge ("positive" knowledge) is derived from sensory experience as interpreted by logic and reason. It is thus based on observation of natural phenomena as processed through science and the scientific method. In contrast to idealist philosophies (from Plato onward), which see certitude only in *a priori* knowledge, positivism recognizes only *a posteriori* knowledge as certain.

Related to his positivism, Comte created philosophies of mathematics, physics, chemistry, and biology, which made him the first modern philosopher of science. On historical, "evolutionary" grounds, he advocated the necessary replacement of metaphysics by the scientific method, in which theory was always grounded in, and in turn guided, empirical observation. Indeed, Comte's "Law of Three Stages" held that society's quest for truth passed through three stages, beginning with the theological, moving through the metaphysical, and culminating in the positive.

Auguste Comte was born in Montpellier on January 20, 1798 and won a place at the École Polytechnique in Paris in 1814. Restored to power after the fall of Napoleon I, the Bourbons shuttered the Polytechnique in 1816. Cast adrift, Comte met the economic and political theorist Henri de Saint-Simon the following year and was appointed his secretary. Through this connection, Comte was admitted into the world of politics and wrote a number of articles, which gained him rapid fame.

He left Saint-Simon's service, married a seamstress, Caroline Massin, and, in April 1826, began teaching a *Course of Positive Philosophy*, which attracted, among others, leading scientists of the early nineteenth century. At the height of his early recognition, however, he suffered a nervous breakdown as he was assailed by fantastic fears of his wife's infidelity. It was 1829 before he resumed offering the *Course of Positive Philosophy.*

Over the next thirteen years, Comte published the course in six substantial volumes, which was followed by *Elementary Treatise on Analytic Geometry* (1843) and *Philosophical Treatise on Popular Astronomy* (1844), which drew on his teaching of Parisian laborers. This same year, he also published *Discourse on the Positive Spirit,* which ventured from the philosophy of science into moral and ethical philosophy.

In 1844, Comte added a *System of Positive Polity* to his *Positive Philosophy* course, which already included the evolution of humanity. From this, he went on to found the Positivist Society in 1848, published the *General View of Positivism*—inspired by the liberal revolutions that swept Europe in that year—and, in 1849, founded the Religion of Humanity. During 1851–1854, Comte published, in four volumes, his *System of Positive Polity*, taking time in 1852 to write *Catechism of Positive Religion.*

Comte died on September 5, 1857, on the verge of beginning a new work, *Treatise of Universal Education.*

Confucius

Rooted in ancient Chinese religious, philosophical, and political traditions, Confucianism emerged as body of philosophical thought through the teachings of Confucius, who saw himself not as an original philosopher, but as a faithful transmitter of Shang (ca. 1600-1046 BC) and Zhou (ca. 1046-256 BC) theology and ethics.

Like any complex and nuanced theological or philosophical body of thought, Confucianism defies easy characterization. Its essential tenets are these:

- An emphasis on the received wisdom of revered teachers of the past. Discovery and innovation are not Confucian values. Rather, the cornerstones of the Confucian approach are precedent and universality, which are to be applied to create self-improvement.
- Adherence to two basic doctrines: *Zhong,* faithfulness to self and humanity, and *Shu,* "cherish the heart as if it were your owner."

- Social order is created not by laws but by morality. Laws seek to maintain order through external punishment, whereas morality maintains order through inner shame.
- Look to the precedents and wisdom of the past to guide benevolence, moderation and harmony with nature, filial piety, and the "rectification of names"—the recognition of the nature of things by naming them correctly.
- In contrast to Taoism, which seeks the *natural* way, Confucianism seeks the *social* way.

Confucius was born on September 28, 551 BC in Zou, in the state of Lu (present-day Shandong, China), the son of a local garrison commander, Kong He. Kong died when the boy was just three years old, leaving him to be raised in poverty by his mother, Yan Zhengzai. Confucius had the early education suited to commoners, though he had been born into a class intermediate between the common folk and the aristocracy. He came of age during a period of intense political and ideological ferment and achieved some political influence through his teachings, which were highly regarded.

About 497 BC, Confucius left a ministerial position with the ducal court of the state of Lu and commenced a series of journeys through northeast and central China, visiting the courts of Wey, Song, Zheng, Cao, Chu, Qi, Chen, and Cai. In each, he offered counsel based on his beliefs concerning political reform. He was heard but was unable to persuade any of the rulers to implement his principles.

Confucius returned to Lu in his sixty-eighth year at the behest of Chief Minister Ji Kangzi. He taught seventy-two or seventy-seven disciples in the "old wisdom," drawing on texts known as the Five Classics. At the same time, he often acted as an official advisor on matters of governance and justice. He died in 479 BC, at the age of 71 or 72.

Confucius' disciples were faithful in disseminating their master's teachings, which they digested into a set of rules and practices called the *Analects*. Zisi, the philosopher's grandson, continued to conduct his philosophical school, whose students included many who served in the royal courts in China. This established Confucianism widely.

Two of the most important followers of Confucianism, Mencius and Xun Zi, wrote important versions of the master's teachings, but approached them so differently from one another that it is difficult to assess their purity. Mencius (who flourished in the fourth century BC) emphasized the goodness of humanity as the basis of intuitional ethics. Xun Zi (third century BC) focused on the more materialistic and pragmatic dimensions of Confucian thought. In his version, morality was deliberately imposed on society through reverence for tradition and strict training. The works of Mencius and Xun Zi were eventually assembled with the Analects to represent the legacy of Confucianism.

Through time and the reigns of different dynasties, Confucianism was repeatedly adapted, modified, and distorted to suit changing contexts. Knowledge of the ancient philosopher first reached the West in the sixteenth century when Jesuit missionaries translated the Confucian texts into European languages. Such Confucian movements as New Confucianism surfaced in the twentieth century and influenced Mao Zedong other revolutionaries, but the philosopher fell out of favor during Mao's Cultural Revolution (1966-1976). As a body of political philosophy, Confucianism was increasingly denounced for its adherence to tradition, its close-mindedness, and a general resistance to modernization. Nevertheless, Confucius and his thought remain of great interest to contemporary philosophers and scholars, in such Asian nations as Korea, Japan, and Vietnam, as well as in the West.

Crescas, Hasdai

Rabbi Hasdai Crescas, who led the Jewish community in fourteenth- and early fifteenth-century Aragon, was revered as a great rabbinic authority. He wrote a philosophical polemic refuting Christian principles and, more importantly, *Or Adonai* (also known as *Or Hashem* or *The Light of the Lord*), a philosophical rebuttal of Aristotelian rationalism in the theology of Maimonides and Gersonides. *Or Adonai* is, in effect, a critique of Aristotelian rationalism itself and, as such, anticipates the seventeenth-century work of Baruch Spinoza, who was influenced by the example of Crescas.

Crescas used Neoplatonic idealism as a counter to Aristotle, arguing that rationalism is inadequate to understanding the world. In the course of the critique, Crescas provided a definition of the infinite in terms of both logical and mathematical principles, a definition of matter, a definition of place, a discussion of free will, and a platonic discourse on the essence of the soul and its status in the afterlife. All contribute to his defense of traditional Jewish theology.

Hasdai Crescas was born about 1340 in Barcelona into a family of merchants and rabbis. He became a renowned Talmudist before leaving Barcelona to accept the office of crown rabbi of Aragon. He became a teacher—his most famous student was the philosopher Joseph Albo—and despite his political prominence was imprisoned on a false charge of host desecration in 1378. In 1391, his only son was killed an anti-Semitic massacre in Barcelona. Revered as the spiritual head of Spanish Jewry, he died at the end of 1410 or in January of 1411.

Davidson, Donald

Born on March 6, 1917, in Springfield, Massachusetts, Donald Davidson was educated at Harvard University, primarily in literature and classics, graduating in 1939. He went on to earn a master's degree in classical philosophy in 1941 but interrupted his studies when he enlisted in the US Navy during World War II, serving from 1942 to 1945. He returned to Harvard after the war, resuming his study of classical philosophy and earning a Ph.D. in 1949 with a dissertation on Plato's "Philebus."

Even as he completed his dissertation, Davidson, inspired by the Harvard logician and philosopher Willard Van Orman Quine, whom he had met in 1939, departed from the historical study of philosophy to engage in original analytical philosophy. He taught at Queen's College in New York before moving on to Stanford University (1961–1967), Princeton University (1967–1970), Rockefeller University (1970–1976), and University of Chicago (1976–1981). From 1981 until his death, from cardiac arrest following knee surgery on August 30, 2003, he was a professor at University of California, Berkeley.

From the early 1960s until the end of his life, Davidson wrote papers—and one posthumously published book—that have been influential in epistemology, semantic theory, and ethics. His subject was always the relationships between mind and action, ontology and logical form, meaning and truth, and knowledge and belief. Yet he was a singularly difficult philosopher, in part due to the terse manner of his writing but also because he rarely settled on a "final" answer. He refused to accept the rejection of objective truth as a requirement for philosophy and, along with this, he rejected the views of both skeptics and relativists. At the same time, he could embrace neither realism nor anti-realism, rejecting both as incompatible with his conception of the holistic character of knowledge and belief. In the end, Davidson was unwilling to settle into any fixed classification imposed by the available standard philosophical categories.

Democritus

His contemporaries—he was born about 460 BC in Abdera, Thrace—called him the "laughing philosopher" because, in ethics and politics, he placed great value on optimism and cheerfulness. Modern historians of philosophy and science remember him as the first to establish the atomic—or atomist—theory, which he built upon the foundation of his teacher Leucippus. Going hand in hand with this materialist view of the world was Democritus' empiricism, which has led many to dub him the "father of modern science."

Democritus theorized that atoms are the smallest bodies from which everything in the world is composed. While physically indivisible and indestructible, atoms, he believed, were nevertheless divisible geometrically. Between the individual atoms that form everything, Democritus envisioned the empty space of the infinite void through which the atoms continuously move. He attributed the characteristics of differing forms of matter—iron, water, air, and so on—to differing characteristics of the atoms that make them up. Iron atoms were strong and solid, their surface equipped with hooks that create strong bonds. Water atoms were slippery in nature, and the atoms of air were light and whirling. Democritus' universe of atoms and voids was not teleological. That is, its regularity and patterns were the structural result of the underlying atoms themselves and not the product of a transcendent divine plan.

Little is known of the life of Democritus, but it is generally accepted that he was a citizen of the Thracian city of Abdera, although a dissenting minority suggests he was from Miletus. It is known that his teacher (or, perhaps, colleague) was Leucippus, and some speculate that he was also associated with Anaxagoras. None of Democritus' writings survive.

Diogenes Laertius, the third century AD biographer of the ancient philosophers, compiled an extensive list of works by Democritus in fields ranging from ethics to physics, mathematics, music, and cosmology. Modern scholars have doubts about the authenticity of his ethical works, and all that is known of his writing comes from the reports of others, including Aristotle, a critic of his views, but one who devoted a monograph to him, of which only quotations by third parties survive.

Related to Democritus' theory of atomism is his theory of perception, which holds that *eidôla* (images) are exquisitely thin layers of atoms, which continually slough off from the surfaces of things, are carried through the air, and enter the eye, where their impact causes the sensation of sight. Atomists following Democritus theorized that these atomic films contract and expand. The expanded films are too large to enter the eyes, so that only the contracted films can be visually perceived.

Aristotle reports that Democritus envisioned the soul (*psyche*) as composed of fire atoms. This is consistent with the ancient equation of life with heat and with the notion, also popular in antiquity, that the soul was responsible for motion in living beings. No atoms, they argued, are more mobile than those of fire. Apparently, Democritus believed that the movement of the fire atoms of the psyche was also responsible for thought, so that his theory of knowledge holds that the phenomena of thought are caused by images that impinge from the outside. He further held that perception is due, essentially, to bodily changes caused by external influences.

Ancient authorities ascribe various works of mathematics to Democritus, along with treatises on biology and cosmology. None of these survive, except for the geometric principle that cones whose base and height are the same have one-third the volume of a cylinder of the same base and height. Similarly, a pyramid whose base and height are the same have one-third the volume of a prism with the same base and height.

As for the philosopher's ethics and politics, all that survives are individual maxims, whose authorship is disputed and whose intellectual relation to one another is doubtful. In short, Democritus left no systematic philosophy of ethics or politics. He is believed to have died at about ninety, which would have been approximately in the year 370 BC.

Derrida, Jacques

Born on July 15, 1930, in the French Algiers suburb of El-Biar, Jacques Derrida founded the critical method known as "deconstruction," which has been applied primarily to literary texts but is applicable to texts in many disciplines as well as to institutional and cultural structures of all kinds, especially political institutions.

Deconstruction argues that language, especially as applied to ideal concepts, is complex and indeterminate. As an analytical and critical method, therefore, deconstruction examines the surface of a text or the visible structure of an institution on the assumption that in appearance is to be found the closest thing to the essence of the work under consideration. Thus, deconstruction has had great influence on literary criticism and literary theory, as well as linguistics, law, history, anthropology, sociology, psychoanalysis, feminism, and LGBT studies. In the context of philosophy, deconstruction has implications for epistemology, ontology, ethics, aesthetics, and hermeneutics.

Derrida was born into a Sephardic family and, during World War II, was expelled from the lycée in accordance with the pro-Nazi antisemitic laws of the French Vichy regime in Algeria. He nevertheless became enthralled with the works of philosophers and literary writers and, after the liberation, was able to continue his lycée education in Algiers and then, after he moved in 1949, in Paris. He was admitted to the École Normale Supérieure in 1952, where he became acquainted with the Marxist philosopher Louis Althusser. Derrida wrote his master's thesis on the phenomenologist Edmund Husserl and studied at Harvard University during 1956–1957. From 1960 to 1964, he taught philosophy at the Sorbonne and received an appointment to the philosophy faculty of the École Normale Supérieure in 1964, which he held through 1984.

In 1967, Derrida published his first three books, all highly influential, *Writing and Difference*, *Speech and Phenomena*, and *Of Grammatology*. He was appointed Professor of the Humanities at the University of California, Irvine, in 1986 and taught there until shortly before his death on October 9, 2004.

The concept of deconstruction proved to be not merely controversial but divisive. It became a crux of singularly bitter dispute between the "analytic" philosophers (mostly based in the United States and Britain) and the "continental" philosophers (mostly associated with Europe). When the University of Cambridge became in 1992 one of numerous distinguished institutions to award Derrida an honorary doctorate, a number of the most eminent "analytic" philosophers, among them Willard Van Orman Quine, Ruth Barcan Marcus, and David Malet Armstrong, wrote a joint letter of protest, arguing that "Derrida's work does not meet accepted standards of clarity and rigour" and was based on "semi-intelligible attacks upon the values of reason, truth, and scholarship." Derrida succumbed to pancreatic cancer and died during surgery for the condition, in Paris, on October 9, 2004.

Descartes, René

René Descartes was known among his seventeenth-century contemporaries chiefly as a mathematician and only secondarily as a natural philosopher—who developed novel theories of physics and of biology—a philosopher of mind, and a metaphysician. Perhaps the most salient feature of his theory of mind is that it was aboard the body but not part of the body. It guided a person as a "pilot" guides a ship. This conceptualization proved extraordinarily influential and durable, establishing in Western philosophy and psychology the dualism of mind and body virtually as an axiom.

Descartes' single most celebrated philosophical utterance, *Je pense, donc je suis,* even better known in its Latin translation, *Cogito, ergo sum* ("I think, therefore I am"), has been used as a sovereign retort to the radical doubt of Skepticism. The very act of thought is taken as proof of existence and therefore lays a solid foundation for the possibility of knowledge. Descartes explained more fully: "We cannot doubt of our existence while we doubt." In effect, Descartes supplied a fundamental element of Western philosophy.

Indeed, thinkers in every age found something in Descartes to use or to dispute. In the seventeenth century, his natural philosophy was the basis for an entire philosophy of science, and so, Descartes is regarded as one of the fathers of modern science. In the eighteenth century, his theories of physiology and psychology became his chief legacy. In the nineteenth century, his physiology was appreciated for its mechanistic bent, essentially envisioning both animal and human bodies as machines, governed by physical laws. Philosophers in the twentieth century saw in him a model philosopher, in that he managed to be culturally engaged. They did, however, increasingly question the absolute nature of his mind-body dualism. Indeed, through the centuries, Descartes served as something of an intellectual mirror, in which thinkers saw perhaps as much of themselves as they did of him. His spirit was alternatively a fresh intellectual breeze, liberating modern philosophy from slavish adherence to Aristotle, and an icy wind bringing a cold, reductive rationalism.

René Descartes was born on March 31, 1596, in La Haye, France, into a family of doctors and lawyers. His early education was at a Jesuit college in La Fléche, where he studied grammar, rhetoric, arithmetic, music, geometry, astronomy, metaphysics, natural philosophy, and ethics. Descartes is known to have disdained what he deemed as impractical subjects but did have a pronounced affinity for the mathematical curriculum.

He completed his schooling at La Fléche in 1614 and received a degree in civil and canon law from the University of Poitiers. In 1618, he volunteered to serve in the army of Maurice of Nassau and became acquainted with the Dutch philosopher Isaac Beeckman, who reawakened in Descartes his earlier interest in philosophy and mathematics. Under Beeckman's guidance, Descartes began applying mathematics to music and to mechanics. In 1619, he left the service of Maurice and joined the army of Maximilian of Bavaria. While stationed at Ulm, he reported experiencing three dreams, which inspired him to formulate a new methodology of scientific inquiry. Beyond this, the dreams were also the start of a philosophy that sought to unify the sciences.

While struggling toward the methodology, Descartes made practical discoveries in optics, discovering the law of refraction in 1626. Three years later, he completed *The World,* which applied mechanistic physics to many natural phenomena. In 1637, he completed *The Discourse on Method*, by which he defeated skepticism and radical doubt precisely by beginning at the position of doubting everything and working toward proof and belief. Among other things, the *Discourse* is considered foundational to natural science.

Meditations on First Philosophy was published in 1641 and laid out Descartes' metaphysics, which is founded on the existence of God and the immortality of the soul. To this day, *Meditations* is regarded as a kind of philosophical guidebook. Not only did Descartes begin with all "things that can be called into doubt," he solicited from others objections to his positions and then defended those positions against them. The result was a set of meditations on the nature of mind, on the existence of God, of truth and falsity, on the essence of material things, and on the "real distinction between mind and body."

A friendship and correspondence begun in 1643 with the brilliant Princess Elizabeth of Bohemia so influenced his next book, *Principles of Philosophy*, that he dedicated it to her. Elizabeth's questions to him regarding free will, the passions, and morals inspired his 1649 *The Passions of the Soul.*

Descartes accepted in 1649 an invitation to join the entourage of Queen Christina's court in Stockholm, Sweden. It proved a tragically brief residence, however, as he succumbed to pneumonia on February 11, 1650.

Dewey, John

With William James and Charles Sanders Peirce, John Dewey was a founder of pragmatism, a uniquely American philosophy. Rejecting the traditional philosophical conception of thought as a function representing or mirroring reality, pragmatism conceives of thought (and language) as an instrument for problem solving, prediction, and action. The pragmatist views the traditional objects of philosophical contemplation, such as meaning, knowledge, and belief, from the point of view of their uses. As Peirce put it, "Consider the practical effects of the objects of your conception. Then, your conception of those effects is the whole of your conception of the object."

Dewey was a practical philosopher, a practitioner of applied philosophy, who developed important theories of education, psychology, and democratic government. He also pursued more traditional philosophical topics, including in the fields of logic, ethics, epistemology, metaphysics, the philosophy of religion, and even aesthetics. But his consistent position was that philosophy had become a jejune technical pursuit divorced from social and cultural engagement. He proposed reforming philosophy into a discipline dedicated to "education for living."

John Dewey was born in Burlington, Vermont, on October 20, 1859. Brought up in the Congregationalist Church, he attended public schools and enrolled in the University of Vermont at fifteen. After graduating in 1879 at nineteen, he taught high school for two years and then returned to Vermont to study philosophy privately with Henry Augustus Pearson Torrey, an Intuitionist with a passion for Kant. Dewey next enrolled in the graduate philosophy program at Johns Hopkins University in 1882 and resolved to reconcile Neo-Hegelian idealism, Darwinian biology, and experimental psychology into a new psychology and a new philosophy. His objective was to synthesize the biological, functional, and materialist Darwinian pole with the creative and spiritual pole of idealism. He saw Hegel's dialectical process as a way of synthesizing matter and spirit, the divine and the human.

Dewey developed a powerful reputation as a philosopher and psychologist through engagements at the University of Michigan, University of Minnesota, and the University of Chicago, where he was appointed chairman of the Philosophy Department, which, conveniently for him, encompassed Psychology as well as Pedagogy. This put Dewey in a unique position to apply philosophy practically. With George Herbert Mead, Harvey A. Carr, and James Rowland Angell, Dewey fostered development of the so-called Chicago School, advocating "psychological functionalism," which focuses on the utility and purpose of behavior modified in an evolutionary manner over years of human experience. This led to Dewey's work in educational theory. He founded at the University of Chicago the Laboratory School, which became a renowned vehicle for testing both psychological and educational theories. He also engaged in political and social causes and became a friend and colleague of Jane Addams and supported her Hull House movement in social work.

In 1904, disputes involving the Laboratory School prompted Dewey to leave Chicago and become a professor in the philosophy department of Columbia University in New York City, where he also worked closely with Columbia's distinguished Teacher's College.

Dewey's philosophical orientation can best be understood through his approach to epistemology—a field he preferred to call "theory of inquiry." His belief was that the tendency of philosophy had been to mystify thought and its relevance to the world. Dewey embraced a Hegelian view, arguing that the world does not stand apart from thought but is in fact the objective manifestation of thought and is therefore defined by thought. In the course of his work, however, he revised this initial idealistic view and instead proposed that a valid theory of knowledge had to start with a consideration of the development of knowledge as an adaptive response to the environment aimed specifically at constructively restructuring that environment. Indeed, Dewey came to see thought as the product of an interaction between organism and environment. Knowledge, in this view, was the instrument by which people could strive to guide and control the interaction with the environment. This view was set out in "The Reflex Arc Concept in Psychology" (1896) and developed further in *Studies in Logical Theory* (1903).

Dewey extended his "naturalistic" views on epistemology and logic to metaphysics. Concluding that the aim of traditional metaphysics was to find an immutable cognitive object as the foundation for knowledge, Dewey countered that knowledge is the product of activity intended to fulfill human purposes; therefore, the truth of a belief ("knowledge") is discovered by the consequences of its practical employment, not by an abstruse analysis of its ontological origins. His 1908 article "Does Reality Possess Practical Character?" addressed this redefinition directly.

Dewey's pragmatic philosophy—with respect both to epistemology and metaphysics—lent itself naturally to ethics and social theory, which Dewey saw as rich fields for the practical application of philosophy. Both moral and social problems, as Dewey saw them, begged for answers that guide human action to achieve socially defined productive ends, which manifest themselves in a satisfying life. From this basis, he went on to discuss the nature of democracy and democratic society, thereby seamlessly extending his pragmatism into political philosophy.

In 1931, Dewey delivered the William James Lectures at Harvard University in what was a new field for him, aesthetics. The lectures became one of Dewey's most widely read and influential books, *Art as Experience*, which argues that the roots of aesthetic experience are to be found in commonplace human experience as a coalescence of meanings and values drawn from previous experience *and* present circumstances.

Dewey's career as philosopher is enviable in the degree to which he engaged culture at every level, giving philosophy a popular relevance that is rare in the modern world—perhaps rare at any time. Dewey lived a long life, dying on June 1, 1952, at the age of ninety-two.

Dharmakirti

Active in the sixth or seventh century, Dharmakirti was born, of the Brahmin caste, in southern India and is central to epistemological thought in Buddhist philosophy. His *Pramanavarttika* is considered the primary text on *pramana* ("valid knowledge instruments"). He is also regarded as a key theorist of Buddhist atomism. After some 1,400 years, his *Pramanavarttika* is still widely studied in Tibetan Buddhist monasteries.

Dharmakirti's epistemology seeks to establish a theory of logical validity and certainty based on causality. He identifies only two valid instruments of *knowledge*: perception and inference. He defines *perception* as non-conceptual knowledge bound by causality. He defines *inference* as conceptual, reasonable, and linguistic. Although Buddhist scripture must be relied upon when considering such inaccessible things as the laws of karma, it is not an infallible source of knowledge, unlike perception and inference.

Dharmakirti's epistemology must be apprehended in terms of his nominalist metaphysics, which denies the existence of universals as well as abstract objects. Dharmakirti asserts that the real is perceived only in its momentary particulars and that any concept of the universal is a fiction.

Both Dharmakirti's epistemology and metaphysics relate to his belief in the theory of consciousness proposed by the sixth-century Buddhist logician Dignaga, namely that consciousness is non-conceptually reflexive, such that an act of intentional consciousness is aware of itself as being aware. Consciousness is thus self-illuminating, and an apparent object of cognition is neither external nor separate from the cognitive act. In this context, he wrote *Substantiation of Other Mindstreams,* arguing that "mindstream" has neither beginning nor end and yet exhibits a temporal sequence.

Dharmakirti's most durable influence has been on the philosophical dimensions of Tibetan Buddhism. Of his life, virtually nothing known.

Diderot, Denis

Born in Langres, Champagne, on October 5, 1713, Denis Diderot was educated at the local Jesuit college, which granted him a Master of Arts degree in philosophy in 1732. From here, he continued his studies at Collège d'Harcourt, University of Paris, with the intention of entering the clergy but instead enrolled in the Paris Law Faculty. This path proved abortive, and, abandoning the law, Diderot set up instead as an independent author and translator. Infuriated, his father disowned him. So, the young man went about living by his wits in Paris. He met Jean-Jacques Rousseau in 1742, who became a significant influence on him.

After writing several translations, Diderot published in 1746 *Peneés philosophiques* (*Philosophical Thoughts*), his first original work, in which he argued for a synthesis of feeling and reason to create harmony. This was followed the next year by *Promenade du sceptique* (*The Skeptic's Walk*), a dialogue among a deist, atheist, and pantheist on the nature of God. The deist presents the argument that evidence of design in the universe supports the existence of an intelligent creator. He is countered by the atheist, who argues that science, especially chemistry and physics, account for the "design" of the universe more adequately, whereas the pantheist argues for a cosmic unity of mind and matter in the universe, which is God. The manuscript was not published until 1830, perhaps having been suppressed by police order.

In 1748, Diderot wrote a novel as a money-making endeavor. *Les bijoux indiscrets* (*The Indiscreet Jewels*) is a racy fantasy about a magical ring that, when pointed toward them, compels women to confess their sexual experiences while also rendering the wearer invisible. Yet Diderot also manages to digress into discussion of music, literature, and philosophy—the latter in the form of a dream in which a child named "Experiment" grows to gigantic proportions and smashes an ancient temple called "Hypothesis."

In 1749, he published *Lettre sur les aveugles* (*Letter on the Blind*), an epistemological work exploring and supporting John Locke's theory of knowledge—knowledge is acquired through the senses—and its relation to reason. This rapidly launched him into the inner circle of French intellectuals but also provoked his imprisonment for three months at Vincennes. Released through the influence of Voltaire's friend Madame du Chatelet, he became associated with the leading lights of French revolutionary thought.

In 1751, Diderot collaborated on the creation of the *Encyclopédie* with the philosopher Jean le Rond d'Alembert, which was published progressively through 1772 and epitomized French thought of the Enlightenment. Monumental though the *Encyclopédie* was, Diderot profited little from it, and, impoverished, arranged to sell his personal library to Empress Catherine the Great of Russia in 1766. She purchased it but granted him use of the books as long as he lived, and gave him a yearly salary, of which she advanced him 50,000 livres, representing fifty years of employment. In 1773, Catherine called him to St. Petersburg for the purpose of intellectual conversation, after which he returned to France. In 1784, learning that Diderot was ailing, Catherine financed a retirement in a luxurious suite in Paris. He died on July 31, 1784, just two weeks after moving to his new home.

Diogenes of Sinope

Born about 412 BC in the Ionian Black Sea colony of Sinope, Diogenes was a founder of Cynic philosophy and by far the most famous of the Cynics—ascetics, who believed that the purpose of life was to live naturally and virtuously, shunning power, fame, and wealth—indeed, all material possessions.

Perhaps a student of the orator and friend of Socrates, Antisthenes (ca. 441-366 BC), Diogenes philosophized but may have written none of it down. At least nothing of his work survives. He is known only through stories that depict him as debating, variously, the likes of Alexander the Great and Plato.

It is believed that Diogenes fled (or was exiled from) his native Sinope after having defaced some of the colony's coinage. He took refuge in Athens, where—in the most famous story concerning him—he took up residence in a *pithos,* or tub.

Plato famously characterized the philosophy of Diogenes as the work of a "Socrates gone mad." He was notoriously scornful of all convention, was ashamed of nothing, and believed that his shamelessness was in harmony with both nature and reason. He scoffed at accusations of his being a madman by pointing out that if a person walked about with his middle finger extended, he would be called mad. If, however, he extended his little finger, no one would think anything of it. It was all a matter of convention, to which people were unnaturally wedded.

Diogenes believed that reason should guide all conduct. Otherwise, one would be reduced to level of an animal in need of a leash. He was harshly critical of Plato and famously mocked his definition of a human being as an animal that stood on two legs and lacked feathers. He rebutted this definition by plucking a chicken and displaying it as Plato's human being. He was equally harsh on Platonic ethics, which he dismissed as mere theory. Diogenes, in contrast, was said to have walked about—in daylight—with a lamp, proclaiming that he was in search of a human being—by which he meant a being who acted in accordance with reason and was thus virtuous.

Reportedly, Diogenes died in Corinth about 323 BC, when he would have been in his late eighties or early nineties.

Emerson, Ralph Waldo

In his native United States, Emerson became more revered as a literary figure—an essayist and poet—than as a philosopher, but his founding role in Transcendentalism drew admiration from the likes of Friedrich Nietzsche and other philosophers. Transcendentalism may be regarded as an American branch of British and German early nineteenth-century Romanticism, albeit influenced by Unitarian Christianity. In terms of ethics, it regarded human beings as inherently good. In terms of metaphysics, it regarded nature as inherently good but subject to corruption by some of society's institutions. For this reason, the ideal man or woman was of independent mind and, to use Emerson's own term, was "self-reliant." In terms of theology, Transcendentalism was tinged with pantheism; that is, the Divine was deemed immanent in natural creation, and God could be best known through His natural works.

Ralph Waldo Emerson was born on May 25, 1803, in Boston, the son of a prominent clergyman. He entered Harvard when he was fourteen, graduated, taught at a school run by his brother, and, in 1825, enrolled in the Harvard Divinity School. His true education, however, was earned in the voluminous reading he did on his own, devouring volumes of history, literature, philosophy, and theology. He was so intense a student that both his general health and his eyesight suffered.

In 1829, he became junior pastor at Boston's Second Church, resigning in 1832 because he objected to the practice of the Lord's Supper, or Eucharist. In 1836, Emerson self-published a long essay titled *Nature*, which laid out the fundamentals of American Transcendentalism. The next year, he delivered "The American Scholar" as a Phi Beta Kappa address at Harvard, a plea for American intellectuals to break free of the prejudices of the Old World and create a literature, art, and philosophy of and for the New World. His "Harvard Divinity School Address," delivered in 1838, was so radical in its religious views—savoring as it did of both pantheism and Deism—that he was not invited to speak again at Harvard for twenty-nine years.

Having essentially renounced both the pulpit and academia, Emerson found himself pressed for a living and embarked on a distinguished and spectacularly successful career on the lecture circuit, beginning in 1839. For the next four decades, he did what few philosophers have been able to do. He made philosophy both public and popular.

From 1840 to 1844, Emerson edited *The Dial* with fellow Transcendentalist Margaret Fuller. He drew upon his lectures to create two distinguished and popular sets of essays, *Essays: First Series* (1841) and *Essays: Second Series* (1844). These established him as a philosopher. With his financial fortunes on the rise, Emerson in 1844 bought land on the shore of Walden Pond, on which he allowed the naturalist and philosopher Henry David Thoreau (1817-1862) to build a rude cabin, which inspired Thoreau's masterpiece, *Walden* (1854), a practical experiment in living "authentically" and according to the Transcendental tenet of self-reliance.

Inspired by the experimental quasi-utopian collective at Brook Farm, Emerson assembled around himself in Concord, Massachusetts, an informal community of kindred spirits including Thoreau, the novelist Nathaniel Hawthorne, the philosopher and social reformer Margaret Fuller, reformer Bronson Alcott, and the minor New England poet Ellery Channing. During this period, Emerson became an outspoken abolitionist, adding slavery to his menu of lecture subjects. He wrote and lectured well into the 1870s, but his final years were marked by an intellectual decline suggestive of dementia. He died on April 27, 1882, in his Concord home.

The core of Emerson's Transcendentalism is found in his 1836 *Nature,* in which he portrays nature as the perfect medium through which the divine is communicated to humanity. He spoke of an existential epiphany evoked by the natural environment, in which he felt himself become a "transparent eye-ball ... through which ... the currents of Universal Being circulated." Thus, nature, properly experienced, transports one to realms beyond nature, which Emerson implied were divine. Within nature, the individual becomes one with the experience of nature, and the seer becomes the actions of seeing. "I am nothing," he writes. "I see all."

Emerson proposed, in "The American Scholar," that the philosopher should evolve himself into a new species of humanity, "Man Thinking." His thought, however, was to be liberated from secondhand book knowledge: "Only so much do I know, as I have lived." The true philosopher should live an active and self-reliant intellectual life that opens his mind to the "Divine Soul." The *American* scholar, he proposed, will create in America, "for the first time" in history, a "nation of men."

Throughout his essays collected in 1841 and 1844, Emerson fused philosophy and poetry. Although he wrote verse and was widely recognized as an important American poet, his philosophical prose is more provocative and original in its use of metaphor. Indeed, perhaps no nineteenth-century philosopher has so effectively bent literature to philosophic ends or so skillfully used philosophy to produce literature.

Empedocles

Active in the mid-fifth century BC, Empedocles of Acragas was one the most important of the Pre-Socratic philosophers and the last Greek philosopher to write in verse. He is best known for his theory of the four elements—air, water, earth, and fire—of which everything is made, and for the two "active principles," the divine powers Love and Strife, a controlling opposition that influenced subsequent philosophers, physicians, mystics, cosmologists, and theologians. Empedocles may be considered a transitional figure in ancient philosophy, inhabiting an intellectual landscape between *mythos* (religion) and *logos* (science).

Born about 494 BC, in Acragas—modern Agrigento, Sicily—Empedocles was among those portrayed in Diogenes Laertius's *Lives and Opinions of Eminent Philosophers*, a work from the third century AD. Unfortunately, the accounts in this volume are often of more fictional than historical interest. It is believed, however, that Empedocles was born to an aristocratic family, studied philosophy with Parmenides of Elea, and became an intellectual follower of Anaxagoras and Pythagoras. He may have been a talented political orator, an opponent of tyranny, and an advocate of democracy. Aristotle (in the *Sophist*) credits him with having invented rhetoric. Other sources report his having been a prominent physician, who founded a school of medicine in Sicily. Legendary history reports his suicide, about 434 BC, by leaping into an erupting Mt. Aetna.

Fragments of papyrus text have been attributed to Empedocles, but it is only Diogenes Laertius who attributes to him two philosophical poems, *Purifications* and *On Nature.*

Purifications may be a fragment of Empedocles' philosophical system or it may merely be a fragment of a treatise on ritual purification. Most modern scholars believe it is, in fact, a fragmentary part of *On Nature,* which did outline his philosophical system. In its intact form, this work apparently accounted for the nature and history of the universe, including the four elements, and also outlined theories on causation, perception, and thought, with additional observations on various terrestrial phenomena and biological processes. What is clear is that Empedocles combined a mystical belief in the Orphic mysteries with a scientific approach to what we might call a proto-physics.

Empedocles held that the four elements were the fundamental and unchangeable foundation of reality, which were transfigured into a succession of worlds by the force of Love and Strife. Thus, each world was the product of what he called the "unity of opposites."

The four elements are the constituents of a system in which nothing ever came into being. That is, all change is the result of the juxtaposition of unchangeable elements with other unchangeable elements. This cosmological and metaphysical explanation was so compelling that it held sway in Western thought for some two millennia. The four elements are not inert within themselves but are eternally and perpetually brought together and parted from one another by Love and Strife, which are the two divine creative powers. The four elements are the material of the universe, and Love and Strife bring about their variation and their harmony.

Empedocles theorized that there was a golden epoch in the history of the universe, in which the four elements coexisted with Love and Strife in a peaceful condition of restful inertia, taking the form of a perfect sphere. Love reigned within the sphere, while Strife stood sentinel at its edges. This so-called Sphere of Empedocles embodied pure existence, which, in turn, was a manifestation of God. Empedocles held that the universe was cyclical and would return to the balanced state for a time.

By way of explaining the separation of the elements, Empedocles developed a cosmogony accounting for the formation of earth and sea, of sun and moon, and the atmosphere. He extended the account to the origin of life and human physiology. Some consider this a distant adumbration of Darwinian evolution. Likewise, his theory of light and vision—we see objects because light streams out of our eyes and touches them—served as the basis for the work of Euclid and others. Empedocles not only discussed perception and sensation, he extended these subjects into the realm of epistemology, arguing that our senses are narrow and cannot alone lead us to truth, which is the province of the philosopher.

Engels, Friedrich

Philosophy is not a field renowned for collaboration, so Friedrich Engels may be the most prominent collaborator in the history of philosophy. He is known primarily for having developed, with Karl Marx, so-called Marxist theory, the political and economic doctrine that gave rise to communism. His first collaborations with Marx produced *The Condition of the Working Class in England* (1845) and *The Communist Manifesto* (1848). Engels's financial support of Marx enabled that philosopher to research and write the massive *Das Kapital*. The work was unfinished at the time of Marx's death, and Engels edited its second and third volumes. He also edited Marx's notes on the *Theories of Surplus Value*, which were later published as a "fourth volume" of *Das Kapital*.

Engels was born in Barmen, Germany, on November 28, 1820, to a prosperous manufacturer. He followed in his father's footsteps, but even as he enjoyed success in commercial ventures, Engels began writing radical and socialist newspaper articles. He worked in Bremen as a clerk and served as a volunteer in the army in 1842 before spending two years in Manchester,

England, working in a cotton mill that his father co-owned. He left this employment in 1844 to write for the *Deutsch-Französische Jahrbücher*, which was published by Arnold Ruge and Karl Marx in Paris. Later in the year, he returned to Barmen and, in 1845, began addressing communist meetings in Elberfeld. With Marx, he joined the clandestine Communist League in 1846, under the auspices of which he collaborated with Marx on the *Communist Manifesto*.

During the revolutions of 1848-1849, Engels lived in Cologne, where he wrote for the *Neue Rheinische Zeitung*, which Marx edited. When the government suppressed this publication, he began in 1850 writing for the *Politisch-oekonomische Revue*. That same year, discouraged by the collapse of revolutions throughout Europe, Engels fled to England and rejoined his father's cotton firm in Manchester.

He worked in the family business until retiring in 1869. In 1870, he moved to London, where he drummed up support for the international labor movement. Engels became an internationally prominent advocate of Marxian communism, which he opposed to the emerging political philosophy of anarchism.

In addition to his collaborations with Marx, Engels wrote *The Peasant War in Germany* (1850) and *Herr Eugen Dühring's Revolution in Science* (1878), a critique of the work of the anti-Marxist philosopher Eugen Dühring. The book is notable for Engels's skillful application of Marxian dialectic to modern science and mathematics. *Socialism: Utopian and Scientific* (1880) was a critique of utopian socialists and socialism and achieved a surprising popular success. In 1883, Engels began writing *Dialectics of Nature,* which applied Marxian concepts to natural science, but the manuscript was left unfinished at the time of his death, August 5, 1895.

Epictetus

Born AD 50 at Hierapolis, Phrygia, Epictetus was a stoic philosopher, who studied in Rome (apparently while in servitude) and subsequently taught in his own school at Nicopolis, Greece. None of his works survive, and, in fact, it is doubtful that he wrote any philosophical texts. All we know of his philosophy comes from two texts composed by Arrian, his student. The *Discourses* are dialogues between Epictetus and his students, and the *Handbook* is derived from the *Discourses* and has been studied as a summary of the philosopher's version of Stoicism. Both works are devoted solely to Epictetus' views on Stoic ethics, omitting mind, logic, and physics.

Epictetus' ethics were typical of Stoicism, emphasizing the goal of achieving *eudaimonia* (flourishing happiness) through a virtuous life founded on reason, which the Stoics defined as living according to nature. As they saw it, to achieve the status of a Stoic *sophos* (wise person), the aspirant must learn what is within a human being's power and what is not. The aspirant must also understand the correct use of *phantasiai,* or impressions. The good is defined simply as acting from virtuous motives. The bad is acting from vicious motives.

Rationality is a fragment of divinity, which the Epictetus conceived of as a rarefied fiery air suffusing all creation.

Epictetus apparently came to Rome as the slave of a wealthy master, Epaphroditus, who had been the administrative secretary to the Emperor Nero. Even while still enslaved, Epictetus studied under the Stoic teacher Musonius Rufus. Ancient sources record that Epictetus' master, one Epaphroditus, once tortured him by twisting his leg. The young Stoic endured the pain and did not protest, except to remark that if he continued to twist, his leg would break. When that indeed happened, Epictetus calmly remarked, "There, did I not tell you that it would break?" According to some sources, the incident left the philosopher lame lifelong.

Epictetus was emancipated, but, in 89, was banished from Rome with other philosophers by order of Emperor Domitian. This prompted his removal to Nicopolis, where he opened his own school, which flourished. He died about AD 135.

Epicurus

A major figure of the Hellenistic period of philosophy (the roughly 300 years following 322 BC, the year of Aristotle's death), Epicurus was a materialist in metaphysics, an empiricist in epistemology, and a hedonistic in ethics. Indeed, the modern English words *epicure* and *epicurean*—denoting a discriminating devotion to sensual pleasure, especially relating to food and drink—are derived from the philosopher's name.

Epicurus was an atomist, who believed that everything consisted of indivisible units of matter flying through the void. He believed all natural phenomena were explicable in atomic terms. Born about 341 BC, some seven years after the death of Plato, Epicurus rejected the concept of Platonic forms, the existence of an immaterial soul, and, while he accepted the existence of the gods, he argued that they have no influence on human life. In terms of epistemology, he spurned skepticism and believed that knowledge was gained via the senses, which he accepted as reliable. He taught his students that human beings acted solely to attain pleasure—which created the desired state of tranquility. Yet he did not advocate what is today commonly meant by hedonism, the indiscriminate lusting after pleasure. True pleasure—tranquility—was achieved by deliberately limiting one's own desires and overcoming fear of the gods and of death. It was this principle of freeing oneself from fear that attracted many to become Epicureans long after the philosopher died.

Born (or at least raised) on Samos, an Athenian island colony in the Mediterranean, he was about nineteen when Aristotle died. He studied with followers of Democritus and Plato, whose most essential ideas he nevertheless rejected. Epicurus founded philosophical schools in Mytilene and Lampsacus, leaving these in 306 BC to settle in Athens, where he created the Garden, a philosophical commune and school. Here, Epicurus' students endeavored to put the master's teachings into practice. Both the Garden and Epicureanism survived the philosopher's death, from kidney stones, about 271 or 270 BC.

For many years, Epicureanism and Stoicism vied with one another to become the dominant school of philosophical thought in the Hellenistic world. With the emergence and rise of Christianity, Epicureanism fell out of favor and went into decline or was actively suppressed. Elements of Epicureanism were revived during the Renaissance and later as part of a rebellion against what was perceived as the excessively mechanistic explanations of natural phenomena offered by Aristotelianism. Although Epicurus wrote plentifully, virtually nothing of his work survives. Most of it was likely destroyed by Christian authorities.

In metaphysics, Epicurus' atomism is his most important contribution. He based his argument for atoms on two observable facts: we clearly see bodies in motion, and we know that nothing comes from nothing. That bodies move proves the existence of empty space or a void. Since the bodies we see are all divisible into smaller pieces, they must be made up of still smaller pieces. Epicurus rejected that the breakup of bodies could proceed infinitely because, if this were the case, matter would dissolve into nonexistence. Moreover, nature is orderly and, therefore, must be built ultimately on indivisible units of matter.

Epicurus' belief that nothing comes into existence from nothing implies that the universe is infinite, with neither beginning nor end. This includes atoms. He distinguishes, however, between the universe and the cosmos, which exists within the universe as a temporary assemblage of atoms that came together at some time and will disassemble at some time. Moreover, our cosmos is only one of an infinite number, all of which, as assemblies of atoms, are temporary.

Epicurus argued for the infinity of the universe based on what we might call a thought experiment. If the universe were finite, you could reach its edge, extend your fist, and the location of your fist would be, *ipso facto*, the new limit of the universe. This only proved the infinity of the universe since the process could be repeated infinitely. Because the universe is infinite, the number of atoms must also be. The proof of this is that, in an infinite universe, the population density of a finite number of atoms in a given region would necessarily be zero, which would mean that no bodies (agglomerations of atoms) could exist. Our senses reveal that such bodies do exist; therefore, the number of atoms must be infinite. Indeed, their infinitude proves the infinity of the universe, since, if the void had a limit, the infinite number of atoms would fill all space and therefore be unable to move.

Epicureanism has incurred charges of atheism. Yet Epicurus himself asserted his belief in gods, arguing, however, that they have no care for or influence over human life because, if they did, they would be themselves imperfect in that they could enjoy no tranquility. It is not that the gods turn their back on humanity, however, but that they are simply unaware of it.

Epicurus formulated what philosophers call an identity theory of mind, in which mind is identified as an organ of the chest, which is the seat of the emotions. As a materialist, Epicurus was eager to define mind as bodily and offered as proof of this the fact that mind clearly interacts with the body—so must of a bodily nature itself. This stood in opposition to the idealism of Plato, who argued for the complete non-corporeality of mind.

Since mind is bodily, the process of thought is an atomic process, the atoms of mind creating four categories of particle: fire, air, wind, and a "nameless element" of supreme fineness. Since mind is matter, death must be annihilation. This assertion allowed Epicurus to nullify fear of death, which he defined as fear of a hellish afterlife. If death is annihilation—the dispersal of atoms—there is no organ to experience the effect of death and, therefore, no reason to fear it.

Epicurean ethics assigns fundamental value only to one's own pleasure. Nevertheless, the philosopher taught the wisdom of leading a somewhat ascetic life as a means of ensuring that achieving tranquility would always be feasible since desires would be limited. Epicurus also proposed that the highest good is what is valued for its own sake and proposed (as did Aristotle) that happiness (defined essentially as tranquility) is the greatest good. Epicurus defined justice as a social compact, an agreement "neither to harm nor be harmed." This and a need to be protected from the dangers of the wild motivated the creation of communities.

Fichte, Johann Gottlieb

The life of Johann Gottlieb Fichte spanned the development of German Idealism between the death of Kant and the emergence of Hegel. He was thus a major figure during the German Romantic Movement in philosophy and literature and was highly regarded in his own day. Until recently, modern students of philosophy tended to relegate him to a transitional role between two giants of German philosophy, Kant and Hegel, but, to-day, Fichte has increasingly emerged as a great philosopher in his own right.

Born in Saxony on May 19, 1762 into to a family of impecunious ribbon makers, Fichte secured the patronage of a Saxon nobleman who financed both his preparatory education and his subsequent study at the universi-ties of Jena and Leipzig—at least up to a point. The young man set out to earn a degree in theology, but, about 1784, left the university because he ran out of money. He supported himself for some years as an itinerant tu-tor. His vocational travels took him to Zurich, where he met Johanna Rahn, whom he subsequently married.

Hired in 1790 to tutor a university student in Kantian philosophy, Fichte immersed himself in that philosopher's work. Whatever effect this had on his student, it profoundly transformed Fichte, who rejected deter-minism or, rather, prompted him to reconcile freewill and determinism in the manner of Kant's categorical philosophy.

Armed with his new enlightenment, Fichte journeyed to Königsberg to meet personally with Kant. His discussion with the master, on July 4, 1791, did not impress Kant. Undaunted, Fichte wrote an essay on the relation of Kant's critical philosophy to divine revelation. The work won Kant over, and the philosopher persuaded his own publisher to publish Fichte's *An Attempt at a Critique of all Revelation* in 1792. Although Fichte based his work on Kant's dictum that religious belief must hold up under rational ethical scrutiny, Fichte was more radical than his mentor. He concluded, in effect, that Christianity did not meet the test of rational scrutiny, espe-cially because original sin is incompatible with the ethical standard of hu-man justice supported on moral law.

Continuing to support himself by tutoring. Fichte published *Contribution to the Rectification of the Public's Judgment of the French Revolution*, which cemented his reputation as a radical political philosopher. He married in

October 1793 and accepted in May 1794 the chair of the philosophy department of the University of Jena.

During his tenure at Jena, 1794-1799, Fichte wrote his most important works. He developed a professional persona less as a philosopher than as a scholar in the public service. As he argued in a popular series entitled "Some Lectures Concerning the Scholar's Vocation," the task of the philosopher was to offer rational guidance toward the creation of a free, harmonious society and to be, in short, a teacher of humankind as it struggled toward perfection.

Fichte developed a philosophical system he called the *Wissenschaftslehre,* sometimes translated as "science of knowledge" but usually left in the original German. Thus, the translation of his 1795 exposition of his system was titled *Foundations of the Entire* Wissenschaftslehre. The book argued that all truly philosophical thought must be grounded in epistemology and phenomenology. Experience, Fichte argued, rests on an "Absolutely Unconditioned Principle," namely *The I posits itself.*

In some ways, Fichte spent the rest of his career explaining and justifying his philosophical system, and one such work, *The Vocation of Man*, published in 1799, defined the human intellectual journey as a progress from doubt to knowledge and from knowledge to faith. It was widely received as Fichte's most important literary work. In 1806, he attracted much attention with the publication of a series of lectures titled *The Characteristics of the Present Age,* which analyzed the Enlightenment, defining it in terms of general human intellectual evolution but also noting that it fell short of the highest aspect of the life of reason, namely the attainment of rational belief in the divine order of the universe. *Characteristics* was followed, also in 1806, by *The Way Towards the Blessed Life,* exploring the possibility of a union between the finite self-consciousness and the infinite self, namely God.

In 1810, Fichte assumed the chairmanship of philosophy faculty of the newly founded University of Berlin, of which he became rector the following year. In 1813, when the German Campaign was fought against Napoleon in the War of the Sixth Coalition, Fichte abruptly left academe to fight in the "War for Liberation." He contracted a fever, from which he died on January 29, 1814.

Foot, Philippa

Philippa Foot was a founder of modern virtue ethics, a theory of normative ethics that focuses on the outcomes of action and is founded in Aristotelian ethics. She devoted her career exclusively to moral philosophy, including issues in metaethics, moral psychology, and applied ethics. Foot is perhaps most widely known for having formulated the Trolley Problem, which asks why it is deemed permissible to steer a trolley aimed at five people toward one person but is deemed impermissible to kill one healthy man for the purpose of using his organs to save five people who would otherwise die.

Born Philippa Judith Bosanquet on October 3, 1920, in Owston Ferry, Lincolnshire, Foote grew up in Kirkleatham, North Yorkshire, England. Her mother, Esther, was a daughter of President Grover Cleveland, and her father, William, ran a major Yorkshire steel works. Foot studied philosophy, politics, and economics at Somerville College, University of Oxford, where her first tutor was philosopher and theologian Donald MacKinnon and where she met Iris Murdoch and a small group of other female philosophers. After earning a BLitt in 1942, with a thesis on Kant, she worked in London during the remainder of World War II. At war's end, she married military historian M. R. D. Foot, from whom she was divorced in 1960.

After the war, Foot also returned to Somerville as a teacher and began a fellowship there in 1949. In 1969, she came to the United States and, until 1976, held visiting professorships at the Universities of California—first at Los Angeles and then at Berkeley—and at the University of Washington, Princeton University, Stanford University, and the City University of New York. In 1976, she became a professor at University of California, Los Angeles, from which she retired in 1991. Returning to Oxford, she completed a monograph titled *Natural Goodness*. She died on her ninetieth birthday, October 3, 2010.

Philippa Foot's career as a moral philosopher can be said, quite simply, to have been driven by the question, "Why be moral?"

In her early years, the answer was that the "received virtues"—courage, temperance, justice, and the like—were cultivated rationally. It was therefore rational to act according to them. In short, moral judgment is associated with rationally cultivated traits, including virtues. This sets "just action" apart from other forms of action.

As she matured, Foot argued differently, defining morality as a system of hypothetical imperatives and concluding that just and benevolent acts turn on contingent motivations. Paraphrasing Kant, she observed: "we are not conscripts in the army of virtue, but volunteers."

Later in life, as she wrote in *Natural Goodness*, practical reason emerged as the overriding driver of moral action. Dissatisfied with both Kantian and utilitarian ethics, Foot defined a form of evaluation that predicates goodness and defect only to living things. She argued that moral evil is a natural defect. From this point of view, she explored practical rationality, erring conscience, and the relation between virtue and happiness, concluding the book with a critique of Nietzschean immoralism.

Foucault, Michel

Educated primarily as a philosopher, Michel Foucault produced work so broadly trans-disciplinary that perhaps its most controversial aspect is the debate over whether it even is philosophy. He himself once described his chief interest as working toward a historical account of the production of truth. Although he wrote abundantly, his life was cut short by AIDS at the age of fifty-eight, and it cannot be said that he ever completed the "historical account" he identified as his intended project. In the end, he may be best described as a philosophically oriented historical researcher or, perhaps, historically oriented philosophical researcher.

Foucault was a French structuralist and, subsequently, poststructuralist. A leading theme in French intellectual pursuits by the early 1960s, structuralism is an approach to the study of the elements of culture by defining a given element's relationship to a bigger, more encompassing system or structure. The challenge is to discover the structures that underlie all human thought and cultural activity. It is, in fact, the relations among the various phenomena of human life that constitute a structure transcending the local in time and place and revealing constant laws of human cultural activity. Poststructuralism is a reflective, critical approach to structuralism, which rejects aspects of structuralism—most importantly the idea of "constant laws"—yet builds upon other structuralist insights into the relationship among various human phenomena and their symbolic representation in language and other signs. Thus, Foucault most often sought to understand the leading ideas that shape culture in the present by understanding the function of these ideas in history. This required using history to trace the changes in the function of each major idea.

Michel Foucault was born Paul-Michel Foucault on October 15, 1926, in Poitiers, France. His father was a surgeon and the son of a physician, and his mother was the daughter of a surgeon. Educated in Poitiers during the Nazi occupation, Foucault gravitated toward philosophy in defiance of his father, who wanted him to pursue medicine. Immediately after the end of World War II, Foucault moved to Paris and studied with the French Hegelian, Jean Hyppolite. In 1946, he was enrolled in the prestigious École Normale Supérieure d'Ulm as the student of Maurice Merleau-Ponty and the mentee of Louis Althusser. He qualified both in philosophy and in psychology.

In 1951, Foucault aggregated in philosophy from the École Normale, in which he also taught psychology. Among his most renowned students was Jacques Derrida, who would subsequently become a philosophical rival. In 1955, Foucault became a director of the Maison de France at the University of Uppsala, Sweden, leaving that post in 1958 to become a French cultural attaché in Poland. In 1959, he moved to the Institut Français in Hamburg. During this peripatetic period, he wrote a doctoral thesis on the history of madness, which he revised into a book, *Madness and Civilization,* published in 1961. By this time, he returned to France, teaching psychology in the philosophy department of the University of Clermont-Ferrand—commuting to classes from Paris.

Foucault formed a close relationship with the militant leftist Daniel Defert, with whom he would form a partnership that lasted the rest of Foucault's life. In 1964, Defert went to Tunisia to serve eighteen months of compulsory military duty. Foucault visited him during this time, and in 1966 assumed the chairmanship in the department of philosophy at the University of Tunis.

Foucault published *The Order of Things* in 1966, a study of the history of the so-called human sciences, essentially the disciplines devoted to philosophy, biology, and culture. Despite its volume and obscurity, the book became a bestseller and catapulted Foucault to the status of intellectual celebrity. Returned to France in 1968, Foucault built and then presided over the philosophy department of the new experimental university at Vincennes in Paris. Working in the aftermath of the student uprising of 1968, Foucault built a militantly Marxist department, which briefly lost its official accreditation. By this time, 1970, Foucault had been elected to a chair in the Collège de France, a lifetime appointment. This occasioned a series of annual lectures.

Foucault became a political activist in the early 1970s and then retreated into journalism. By the end of the decade, he spent much of his time teaching in the United States. He was terminally ill with AIDS in 1984 as he finalized a work on ancient sexuality, which was published posthumously. He had already written and published the introductory volume of *The History of Sexuality.* He died, in Paris, on June 26, 1984.

Frege, Gottlob

Gottlob Frege was a mathematician, logician, and philosopher who may be deemed the father of modern logic and analytic philosophy. More than any other figure of the late nineteenth century and early twentieth, Frege defined an approach to logic radically different from the Aristotelian tradition that had held sway in antiquity and since the rediscovery of Aristotle in the Middle Ages.

Frege invented modern quantificational logic, in which symbols are used to create a fully axiomatic system of logic. As Frege injected mathematics deeply into logic and analytical philosophy, so he injected logicism into the philosophy of mathematics, arguing that mathematical truths are logical truths rather than psychological or formal truths. Frege did not abandon the philosophy of language, however, but developed a theory of meaning based on a distinction between the sense and the reference of linguistic expressions. In the history of philosophy, Frege is frequently cited as the founder of analytic philosophy, which he regarded as an alternative to prevailing German Idealism. To this day, the mainstream of philosophy is divided—often rancorously—between Continental philosophy (German Idealism, phenomenology, existentialism, structuralism, post-structuralism, and the like) and analytic philosophy (emphasizing formal logic, mathematics, and aspects of linguistics).

Frege was born on November 8, 1848 in Wismar, Germany. After study in the Wismar Gymnasium, Frege enrolled at the University of Jena in 1869, studying chemistry, philosophy, and mathematics. After his fourth semester, he transferred to the University of Göttingen, where he studied mathematics, physics, and the philosophy of religion. He received his Ph.D., having written a dissertation titled "On a Geometrical Representation of Imaginary Figures in a Plane," and became a lecturer at the University of Jena in 1874. He spent his entire academic career there.

In 1879, Frege published *Concept-Script: A Formula Language for Pure Thought Modeled on That of Arithmetic*, which presented his new method for constructing a logical language. His purpose was mainly to demonstrate that all the truths of arithmetic could be derived from purely logical axioms, an argument he presented in his 1884 *Foundations of Arithmetic.* He went on to attempt to derive the basic laws of arithmetic within his logical language, but, by the late 1880s and early 1890s, he turned to developing theories concerning the nature of language, functions and concepts, and philosophical logic. These were published in such articles as "Function and Concept" (1891), "On Sense and Reference" (1892), and "On Concept and Object" (1892).

Frege's new linguistic insights prompted him to revise, in 1893, his work on logic and the foundations of mathematics as *Basic Laws of Arithmetic.* Here he introduced his new logical language and applied it to the definition of the natural numbers and their properties. His aim was to make this the first of a three-volume work; in the second and third volumes, he would move on to the definition of real numbers, and then on to demonstrations of their properties.

Like much of his work, *Basic Laws of Arithmetic* met with incomprehension from his contemporaries. Nevertheless, he published a second volume of *Basic Laws* at his own expense in 1902. The book was not yet off the press when he received a letter from Bertrand Russell, who had devised a proof of a contradiction in the logical system of the first volume of *Basic Laws*. "Thunderstruck," as he put it, Frege wrote an appendix to the second volume in response to Russell. He then went on to write on the logical foundation of Geometry (1903-1906) but suffered a fallow period and retired from teaching in 1918. He wrote several works on thought before returning in 1924 to the foundations of arithmetic—this time based on Kant's notions of pure intuitions of space. He died, on July 26, 1925, before he published on this departure from logic.

Gersonides

A controversial figure in the history of Jewish philosophy, Gersonides is best known for his *Milhamot Ha-Shem* (*The Wars of the Lord*), written in 1329, which likely exerted an influence on such later giants as Gottfried Wilhelm Leibniz and Baruch Spinoza.

At bottom, Gersonides' great project was to reconcile the rational human faculty with God, based on the proposition that reason is God-given and therefore a legitimate faculty through which to understand the Creator. As a religious philosopher, then, Gersonides developed a defense of rationality in religion.

Born Levi ben Gerson in Provence in 1288, Gersonides may have been the son of Gershom ben Salomon de Beziers, a man of sufficient prominence to earn mention in contemporary medieval histories. As Spanish tolerance of Jews declined, Provence became a magnet for Jewish intellectual culture, the Avignon popes maintaining a lenient policy toward the Jews.

Gersonides spoke Provençal but wrote in Hebrew. His knowledge of Aristotle came largely via Averroes, and his command of Latin may have been uncertain and limited to a reading knowledge. In any case, all his quotations from Averroes and Aristotle are in Hebrew. It is also likely that he read Averroes in Hebrew translation from the Latin.

By trade, Gersonides was likely a moneylender. He died on April 20, 1344.

Gersonides wrote commentaries on Aristotle or, more accurately, commentaries on Averroes's commentaries on Aristotle. He also wrote on questions of mathematics and science. His 1321 *Maaseh Hoshev* ("A Work of Calculation") dealt with arithmetical operations and may be the earliest introduction of proof by mathematical induction. He wrote *On Sines, Chords and Arcs* (a work on trigonometry) in 1342 and *The Harmony of Numbers* the following year, an exploration of "harmonic numbers." His "Jacob's staff" was an instrument for measuring the angular distance between celestial objects and was a significant contribution to medieval astronomy. He created a geometrical model for the motion of the moon and developed a theory of the nature of the sun. Using a camera obscura, he made other astronomical observations.

Gersonides was an astrologer as well and proposed a non-supernatural explanation of how astrology works by citing the medieval idea that all earthly occurrences depend on the heavens. Despite his willingness to venture into astrology, he was the only astronomer before modern times who correctly estimated stellar distances. In contrast to his contemporaries, who speculated that the stars were distributed on a rotating sphere a short way beyond the outer planets, Gersonides estimated the distances to be far greater—some ten billion times greater.

His astronomical breakthrough was a refutation of the Ptolemaic solar system based on the flaws he observed in Ptolemy's complex epicyclic corrections. He was unable, however, to improve on the Ptolemaic model.

His most original work of philosophy, *The Wars of the Lord*, was written over a dozen years between 1317 and 1329. He modeled it after Maimonides's *Guide for the Perplexed* and covered the doctrine of the soul, in which he presented a theory of impersonal reason mediating between God and man and developed an explanation of how acquired intellect was developed in humanity. Gersonides wrote of God's knowledge of facts and providence, advancing the theory that God does not decide individual facts but creates a general providence of celestial substances, of spiritual hierarchy, creation, and miracles.

In stark contrast to other medieval Jewish thinkers, Gersonides denied that God possesses complete foreknowledge of human acts. Thus, the philosopher elevates the status of free will. He proposed that the soul is composed of an inborn material intellect and an acquired intellect. The first gives people the capacity to understand and learn. This material intellect dies with the body. Acquired intellect, however, survives death and contains the knowledge acquired during one's lifetime.

Gödel, Kurt

Mathematician and analytic philosopher Kurt Gödel stands as the third in a triumvirate of history's great logicians, alongside Aristotle and Gottlob Frege. Among twentieth-century analytical philosophers, his peers in influence are Alfred North Whitehead, Bertrand Russell, and David Hilbert. His breakthrough contributions were two "incompleteness theorems," which constitute the key theorems of mathematical logic. Published in 1931, they demonstrate the limitations of axiomatic systems capable of modeling basic arithmetic.

The first of these theorems holds that no consistent system of axioms whose theorems can be listed by an algorithm can prove all truths about the arithmetic of natural numbers. That is, in any such consistent formal system, true statements about natural numbers exist but are unprovable within the system. The second incompleteness theorem extends the first, showing that the system cannot demonstrate its own consistency.

Taken together, the incompleteness theorems have implications beyond arithmetic in demonstrating the limitations of all formal systems. The theorems are consistent with the work of Alfred Tarski (the "undefinability theorem" demonstrating the formal undefinability of truth), Alonzo Church (his proof that David Hilbert's *Entscheidungsproblem*—"decision problem"—is unsolvable), and Alan Turing (there is no algorithm to solve the halting problem in computability theory).

The incompleteness theorems called into question logicism as proposed by Frege and Russell and have implications for the nature of human intelligence versus machine intelligence. Finally, the incompleteness theorems have been applied beyond mathematics and classical logic to the analysis of proofs in other fields.

Kurt Gödel was born on April 28, 1906 in Brünn (modern Brno, Czech Republic), the son of a prosperous businessman and a brilliant mother, who remained an enduring influence. A sickly child, Gödel nevertheless was a brilliant student, who, on graduation from the gymnasium in Brno, enrolled in the University of Vienna in 1924. He began studying physics but soon turned to mathematics, earning in 1929 a doctorate in that field, with a dissertation that became the basis of his incompleteness theorems.

At university, Gödel became an important figure in the so-called Vienna Circle, which was associated with the founding of logical positivism, which asserted that only statements verifiable through direct observation of logical proof are meaningful. During the 1930s, Gödel not only published his incompleteness theorems (1931), but joined the faculty of the University of

Vienna (1933) and made breakthroughs in set theory, modal and intuitionistic logic, arithmetic, first-order logic (predicate calculus), the length of proofs, and differential and projective geometry.

During the rise of Hitler, Gödel lost his position at the university and, in 1939, was pronounced fit for military service. With his wife, he left Austria for the United States in 1940 and received an "ordinary member" appointment to the Institute for Advanced Study at Princeton University. He was not made a "permanent member" until 1946 and was appointed a professor in 1953. Both Gödel and his wife were naturalized as American citizens in 1948.

At the Institute, Gödel formed a close personal and professional relationship with fellow European refugee Albert Einstein. He produced important papers in philosophy and mathematics, including work on Russell's mathematical logic, Cantor's Continuum Hypothesis, and, most notably, the relationship between Relativity Theory and Idealistic Philosophy. In 1949, he published "An Example of a New Type of Cosmological Solutions of Einstein's Field Equations of Gravitation," based on his work on rotating universes in relativity.

He turned somewhat from mathematics to philosophy during the 1950s, delivering a landmark lecture at Brown University, "Some Basic Theorems on the Foundations of Mathematics and Their Philosophical Implications," in 1951 and left in manuscript a work on phenomenology. His final years were marked by psychological problems, and the cause of his death, at Princeton, January 14, 1978, was ascribed to "starvation and inanition, due to personality disorder."

Goethe, Johann Wolfgang

A polymath active in the realms of literature—including poetry, fiction, and drama—diplomacy, government administration, and science ("natural philosophy"), Goethe created a career not easily categorized. By volume and influence, he is best known as a literary figure, but his literary works have a compelling philosophical basis, especially with respect to ethics, religion, and politics. In addition, his extensive work in science—or natural philosophy, as it was still called at the time—has strong implications for philosophy, particularly in the areas of phenomenology and epistemology.

Goethe's life is well known and has been extensively studied and written about. The essential facts follow. He was born on August 28, 1749 in Frankfurt, the son of a wealthy attorney married to the daughter of the Bürgomeister. Goethe enrolled in Leipzig University in 1765 and then traveled to Strasbourg for legal studies, which he completed in 1770-1771. His prolific and prodigious literary career began early, in 1769, with a play, *Die Laune des Verliebten* (*The Mood of the One in Love*), which was followed in 1773 by his first notable drama, *Götz von Berlichingen.* The next year came his initial literary breakthrough with the romantic novel, *Die Leiden des jungen Werthers* (*The Sorrows of Young Werther*), a work that embodied the Sturm und Drang (Storm and Stress) prelude to the Romantic era in European literature, art, and thought. It both created a popular sensation in Europe and became the subject of much philosophical discussion of an existential direction, relating mainly to the question, "What is the purpose of life?"

On the strength of what Goethe had achieved with *Werther,* Duke Karl August invited him to Weimar to serve in his court as an adviser and administrator. He would remain in Weimar for the rest of his life.

During 1786-1788, Goethe toured Italy, an experience that fired his imagination and turned it toward the classical era. During 1787-1789, he produced three major dramas, all landmarks of German literature, *Iphegenie auf Tauris* (*Iphigenia in Tauris,* 1787), *Egmont* (1787), and *Torquato Tasso* (1789).

Beginning in 1791, Goethe increasingly devoted himself to scientific studies while also approaching the epoch of his greatest literary achievement. In 1794, he began a friendship with the playwright and aesthetician Friedrich Schiller, which lasted until Schiller's death in 1805 and was an enduring inspiration to Goethe in his literary output. In 1796, he published the novel *Wilhelm Meisters Lehrahre* (*Wilhelm Meister's Apprenticeship*), followed in 1797 by a long poem, *Hermann und Dorothea.* During 1808-1831, he wrote one of the great autobiographies in world literature, *Dichtung und Wahrheit* (*Poetry and Truth*), which is also of philosophical interest, especially with respect to the roles of intuition and rationality in the acquisition of knowledge. In 1829, Goethe published the second part of *Wilhelm Meister,* titled *Wilhelm Meisters Wanderjahre* (*Wilhelm Meister's Journeyman Years*).

Early in his career, in 1770, Goethe published *Faust, Part I,* in itself a complete epic poem. In 1832, *Faust, Part II* was posthumously published. Together, these works constitute not only Goethe's signature masterpiece but what many readers and critics consider the greatest poetic work ever published in the German language. Like all great works of literature, there is in *Faust* the most profound philosophy. It may be viewed as a phenomenology of experience itself—of the bases of religion, ethics, and knowledge, and of the balance of knowledge and ethics.

Goethe died, of heart failure, on March 22, 1832, his last words (reportedly) being "*Mehr Licht!*" ("More light!"). He was buried in the Ducal vault of Weimar, beside the body of Friedrich Schiller.

As a natural philosopher, Goethe studied morphology (form and structure of organisms), optics, and anatomy. He wrote *Metamorphosis of Plants* in 1790 and *Theory of Colors* in 1810. As a scientist, philosopher, and Romantic, Goethe sought to reconcile rational inquiry with knowledge that transcended rationality. In effect, he took up the epistemological problem Immanuel Kant had addressed, reconciling the validity of knowledge derived by reason with the German Idealism of Fichte, Hegel, and Schelling to bridge the divide between sensual reality and the super-sensual realm beyond it. Later, in the America of Emerson, this would produce the philosophical school known as Transcendentalism.

In his study of natural science, beginning with botany, Goethe sought to infuse the mechanical rationality of taxonomy with an approach that engaged humanity with nature, the interrelation of nature and natural historical change, and the role of the observer's sensibilities intuition, emotions, and imagination. He advocated the role of a scientific experimenter as humane and life-affirming, with the objective not merely of describing anatomy or taxonomy but of entering into the living essence of what was observed in the natural world. By so doing, Goethe believed that the natural philosopher could penetrate the surface and reach the *Ur-phänomen,* the ur-phenomenon, which would reveal a new vision of natural order and obedience to natural law.

Gorgias

Gorgias, with Protagoras, represents the first generation of Sophists, Pre-Socratic philosophers who used philosophy and rhetoric to acquire valid knowledge. Gorgias was born about 483 BC in Leontinoi, an eastern Sicilian colony allied with Athens. Gorgias had an uncle who was renowned as a physician and with whom he sometimes traveled. He likely studied under Empedocles of Acragas (c. 490– c.430 BC) and perhaps also under the rhetoricians Corax of Syracuse and Tisias.

Gorgias may have been active in politics. It is known that, in 427 BC, he was sent to Athens to seek Athenian protection against Syracusan aggression, and, after this year, he settled in mainland Greece, living in Athens, Larisa, and perhaps elsewhere as well. He made his living primarily as a teacher of rhetoric, Aristotle reporting that his most illustrious student was the rhetorician Isocrates. Gorgias' was a stylistic influence on the rhetoric of the historian Thucydides, the playwright Agathon, and the physician Hippocrates.

Possibly credible legend has it that Gorgias lived to be 108 and profited handsomely from plying his trade as a rhetorician-philosopher. He reportedly died at Larissa, Thessaly, in 375.

The philosophy of Gorgias is not extensively understood, largely because most of his writings have been lost. What survives was heavily edited and redacted by copyists who lived long after him. Moreover, while modern philosophers prize precise and economical prose, Gorgias employed elaborate and often ambiguous, similes and metaphors—and even puns—as well as apparent satire and sarcasm. He rarely made straightforward philosophical propositions but often wrote in ways verging on satire. Where most philosophers strive to create systemic consistency, Gorgias freely contradicts himself. For these reasons, some have characterized him as a Nihilist, though most modern commentators reject this characterization.

The most important philosophical work of Gorgias, *On the Non-Existent,* appropriately enough no longer exists. As far as can be concluded from mentions of and quotations from this work, it was an extreme skeptical view of epistemology, arguing that nothing exists, but even if something did exist, nothing can be known about it, and even if something can be known about it, knowledge about it cannot be communicated, but even if it can be, it cannot be understood. True objectivity, Gorgias seems to have argued, is impossible because the mind cannot be separated from the human being who possesses it.

In the nineteenth century, Georg Wilhelm Friedrich Hegel attempted to revive interest in and respect for the Sophists, including Gorgias. There is, however, a sound reason why the word *sophistry* came into the English language to describe the use of deceptive and fallacious argument. For many of Hegel's contemporaries, the Sophists were in deep disrepute. Far more recently, however, post-Structuralist philosophers have been revisiting Gorgias and have found value in his extreme brand of skepticism when it comes to examining the value of language and its tenuous relation to truth.

Halevi, Judah

A Spanish Jew, Judah Halevi (Yehuda Halevi) was a physician, poet, and philosopher. His most enduring fame is as Hebrew poet, and much of what he composed in the eleventh century is still present in modern Jewish liturgy. As a philosopher, he is known for *The Kuzari,* which posits that religious fulfillment is possible only in the presence of God, and God's presence is to be felt most in Israel.

Born in Toledo, Spain, in 1075 or 1086, Halevi journeyed to the Holy Land (the Crusader Kingdom of Jerusalem) in 1141, only to die shortly after his arrival.

In his youth, Halevi left his native Toledo and traveled to Granada, at the time the focal point of Jewish intellectual life. There he came under the mentorship of Moses Ibn Ezra. He was educated in Jewish scholarship, Arabic literature, and (in Arabic translation) Greek philosophy and science. He became a physician of high reputation and may have served the court in Toledo as a physician. In any event, his medical work kept him so busy that he complained of having too little time to devote to scholarship. Halevi wrote prose in Arabic and reserved Hebrew for his poetry. The most prolific of Hebrew poets of the period, he is still regarded as the greatest of the Middle Ages.

Halevi was adequately assimilated into Spanish culture but, as an observant Jew, felt it incumbent upon himself to end his days in Israel. At an earlier point in his life, he saw in philosophy an alternative to religion as a path to the truth. But he came to believe that only faith and revealed religion would bring him enlightenment. Moreover, the God of Israel was most strongly manifested in Israel, and so he embarked, arriving in the port of Alexandria on September 8, 1140, where he met with a warm welcome. From here, he journeyed to Cairo, where highly placed friends tried to persuade him to take up residence. Instead, he returned to Alexandria, from which he sailed to Israel on May 14, 1141. Sometime during the summer, he died—probably after having reached Palestine. Legend has it that he was run over by an Arab horseman almost immediately on his arrival in Jerusalem.

His most important philosophical work, *The Kuzari*, was written in large measure to liberate Judaism from philosophy. The work presents his argument that reason (philosophy) alone is insufficient to the attainment of truth and only religious tradition and faithful devotion lead to revelation. In the Kuzari, he expounded on this thesis and defended Judaism against the attacks of non-Jewish philosophers, including those adhering to Aristotelean logic.

Hegel, Georg Wilhelm Friedrich

Georg Wilhelm Friedrich Hegel (1770-1831) may justly lay claim to being the archetypal German philosopher of the early nineteenth century. The exemplar par excellence of German Idealism, he was also an incredibly ambitious thinker, who firmly believed that his own philosophical system was the historical culmination of philosophy itself. He took a holistic and encyclopedic approach to philosophy, dividing the entire subject into three massive segments: the Science of Logic, the Philosophy of Nature, and the Philosophy of Spirit. All are challenging, but what remains of greatest interest to modern philosophers is how Hegel applied his philosophy to analyze history, society, and the state, all of which he classified under the rubric of Objective Spirit.

In terms of the history of philosophy, Hegel's most enduring contribution is in his description of idealism, or "absolute idealism," by which he sought to resolve subject-object dualism as well as the dualism of mind and nature. He is widely credited with the philosophical process of thesis, antithesis, and synthesis—which he thoroughly exploited, though the phrase itself originated with Johann Gottlieb Fichte. Still, no philosopher has taken it quite so far as Hegel, who synthesized such oppositions as necessity and freedom and immanence and transcendence.

G. W. F. Hegel was born in Stuttgart on August 27, 1770, into the family of a government officer in the service of the Duke of Württemberg. After graduating from the Royal High School in Stuttgart in 1788, he entered a seminary in Tübingen, where he befriended the Romantic poet Friedrich Hölderlin and philosopher Friedrich Schelling. He earned a master's degree in 1790, became the private tutor to a Swiss family in Berne (1793-1796), and, in 1797, began another engagement as a tutor in Frankfurt. His earliest writings, on religion, date from this era.

In January 1801, Hegel secured a position as *Privatdozent* (unsalaried lecturer) at the University of Jena, where Schelling was a professor. With him, Hegel began publishing the *Critical Journal of Philosophy*. He became a professor at Jena in 1805 and, two years later, published his first major book, *Phenomenology of Spirit*. Unfortunately, at precisely this time, Napoleon occupied Jena, bringing about the closure of the university. To make ends meet, Hegel found employment as editor of *Die Bamberger Zeitung*, a Bamberg newspaper. After a year of this work, Hegel moved to Nuremberg in 1808 to become headmaster of a *Gymnasium*. He also taught philosophy there.

Hegel spent eight years at the Gymnasium, married, and started a family. In 1816, he published the three-volume *Science of Logic* and became professor of philosophy at the University of Heidelberg. While holding this post, he published *Encyclopedia of the Philosophical Sciences in Outline* in 1817.

In 1818, Hegel moved to the University of Berlin as professor of philosophy and spent the rest of his life at this institution. He became closely associated with the Prussian government and turned his formidable philosophical apparatus to questions of governance, ethics, and politics. At the same time, he lectured on a broad array of philosophical topics, including art, history, religion, and the history of philosophy itself. He earned a degree of popular renown rare for a philosopher and was ensconced in the Prussian Ministry of Education.

In 1821, Hegel published the *Philosophy of Right,* was elected Rector of the University of Berlin in 1830, and, on November 14, 1831, succumbed to cholera.

Central to the philosophy of Hegel is the principle that only the rational is real. That is, reality is capable of being expressed in rational categories within absolute idealism. Each philosophical concept can be defined based on experience, which follows the triad of thesis, antithesis, synthesis. The concept of liberty, for example, begins as license—unrestrained action. In the course of history, it is acted upon by restraint in the form of law or tyranny. At the highest state of social evolution, liberty is synthesized with restraint to create liberty in law (synthesis). Hegel held that philosophy could explain reality in terms of time (history) through this triadic process. Hegel called the first stage of the triad *An-sich* ("in itself"). The second stage was the "sublation" (or even annihilation) of the first, a stage called *Anderssein* ("out of itself"). The third stage, the synthesis, is the return of the *An-sich* in a higher, truer fuller form, the *An-und-für-sich* ("in and for itself").

The triad meshes with the idea of the dialectic as the fundamental pattern of thought: thesis, antithesis, and synthesis. In this way, it can be applied throughout the intellectual realm to describe reality in the dimension of progression through time. Thus, Hegelian philosophy has had a strong influence on historiography and, most notably, on economic and political movements such as Marxism, to which the view of history as a progress away from self-interest and then national interest to class-based interest is a central tenet.

As a philosopher, Hegel used the dialectic to arrive at a true appreciation of the world—that is, from an ideal perspective. Like Immanuel Kant, he believed that our senses deliver to us a virtual representation of an ideal reality. In contrast to Kant, Hegel believed that the ideas we form about the world are social and thus shaped by others. We therefore participate in the *Geist* (spirit) that is the collective consciousness of one's society. This *Geist* evolves in precisely the manner of a philosophical dialectic, from thesis to antithesis to synthesis. This, in fact, is the intellectual content of history. Indeed, because this dialectical succession is logical, the course of history can be properly interpreted only through logic alone.

Although the triad and the dialectic can be applied to understanding any aspect of reality, Hegelianism has been most influential in understanding history and, more specifically, social history. *Geist* is the self-awareness, within each individual, of society. Consciousness of an object necessarily implies consciousness of a subject—that is, self-consciousness. Self-consciousness involves not only a subject and an object but other subjects as well, so that individuals become aware of themselves through the eyes of another. This is the basis of social organization as well as lordship and subjugation. Finally, Hegel posited that the evolved society exhibits ethical life as a cultural expression of the Geist, creating individual liberty within the perceived bonds of a society.

Heidegger, Martin

Martin Heidegger was a philosopher engaged most deeply in ontology, the nature and study of being. His central work, *Being and Time* (1927), investigates being (*Sein* in German) by means of a phenomenological analysis of human existence (*Dasein*) through such human themes as mortality, anxiety, temporality, and historicity. During the 1930s and 1940s, however, he changed his focus (in what Heidegger scholars call "die Kehre," the turn) to the role language plays as the vehicle through which the question of being is unfolded. His questions shifted from *being* in the world to *doing time* in the world. And he found modern Western society wanting in this doing of time. He criticized technological culture as inherently nihilistic. His desire was to refresh philosophy by reaching back to Pre-Socratic traditions to revive the Greek experience of wonder in being.

Heidegger inspired modern thought in phenomenology, existentialism, hermeneutics, political philosophy, psychology, and theology. He was critical of both traditional metaphysics and more recent positivism, rejecting the mechanistic tendencies of technology and analytical philosophy. This was an inspiration to such postmodernist Continental philosophers as Jacques Derrida and Michel Foucault. What even some of his most enthusiastic acolytes could not forgive, however, was Heidegger's involvement in the Nazi movement. He was both a supporter and member of the Nazi Party.

Martin Heidegger was born on September 26, 1889 in Messkirch, Germany, where his father was sexton in the local Catholic church. Young

Heidegger began to prepare for the priesthood and, in 1903, enrolled at the high school in Konstanz, under a Church scholarship. In 1906, he moved to Freiburg, where a reading of Franz Brentano's *On the Manifold Meaning of Being according to Aristotle* inspired his interest in philosophy. He became a Jesuit novice in 1909, but ill-health necessitated his discharge from the order. He enrolled in Freiburg University, as a theology student but left the seminary in 1911 and definitively ended his training as a priest, turning instead to philosophy, mathematics, and science.

He came under the influence of Edmund Husserl and completed his doctorate in 1913. Conscripted into the army at the start of World War I in 1914, he was soon discharged because of his perilous health. In 1915, he was appointed a *Privatdozent*, lecturer, at Freiburg, teaching Aristotelian and scholastic philosophy. In 1916, he joined the Freiburg faculty as a junior colleague of Edmund Husserl, married one of his students, served briefly in the German military meteorological service, and returned to Freiburg immediately after the war. Formally announcing his break with Catholicism in January 1919, he was appointed Husserl's assistant and began his teaching career in earnest, lecturing on phenomenology and Aristotle. His originality earned wide acclaim.

In 1923, Heidegger was appointed associate professor at Marburg University and taught courses on the history of philosophy, time, logic, phenomenology, Plato, Aristotle, Aquinas, Kant, and Leibniz. It was in 1927 that, under academic pressure, he released his still unfinished *Being and Time* for publication. It was instantly recognized as a breakthrough and earned Heidegger promotion to a full professorship at Marburg. On Husserl's retirement, he succeeded to the chairmanship of the philosophy department at Freiburg University.

In 1929, Heidegger published two essays and a book: "What is Metaphysics?," "On the Essence of Ground," and *Kant and the Problem of Metaphysics*, which demonstrated his journey from neo-Kantianism to an original view of phenomenological ontology.

Heidegger was largely apolitical until April 21, 1933, when the faculty elected him rector of the University of Freiburg. He later claimed that he believed he could use this post to influence the course of the Nazi Party, so he joined the party on May 3. On May 27, in his inaugural rectoral address, he seemed to express frank support for Hitler, and, during his rectorship, he made several speeches in support of the party—only to resign as rector on April 23, 1934 and withdraw from politics entirely. His work became vaguely anti-Nazi after this point, and in 1944, the university sought to humiliate him by sending him to the Rhine to dig trenches. After the war, only his original support for the Nazis was remembered, and he was not only dismissed as chair of the Freiburg philosophy department in 1946 but barred from teaching. This ban was lifted in 1949.

The 1930s were fateful for another reason, as Heidegger underwent "the turn" (*die Kehre*) and began to devote himself to philosophical and literary exegesis in search of "the essence of truth." He became increasingly interested in Nietzsche as part of his rejection of traditional Western metaphysics and then sought a rebirth of modern philosophy by going back to its Pre-Socratic roots.

Heidegger died on May 26, 1976, in Freiburg.

Heraclitus of Ephesus

A native of Ephesus, a major city on the Ionian coast of Asia Minor, Heraclitus was born about 535 BC. His controlling philosophical tenet was the unity of experience in a universal system of balanced exchanges. For Heraclitus, the common denominator of existence was change, a law of nature that is also a moral law for humanity. Indeed, Heraclitus was the first Western philosopher to posit a metaphysical and moral connection between physical reality and human beings.

Virtually nothing is known of the life of Heraclitus other that he lived in Ephesus and, despite Plato's belief that he wrote after Parmenides, it is more likely that he predated him. Heraclitus was as much a critic as he was a philosopher. Not only did he criticize the likes of Pythagoras and Xenophanes, but he scorned myth makers such as Homer and Hesiod.

Not surprisingly, Heraclitus saw most of his fellow creatures as ignorant and incapable of deep comprehension. He characterized the mass of humanity as sleepwalkers through life. Nevertheless, he did believe that the right message was capable of bringing enlightenment, even to the dense mass of humanity. He had a great faith in language as the vehicle by which humanity would learn that all things are one.

Both Plato and Aristotle disdained Heraclitus's views as radical to the point of incoherence. He is best known for his doctrine of change—everything is constantly changing—and for the idea that opposite things are identical, which means that everything is and is not at the same time.

In fact, his concept of the system of the universe was more subtle and idealist. True, reality is characterized by Universal Flux and the Identity of Opposites. In his famous river metaphor, Heraclitus declared, "On those stepping into rivers staying the same other and other waters flow," a statement Plato recalled as a metaphor likening existence to the flow of a river. "He says," Plato wrote, "you could not step twice into the same river." The full meaning of Heraclitus' statement is not that rivers are ephemeral, subject to continual change, but that they can stay the same over time—except that their waters continually change. So, the point is less that everything changes than it is that the change of *some* things enables the continued existence of *others*. Change in the elements supports the durable constancy of higher-level structures. More difficult is the doctrine of the Identity of Opposites. He stated, "God is day night, winter summer, war peace, satiety hunger." Existence contains its opposite.

Heraclitus did not preach a universal flux, but, rather, a universal *law* of flux. He did not claim the Identity of Opposites, but the *Transformational Equivalence* of Opposites. Heraclitus called the world an "ever-living fire" observing: "all things are an exchange for fire, and fire for all things, as goods for gold and gold for goods." Fire is constantly changing, but the processes it drives do not change. The Law of Transformations is itself constant.

Heraclitus drew his metaphysical conclusions from physical theory. His theory of the "kosmos" (the first time the word was used in philosophy) is that the universe was not created but "it ever was and is and will be: everliving fire, kindling in measures and being quenched in measures." He speaks of how fire is transformed into water (the "sea"), half of which transforms back into fire (so-called, "firewind") and half into earth. There is, then, a sequence of elements: fire to water to earth, all interconnected.

Heraclitus was above all a philosopher of nature, but he was also a metaphysician, who struggled to define the soul, and a moralist and philosopher of society and law, arguing that the human cosmos is like the natural cosmos in that both reflect an underlying order.

Heraclitus died, in Ephesus, in about 475 BC.

Hilbert, David

Although identified primarily as a mathematician who made several fundamental breakthroughs in the field, David Hilbert's work in proof theory and other aspects of mathematical logic have given him a significant place in logic and analytical philosophy. Of central importance was "Hilbert's Program," a call to formalize all mathematics in axiomatic form, thereby bringing mathematics and philosophy under the same intellectual umbrella.

David Hilbert was born in Prussia (either in Königsberg or Wehlau [modern Znamensk]) on January 23, 1862. He enrolled in the Friedrichskolleg Gymnasium in 1872 but in 1879 transferred to the more science-intensive Wilhelm Gymnasium, from which he graduated. He then enrolled in 1880 at the University of Königsberg, from which he earned a doctorate in 1885, with a dissertation titled "On the Invariant Properties of Special Binary Forms, in Particular the Spherical Harmonic Functions." The university appointed him a *Privatdozent* (lecturer), a post in which he served from 1886 to 1895 before being appointed Professor of Mathematics at the University of Göttingen. Hilbert remained at that institution for the rest of his life and was instrumental in elevating it to recognition as the foremost center of mathematics in the world.

From 1925 until the end of his long life, Hilbert suffered from debilitating pernicious anemia, which diminished his creativity. He died on February 14, 1943, having lived long enough to witness the dismantling of Göttingen's mathematics department by the Nazi purge of Jewish faculty.

In the early 1920s, Hilbert published his proposal to formalize all of mathematics in axiomatic form, together with a proof that the axiomatization of mathematics is consistent. This bold step forward in epistemology and mathematics was known as Hilbert's Program. Eminent logicians, including Paul Bernays, Wilhelm Ackermann, John von Neumann, and Jacques Herbrand, were drawn into the work of furthering Hilbert's Program. But in 1930-1931, Kurt Gödel published his two "incompleteness theorems," which demonstrated that even elementary axiomatic systems such as Peano arithmetic are either self-contradicting or contain logical propositions that are impossible to prove or disprove. To many, this seemed the death blow to Hilbert's Program—and to what might have been a major pillar of epistemology. Still, Hilbert's work has continued to drive the development of proof theory, one of the central interests of analytic philosophy.

Hobbes, Thomas

Product of the seventeenth-century Enlightenment, Thomas Hobbes is justly remembered as the founder of modern political philosophy. In an eloquent and systematic manner, he defined all the principal issues of political debate. Although he concluded that the challenges posed by human beings as social animals dictate that the best government is that ruled by an absolute sovereign, his arguments were never arbitrary, and they have remained relevant both in historical and contemporary terms—even when democracy is generally accepted as the most desirable form of government.

Hobbes accepted nothing on faith and took nothing for granted but, rather, set out to justify authority, lay out the parameters of social and political inequality, and question the limits of authority based on religion.

Hobbes confronted the issue of human rights but, unlike John Locke or (later) Thomas Jefferson, also deeply questioned who determines these rights, who enforces them, and how. In the end, he created a picture of politics and society as an arena of power countervailing power. In addition to emerging as the archetypal political philosopher, Hobbes made important contributions to philosophy in general as well as mathematics (geometry), physics (the nature of gases), ethics, law, theology, and the philosophy of history.

He was born on April 5, 1588 in Malmesbury, Wiltshire, England, the son of a Church of England clergyman. Educated at Magdalen Hall, Oxford, from which he received a B.A. in 1608, he tutored William Cavendish (future second earl of Devonshire), whose family became Hobbes's loyal patrons.

His pupil in tow, Hobbes toured Europe during 1610, and in 1629 published his first book, a translation of Thucydides. He toured Europe again, in 1629-1630 and 1634-1637, and developed a consuming interest in Euclidean geometry. In Florence, he met Galileo Galilei, whose theories he embraced.

Hobbes was an ardent monarchist, whose early political works—circulated in manuscript in 1640 and published in 1650 as *Of Human Nature* and *De Corpore Politico (Of the Body Politic)*—defended the concept of absolute monarchy. This put him in danger during the English Civil War (1642-1651), and he took flight to Paris to escape the wrath of the parliamentarians. It was here that he wrote his masterpiece of political philosophy, *Leviathan* (1651). His view of humanity boiled down to a bitter kernel. The life of members of the human race is "solitary . . . nasty, brutish, and short," and the condition of humanity is that of "war of everyone against everyone." For this reason, only absolute authority can save humanity from itself.

The irony of Hobbes's intellectual life was that his advocacy of absolute monarchy enraged advocates of republican models of state while his relentlessly materialist philosophy offended royalists and church alike. He lived to see his major works excoriated by all sides and banned. Hobbes died at Hardwick, Derbyshire, on December 4, 1679.

A philosophical and literary masterpiece, *Leviathan* applies the paradigm of a geometric proof, grounded in first principles and established definitions, to advance Hobbes's argument stepwise. He had decided on this method of proceeding after discussion with no less a figure than Galileo, deciding that conclusions derived by geometry cannot be disputed because each step in the argument is itself indisputable. So, beyond the value of

Leviathan as a political and sociological analysis, it is also a massive experiment in the application of mathematical logic to issues of ethics and human conduct.

His argument is that civil peace and social unity are best achieved in a commonwealth founded on a social contract—yet governed by a sovereign empowered with absolute authority to protect the commonwealth and provide for the common defense. Hobbes conceived of the commonwealth as what he called an "artificial person" and the body politic, in consequence, an emulation of the human body. Indeed, the Leviathan of the book's title is a reference to the monstrous sea creature that appears in the Bible, which Hobbes illustrates in the frontispiece to the first edition of his book. It is a gigantic human form representing the state, and it is constructed of the bodies of the state's citizens—with the absolute sovereign as its head.

Does Hobbes love this monster? No. But he posits its necessity for preserving peace and preventing civil war.

The work is divided into four books: "Of Man," "Of Common-wealth," "Of a Christian Common-wealth," and "Of the Kingdome of Darknesse." The entire philosophical framework is presented in Book I, and the other three books elaborate on it. Hobbes begins with first principles, a consideration of the elementary motions of matter. He goes on to argue that every aspect of human nature can be derived using arguments made from materialist principles. He then establishes the natural condition of mankind as violent and dominated by fear. In this "state of nature," the prevailing condition is the "war of every man against every man." Each seeks to destroy the other. So intolerable is this condition that human beings seek peace through government. Hobbes sets out to demonstrate that the best form of government capable of achieving and keeping peace is to erect a Leviathan via social contract.

Hume, David

The Scots philosopher David Hume was among the towering intellects of the eighteenth century and drew both admiration and condemnation—but always great interest—for his relentlessly skeptical approach to the entire range of subjects suited to philosophical inquiry.

As an epistemologist, he seems strikingly modern, arguing that personal identity itself is a kind of fiction because there is, in fact, no permanent self that is continuous through time. In examining commonsense notions of causality, he argued that our concept of cause and effect is not the product of observation but of unexamined habits of thinking. Moreover, he rejected reason as a reliable guide to reality and truth because reason is inherently contradictory. He argued that it is through congenital, inborn, natural beliefs that we are even capable of finding our way through life.

He rejected the miraculous in religion, arguing that belief founded on miracles is unreasonable. At the same time, he criticized the contention that the existence of God was provable through arguments based on design or causality. He defended the notion that popular religious beliefs are not the product of divine revelation but of irrational human psychology. Hume, however, was far less interested in questioning religion and the validity of divine revelation than he was to make philosophy entirely independent from religion or, for that matter, psychology. Indeed, he liberated morality itself from God and religion by proposing a secular morality based on motivation by anticipated outcomes. One acts in ways calculated to achieve useful or pleasing outcomes. This was the foundation of his concept of utility as a criterion for ethics and morals and anticipated the later utilitarianism of Jeremy Bentham and John Stuart Mill. Hume even ventured into the philosophy of aesthetics, arguing that human nature is defined by a common standard of aesthetic taste, and although he was an intellectual progressive, Hume's political philosophy embraced the conservative view that governments are best run by strong monarchs.

David Hume was born on April 26, 1711 in Edinburgh, Scotland. A prodigy, he enrolled at Edinburgh University when he was just twelve and then traveled to France in 1734. He lived with Jesuits at La Flèche and wrote A *Treatise of Human Nature* (1739-1740). Taken aback by criticism of this book, he withdrew to his family's estate in Berwickshire and wrote *Essays Moral and Political* (1741-1742), which was highly successful.

Hume served as judge advocate to General James St. Clair on a diplomatic mission to France in 1746 and then traveled with his entourage to Vienna and Turin during 1748-1749. In the meantime, he revised the ill-fated *Treatise of Human Nature* as *Enquiry Concerning Human Understanding* in 1748. The book begins with an introduction to philosophy itself and goes on to analyze the "origin of ideas" and the "association of ideas." From this basis, Hume develops his skepticism regarding human understanding, casting doubt on whether inductive reasoning leads to knowledge (truth). Having immersed his readers in skepticism, Hume then rescues them with a "skeptical solution" to the doubt created by skepticism. Next, he investigates the roles of custom, belief, and probability as sources of knowledge. This is empirical epistemology. To address its shortcomings, which are dead ends in his skeptical view, Hume devotes the second part of his book to applied epistemology, which verges on what would emerge in the nineteenth century as pragmatism.

In the 1750s, Hume settled in Edinburgh and turned from the philosophy of mind and epistemology to ethics and political philosophy with his *Enquiry Concerning the Principles of Morals* (1751) and *Political Discourses* (1752). From these works, he turned to history with a massive *History of England, on which he labored from* 1754 to 1762. It became the standard English history for decades.

Hume died in Edinburgh on August 25, 1776, having not only transformed philosophy in England but having generally recast Enlightenment thought throughout Europe and the emerging United States. Although John Locke's combination of idealism and skepticism was highly influential and comported well with the humanistic liberalism that helped drive the American Revolution and other radical movements, Hume's logical rigor proved more durable among philosophers. Locke may have influenced the likes of Thomas Jefferson and the other American founding fathers, but Hume exerted a powerful posthumous influence over the coming nineteenth century, proving the foundation for both positivism and utilitarianism.

Husserl, Edmund

Born in Prossnitz, Moravia (today part of the Czech Republic) on April 8, 1859, Edmund Gustav Albrecht Husserl is widely considered the father of modern phenomenology, the philosophical effort to describe experience and the phenomena of experience without the theoretical apparatus of metaphysics. Husserl sought to make philosophy the equivalent of a unique science, of which phenomenology, as the science of consciousness, was the core. This intellectual project required the renunciation of naturalism—that is, the idea that all things are aspects of the world of nature and can therefore be studied by the methods of the existing sciences. Husserl countered that consciousness is different from nature and must therefore be studied by different methodologies. In radical contrast to the scientific study of nature, phenomenology does not rest on large amounts of data that, by induction, are related to some general theory. Instead, phenomenology looks at individual examples of experience without theoretical presupposition and then discerns what is essential to these experiences. This is known as the phenomenological method, in contrast to the scientific method, and it has greatly influenced modern philosophy and psychology.

Husserl was the son of a prosperous Jewish clothing merchant, who used his wealth to send the ten-year-old boy to the *Realgymnasium* in Vienna for a classical German education. At the end of his first year, in 1870, Husserl transferred to the *Staatsgymnasium* in Olmütz, and, on graduation in 1876, enrolled in the University of Leipzig. He studied mathematics, physics, and philosophy before transferring to Berlin in 1878 for further studies in mathematics. He went on to earn a doctorate in mathematics from the University of Vienna in 1883. He briefly taught in Berlin but returned to Vienna in 1884 to attend Franz Brentano's lectures in philosophy. Two years later, in 1886, he enrolled at Halle to study psychology, writing his *Habilitationsschrift* (the examination that certified him to teach at the university level) on number theory.

Granted the post of *Privatdozent* (lecturer) at Halle, he married Malvine Charlotte Steinschneider (with whom he would have three children). Before he left Halle in 1901, Husserl wrote *Philosophie der Arithmetik* (1891) and two volumes of *Logical Investigations* (*Logische Untersuchungen*), which came out in 1900 and 1901. He moved to the faculty at Göttingen, where he taught for sixteen years and fully developed his formulations of phenomenology in his *Ideen zu einer reinen Phänomenologie und phänomenologischen Philosophie* (*Ideas Pertaining to a Pure Phenomenology and to a Phenomenological Philosophy*).

The Great War (World War I) disrupted the Göttingen faculty, and Husserl's son Wolfgang was killed at the Battle of Verdun. This sent Husserl into a year of mourning, but in 1916 he accepted a professorship at Freiburg im Breisgau, where he spent the remainder of his professional life, which was devoted to phenomenological research. He died of pleurisy on April 27, 1938.

Husserl devoted his mature years to researching the essential structures of consciousness with the goal of understanding how the world of objects—and our perception of them—can be reconceived apart from the traditional "natural standpoint." Instead, Husserl proposed looking at objects by studying how we, as beings intentionally directed toward them, "constitute" them in consciousness. Viewed from the phenomenological perspective, objects cease to be "external" and instead become sets of perceptual and functional aspects that imply one another under the idea of a given "type." Objects are real but not as things in themselves so much as exemplars of an essence created by the relation between the object and the perceiver.

Husserl's goal was to reach an understanding of the world of appearances and objects by identifying the universal and invariant features of how objects are perceived. In his most mature conception of phenomenology, Husserl became a transcendental idealist, concerned with Intersubjectivity—specifically how communication about a particular object can be assumed to refer to the same ideal entity.

Husserl believed that phenomenology provided scientific inquiry—primarily in the field of psychology—with a new tool that allowed the natural attitude to be "bracketed," so that relation of object to subject could be more reliably studied. Husserl postulated that mental and spiritual reality was independent of any physical basis. Phenomenology, therefore, made the *spirit* an object of systematic scientific study. This, he believed, created a "total transformation of the task of knowledge."

Ibn Ezra, Abraham

Born between 1089 and 1092 in Tudela, Spain, Abraham Ibn Ezra claimed Córdoba as his birthplace. Other than these conflicting facts, little is known of Ibn Ezra's family, although he himself mentions having a wife and five children, one of whom, Isaac, became a celebrated poet. Ibn Ezra was a friend of Judah Halevi, one the great philosophers of Jewish Spain. Ibn Ezra traveled widely over some thirty years, venturing as far as Baghdad. He wrote poetry, composed a distinguished series of Torah commentaries, translated the works of the grammarian and biblical exegetist Judah ben David Hayyuj from Judeo-Arabic to Hebrew, and composed important biblical commentaries. He died between 1164 and 1167.

In addition to his theological works, Ibn Ezra published extensively in science, but his most significant contributions to philosophy are his approach to biblical criticism (hermeneutics) and *Yesod Mora Vesod Hatorah* of 1158, a book on the structure and reasons for the Biblical commandments. No less a figure than Baruch Spinoza cited Ibn Ezra as support for his contention that the Pentateuch was not written by Moses, but by another who lived much later. As a philosopher of religion, Ibn Ezra was Neoplatonic in orientation, avoiding Kabbalistic interpretation of scripture, struggling to divine the most literal sense of the word, and always stressing rationalism in his approach to scripture.

Gabirol, Solomon Ibn (Avicebron)

Born in Málága, Andalusia, in 1021 or 1022, Solomon Ibn Gabirol was a poet and Neoplatonic Jewish philosopher. Until well into the nineteenth century, he was known only by his Latinized name, Avicebron, and was assumed to have been either an Islamic or a Christian scholar. His great contribution to philosophy is his argument that everything, including the intellect and the soul, is composed of matter and form—a version of Aristotle's hylomorphism.

Gabirol seems to have been financially well off but nevertheless suffered a hard life in that he was lonely, cursed with ill health, and fell afoul of powerful foes. He may have been afflicted by lupus vulgaris, a form of cutaneous tuberculosis that left him disfigured. He was also beset by what another Jewish-Spanish philosopher, Moses ibn Ezra, called an "irascible temperament" and "could [not] rein [in] the demon that was within himself." His discourse was often sarcastic and mocking.

In Zaragoza, to which he moved in his teens, Gabirol's mocking wit won him powerful enemies, and he was forced to interrupt his studies in the Talmud, grammar, geometry, astronomy, and philosophy until he found a patron in Samuel ibn Naghrillah, the grand vizier to the kings of Granada. Before long, however, Gabirol managed to alienate him as well, and, having done this, became an itinerant poet-philosopher before dying young (in 1050, 1058, or 1070), possibly the victim of murder.

His chief work, *Fons Vitae* (*Source of Life*), which he wrote in Arabic and that was later translated into Hebrew and then into Latin, is a Neoplatonic philosophical dialogue between "master" and "disciple" on the nature of God's creation and how understanding our own nature (what we are) can enable us to discover our purpose and thus live, with meaning, accordingly. He saw all existence as being reducible to three categories: God; matter and form (that is, creation); and will, the latter functioning as an intermediary between the first two categories.

Ibn Tibbon, Samuel

Samuel ben Judah ibn Tibbon was born about 1150 in Lunel, in the Languedoc region of what is today France. Best known as a translator of rabbinic literature from Arabic to Hebrew, he was also an important Jewish philosopher.

His principal theological work was a commentary on Ecclesiastes and a philosophical-exegetical monograph entitled *Ma'amar Yiqqawu ha-Mayim*. The latter work, which may be translated as *Treatise on "Let the waters be gathered" (Gen 1:9)*, was written perhaps in 1221 or 1231. Like some of Ibn Tibbon's other writing, it is clearly inspired by Maimonides' *Guide for the Perplexed*, and it uses the verse from Genesis to explore a unique cosmological question: Why is the earth *not* covered entirely by water? It finds the answers to this question in a rational exegesis of other portions of the Old Testament, namely verses from Genesis, Isaiah, Ezekiel, Job, and the Book of Psalms.

Samuel ibn Tibbon was one of the great masters of medieval Jewish philosophical exegesis of Scripture. His work is a kind of model of this analytical and argumentative hermeneutic technique, useful in theology and the philosophy of religion alike. In Ibn Tibbon's hands, it also became a bridge to profound issues of creation and cosmology.

Ibn Tibbon's father, Judah ben Saul ibn Tibbon, gave him a full traditional Jewish education in the rabbinic literature. He also sought for him other teachers in Lunel to school him as a physician and to impart to him other important knowledge from the secular realm.

Samuel ibn Tibbon was married and had children. We know that his son, Moses ibn Tibbon, translated religious and philosophical works from Arabic to Hebrew. Samuel was widely traveled. He lived in several towns in the south of France, including Béziers and Arles, and he sojourned in Barcelona, Toledo, and Alexandria during 1210–1213. His final permanent residence was in Marseilles, where he died about 1230. His corpse was carried to what was then the Kingdom of Jerusalem and was buried in Tiberias.

James, William

One of the most original and approachable of philosophers, William James was instrumental in founding and establishing Pragmatism, which embraces language and thought as the means of problem solving and prediction. In this, it breaks with other, earlier schools of philosophy, which define thought as a means of representing or even mirroring reality. Pragmatism works backward from outcomes, arguing that most philosophical questions, including those concerning the nature of knowledge, meaning, belief, and science, are best answered by evaluating outcomes, practical applications, successes, and failures. Pragmatism was, however, only one dimension of the breadth of James's philosophical interests. He also made basic contributions in the areas of logic, metaphysics, mind, ethics, religion, philosophy of science, and even aesthetics.

William James was born in New York City on January 11, 1842 to the Swedenborgian philosopher Henry James Sr. and was the elder brother (by one year) of the novelist Henry James. Educated in the US and Europe, James studied art under William Morris Hunt before turning to science and entering the Lawrence Scientific School of Harvard University in 1861. From here, he went on to Harvard Medical School. After accompanying the great naturalist Louis Agassiz in an exploration of the Amazon in 1865 and studying in Germany during 1867-1868, he took his MD degree in 1869.

Instead of practicing, however, he taught physiology, psychology, and, ultimately, philosophy at Harvard in a career that spanned 1872 to 1907.

He married Alice Howe Gibbons in 1878 and had four children with her. The milestones of his illustrious career are marked chiefly by his books, which were read not only in academia but by a far wider audience. They include *The Principles of Psychology* (1890), *The Varieties of Religious Experience* (1902), *Pragmatism: A New Name for Some Old Ways of Thinking* (1907), *The Meaning of Truth* (1909), *A Pluralistic Universe* (1909), and *Essays in Radical Empiricism* (1912). He died on August 26, 1910.

James was a great psychologist, who would be remembered as such had he not gone on to work in philosophy, a field he found more intellectually congenial. His philosophical efforts in psychology were aimed primarily at aiding the full transformation of psychology into an independent science of mental phenomena and states of consciousness, including thoughts, feelings, desires, and volitions. He defined thinking in terms of five characteristics:

1. All thought is owned by some personal self.
2. It is a stream of consciousness and never static.
3. There is a continuity of the thought stream through its shifting foci.
4. Thought generally deals with objects independent of consciousness itself. The implication of this is that two minds *can* experience common objects.
5. Consciousness chooses the objects in which it is interested.

James regarded the self as something that can be viewed as the object or the subject of thought. The first view is the empirical self ("me"); the second is pure ego ("I"). The *me* is defined in material, social, and spiritual terms, whereas the *I* is identifiable with the soul (as understood in traditional metaphysics) and therefore cannot be an object of science.

James saw a progression from sensation to perception to imagination to belief. He believed that human beings share primitive instincts—fear, some desires, and certain forms of sympathy—with other animals. These instincts are inborn. In addition, some emotions are learned behaviors. Most provocatively, James argued that while common sense suggests that perceptions trigger emotional responses, eliciting bodily expressions, the actual sequence is perception, followed by expression, followed by emotional feeling. By way of illustration, James asked us to suppose we see a bear. We respond not with fear that causes us to run, but we have a physical reaction (we tremble) and take a volitional action (we run) but only after we experience the sensation (trembling) and take the action (running) do we feel the emotion (fear). That is, we do not run because we are afraid but we are afraid because we run. The implication is that cognition is not confined to a Cartesian mind separate from the body but is, in fact, embodied, distributed throughout the organism.

In the area of epistemology, James repudiated rationalism and *a priori* truths. He instead embraced empiricism, which he used in his adaptation of William Sanders Peirce's original conception of Pragmatism. James envisioned the pragmatic epistemological approach as a compromise between idealism and empiricism. As he formulated it, pragmatism is grounded in the empirical but accommodates the spiritual, moral, and religious. The compromise is enabled by focusing on outcomes—outputs—rather than theoretical or ideal inputs and *a priori* assumptions. Before investing time and effort seeking the meaning of any phenomenon, we should ponder what practical benefit the answer would provide.

Pragmatism defines truth as a true idea or belief that can be incorporated into our ways of thinking such that it can be validated by experience. Truth must be true in three dimensions: with respect to matters of fact, valid relations of ideas (mathematical truth), and in relation to the entire set of truths to which we are committed. All existential truths are revisable based on new experience. Thus, truth is inherently relative—an idea that created great controversy, which James addressed in *The Meaning of Truth*.

James devoted special attention to religious belief and wrote one of the great works on the philosophy of religion, *The Varieties of Religious Experience.* Asserting that, by definition, we do not naturally experience the supernatural, James thought of faith as a failure of knowledge. Yet he admitted that faith is pragmatically meaningful to a great many people. He identified a "Will to Believe," which substituted religious faith for knowledge when conclusive logical argumentation or scientific evidence is unavailable. Faith, therefore, performs an essential function that permits belief and action even when empirically based knowledge is unavailable.

James went on to develop a philosophy of religion, which he expounded in *The Varieties of Religious Experience.* He defined religion as the experiences of human beings insofar as they perceive themselves related to whatever they deem divine. Religion is not dependent on the existence of a transcendent, monotheistic God and does not required the presence of a religious community.

The scope, depth, and intellectual generosity of James's philosophy, coupled with the literary eloquence with which he expressed it, elevated him to the position of "father of American psychology." Arguably, he remains the single most influential American philosopher as well.

Kant, Immanuel

Kant brought eighteenth-century Western philosophy to a new height of ambition. He saw his task, as a philosopher, to answer three essential questions: "What can I know? What should I do? What may I hope?" He approached these questions through "transcendental idealism," which is founded on the idea that we live in a world consisting of what we are capable of experiencing through our senses (the natural world) and what we cannot experience sensually (the "supersensible" realm of the soul and God). True knowledge of the supersensible is impossible. All we know comes from things we can experience.

"What can I know?" The directly observable world. The realm beyond the physical, the realm contemplated in metaphysics, we cannot know.

"What should I do?" is answered via Kant's ethics, which center on his concept of a "categorical imperative," a universal ethical principle holding that one must respect the humanity in others and that one must act according to rules that could apply to everyone. Because moral law is a truth of reason, all rational creatures are bound by the same moral law. *What, then, should I do?* Act rationally, in accordance with universal moral law.

Kant's ethics form a bridge between knowledge and belief. The philosopher argues that his theory of ethics requires *belief* in free will, God, and the immortality of the soul. Of none of these can we have *knowledge*; however, to contemplate the categorical imperative of the universal moral law justifies *belief* in them. Thus, in default of knowledge, we are permitted a rational faith, and this is the answer to "What may I hope?" We are justified in hoping that there is a God and that our souls are immortal.

Kant's body of epistemological and ethical philosophy would have been an ample achievement for any philosopher, but he also created a brilliant and still-relevant theory of aesthetics, a theory of knowledge that continues to be foundational to analytic philosophy, a political theory that remains useful, and contributions to cosmology that retain relevance even in our era of advanced astrophysics.

Immanuel Kant was born on April 22, 1724 in Königsberg, Prussia (modern Kaliningrad, Russia). His parents were pietist Lutherans, a devotion against which young Kant rebelled. He studied at the Collegium Fridericianum in Königsberg and then the University of Königsberg, embarking on a course in the classics but soon focusing instead on philosophy.

Following the death of his father in 1746, Kant left the university and hired out as a private tutor for several prosperous families. In 1754, he became a *Privatdozent* (lecturer) at the University of Königsberg and made his living by this means until 1770. During this early period of his academic career, Kant published essays, wrote on astronomy, physics, and earth science, and began probing the limits of rationalism. His career goal was to be appointed Professor of Logic and Metaphysics at Königsberg, which he attained in 1770.

Shortly after he became a professor, Kant was deeply disturbed by the radical skepticism of David Hume's empirical philosophy. Anxious to write a response to Hume, Kant embarked on his first masterpiece, *Critique of Pure Reason,* which was published in 1781. This was followed in 1783 by *Prolegomena to Any Future Metaphysics*, in effect a retrospective introduction to the *Critique.* He published *Groundwork for the Metaphysics of Morals* in 1785 and *Critique of Practical Reason* in 1788. In 1786, he turned to the philosophy of science with *Metaphysical Foundations of Natural Science* and revised the *Critique of Pure Reason* in 1787. The *Critique of the Power of Judgment* appeared in 1790.

Less well-known works include *Religion within the Bounds of Bare Reason* (1793), *Towards Perpetual Peace* (1795), *Metaphysics of Morals* (1797), and *Anthropology from a Pragmatic Point of View* (1798). He was at work on a book intended to bridge philosophy and physical science, but old age impaired his thought processes, and the work was left very much unfinished and published in that incomplete form as *Opus Postumum.* He died on February 12, 1804.

The concepts of transcendental idealism and the categorical imperative are the two greatest pillars of Kant's thought.

Transcendental idealism is Kant's theory of the relation between the mind and its objects. There are three theses: First, appearances (things as they appear, or *Ding für Uns*, the thing for us) are distinct from things as they are in themselves (*Ding an Sich,* the thing itself). Second, space and time are *a priori.* They are subjective conditions that pertain to appearances, not to things in themselves. Third, we can know (have "determinate cognition of") only that which can be experienced—in other words, only appearances and not things in themselves. Transcendental idealism implies that the objects of experience are mind-dependent

To this day, Kant's distinction between the *Ding für Uns* and the *Ding an Sich* remains a subject of philosophical controversy. Some see the distinction in metaphysical and ontological terms. Appearances constitute one world (set of entities), and things in themselves are ontologically distinct from these, effectively constituting another world. Others argue that the distinction between appearances and things in themselves is to be understood in epistemological terms. The two are ontologically identical, this argument runs, the phrase "in themselves" meaning nothing more than "not considered in relation to human perceivers."

To turn to the other great pillar of Kant's thought, the categorical imperative, we must first understand what Kant means by an imperative. It is a principle that commands an action. Most imperatives are "hypothetical," functioning as commands only if certain conditions are met. *If* you want to become a successful banker, *then* you must establish a reputation for integrity and trustworthiness.

Because hypothetical imperatives are conditioned on desires and desired outcomes, they are not evidence of an unconditionally good will. For this, Kant's ethics calls for a "categorical imperative." In contrast to a conditional hypothetical imperative, a categorical imperative is universal, without condition. There is no if/then but merely *do this*. The categorical imperative is without determinate content and is therefore purely formal and universally binding. To act morally, one must act in conformance with a categorical imperative—that is, to "act only in accordance with that maxim through which you can at the same time will that it become a universal law."

Kant was the major influence on the philosophers of German Idealism but has also influenced virtually every major philosopher since the end of the eighteenth century. Beyond this, he has been a major influence on moral and political thought and in such diverse scientific fields as physics, sociology, and psychology.

Kaspi, Joseph

Born Abba Mari ibn Kaspi about 1280 in Arles, Provence, Joseph Kaspi was a rabbinical author who wrote numerous commentaries on the Old Testament. In these, he drew upon philosophy and logic to define his method of exegesis.

Kaspi traveled widely in search of knowledge, getting as far as Egypt in 1314 but suffering disappointment at finding "no scholars" there. He lived in several towns in Arles and in various Spanish locations, including Perpignan, Barcelona, Majorca, Valencia, and Tudela. He died in Majorca in 1345.

While he was in Spain, Kaspi wrote (among other things) three books on logic and linguistics. He read such philosophers as Maimonides and Samuel ibn Tibbon as well as Plato, Aristotle, Averroes, Avicenna, Boethius, and others. He approached the traditionally scholarly work of biblical exegesis with an eminently philosophical purpose, namely to bring to light the "real intention of the author of the book"—even, perhaps especially, when that author was God Himself.

He compared the act of interpretation to prophesy. For him, hermeneutics was dedicated less to "decoding" the author's writing than it was to increasing the understanding of the reader. At the same time, Kaspi stressed the importance of logic in interpretation. He defined two functions for logic. First, logic determines the correctness of things; it defines the correct way of thinking. Second, logic determines the proper use of language by aligning proper expression with laws of universal syntax that transcend any particular language. Kaspi faulted many Biblical scholars for misinterpreting Scripture because they failed to use logic, which he believed was indispensable to discovering truth. He viewed verbal expression as creating a match between "external" and "internal" speech, thereby revealing hidden thought.

Kierkegaard, Søren

Søren Kierkegaard was born on May 5, 1813 in Copenhagen, the son of a wealthy wool merchant. He studied at Copenhagen University during 1830-1840 and wrote a doctoral dissertation titled *On the Concept of Irony with Continual Reference to Socrates,* which his examiners admired yet dismissed as insufficiently formal for an academic thesis. He was nevertheless awarded the equivalent of a master's degree.

A year after taking his degree, Kierkegaard broke off his engagement to Regine Olsen, the beautiful and intelligent daughter of a Danish councilor of state. Clearly, Kierkegaard loved her but decided that his "melancholy" nature made it wrong for him to marry her. The broken engagement would haunt him and his philosophical works for the rest of his life.

After breaking the engagement, Kierkegaard spent two years in Berlin and then returned to Copenhagen in 1843. He wrote *Either/Or* (1843), which investigated problems of "aesthetic" versus "ethical" consciousness. This book may be the first work of existentialist philosophy, that is, a philosophical inquiry into how one lives as a single individual, grappling with concrete human reality, making life choices, deciding on commitments, and defining one's relationship to God.

The first part of *Either/Or* deals with aesthetic experiences, the second part with ethics. Through fictitious narrators, Kierkegaard discusses how both love and the arts inspire the imagination, which produces aesthetic pleasure. The counterargument is that living an ethical life creates a happiness that cannot be achieved through the aesthetic life. The curse of the aesthetic life is repetition, which inevitably dulls pleasure and creates boredom, the most common, and painful, human state. Ultimately, the debate between the aesthetic and ethical ways of life is adjudicated in a concluding sermon, "The Edification Which Lies in the Fact that in Relation to God We Are Always in the Wrong." Humans, the sermon declares, whether the choices they make are motivated by aesthetics or ethics, are never in the right. The only escape is to accept that God is always right. Attempt to do God's will, and you will avoid unhappiness.

Later in 1843, Kierkegaard published *Fear and Trembling*, in which he extended the array of philosophical/psychological categories he explored—anxiety, despair, melancholy, repetition, inwardness, irony, existential stages, inherited sin, teleological suspension of the ethical, Christian paradox, the absurd, reduplication, universal/exception, sacrifice, love as a duty, seduction, and the demonic—to the subject of religious faith as an absolute relation of the individual with God. In a remarkable exegesis of Genesis 22, Abraham's near-sacrifice of his son, Isaac, Kierkegaard wrote of the teleological suspension of the ethical (in which religious faith enables one to believe that an unethical action—the murder of one's son—will result in a better end) and an acceptance of the absurd: the conflict between the urge to seek inherent value and meaning in life and the conviction of life's purposelessness.

In 1849, Kierkegaard published *The Sickness unto Death*, a work of Christian existentialism in which the concept of sin is wholly defined as the sin of despair. A person is "in despair" if he fails to align himself with God or God's plan for him. He loses not only God but himself—or, more accurately, his self. He is lost between the finite and the infinite as well as the possible and the necessary. Because human beings are reflective and self-conscious, they require being both conscious of the self and conscious of being grounded in love—the creator, which is God. To deny the self or the power that creates and sustains the self is to fall into the sin of despair.

Kierkegaard was a sincere believer, who nevertheless was perpetually unsure of his faith. He believed that human beings are by nature self-reflective and that Christianity, in fact, demands self-examination and an existential transfiguration toward an absolute relation to the absolute—that is, God. He came to feel that conventional theology wrongly mediated and thus diluted this relationship, and for that reason Kierkegaard began an increasingly public and rancorous attack on the Danish People's Church, the state church of Denmark. He accused that institution of essentially failing to facilitate the spiritual life of the individual who was looking to find a direct relationship with God. As the attacks became progressively more strident, he accused the Church of attempting to replace the "single individual" with "the crowd." The dispute consumed the philosopher utterly, and in September 1855 he suffered a collapse on the street and was hospitalized. Kierkegaard never recovered. He died in Frederik's Hospital on November 11, 1855.

Kripke, Saul

Saul Aaron Kripke was born on November 13, 1940, in Bay Shore, New York. His father was a rabbi, and his mother a writer of Jewish educational books for children. Kripke grew up in Omaha, Nebraska, where his father led Beth El Synagogue, the city's only Conservative congregation. He was educated in Omaha public schools and was self-taught in Ancient Hebrew by age six, read Shakespeare's complete works at nine, and read Descartes and was solving complex math problems during elementary school. At seventeen, he wrote a completeness theorem in modal logic, which was published the following year.

He graduated from high school in 1958 and enrolled at Harvard University, from which he graduated summa cum laude in 1962 with a bachelor's degree in mathematics—his only earned academic degree. He received a Fulbright Fellowship and was appointed to the Society of Fellows in 1963.

Kripke taught briefly at Harvard but in 1968 began teaching at Rockefeller University in New York City, remaining with this institution until 1976. In 1978 he accepted a chaired professorship at Princeton University and in 2002 began teaching at the CUNY Graduate Center. He was appointed a distinguished professor of philosophy there in 2003. He holds numerous honorary degrees, is a member of the American Philosophical Society, an elected Fellow of the American Academy of Arts and Sciences and was a Corresponding Fellow of the British Academy. He was awarded the Schock Prize in Logic and Philosophy in 2001.

Kripke is best known for his work in mathematical logic, modal logic, philosophy of language, philosophy of mathematics, metaphysics, epistemology, and recursion (computability) theory. "Kripke semantics" is named for him. It is a form of relational, or frame, semantics and is a formal semantics for application to non-classical logic systems, which Kripke created during the late 1950s and early 1960s in collaboration with André Joyal.

Originally intended for application to modal logics—that is, to represent statements concerning necessity and possibility—Kripke semantics has also been used in intuitionistic logic and other non-classical systems.

In addition to his work in logic, Kripke is credited with stimulating a revival in metaphysics by positing that necessity is inherently a metaphysical notion distinct from the epistemic notion of *a priori*. He argues that there are necessary truths that are known *a posteriori*, such as the statement that water is H_2O. This led in 1970 to a Princeton lecture series, which was published ten years later as a book, *Naming and Necessity*. In this work, he attacked the Frege-Russell descriptivist theory of names (the idea that the semantic content of a proper name is identical to the descriptions associated with it by speakers) and proposed instead a causal theory of reference, in which a name refers to an object by virtue of a causal connection with the object as mediated through communities of speakers.

Kripke further contributed to the philosophy of language by proposing an original interpretation of Ludwig Wittgenstein's philosophy in *Wittgenstein on Rules and Private Language* (1982), contending that Wittgenstein's posthumously published *Philosophical Investigations* is based on a rule-following paradox that militates against the possibility of ever following rules in the use of language.

In his 1975 article "Outline of a Theory of Truth," Kripke proposed a formal alternative to Alfred Tarski's "orthodox" theory of truth. By letting truth be a partially defined property over the set of grammatically well-formed sentences in a language, Kripke demonstrated that a language can consistently contain its own truth predicate, a possibility Tarski categorically denied.

Kuhn, Thomas

Trained as a physicist, Thomas Kuhn became a philosopher of science, producing his best-known work in 1962, *The Structure of Scientific Revolutions*, which, among other things, put the history of science in a new light and introduced the concept of the "paradigm shift" into both history and intellectual history.

Kuhn was born in Cincinnati, on July 18, 1922, the son of an MIT-trained hydraulic engineer. He was educated at the progressive Lincoln School in Manhattan and the equally progressive Hessian Hills School in Croton-on-Hudson before prepping at Solebury School (New Hope, Pennsylvania) and Taft School (Watertown, Connecticut). In 1940, Kuhn enrolled at Harvard, studying philosophy before embarking on a physics major. After graduating *summa cum laude* in 1943, Kuhn worked at the Radio Research Laboratory in the war-related field of radar counter-technology. He went abroad to do work with the U.S. Office of Scientific Research and Development and began reading books on the philosophy of science.

After World War II, Kuhn received a master's degree (1946) and a Ph.D. (1949) in physics, both from Harvard. He came to realize, however, that his own ideal orientation to science was through philosophy, and in the 1950s, Kuhn began pioneering the field of the history of science. He concluded that scientific change was not simply a uniform process of new knowledge accreting over old but was a process of "normal" change that alternated with "revolutionary" change. He developed the idea of the paradigm shift, which created revolutionary change by disrupting accumulated knowledge as much as it added to it. Indeed, what came to be called "Kuhn-loss," the forgetting of seemingly outmoded scientific knowledge in the face of a paradigm shift, became recognized as a research phenomenon to be contended with.

Kuhn wrote of the sociological dimensions of scientific progress, namely the need for a scientific community with shared theoretical beliefs, values, and even techniques. He also wrote of the inherent tension in science between the conservatism imposed by the scientific method, on the one hand, and the intense drive toward continual innovation on the other. He focused on the role of the anomaly in science, and how the first inclination of the scientific community is to ignore or explain away anomalies. Only those that undermine "normal" science persist and develop into paradigm shifts, a revision of the entire disciplinary matrix of science.

In contrast to traditional philosophy, which characterizes itself as a quest for truth, Kuhn rejected a teleological view of science and saw it instead as evolutionary, a response to challenges presented by the environment rather than a progress toward some perfection. Kuhn was diagnosed with lung cancer in 1994 and died two years later, on June 17, 1996.

Laozi (Lao Tzu)

Laozi is not a proper name but an honorific meaning "Old Master." It is applied to a semi-historical, semi-legendary, or perhaps wholly legendary philosopher credited as the founder of philosophical Taoism. Insofar as Laozi may be a historical figure, he is believed to have flourished between the sixth and fourth centuries BC.

Taoism, the quasi-religious philosophical tradition with which Laozi is associated, emphasizes living in harmony with the *Tao* (*Dao*), the combined source, pattern, and substance of all that is. The short book said to have been written by Laozi is itself called the *Laozi* or *Tao Te Ching* (*Daodejing*). It is a cosmogony in which the *Tao* is described as the source/ideal of all existence. Tao is invisible but not transcendent. Powerful yet humble, it is the root of all things. Human beings, possessed of desire and free will—the ability to alter their very own nature—are free to act unnaturally, thereby disrupting the balance of the Tao. *Tao Te Ching* was written to guide students back to the natural state of harmony.

Laozi—both the (putative) person and the book—became the authority on which many non-Confucian sages drew for inspiration and guidance. The work has been especially influential on political theory, advocating humility and restraint in leadership. Without doubt, Laozi advocates limited government, even to the point of anarchy. Contemporary Libertarians have also claimed Laozi as a spiritual and intellectual forebearer.

Leibniz, Gottfried Wilhelm

One of the signature minds of the Enlightenment, Gottfried Wilhelm Leibniz is celebrated as the man who cofounded calculus with Isaac Newton, albeit independently from him. He is also remembered as a metaphysical idealist in philosophy, who theorized that reality is composed of spiritual non-interacting "monads," which have created, of necessity, the "best of all possible worlds."The core of Leibniz's philosophy concerns our method of reasoning, which is based on two principles. The principle of contradiction deems every contradiction to be false; that is, a thing cannot be both *x* and *not x* at the same time. This affirms Aristotle. The second principle is that of sufficient reason: We can find no true or existent fact, no true assertion, without there being a sufficient reason why it is thus and not otherwise—although most of these reasons cannot be known to us. In short, there is nothing without reason or cause.

Related to the principle of sufficient reason is a third principle, the principle of the best, which holds that rational beings always choose and act for the best. Reason, therefore, is teleologically oriented toward goodness, and goodness provides the sufficient reason for rational choice. Leibniz sees the principle of the best as operating—differently—in both God and man. God, an absolutely perfect being, always knows what is best and acts accordingly. Human beings are imperfect and their knowledge thus limited, yet they always act according to what seems (from their limited perspective) best.

Three more principles are central to Leibniz's philosophy.

The predicate-in-notion principle holds that in any true, affirmative proposition, the predicate is contained in the subject. The principle of the identity of indiscernibles holds that any two objects sharing all properties are in fact the same, identical object. Each individual object contains *some* individuating characteristic. Individuation is intrinsic to the individual. Finally, the principle of continuity holds that nothing takes place suddenly: nature never makes leaps. Thus, all change is continuous. This principle is essential to Leibniz's development of the infinitesimal calculus and is also significant for his metaphysics and epistemology.

Leibniz was born on July 1, 1646, in Leipzig, Germany, the son of a professor of moral philosophy at the University of Leipzig. Young Leibniz enrolled in that university in 1661 and studied briefly as well at the University of Jena in 1663. From here, he pursued a law degree and earned a doctorate from the University of Altdorf in 1666. During this latter period, he wrote a bachelor's dissertation, *A Metaphysical Disputation on the Principle of Individuation*, as well as *A Dissertation on the Art of Combinations* (a treatise on combinatorial logic) and works on legal theory.

In 1668, Leibniz was employed by the Catholic court of the Prince-Archbishop of Mainz to reform legal codes and statutes. He was tasked by the Mainz court with working on the most important philosophical and theological questions of the day and laid the groundwork for a book on the Eucharist and a modern philosophy in harmony with Christian theology. Although the latter opus was never fully realized, Leibniz did write, during 1669-1671, *Elements of Natural Law*, *Theory of Abstract Motion*, and *New Physical Hypothesis*. The last is a rebuttal of Thomas Hobbes's materialist view of the philosophy of mind. In the hindsight of maturity, Leibniz found all these youthful physical works unimpressive, but they attest nevertheless to the remarkable diversity of his interests.

In 1672, while on a diplomatic mission to Paris, Leibniz had access to the unpublished writings of Descartes and Pascal, met with leading Parisian intellectuals, and studied mathematics under the great Dutch mathematician Christiaan Huygens. He also twice visited London (1673 and 1676), meeting with mathematicians and physicists of the Royal Society. In 1676, he visited The Hague, where he met with Baruch Spinoza.

By 1675 he had fully developed his infinitesimal calculus, for which he became widely known. In 1672-1673, he wrote *Philosopher's Confession* in refutation of determinism and in an effort to justify or rationalize the existence of evil in the best of all possible worlds.

In 1676, Leibniz became court librarian to Duke Johann Friedrich of Hanover, publishing in his spare time essays on mathematics, epistemology, and physics. His *Discourse on Metaphysics* (1686) developed a philosophy reconciling physical substance and physics with God's role in the universe. In 1695, he published the first part of his *Specimen of Dynamics* and his *New System of Nature,* both works on physics. In 1703, he began writing *New Essays on Human Understanding,* a response to Locke's *Essay on Human Understanding.* His *Theodicy* of 1710 defended his provocative thesis that we live in best of all possible worlds. Four years later, he wrote *Monadology,* a comprehensive summary of his philosophy. He died, in Hanover, on November 14, 1716.

Leucippus

Remarkably little is known of Leucippus, who is generally credited with having founded atomism in Greek philosophy. Except for this historical distinction, there is little evidence to show how Leucippus' concept of atoms differs from the more famous example of Democritus, with whom he was associated.

Leucippus may have been born in Elea, Abdera, or Miletus some time during the fifth century BC. He was reportedly a student of Zeno, who was a follower of Parmenides. Just how Leucippus worked with Democritus is subject to much controversial speculation. Indeed, Epicurus may have denied the very existence of Leucippus. Yet Aristotle credits him with laying the foundation for atomism.

The atomist doctrine ascribed to Leucippus holds that the universe consists of just two elements, "the full" (or "solid") and "the empty" (or "void"). Both these elements are infinite and constitute all that is. Change, in this system, occurs only at the level of appearances, the ultimate constituents of being remaining changeless, only rearranging themselves into new combinations. As for the void, this was necessary to allow motion, and Leucippus purportedly argued that atoms are always in motion, an idea with which Aristotle found fault because Leucippus failed to account for what force produces the motion.

Leucippus formulated a cosmology in which worlds are formed by groups of atoms that coalesce in a cosmic whirl. This forces the atoms to separate out and sort themselves by like kind. The circling atoms create a membrane of atoms, which encloses others within it. The outer membrane acquires additional atoms, which take flame as they revolve. In this way, the stars were formed, with the burning sun in the outermost circle. Worlds are also formed, develop, and perish in this same process of coalescence and whirling.

Although Leucippus' cosmology seems mechanical, a quotation that has come down from him declares that nothing happens in vain but everything proceeds from *logos* and by necessity. The introduction of *logos* suggests regulation by reason, which certainly has no place in Democritus' atomism. The interpretation of the *logos* quotation remains unresolved.

Locke, John

Born on August 29, 1632, in Wrington, Somerset, England, John Locke was educated at Westminster School (1647-1652) and Christ Church, Oxford, from which he received a B.A. in 1656 and an M.A. in 1658. He joined the faculty there as a lecturer in Greek, rhetoric, and philosophy, serving during 1661-1664 while pursuing further studies in the sciences, with a concentration in medicine.

Locke was befriended by Lord Ashley (Sir Antony Ashley Cooper, future earl of Shaftesbury), whose advisor he became and under whose patronage he was appointed to several public offices. In 1668, Locke was elected a fellow of the Royal Society. He traveled and studied in France during 1675-1679 and subsequently followed Shaftesbury (fallen from royal favor) into exile in Holland. Locke lived there during 1683-1689, writing his *Essay Concerning Human Understanding*, which was published in 1690 after his return to England upon the accession of William III to the English throne.

The *Essay* created a sensation, which made Locke famous throughout Europe, and although he is most celebrated for this work, he wrote three others of significant philosophical importance: *Two Treatises on Government* (1690), *Some Thoughts Concerning Education* (1693), and *The Reasonableness of Christianity* (1695). He died, a childless bachelor, on October 28, 1704 in High Laver, Essex, England.

Locke essentially founded the Enlightenment as it was manifested in England and France. His work exercised a profound influence on virtually all subsequent philosophy and political theory, serving most famously as a model for Thomas Jefferson's draft of the American Declaration of Independence (1776).

Locke's philosophy was foundational in many respects. He was the first to define the concept of *self* as a continuity of consciousness, and, in contrast to Descartes, held that the human mind was at birth a blank slate (*tabula rasa*), void of pre-existing concepts or innate ideas. Knowledge, he postulated, was derived exclusively through experience as conveyed via sense perception. Thus, he held that knowledge is the product of empiricism. This led him to articulate a key tenet of the scientific method, whereby an assertion must be capable of repeated testing and that no assertion is immune from disproof by empirical means.

An Essay Concerning Human Understanding put forward the picture of the mind at birth as a blank slate on which experience "writes." This was the source and model of empiricism in modern philosophy and was a driving influence on the likes of David Hume and George Berkeley. The *Essay* is divided into four books, the first of which refutes the notion of innate ideas. Book II develops Locke's own theory of ideation, including a remarkable distinction between passively acquired "simple ideas" (such as colors, tastes, and shapes) and actively constructed "complex ideas." This latter category includes causes and effects, numbers, abstract concepts, and ideas concerning substances, identity, and diversity. Book II also presents Locke's provocative definition of self as a continuity of consciousness. In Book III, Locke explores language, and in Book IV addresses the nature of knowledge, including such categories as intuition, morals, science, faith, opinion, and mathematics.

Locke's *Two Treatises of Government* presents a critique of patriarchalism as government on false principles (the first treatise) and counters with "true original" government in the second treatise. The basis for this is the concept of natural rights and a theory of contract.

Some Thoughts Concerning Education was deemed, on its publication in 1693, the most important philosophical work on education in England and was quickly and widely translated. Locke created a progressive theory of education founded on his empirical view that all knowledge is acquired through experience. He addressed the connection between body and mind, the use of education to instill virtue in children and the connection of virtue to reason, and he prescribed a quite specific curriculum for schools.

Finally, in *The Reasonableness of Christianity,* Locke presented an argument justifying the Bible in its entirety as perfectly consonant with human reason. It is thus a conservative, even conventional view of religion. Nevertheless, Locke advocated here a liberal toleration of a wide range of religious beliefs—including the doctrine of religious freedom—but drew the line at atheism, arguing that denying the existence of God catastrophically undermines the social order.

Lucretius

Known at least as much for his literary merits as for his Epicurean philosophy, Titus Lucretius Carus left to posterity only one known work, *De rerum natura* (*On the Nature of Things*), a poem of some 7,400 lines in dactylic hexameter, which brought Epicurean philosophy to Roman readers. While the subject is didactic, the verse is eminently poetic, rich with metaphor and considerable beauty of language.

As philosophy, the work offers the theory of atomism, a disquisition on mind and soul, an account of sensation and thought, and the evolution of the world and the multitudinous phenomena associated with it. *De rerum natura* also ventures beyond this planet to explain various celestial phenomena. As Lucretius describes it, the universe operates on certain physical principles and is guided not by the traditional Roman gods and goddesses but by *fortuna,* chance.

Lucretius takes an evolutionary view not only of cosmology but of human historical and cultural development. He discusses man's mastery of materials, tools, and weapons, beginning in prehistory and proceeding to the present. He portrays an evolution of hands, nails, and teeth as the first weapons to stones, branches, and fire and thence to the use of metal in fashioning more destructive weapons as well as useful tools and agricultural implements.

Of special interest is Locke's panoramic presentation of human social evolution, from a bestial and nomadic state, through a period of huts and rudimentary clothing, to the emergence of families and city-states. He does not credit the genius of humankind with learning the art of smelting (the use of heat to extract metal from ore) but sees it as a development that resulted from an accidental fire, perhaps created by lightning. Lucretius is believed to be the first writer to theorize that humanity evolved in part through successive ages dominated first by the use of wood and stone, followed by copper and bronze, and, lastly, iron. The theory was not popular until the Danish antiquarian Christian Jürgensen Thomsen (1788-1865) systematized it as the "three ages" of man in 1834.

Born about 99 BC, Lucretius died about 55 BC.

Machiavelli, Niccolò

Born on May 3, 1469 in Florence, Italy, Machiavelli is most famous for *Il Principe* (*The Prince*), which he wrote in 1513 and dedicated to Lorenzo di Piero de' Medici, a work that has earned him the title of father of modern political philosophy.

Machiavelli was the son of an impoverished lawyer named Bernardo Machiavelli. In 1498, the young man advanced in the government of the Florentine Republic, becoming head of the second chancery after the execution of Cirolamo Savonarola. As secretary to the magistracy of the *Signoria* (Florentine grand council) during 1500-1502, Machiavelli became intimately involved in the complex workings of diplomacy and power politics. After Piero di Tommaso Soderini (1450-1522) was elected *gonfalonier* (chief executive) for life, Machiavelli became his principal assistant in 1502. In this capacity, he crafted and engineered passage of a militia law that created a 10,000-man citizen army for Florence in December 1505. The following year, he became secretary to the Council of Nine, the body that controlled the militia. He personally commanded the militia in operations against Pisa and was instrumental in forcing that city to surrender on June 8, 1509.

Machiavelli went on to play a leading role in the diplomatic and military maneuvering preparatory to the War of the Holy League during 1510-1511 but was ejected from his offices after Florence fell to a Papal-Spanish army and the Medici were restored to power in 1512. Cast into prison and tortured there on suspicion of sedition and treason, he was at length released for lack of evidence.

He composed *The Prince* but retired from public life in 1513, living on his modest estate, Sant'Angelo, just outside Florence. While *The Prince*, composed at the beginning of this period, is his most famous work, he devoted the succeeding fourteen years to study and writing, producing *Discourses on Livy* (1516-1519) and *The Art of War* (1520), as well as a number of plays, works of fiction, and poems.

During the 1520s, Machiavelli won favor with Cardinal Giulio de' Medici, through whom he obtained the post of official historian of Florence in November 1520. During the period of this appointment he wrote *The History of Florence* (1521-1525) while also serving on numerous minor diplomatic missions. Appointed secretary to the inspectors of fortifications in April 1526, he marched with the Papal army in 1526-1527, returning to Florence after the sack of Rome in May 1527. Unable to find a place in the new republican government that had replaced the Medici in Florence, Machiavelli declined in health and died on June 21, 1527.

The Prince lays out the tasks of a "new"—that is, non-hereditary—prince, who must hold his freshly acquired power by building his state on an enduring political structure to create needed stability and security. This public benefit may require personally unscrupulous actions, which the prince should make boldly on the assumption that it is better to be feared than loved. Whereas a loved ruler holds power through the people's sense of obligation toward him, the feared leader wields the more compelling motive of fear of punishment.

Machiavelli postulated that the "necessity" of acquiring and holding power to create a stable state requires the systematic and methodical application of brute force and deceit. All comers who challenge the prince's power make themselves liable for their own destruction. Machiavelli championed the notion of strategic overkill. To block others' ascension to power, he advocated killing not merely the rival but his family, members of which might claim revenge or right of rule through inheritance. When power is at stake, the ends unconditionally justify the means, even to the point of genocide.

The amoral elevation of power—and stability—over all other considerations earned the philosophy of *The Prince* the adjective *Machiavellian*. At one point, the Catholic Church banned the book. The rising Humanists of the Renaissance, Erasmus among them, condemned it bitterly as well. The book has come to define political "realism" versus political "idealism," as presented by the likes of Plato and Aristotle.

Maimonides (Moses ben Maimon)

Maimonides codified Jewish law, shaped in the Middle Ages a large body of Jewish thought, and was a provocative philosopher, whose views on the relation of reason to revelation stirred controversy among his contemporaries and continues to do so today. His influence extended not only to Jewish theology and philosophy but to the philosophy of such diverse thinkers as Aquinas and Leibniz.

Born in Córdoba, Spain, in March or April 1135, Maimonides soon fled growing anti-Semitic persecution, finally settling in North Africa. Maimonides briefly visited the Holy Land but spent much of his mature career in Fostat, the "Old City" of Cairo. Throughout his early struggles, Maimonides and his family depended on the income produced by his younger brother, a merchant. When the brother was lost at sea, Maimonides, seeking a living, turned to the practice of medicine, becoming physician to the Grand Vizier of Egypt. During this time, he wrote major works on Jewish law but refused payment for them on the grounds that the work was a sacred duty.

Maimonides also wrote on medicine and science. He produced *Mishneh Torah*, a still-influential codification of Jewish law, but his *Guide for the Perplexed,* written about 1190, in Arabic using the Hebrew alphabet, is his philosophical masterwork, a bold endeavor to reconcile Aristotelian rationality with rabbinical theology.

The first of the *Guide*'s three books begins with an argument against anthropomorphism in the conception of God. In support of his argument,

Maimonides conducts an intensive hermeneutic analysis of Scripture to prove the incorporeality of God and, what is more, the philosophical concept that God cannot be described in any positive terms at all but only in negatives—what God is not.

Book Two opens with an essentially Aristotelian cosmology, which argues against Aristotle's view that the universe is eternal but which appropriates Aristotle's proofs of the existence of God, especially the concept of God as the Prime Mover. Maimonides goes on to associate natural forces and the heavenly spheres with the idea of angels as forms of pure intelligence.

Book Two includes a discussion of prophecy, which Maimonides defines in unorthodox terms as a vision interpreted through a prophet's intellect. Maimonides holds that many aspects of prophesy are metaphors, as in the narratives of God speaking with a prophet. Moreover, he concludes that all prophesy, save that of Moses, is the product of natural law. He goes on to describe eleven hierarchical levels of prophecy, with that of Moses being beyond the highest and closest to God.

Book Three begins with an exegesis of the Chariot in Ezekiel. Maimonides explains the mystical elements of this material with reference to cosmology—the Spheres, the elements, and the Intelligences. This is followed by an analysis of the moral aspects of the universe, including the problem of evil, trials and tests (citing Job and the story of the binding of Isaac), and the topics of providence and omniscience.

Book III ends with the idea of achieving a perfect and harmonious life through the correct worship of God, which is attained when one correctly understands the rational philosophy that supports Judaism.

A measure of the *Guide*'s power as philosophy is the mixed reception it received and continues to receive, with some greeting it as a much-needed intellectual and spiritual triumph and others branding it as the vision of a heretic. The *Guide* was frequently banned and even burned. As Aristotelian thought has receded into historical perspective, Maimonides' place as the archetypal Jewish philosopher has become secure and authoritative. It continues to be much studied, especially among the Orthodox. The philosopher's death, on December 12, 1204, in Fostat, was widely mourned by Jews as well as Muslims, who respected him as physician and a thinker.

Mao Zedong

Mao Zedong was born on December 26, 1893, in Shaoshan, Hunan, the son of a land-owning and prosperous peasant family. At the local elementary school, he received a classical Chinese education, which included liberal exposure to Confucian philosophy and literature. He left school in October 1911, after forces under Sun Yat-sen overthrew the Ch'ing (or Manchu) dynasty. He attended a commercial school during 1912-1913 and during 1913-1918 lived in Changsha, where he attended the local normal school. In 1919, he became a teacher at the Changsha Normal School, and in 1921 served as Hunan's chief delegate to the founding congress of the Chinese Communist Party (CCP). He rose through the ranks of the party and emerged as a leader of the resistance against the Japanese invaders during World War II and in the Chinese Communist Revolution of 1945-1950, which resulted in the proclamation of the People's Republic of China on October 1, 1949.

Mao's intellectual development embodied a strong element of political philosophy, beginning with his embrace of Marxism during 1920-1926. While Mao was enthusiastic about Karl Marx's socioeconomic explanation of political change, he believed that educating people about Marxism was not sufficient to bring about regime change without the violent overthrow of the current political leaders, which would create a vacuum that Communism would replace.

From 1927 to 1935, Mao moved away from classical Marxism and created what would come to be called Maoism. Mao continued to write about the "Marxist method of political and class analysis," but he was concerned to close the gap between revolutionary ideology and conditions that continued to create counterrevolutionary opposition. Accordingly, during the period 1936-1940, he began to formulate an application of Marxist theory that, as he saw it, was uniquely suited to the Chinese situation. Marxism was tailored to industrialized nations and targeted industrial workers as the revolutionary vanguard. Mao adapted this political philosophy to China's essentially agricultural or pre-industrial society, targeting the peasanty, not the proletariat, as the revolutionary vanguard.

During 1940-1949, which included World War II and the beginning of the Cold War that followed, Mao redefined his philosophical relation to classical Marxism, explaining that "The target is the Chinese revolution, the arrow is Marxism–Leninism. We Chinese communists seek this arrow for no other purpose than to hit the target of the Chinese revolution and the revolution of the east." Thus, Marxism was but a weapon, a means to an end—the end being a Maoist revolution. This he increasingly defined as an abandonment of Marxist revolutionary theory (which Mao derided as dogmatic) and an embrace instead of empirical pragmatism guided by ideological commitment.

The post-revolutionary period, 1949-1976, confirmed Mao in his revisionist application of Marxism as Maoism. His chief project came to be the resolution of the contradiction between subjective thought (idealism) and objective reality (materialism). Marx would have seen this as a Hegelian instance of thesis meeting antithesis and creating synthesis. Maoism required, more simply, accepting the subject-object, idealist/materialist contradiction as a universal principle underlying all great processes of development. Accepting a core of contradiction proved increasingly difficult, however, and in 1966, Mao launched the Cultural Revolution aimed at purging remnants of capitalism and traditionalism from Chinese society through relentless agitation and violence.

Marx, Karl

At the funeral of Karl Marx, who died on March 14, 1883, poor and mostly forgotten, his friend and collaborator Friedrich Engels (1820–1895), coauthor of *The Communist Manifesto*, delivered a eulogy. It is a fair statement of what would prove to be the magnitude of this economist-philosopher's disruptive transformation of social thought:

> Just as Darwin discovered the law of development of organic nature, so Marx discovered the law of development of human history: the simple fact, hitherto concealed by an overgrowth of ideology, that mankind must first of all eat, drink, have shelter and clothing, before it can pursue politics, science, art, religion, etc.; that therefore the production of the immediate material means, and consequently the degree of economic development attained by a given people or during a given epoch, form the foundation upon which the state institutions, the legal conceptions, art, and even the ideas on religion, of the people concerned have been evolved, and in the light of which they must, therefore, be explained, instead of vice versa, as had hitherto been the case.

It is significant that Engels compared Marx to Charles Darwin, who explained biological evolution, but it was even bolder for Engels to go on to compare Marx with Isaac Newton. Like Newton, Marx "discovered the special law of motion," a law "governing the present-day capitalist mode of production, and the bourgeois society that this mode of production has created." This was a reference to the concept of "surplus value," which Marx defined as the increase in the value of capital that results when workers add their labor to it. This "surplus value" is commonly called *profit*, and it is entirely appropriated by the capitalist when the products of labor are sold. In societies in which capitalists own the means of production, workers are exploited by being deprived of any share of the surplus value they create. Thus, the foundation of capitalist civilization is theft and therefore inherently corrupt.

Engels celebrated Marx as a scientist. In a sense, he was what scientists were commonly called even in the nineteenth century—a natural philosopher. Today, he is considered a political philosopher, a philosopher of economics, and a philosopher of history. But Engels's identification of him as a natural philosopher was also accurate, since Marx's philosophy put the analysis of politics, economics, and history on a par with natural science. Thus, Marx was a truly transformative philosopher. Even more, his philosophical work had an impact on the "real" world—the world of politics and economics—that the intellectual and imaginative products of few thinkers ever achieve. He created global revolution and laid the ideological foundation of communism, a political philosophy that argued for an end to nations and nationalities and the beginning of a global commonwealth based on the universal value of labor.

Karl Heinrich Marx was born on May 5, 1818, into a middle-class family in Trier, Germany. His parents were descended from rabbis, but his father, Heinrich, sought baptism as a Lutheran to retain his position as a prominent attorney. Marx set out to emulate his father, enrolling in the Faculty of Law at the University of Bonn. He also became engaged to Jenny von Westphalen, daughter of Baron von Westphalen, who was highly placed in Trier society. But a reading of the works of Claude Henri de Rouvroy, comte de Saint-Simon (1760–1825), a political philosopher who predicted social evolution toward equality based on a universal, international union of working people, stirred his political consciousness. He left the University of Bonn and the study of law to study philosophy at the University of Berlin, where he became a devotee of Georg Wilhelm Friedrich Hegel (1770–1831), especially his analytical method of thesis, antithesis, and synthesis and his concept of the master-slave dialectic. Marx became active in the Young Hegelian movement, which was opposed to Christianity and the Prussian autocracy.

Alignment with the Young Hegelians disqualified Marx from an academic career, so he turned to journalism, becoming the editor, in October 1842, of the *Rheinische Zeitung*, a liberal newspaper based in Cologne. When his articles offended the Prussian government, the authorities shut down the newspaper, which sent Marx in flight to Paris. There, he edited the short-lived *Deutsch-Französische Jahrbücher*, which combined the interests of French socialists and radical German Hegelians. He also became a communist and developed a humanist version of communism based on contrasting the alienated nature of labor under capitalism with the engaged state of labor as it would be under communism. In Paris, Marx met Engels, with whom he developed a lifelong friendship and intellectual collaboration.

Marx was so vocal in his radicalism that the French government expelled him at the end of 1844. With Engels, he moved to Brussels, where he began studying history in the light of economic theory and Hegelian philosophy. This led him to develop one of his key philosophical concepts, "materialism." As explained in *The German Ideology* (composed at this time but published posthumously), materialism viewed history as being created by "the material conditions determining . . . production."

In Brussels, he also joined the Communist League, and when members convened in London at the end of 1847, they commissioned Marx and Engels to write a declaration of their organization's position. This was *The Communist Manifesto* of 1848, the very year in which all Europe was swept by a tidal wave of revolution, in part driven by Marx's journalism and intellectual presence.

Marx moved back to Paris and then returned to Germany, where he founded, again in Cologne, the *Neue Rheinische Zeitung*, which took a radical democratic line against the Prussian autocracy. The paper was quickly shuttered, and Marx fled to London in May 1849. Rejoining the Communist League, he wrote two long pamphlets on the 1848 revolution in France and its aftermath, *The Class Struggles in France* and *The 18th Brumaire of Louis Bonaparte*. He argued that the revolution would come, just as soon as some crisis ignited it. In the meantime, he and his family—his wife, Jenny, and their four children—lived in abject poverty in London's Soho.

Marx began work on a radical and comprehensive study of political economy, hoping to articulate the nature of the coming revolutionary crisis. By 1857, he had produced a manuscript of 800 pages, which he called the *Grundrisse* ("Outlines") of what he projected as a study of the nature of capital, real property, wage labor, the state, foreign trade, and the world market. Laying aside the *Grundrisse*, however, he turned to writing *Theories of Surplus Value*, a three-volume essay in political philosophy, including extensive analyses of the father of capitalist economic theory, Adam Smith (1723–1790), and David Ricardo (1772–1823), one of the founders of classical economics.

In 1867, Marx began mining the material in *Grundrisse* and wrote the first volume of his masterpiece: *Das Kapital* (*Capital*). It was nothing less than a materialist history of Western civilization. The next two volumes, which with the first comprised the complete book, were essentially finished during the 1860s, but Marx would not let them go, and they were published posthumously.

In *Capital*, Marx developed his philosophical analysis of the relationship of labor to capital and his theory of surplus value, which explained the historical oppression of the proletariat (working classes) by the bourgeoisie (capitalists). *Capital* predicted the inevitability of the collapse of industrial capitalism due to the inescapable decline in the rate of profit built on surplus value. Marx envisioned social conflict as the playing-out on the world stage of Hegel's process of *thesis* versus *antithesis*. What Marx saw as the crisis of this conflict, a crisis that history itself made inevitable, was the *synthesis* that would bring an end to industrial capitalism.

Marx became thoroughly obsessed with *Capital* and its role in guiding a global revolution. In the meantime, he struggled with other writing projects to keep his impoverished family afloat. He devoted much time and effort to the First International Workingmen's Association—more simply, the First International—to whose General Council he was elected when it was founded in 1864. He became caught up in its internal struggles and the rapid decline of the organization that followed. He saw a ray of hope in the Paris Commune of 1871, but it proved fleeting, and from the early 1870s, Marx was afflicted with deteriorating health. He died in relative obscurity, but the faithful Engels enabled the publication of the complete *Capital,* which become a philosophical handbook of the communist revolutions that swept through the twentieth century. For a time, during that epoch, half of the world lived under governments proclaiming themselves "Marxist."

Melissus of Samos

The last of the Eleatic philosophers—Pre-Socratics active in Elea (modern Velia, Italy) early in the fifth century BC—Melissus of Samos, along with Zeno and Parmenides, argued that reality is eternal: ungenerated, indestructible, indivisible, changeless, and motionless. Going beyond Parmenides, Melissus argued that it is also infinite in every direction and, therefore, unitary: one.

All that remains of Melissus' work is *On Nature,* fragmentarily preserved in a few summaries and in commentaries on Aristotle by Simplicius of Cilicia (c. 490-c. 560). Moreover, little is known of his life. It is believed he was born about 500 BC, but his death date is entirely a mystery. Plutarch, in his *Life of Pericles,* notes that Melissus commanded the Samian fleet in the Samian War (440-439 BC).

From what fragments we have of *On Nature,* we can conclude that Melissus' concept of the universe was infinite and (in contrast to Parmenides) wholly unlimited. Moreover, while Parmenides conceived of being as a timeless present, Melissus described it as eternal. Melissus calls *being* "The One" and tries to create a conceptual timeline for its eternal nature. That is, he argues that whatever comes to be must have a beginning, but The One did not come to be, so cannot have a beginning and is therefore eternal in that it has always existed in the past. Moreover, that which has a beginning must also have an end. Because The One had no beginning, it will not end but will always exist in the future.

Parmenides defines eternity as an eternal present; that is, only the moment exists. In contrast, Melissus conceptualizes eternity as an infinity of moments. Critics of Melissus fault his reasoning on a deductive basis in that he does not solve all the formal problems created by arguing for a changeless, motionless, infinite *succession* of moments, a position that poses inherent self-contradiction.

Among Melissus' sharpest critics was Aristotle, who cited invalid arguments proceeding from false assumptions. Nevertheless, Melissus' philosophy was influential on atomism and was the representation of Eleatic philosophy used in the writings of Plato and Aristotle.

Mencius (Mengzi)

Considered by many the "Second Sage," after Confucius, his intellectual progenitor, Mencius was a counselor during the Warring States period of Chinese history (475-221 BC) and is best known for his theory that human beings are essentially good, but that their goodness requires deliberate cultivation. His political philosophy was founded on a concept of servant leadership by which rulers had always to justify the legitimacy of their authority through benevolence toward their subjects.

Mencius, whose birth name was Mengzi or Meng Ke, was born in 372 BC in Zou (modern Zoucheng, Shandong, China) and earned a reputation as a traveling interpreter of Confucianism. He was a government official in the State of Qi from 319 to 312 BC but retired from public life when he came to believe that his counsel had no effect on the world around him. He died in 289 BC and is buried in "Mencius Cemetery" near the city of Zoucheng.

Mencius' philosophical writings cover three broad areas: theodicy, government, and human nature.

Mencius' theodicy, his vindication of God's goodness in the context of the existence of evil, tracks closely with that of Confucius. *Tian* (God) links the deity with both fate and nature and can be used to justify aspects of rule. As Mencius conceives it, Tian is both extrahuman and absolutely powerful. Aligned with the morally good, Tian nevertheless relies on human beings to manifest its will on earth. This is the basis of Mencius' justification of the ways of Tian to man.

Mencius' philosophy of government flows from his theodicy. Earthly rulers are the human agents of the will of Tian. This said, the satisfaction of the people is the earthly measure of a ruler's legitimacy—the source of his moral right to rule. This position, however, is compatible with a government presided over by a benevolent despot.

In terms of human nature, Mencius believed that its essence was goodness, which he defines in three philosophical dimensions: teleology, theory of virtue, moral psychology.

In teleological terms, Mencius sees human nature as motivated by empathy, the existence of a consciousness that feels for others. He bases this assumption on experience and reason. The distress of a child, he notes, is almost invariably answered by selfless aid from adults. This demonstrates the quality of empathy. He reasons that, in the absence of empathy, a person is not human.

Empathy—the "heart-mind" that feels for others—produces four cardinal virtues: sympathy, shame, deference, and judgment, which give rise to the "sprouts" of co-humanity, rightness, ritual propriety, and wisdom. His explanation is a compound of a kind of physiology of vital energy (*qi*) and mysticism, which may have been related to a yoga-like meditative regimen of positive self-cultivation aimed at developing one's heart-mind. Through its proper development, Mencius asserts, one comes to know one's own nature and, through this self-knowledge, comes to know Tian.

Mill, John Stuart

John Stuart Mill was a prolific Victorian philosopher, who wrote in the fields of logic, epistemology, economics, social and political philosophy, ethics, metaphysics, religion, and current affairs. He was most influential for his elaboration of the philosophy of Jeremy Bentham into what Mill termed Utilitarianism, which is the title of one of Mill's major works. Additional major treatises include *A System of Logic*, *Principles of Political*

Economy, On Liberty, The Subjection of Women, Three Essays on Religion, and his *Autobiography.*

Mill was born on May 20, 1806 in London, the son of historian and economist James Mill, who was a close associate of Jeremy Bentham, with whom he collaborated in the development of utilitarianism. The senior Mill was a founder of philosophical radicalism, which rejected philosophical—and legal—naturalism and supported Bentham's utilitarian philosophy.

John Stuart's father gave him a thorough and greatly accelerated education, and in 1820-1821, the young Mill spent a year of study in France with the family of Jeremy Bentham's brother, Sir Samuel Bentham. He then read law preparatory to taking a position under his father at East India Company in 1823. He rose rapidly to the position of chief examiner.

In 1822, under the sway of Bentham's doctrines, John Stuart Mill founded the Utilitarian Society, a political and philosophical discussion group and assumed the de facto leadership of the philosophical radicals. During this period, he wrote for the leading periodicals and, years later, published his *System of Logic* (1843), *Principles of Political Economy* (1848), *On Liberty* (1854), and *Considerations on Representative Government* (1861). Much of the writing elaborated on utilitarian theories of ethics, government, and economics, injecting into Victorian politics a new emphasis on the role of government in addressing human needs and human welfare.

As a social reformer, Mill was greatly influenced by his wife, the former Harriet Hardy, widow of John Taylor, and a feminist. She and Mill married in 1851, and she died in 1858. Later, as a member of House of Commons during 1865-1868, Mill voted with the radicals and, in *The Subjection of Women* (1869), presented a cogent argument for equality of the sexes.

Mill retired to Avignon, France, where he completed his *Autobiography,* which revealed both his unorthodox education and the emotional toll of his intellectual exertions. The book was published posthumously in 1873, his having died on May 8 of that year.

Of his primarily philosophical works, his first major book was his 1843 *A System of Logic,* which is a key contribution to the philosophy of science and is an empirical justification for Mill's own moral philosophy. He formulates five principles of inductive reasoning ("Mill's Methods"), the direct method of agreement, the method of difference, the joint method of agreement and difference, the method of residue, and the method of concomitant variations.

In 1859 came his iconic *On Liberty,* in which Mill defines the nature and limits of the power that society may legitimately exercise over the individual. He identifies the struggle between liberty and authority as the driver central to much of history and sees it as a contest between subjects or between some classes of subjects and the government. He defines the concept of social liberty as protection from political tyranny, which includes the tyranny of the majority. Liberty itself is the right of the individual to be free to do what he or she wishes, provided that it harms no one. This liberty extends to freedom of speech, which, Mill argues, is essential to advancing society. His confident belief is that the public will ultimately "filter" the wrong and the harmful from speech. The limit of free speech and of individual liberty is defined by the "harm principle." A government may act to suppress the liberty of an individual insofar as doing so prevents harm to others.

In 1863, Mill's *Utilitarianism* set forth what is generally regarded as the most complete and refined exposition of the Utilitarian philosophy and ethics. He not only defined the philosophy but argued that it was, quite simply, the best theory of ethics, and he set out to defend it against a wide range of attacks and criticisms. The book was instrumental in popularizing the Utilitarian point of view and had great influence over political scientists, government, and politicians.

While Mill's *Principles of Political Economy* (1848) is claimed chiefly by economists rather than philosophers—it is, after all, a comprehensive textbook of economics—its holistic view of production, distribution, exchange, and the roles of society and government in these matters is very different from the economics textbooks of today. In place of mathematically supported discussion of the mechanics of economics, Mill adopts a sweeping intellectual view with a vision and even a grandeur that characterizes the work of some of history's great philosophers.

Mill was the embodiment of the practitioner of applied philosophy and stands as one of the foundational philosophers of both Utilitarianism and liberalism in modern Western thought.

Montaigne, Michel de

Born on February 28, 1533 at Chateau de Montaigne, near Bordeaux, Michel de Montagne is more widely known as a literary figure, the originator of the prose essay, than as a philosopher, but his three books of essays are, in fact, an intellectual venture into free judgment, skepticism, and relativism. The foundation of all the essays is an attempt to answer one of the most basic of philosophical questions, *What do I know?* It was his extremely skeptical version of *What is truth?*

Montaigne grew up in a merchant family only recently ennobled and was taught to speak Latin before French. He studied at College de Guyenne at Bordeaux during 1539-1546 and then embarked on the study of law. He became a judge in Bordeaux, serving on the bench from 1555 to 1570. In 1569, a year before he retired from his judicial post, he published a translation of *Theologia Naturalis* of the fifteenth-century Catalan philosopher Raymond of Sabunde (1569). From 1572, he wrote his *Essays, the* first of books I and II appearing in 1580, and the final revised edition of books I, II, and III posthumously, in 1595.

Montaigne served as mayor of Bordeaux from 1581 to 1585 and was occasionally an ambassador for Henry of Navarre. He died, at Montaigne, on September 13, 1592.

The *Essays*—in French, *essais* means "attempts"—are efforts at self-description and, as such, appear to move in a stream-of-consciousness manner from one topic to another. Yet even as he seems to write about random things, Montaigne discuses each with great coherence of thought. Two themes are common to virtually all the essays: skepticism and relativism. Both themes are inherently subversive of much received wisdom, such as the superiority of European culture versus primitive or barbaric peoples or the superiority of human beings to animals.

In his "Apology for Raymond of Sabunde," Montaigne explores skepticism in the form of Pyrrohnism (the fourth century BC philosophy of Pyrrho), which posits the suspension of judgment because certainty in knowledge is unattainable. Montaigne struggled to find in Pyrrohnism a way to cope with the uncertainty of knowledge through attaining *ataraxia,* a state of equanimity that enables *eudaimonia,* or happiness. Thus, while the question "What do I know?" was essentially unanswerable, it did launch Montaigne on an effort to find a viable way of life despite uncertainty. This has given his work not so much a timeless quality as a modern, existential quality, and Montaigne has exerted an influence on the diverse likes of Francis Bacon, René Descartes, Blaise Pascal, Jean-Jacques Rousseau, Albert Hirschman, William Hazlitt, Ralph Waldo Emerson, Friedrich Nietzsche, Stefan Zweig, Eric Hoffer, and Isaac Asimov.

Montesquieu, Charles-Louis de Secondat, Baron de La Brède et de Montesquieu

Montesquieu was born at Chateau de La Brède, near Bordeaux on January 18, 1689, into a noble family of lawyers. From 1700 to 1705, he attended Oratorian College de Juilly, and then studied law in Bordeaux from 1705 to 1708 and in Paris from 1708 to 1713. He served in the *parlement* of Bordeaux from 1714 to 1726, and in 1716 was elevated to membership in the Académie de Bordeaux.

Prior to the publication of his most celebrated literary work, *Persian Letters* (1721), a satirical epistolary novel on the philosophical theme of the virtual impossibility of self-knowledge, Montesquieu devoted himself mainly to scientific research. After the novel made him a celebrity, he became a fixture in Parisian intellectual circles and the social establishment. In 1728, he was elected to L'Académie française and launched himself on a tour of the Continent (1728-1729) and a two-year sojourn in England (1729-1731).

After returning to France, he spent most of his time at his ancestral seat, La Brède, researching and writing his monumental history, *Considerations on the Causes of the Greatness of the Romans and Their Decline* (1734) and his philosophical masterwork, *The Spirit of the Laws* (1748). This latter work sets out to explain the nature and basis of laws and of social institutions.

Montesquieu begins by contrasting physical laws, which are decreed and upheld by God, with laws and social institutions created by imperfect and utterly fallible human beings, who are not only subject to error but are driven by "impetuous passions." Thus, from a philosophical point of view, the project of *The Spirit of the Laws* seems impossible, given the experience of humanity as recorded in a catalog of human folly. Without denying human fallibility, Montesquieu argues that the chaos of human laws and social institution is only apparent, and that these things are far more comprehensible than is apparent.

Montesquieu holds that the underlying spirit of the laws can be understood only if one accepts that, properly conceived, laws are adapted to the people for whom they are created, and not just that, but to the nature of each government, the climate of the country, the quality of its soil, its geography, and the principal occupation of its people. The laws and institutions should be related to "the degree of liberty which the constitution will bear" and to the prevailing religion of the people as well as to "their inclinations, riches, numbers, commerce, manners, and customs." Understand all the characteristics of the people for whom a set of laws is framed, and the spirit that animates them becomes thoroughly comprehensible.

Montesquieu believed that one needed to understand the spirit of the laws in relation to a particular people and place rather than attempt simply to graft one set of utopian laws onto everyone everywhere. He was concerned to discourage misguided attempts at absolute reform. Montesquieu was by no means a utopian philosopher, but he believed that a proper government is stable and non-despotic, giving law-abiding citizens a high degree of freedom in harmony with the specific conditions of the country and its culture.

Montesquieu would have bristled at any attempt to classify him as radical, yet his view of laws and society was radically relativistic, and he denied, in matters of human law, most absolutes. This made him a highly controversial figure, and he was thus obliged to spend the last seven years of his life defending *The Spirit of the Laws* against politicians on both the right and the left and from attacks by the Roman Catholic Church, which placed the book on its infamous Index of Forbidden Books. He died, in Paris, of fever on February 10, 1755.

Moore, G[eorge] E[dward]

Born on November 4, 1873, in London, G. E. Moore enrolled in Trinity College, Cambridge to study classics but met Bertrand Russell, then a philosophy student two years ahead of him, and Philosophy Fellow J. M. E. McTaggart. Both encouraged Moore to pursue philosophy, which he immediately added to his classics focus. In 1896, he graduated with a First Class degree in philosophy and emulated both Russell and McTaggart by winning, in 1898, a Fellowship at Trinity College. This enabled him to continue studying philosophy there.

Moore moved steadily away from British idealism and toward the analytic tradition, taking Russell with him. Moore's fellowship ended in 1904, and in 1911 he was appointed to a lectureship at his alma mater. Except for an American sojourn during 1940-1944, he lived and worked in Cambridge for the rest of his life and career.

Moore began editing *Mind*, the preeminent British philosophical journal, in 1921 and, four years later, was appointed a full professor. He was now widely regarded as the most important British philosopher of the age. When Ludwig Wittgenstein returned to Cambridge after 1929, the university became peerless as a world-renowned center of philosophy. Moore retired as a professor in 1939 and was succeeded by Wittgenstein. Moore stepped down as editor of *Mind* in 1944.

Moore was a true humanist intellectual, who was associated with London's celebrated Bloomsbury Group, which included the literary luminaries Lytton Strachey, E. M. Forster, and Virginia and Leonard Woolf, as well as the great economist John Maynard Keynes. As a philosopher, Moore was best known for his work in ethics, publishing in 1903 *Principia Ethica,* which set out to prove that "good" is essentially impossible to define. In this, he coined the term "naturalistic fallacy" to describe the consequences of confusing the use of a term in a specific argument with the definition of the term in all arguments. While it is possible to define a certain thing as good, the property of goodness itself remains indefinable. He went on to argue that good is a non-natural property and thus not within the bounds of natural science. Questions of goodness, therefore, could be answered only by appeal to what Moore described as "moral intuitions."

Moore stood against both idealism and skepticism, arguing in his influential 1925 essay "A Defence of Common Sense" that neither idealists nor skeptics could provide reasons for accepting that their metaphysical premises with respect to the external world were more plausible than the force of common sense. He formulated "Moore's paradox," in which certain statements that are paradoxical and appear absurd nevertheless can be true, are logically consistent, and are not contradictions. For instance, the sentence "It is raining, but I don't believe it is raining" can be true, is not logically inconsistent, and is not contradictory. Philosophy has yet to provide an explanation for the paradox.

As an advocate of commonsense concepts, Moore cast a fresh light on ethics as well as epistemology and metaphysics, at once defining the limitations of philosophical idealism while simultaneously elevating the human mind to the status of an organ quite sufficient to understanding the world external to it. He died on October 24, 1958.

Murdoch, Iris

Best known as a novelist who wrote powerful works on themes of feminism, sexual politics, and morality—including *The Bell* (1958), *A Severed Head* (1961), *The Red and the Green* (1965), *The Nice and the Good* (1968), *The Black Prince* (1973), *Henry and Cato* (1976), *The Sea, the Sea* (1978, Booker Prize), *The Philosopher's Pupil* (1983), *The Good Apprentice* (1985), *The Book and the Brotherhood* (1987), *The Message to the Planet* (1989), and *The Green Knight* (1993), among others—Iris Murdoch was trained as a philosopher and is today widely recognized for her work in ethics and morality as well as on the philosophy of Aristotle and Plato.

Born in Phibsborough, Dublin, Ireland, on July 15, 1919, Murdoch was the only child of a civil servant father and a mother who had been trained as a singer. Murdoch moved with her parents to London, where she grew up and was educated in progressive independent schools before entering Somerville College, Oxford. Here she studied a combination of classics, ancient history, and philosophy. After leaving Oxford with a first-class honors degree in 1942, Murdoch worked for the treasury, leaving that position in June 1944 to work for the United Nations Relief and Rehabilitation Administration (UNRRA) in London, Brussels, Innsbruck, and Graz, Austria. She entered graduate school at Newnham College, Cambridge (1947-1948) and was made a fellow of St Anne's College, Oxford, where she taught philosophy from 1948 to 1963. From 1963 to 1967, she taught part-time in the General Studies Department of the Royal College of Art.

Murdoch married literary critic, novelist, and Thomas Warton Professor of English at Oxford University John Bayley in 1956. Their marriage was "open," with Murdoch engaging in numerous sexual relationships with both men and women. Murdoch received multiple honors, including Commander of the Order of the British Empire (1976), Dame Commander of Order of the British Empire (1987), and election as a Foreign Honorary Member of the American Academy of Arts and Sciences (1982). She was awarded honorary degrees by numerous universities. Diagnosed with Alzheimer's disease in 1997, she died in 1999 in Oxford.

As a moral philosopher, Murdoch took a real-world, or naturalist, approach, which admitted the existence of humility, generosity, and other laudable characteristics and behaviors. She rejected David Hume's moral empiricism, which essentially divorced morality from reason. She was influenced by Simone Weil's theory of "attention" as a contemplative practice conducive to moral action. She also harked back to Plato's concept of good as a real force by which the inner life can be externalized as moral action.

Nietzsche, Friedrich

Friedrich Wilhelm Nietzsche was born on October 15, 1844 in Rocken, Saxony, the son of a Lutheran pastor. He studied classical philology at the universities of Bonn and Leipzig and was appointed to a professorship at the University of Basel in 1869. While living there, he became an intimate of the composer Richard Wagner, whose achievements in music and poetic expression Nietzsche extolled in his first book, *The Birth of Tragedy from the Spirit of Music* (1872). Seven years later, Nietzsche publicly broke with Wagner after the composer established an anti-Semitic cult at Bayreuth, the seat of his operatic production and performances. The break occupied Nietzsche lifelong and resulted in his long aesthetic and moral essay, *Nietzsche contra Wagner* (1889).

Chronically plagued by ill health, Nietzsche resigned from the University of Basel in 1879 and became an ascetic and solitary philosopher, famed for his critical rejection of Christianity (as a "slave religion") and middle-class morality in general, which he proposed to displace with his concepts of the "will to power" and the Superman (*Übermensch*), in effect, a higher form of humanity, transcending ordinary religion and morality in a world in which "God is dead." In his most popular book, *Thus Spake Zarathustra* (1883-1884), Nietzsche sought to redefine his essentially nihilistic world view as an opportunity for humanity to make an evolutionary leap.

In all his major works, beginning with *Zarathustra*, and progressing through *Beyond Good and Evil* (1886), *The Genealogy of Morals* (1887), *Twilight of the Idols* (1888; published,1889), *Antichrist* (1888; published, 1895), and *Ecce Homo* (1888; published, 1908), Nietzsche developed the intellectual framework of his rejection of Christian and middle-class morality and fashioned the concepts of the "will to power" and the Superman. These concepts were evolved within a worldview he called "eternal return," the idea that our reality is eternally self-creating and self-destroying, which introduced the most profound degree of nihilism in a philosophy that denied a *telos*, or end goal.

The philosopher decayed mentally beginning in 1889, possibly as a result of syphilis but more likely due to an inherited stroke disorder and perhaps a brain tumor (meningioma). Left to the care of his mother in his final years, he succumbed to pneumonia on August 25, 1900.

Largely unrecognized during most of his life, Nietzsche developed concepts that became hallmarks of twentieth-century philosophy, including the "death" of God, the condition of nihilism, the will to power (as the key to human behavior), the idea of the Superman, perspectivism (versus an absolute concept of truth and ethics), and the concept of eternal return. All exerted a profound, at times intoxicating, influence over intellectuals, artists, writers, philosophers, and—with infamous results—political leaders. His concept of the Superman in particular was hijacked by fascists and Nazis, including Adolf Hitler, as a philosophical justification for opposition to democracy, "ordinary" morality, and, indeed, basic human rights. Most notably, Hitler grafted elements of Nietzsche's thought onto an elaborate Nazi political and mythological dogma. As a result, Nietzsche's legacy in the late twentieth century and into our own time has been deeply stained, albeit through no fault of his own.

Ockham, William of

William of Ockham (William Ockham, William of Occam) was born about 1285, most likely in the small Surrey (England) village of Ockham. He was a Franciscan monk and scholastic philosopher who was critical of the philosophy of Thomas Aquinas. Aquinas sought to reconcile reason with faith and was thus embraced by the Catholic Church, which canonized him while condemning Ockham.

Ockham is best known for the concept of "Ockham's (or Occam's) Razor," a principle of simplicity intended to cut through unnecessary hypotheses. Ockham's Razor has been popularized to mean "the simplest solution (or explanation) is most likely the right one." In fact, Ockham did not propose quite so sweeping a declaration but held that in solving problems, entities should not be multiplied without absolute necessity. Even more precisely, his rule of thumb was that in judging competing hypotheses about the same prediction, choose the solution that makes the fewest assumptions.

As a metaphysician, Ockham was a nominalist, one who believed that such universal essences as "humanity" or "blackness" did not inhere in their object but were no more or less than cognitive concepts. As an epistemologist, Ockham argued for a direct realist empiricism, the idea that humans perceive objects through intuitive cognition, without the aid or intervention of innate ideas. Such perceptions of external reality produce all our abstract concepts and provide knowledge of the world. As a logician, Ockham embraced what modern philosophers call a supposition theory, arguing that words have meaning in a mental language. As a theologian, Ockham held that belief in God is a matter of faith, not knowledge. This went against the discourse of Aquinas, who argued that faith and reason are not mutually inconsistent. Rejecting any notion of the scientific validity of theology, Ockham held that scientific proofs of the existence of God were invalid. In connection with ethics, Ockham rejected the notion that God wills a thing because it is good and instead held that a thing is good because God wills it. In political philosophy, however, Ockham championed the ideas of natural rights, separation of church and state, and freedom of speech.

Little is known about William of Ockham's life, other than he was likely born in Ockham, twenty-five miles southwest of London, also likely spoke Middle English but wrote exclusively in Latin. He became a Franciscan and was educated at a Franciscan house, from which he went on to Oxford University with the intention of obtaining a degree in theology. He failed to complete the degree, because he was forced to leave in response to a 1323 summons to the papal court, which was at the time in Avignon, France. The charge was heresy—largely for his opposition to Aquinas and his argument for the essential incompatibility of faith and reason. While the papal court investigated, he was held four years in Avignon under house arrest.

Persuaded that the papacy was corrupt, he fled with other Franciscans then under trial on May 26, 1328. They found refuge in the court of Louis of Bavaria. Although excommunicated, Ockham and his fellow Franciscans escaped capture.

Louis lost his bid to attain empire and retreated to Munich, where Ockham, as part of his entourage, spent the rest of his life, much of which was consumed in writing anti-papal treatises. He died between 1347 and 1349, outcast by and unreconciled with the Catholic Church.

Parmenides of Elea

Parmenides of Elea, a Pre-Socratic, was the first philosopher to explore the nature of existence itself, thereby laying claim to the title of the "Father of Metaphysics." Since he also was the first to argue deductively, employing *a priori* arguments, he may have a claim as well to edging out Aristotle as the "Father of Logic." Finally, Parmenides is commonly assumed to have been the founder of the Eleatic School, which encompassed those Pre-Socratics who argued for the singular and unchanging nature of reality. As some subsequent interpreters of Parmenides have suggested, the Eleatics espoused a theory that only one "thing" actually exists.

Those who credit Parmenides with this theory also see him as an epoch-making figure in the history pf philosophy, one who challenged the systems of all his predecessors and laid down before those who would follow him a set of metaphysical criteria any proposed system must satisfy.

Parmenides left—and perhaps wrote—only one work, a poem known as *On Nature*, but probably not given that title by the author. As with so much of the work of the Pre-Socratics, *On Nature* is known only through fragmentary quotations found in the work of other, later authors. By way of conjectural reconstruction, the poem is assumed to have been in three parts, "Proem," "Reality" (*Alétheia*), and "Opinion" (*Doxa*).

"Proem" depicts a young pilgrim in search of enlightenment, who embodies traditional Greek religious beliefs. "Reality" develops epistemic guidelines for philosophical inquiry, which culminates in the metaphysical claim for which Parmenides is best known, namely, that which is cannot be in motion, change, come-to-be, perish, or lack uniformity. "Opinion" is an account of the world in terms of theogony and cosmogony. Strangely, the engine of these processes, theogony and cosmogony, consists of motion, change, and the other phenomena Parmenides argues against in "Reality." A further contradiction comes in the "Opinion" section, which cites various claims—such as, *the moon reflects the light of the sun*—which, although manifestly true, are offered as examples of the mistaken opinions of mere mortals. These logical problems vexed no less a figure than Plato, who concluded that it might be impossible to understand Parmenides' work.

It is believed that Parmenides was born about 515 or 540 BC, and it is known with certainty that his place of birth was Elea, a Greek settlement along the Tyrrhenian coast of the Apennine Peninsula, south of the Bay of Salerno. He may or may not have been the personal teacher of Zeno of Elea (490-430 B.C.E), but his death date is entirely unknown.

Pascal, Blaise

Blaise Pascal was born in Clermont, Auvergne, France on August 19, 1623, the son of a magistrate of an old ennobled family. After Pascal's mother died, father and son moved in 1631 to Paris, where the senior Pascal educated his son. The youngster showed a remarkable aptitude for mathematics, and at sixteen wrote a treatise on conic sections. In 1646, two family friends, both ardent Jansenists—Catholic followers of Cornelius Jansen (1585-1638), whose theology emphasized original sin, divine grace, and predestination—converted young Pascal to their beliefs, which ran contrary to free will.

Pascal's father died in 1651, which began for young Pascal a period of intense scientific and social activity culminating in what he described as an "ecstasy" on the night of November 23, 1654. This moved him to associate himself with Port-Royal, a convent of the Jansenists, for which he wrote the eighteen *Provincial Letters* (*Lettres provinciates,*1656-57), a polemic against Jesuit casuistry—the use of exceedingly complex reasoning to justify a variety of what the Jansenists considered immorality and sin.

From 1659 on, Pascal suffered from an increasingly painful illness, which only intensified his habitually ascetic lifestyle. Often, he turned away physicians by telling them that sickness was the natural state of Christians. By the early 1680s, his condition worsened, and he died on August 19, 1682, at the age of thirty-nine. Records of an autopsy are suggestive to modern physicians of such diverse diagnoses as tuberculosis, stomach cancer, and brain damage.

In his brief life, Pascal was prolific in scientific, mathematical, literary, and philosophical activity. As a scientist, he contributed to the fields of hydrodynamics and hydrostatics and produced two practical inventions, the syringe and a hydraulic press. Based on experimentation, he also advanced the idea of the existence of a vacuum, which his contemporaries, adhering to Aristotle, believed impossible.

In mathematics, he created the so-called Pascal's triangle, a tabular representation of binomial coefficients, and advanced the mathematics of probability. In so doing, he laid the groundwork for calculus as subsequently formulated by Gottfried Wilhelm Leibniz.

In his *De l'Esprit géometrique* (*Of the Geometrical Spirit*), he explored the philosophy of mathematics, arguing that geometry was the nearest possible approach to ascertaining first principles and thereby discovering truths. In other mathematical work, he investigated the validity and limitation of axioms.

In philosophy, the *Provincial Letters* went beyond theology to explore the limits of reasoning as a means of attaining truth. Theology was also the motivation for Pascal's greatest literary and philosophical work, *Pensées* (*Thoughts*). This collection of fragments, considered by many the greatest example of seventeenth-century French prose, was intended to be part of a book to be titled *Apologie de la religion Chrétienne* (*Defense of the Christian Religion*), but Pascal died before he could complete the work or, indeed, assemble any part of it into the planned work.

Pensées is a theological and philosophical attempt to explain the paradoxical relationship of man and God. While the existing work is fragmentary, what becomes clear in reading it is that, as philosophy, it is an attempt to summon up the contradictory approaches of Pyrrhonism—a philosophy based on the fourth-century BC Greek philosopher Pyrrho, which argues for "epoché," a suspension of judgment regarding all non-evident propositions—and Stoicism, the philosophy of Zeno of Citium and Epictetus, which argues for liberation from desire for pleasure and fear of pain. With these two contradictory approaches established, Pascal argues that a thinking person would invariably feel confused to the point of desperation, which is the ideal condition in which to accept belief in God.

Although fragmentary and inherently non-systematic, the *Pensées* have exerted a powerful and enduring influence on the philosophy of religion and on Christian theology. Most famous among the many epigrammatical passages in the work is "The heart has its reasons which reason knows nothing of" ("Le cœur a ses raisons que la raison ne connaît point.").

Peirce, Charles Sanders

Although William James is most commonly associated with the philosophical school known as Pragmatism, its earliest apostle was Charles Sanders Peirce, who was James's good friend and intellectual influence. The third exponent of Pragmatism, John Dewey, was Peirce's student.

As developed by all three philosophers, Pragmatism defines the meaning of any concept in terms of the concept's practical outcomes. Thus, any concept is meaningful only insofar as it has an experiential effect on us—on our actions, our conduct, or our intellectual inquiries. Peirce applied this to the scientific method, concluding that it was the only valid means of attaining truth in the human progress toward knowledge.

Peirce was born on September 10, 1839, in Cambridge, Massachusetts. His father, Benjamin, was an eminent mathematician and astronomer, and his mother, Sarah, the daughter of Senator Elijah Hunt Mills. Intellectually indulged by his doting father, Peirce became an original thinker but also one who had nothing but contempt for middle-class morality and establishment institutions. This was destined to make his road in life most difficult.

In 1859, Peirce managed to graduate from Harvard College, a lowly 79th out of a class of 90. He went to work for the United States Coast Survey and then, encouraged by his father, enrolled in the Lawrence Scientific School of Harvard, earning a bachelor's degree in chemistry in 1863. While he made some contributions to science, he was not by temperament a scientist but was far more interested in logic and method. This led him to develop Pragmatism.

Peirce came to believe in the importance of language and symbols—semiotics—in logic, and he early on concluded that classical deduction and induction were insufficient to account for the entirety of reasoning. He proposed that inquiry must include the invention and discovery of ideas, which he called "abduction." While Peirce departed radically from many of the roots of philosophy as it existed in the mid-nineteenth century, he absorbed the logical systems of George Boole and Augustus De Morgan, and was enthralled with Friedrich Schiller and Immanuel Kant. From these sources, Peirce created a triadic theory of elementary conceptions—*I*, *It*, and *Thou*, which became *Firstness, Secondness,* and *Thirdness*, experiential "categories" corresponding to ideas, chance, and possibility; singularity, discreteness, and the quality of this; and generality, continuity, and the quality of all.

Peirce gave a successful series of Harvard lectures on British logicians in 1869, but his personality clashed with that of the university president, Charles W. Eliot, who rejected his 1871 application to teach philosophy. Nevertheless, he wrote innovative essays, including "On a New List of Categories" (1867) and several epistemological articles, all published in the *Journal of Speculative Philosophy* during 1868-1869. These impressed a small group of philosophers, William James among them. In his epistemological articles, Peirce developed a semiotic alternative to Cartesian and empiricist epistemology, which led to his concept of "fallibilism," the hypothesis that human beings cannot attain certitude and that "knowledge is never absolute but always swims, as it were, in a continuum of uncertainty and of indeterminacy." This led to the formulation of Pragmatism as a way out of the corner into which fallibilism backs any seeker of truth.

Peirce became a founding member or the Metaphysical Club in Cambridge, whose other members included William James, Oliver Wendell Holmes, Jr., and the philosopher Chauncey Wright. It was in this forum that Peirce formally introduced Pragmatism, which was most fully articulated in his papers, "The Fixation of Belief" (1877) and "How to Make Our Ideas Clear" (1878).

In 1879, Peirce finally obtained a substantial academic appointment, to Johns Hopkins University, but failed to achieve tenure. Still, he continued his research and writing, publishing (with his students) *Studies in Logic* (1883) and proposing the then-innovative notion of subliminal perception. Among his Johns Hopkins students was John Dewey.

Peirce's rise at Johns Hopkins was cut short in 1884 when he was dismissed as a lecturer on moral grounds, which may have been associated with emotional problems and, possibly, drug addiction. His marriage had ended in divorce the year before, and his bread-and-butter position at the Coast Survey was not going well. Fortunately, he inherited a small amount of money. Unfortunately, he spent much of it on building an elaborate home, *Arisbe*, in Milford, Pennsylvania. He managed to write a new book, *A Guess at the Riddle*, based on his work on categories, but was unable to find a publisher.

In 1891, he was dismissed from the Coast Survey, sunk deeper and more desperately into debt, and, in 1895, fled Milford just ahead of his creditors. He eked out a meager living as an occasional writer in New York City. In 1903, he applied for a grant from the Carnegie Institution and was rejected. William James organized financial support from a circle of friends and, more important, secured some lecture work for him at Harvard in 1903. This stimulated more writing on Pragmatism, which, in fact, amounted to a large cache of mostly unpublished manuscripts. Death came, from cancer, on April 19, 1914. In large part, thanks to the philosopher Josiah Royce, Peirce's papers were preserved, collected, sorted, examined, and, beginning in the 1930s, slowly published. Many, however, have yet to be issued.

Philo of Alexandria

Philo of Alexandria was a Hellenized Jew, also known as Judaeus Philo, who used philosophical allegory to harmonize the Torah with Greek philosophy. More specifically, he applied Stoic philosophy to traditional Jewish scriptural exegesis. This work subsequently influenced several fathers of the Christian Church, and it is possible that Philo's concept of *Logos*, as God's creative principle, was directly absorbed into early Christian theology.

Philo was probably born about 20 BC in Alexandria, Egypt, which was at the time part of the Roman Empire. His familial heritage was noble. He is known to have visited the Second Temple at least once and was a contemporary of Jesus. Philo's education combined Roman and Hellenistic traditions with some aspects of ancient Egyptian culture and, importantly, the traditions of Judaism. His death date is uncertain other than it must have occurred after A.D. 41.

Philo lived in an age of active Jewish-Hellenistic syncretism, and he dedicated himself to synthesizing Plato and Moses into a single, unified philosophical system. In this, he was guided by Aristotelianism and Stoicism as well as by mostly traditional Jewish theology. His starting place was always the Torah, which he took as the baseline of religious truth as well as truth in general. He held that the Greek philosophers borrowed from the Bible, and he interpreted scripture allegorically to support this contention. As he saw it, the characters in Scripture symbolize aspects of the human being, and biblical stories are illustrative of the human experience.

His concept of God is as a transcendent non-anthropomorphic entity without physical features or emotional qualities. God exists beyond time and space and makes no special interventions into the world. God's existence alone is certain and is without predicate. Like Plato, Philo sees matter as transitory and illusory, with reality inhering in the ideal. Humankind consists of mind/spirit and a soul within a body. God created and governs the world via mediators, among which *Logos* is next to God, functioning as the demiurge of the world. Logos is, in effect, the firstborn son of God and functions as the mind of the Eternal. Logos is an entity neither created nor uncreated and thus occupies a middle position between God and Man. The power of Logos flows from God and is not autonomous.

Philo is credited as the first philosopher to identify Plato's "Ideas" with the Creator's thoughts, which are the content of Logos. Logos is an advocate for humanity as well as God's liaison with world. Logos orders the human mind, providing right reason, which is the infallible source of law.

Plato

With his teacher, Socrates, and his student, Aristotle, Plato is one of the triumvirate of Greek philosophers who are credited not only as seminal in creating the discipline of philosophy, but of being among the creators of the Western tradition of thought. Moreover, as the founder of his famed Academy, Plato may be considered the creator of the world's first institution of higher education.

Plato was born about 428 BC in Athens. His family was prominent and aristocratic, and Plato himself was attracted to a career in politics, but developments in Athens prompted him to change course. To begin with, Athens fell victim to the terroristic reign of an oligarchy, which was replaced by a democratic government that nevertheless condemned his friend and mentor Socrates to death. After that event in 399 BC, Plato left Athens and traveled widely. He visited the court of Dionysius I, tyrant of Syracuse, in 387 and endeavored to teach the royal family the principles of philosophical rule. He made two more trips to Sicily, in 367 and 360, but failed to make a dent with his attempts at educating them. He did, however, have epoch-making success with his Academy, which he founded in Athens in 387. It was around this institution that his life revolved until his death in 347. Not only did he cultivate the minds of his students, in the process creating a great philosophical legacy, it was in the Academy that he wrote his twenty-five *Dialogues* and thirteen *Letters* (the authenticity of which is disputed).

The dialogues cover a very wide range of material, addressing the philosophy of justice (*Republic, Gorgias*); epistemology and knowledge (*Theaetetus*); and religion (*Euthyphro*). Others deal with relationships among various things. In *Protagoras,* it is the relationship of virtue to knowledge; in *Phaedo,* between body and soul.

The great philosophical method common to all the *Dialogues* is the use of question and answer to discover truth. Additionally, in all but one of these works, Socrates is the principal interlocutor. Plato, the author, never steps from behind the curtain. One acute side effect of this is that we do not know which philosophical concepts are original to Plato and which belong properly to Socrates. Most important is the Theory of Ideas, the philosophical concept conventionally attributed to Plato that argues the ultimate unreality of the world and ultimate reality of ideas. Generation upon generation of philosophers have identified the Theory of Ideas as Plato's single greatest contribution to philosophy—and yet the theory is brilliantly contested from within several of the *Dialogues,* so that it remains a titanic point of controversy in philosophy. And even this most "Platonic" of Plato's theories is attributed—by Plato—to Socrates and not to himself.

Plato is associated with several philosophical doctrines that have exerted a powerful influence over Western thought. The first is that the world as conveyed to us by our senses is inherently flawed and stands as a screen between our minds and the true realm of "Forms" or "Ideas," which are perfect and, because they are perfect, real. Plato recognized certain abstract objects—such as being, goodness, beauty, likeness, sameness, difference, change, and changelessness—as, in their approach to Ideas or Forms, *nearly* perfect.

Thus, for Plato, reality was bifurcated between the flawed information conveyed by our senses and the perfect information that could be apprehended by the properly educated mind. Virtually all Plato's philosophical works revolve around this duality of vision. As a matter of seeking truth and acting ethically, Plato urged his readers to transform their values by embracing the Forms and rejecting as defective and lesser the phenomena of the physical world.

For Plato, the soul held a special place in his bifurcated view of reality. It does not depend on the body for its functioning and works most efficiently when it is free from attachment to the physical world. The soul functions as the repository of Forms, carrying them into life after birth separates the soul's possessor from them. The soul can know the good, which is to be found in the *Form* of the good.

All that Plato wrote, except for *Laws,* is dominated by his late teacher, Socrates. Because Plato knew and revered Socrates as his mentor, he is assumed to be providing insight into him as he portrays Socrates in his works. How much of the philosophy spoken by the Socrates "character" in the *Dialogues* indeed originated with Socrates and how much is the invention of Plato cannot be determined. So, at best, the intellectual portrait of Socrates Plato creates in *The Republic* and other works is an evocation and, likely, a blend of Socrates and Plato. Modern philosophers assume Plato is using Socrates as his mouthpiece because he was widely respected and revered. No modern philosopher has expressed the belief that Plato has transcribed the words of Socrates with literal accuracy.

In his own time, Plato's greatest contribution to the civilization around him may well have been his effort to educate a generation of statesmen with the noble objective of producing the Philosopher King, the ideal ruler. To posterity, Plato left the great philosophical (and educational) method of the Socratic dialogue, by which truth is arrived at through progressively deeper questioning. At the heart of his philosophy is idealism, which holds that only Ideas (Forms) contain the true nature of things as physical form cannot. This notion animated Western thought for some 2,400 years. Plato died, perhaps in his sleep, in his ninth decade, in 348 or 347 BC.

Plotinus

The founder of Neoplatonism, Plotinus developed a metaphysics consisting of three elements: the One, the Intelligence, and the Soul. From these "emanate" all existence, such that intellectual contemplation produces reality itself.

Beyond his metaphysics and cosmology, Plotinus theorized that the mind orders the objects of its perception and does not passively receive the sensual information of experience. His metaphysics also produced a philosophy of ethics, in which the soul is divided into a higher and lower soul. The higher is divine, whereas the lower is the locus of the personality, including its passions and vices. Ethics ultimately exists in the lower soul's ascent to a union with the higher soul.

Plotinus was born in A.D. 204 or 205 in Egypt. The city of his birth is unknown, but he lived for a time in Alexandria, where he sampled the lectures of a variety of philosophers. He was displeased with all except for one, Ammonius Saccas, who served as his teacher until 242. In that year, he joined Emperor Gordian on an expedition bound for Persia, where Plotinus hoped to find more useful philosophers from whom to learn. When Gordian was cut down by an assassin, Plotinus settled in Rome, where, at age forty, he founded his own school of philosophy.

Plotinus had been teaching in Rome for some twenty years when a student, Porphyry, persuaded him to organize his treatises into a book, the *Enneads,* which Porphyry edited after Plotinus's death in 270 at Campania.

The One, Plotinus's leading metaphysical principle, is derived from Plato's concept of the *Idea* or *Form* as reality. Plotinus argued that Plato's Forms all partake of the nature of the One, which ensures that they do not fall into eternal disunity. If this were to happen, "necessary" (absolute) truth would cease to exist because there would be no ultimate reality to which all truth must relate. Plotinus argued that the human intellect functions to make distinctions among the Forms, which are united in the One. Thus, Intelligence is the principle of essence or "whatness." Finally, the Soul is the principle of desire for objects external to it, such as food, knowledge, procreation, and so on.

Plotinus is also well known for his early treatise, "On Beauty," which, he argues, consists of images of the Forms that are eternally present in the Intelligence. Emulating Plato's *Symposium*, Plotinus creates a hierarchy of beauty up to and above objects, culminating in the Forms themselves. The ultimate source of beauty, therefore, is the Good, the beauty of which is in the virtual unity of the Forms. Because Beauty ultimately causes the complexity of intelligible reality, it delights us.

Poincaré, Henri

Henri Poincaré has been called the "last polymath." Although he is most celebrated for his fundamental contributions to mathematics, he was also a theoretical physicist and a philosopher, with emphasis on the philosophy of mathematics and science.

As a philosopher of mathematics, Poincaré criticized logicism—the idea that mathematics is merely an extension of logic and is therefore both modeled on and largely or wholly reducible to logic. To this he opposed a form of intuitionism, arguing that the essence of mathematics is internal constructive human mental activity rather than the discovery of external principles inhering in objective reality. More accurately, perhaps, Poincaré may be credited with attempting to navigate a third way, between the extremes of logicism and intuitionism. Related to this is his articulation of the concept of geometric conventionalism, in which he argued that geometric theories do not express inherently true or false propositions. Along with this, he rejected Euclidian geometry to the extent of arguing that it should not be taken as an *a priori* truth. Rather, he advocated a pragmatic view in which geometric axioms should be embraced only for the results they produce rather than for their apparent correlation with human intuitions about the external world.

Jules Henri Poincaré was born on April 29, 1854 in Nancy, France, where his father was a professor in the School of Medicine at the University of Nancy. In 1873, Poincaré entered the École Polytechnique, from which he graduated in 1875 and entered the École des Mines. He briefly became a mine inspector, but soon left after being hired to teach differential and integral calculus at the University of Caen. In 1880, his paper on the theory of differential equations won the grand prize in mathematics of the Academy of Sciences in Paris. The work was based on non-Euclidian geometry, at the time a wholly speculative field, and in 1881 he was appointed to the faculty of sciences at the University of Paris. Here, he was given the chair of mathematical physics and probability (1886) and the chair of mathematical astronomy and celestial mechanics (1896). In 1902, he was appointed professor of theoretical electricity at the Bureau de Poste et Télégraph and, two years later, became professor of general astronomy at the École Polytechnique.

In 1889 Poincaré earned lasting renown—and won a prize from the King of Sweden—for his work on the stability of the solar system, in which he showed that the three-body problem of classical mechanics is not integrable. That is, its general solution cannot be expressed in terms of unambiguous coordinates and velocities of the bodies. This breakthrough was recognized as the most important insight into celestial mechanics since Isaac Newton. Moreover, the three-body problem paper has proven critical to the field of topology and is considered a founding document in chaos theory.

Poincaré, a member of the French Academy of Sciences since 1887, became its president in 1906 and, two years later, was elected to the Académie Française. He died on July 17, 1912 in Paris from a surgical complication. His cousin, Raymond Poincaré, was the president of the Republic of France during the eventful period of 1913 to 1920.

Popper, Karl

Born in Vienna on July 28, 1902, Karl Raimund Popper was one of the great philosophers—and among the most important philosophers of science—of the twentieth century. He was also a philosophical champion of liberalism and a proponent of an "open society." He called himself a critical-rationalist and opposed skepticism, conventionalism, and relativism in science.

Born into a Jewish family, he did not follow his father into the law, but both parents instilled in him an interest in the classics, philosophy, and music. In graduate school, Popper chose the history of music as a second subject for his Ph.D. examination.

Popper was educated at the *Realgymnasium*, which he left to attend the University of Vienna in 1918, although he did not formally enroll until four years later. In his young manhood, he was a Socialist and, for a time, a Marxist. Soon disillusioned with Marxism, however, he turned to Freud and Adler and fell under the spell of Albert Einstein. The great virtue of Einstein, he came to believe, was that his major theories were testable and falsifiable, whereas the work of Marx, Freud, and Adler were testable only by way of confirmation.

Popper did not leap into an academic career but trained as a cabinetmaker, earned a primary school teaching diploma (1925), and a secondary school qualification to teach mathematics and physics (1929). In the meantime, he studied at the doctoral level in the Department of Psychology at the University of Vienna and was awarded a Ph.D. in 1928 for his dissertation *Die Methodenfrage der Denkpsychologie* (*The Methodological Question of Thought Psychology*). He questioned the validity of psychology as a science, focusing on issues of method and objectivity.

In 1937, Popper accepted a position teaching philosophy at the University of Canterbury, New Zealand, which would become his sanctuary through World War II. In 1938, annexation of Austria (*Anschluss*) prompted Popper to address problems in social and political philosophy, which resulted in the 1945 publication of *The Open Society and Its Enemies*, a critical condemnation of totalitarianism.

In 1946, Popper moved to London to teach at the London School of Economics and, three years later, was appointed professor of logic and scientific method at the University of London. He launched into an extraordinarily prolific writing career and in 1959 published his first seminal treatise in the philosophy of science, *The Logic of Scientific Discovery*.

Popper viewed science—and epistemology—from what he called the perspective of "critical rationalism," thereby rejecting the empiricism of the Kantian tradition, which assumed that basic statements are infallible. He argued such statements were no more than descriptions in relation to a theoretical framework and that scientific theories are abstract, capable of only indirect testing by evaluation of their implications. From this, he concluded that all human knowledge is ultimately hypothetical. With respect to science, no amount of positive experimental outcomes can confirm a theory; however, a single counterexample is definitively falsifying. He cautioned that the falsifiable nature of a given theory did not imply that the theory was false, but could be shown to be false, by observation or by experiment. Thus, Popper concluded, there is a vast logical asymmetry between verification and falsifiability. This condition formed the core of Popper's philosophy of science.

Popper posited falsifiability as the criterion of "demarcation" between a genuine and a non-genuine scientific theory. A theory is scientific only if it is falsifiable. Thus, psychoanalysis and other putative sciences did not merit a claim to being deemed scientific. Their theories are not falsifiable. Popper came to recognize a kinship between his standard of falsification and Charles Peirce's nineteenth-century doctrine of fallibilism.

Falsification led Popper to explore—he claimed, to solve—the philosophical problem of induction. There is no deductive proof that the sun will rise, yet, based on induction, one can formulate a theory that every day the sun will rise. Should it fail to rise someday, the theory will be falsified—but, until that day, there is no compelling reason to reject the assumption of its truth. Induction cannot be logically justified. In this, Popper agreed with David Hume. But that is no reason to spurn induction, which is invaluable.

Popper applied falsification to *The Open Society and Its Enemies* and *The Poverty of Historicism* (1957) to critique historicism as a theory that history necessarily develops according to knowable general laws toward a determinate end. Not only is this invalid, he argued, but it is morally corrupt in that it justifies authoritarianism and totalitarianism.

As a metaphysician, Popper argued that the search for truth is a compelling motive for scientific discovery. In *Objective Knowledge* (1972), he argued that scientific knowledge approaches objectivity once it is stated in language, which transforms it into an entity that evolves through critical selection as the meaning of truth becomes a matter of how the theory corresponds to facts. Popper proposed three worlds: World One consists of the physical world or physical states. World Two is the world of mind, including mental states, ideas, and perceptions. World Three is the body of knowledge—in other words, the products of World Two made physically manifest in the things of World One. Popper argued that World Three was the product of individual human beings and therefore has an existence independent of any individually known subjects. World Three exerts an influence as strong as that of World One, so that the knowledge in any individual mind owes at least as much to the cumulative store of human knowledge made manifest as it does to the individual's direct experience. For this reason, the growth of knowledge may be considered a function of the independent evolution of World Three.

Popper's long, distinguished, immensely productive life ended on September 17, 1994, when he succumbed to complications of cancer, in London, at the age of ninety-two.

Prodicus of Ceos

Prodicus of Ceos was born about 465 BC in Ioulis on the island of Ceos and was one of the first generation of Sophists. He was noted for teaching linguistics and ethics and for his naturalist approach to the philosophy of religion.

Prodicus served Ioulis as its commercial ambassador to Athens, where he was admired as an orator. He became sufficiently prominent in that city to attract the attention of Plato (who mentions him in the *Protagoras*) and the playwright Aristophanes (in the *Clouds* [423 BC] and *The Birds* [414

BC]). In Athens, he taught the orators Theramenes and Isocrates. He may also have traveled to Thebes and Sparta, where he delivered lectures. According to Plato (in the *Apology*), Prodicus was deemed competent to instruct the youth in any Greek city.

Plato, who had general contempt for the Sophists, mentions (in the *Dialogues*) Prodicus with at least a modicum of respect. Aristophanes treats him more favorably in *The Clouds* than he does Socrates.

Plato portrayed Prodicus as chiefly a philosopher of ethics, but, in fact, he devotes more space to discussing Prodicus' ideas on language, especially the importance of the correct use of names and words and in articulating the distinctions among words closely related in sense.

Like other Sophists, Prodicus framed religion in naturalist terms. He saw the gods as personifications of the sun, moon, rivers, suggesting that these things related to "the comfort of our life." His naturalist view of God was tinged with atheism. Prodicus was not a pantheist, but believed that the variety, bounty, and beauty of nature prompted humanity to interpret elements of the natural world as embodiments of the godhead. The philosopher died about 395 BC.

Protagoras

The subject of an eponymous Platonic dialogue, Protagoras was a Sophist whom Plato credits as the originator of the role of the professional sophist (one who reasons with complexly fallacious arguments). Plato also noted Protagoras' most controversial and (still) most widely quoted aphorism: "Man is the measure of all things." This Plato understood to mean that truth is not absolute but is that which people generally deem as true. This may well be the crux of Protagoras' epistemology, which held that truth was relative to the individual and not based on some objective "given" independent of human perception and interpretation.

Born in Abdera, Thrace, Protagoras may have begun his working life as a porter. At least, it was reported that the philosopher Democritus saw him carrying a load of wood tied with cord. The skill with which Protagoras had tied the load together—seemingly with geometric precision—led Democritus to remark that the man was a mathematical genius. Accordingly, he took Protagoras into his household and tutored him in philosophy. Eventually, Protagoras became renowned in Athens and was befriended by no less a figure than Pericles.

In point of fact, Protagoras cared little about mathematics and had only skepticism about applying theoretical mathematics to the physical world.

At best, he believed mathematics was an art—with little practical purpose. He was far more interested in ethics, virtue, and political life and debated over whether virtue could be taught. He was interested in education generally and pragmatic education in particular, including the teaching of how to properly manage one's own affairs and household as well as how to lead and manage public affairs.

Like his fellow Sophist Prodicus, Protagoras placed special emphasis on the correct use of words and contemplated the gap between their literal meaning and the author's (or speaker's) intention. He was interested in formulating a methodology for teaching usage that could be applied to the creation and interpretation of laws and other written documents in the Athenian courts. According to Diogenes Laërtius, Protagoras ultimately compiled a taxonomy of speech acts, including assertion, command, question, answer, and so on. He was also a teacher of rhetoric and argumentation, who was among the first to compete in the rhetorical contests associated with the Olympic games.

His theory of argumentation was that, on any issue, there are two opposing *logoi* (arguments), and this is associated with the philosophy of relativism, which he is often credited with originating and for which Plato, in *Protagoras,* condemns him.

As a philosopher of religion, Protagoras was either agnostic or atheistic. Ascribed to him is the ultimate agnostic position, reportedly articulated in a lost work titled *On the Gods*: "Concerning the gods, I have no means of knowing whether they exist or not, nor of what sort they may be, because of the obscurity of the subject, and the brevity of human life."

The date of the philosopher's death is conjectural at about 420 BC, when he was approximately seventy years old.

Proudhon, Pierre-Joseph

Pierre-Joseph Proudhon was born on January 15, 1809 in Besançon, France. He gained enduring fame as the "father" of anarchism and was, in fact, the first person to use the term "anarchist" to describe himself. In terms of a fuller philosophy, he created a subset of anarchism he called mutualism, a form of socialism in which free markets exist with usufructs (the common ownership of property). Indeed, Proudhon is best known for the slogan, "Property is theft!" contained in his first book, *What Is Property? Or, an Inquiry into the Principle of Right and of Government* (1840).

Proudhon was born into a working-class family, the son of a brewer and barrel maker. As a boy, he helped out in the family tavern. He did not attend school but was taught to read by his mother, who, with the aid of a friend, was eventually able to gain his admission to the city college of Besançon.

In 1827, Proudhon apprenticed to a printer, who printed mainly Christian books. Proudhon read them voraciously, which led to his ultimate rejection of Christianity and, in fact, all religion. He rose rapidly in the printing trade and, through this profession, met in 1829 the utopian philosopher Charles Fourier, the printing of whose *Le Nouveau Monde Industriel et Sociétaire* (*The New World of Industry and Society*) Proudhon oversaw. Inspired, Proudhon became increasingly interested in political philosophy.

In 1830, Proudhon qualified as a journeyman compositor but was unable to find steady employment. Gustave Fallot, a philologist and librarian who befriended Proudhon, offered to finance his further education if he came to Paris to study philosophy. After walking to Paris from Besançon, he moved in with Fallot in the Latin Quarter until a cholera outbreak forced him back to Besançon. He attempted to start his own printing business in 1838, failed, and applied for a special grant that financed study at the Academy of Besançon. The following year, he won a prize for an essay that adumbrated much of his mature revolutionary philosophy. In 1840 came *What Is Property?* And, in 1846, *The System of Economic Contradictions, or The Philosophy of Poverty.*

In the 1846 book, Proudhon claimed that economics could be understood only in the context of metaphysics, arguing that divinity is the core concept in Economics and that to study the laws of labor and exchange is to become a metaphysician. Economic science, he declared, "is necessarily a Theory of Knowledge, a Natural Theology, and a Psychology."

Yet Proudhon resisted straying into the purely theoretical and worked toward the creation of workers' associations and cooperatives as the practical means of implementing mutualism, the abolition of both private and government ownership of property and other capital assets in favor of these being shared jointly by peasants and workers themselves.

Proudhon played no role in instigating the Revolutions of 1848, but he did participate in the February Revolution in France. Disappointed by the outcome, he published in 1849 *Solution of the Social Problem*, which was a program of mutual financial cooperation among workers. His objective was to transfer control of major economic relations from capitalists to workers. Arguing that "Anarchy is order without power," he sought to implement his philosophy by creating a French national bank funded by an income tax on capitalists. The bank would function to provide to the masses interest-free loans, using exchange notes in place of gold-based currency.

In the wake of the 1848 revolutions, during the Second French Republic (1848–1852), Proudhon made less impact as a philosopher than as a journalist and polemicist. In 1849, however, he was arrested for insulting President Louis-Napoléon Bonaparte and was incarcerated from 1849 to 1852. In 1858, he voluntarily exiled himself to Belgium, where he lived until 1863, when he returned to France. He died two years later, on January 19, 1865.

Putnam, Hilary

Born in Chicago, on July 31, 1926, to a father who taught Romance languages and wrote for the *Daily Worker*, Putnam grew up there, in France, and in Philadelphia. In the latter city, he attended Central High School and was a friend and classmate of Noam Chomsky. As an undergraduate, Putnam studied philosophy at the University of Pennsylvania and did graduate work in philosophy at Harvard University and UCLA, from which he received a Ph.D. in 1951, writing a dissertation titled *The Meaning of the Concept of Probability in Application to Finite Sequences*.

Putnam taught at Northwestern University (1951–1952), Princeton University (1953–1961), and MIT (1961–1965), before moving to Harvard in 1965. He was married to philosopher Ruth Anna Putnam, who taught philosophy at Wellesley College. At Harvard, Putnam was a political activist and, beginning in 1968, was the faculty advisor to the Students for a Democratic Society (SDS).

Putnam retired from teaching in 2000 but served Harvard as the Cogan University Professor Emeritus and was a founding patron of Ralston College, which has yet to open its doors. He died on March 13, 2016 at the age of eighty-nine.

Putnam is best known for his work in the philosophy of mind and, within this field, for his hypothesis of multiple realizability, which holds that mental states are distinct from and cannot be reduced to physical states. The thesis has been used both to support and attack machine-state functionalism (essentially the equivalency of the human mind and the Turing machine theoretical computer). Machine-state functionalism was an early position of Putnam's, but he abandoned it along with other computational theories of mind by the 1980s because it failed to account for certain intuitions with respect to the externalism of mental content. It is, in fact, a hallmark of

Putnam's work that he never manifested any loyalty to a philosophical position, including his own.

Related to his work on the philosophy of mind is his work in the field of philosophy of language, especially semantic externalism, which holds that meaning does not inhere solely within the mind. He developed this in the so-called Twin Earth thought experiment. He proposed Twin Earth on which all is identical to Earth, except that its bodies of water are filled with "XYZ" as opposed to H_2O. Thus, when Fredrick, a resident of Earth, uses the word *water*, it has a different meaning from the Twin Earth word *water* even as used by his identical twin, Frodrick. Because Fredrick and Frodrick are indistinguishable, the meaning of *water* cannot be determined solely by what is in their minds but must be determined with reference to the external. Semantic externalism, it is said, triggered an "anti-subjectivist revolution" among philosophers.

In the philosophy of mathematics, Putnam collaborated with Willard Quine on the Quine–Putnam "indispensability argument" for the necessity of ontological commitments to mathematical entities. Putnam believed that mathematics, like other empirical sciences, uses strict logical proofs as well as "quasi-empirical" methods, which produce knowledge that is conjectural yet still useful in developing mathematical ideas.

As an epistemologist, Putnam developed the "brain in a vat" thought experiment, arguing against the notion that one can coherently suspect one is a disembodied brain placed in a vat by a mad scientist. The reasoning is semantic. Words refer to things and experiences. If every experience is received through wiring by a disembodied brain in a vat, the idea of "brain" held by a brain in a vat does not refer to a "real" brain within a person, since the brain in a vat has no experience of such a thing. Thus, knowledge depends on factors external to the mind and cannot be determined internally exclusively.

Pyrrho

Born about 360 BC in Elis, on the Peloponnese, Pyrrho was the founder of the Greek philosophical school of skepticism known to moderns as Pyrrhonism. This school holds that philosophy has yet to find truth regarding non-evident matters and concludes that it may be impossible to do so. This being the case, Pyrrhonism contends that arguments can nevertheless be made, speculatively, and their validity can be decided by suspending judgment (the suspension is called *epoché*). This enables a state of equanimity (*ataraxia*), which, in turn, empowers the philosopher to attain *eudaimonia* (happiness). Another term for the key assumption of Pyrrhonism is fallibilism, the assertion that every object of human knowledge involves uncertainty.

Tradition holds that Pyrrho embraced his own philosophy enthusiastically, carrying his skepticism to such an extreme that his friends had constantly to attend him, lest he be run over by carriages, whose existence he doubted. This legend is likely spurious, since Pyrrho is also said to have lived in solitude—though he was apparently unaffected by fear, joy, grief, or bodily pain.

He was said to have been subtle in argument, and he was so highly respected that he was named to the office of chief priest and was exempted from taxation. Pyrrho left no writings, and all that is known of his philosophy comes via his disciple Timon of Phlius. Pyrrho is believed to have died about 270 BC.

Pythagoras

Most widely known as a mathematician and the creator of Pythagorean geometry, the originator of the Pythagorean theorem, Pythagorean tuning, identification of the five regular solids, the Theory of Proportions, and the theory of a spherical earth, Pythagoras was born about 570 BC in Samos. Little is known of his life, and he left no writing.

It is known that he founded at Croton (in southern Italy) a society that was both a religious community and a school of science. Eventually, suspicions formed as to the activities of the society, which was attacked, forcing Pythagoras to flee Croton for Metapontum, where he died about 495 BC. (Some versions of this account hold that he died in Croton.)

Beyond mathematics, the nature of the philosophical teachings of Pythagoras are uncertain. Associated with him is a theory of there being three classes of men. Those of the highest class are lovers of wisdom, below this are lovers of honor, and, at the bottom, are lovers of gain. This may be associated with a theory of a tripartite soul, which is attributed to Pythagoras as well as to Plato.

Pythagoras believed in metempsychosis, the doctrine of rebirth or transmigration of souls after death. While the body is mortal, the soul is immortal and is transmigrated from the dead body to a new incarnation. The belief seems to have come, in part, from Pythagoras' claim that he could remember past incarnations of his soul.

As a cosmologist, Pythagoras apparently embroidered upon the cosmogony of Anaximenes, contributing to it the idea that the universe (the

"Unlimited") is as infinite as air but is given form by Limit. Limit, in turn, may be defined by certain numerical ratios, such as those that determine the concordant intervals of the musical scale. Pythagoras held that the practice of medicine was also defined by Limits in the form of opposites, such as the hot and the cold and the wet and the dry. The wise physician is learned in the blending of these opposing Limits to produce effective treatments. Pythagoras and his followers believed the human body was strung like an instrument to a certain pitch of hot versus cold and wet versus dry. Tuning for proper health was similar to tuning for harmonious and melodic music.

Pythagoras concluded that numbers were the key to all forms in the universe. They represented the form-giving Limits to the Unlimited, and his mathematics was, in effect, a cosmic numerology, which had metaphysical and mystical purpose but little or no practical application. His early disciples represented numbers and their properties through dots arranged in various patterns, including the triangular tetractys, which became a sacred symbol to those who lived in the Croton community Pythagoras founded. Here, evidently, philosophy merged seamlessly into a religion.

Quine, Willard Van Orman

Considered among the most influential of twentieth-century philosophers, Willard Van Orman Quine was a logician and analytic philosopher, who argued against logical empiricism, or logical positivism, the notion that the only factually valid knowledge is scientific. He was born on June 25, 1908, in Akron, Ohio, the son of Cloyd Robert Van Orman, founder of the Akron Equipment Company, which produced tire molds, and Harriett E. Van Orman, a schoolteacher.

Quine earned a B.A. in mathematics from Oberlin College in 1930 and a Ph.D. in philosophy from Harvard University just three years later, in 1932, working under Alfred North Whitehead. A fellowship permitted him to travel to Europe during 1932-1933, where he met leading Polish logicians and some of the Vienna Circle, including Rudolf Carnap.

During World War II, Quine lectured in Brazil (in Portuguese) on logic and served in the United States Navy as an intelligence officer decrypting messages intercepted from German submarines. Quine's academic career was spent at Harvard University, and from 1956 until 1978, he held the Edgar Pierce Chair of Philosophy there. As a professor, he taught logic and set theory, arguing that first-order logic was the only kind worthy of being called logic. He developed New Foundations, his own system of mathematics and set theory and, with Hilary Putnam, developed the "Quine–Putnam indispensability thesis," which argued for the reality of mathematical entities. Nevertheless, he also argued that philosophy is not conceptual analysis but, continuous with science, the abstract branch of the empirical sciences. His work in epistemology was aimed at showing how humankind had developed scientific theories based on little sensory data. At the same time, he championed ontological relativity in science, the so-called Duhem–Quine thesis.

He is best known for his papers "On What There Is," which presented Quine's dictum of ontological commitment, "To be is to be the value of a variable," and "Two Dogmas of Empiricism," which rejected positivism in favor of semantic holism, the theory that any part of language can be understood only via its relations to larger segments of language as previously understood. In *The Web of Belief* (written in 1970 with J. S. Ullian), he further extended holism into coherentism, which implies that justification of a belief must be made within the context of a system of beliefs that cohere with one another. Earlier, in *Word and Object* (1960), he introduced his indeterminacy of translation thesis, in which he distinguished three semantic indeterminacies: inscrutability of reference, holophrastic indeterminacy (indeterminacy of sentence translation), and underdetermination of scientific theory (or confirmation holism—the idea that no theory can be tested except when embedded in a context of other hypotheses).

As a logician, Quine confined logic to first-order logic and thus to truth and falsity under any universe of discourse. He was a champion of the application of the formal logic of philosophy and mathematics, and he maintained that mathematics required set theory, which was distinct from logic.

In the field of contemporary metaphysics, he developed abstract object theory—abstract objects having no physical referents—and he rejected the validity of analytic statements even as he affirmed their essential circularity. Ultimately, he concluded that there is no distinction to be made between universally known collateral information and analytic truths.

Extending metaphysics to epistemology, Quine argued against normative epistemology and advocated replacing it with an empirical study of what sensory inputs produce what theoretical outputs. In effect, then, he extended epistemology into the psychological field of behaviorism, a notion that proved tremendously controversial. Quine died, in Boston, on December 25, 2000, at the age of ninety-two.

Rousseau, Jean Jacques

Jean Jacques Rousseau was born on June 28, 1712, in Geneva, Switzerland, the son of a watchmaker. His mother died shortly after his birth, and young Rousseau served two apprenticeships before leaving Geneva in 1728 to wander through southeastern France and northern Italy. He worked, catch as catch can, as a servant, music teacher, and tutor, returning frequently to Annecy, a French town some twenty miles south of Geneva, to see his patroness and (later) mistress, Mme. Louise Eleonore de Warens.

Rousseau arrived in Paris in 1742 and, the next year, published *Dissertation on French Music*, which was well received. He secured an appointment as secretary to the French ambassador to Venice and then returned to Paris in 1744, beginning a lifelong relationship with Thérèse Levasseur, with whom he had five children. During this time he also became associated with Denis Diderot, cofounder and chief editor of the great *Encyclopédie*, and contributed work to the project.

In 1749, his *Discourse on the Arts and Sciences* won first prize (1749) at Academy of Dijon, making him famous overnight. His first truly philosophical work, the book argues that the arts and sciences corrupt morality. Put another way, Rousseau held that civilization itself is destructive to human beings. This idea became foundational to the vast Romantic movement that swept Western art, literature, and thought through at least the first third of the nineteenth century.

In 1755, a sequel to *Discourse on the Arts and Sciences* titled *Discourse on the Origin and Basis of Inequality among Men* further developed the notion that man in the "state of nature" is superior to man in the state of civilization by explaining how the development of the concept of private property is the original sources of all inequality and, thus, all injustice. Taken together, the two discourses may be seen as a philosophical speculation on the perfectibility of humankind.

In counterpoint to his philosophical output, Rousseau composed a successful opera, *Le Devin du village* (*The Village Soothsayer*, 1752), which became a favorite of King Louis XV. Returning to Geneva, he wrote a best-selling and very influential epistolary novel *La Nouvelle Heloise* (*Julie; or the New Heloise*, 1761), which developed his moral philosophy further, exalting the ethics of personal authenticity over rational moral principles. This extraordinarily influential work was followed in 1762 by *Emile,* an anti-intellectual treatise maintaining that the sole purpose of education should be to teach men to live. *La Nouvelle Heloise* was condemned by the

Roman Catholic Church, and both *Emile* and *The Social Contract* (1762) provoked official censorship.

The Social Contract argued against the divine right of kings and held that the only "legitimate" government is one in which the people—men and women—are sovereign. The book inspired political reforms throughout Europe and played a direct role in motivating the French Revolution. It also prompted Rousseau to move from one country to another throughout 1762-1779. He was living in England when he wrote his extraordinary *Confessions* (1766-1769; published posthumously in 1782), which inspired other such revelatory autobiographies by the likes of Goethe, Stendhal, De Quincey, and Casanova.

After his return to Paris in 1770, Rousseau earned a living as a music copyist and wrote *Dialogues* (1774) and *Reveries of the Solitary Walker* (*Les Rêveries du promeneur solitaire*), a contemplative valediction, which, left unfinished, is a work of profound resignation. Rousseau died on July 2, 1778, at sixty-six, in Ermenonville, France.

Royce, Josiah

Josiah Royce was the principal philosopher of absolute idealism, a philosophy associated in Europe with the German G. W. F. Hegel and the British philosopher F. H. Bradley. Royce's metaphysics was thus founded on the view that all aspects of reality are unified in the thought of a single all-encompassing consciousness. In addition to his American advocacy of absolute idealism, Royce contributed to the fields of ethics, community, religion, and logic. His most influential books are *The Religious Aspect of Philosophy* (1885), *The World and the Individual* (1899–1901), *The Philosophy of Loyalty* (1908), and *The Problem of Christianity* (1913).

Royce was a friend of William James, with whom he carried on a vigorous yet congenial dispute dubbed the "Battle of the Absolute." Both philosophers were enriched by the long dialogue, and Royce ultimately modified absolute idealism into what he called "absolute pragmatism," which was grounded, somewhat surprisingly, in semiotics. Rejecting his own advocacy of the "absolute mind" concept, Royce reimagined reality as a realm of ideas and signs, which come into being through the interpretation of an infinite community of minds. In turn, these very minds, along with the community they constitute, may also be interpreted semiotically, as signs. All of Royce's philosophical positions relate to his metaphysics and thus create a cohesive philosophical vision.

Josiah Royce was born on November 20, 1855, in Grass Valley, California. His mother, Sarah Eleanor Bayliss Royce, was a devout Christian and the local schoolteacher. She conducted her son's early education before he began, at eleven, attending school in San Francisco. In 1875, he graduated from the University of California, with a B. A. in Classics. He went to Germany to study philosophy in Heidelberg, Leipzig, and Göttingen, returning after a year to enter Johns Hopkins University, from which he was awarded a Ph.D. in 1878.

Although his doctorate was in philosophy, Royce taught composition and literature at the University of California, Berkeley, from 1878 to 1882. He did, however, publish in philosophy during this period, including a textbook on logic (*Primer of Logical Analysis*). He married in 1880 and had, with Katherine Head Royce, three children. His first son was newborn when, in 1882, he accepted Harvard University's offer to replace William James during James's one-year sabbatical. He resigned from the University of California to accept the temporary appointment, which became a three-decade Harvard career, during which he taught the likes of T. S. Eliot, George Santayana, and W. E. B. Du Bois.

Royce was a prolific and diverse writer. His *Religious Aspect of Philosophy* (1885) was based on his insight that, for the concepts of truth and error to be meaningful, there must be an Absolute Knower, an infinite mind encompassing the totality of all truths and possible errors. A year after his breakthrough philosophy book, he published *History of California* (1886) and, in 1887, a novel. This span of intense work brought about a so-called nervous breakdown in 1888, which prompted his taking a long sea voyage.

Recovered, Royce was appointed professor of History of Philosophy at Harvard in 1892 and chaired the Department of Philosophy from 1894 to 1898, establishing himself as a leading American philosopher with public lectures and books, including *The Spirit of Modern Philosophy* (1892) and *The Conception of God* (1895).

In 1898, Royce, like James, was profoundly influenced by Charles S. Peirce's lecture series "Reasoning and the Logic of Things." Invited to deliver the Gifford Lectures at the University of Aberdeen in 1899 and 1900, Royce was motivated to write what he considered the definitive expression of his metaphysics, *The World and the Individual* (1899–1901). The lectures and the book required him to perfect his philosophical theories in detail, and his achievement was recognized by the American Psychological Association in 1902 and the American Philosophical Association, both of which elected him their president in 1902 and 1903, respectively.

While *The World and the Individual* met with nearly universal praise, Peirce found fault with Royce's use of logic. Unoffended, Royce threw himself into the study of mathematical logic, with an eye toward revising his views. Indeed, from 1900 onward, he increasingly relied on logical and mathematical concepts as the foundation for his metaphysical work. At the same time, he increasingly emphasized that philosophy must be an instrument for understanding the most basic phenomena of life, including the nature of society, religious experience, ethical action, suffering, and the persistence of evil. In 1908, he published *The Philosophy of Loyalty*, an example of practical philosophy in the form of applied ethics. That same year, his collection of essays, *Race Questions, Provincialism, and Other American Problems*, appeared and was followed in 1911 by *William James and Other Essays on the Philosophy of Life*. His final work, *The Hope of the Great Community*, was published in 1916, after his death on September 14 of that year. It grappled with global politics and the Great War (World War I), then in its second year.

Russell, Bertrand
Bertrand Arthur William Russell, 3rd Earl Russell, was among the most famous and most quoted intellectuals of the twentieth century. Earning distinction in the fields of mathematics, logic, history, social criticism, political activism, and literature (winner of the Nobel Prize for literature), he was also one of the century's leading philosophers. With Gottlob Frege, G. E. Moore, and Ludwig Wittgenstein (his protégé), he led what has been called the "revolt against idealism" and founded analytic philosophy.

Preeminent among twentieth-century logicians in his day, Russell collaborated with Alfred North Whitehead in writing the magisterial *Principia Mathematica* (published in 1910, 1912, 1913, and in a second revised edition in 1925-1927) in an effort to establish a logical basis for mathematics. In philosophy proper, Russell's 1905 "On Denoting" (published in the journal *Mind*) advanced the theory that denoting phrases (semantically complex expressions that can serve as the grammatical subject of a sentence) have no meaning in themselves, "but every proposition in whose verbal expression they occur has a meaning." This led to the descriptivist theory of names, which holds that for every proper name, there is some collection of descriptions associated with it that constitute the meaning of the name. This theory is considered a paradigm of philosophy and is representative of a whole range of Russell's thought, which has influenced everything from logic and mathematics to cognitive science, computer science, epistemology, the philosophy of language, and metaphysics.

Bertrand Russell was born May 18, 1872 in Trellech Monmouthshire, Wales, into a liberal-leaning aristocratic family. He was raised largely by his grandparents after his father's death and was from youth afflicted with depression. His absorbing passion for mathematics helped him to overcome suicidal thoughts, and he entered Trinity College Cambridge in 1890 on a mathematics scholarship. He married Alys Smith in 1894—the first of four marriages, all in varying degrees unhappy, prompting him at last to advocate "free love."

Principia Mathematica was published in 1903 and catapulted him to international fame, leading to his elevation as a fellow of the Royal Society in 1908. As a lecturer at Cambridge University, he met Ludwig Wittgenstein, who became an associate and a protégé. During World War I, Russell's vigorous pacifism led to his dismissal from Trinity college in 1916 and a six-month term in prison. In 1920, after the war, he visited Russia, hoping to have his hopes for the positive effects of the Communist revolution confirmed, only to experience disappointment, which led him to write *The Practise and Theory of Bolshevism*, a condemnation of Communism. Similarly, the outbreak of World War II compelled Russell to suspend his pacifism because he believed fighting the evil of Hitler justified going to war. In 1945, his *History of Western Philosophy* became a bestseller, earning him yet greater fame and providing a substantial income for the rest of his long life. Russell continued to write and eloquently resumed his pacifist stance. He succumbed to influenza on February 2, 1970 at the age of 97.

Russell's greatest impact on philosophy was his foundational work on analytic philosophy, which steered both British and American twentieth-century philosophical thought away from the idealism of so-called "Continental philosophy." But, in truth, he made important contributions to every major field of philosophy except for aesthetics. Moreover, despite his embrace of analytics, he advocated what he called the "Will to Doubt," arguing that all "our beliefs ... have at least a penumbra of vagueness and error" and "increasing the degree of truth in our beliefs" requires "hearing all sides, trying to ascertain all the relevant facts, controlling our own bias by discussion with people who have the opposite bias, and cultivating a readiness to discard any hypothesis which has proved inadequate."

Russell's influence on twentieth-century philosophy is matched only by his impact on logic and mathematics—and, more precisely, mathematical logic. He also proposed in a series of 1918 lectures, "The Philosophy of Logical Atomism," the concept of an ideal language by which human knowledge could be reduced to terms of "atomic" propositions and their truth-functional "compounds." This was Russell's most extreme expression of radical empiricism, requiring every meaningful proposition to refer directly to known objects. While Russell later retrenched from the extremism of logical atomism, he continued to advocate breaking everything down to the simplest possible components.

Saadya (Saadya Gaon)
Born in Fayyûm (upper Egypt) in 882, Saadya was the first major rabbinical writer to work in Arabic and is the father of Judeo-Arabic literature. He was a Hebrew linguist and philosopher, whose *Book of Beliefs and Opinions* was the first truly systematic attempt to synthesize aspects of Jewish theology with aspects of Greek philosophy. As a translator and theologian. He left two Arabic translations of the Bible, a Biblical commentary in Arabic (most of it lost), a Hebrew dictionary, liturgical poetry, and a Jewish book of prayer.

As a philosophical theologian, Saavya combined a commitment to reason with a belief in revelation. Together, these guided both knowing and morality. He considered and discussed the difference between "laws of reason" and "laws of revelation," arguing for the validity of both. His philosophy of religion, as expressed in the *Book of Beliefs and Opinions* (compiled in 933 and variously revised) endeavored to demonstrate harmonious parallels between the truths delivered to the Israelites by divine revelation and conclusions reached by way of rational argument. Saadya asserted the necessity of reason even in the context of faith and revelation.

Saadya was so revered in his own time that David ben Zakkai, exilarch (leader of the Jewish community in Babylon) appointed him Gaon (head of the academy), the first foreigner ever to be so appointed. Saadya died in Baghdad in 942.

Santayana, George
Born in Madrid, Spain, on December 16, 1863, George Santayana was a philosopher, poet, and literary and cultural critic. In 1872, his family brought him to the United States to be educated with three children from his mother's previous marriage. He attended Boston Latin School and Harvard, earning a B.A. in 1886, and then studied two years at the University of Berlin before returning to Harvard, from which he received an M.A. and, in 1889, a Ph.D. Santayana was a member of the Harvard philosophy department from 1889 to 1912, when fellow faculty members included William James, Josiah Royce, and George H. Palmer. Among his students were

T. S. Eliot, Conrad Aiken, and future U.S. Supreme Court associate justice Felix Frankfurter.

Santayana may be best remembered as a revisionist American literary historian and critic, but he was also a major figure in American philosophy. *The Sense of Beauty* (1896), his debut book, is considered the first important philosophical work on aesthetics written in the United States. In it, he argues that beauty is essentially a human sensual experience, and while this viewpoint has been influential on the field of aesthetics, Santayana himself subsequently rejected it.

Of far greater importance is *The Life of Reason*, which was published in five volumes during 1905–1906 and is devoted to the application of reason to moral philosophy. Santayana did not publish another major philosophical work until *Skepticism and Animal Faith* in 1923. This functioned as a sort of prolegomenon to his most original work, *The Realms of Being*, consisting of four volumes published between 1927 and 1940. The work is a major foray into ontology, which Santayana divides into four realms—essence, matter, truth, and spirit—corresponding to his four volumes.

The Realms of Being confirms Santayana's skepticism. He held that knowledge is faith in the unknowable and that, ultimately, matter is the only reality. He was raised a Catholic, but by adulthood, became an atheist and came to believe that religion was essentially the product of imagination.

Santayana left the United States in 1912 and lived in France, Spain, and England until the end of World War I, when he settled in Rome. During World War II, he took refuge in a Roman convent and continued to live there until his death on September 26, 1952. Beyond his philosophical works, Santayana produced distinguished literary writing, including a novel, *The Last Puritan* (1935); a play, *Lucifer* (1899); and a three-volume autobiography, *Persons and Places* (1944), *The Middle Span* (1945), and *My Host the World* (published posthumously in 1953). He wrote poetry—*Sonnets and Other Verses* (1894) and *A Hermit of Carmel and Other Poems* (1901)—and works of literary and social criticism. The latter includes *Three Philosophical Poets: Lucretius, Dante and Goethe* (1910), *Egotism in German Philosophy* (1916; revised, 1940), and *Character and Opinion in the United States* (1920).

Sartre, Jean-Paul

Jean-Paul Sartre achieved rare fame for a philosopher. Indeed, to many, he was and remains the archetypal—or perhaps stereotypical—philosopher of the twentieth century. His fame rests on Existentialism and the

Existentialist movement, which he fashioned into what some consider the representative philosophy of the twentieth century.

Born on June 21, 1905, in Paris, Sartre was the only child of Jean-Baptiste Sartre, a naval officer, and Anne-Marie Schweitzer. Sartre became interested in philosophy after reading Henri Bergson's "Time and Free Will" when he was a young man. He earned a master's degree in philosophy at the École Normale Supérieure, where he also met Simone de Beauvoir, then a student at the Sorbonne. The two became lifelong partners, albeit hardly monogamous. Their unconventional lifestyle became a dimension of their challenge to the norms of "bourgeois" society.

During World War II, Sartre was conscripted into the French army in 1939. Captured by German troops in 1940, he was held for nine months as a POW. A civilian by 1941, he taught at Lycée Pasteur and became active in the French underground as a founding member of the clandestine group Socialisme et Liberté and was a contributor to *Combat,* the newspaper (edited by Albert Camus) of the Resistance. During the war, he also wrote *Being and Nothingness: An Essay on Phenomenological Ontology* (1943), his key expression of Existentialism, in which he made the central claim of this philosophy: "existence precedes essence," thus standing on its head the traditional view that the essence, or nature, of a thing is more fundamental than the thing's mere existence. From this reversal flowed Sartre's ontological theories, including his contention that humans create, through consciousness, their own identity, values, and purposes in life because human beings possess no inherent value or even identity.

In Existentialism, ontology is distinct from metaphysics, mainly because it is descriptive rather than causally explanatory, which is the province of metaphysics. Sartre essentially rejected the validity of explanation in a strictly philosophical sense. Nevertheless, in his political philosophy, he dealt extensively in causal explanation. This aspect of his thought merged with his postwar leftist activism, although he found Marxism flawed as a philosophical position if not as a political and social guide. He also ventured outside of philosophy into psychology in his detailed exploration of the phenomenology of consciousness, arguing in his *The Psychology of Imagination* (1940; also titled *The Imaginary*) that imagination, in contrast to perception (in which intention plays only a subordinate role), is highly intentional and, in effect, frees human beings from ontology. Sartre extended this liberating intentionality to emotions as well. Thus, his psychology circled back from psychology to philosophy in an argument that freedom is ontological. Humans are free because they are not a self or, as

Sartre put it, an "in-itself," but, rather, a presence-to-self. In effect, then, we are all "other" with respect to ourselves.

Sartre was an ethical philosopher, who argued for individual moral responsibility based on "authenticity," which he defined as the degree to which one's actions flow from or are congruent with one's beliefs and desires irrespective of external pressure or coercion.

Sartre wrote plays and novels, including the drama *No Exit* (1944) and the novel *Nausea* (1938), both "existential" in theme and content, and he also made forays into aesthetics, most notably in his 1947 essay collection titled *What Is Literature?* He defined literary writing as a form of "acting in the world," which, like other action, produces effects for which the actor (author) must assume responsibility. Sartre believed that literature and other aesthetic work had significant power. Rejecting the "art for art's sake" aesthetic standard, he argued that art should address social, political, and moral issues of importance.

In 1964, Sartre was awarded the Nobel Prize in Literature, which he declined because he refused all official distinctions on principle as a compromise of his authenticity. During the 1970s, he was plagued by ill health exacerbated by overwork, the use of amphetamines, and an addiction to cigarettes. He died on April 15, 1980 from pulmonary edema and was buried at Montparnasse Cemetery. When Simone de Beauvoir died six years later, she was buried in the same grave.

Saussure, Ferdinand de

Ferdinand de Saussure was a Swiss linguist, semiotician, and philosopher of language. He was a founding father of twentieth-century linguistics and may be considered, with Charles Sanders Peirce, a founder of semiotics.

Saussure approached language as both a system of signs (a semiotic system) and a social phenomenon (a product of the language community). The methodology he created to study language from these dual perspectives provided the basis of structuralism, which a later generation of philosophers, semioticians, linguists, and anthropologists, such as Roland Barthes, Jacques Lacan, and Claude Lévi-Strauss, applied to such fields as literature, psychoanalysis, popular and commercial culture, and anthropology.

Born in Geneva on November 26, 1857, Ferdinand de Saussure was the son of a mineralogist, entomologist, and taxonomist. He enrolled in the Institution Martine in 1870 and, on graduation, continued his studies at the Collège de Genève before entering the University of Geneva, where he studied Latin, Ancient Greek, and Sanskrit. In 1876, he entered the University of Leipzig for graduate work, publishing just two years later *Mémoire sur le système primitif des voyelles dans les langues indo-européennes* (*Dissertation on the Primitive Vowel System in Indo-European Languages*). Moving on to the University of Berlin, he studied Celtic and Sanskrit, and then returned to Leipzig to defend his doctoral dissertation on a topic in Sanskrit linguistics. He was awarded the Ph.D. in 1880.

Saussure lectured at the University of Paris on Sanskrit, Gothic, and Old High German. Beginning in 1881, he taught at the École Pratique des Hautes Études, in Paris, remaining there for eleven years, during which he was honored with the title of Chevalier de la Légion d'Honneur. Offered a professorship at the University of Geneva in 1892, he returned to his native country and taught Sanskrit and Indo-European there until his death on February 22, 1913.

It was during this final period that he first offered his Course of General Linguistics, which helped to transform the field when the lectures were collected and posthumously published in 1916 as the *Cours de linguistique Générale.*

Saussure was able to reconstruct theoretically the Proto-Indo-European language vocalic system, which greatly aided the study of ancient languages, including the decipherment of Hittite. His contributions to general linguistic theory, however, made an impact far beyond philology and linguistics. His two-tiered conception of language, which he viewed as the *langue* (the abstract, invisible layer of language) and the *parole* (spoken speech), was the basis of a broader theory of structuralism, which emerged in the work of anthropologist Claude Levi-Strauss, who analyzed myths on the theory that all have an underlying pattern driving their structure and making them myths as opposed to mere tales. Following Levi-Strauss, structuralism has been applied to many other fields of study.

For Saussure, the linguistic sign was the organizing principle of linguistic structure. He embarked on an analytical inquiry into how arbitrary signs, sounds of distinct phonological shape, evolve into meaning via grammatical structure. This was the inquiry he developed in the lectures that constituted the Course in General Linguistics. He approached language as "a system of signs that expresses ideas" and thus evolved semiology, the science devoted to the study of the life of signs within society. This has proved to be a fruitful basis for the development of a philosophy of language and, by extension, the fields of epistemology and ontology as applied to language.

Schleiermacher, Friedrich

Friedrich Daniel Ernst Schleiermacher was a theologian and philosopher who struggled to reconcile Protestantism with Enlightenment thought and effectively founded the modern field of hermeneutics, shifting away from traditional methods of interpreting biblical and classical texts to focusing, more philosophically and philologically, on how people understand texts.

Born on November 21, 1768 in Breslau, Germany, into the family of a clergyman of the reformed church, Schleiermacher was educated in schools of the Moravian Brethren (Herrnhuter) but enrolled in the far more liberal University of Halle in 1787 and studied theology, philosophy, and classical philology. After passing his theological examinations in 1790, he worked as a private tutor for a time and wrote critical essays on Kant, including "On the Highest Good" (1789), "On What Gives Value to Life" (1792–1793), and "On Freedom" (1790–1793). He also wrote on Spinoza, evolving a neo-Spinozistic monist philosophy, which would figure in his 1799 book devoted to the philosophy of religion, *On Religion: Speeches to Its Cultured Despisers.*

From 1794 to 1796, Schleiermacher was a pastor in Landsberg, moving to Berlin in 1796 to serve as a hospital chaplain. In this city, he met brothers Friedrich and August Wilhelm Schlegel and became interested in the developing romantic movement in German philosophy. He grew increasingly progressive, publishing in 1798 the quasi-feminist "Idea for a Catechism of Reason for Noble Ladies." His fellow romantics encouraged his 1799 *On Religion: Speeches to Its Cultured Despisers*, which argued that the immortality of the soul and even the existence of God are inessential to religion, asserting further that the world offers an endless variety of equally valid forms of religion. He also openly advocated granting the Jews of Prussia full civil rights.

Schleiermacher embarked on the ambitious project of translating Plato's dialogues, and the translations, which were published between 1804 and 1828, are widely considered masterpieces. In 1804, he began teaching at Halle University, earning more than local notoriety for his lectures on ethics and on hermeneutics. During the Napoleonic Wars, he left French-occupied Halle and, inspired by German nationalism, promoted resistance to the French occupation. He served as a preacher at the Dreifaltigkeitskirche during 1808-1809, was appointed professor of theology at the University of Berlin in 1810, and, the next year, was inducted into the Berlin Academy of Sciences.

The Academy served as a platform from which Schleiermacher lectured. His lectures on ethics, translation, dialectics, and Leibniz's idea of a universal language were especially important. He published *The Christian Faith* in 1821-1822, a work of systematic theology. It was his last major book. He died of pneumonia on February 12, 1834.

Today, Schleiermacher is studied mostly for his philosophical works on language, hermeneutics, and translation. He believed language was social in nature and that language did not merely transcribe thought but actively infused it. Indeed, he identified thought closely with linguistic expression. He emphasized word usage, not the referents of words, as the core of linguistic meaning, and he stressed the importance of understanding language in terms of historical periods and cultures.

As a philosopher of mind, Schleiermacher argued for the dependence of mind on body and saw the mind as a force. He thus stood in opposition to Descartes. His theory of hermeneutics combined his conceptualization of language and mind, and he argued that thought is virtually identical with language and that meaning inheres in word usage. All interpretation is effectively an act of translation because there are profound linguistic and intellectual differences between people. Adherence to doctrine impedes rather than facilitates both interpretation and translation. Indeed, Schleiermacher argued that interpretation is a far more difficult task than is commonly assumed. Whereas the mass of people believe that understanding occurs as a matter of course, Schleiermacher contended that misunderstanding occurs as a matter of course. Understanding, therefore, cannot be assumed but must be actively sought and willed at every turn.

His hermeneutic process was grounded in distinguishing between the *meaning* of a text and the question of its *truth*. It is best to interpret a text without assuming its truth. Moreover, interpretation is contextual and requires a thorough knowledge of the historical period within which the text was composed. Interpretation is a coin with two sides—the linguistic and the psychological. Linguistic interpretation is concerned with what is shared in a language, whereas psychological interpretation focuses on what is distinctive to a particular author.

As varied as Schleiermacher's intellectual interests were, it is liberalism that ultimately united them. Whether in theology or hermeneutics, Schleiermacher rejected absolutism and leavened all definitions with an appreciation of context. Often called the "Father of Modern Liberal Theology," Schleiermacher was an early liberal voice in philosophy as well.

Schopenhauer, Arthur

Born in Danzig (now Gdansk, Poland) on January 22, 1788, Arthur Schopenhauer is most famous for *The World as Will and Representation*

(1818; expanded in 1844), a major phenomenological text that describes the phenomenal world as the product of a metaphysical will. Schopenhauer developed Immanuel Kant's idealism into an atheist metaphysics (and concordant ethics) that overturned Kant and German idealism generally. His orientation toward the world was pessimistic, and, indeed, Schopenhauer has become a kind of byword for pessimism. His work influenced philosophers, literary figures, and psychologists, among them Friedrich Nietzsche, Ludwig Wittgenstein, Leo Tolstoy, Thomas Mann, Samuel Becket, Sigmund Freud, Carl Jung, and such modern physicists as Erwin Schrödinger and Albert Einstein.

Schopenhauer's father was a prosperous merchant and shipowner, who died, perhaps by his own hand, when Schopenhauer was seventeen. Two years later, the young man left his business apprenticeship and, in 1809, began studies at the University of Göttingen. He started in medicine but, after two years, moved on to philosophy. He enrolled at the University of Berlin, which he attended from 1811 to 1813, hearing lecturers by Johann Gottlieb Fichte and Friedrich Schleiermacher. His studies in Göttingen and Berlin encompassed physics, psychology, astronomy, zoology, archaeology, physiology, history, literature, and poetry, and in 1813 he wrote his doctoral dissertation, titled *The Fourfold Root of the Principle of Sufficient Reason.* This created the kernel of his mature philosophy, which is contained in the sentence, "The world is my representation."

Consciousness, by which such representation is made, is divided between subject and object. The object for the subject is the subject's representation. All our representations are objects for the subject, and all objects of the subject are our representations. The first dimension of the fourfold root of sufficient reason—the concept that everything must have a cause—is becoming, or the law of causality. The second, knowing, is the conceptual representation. The third is being in space and time, which shows that the existence of one relation implies the other. The fourth aspect deals with willing, or actions, and is the law of motivation.

Awarded his doctorate by the University of Jena, Schopenhauer moved to Dresden in 1814 and, by 1818, developed the Fourfold Root concept into his magnum opus, *The World as Will and Representation,* which argues that the world we experience is a representation dependent on the cognition of the perceiving subject. It is not a world that exists in itself, independently of the representation. Our so-called knowledge of objects, therefore, is thus a knowledge of phenomena and not things-in-themselves. The thing-in-itself, Schopenhauer argues, is "will," which is an unconscious, blind, aimless striving without knowledge and outside of space and time. The world as representation is thus a cognitive objectification of the will.

In 1818, Schopenhauer secured a lectureship at the University of Berlin, but he enjoyed little success in academia. After drifting from one opportunity to another, he moved to Frankfurt-am-Main, and then to Mannheim, before settling, in 1833, permanently in Frankfurt. Schopenhauer lived a solitary life of study and continued to write, producing in 1836 *On the Will in Nature*, which attempted to synthesize his metaphysical views with recent advances in science. He also developed an intense interest in Sinology (Chinese studies) and parapsychology.

In 1839, Schopenhauer published an essay titled "On the Freedom of Human Will," which won a prize from the Royal Norwegian Society of Sciences and Letters in Trondheim. This was followed in 1840 by "On the Basis of Morality," which was not well received. Nevertheless, he did begin to receive wider recognition, and by the time *The World as Will and Representation* appeared in a third edition in 1859, he was reasonably famous. He died on September 21, of the following year.

Schopenhauer's ethics flows from his metaphysics. He argues that no individual human actions are free because they are events in the world of appearance and therefore subject to the principle of sufficient reason. That is, one's actions are a necessary consequence of motives and the given character of the individual. "A man," he said, "can do as he will, but not will as he will." Thus, Schopenhauer's ethics is governed by a limiting necessity, and our salvation from this state lies only in the metaphysical realization that true free will and individuality are merely illusions.

Schopenhauer's metaphysics also extended to a philosophy of aesthetics. He saw the greatest art as portraying the world as objectively as possible, and he believed the function of art was to escape the pain of "willing"—that is, of desire and craving—through aesthetic contemplation, a state in which subject and object are at last no longer distinguishable.

Schopenhauer is infamous among some for what is described as his misogyny, and he did object to what he deemed the male's "reflexive" reverence for women, whom he believed were inherently "childish, frivolous and short-sighted" and intended "by nature ... to obey."

Seneca

Lucius Annaeus Seneca was born about 4 BC in Cordoba, Hispania (modern Spain) and was a dramatist as well as a Roman Stoic philosopher. The son of a rhetorician, he left Cordoba for Rome as a child and was trained there in law, rhetoric, and philosophy. As a young man, he earned fame as an orator but in AD 41 was banished to Corsica by Emperor Claudius. Agrippina, the mother of Nero, engineered Seneca's recall to Rome so that he could serve as her son's tutor.

When Nero ascended the throne in 54, Seneca served alongside Sextus Afranius Burrus as the young emperor's adviser. Indeed, thanks to his advisors, for the first few years of his reign, Nero managed to provide a decent government. With the death of Burrus in 62, however, Seneca's influence over Nero rapidly declined, and he effectively retired. Implicated (probably unjustly) in an assassination plot against the emperor, Seneca obeyed Nero's order to commit suicide, which he did by opening his veins in 65.

As a practicing politician, Seneca was both greedy and corrupt, but as a philosopher, he expressed the Stoic creed in moral essays collected in *Epistulae Morales ad Luclilium (Moral Epistles to Lucilius)* and in his nine tragedies, the best known of which are *Medea, Thyestes,* and *Hercules Furens.* His dramatic works exerted a powerful influence on the development of Renaissance tragedy, and his philosophical works were central to the revival of Stoic concepts in the Renaissance. Even today, many philosophy students form their ideas of Stoicism based on Seneca rather than on the Greek originators of the philosophy, whose writings survive—when they do at all—largely in fragmentary form.

Because Seneca's political career was turbulent and hazardous, his philosophical writings have often been taken as autobiographical, especially in his development of the Stoic ideal of finding consolation in philosophy. In addition to the *Moral Epistles,* Seneca wrote *Naturales quaestiones,* a work of natural philosophy—a subject rarely explored by the Roman philosophers. But it is for his exposition of Stoic ethics in *Moral Epistles* that Seneca is most remembered as a philosopher. He articulated the principles that philosophy is consolation for the suffering of life; that the task of a truly moral man is to suppress or at least moderate such destructive passions as anger and grief; and that the ultimate objective of the contemplative life is preparation for facing death. In the *Moral Epistles,* he extols a willingness to suffer poverty (something he never himself did), and celebrates the power of clemency and forgiveness, the importance of friendship, and the need for altruism. Seneca grounded his Stoic ethics in a belief that the universe is controlled by a rational providence, which demands reconciliation to individual adversity.

Smith, Adam

Although economists claim him as their own, Adam Smith was an important social and moral philosopher, the author of *The Theory of Moral Sentiments* (1759), which articulated the methodological, psychological, social, and ethical assumptions underlying his masterpiece of economics, *The Wealth of Nations* (1776).

The 1759 volume is a critical analysis of moral thought as it existed in the mid-eighteenth century. Smith argues that conscience is the product of social relationships through which human beings seek empathy, or what Adams describes as "mutual sympathy of sentiments." It is this quest that explains how humans, who come into the world without natural moral sentiments, acquire them. The experience of life includes the observance of the behavior and actions of others and the judgments people form of one another. What we perceive from the judgment of others incentivizes each of us to find the "mutual sympathy of sentiments."

What is compelling about *The Theory of Moral Sentiments* is the explanation of human emotions and drives that tend to hold self-interest in check. Indeed, an alternative definition of the "moral sentiments" might be as the faculty of human behavior that restrains self-interest. *The Wealth of Nations,* in contrast, returns to self-interest, revealing it as the moral engine behind free-market capitalism, the "invisible hand" that determines the wealth of nations.

Adam Smith was born in Kirkcaldy, Fife, Scotland, the son of the local comptroller of the customs, who died some six months before his son's birth. Although the exact date of his birth is not known, Smith was baptized on June 5, 1723. Little is known about his childhood, but at fifteen he enrolled at Glasgow University, where he studied moral philosophy under Francis Hutcheson. He entered Balliol College, Oxford, in 1740 but left in 1746, before his scholarship ended.

He found a patron in Henry Home, Lord Kames, and, in 1748, began delivering public lectures in Edinburgh, including among his subjects the economic philosophy of "natural liberty." In 1752, Smith was appointed professor of logic at Glasgow University and soon was awarded the chair of moral philosophy. He lectured on rhetoric, ethics, jurisprudence, and political economy. His 1759 *Theory of Moral Sentiments* generally established his reputation as a philosopher.

In 1763, Smith resigned his professorship to take up a more remunerative post as tutor to the Duke of Buccleuch, with whom he traveled during 1764-1766, mostly in France. On his return to Scotland, he devoted himself chiefly to writing *The Wealth of* Nations, which was published in 1776. Two years later, he received a sinecure as commissioner of customs in Scotland and lived with his mother in Edinburgh. He died in that city on July 17, 1790 from what is described only as a "painful illness."

Socrates

As a historical and cultural presence, no philosopher is more important than Socrates. Sufficient sources exist, especially Plato, to give us confidence that there was, in fact, a Greek philosopher from Athens named Socrates. In all but one of Plato's *Dialogues*, Socrates is the central character and source—or at least mouthpiece—of philosophical doctrine. If his role in these writings reflects historical fact and accurately expresses Socrates' life and philosophy, then he deserves to be counted as one of the principal founders of Western philosophy and, indeed, Western thought. Even more significantly, at least for the discipline of philosophy, he deserves to be identified as the first moral philosopher in the Western tradition.

This said, Socrates exists today as a shadow, who apparently left no writings—certainly none survive—and is therefore known only through the accounts of several classical writers, paramount among them two of his students, Xenophon (c. 430-354 BC) and Plato. If we could accept Plato's *Republic* and the other *Dialogues* as essentially accurate transcriptions of Socrates' philosophy, we would be able to credit him in detail with a trove of contributions to ethics and epistemology and with essentially laying the foundation of Western philosophy. But the fact is that the Socrates we know is more accurately called the "Platonic Socrates." He and his thought exist for us somewhere on a spectrum that spans transcription on one end and fiction on the other. Perhaps Plato gives us a highly faithful representation of the historical Socrates, or perhaps he puts his own words into the mouth of an essentially fictional character. Most likely, the *Dialogues* are, like all memoirs, a synthesis of recollection and invention.

In short, we must accept that the only source of Socratic philosophy is Plato and leave it at that. Thus, in this book, the entry on Plato is the place to find a discussion of the philosophy of Socrates.

Importantly, the name of Socrates has been lifted to identify two methodological concepts that figure importantly in philosophy and rhetoric. These are "Socratic irony," which is feigning ignorance as a means of confuting a rhetorical or philosophical adversary, and the "Socratic method," a cooperative argumentative dialogue between or among individuals, which consists of asking and answering questions that stimulate critical thinking and therefore extract ideas and assumptions through the evolution of the resulting discourse.

The description of "Socratic irony" is based on an observation or assertion that Socrates was a master at convincingly pretending to know nothing of a topic under discussion and to use that feigned ignorance to draw out from his adversary nonsensical or erroneous arguments. This form of rhetorical jiujitsu effectively prompted the adversary to confute or even refute himself.

The "Socratic method" is much more profound because it is far more than a rhetorical tactic. It is driven by a key epistemological assumption that knowledge ("truth") is either discovered or created in thought that is expressed in language, the expression created by the dialogue of multiple minds over the span of the dialogue. Truth thus emerges through a progressive combination of hypothesis creation, hypothesis testing, and hypothesis elimination.

As for the life of Socrates—bearing in mind that while accounts are relatively plentiful, considering he was a figure from antiquity, they do not extensively corroborate one another—the consensus is that he was born about 469 BC in Athens and died there in 399 BC. He was the son of Sophroniscus, a sculptor, and Phaenarete, a midwife. The family was well-to-do but not wealthy. Late in his life, he married Xanthippe, who (tradition has it) was a notorious shrew. The marriage produced three sons, none of whom achieved fame.

It is believed he developed an interest in science as a young man and became the student of the physicist Archelaus of Miletus. He fought with distinction as a hoplite in the Athenian army and may have participated in combat at Samos (441-440) and at the Battle of Potidaea (432-430). In this engagement during the Peloponnesian War, he reputedly saved the life of the controversial general Alcibiades. Socrates, it is said, also fought at Delium (424) and Amphipolis (437-438).

Socrates never sought or held public office but nevertheless believed that no citizen had the right to refuse public duty. He served on the Boule, also known as the Council of 500, during 406-405 and was the only councilor who stood against the condemnation of the Athenian generals accused of wrongdoing at the Battle of Arginusae (406). In 404, he defied the orders of the Thirty Tyrants (the pro-Spartan oligarchy installed in Athens after defeat in the Peloponnesian War) to make a politically motivated arrest of those generals.

In 399, Socrates was tried for the crime of "impiety" and convicted of religious heresies and corrupting the Athenian youth. Sentenced to death, he declined an escape plan offered by his friend Crito and instead drank hemlock to carry out, by suicide, the penalty levied against him.

Spinoza, Baruch

The most radical philosopher of the seventeenth century, Baruch Spinoza strikes modern readers as almost stunningly modern. In his own day, his philosophy was sometimes labeled "Spinozism" and described a monism in which God is defined, impersonally, as a singular and self-subsistent "substance," containing within itself both matter and thought.

In many respects, Spinoza was a philosopher of his age. He drew on Descartes for much of his epistemology and metaphysics and on Hobbes (as well as the ancient Stoics) for his ethics. His rational approach to religion was a well-established Jewish hermeneutic tradition. Yet he directed all these streams to a naturalistic view of God, strikingly impersonal, and conducive to a liberal approach to moral and political philosophy.

He was born Baruch Espinosa in Amsterdam, Dutch Republic, on November 24, 1632 and was a Jew of Portuguese Sephardic descent. Although best known today as Baruch Spinoza, he signed his learned Latin and Dutch works "Benedictus de Spinoza."

The middle son in a prominent family, he was educated at Talmud Torah school of Amsterdam and was likely destined for a career as a rabbi but withdrew from the school when he was seventeen so that he could help run his family's importing business. On July 27, 1656, when he was in his twenties, the Sephardic community of Amsterdam effectively excommunicated him, issuing a *herem* for his "abominable heresies." Although he had yet to publish his philosophical treatises, he must have already given voice to his rejection of the providential and transcendent God of Abraham as described in the Old Testament. Along with this, he may also have discussed his notion that the Law—Torah—was not given by God and was therefore not binding on Jews.

By 1661, he had abandoned Judaism and left Amsterdam to take up residence in Rijnsburg, near Leiden. He began composing *Treatise on the Emendation of the Intellect*, a work on epistemology and philosophical method (published posthumously in 1677). He then moved to Voorburg, near The Hague, and wrote a critical commentary on Descartes' *Principles of Philosophy* (1663).

At this point, Spinoza was also composing his *Ethics*, which he temporarily laid aside to write *Theological-Political Treatise* (*Tractatus Theologico-Politicus*), which he published anonymously in 1670. Drafted in response to the encroachment of the Dutch Reformed Church on religious freedom and freedom of thought and expression, this work critically examines both contemporary Judaism and Christianity and the Scriptures on which both are based. Arguing for democracy and freedom of speech and religion, Spinoza proposes that the cardinal duty of the state is to guarantee liberty.

Spinoza made his living as a lens grinder and, from 1670 on, enjoyed a modest pension funded by two friends. Offered the chair of philosophy at the University of Heidelberg, he declined, preferring to work as what today would be called an independent scholar. He corresponded with the likes of Christiaan Huygens and Gottfried Leibniz. He died, in Voorburg, on February 21, 1677, at the age of forty-four.

Spinoza's most radical and inflammatory argument is that while God exists, it is as an entity both abstract and impersonal. A monist, he argued that everything in the universe is one substance (Reality) and that "God" and "Nature" are merely two terms for the same thing. All the varied entities found in nature are "modes," modifications flowing from the One.

God—the One, the universe—has infinite attributes, but Spinoza identifies the two most salient as *thought* and *extension.* In this way, the mental and physical realms are intertwined in that they derive from the same One. While Spinoza distinguishes mental and physical effects on the human mind, he denies the Cartesian mind-body dualism, arguing that the universal Substance flows through body and mind alike.

In Spinoza's universe, God does not rule providentially but is, in fact, one with a deterministic system in which God could not have produced things in any other way but that in which they exist. Thus God is not transcendental with respect to the universe, and everything that happens, has happened, or will happen is the product of a chain of cause-and-effect that neither God (the Creator) nor human beings can change. Thus, prayer is in vain. Nevertheless, knowledge of God enables people to formulate the best response to the world around them.

Where does this leave ethics? Spinoza's determinism is so thoroughgoing that morality and ethical judgment eventuating in choice are based on an illusion. Blame and praise are alike ideals—more accurately, ideations—without basis in the real world. Ethics, therefore, must be based on a kind of Stoicism, with philosophy serving a therapeutic role by guiding people to happiness defined as moderating passion and reducing needs. Reason, Spinoza believed, could not simply overcome emotion. Only a stronger emotion could overcome a prevailing emotion. He therefore argued that "active" emotions—capable of rational understanding—could be used to overcome "passive" emotions, which were incapable of being understood. Do this, and a degree of happiness might be attained.

Good and evil, Spinoza, argued, are not intrinsically good or evil because everything proceeds from a determined necessity and is therefore perfect. We call some things good and some evil because they are either good or evil relative to humanity. With respect to the universe, however, all is necessary and therefore prefect. This being the case, the loftiest human virtue is knowledge of God or, what is precisely the same, knowledge of nature or the universe.

Thales of Miletus

Throughout centuries of Western letters, science, and philosophy, the name of Thales appears with astounding persistence. He is seen as having innovated thought itself, essentially beginning the replacement of mythology with philosophy and science.

Clearly a man of infinite curiosity in many fields, Thales is credited with the discovery of Ursa Minor, he made early observations in electricity, was an important pre-Euclidian mathematician (formulating applications later developed by Euclid), invented a primitive telescope, investigated the nature of the seasons, and observationally calculated the solstice. In short, he was a principal progenitor of "natural philosophy," the precursor of modern science, and was cited by Plato as one of the Pre-Socratic philosophers who constituted the "Seven Sages" of Ancient Greece.

His most immediate effect was on his fellow Pre-Socratics, who, following him, turned away from mythology and toward the careful observation of nature. Thales explained nature as embodying a unity that flowed from the existence of a single elementary material substance, which, Thales argued, was water.

The philosopher was born into a prosperous family in Miletus probably in 624 BC. At the time, Miletus was among the wealthiest and most influential of the Greek city-states. At this early epoch, however, Greek civilization trailed the cultures of Babylon and Egypt, and it is believed that Thales traveled to both regions for study, bringing back with him advanced knowledge in mathematics, astronomy, and commerce. Indeed, Thales' first vocation was that of merchant, most likely working within his family's business.

Some believe that Thales abandoned a lucrative commercial career after he studied in Egypt and decided to set up as a natural philosopher. He accurately predicted the solar eclipse of May 28, 585 BC and (according to Aristotle) was the first philosopher known to have inquired into the basic element of the universe—its "First Cause." His answer, water, came in part because of its ability to change form and to move yet remain, in its essence, unchanged.

There is no surviving text by Thales, and the sum of his thought is contained in what others wrote about him. Thus, it is difficult to definitively separate his empiricism from the quotation Aristotle cites: "All things are full of gods." From this, Aristotle concluded that Thales supposed the soul was the cause of movement. Thales, according to Aristotle, pointed to the magnetic lodestone and declared that it was endowed with a soul because it causes iron to move. Whether justifiably or not, Plato appropriated "All things are full of gods" as proof that Thales was an idealist akin to himself.

Thales founded a philosophical school, known as the Milesian School, and likely similar in purpose if not spirit to Plato's much later Academy. Still, he apparently found himself repeatedly called upon to defend philosophy, which paid poorly if at all, as a profession. Aristotle related that, in response to a criticism of his poverty, Thales applied his astronomical observations to a prediction of a bumper olive crop. He borrowed enough money to commandeer all the olive presses in Miletus and Chios and, when a large crop did in fact come in, he hired out the presses he controlled at substantial profit. This, he said, was a demonstration that philosophers could be rich ... if they wanted to be.

Thoreau, Henry David

Second only to his friend and quasi-patron Ralph Waldo Emerson, Henry David Thoreau was a founding figure in the Transcendentalist movement, the American translation of the German Romanticism of Johann Gottfried Herder and Friedrich Schleiermacher combined with the radical skepticism of Englishman David Hume. The Transcendentalists were forward-looking, politically and socially activist (they were ardent abolitionists in the years preceding the Civil War), and utopian in outlook. Iconoclastic, the Transcendentalists were critical of the conformity of contemporary American society and its slavish imitation of European aesthetics and social mores. Emerson and Thoreau led the way in advocating what the twentieth-century Existentialists called "authenticity" and what Emerson called an "original relationship" with nature. They attempted to enact their beliefs in such social experiments as the commune of Brook Farm and the experience of solitude in nature at wooded Walden Pond.

Henry David Thoreau was born on July 12, 1817, in Concord, Massachusetts, the son of a pencil factory owner. He was educated at

Concord Academy, at which he learned surveying before enrolling at Harvard College, where he studied classics and Eastern languages. He graduated with B.A. in 1837.

Thoreau returned to Concord after college and began a remarkable *Journal*, which ran to fourteen posthumously published (1906) volumes. He never married and worked briefly as a schoolteacher, a surveyor, and a handyman as well as an occasional public lecturer. He was befriended by Ralph Waldo Emerson, who took him in to live with his family during 1841-1843 and 1847-1848. He was a featured contributor of essays to the *Dial*, a Transcendentalist periodical, and from July 1845 until September 1847 he embarked on what he called an experiment in living deliberately—in paring down life to its essentials and doing so in the quiet surrounds of nature. He built a hut on land owned by Emerson beside Walden Pond. He studied nature with the keen eye of a naturalist, and, at Walden, he wrote his first book, *A Week on the Concord and Merrimack Rivers* (1849), based on an excursion he and his brother John had made ten years earlier. He also took voluminous notes at Walden for what became his magnum opus, a philosophical memoir titled *Walden, or Life in the Woods*, which was published in 1854.

Thoreau's writing was little read during his brief life, but he is remembered today as one of the creators of the so-called American Renaissance in literature—a group that includes Emerson, Nathaniel Hawthorne, Herman Melville, Walt Whitman, and Emily Dickinson. He transformed Transcendentalist philosophy into literature and is one of the world's great memoirists and nature writers. Trips to Cape Cod and Maine provided the material for *The Maine Woods* (1864) and *Cape Cod* (1865), two more Transcendentalist contemplations of nature.

As a social philosopher, he was the champion of civil disobedience, which he applied to peacefully defiant protest against the United States-Mexican War (1846-1848), which Thoreau and most of his circle saw as unjust to Mexico and as a craven attempt to acquire more territory to create more states for the expansion of slavery. His 1849 essay, originally titled "Resistance to Civil Government" but better known as "Civil Disobedience," defined this form of protest and inspired, in coming generations, the likes of Mohandas Gandhi, Martin Buber, Martin Luther King Jr., and others.

Thoreau contracted tuberculosis in 1835 and experienced periods of remission alternating with spans of illness. By 1861, he understood that his condition was terminal but kept writing. His friends marveled at the tranquility with which he accepted his approaching end, which came at the age of forty-four on May 6, 1862. Before he passed, he uttered, "Now comes good sailing," adding two cryptic words, "moose" and "Indian," the significance of which has been the subject of considerable scholarly speculation.

Turing, Alan Mathison

Alan Mathison Turing framed the theory of modern computing with both his "Turing machine" thought experiment and his pioneering work on artificial intelligence. The paradigm-shifting technological impact of this work is apparent everywhere in modern civilization. In terms of metaphysics and the philosophy of mind, Turing explored and defined the border between human and artificial intelligence.

Turing was born on June 23, 1912, in London, the son of a civil servant in the Indian service. Enrolled at the age of six in St. Michael's Day School, he was immediately recognized as a gifted student and attended Hazelhurst Preparatory School and Sherborne School, which positioned him for admission in 1931 to King's College, Cambridge, from which he graduated in 1934 with first-class honors in mathematics.

In 1936, Turing published "On Computable Numbers, with an Application to the *Entscheidungsproblem*." Posed by the German mathematician David Hilbert in 1928, the *Entscheidungsproblem* ("Decision Problem") asked: Is there an algorithm that, when fed any statement in the language of first-order arithmetic, determines in a finite number of steps whether or not the statement is provable using the usual rules of first-order logic? In 1931, the mathematician Kurt Gödel presented a formal mathematical proof that no such algorithm exists; Turing reached the same answer, not through formal math, but by a thought experiment in which a hypothetical "universal computing machine" (what others later called a "Turing machine") serves as a device capable of performing any mathematical computation that could be represented by an algorithm. He argued that such an imagined computer would be unable to answer the *Entscheidungsproblem* in the affirmative, but, more important, he demonstrated that it could perform any calculation capable of being represented by an algorithm.

Thus, Turing conceptualized a universal computer as a mathematical abstraction of an entity capable of reading from, writing on, and moving forward and backward an indefinite tape, thereby providing a model for computer-like procedures. The behavior of a Turing machine is specified by listing an alphabet (that is, a collection of symbols read and written), a set of internal states, and a mapping of an alphabet and internal states, all of which determine what the symbol written and the tape motion will be, and also what internal state will follow when the machine is in a given internal state and reads a given symbol. Later, in a 1948 essay, "Intelligent Machinery," Turing provided a less abstract physical visualization of such a machine. It consisted of:

> an unlimited memory capacity obtained in the form of an infinite tape marked out into squares, on each of which a symbol could be printed. At any moment there is one symbol in the machine; it is called the scanned symbol. The machine can alter the scanned symbol, and its behavior is in part determined by that symbol, but the symbols on the tape elsewhere do not affect the behavior of the machine. However, the tape can be moved back and forth through the machine, this being one of the elementary operations of the machine. Any symbol on the tape may therefore eventually have an innings [turn at bat, in cricket].

The physical components of the machine, as Turing imagined it in 1948, corresponded to the major components of any modern digital computer.

From 1936 to 1938, Turing studied at Princeton University under the American mathematician and philosopher Alonzo Church, who also addressed the *Entscheidungsproblem*, but did so mathematically. Princeton awarded Turing a Ph.D. in 1938. His dissertation, *Systems of Logic Based on Ordinals*, further developed the theoretical science behind computing by introducing the concept of relative computing, which carried computer theory beyond problems that could not be solved by Turing machines. While he was at Princeton, Turing also took the fateful step of studying the practical application of theoretical mathematics to cryptology, in the process actually constructing most of an electro-mechanical binary multiplier, a device capable of multiplying binary (base 2) numbers. This was a practical implementation of the arithmetical basis of digital computing.

Turing returned to England and King's College in 1938. At the outbreak of World War II in September 1939, he volunteered his services at the headquarters of the Government Code and Cipher School at Bletchley Park, Buckinghamshire. Working with an elite cryptography team, Turing broke the ciphers produced by the hitherto unbreakable German "Enigma" encryption and decryption machines. This gave the Allies an indispensable edge in World War II combat operations, especially on the waters of the North Atlantic.

While laboring to crack Enigma, Turing realized that the Germans had not considered one unique weakness of a machine-generated cipher, which is that, while impervious to human code breakers, it could be broken by another, properly programmed, machine. Drawing on his experience at Princeton, Turing supervised the design and construction of radically new codebreaking machines called Bombes. They were a series of early electro-mechanical computers, which, by 1942, enabled British cryptanalysts to decode some 39,000 intercepted Enigma messages each month. Later in the war, this monthly volume rose to an astounding 84,000 messages. For his contribution to the British war effort, Turing was made an officer of the Order of the British Empire (OBE).

After the war, in 1945, Turing joined the National Physical Laboratory (NPL) and began to design a fully electronic computer. His design for the Automatic Computing Engine (ACE) was a nearly complete plan for an electronic stored-program general-purpose digital computer. But his superiors considered it unbuildable and Turing resigned from NPL to become deputy director of the Computing Machine Laboratory in Manchester. There he designed the programming system for the Mark I, the world's first commercially available electronic digital computer.

Now a full-fledged philosopher of computer science, Turing published "Computing Machinery and Intelligence" while he was on the faculty of the University of Manchester in 1950. He considered the question "Can machines think?" Finding that "thinking" was a concept almost impossible to meaningfully define, he tried a less ambiguous question, asking if there are "imaginable digital computers" that could excel in the "Imitation Game."

In this parlor game with three players, player A is a man, player B is a woman, and player C, the interrogator, may be of either sex. Player C cannot see players A or B and can communicate with them only through written notes. By asking questions of A and B, C tries to determine which is the man and which is the woman. Player A is assigned to trick the interrogator into making the wrong decision, while player B attempts to assist the interrogator in making the right one. In the end, Turing concluded that it is impossible to argue definitively against the proposition that machines can think. This "proof" is foundational to the philosophy, science, and technology of artificial intelligence (AI).

In 1951, Turing was made a fellow of the Royal Society, but less than a year later, he was arrested and tried on charges of homosexuality—then a crime under British law—and sentenced to a year of hormone therapy ("chemical castration") in lieu of prison. In the depths of the Cold War, the

British government also judged him to be a significant security risk, his homosexuality making him vulnerable to blackmail by Communist agents. He was stripped of government security clearances but allowed to retain his academic position at the University of Manchester as the institution's first reader in the Theory of Computing. Made ill by the hormone treatments, he grew despondent. On June 7, 1954, he was found dead in his bed, the victim of cyanide poisoning. His death was ruled a suicide.

Venn, John

Born on August 4, 1834 in Kingston upon Hull, Yorkshire, John Venn was a British mathematician, logician, and philosopher. He is most widely remembered for developing the Venn diagram, which is a simple way of showing all possible logical relations between a finite collection of sets. Venn diagrams have been used in math and logic education as well as in the development of set theory, probability, logic, and computer science.

Beyond the Venn diagram, John Venn wrote a major book on probability, *The Logic of Chance* (1866), which put forth a frequency theory of probability, proposing that probability should be determined by how often a certain thing is forecast to occur rather than left to various attempts at guesswork, no matter how "educated." The very idea that "chance" admits of "logic" has profound epistemological implications.

In 1881, Venn published *Symbolic Logic,* an advance in this field that built on the theories of George Boole. It was in the context of this work that Venn introduced the diagraming tool that would come to be named for him.

John Venn's father, Rev. Henry Venn, was rector of the parish of Drypool in Yorkshire, and his son was the descendent of generations of evangelicals. This—and the death of his mother when he was only three—made for a stern upbringing. In September 1864, he was sent to London with his brother Henry to attend Sir Roger Cholmeley's School (today known as the Highgate School). He subsequently transferred to Islington proprietary school before entering Gonville and Caius College, Cambridge, in October 1853.

Venn received a degree in mathematics in 1857 and became a fellow. In 1859, following family tradition, he took orders as an Anglican priest and served at the church in Cheshunt, Hertfordshire, and then in Mortlake, Surrey. In 1862, however, he returned to Cambridge as a lecturer in moral science while also studying and teaching logic and probability theory. In 1869, he began giving intercollegiate lectures, and it was sometime during this activity that he developed the diagramming method later named for him.

In 1883, Venn resigned from the clergy because, he declared, Anglicanism was incompatible with his philosophical beliefs. Shortly after this, he was awarded a Sc.D. by Cambridge and elected a Fellow of the Royal Society. Venn's thriving academic career was crowned by his election to the presidency of Gonville and Caius College in 1903. He held that post until his death on April 4, 1923.

Voltaire (François-Marie Arouet)

Philosopher, historian, poet, dramatist, novelist, wit, and advocate of freedom of speech and religion, Voltaire was the embodiment of the Enlightenment. He was born François-Marie Arouet in Paris on November 21, 1694. The son of a lawyer, he was educated at the Jesuit College of Louis-le-Grand, where he gave rein to a remarkable ability to make influential lifelong friendships among the young dukes and marquises who were his classmates. He studied classics and veered sharply away from his father's profession to embrace instead a literary career.

Following the stage triumph of *Oedipe* (1718), his first tragedy, he adopted the pseudonym of Voltaire. After he was twice unjustly imprisoned in the Bastille and then forced into exile to England (1726-1728), there awakened in him a passion for justice. Nevertheless, he made good use of his English exile by allowing himself to come under the influence of the works of Newton and Locke. In 1733, he published, in England, *Letters on the English*, which were subsequently published in France in 1734. The French crown took the work as an attack on itself and publicly burned the books.

Voltaire lived with his mistress Émilie, marquise du Chatelet at her husband's estate in Cirey, until her death in 1749. While living with her, he wrote a study of Isaac Newton, several plays, and commenced an important correspondence with the future Emperor Frederick the Great of Prussia. In the meantime, Madame de Pompadour, mistress of Louis XV, intervened with the king to win him favor in Versailles, and Voltaire was suddenly appointed royal historiographer and gentleman of the king's bedchamber. He was also made a member of French Academy. He took up residence from June 1750 to May 1753 at the court of Frederick the Great but left after a dispute—which was subsequently resolved, whereupon the two figures resumed their former correspondence.

While pursuing the literary life, Voltaire proved himself a savvy investor and moneylender to the wealthy. He amassed a substantial fortune and purchased in 1758 Les Delices near Geneva, followed by the estate of Ferney across the Swiss border in France. Here he lived in great luxury, holding court to which the eminent men and women of Europe flocked. Yet he also worked diligently, writing articles for the great *Encyclopédie* and novels—the most celebrated of which was *Candide* (1759)—as well as plays. He also undertook the labor of editing the works of the tragedian Pierre Corneille (1606-1684).

Even from the lap of luxury, Voltaire became a literary activist, writing—anonymously, for the most part—appeals on behalf of the underprivileged majority of France. He left Ferney in February 1778 and lived in Paris until his death, at age eighty, on May 30, 1778.

Besides *Candide,* Voltaire wrote other major literary works, including the tragic dramas *Brutus* (1730), *Zaire* (1732), *Merope* (1743), and *Irene* (1778) and the novel *Zadig* (1747). His major philosophical books include the *Dictionnaire philosophique* (1752), an alphabetically arranged encyclopedia of reasoned articles mostly analytically criticizing such institutions as the Roman Catholic Church, Judaism, and Islam. The *Dictionnaire* is a work of moral philosophy and critical of the concept of God generally and of Christianity in particular.

Other philosophical works include *Treatise on Tolerance* (1763), an argument in favor of religions toleration; *Idées républicaines* (1765), an argument defending free thought and free expression; *The Philosophy of History* (1765), which defined the study of history as a philosophical discipline; and *Des singularités de la nature* (1768), largely a defense of the existence of a supreme being who created nature to benefit humanity.

Voltaire regarded philosophy and writing as forms of action, much as Jean-Paul Sartre would in the twentieth century. He was an acute social critic and advocate of reform, who delighted in deconstructing the institutions of his age, especially the Catholic Church and the clergy. He had no direct quarrel with monarchy as an institution, and, indeed, was very skeptical of the judgment of the common people in great affairs. Nevertheless, he espoused and argued in support of "natural religion" and believed that organized religion and priesthoods should be done away with. He opposed religious intolerance and passionately advocated for equality under law. Until this measure of justice could be won, however, he counseled maintaining a philosophy of stoic endurance.

Warnock, Mary

Helen Mary Warnock, Baroness Warnock, was born Helen Wilson on April 14, 1924, in Winchester, England, the youngest of seven children. Her father, Archibald Edward Wilson (1875-1923), housemaster and German tea cher at Winchester College, died before her birth, and she was raised by her mother and a nanny.

Inherited wealth enabled Warnock to enjoy a fine education, including, in 1942, at Lady Margaret Hall, Oxford, where she studied classics. From 1949 to 1966, Warnock was a fellow and tutor in philosophy at St Hugh's College, Oxford while her husband, Geoffrey Warnock, was a fellow of Magdalen College. She participated in philosophical radio debates broadcast on the BBC Third Programme and was invited to write on contemporary ethics for a popular series published by Oxford University Press. This led her to the study of Jean-Paul Sartre and Existentialism and prompted her to publish three books on Existential philosophy between 1963 and 1970.

While Talbot Research Fellow at Lady Margaret Hall during 1972-1976, Warnock published a book titled *Imagination* (1976) and then worked at St. Hugh's College as senior research fellow from 1976 to 1984, becoming an honorary fellow of the college in 1985 and mistress of Girton College, Cambridge from 1984 to 1991.

Warnock retired from teaching in 1992 but continued to write prolifically, publishing *The Uses of Philosophy* (1992), *Imagination and Time* (1994), and *An Intelligent Person's Guide to Ethics* (1998). She delivered the Gifford Lectures, entitled "Imagination and Understanding," at the University of Glasgow in 1992.

Warnock is an example of a philosopher who extensively applied her philosophical perspective to public service and the creation of public policy. Her interest in the philosophy of education led to her appointment in 1974 to chair a government inquiry on special education, and her 1978 report drove radical change in the field by emphasizing teaching learning-disabled children in mainstream schools.

From 1979 to 1984, Warnock served on a Royal Commission on environmental pollution and, during 1982-1984, chaired the Committee of Inquiry into Human Fertilisation and Embryology. Her report prompted passage, in 1990, of the Human Fertilisation and Embryology Act, which regulated human fertility treatment and experiments using human embryos. The act requires licensing for such procedures as in vitro fertilization and bans research on human embryos more than fourteen days old. During 1984-1989, Warnock chaired a Home Office Committee on animal experimentation. She subsequently served on an advisory panel on spoliation, and, in 2008, created controversy by proposing that people with dementia should be permitted an assisted suicide if they believed they presented a burden "to their family or the state." Warnock died on March 20, 2019, at the age of ninety-four.

Whitehead, Alfred North

Alfred North Whitehead is among the best-known mathematicians and most celebrated philosophers of the first half of the twentieth century. He is famed for developing the early phases of the analytic philosophy movement and for his work as a mathematician, a mathematical logician, and as a philosopher of science. He went on to develop "process philosophy," which also spawned "process theology." As a mathematician and logician, he collaborated with Bertrand Russell on the monumental three-volume *Principia Mathematica* (1910, 1912, 1913).

Whitehead was born February 15, 1861, in Ramsgate, Isle of Thanet, Kent, England, the son of a clergyman. He entered Trinity College, Cambridge, in 1880 with a scholarship in mathematics and was elected to membership in the elite Apostles discussion club in 1884. Graduating with a B.A. in mathematics that year, he was elected a Fellow in Mathematics at Trinity College.

In 1890, he met Bertrand Russell, his future collaborator, and married Evelyn Wade. Elected a Fellow of the Royal Society in 1903—in recognition of his work on universal algebra, symbolic logic, and the foundations of mathematics—he resigned from Cambridge in 1910 and moved to London, where, in 1911, he was appointed Lecturer at University College London. The following year, he was elected president of both the South-Eastern Mathematical Association and the London branch of the Mathematical Association, and in 1914 was appointed Professor of Applied Mathematics at the Imperial College of Science and Technology. In 1915, he was elected President of the Mathematical Association for 1915–1917.

Whitehead met Albert Einstein in 1921 and, in 1922, was elected president of the Aristotelian Society for 1922–1923. It was the prospect of mandatory retirement that prompted Whitehead to leave England and accept an appointment at Harvard University in 1924. This move was especially propitious in that it took him out of an academic milieu in which he was recognized essentially as a mathematician and put him in a place where he could be a philosopher. Just one year after his arrival, Whitehead delivered Harvard's prestigious Lowell Lectures, which became the 1926 book *Science and the Modern World.* This was followed in 1927-1928 by the Gifford Lectures at the University of Edinburgh, which resulted in *Process and Reality* (1929), a kind of prelude to his 1933 *Adventures of Ideas.* Together, these three volumes constitute his metaphysics, which rejected fragmentation of the world into objective facts and subjective values.

Whitehead sought to harmonize the abstractions of science with those of art, morals, and religion—and to do so in harmony with the intuitions offered by human experience. This led to his most original philosophical concept, an ontology defined as "process philosophy." It is an ontology of becoming, which identifies metaphysical reality with change. Process philosophy is a departure from earlier concepts of change as illusory or accidental and instead regards change as the very foundation of reality, which Whitehead defined as a process of becoming.

From Whitehead's new metaphysics, others—including Charles Hartshorne and John B. Cobb—developed the influential concept of process theology, which conceives of God not as unchanging and remote from change, but as affecting and affected by temporal processes. Thus, while God is eternal (in that He will never die), immutable (in that He is always and forever good), and impassible (in that His eternal aspect is unaffected by actuality), God is also temporal, mutable, and passible.

Asked to define religion, Whitehead replied that "Religion is what the individual does with his own solitariness. It runs through three stages ... the transition from God the void to God the enemy, and from God the enemy to God the companion." This definition, which took religion out of the traditional realm of group consensus and celebration and applied it to the solitary individual, seemed to many especially suited to life in the twentieth century.

Whitehead served as Professor of Philosophy at Harvard University until his retirement in 1937. In 1931, he was elected a Fellow of the British Academy and, in 1945, was awarded the Order of Merit. He died two years later, on December 30, 1947, in Cambridge, Massachusetts.

Among Whitehead's many students were the mathematicians Bertrand Russell, G. H. Hardy, and J. E. Littlewood; physicists Edmund Whittaker, Arthur Eddington, and James Jeans; economist John Maynard Keynes; and philosophers Susanne Langer, Nelson Goodman, and Willard van Orman Quine.

Wittgenstein, Ludwig

One of the giants of twentieth-century philosophy, particularly in its analytic dimension, Ludwig Wittgenstein has had an enduring impact on work in logic and language as well as on the relationships between aesthetics and culture and between ethics and religion. In the area of mind, his work is relevant to the links between perception and intention.

In the span of his sixty-two-year life, Wittgenstein completed just two books, *Tractatus Logico-Philosophicus,* a 75-page volume published in 1921, and *Philosophical Investigations,* published posthumously in 1953. Some additional 20,000 pages of manuscript were found among his personal papers when he died of metastasized prostate cancer on April 29, 1951. Some of this material has been edited and published, and much of the rest is accessible digitally via the Wittgenstein Archives at the University of Bergen (http://wab.uib.no/wab_nachlass.page/). Philosophers continue to pore over this work.

Many students of Wittgenstein's philosophy judge that his thought is defined by his two main works. The period marked by the *Tractatus* concerns the application, through language, of modern logic to metaphysics for the purpose of exploring relations among world, thought, and language. This, in turn, reflects upon the very essence of philosophy. The later *Philosophical Investigations* extends the discussion to a self-reflexive critique of virtually the entire body of traditional philosophy—including Wittgenstein's own *Tractatus.* The result is a resolutely non-systematic approach to philosophy, yet one that does not abandon the endeavor to understand, in philosophical terms, the problems that thousands of years of philosophy have engaged.

Wittgenstein was born on April 26, 1889, in Vienna, the scion of one of the wealthiest industrial families in Europe. After private tutoring and subsequent enrollment in a Realschule at Linz, he studied mechanical engineering at the Technische Hochschule Berlin, from which he graduated in 1908. That year, he enrolled at Manchester University to study aeronautical engineering. A developing interest in the philosophy of mathematics led him to a meeting in 1911 with Gottlob Frege at the University of Jena. Frege recommended that he study at Cambridge with Bertrand Russell. Wittgenstein did just that, working with Russell from 1911 to 1913, when he returned to Austria. The following year, at the outbreak of World War I (1914–1918), he joined the Austrian army. Captured in 1918, he spent the final months of the war in a POW camp.

During the tumult of that first great cataclysm of the twentieth century, Wittgenstein began work on what would become *Tractatus Logico-Philosophicus.* After its publication, he became somewhat unmoored, feeling that his book had solved all philosophical problems. He abandoned philosophy, gave away large sums of money, and pursued miscellaneous vocations until 1929, when he returned to Cambridge and once again immersed himself in philosophy. He now began to look upon *Tractatus* as dogmatic and, throughout the 1930s and 1940s led seminars at Cambridge in which his ideas developed into those posthumously published in *Philosophical Investigations.*

He turned away from formal logic to ordinary language and was on the verge of publishing *Philosophical Investigations* in 1945, only to withdraw it—though not without subsequently authorizing posthumous publication.

The remarkably brief *Tractatus* consists of seven propositions and virtually no arguments. Its primary objective was to define the relationship between language and reality and then to define the limits of both knowing and science. He defined the world as the totality of facts rather than of things, proposing that the facts in logical space constitute the world. He went on to develop an atomistic epistemology in which the world consists of the totality of interconnected atomic facts and in which all propositions make "pictures" of the world. These pictures are beyond the competence of language to describe, and because a thought is a "proposition with a sense," most philosophical propositions are not false but literally nonsensical. Indeed, the deepest problems are not problems at all, but failures to understand the logic of language. So, Wittgenstein concluded, philosophy attempts to say something where nothing can be properly said. The alternative to this futile endeavor is a logical statement of a proposition in the form of a truth function. Beyond this, Wittgenstein suggested, it was impossible to progress. "Whereof one cannot speak, thereof one must be silent," Wittgenstein wrote as his seventh and final thesis.

Philosophical Investigations rejected the assumption that underlay *Tractatus,* namely that the task of logical analysis is to discover the elementary propositions, whose form was not yet known. *Philosophical Investigations* moves from the "dogmatism" of this assumption—away from logic—and toward ordinary language. Ultimately, Wittgenstein came to look at philosophy in a new way, as an embrace of language used as a kind of disciplined intellectual therapy.

Perhaps fittingly, Wittgenstein's posthumous reputation remains unsettled. Some see him as having defined the limits of philosophy and of logic and of thought itself, while others have dismiss his work as ultimately obscurantist and even trivial. And yet even his critics do not deny the enduring importance of Wittgenstein's challenge to philosophy and expression.

Xenophanes

Born about 570 BC in Colophon, Ancient Greece, Xenophanes was a poet, epistemologist, metaphysician, and theologian. He is best known for his criticism of anthropomorphism in religion and for his forays into monotheism. His reflections on epistemology are also of importance, and, if Plato and Aristotle are correct, he, and not Parmenides, may deserve credit for founding Eleatic philosophy—the view that reality, changeable appearances notwithstanding, is a changeless "One." In his own time, he was best known as an itinerant poet, a "rhapsode," who criticized other poets' tales of the gods.

What is known of his life comes from Diogenes Laertius, who reported that Xenophanes had been born in Colophon and was active during the sixtieth Olympiad—540–537 BC. For some reason, he was "banished from his native city" and thus settled in Elea (in Italy), also living for a time in Zancle and Catana (in modern Sicily). His verse (which survives almost exclusively in attributed fragments) attacked both Hesiod and Homer for their anthropomorphism of the gods.

It is believed that Xenophanes was the first Greek philosopher to offer some systematic account of the nature of divinity and also to adumbrate monotheism in a fragment that mentions "One god greatest among gods and men, / Not at all like mortals in body or in thought."

Xenophanes also offered social criticism, making remarks on proper conduct at symposia and what constitutes personal excellence. He also discusses human foibles. He counsels moderation in life, condemns the pursuit of luxuries, and criticizes the honor accorded wealth and power versus the scant recognition virtue commands. His forays into epistemology emphasize the subjectivity of human taste. "If god had not made yellow honey," he wrote, "[people] would think that figs were far sweeter." Thus, judgment is subjective, limited and conditioned by personal experience, and knowledge therefore uncertain.

Xenophanes made several observations relevant to natural philosophy and has been credited by some with viewing the earth as the *archê* ("first principle") of all things, with describing the sea as a container of many mixtures, and with observing that the soul is composed of earth and water. In short, to him is ascribed a "two-substance theory" of metaphysics, in which all things are either earth, or water, or earth variously combined with water. Xenophanes vividly describes the sea as

> ... the source of water and of wind,
> For without the great sea, there would be no wind
> Nor streams of rivers, nor rainwater from on high
> But the great sea is the begetter of clouds, winds, and rivers.

He saw in clouds an explanation the origin of the sun and the stars (burning clouds) and the moon (a compressed cloud).

Fragments attributed to Xenophanes pose such epistemological questions as

- "How much can any mortal being hope to know?"
- "Does truth come to us through our own efforts or by divine revelation?"
- "What role do our sense faculties play in the acquisition of knowledge?"

Xenophanes wrote that "no man has seen nor will there be anyone who knows about the gods and what I say about all things" and goes on to observe, "But opinion is allotted to all." He does not, however, condemn "opinion," which he sees as essentially better than no knowledge at all and, in fact, worthy of being "believed as like the realities…" The philosopher died about 475 BC.

Zeno of Citium

Zeno of Citium was born in Citium, Cyprus, about 334 BC, and is considered the founder of Stoicism, a philosophy he taught in Athens from around 300 BC until his death, about 262 BC. Zeno's Stoicism was founded on the moral ideas of the Cynics and set as the goal of existence living a life virtue, which he defined as a life in harmony with nature.

What is known about Zeno's own life comes from Diogenes Laërtius' *Lives and Opinions of Eminent Philosophers*, written in the third century AD. Diogenes records that Zeno became interested in philosophy after an oracle responded to his question about how he should lead the best life with the advice that he should "take on the complexion of the dead." This advice did not immediately set him on a course toward becoming a philosopher. Instead, he became a merchant and grew wealthy. He suffered a shipwreck, which landed him not far from Athens, where he visited a bookseller. He purchased Xenophon's *Memorabilia* and was so taken by the material he found there on Socrates that he asked the bookseller where men like Socrates could be found. This led to a meeting with Crates of Thebes, a celebrated Cynic, and Zeno became his pupil.

Zeno studied with others as well, including the Platonists Xenocrates and Polemo. He then began teaching in the Agora of Athens and soon accumulated disciples of his own. Originally, they were known as the Zenonians, but later were called the Stoics, after the *Stoa Poikile*, the colonnade at the

Agora where poets and philosophers gathered. Zeno declined the honor of Athenian citizenship when it was offered to him, lest he appear unfaithful to Citium.

Diogenes Laërtius reports that Zeno died after he tripped, fell, and broke his toe. He struck the ground with his fist and spoke a line from *Niobe* (a lost play be Aeschylus): "I come, I come, why dost thou call for me?" With that, he held his breath and died—about 262 BC.

Zeno's logic was faulted by Cicero as inferior to that of his predecessors. Nevertheless, Zeno laid out his method clearly. Stretching out his fingers, he showed the palm of his hand. "Perception is a thing like this." he explained. Closing his fingers a little, he defined "Assent ... like this." Next, he completely closed his hand and exhibited his fist. "This," he explained, "is Comprehension." Finally, he took his right fist into his left hand, squeezed, and proclaimed it Knowledge.

As to physics, Zeno believed that the universe is God, which is a divine reasoning entity, of which all the parts belong to the whole. Into this pantheistic vision, Zeno imported the physics of Heraclitus, arguing that the universe contained a divine fire, which foresees all and produces all. The divine fire, which is also called the *aether*, is the foundation of all that happens in the universe. Thus, the primary substance of the Universe is derived from fire, becomes air, and then water. Next, the thicker portion of the water becomes earth and the thinner becomes air once again—before it finally rarefies back into fire. The souls of individuals are of the same fire as the world-soul.

Zeno's ethics rested on a single good, which is the goal to which a man should strive. By using right reason, which coincides with Universal Reason (Logos), a person becomes one with everything.

Zeno of Elea

Born about 495 BC in Elea, Zeno of Elea was a Pre-Socratic philosopher known for his paradoxes. Aristotle further credits him with inventing the dialectic.

No less a figure than Bertrand Russell called Zeno's paradoxes "immeasurably subtle and profound." The most important of the paradoxes purport to show that motion is impossible by revealing contradictions in assumptions regarding motion. Another paradox purports to invalidate the commonsense assumption that the world contains many things. The motive for Zeno's paradoxes is disputed, but it is traditionally believed that they were intended to defend the monistic views of his mentor, Parmenides.

Plato's *Parmenides* dialogue and Aristotle's *Physics* both mention Zeno of Elea. Plato writes that he visited Athens in company with Parmenides. Dates mentioned in Plato's account suggest that Zeno was born about 490 BC. The third century AD biographer Diogenes Laërtius, in his *Lives and Opinions of Eminent Philosophers*, reports that Zeno was the *natural* son of Teleutagoras and the *adopted* son of Parmenides. He was arrested—perhaps even killed—by Nearchus, the tyrant of Elea, for conspiring to overthrow him. Under torture, Zeno refused to reveal the identities of his coconspirators but told Nearchus that he had a secret to reveal. When the tyrant leaned in close to hear him, Zeno bit his ear. (Another account says that he bit off his nose.) Whatever the cause of his death, Zeno of Elea is believed to have died about 430 BC.

The most famous paradoxes of Zeno include:

1. The Dichotomy paradox: That which is moving must arrive at the half-way stage before it reaches its goal. But before it can get half-way, it must get a quarter of the way. Indeed, the fractions may be split infinitely, so that it becomes impossible to complete or begin any journey. Motion, therefore, is an illusion.
2. Achilles and the tortoise: The quickest runner can never overtake the slowest, when that runner is given a head start, because the pursuer must first reach the point whence the pursued started, so that the slower must always hold the lead.
3. The arrow paradox: For motion to occur, an object must change the position which it occupies, but, in any given instant (a durationless point) of time, the arrow is neither moving to where it is nor to where it is not. It cannot move to where it is because it is already there. At every instant, therefore, no motion occurs. If everything is without motion at every instant, and if time is composed of instants, motion is impossible.

13

Short Summaries of Important Books, Papers and Fictional Writings in Philosophy

Ancient Philosophy

Heraclitus of Ephesus, *Fragments*
Epicurus, *On Nature*
Plato, *Apology*
Plato, *Crito*
Plato, *Euthyphro*
Plato, *Gorgias*
Plato, *Protagoras*
Plato, *Cratylus*
Plato, *Meno*
Plato, *Phaedo*
Plato, *The Symposium*
Plato, *Parmenides*
Plato, *Theaetetus*
Plato, *Phaedrus*
Plato, *Laws*
Plato, *The Republic*
Plato, *Timaeus*
Aristotle, *Organon*
Aristotle, *Physics*
Aristotle, *Metaphysics*
Aristotle, *On the Soul*
Aristotle, *Nicomachean Ethics*
Aristotle, *Politics*

Aristotle, *Rhetoric*
Aristotle, *Poetics*
Lucretius, *On the Nature of Things*
Cicero, *On the Commonwealth*
Cicero, *On the Laws*
Seneca, *Letters from a Stoic*
Marcus Aurelius, *Meditations*
Epictetus, *Discourses*
Epictetus, *Enchiridion*
Sextus Empiricus, *Outlines Of Pyrrhonism*
Plotinus, *The Enneads*
Porphyry, *Isagoge*
Hermes Trismegistus, *Corpus Hermeticum*

Medieval Philosophy

St. Augustine of Hippo, *Confessions*
St. Augustine of Hippo, *The City of God*
Proclus, *Elements of Theology*
Damascius, *Problems and Solutions Concerning First Principles*
Boethius, *The Consolation of Philosophy*
Johannes Scotus Eriugena, *Periphyseon*
Avicenna, *The Book of Healing*
Avicenna, *Proof of the Truthful*
Moses Maimonides, *Guide for the Perplexed*
Moses Maimonides, *Mishneh Torah*
Saadia Gaon, *Emunoth ve-Deoth*
Al-Ghazali, *The Incoherence of the Philosophers*
Averroes, *The Incoherence of the Incoherence*
Anselm, *Proslogion*
St. Thomas Aquinas, *Summa Contra Gentiles*
St. Thomas Aquinas, *Summa Theologica*
John Duns, *Ordinatio*
William Ockham, *Summa Logicae*

Early Modern Philosophy

Desiderius Erasmus, *The Praise of Folly*
Niccolò Machiavelli, *The Prince*

Niccolò Machiavelli, *Discourses on Livy*
Michel de Montaigne, *Essays*
Francis Bacon, *Novum Organum*
Hugo Grotius, *De Jure Belli Ac Pacis*
René Descartes, *Rules for the Direction of the Mind*
René Descartes, *Meditations on First Philosophy*
René Descartes, *Discourse on the Method*
René Descartes, *Principles of Philosophy*
Baruch Spinoza, *Ethics*
Gottfried Leibniz, *Discourse on Metaphysics*
Gottfried Leibniz, *Monadology*
Gottfried Leibniz, *New Essays on Human Understanding*
John Locke, *Two Treatises of Government*
John Locke, *An Essay Concerning Human Understanding*
Jean-Jacques Rousseau, *Discourse on the Arts and Sciences*
David Hume, *An Enquiry Concerning the Principles of Morals*
Jean-Jacques Rousseau, *Discourse on the Origin and Basis of Inequality Among Men*
Adam Smith, *The Theory of Moral Sentiments*
George Berkeley, *A Treatise Concerning the Principles of Human Knowledge*
Gottfired Leibniz, *Théodicée*
David Hume, *A Treatise of Human Nature*
David Hume, *An Enquiry Concerning Human Understanding*
Charles de Secondat, Baron de Montesquieu, *The Spirit of the Laws*
Jean-Jacques Rousseau, *Emile, or On Education*
Jean-Jacques Rousseau, *The Social Contract*
Voltaire, *Treatise on Tolerance*
Immanuel Kant, *Critique of Practical Reason*
Immanuel Kant, *Critique of Pure Reason*
Thomas Reid, *Inquiry into the Human Mind on the Principles of Common Sense*
Adam Smith, *The Wealth of Nations*
Jeremy Bentham, *An Introduction to the Principles of Morals and Legislation*
Edmund Burke, *Reflections on the Revolution in France*
Julien Offray de La Mettrie, *Man a Machine*
Immanuel Kant, *Critique of Judgment*
René Descartes, *Passions of the Soul*

Thomas Hobbes, *Leviathan*
Blaise Pascal, *Pensées*
Baruch Spinoza, *Tractatus Theologico-Politicus*
Immanuel Kant, *Groundwork of the Metaphysic of Morals*
Marquis de Condorcet, *Sketch for a Historical Picture of the Progress of the Human Mind*
Sophie de Condorcet, *Letters on Sympathy*
Thomas Paine, *Rights of Man*
Mary Wollstonecraft, *A Vindication of the Rights of Women*
Johan Gottlieb Fichte, *Foundations of the Science of Knowledge*

Nineteenth-Century Philosophy

Georg Wilhelm Friedrich Hegel, *Phenomenology of Spirit*
Georg Wilhelm Friedrich Hegel, *Science of Logic*
Georg Wilhelm Friedrich Hegel, *The Philosophy of Right*
Georg Wilhelm Friedrich Hegel, *The Philosophy of History*
Arthur Schopenhauer, *The World as Will and Representation*
Auguste Comte, *Course of Positive Philosophy*
Søren Kierkegaard, *Either/Or: A Fragment of Life*
Søren Kierkegaard, *Fear and Trembling*
Søren Kierkegaard, *Concluding Unscientific Postscript to Philosophical Fragments*
Søren Kierkegaard, *The Concept of Anxiety*
Max Stirner, *The Ego and Its Own*
Karl Marx and Friedrich Engels, *The Communist Manifesto*
Karl Marx, *Das Kapital* (*Capital*)
John Stuart Mill, *On Liberty*
John Stuart Mill, *Utilitarianism*
John Stuart Mill, *The Subjection of Women*
Herbert Spencer, *System of Synthetic Philosophy*
Henry Sidgwick, *The Methods of Ethics*
Friedrich Nietzsche, *On the Genealogy of Morals*
Friedrich Nietzsche, *Beyond Good and Evil*
Henri Bergson, *Time and Free Will*
Henri Bergson, *Matter and Memory*

Phenomenology and existentialism

Edmund Husserl, *Logical Investigations*
Max Scheler, *Formalism in Ethics and Non-Formal Ethics of Values*
Martin Buber, *I and Thou*
Martin Heidegger, *Being and Time*
Edmund Husserl, *Cartesian Meditations*
Alfred Schutz, *The Phenomenology of the Social World*
Albert Camus, *Myth of Sisyphus*
Jean-Paul Sartre, *Being and Nothingness*
Maurice Merleau-Ponty, *Phenomenology of Perception*
Jacques Maritain, *Existence and the Existent*
Simone de Beauvoir, *The Second Sex*
Emmanuel Levinas, *Totality and Infinity*
Emmanuel Levinas, *Otherwise than Being*
Jean-Luc Marion, *Being Given: Toward a Phenomenology of Givenness*
Thomas Nagel, *The View from Nowhere*
Roger Penrose, *The Emperor's New Mind*
Daniel Dennett, *Consciousness Explained*
David Chalmers, *The Conscious Mind*

Hermeneutics and Deconstruction

Hans-Georg Gadamer, *Truth and Method*
Hans-Georg Gadamer, *Philosophical Hermeneutics*
Paul Ricœur, *Freud and Philosophy: An Essay on Interpretation*
Jacques Derrida, *Of Grammatology*

Structuralism and Post-Structuralism

Georges Bataille, *The Accursed Share*
Michel Foucault, *The Order of Things*
Gilles Deleuze, *Difference and Repetition*
Gilles Deleuze, *The Logic of Sense*
Felix Guattari and Gilles Deleuze, *Capitalism and Schizophrenia*
Jean Baudrillard, *The Mirror of Production*
Michel Foucault, *Discipline and Punish*
Jean Baudrillard, *Simulacra and Simulation*

Critical Theory and Marxism

Gyorgy Lukacs, *History and Class Consciousness*
Herbert Marcuse, *Reason and Revolution*
Theodor Adorno and Max Horkheimer, *Dialectic of Enlightenment*
Herbert Marcuse, *Eros and Civilization*
Jean-Paul Sartre, *Critique of Dialectical Reason*
Herbert Marcuse, *One-Dimensional Man*
Louis Althusser, *Reading* Capital
Theodor Adorno, *Negative Dialectics*
G. A. Cohen, *Karl Marx's Theory of History*
Jürgen Habermas, *The Theory of Communicative Action*
Marshall Berman, *All That Is Solid Melts into Air*

Epistemology

Bertrand Russell, *The Problems of Philosophy*
George Edward Moore, *A Defense of Common Sense*
Jacques Maritain, *The Degrees of Knowledge*
Richard Rorty, *Philosophy and the Mirror of Nature*
Olaf Helmer and Nicholas Rescher, *On the Epistemology of the Inexact Sciences*
Edmund Gettier, *Is Justified True Belief Knowledge?*
Roderick Chisholm, *Theory of Knowledge*
Willard Van Orman Quine, *Epistemology Naturalized*
Peter Unger, *Ignorance: A Case for Skepticism*
Alvin Goldman, *What Is Justified Belief?*
Laurence Bonjour, *The Structure of Empirical Knowledge*
John Hardwig, Epistemic Dependence
Alvin Goldman, *Epistemology and Cognition*
John McDowell, *Mind and World*
David K. Lewis, *Elusive Knowledge*
Alvin Goldman, *Knowledge in a Social World*
Jürgen Habermas, *Truth and Justification*
Timothy Williamson, *Knowledge and its Limits*
Donald Davidson, *Subjective, Intersubjective, Objective*
Hilary Kornblith, *Knowledge and its Place in Nature*
Jonathan Kvanvig, *The Value of Knowledge and the Pursuit of Understanding*

Keith DeRose, *The Case for Contextualism: Knowledge, Skepticism, and Context*
Miranda Fricker, *Epistemic Injustice: Power and the Ethics of Knowing*
Jason Stanley, *Knowledge and Practical Interests*

Metaphysics

Henri Bergson, *Introduction to Metaphysics*
George Edward Moore, *The Refutation of Idealism*
Henri Bergson, *Creative Evolution*
William James, *Pragmatism: A New Name for Some Old Ways of Thinking*
John Dewey, *Experience and Nature*
Alfred North Whitehead, *Process and Reality*
Robin George Collingwood, *An Essay on Metaphysics*
Willard Van Orman Quine, *On What There Is*
Rudolf Carnap, *Empiricism, Semantics, and Ontology*
Willard Van Orman Quine, *Two Dogmas of Empiricism*
David Malet, *Universals and Scientific Realism*
Willard Van Orman Quine, *Theories and Things*
Timothy Williamson, *Modal Logic as Metaphysics*
David Chalmers, *Constructing the World*
Theodore Sider, *Writing the Book of the World*
Stephen Mumford, *Dispositions*
Derek Parfit, *Reasons and Persons*
David K. Lewis, *On the Plurality of Worlds*
Nicholas Malebranche, *Dialogues on Metaphysics*
Anne Conway, *The Principles of the Most Ancient and Modern Philosophy*
Francis Hutcheson, *An Inquiry into the Original of our Ideas of Beauty and Virtue*

Philosophy of Mind

Gilbert Ryle, *The Concept of the Mind*
Wilfrid Sellars, *Empiricism and the Philosophy of Mind*
Herbert Feigl, *The "Mental" and the "Physical"*
David K. Lewis, *An Argument for the Identity Theory*
Jerry Fodor, *The Language of Thought*
Hilary Putnam, *The Meaning of "Meaning"*
Tyler Burge, *Individualism and the Mental*

Jerry Fodor, *The Modularity of Mind: An Essay on Faculty Psychology*
John Searle, *Intentionality: An Essay in the Philosophy of Mind*
Stephen Stich, *From Folk Psychology to Cognitive Science: The Case Against Belief*
Ruth Garrett Millikan, *Language, Thought, and Other Biological Categories: New Foundations for Realism*
Patricia Churchland, *Neurophilosophy: Toward a Unified Science of the Mind-Brain*
Mark Johnson, *The Body in the Mind: The Bodily Basis of Meaning, Imagination, and Reason*
Francisco J. Varela, Evan Thompson, and Eleanor Rosch, *The Embodied Mind: Cognitive Science and Human Experience*
Andy Clark, *Being There: Putting Brain, Body and World Together Again*
Shaun Gallagher, *How the Body Shapes the Mind*
Andy Clark, *Supersizing the Mind: Embodiment, Action, and Cognitive Extension*
David Chalmers, *The Character of Consciousness*
Evan Thompson, *Mind in Life*
Andy Clark, *Surfing Uncertainty: Prediction, Action, and the Embodied Mind*
Thomas Nagel, *What Is It Like to Be a Bat?*
Thomas Nagel, *The View from Nowhere*
Roger Penrose, *The Emperor's New Mind*
William James, *Pragmatism: A New Name for Some Old Ways of Thinking*
Cordelia Fine, *Delusions of Gender: How Our Minds, Society, and Neurosexism Create Difference*

Philosophy of Religion

William James, *The Will to Believe*
William James, *Varieties of Religious Experience*
Aldous Huxley, *The Perennial Philosophy*
Frithjof Schuon, *The Transcendent Unity of Religions*
Alvin Plantinga, *God and Other Minds: A Study of the Rational Justification of Belief in God*
Dewi Zephaniah Phillips, *Religion Without Explanation*
Richard Swinburne, *The Existence of God*
William Lane Craig, *The Kalam Cosmological Argument*
Alvin Plantinga, *Is Belief in God Properly Basic?*

Jean-Luc Marion, *God Without Being*
John Leslie Mackie, *The Miracle of Theism: Arguments for and against the Existence of God*
John Hick, *An Interpretation of Religion: Human Responses to the Transcendent*
William Alston, *Perceiving God*
John L. Schellenberg, *Divine Hiddenness and Human Reason*
William Leonard Rowe, *The Evidential Argument from Evil: A Second Look*
Jay Lazar Garfield, *Empty Words: Buddhist Philosophy and Cross-Cultural Interpretation*
Keith Yandell, *Philosophy of Religion: A Contemporary Introduction*

Philosophy of Science

William Whewell, *The Philosophy of the Inductive Sciences: Founded upon their History*
William Stanley Jevons, *The Principles of Science: A Treatise on Logic and Scientific Method*
Charles Sanders Peirce, *Illustrations of the Logic of Science*
Henri Poincaré, *Science and Hypothesis*
Hermann Weyl, *Philosophy of Mathematics and Natural Science*
Otto Neurath, *Physicalism: The Philosophy of the Viennese Circle*
John Dewey, *Logic: The Theory of Inquiry*
Steven Shapin and Simon Schaffer, *Leviathan and the Air-Pump: Hobbes, Boyle, and the Experimental Life*
Edward Osborne Wilson, *Consilience: The Unity of Knowledge*
Roland Omnès, *Quantum Philosophy: Understanding and Interpreting Contemporary Science*
Karl Pearson, *The Grammar of Science*
Henri Poincaré, *The Value of Science*
Rudolf Carnap, *Logical Foundations of Probability*
Hans Reichenbach, *The Rise of Scientific Philosophy*
Stephen Toulmin, *The Philosophy of Science: An Introduction*
Nelson Goodman, *Fact, Fiction, and Forecast*
Michael Polanyi, *Personal Knowledge: Towards a Post-critical Philosophy*
Karl Popper, *The Logic of Scientific Discovery*
Mario Bunge, *Treatise on Basic Philosophy*
Michael Friedman, *Explanation and Scientific Understanding*

Rudolf Carnap, *Meaning and Necessity: A Study in Semantics and Modal Logic*
John Stuart Mill, *A System of Logic*
Ernest Nagel, *The Structure of Science*
Thomas Kuhn, *The Structure of Scientific Revolutions*
Carl Gustav Hempel, *Aspects of Scientific Explanation*
Bas C. Van Fraassen, *The Scientific Image*
Roy Bhaskar, *A Realist Theory of Science*
Larry Laudan, *Progress and its Problems: Towards a Theory of Scientific Growth*
David Kellogg Lewis, *How to Define Theoretical Terms*
Mark W. Wartofsky, *Models: Representation and the Scientific Understanding*
Carolyn Merchant, *The Death of Nature: Women, Ecology, and the Scientific Revolution*
Wesley Charles Salmon, *Scientific Explanation and the Causal Structure of the World*
Ronald Giere, *Explaining Science: A Cognitive Approach*
David Hull, *Science as a Process: An Evolutionary Account of the Social and Conceptual Development of Science*
Paul Thagard, *Computational Philosophy of Science*
Helen Longino, *Science as Social Knowledge: Values and Objectivity in Scientific Inquiry*
Peter Achinstein, *Particles and Waves: Historical Essays in the Philosophy of Science*
Lorraine Code, *What Can She Know? Feminist Theory and the Construction of Knowledge*
Sandra Harding, *Whose Science? Whose Knowledge? Thinking from Women's Lives*
Paul Thagard, *Conceptual Revolutions*
John Dupré, *The Disorder of Things: Metaphysical Foundations of the Disunity of Science*
Deborah Mayo, *Error and the Growth of Experimental Knowledge*
John Ziman, *Real Science: What it Is, and What it Means*
Patrick Suppes, *Representation and Invariance of Scientific Structures*
Hasok Chang, *Inventing Temperature: Measurement and Scientific Progress*
William C. Wimsatt, *Re-Engineering Philosophy for Limited Beings: Piecewise Approximations to Reality*

Nancy J. Nersessian, *Creating Scientific Concepts*
Heather Douglas, *Science, Policy, and the Value-Free Ideal*
Peter Godfrey-Smith, *Theory and Reality: An Introduction to the Philosophy of Science*
William Bechtel and Robert C. Richardson, *Discovering Complexity: Decomposition and Localization as Strategies in Scientific Research*
Paul Feyerabend, *Against Method*

Philosophy of Biology

Edwin Schrödinger, *What is Life? The Physical Aspect of the Living Cell*
Stephen J. Gould and Richard Lewontin, *The Spandrels of San Marco and the Panglossian Paradigm: A Critique of the Adaptationist Program*
Stephen J. Gould, *The Mismeasure of Man*
David Lee Hull, *Philosophy of Biological Science*
Elliott Sober, *The Nature of Selection: Evolutionary Theory in Philosophical Focus*
Michael Ruse, *Taking Darwin Seriously: A Naturalistic Approach to Philosophy*
Kristin Shrader-Frechette and Earl D. McCoy, *Method in Ecology: Strategies for Conservation*
Elliott Sober, *Philosophy of Biology*
Martin Mahner and Mario Bunge, *Foundations of Biophilosophy*
Kim Sterelny and Paul E. Griffiths, *Sex and Death: An Introduction to Philosophy of Biology*
Sandra Mitchell, *Biological Complexity and Integrative Pluralism*
Daniel C. Dennett, *Darwin's Dangerous Idea: Evolution and the Meanings of Life*
Denis Noble, *The Music of Life: Biology Beyond the Genome*
Samir Okasha, *Evolution and the Levels of Selection*
Elliott Sober, *Evidence and Evolution: The Logic Behind the Science*
Michael Ruse, *The Philosophy of Human Evolution*

Philosophy of Physics

Pierre Duhem, *The Aim and Structure of Physical Theory*
Albert Einstein, *The Meaning of Relativity*
Hans Reichenbach, *The Philosophy of Space and Time*
Arthur Eddington, *Philosophy of Physical Science*

Werner Heisenberg, *Physics and Philosophy: The Revolution in Modern Science*
John Stewart Bell, *On the Einstein–Podolsky–Rosen Paradox*
Lawrence Sklar, *Space, Time, and Spacetime*
Nancy Cartwright, *How the Laws of Physics Lie*
Michael Friedman, *Foundations of Space-Time Theories: Relativistic Physics and the Philosophy of Science*
John Stewart Bell, *Speakable and Unspeakable in Quantum Mechanics: Collected Papers on Quantum Philosophy*
Lawrence Sklar, *Philosophy of Physics*
Lawrence Sklar, *Physics and Chance: Philosophical Issues in the Foundations of Statistical Mechanics*
Jeffrey Bub, *Interpreting the Quantum World*
Roberto Torretti, *The Philosophy of Physics*
Craig Callender and Nick Huggett, *Physics Meets Philosophy at the Planck Scale: Contemporary Theories in Quantum Gravity*
Harvey Brown, *Physical Relativity: Space-time Structure from a Dynamical Perspective*
Laura Ruetsche, *Interpreting Quantum Theories: The Art of the Possible*

Ethics and Value Theory

George Edward Moore, *Principia Ethica*
Gertrude Elizabeth Margaret Anscombe, *Modern Moral Philosophy*
Conrad Hal Waddington, *The Ethical Animal*
Peter Singer, *Famine, Affluence, and Morality*
J. L. Mackie, *Ethics: Inventing Right and Wrong*
Sissela Bok, *Lying: Moral Choice in Public and Private Life*
Alan Gewirth, *Reason and Morality*
Peter Singer, *Practical Ethics*
Alasdair MacIntyre, *After Virtue*
Samuel Scheffler, *The Rejection of Consequentialism*
Derek Parfit, *Reasons and Persons*
Bernard Williams, *Ethics and the Limits of Philosophy*
David Gauthier, *Morals by Agreement*
Peter Railton, *Moral Realism*
Martha Nussbaum, *The Fragility of Goodness*
Paul W. Taylor, *Respect for Nature: A Theory of Environmental Ethics*

Holmes Rolston III, *Environmental Ethics: Duties to and Values in the Natural World*
Susan Hurley, *Natural Reasons: Personality and Polity*
Shelly Kagan, *The Limits of Morality*
Allan Gibbard, *Wise Choices, Apt Feelings: A Theory of Normative Judgment*
Joan Tronto, *Moral Boundaries: A Political Argument for an Ethic of Care*
Annette Baier, *Moral Prejudices: Essays on Ethics*
Michael A. Smith, *The Moral Problem*
Christine Korsgaard, *The Sources of Normativity*
Peter Unger, *Living High and Letting Die*
Thomas M. Scanlon, *What We Owe to Each Other*
Rosalind Hursthouse, *On Virtue Ethics*
Phillipa Foot, *Natural Goodness*
Derek Parfit, *On What Matters*
Allan Gibbard, *Thinking How to Live*
Michael Huemer, *Ethical Intuitionism*
Virginia Held, *The Ethics of Care: Personal, Political, and Global*

Logic and Philosophy of Logic

Charles Sanders Peirce, *How to Make Our Ideas Clear*
Gottlob Frege, *Begriffsschrift*
Kurt Gödel, *On Formally Undecidable Propositions of Principia Mathematica and Related Systems*
Frank P. Ramsey, *Foundations of Mathematics and other Logical Essays*
Alfred Tarski, *The Concept of Truth in Formalized Languages*
Alfred Tarski, *Introduction to Logic and to the Methodology of the Deductive Sciences*
Wilfrid Sellars, *Inference and Meaning*
William Kneale and Martha Kneale, *The Development of Logic*
Saul Kripke, *Semantical Considerations on Modal Logic*
Donald Davidson, *Truth and Meaning*
Willard Van Orman Quine, *Philosophy of Logic*
David K. Lewis, *Counterfactuals*
Susan Haack, *Philosophy of Logics*
Peter Spirtes, Clark Glymour, and Richard Scheines, *Causation, Prediction, and Search*
Robert Brandom, *Articulating Reasons: An Introduction to Inferentialism*

Philosophy of Language

Gottlob Frege, *On Sense and Reference*
Bertrand Russell, *On Denoting*
Ludwig Wittgenstein, *Tractatus Logico-Philosophicus*
Alfred Jules Ayer, *Language, Truth, and Logic*
Ludwig Wittgenstein, *Philosophical Investigations*
Stanley Cavell, *Must We Mean What We Say? A Book of Essays*
Willard Van Orman Quine, *Word and Object*
John Langshaw Austin, *How to Do Things with Words*
John Langshaw Austin, *A Plea for Excuses*
John Searle, *Speech Acts: An Essay in the Philosophy of Language*
Donald Davidson, *Radical Interpretation*
Donald Davidson, *On the Very Idea of a Conceptual Scheme*
Michael Dummett, *Frege: Philosophy of Language*
Herbert Paul Grice, *Logic and Conversation*
Saul Kripke, *Naming and Necessity*
Cora Diamond, *The Realistic Spirit: Wittgenstein, Philosophy, and the Mind*
Robert Brandom, *Making It Explicit: Reasoning, Representing, and Discursive Commitment*
Michael Devitt and Kim Sterelny, *Language and Reality: An Introduction to the Philosophy of Language*

Philosophy of Mathematics

Gottlob Frege, *The Foundations of Arithmetic*
Alfred North Whitehead and Bertrand Russell, *Principia Mathematica*
Eugene Wigner, *The Unreasonable Effectiveness of Mathematics in the Natural Sciences*
Ian Hacking, *The Emergence of Probability*
Imre Lakatos, *Proofs and Refutations*
Mark Colyvan, *The Indispensability of Mathematics*

Synopses of Classic Philosophical Fiction

Saint Augustine, *De Magistro*
Peter Abelard, *Dialogue of a Philosopher with a Jew and a Christian*
Ibn Tufail, *Hayy ibn Yaqdhan*

Judah Halevi, *Kuzari*
Thomas More, *Utopia*
Voltaire, *Zadig*
Voltaire, *Candide*
Jean-Jacques Rousseau, *Julie, or The New Heloise*
James Hogg, *The Private Memoirs and Confessions of a Justified Sinner*
Walter Pater, *Marius the Epicurean: His Sensations and Ideas*
Thomas Carlyle, *Sartor Resartus*
Johann Wolfgang von Goethe, *Wilhelm Meister's Apprenticeship*
Fyodor Michailovich Dostoevsky, *Crime and Punishment*
Leo Tolstoy, *War and Peace*
Giacomo Leopardi, *Operette Morali*
Robert Musil, *The Man Without Qualities*
Milan Kundera, *The Unbearable Lightness of Being*
Aldous Huxley, *After Many a Summer*
Aldous Huxley, *Island*
C. S. Lewis, *The Space Trilogy*
Søren Kierkegaard, *The Seducer's Diary*
Friedrich Nietzsche, *Thus Spoke Zarathustra: A Book for All and None*
Leo Tolstoy, *Resurrection*
Samuel Beckett, *Waiting for Godot*
Louis-Ferdinand Céline, *Journey to the End of the Night*
Marcel Proust, *In Search of Lost Time* (*Remembrance of Things Past*)
Antoine de Saint-Exupéry (Antoine Marie Jean-Baptiste Roger, comte de Saint-Exupéry), *The Little Prince*
André Malraux, *Man's Fate*
Thomas Mann, *The Magic Mountain*
Franz Kafka, *The Trial*
George Orwell, *Animal Farm*
B. F. Skinner, *Walden Two*
George Orwell, *Nineteen Eighty-Four (1984)*
Anthony Burgess, *A Clockwork Orange*
Philip K. Dick, *Do Androids Dream of Electric Sheep?*
Philip K. Dick, *A Scanner Darkly*
Philip K. Dick, *Valis*
Jean-Paul Sartre, *Nausea*
Ralph Ellison, *Invisible Man*
Simone de Beauvoir, *She Came to Stay*
Raimon Fosca, *All Men Are Mortal*

Osamu Dazai, *No Longer Human*
Walker Percy, *The Moviegoer*
Yukio Mishima, *The Sailor Who Fell from Grace with the Sea*
José Lezama Lima, *Paradiso*
Robert Pirsig, *Zen and the Art of Motorcycle Maintenance*
Renata Adler, *Speedboat*
David Markson, *Wittgenstein's Mistress*
Jostein Gaarder, *Sophie's World*
Arthur Asa Berger, *Infinite Jest*
Neal Stephenson, *Anathem*
Giannina Braschi, *United States of Banana*
André Alexis, *Fifteen Dogs*
Joseph Conrad, *Heart of Darkness*
Fyodor Dostoevsky, *The Brothers Karamazov*
James Joyce, *Ulysses*
Franz Kafka, *The Metamorphosis*
Ibn al-Nafis, *Theologus Autodidactus*
William Shakespeare, *Hamlet*
Leo Tostoy, *The Death of Ivan Ilyich*
Sergio Troncoso, *The Nature of Truth*

Leading Authors of Philosophical Fiction

Albert Camus
Marquis de Sade
Franz Kafka
Hermann Hesse
Stanisław Lem
Ayn Rand
Samuel Beckett
Iris Murdoch
Anthony Burgess
Simone de Beauvoir
André Malraux
Fyodor Dostoevsky
Jorge Luis Borges
Umberto Eco
Rebecca Goldstein

Ancient Philosophy

Heraclitus of Ephesus, *Fragments*

Fragments is a collection of an incomplete philosophical treatise written in the sixth century by Greek philosopher Heraclitus of Ephesus. In the book, the philosopher focuses mainly on human affairs, suggesting that everything in the universe is always in a state of flux, so that it is impossible to experience the same thing twice. In addition to stating that everything in the universe originates directly or indirectly from fire, he argues that opposite things are similar and that everything is the same and not the same over time. The author further contends that knowledge is a precious commodity, yet only a few people can grasp the true nature of knowledge. In short, most views of Heraclitus in *Fragments* indicate that he is an unorthodox thinker and a proponent of monism.

Epicurus, *On Nature*

On Nature is a 37-volume philosophical treatise authored in the third century by Epicurus. The book debunks the claim that the gods influence human lives. In this masterpiece, the author explains that the fear of gods and death makes humans anxious. By eliminating this fear, Epicurus thinks that humans will be motivated to pursue pleasures and activities that give them peace of mind. He also insists that pleasure is the highest end a human can achieve, arguing that one should live a life in which pleasure is constant. Epicurus nonetheless emphasizes the dangers of overindulging in excessive pleasures and states that moderation should be practiced at all times. He then goes ahead to reject the concept of an afterlife. According to Epicurus, death is an absence of sensation that causes no pain. In sum, this treatise urges humans to seek pleasure and banish the fear of gods, death, and the afterlife.

Plato, *Apology*

The Apology of Socrates, written in 399 BC, is a Socratic dialogue of a speech of legal self-defense by Plato, a philosopher from Athens. The speech is not an "apology" in the modern understanding of the word. Socrates is not trying to apologize; instead, he attempts to defend himself and his conduct. During the trial, Socrates was charged with corrupting the youth of Athens and for "impiety": believing in new gods not recognized by the state. He was found guilty and is given his choice of penalties. Socrates offered to pay a fine; however, the jury rejected the offer and sentenced him to death after he declined the offer of exile or imprisonment. He accepted the verdict, warning the jurymen who voted against him that, by silencing him, they have harmed themselves more.

Plato, *Crito*

Published around 387 BC, *Crito* is a philosophical dialogue by Greek philosopher Plato. As narrated by Plato, Socrates is incarcerated and is awaiting execution. Crito of Alopece, a wealthy Athenian, learns about his friend's impending execution and desires to help Socrates escape. The main dialogue begins when Crito visits Socrates in prison. The rich man does not want the philosopher to die not only because of their friendship but also because he wants Socrates to give his sons a proper education about the philosophy of life. Besides, Crito fears that Socrates's refusal to leave the prison will be seen as a criticism of himself, as too miserly to save his friend from prison.

Plato depicts the conversation of Socrates and Crito regarding the nature of justice. Their arguments revolve around the social contract theory, one that focuses on the ability of individuals to recognize the legitimacy of the state's authority. More specifically, the debate centers on whether unconditional obedience to leadership authority is good or not for society. Citing the Laws of Athens, Socrates argues that injustice cannot be used to correct justice. He reasons that escaping from prison is not a good option for correcting wrong judgments and that fleeing from prison and becoming a fugitive undermines his moral right to criticize those who violate the laws of Athens. Overall, this philosophical dialogue highlights Socrates's conundrum: if he runs away from prison, he loses his moral rights to pursue justice: but if he stays, he will be executed unjustly.

Plato, *Euthyphro*

Euthyphro is a Socratic dialogue written by Plato, the Athenian philosopher who lived in ancient Greece in the 5th century. It explores the nature of piety and justice, and, in his questioning of Euthyphro, it is also a demonstration of Socratic irony. Socrates refutes definitions of piety that rely on a list of virtuous deeds and pleasing the gods. The latter refutation is now known to philosophers as Euthyphro's dilemma: "Do the gods love the holy act because it is holy? Or are the acts holy because the gods love them?" Euthyphro offers that piety is concerned with looking after the gods, implying that it is an act of sacrifice and prayer. Socrates counters that divine approval is not a universal definition of piety, and the dialogue ends with a definition of piety.

Plato, *Gorgias*

Written by Plato about 380 BC, *Gorgias* is a Socratic dialogue that explores the meaning of rhetoric. The text depicts a conversation among Socrates and a group of rhetoricians: Gorgias, Polus, and Callicles. The text begins with Socrates' inquiry into the nature of Gorgias' art and what the Sophist professes and teaches as a rhetorician. Gorgias describes rhetoric as the effective and persuasive use of language. He contends that oratory skill is of utmost importance, while Socrates argues that rhetoric is mere flattery. Polus, the next Sophist with whom Socrates argues, claims that rhetoric equals power. However, Polus fails to convince Socrates, who accuses him of speechifying instead of answering questions and insists that rhetoricians have no power. After that discourse, the men discuss power, evil and happiness, including the nature of temperance and justice. In his reply, Socrates states that unless rhetoric is used for good, it is of no use. He emphasizes that the chaos in society is generated when people confuse flattery with art, and persuasion with truth.

Another Sophist, Callicles, joins the conversation and begins to undermine Socrates' philosophical views. Unable to convince Calicles, the philosopher realizes that many people will not agree with his theory. Socrates later explains the dialogue with a story about the Homeric description of the passage into the Isles of the Blest and the dark realm of Tartarus. In his narration, people are judged based on the nature of their soul, not by their outward appearance. He concludes that a man who lives a just and good life lives the best life.

Plato, *Protagoras*

Composed about 380 BC by the Athenian philosopher Plato, *Protagoras* is a Socratic dialogue on sophistry and ethics. The conversation, between Socrates and Protagoras, a well-known Sophist, takes place in the presence of the disciples of Protagoras and Athenians of the Socratic circle. The subject is what it means to be a virtuous man. The participants also explore whether virtue is teachable. When Protagoras claims that he could teach one of his students, Hippocrates, to become a better and wiser man, Socrates expresses doubt that one can learn virtue. According to him, all human learning may be the recovery of knowledge already processed by one's immortal soul. Expressing his views in the form of an apologue, Protagoras asserts that, unlike the arts, all men can be taught justice and reverence (political virtue) to a certain degree. In sum, Socrates believes that knowledge is all one needs to live a good life and that every aspect of moral or emotional failure is a cognitive failure.

Plato, *Cratylus*

Cratylus is a philosophical dialogue by Plato, a Greek philosopher, around 360 BC. The philosopher critically examines naming conventions. He begins the dialogue by comparing the creation of a name or a word to a painter's vivid creativity. He then goes on to identify the origin of certain names. According to the philosopher, letters used in a name are used to convey the nature of the item that is named. In addition to that, he explains that some letters are best suited for certain objects or subjects. The scholar argues that names should closely resemble the item that they represent. He asserts that the worst naming convention is to use opposite names for an item. Plato concludes *Cratylus* by stating that, when naming objects, the study of language is not as important as the study of the objects to be named.

Plato, *Meno*

Written in 385 BC, *Meno* is a philosophical dialogue authored by Plato, the Athenian philosopher. Here, Plato attempts to define virtue. *Meno* is different from Plato's other philosophical works on virtue in that it does not extol any particular virtue, but instead analyzes the concept. The dialogue begins by discussing what virtue is and whether it can be taught. Plato later argues that virtues are common to all humans regardless of their age, class, or gender. He also contends that, rather than creating a standard definition for virtue, there should be a set of attributes that makes something a virtue. In the end, the philosopher concludes that there is no satisfactory or unifying definition of virtue.

Plato, *Phaedo*

Phaedo is a philosophical discourse written, in 360 BC, by Plato, the Greek philosopher. Composed immediately after the death of Plato's mentor Socrates, the work articulates four arguments for the immortality of the soul. The first argument is the Opposites or Cyclical argument, which contends that forms are unchanging and eternal, so the soul is imperishable. The second argument is the Theory of Recollection, which states that all humans possess innate knowledge at birth, so the soul must exist before birth. The third argument is the Affinity Argument, which states that the body is visible and mortal, while the soul is invisible and immortal. The fourth and final argument postulates that the soul participates in the Form of Life, meaning it can never die. In the end, the book concludes that the soul is immortal.

Plato, *The Symposium*

Written around 370 BC by the Athenian philosopher Plato, *The Symposium* is a study of love. The author narrates a fictional banquet in which Socrates and other notable figures give a series of speeches on Eros, love. The writer describes various characteristics of love and then explains how powerful love is. Plato then writes about the origin of love, the nature of love, the various kinds of love, how humans express love, the motivations for love, and how love affects human virtue. He goes further, explaining the processes of human love, the concept of love in nature, barriers to love, and non-sexual love. He also introduces the concept of impure or evil love, thus asserting that not all types of love are worthy of praise. In summary, the book illustrates the concept of love from the perspectives of various people in a fictional setting.

Plato, *Parmenides*

Plato's *Parmenides*, written in 370 BC, is a dialogue between Parmenides, Zeno, and Socrates, who critically examine the theory of forms, which states that there is a single, unified, and non-physical form, which all objects and matter merely imitate. The dialogue is largely divided into two parts. In the first part, the philosopher uses the theoretical function of Forms to explain why sensible things have certain properties and then explains why the theory of Forms is inconsistent. In the second part of the dialogue, Plato proposes a method of defending the theory of Forms comprising eight deductions, all of which focus on the consequences of positing the being and non-being of a particular Form. In the end, the book concludes that the proper way to save the Forms is by abandoning the principles that render the theory of Forms inconsistent.

Plato, *Theaetetus*

Theaetetus is a masterpiece written about 369 BC by the Greek philosopher Plato. The dialogue is a discussion between Theaetetus and Socrates about the nature and forms of knowledge. Unsure of what knowledge is, Socrates asks Theaetetus to define and explain it. As Theaetetus cannot define it, Socrates thinks that knowledge is a function of one's perception. Yet he reasons that this definition is not satisfactory. Socrates then defines knowledge as anything that is in a state of flux. He later admits that this definition is not foolproof. After Socrates states the difference between true judgment and knowledge, Theaetetus then proceeds to define knowledge as anything "with an account" that is "knowable." Socrates still faults this definition.

Plato, *Phaedrus*

Written in 360 BC by Plato, *Phaedrus* is a discourse between Phaedrus and Socrates regarding erotic love, rhetoric, and the transmigration of the soul. Sitting under a tree with Socrates, Phaedrus reads the written speech of Lysias. According to the argument of the speech, it is better to be in a sexual relationship with someone who is more in love than with someone who is less in love. Unimpressed with the speech, Socrates describes love as a form of madness that occurs when desire overrides better judgment. Socrates reads the second speech, also known as the Great Speech. In the speech, he talks about the nature of madness, arguing that madness is sometimes good, most especially when the madness of love is designed to benefit a lover. Socrates then proceeds to discuss the nature of soul, arguing that the soul is always in flux. After concluding that the soul is immortal, he ends the dialogue with the nuances of good versus bad writing and the indispensability of the soul in proper rhetoric.

Plato, *Laws*

Written c. 355-c. 347 BC, *Laws* is a philosophical dialogue between Plato, an Athenian Stranger, and two older men. The only Platonic dialogue that does not include Socrates as an interlocutor, *Laws* focuses on the nature of laws in society. Central to Plato's purpose here is to understand who is responsible for creating laws in society and who should take the credit for creating them. Plato talks about many forms of laws, some of which are from divine sources and others from non-divine sources. The philosopher describes what natural right and natural law mean as well as the role of intelligence in establishing laws. Apart from this, he spends effort analyzing the influence of politics, religion, and philosophy in the creation of laws.

Plato, *The Republic*

The Republic by Plato is a Socratic dialogue that aims to clarify the concept of justice from the viewpoint of a just man. Authored in 375 BC, the book defines justice as doing one's duty without encroaching on others' business. Plato argues that in a just state, every individual and class should be mandated to fulfill a set of duties or obligations. In his opinion, this delineation of tasks leads to a harmonious society. The Greek philosopher also points out that people become unjust when their behavioral deficiencies and excesses are not checked. He further emphasizes that an unjust state arises when it fails to provide basic amenities for its citizens. Plato bases his arguments on the hierarchy that exists in the universe, which creates a harmonious whole. He suggests that a just state should also emulate this design and be hierarchal. In sum, individuals should be placed in hierarchy and ranked according to their skills.

Plato, *Timaeus*

Written in 360BC, *Timaeus* is Plato's view on how the universe was created. Plato reasons that the universe was intelligently designed by a divine craftsman who imposed order on an initially chaotic existence. According to the Greek philosopher, the beauty and order of the universe could not have happened without a cause. He believes that the creation of the universe must be the handiwork of a good craftsman desirous of bringing order out of chaos. As Plato puts it, this orderliness not only shows intelligence; it is also a model for humans to emulate. Plato further claims that humans lose their inborn excellence because of environmental and social influence. In conclusion, he thinks that when rational humans seek to understand and emulate the orderliness of the universe, their souls will be restored to its original excellence.

Aristotle, *Organon*

Aristotle wrote *Organon* in 567 BC to tackle issues concerning logic and reasoning. In the book, he proposes a methodology that can help humans learn in any field. First, the Greek philosopher posits that humans can only learn through logic. He then reveals that every field of human knowledge has properties or features that are of a certain kind. Aristotle goes on to state that this is in line with the true reality of nature. Since reality, language, and thought are similar, the philosopher argues that one must carefully consider what to say, as it can help one to understand reality. In the end, Aristotle concludes that it is possible to fully understand the world if one can come up with simple definitions of certain things.

Aristotle, *Physics*

Written around 340 BC by Aristotle, *Physics* is a collection of philosophical treatises that discusses "the study of nature." Consisting of eight books, the work studies the motion of naturally occurring things like plants, animals, humans, and celestial bodies. The philosopher starts by evaluating previous theories on nature. Afterward, he defines matter as the primary substratum of every natural object in existence. Furthermore, he asserts that physics or nature is a source or cause of being moved or at rest. The author then discusses change, the infinite, motion, time, forms, causation, being, continuity, the universe, celestial bodies, relativity, and other phenomena. In summary, *Physics* analyzes nature and its relation to science.

Aristotle, *Metaphysics*

Metaphysics is a philosophical work written by Aristotle, the Greek philosopher, around 350 BC. The work explores the study of "being" and the subject of existence, including the argument for the existence of God or a Supreme Creator. The author starts the book by criticizing and rejecting Plato's theory of Forms, which posits that the physical world is not timeless or absolute. Aristotle then argues that there is nothing like an infinite causal series. According to him, there must be a first cause or a God that was never caused by a previous thing. What's more, the philosopher asserts that the study of qua being is superior to any theoretical science because it evaluates the ultimate cause of existence or reality. In addition to arguing that the fundamental goal of philosophy is to understand being, the writer evaluates the very nature of substance, actuality, potentiality, unity, difference, sameness, and the origin of numbers. Aristotle concludes *Metaphysics* by defining the most divine being as the Unmoved Mover (God), who is the creator of everything in the world yet remain detached from the world.

Aristotle, *On the Soul*

On the Soul is a philosophical treatise by Aristotle, written in 350 BC. The treatise studies the soul in relation to human psychology and biology. The work begins by examining prior literature on the subject of the soul. Then the author gives his own definition, defining the soul as the essence or form of any living thing. He further argues that the soul makes something an organism. Thus, no being can exist without a soul. The writer also talks about the kinds of souls possessed by living organisms and distinguishes among them. He then discusses plant and animal nutrition, reasoning in animals, intellect in humans, and the five senses, with their relation to the soul. Aristotle concludes by arguing that the soul can exist without the body.

Aristotle, *Nicomachean Ethics*

Written by Aristotle in 130 BC, *Nicomachean Ethics* is a philosophical consideration of the highest purpose of man. The philosopher argues that the highest aim of human actions is happiness, which is an end in itself. He then discusses how best to achieve happiness by performing virtuous actions. Aristotle goes further to discuss the various moral virtues and their corresponding vices. According to him, virtue can be defined as the mean between two extremes—excess and deficiency. In addition to asserting that humans are not born with virtues but they can learn how to be virtuous, the philosopher talks about different forms of virtue and the relationship of justice and happiness. Aristotle also touches on the meaning and forms of friendship as well as the driving force behind them. In summary, *Nicomachean Ethics* explains the best ways of using certain ethical virtues to achieve the highest human good, which is happiness.

Aristotle, *Politics*

Written by the Greek philosopher Aristotle in 350 BC, *Politics* is a work on political philosophy that begins with a discussion of the city, or *polis*. Aristotle states that a city is created to achieve happiness, and the foremost community is the polis. Asserting that all humans in a polis are political animals, Aristotle compares the relationship of a monarch and his people to that of a master and his slave. He further contends that monarchs only help their people as long as the people are subservient to them. Aristotle defines citizenship and differentiates the various types of monarchies. The remainder of the book evaluates political theory, types of democracies, types of oligarchies, types of constitutions, government policies, tyranny, and revolution. Aristotle wraps up *Politics* by describing the perfect state, the perfect life, citizens of the perfect state, and how life in the perfect state should be.

Aristotle, *Rhetoric*

Written by Aristotle in the fourth century BC, *Rhetoric* is a masterpiece that explores how to use persuasion in speech. It consists of three books, all of which focus on the art of persuasion. In Book I, Aristotle explains the purpose of rhetoric and describes its major types. In Book II, he discusses the three methods of persuasion a rhetorician should use: emotion, logical reasoning, and character. In Book III, the Greek philosopher acquaints readers with the elements of style and organization and refers them to his own *Poetics* for more information. The three books of *Rhetoric* also depict rhetoric as a skill that everyone should possess. In the end, Aristotle suggests that every speech should be structured in the following order: an introduction, a narrative, an argument, and a conclusion.

Aristotle, *Poetics*

Written in 335 BC, Aristotle's *Poetics* explores the art of poetry through the lens of philosophy. According to Aristotle, humans are naturally attracted to poetry because of their tendency to imitate one another. The Greek philosopher categorizes poetry into dramatic, epic, and lyric. He further classifies drama into satyr play, tragedy, and comedy. He explains that, although the genres imitate life, they differ in the way the story is told or acted, the goodness of the characters, and the melody of the poetry. Aristotle particularly focuses on tragedy in the book. In his opinion, tragedy arouses fear and pity from the audience and creates from these emotions a cathartic effect. Thus, he suggests that a good tragedy should have a plot, character, thought, diction, melody, and spectacle. The philosopher then turns from drama to epic poetry. He reveals that tragedy and epic poetry are similar in many ways, but that, the epic covers a larger action scope and is longer than tragedy. Ultimately, Aristotle concludes that tragedy is a genre superior to epic poetry.

Lucretius, *On the Nature of Things*

Written by Lucretius in the first century BC, *On the Nature of Things* is a didactic poem divided into six books, all of which explain Epicurean philosophy. The author uses metaphors and poetic language to explore many topics, including the nature of atoms, the soul, mind, thought, sensation, space, and nothingness. More specifically, he asserts that the world is composed of innumerable atoms scattered in a vast and endless void. As each atom has its own will and character, Lucretius suggests that one should study them to understand such natural phenomena as rain and earthquake. The philosopher then argues that it is irrational to fear death, which does no more than to erase feelings, whether good or bad. He goes on to explain that the afterlife does not exist because the body and soul live and die together. The book concludes that the universe is guided by chance, not by divine beings.

Cicero, *On the Commonwealth*

Written around 50 BC, *On the Commonwealth,* or *De re publica,* is a philosophical dialogue by Cicero, a Roman statesman and philosopher. Comprising six books, the dialogue focuses on Roman constitutional theory and general politics. The author begins by critiquing the various forms of governments that have ruled Rome. Following this, he examines how the Roman constitution was developed by the Patricians and the Plebeians. The statesman then examines the various types of constitutions and the impact of the constitutions on Roman citizens. According to Cicero, the commonwealth should serve a universal purpose to meet the needs of modern society. In the concluding part of the dialogue, Cicero reveals his expectation of the ideal citizen in government, which is unwavering patriotism.

Cicero, *On the Laws*

On the Laws, or *De Legibus*, is a philosophical political dialogue written by the Roman statesman in 52 BC. Here, Cicero presents his theories concerning the ideal laws of a society. Cicero conceptualizes an ideal Rome in which all political and social classes work together. He then proceeds to highlight the poor sections of the current constitution and suggests suitable reforms. The author seeks reform, not a total rejection of the laws. According to him, human laws can be good or bad, depending on how they conform to eternal, natural laws. The writer goes on to argue that belief in the gods or eternal wisdom must be the foundation for all laws. He ends by presenting his reformed constitution for a new Roman state.

Seneca, *Letters from a Stoic*

Written around AD 65, *Letters from a Stoic* is a collection of 124 letters by Seneca, a Roman Stoic philosopher. The work advocates for a disciplined moral life without vices or excesses. Each letter starts with a story or an observation from everyday life. Seneca then draws out a moral lesson from each story. The letters expound on the joy that wisdom brings. In short, Seneca teaches that virtue is the only good and that vices are the worst evil. What is more, he admonishes that life is short and should therefore be lived well. Seneca asserts that every man must focus on self-improvement and contentment regardless of his station. He also advocates for Stoic asceticism and speaks of the vanity of riches, warning against evil associations and the disadvantages of treating others wrongly. In sum, *Letters from a Stoic* reveals how and why to adopt a Stoic lifestyle.

Marcus Aurelius, *Meditations*

Written about AD 170, *Meditations* is a collection of notes by Marcus Aurelius, the Roman emperor and philosopher, focusing on self-improvement and Stoic philosophy. The collection begins with the emperor thanking those who have positively impacted his life, instilling in him a good character. The author then advocates for maintaining focus without distractions. More specifically, he teaches that a man's mind is his greatest weapon. According to Aurelius, men should avoid indulgence in excessive pleasure, for it will lead to pain and regrets. The philosopher also admonishes men to eschew vices and evil deeds. Apart from advising against repaying evil for evil, Aurelius believes that a man must be rational and clearheaded to overcome adversities. As life is transient and brief, he points out that every man must live an impactful life by finding his place in the universe. In summary, *Meditations* is a book that focuses on how to live a stoic life and how to engage in self-improvement.

Epictetus, *Discourses*

Written about AD 108, *Discourses* is a collection of lectures by Epictetus, a Greek philosopher. The work centers on Stoic philosophy, with the recurring theme of how men focus their attention on what they desire and what they can control. The author classifies philosophy into assent, choice, and desire. Thereafter, he posits that every man is bound by the law of nature, with the universe governed by a divine Providence or God. Epictetus admonishes all men to focus their passions, desires, anxieties, and opinions so that they can be successful. Moreover, he teaches that people must distinguish between what is theirs from what belongs to others. He goes further in an effort to persuade people to speak to others with respect and live freely and happily with others. According to him, hardship is a part of life, and obstacles offer an opportunity to grow. *Discourses* is a work of practical advice on Stoic living.

Epictetus, *Enchiridion*

Published around AD 125, *Enchiridion* is a work of Stoic ethics by Epictetus. Its title, in Ancient Greek, loosely translates as "handbook of life." The book is a compact philosophical guide to attaining happiness and mental freedom, regardless of one's station in life. It contains excerpts from *Discourses*, written by the same author. In *Enchiridion,* the writer teaches that every man should concern himself with matters subject to his control; therefore, men should never let misfortune or suffering disturb their inner freedom and pursuit of their life goals. Epictetus goes on to recommend constant vigilance against judging others and situations wrongly. Also, he emphasizes the importance of reasoning in everything and asserts that every good and bad experience is both beneficial for learning. *Enchiridion* is an abridged practical manual on using the power of focus to attain one's life goal and remain happy regardless of one's circumstance.

Sextus Empiricus, *Outlines of Pyrrhonism*

Greek author Sextus Empiricus' *Outlines of Pyrrhonism* was written around AD 180. In this guide to Pyrrhonic skepticism, the author advises that men should have no fundamental belief about philosophy, science, and theoretical matters. Instead, they must be skeptical and prepared to doubt and question everything because doubt is necessary to establishing truth. The author questions the very rationality of belief, stating that all beliefs are probabilities and that nothing is ever known for certain. According to Empiricus, every argument has an opposing and equal argument, meaning that men must judge nothing and no one. Pointing out that knowledge is unattainable, he reasons that the quest for knowledge is futile. In summary, *Outlines of Pyrrhonism* explains Pyrrhonic skepticism and is an excellent guide for anyone who wants to adopt this philosophy and lifestyle.

Plotinus, *The Enneads*

Published in AD 270, *The Enneads* is a collection of writings by Plotinus, an Egyptian philosopher. There are six "Enneads," each revolving around a different philosophical topic. The first focuses on human ethics. Here, the author writes about virtues, the living being, happiness, dialectics, good, evil, beauty, and nature. The second and third Enneads are devoted to cosmology. In these Enneads, heaven, the stars, providence, eternity, matter, time, guardian spirits, fate, love, actuality, potentiality, sight, relativity, and other phenomena are discussed. The fourth Ennead discusses the soul, highlighting the essence, immortality, and problems of the soul. It also treats memory, sense-perception, and the descent of the soul into the body. The fifth Ennead explains intelligible reality, knowledge, intellectual beauty, and the Forms. Last, in the Sixth Ennead, the philosopher writes about being, numbers, multiplicity of Forms, and the Supreme One.

Porphyry, *Isagoge*

Greek philosopher Porphyry wrote *Isagoge* as a commentary on Aristotle's *Categories* in AD 270. The work is best known for the author's conception of logic in philosophy and for introducing the "Porphyrian Tree," used by taxonomists to classify living organisms. Porphyry discusses philosophical logic, focusing on definition, proof, and the theories of predication. He subsequently breaks down substance into five categories: species, genus, accident, difference, and property. Following this, he introduces the nature of predicables, a term that depicts the classification of relations that may occur when a predicate stands up to a subject. The philosopher later explains the nature of universals, which are what things have in common. Porphyry ends by discussing "the problem of universals," declining to confirm whether universals are real or virtual. In sum, *Isagoge* combines philosophical logic with the biological classification of plants and animals.

Hermes Trismegistus, *Corpus Hermeticum*

Written by Hermes Trismegistus, the Egyptian philosopher in the second century, *Corpus Hermeticum* is a collection of dialogues between the author and a student. The work introduces Hermeticism by discussing various theories on astrology, alchemy, nature, cosmos, the divine, and the mind. Apart from arguing that there is a single, true theology, the philosopher makes two assertions: God is good and God is one. Following this, he writes that all humans, animals, and beings in the universe are subject to the control of the Supreme Being. He goes on to explain his views further, calling for the purification of the soul and obedience to God. According to Trismegistus, angels, elementals, *aeons*, and other beings exist in the universe. He then introduces the concept of "as above, so below," meaning that the earth is a mirror of the heavens. The writer argues that alchemy, astrology, and other fields are subject to divine principles. In his words, God brings good, and demons bring evil.

Medieval Philosophy

St. Augustine of Hippo, *Confessions*

Confessions is an autobiographical work written between 377 and 400 by St. Augustine of Hippo, who lived in Numidia, Roman North Africa. Written during Augustine's first year as a bishop, the book is a meditation on the course and meaning of his life. Each confession begins with praise to God for his grace as the author recalls his childhood, school days, sexual immorality, and intellectual exploration. The theologian further expresses sorrow at the sexual sins of his youth and considers cleansing himself of sexual impurity, an act he believes is as an important prerequisite to baptism. In *Confessions*, Augustine regrets practicing the Manichean religion and astrology, attributing his conversion to Christianity to St. Ambrose's preaching. His writing depicts the influences of resources that have impacted him, such as the Bible, Cicero, Virgil, and Neo-Platonism. The last part of the book describes the author's ongoing study of Scripture, as he accepts his imperfections and offers grateful praise to God.

St. Augustine of Hippo, *The City of God*

The City of God is a Christian philosophical masterpiece written around 412-426 by St. Augustine of Hippo, a theologian and philosopher. It is a defense of Christianity in response to Pagan allegations that the defeat of Rome by the Visigoths in 410 was a consequence of abandoning Roman gods for Christianity. The theologian asserts that the Roman Empire's decline was due to moral decay, arguing that Christianity saved it from utter destruction. The first part of the text is a criticism of Pagan worship and philosophy, which, according to him, is antagonistic to the Christian religion. In the second part, Augustine establishes his own beliefs through an analogy of two cities: the City of God and the City of the World. Using them as symbols of faith versus nonbelief, he details their origin, progress, and destinies. Augustine then asserts that the City of God is a kingdom that will outlast any earthly empire, including Rome. For this reason, the theologian believes that Christians should focus on the heavenly kingdom rather than paying attention to earthly politics.

Proclus, *Elements of Theology*

Elements of Theology is a of 211 propositions on the subject of Neoplatonism by Proclus, a Greek Neoplatonist who lived from 413 to 485. In the first part, Proclus argues that all particular things can be traced to the One.

According to him, without the One, nothing can exist. He further explains the One using such abstract terms as *eternity, infinitude, procession, gradiation, participation*, and *causality*. In the second part of the work, the philosopher discusses three types of causes in reality: souls, intelligence, and gods (*henads*). After writing about the characteristics of souls, intelligences, and gods, Proclus surmises that the three fundamental levels of reality are the Soul, the Intellect, and the One.

Damascius, *Problems and Solutions Concerning First Principles*
The chief work of the Greek philosopher Damascius (c. 458-after 538), *Problems and Solutions Concerning First Principles* is a criticism of Proclus' views on metaphysics. Damascius begins by acknowledging that his understanding of the triad of Being is quite different from that of Proclus in many ways. He then investigates the theory of descent, contending that cause and effect cannot be similar when one order (intellect) produces a different order (soul). Damascius ends the book by pointing out the limitations of dialectic and Proclean metaphysics.

Boethius, *The Consolation of Philosophy*
Written in 523 by scholar and Roman statesman Boethius, *The Consolation of Philosophy* is a philosophical dialogue on early Medieval Christianity. The work is written as a conversation between him and Lady Philosophy while he is incarcerated, awaiting trial for the alleged crime of treason. Boethius is about to write a sad poem when a tall woman (Lady Philosophy) holding books and a royal staff (a symbol for philosophy) arrives to console him. While the author appreciates her visit, he laments the injustice of his sentence and the presence of evil in a world ruled by God. In response, the woman declares that melancholy has caused Boethius to forget his true nature. She further consoles him by pointing out that, contrary to his belief, the wicked are powerless and outward appearance does not determine happiness. In the end, Lady Philosophy persuades Boethius that, since God represents true happiness and perfect good, he should dedicate himself to contemplating the nature of God rather than dwelling on his misfortunes.

Johannes Scotus Eriugena, *Periphyseon*
Written in 867, *Periphyseon* is a philosophical dialogue by Irish philosopher and theologian Johannes Scotus Eriugena. Divided into five books, it focuses on the relationship between God and creation. The author posits four "species": primordial causes, phenomena, and the final species, God, who is

not created. He explains that God, the origin of all things, created the world to manifest his essence in the things he created. The philosopher thinks that creation unfolds the Divine Nature, which corresponds to the Word of God. According to Eriugena, God is the final goal or end of all things in the universe. Eriugena also writes about a cyclical process in which all the things created by God ultimately return to him. At the end of the text, the theologian illustrates that the beginning, the middle, and the end are all one and that humans cannot truly understand this concept due to their limited comprehension.

Avicenna, *The Book of Healing*

The Book of Healing is a philosophical and scientific encyclopedia written between 1014 and 1020 by Muslim philosopher and physician Avicenna. Despite the title, the text does not discuss medicine. Instead, the author's aim in this book is to "heal" the ignorance of the soul. In the text, Avicenna synthesizes Aristotelian, Islamic, and Neoplatonic ideas while examining the existence of God. Using a system known as Avicennian logic, the author starts the first part of the book by exploring what logic entails in Islamic philosophy. Avicenna goes further to discuss the philosophy of science. He then proposes the use of a method of experimentation in scientific inquiries as an alternative to Aristotelian induction. The philosopher also reconciles the ideas of Aristotelianism and Neoplatonism, making Avennism a central authority in philosophy. He proceeds to distinguish between essence and existence, asserting that while existence is contingent or accidental, essence endures without an external force. In summary, *The Book of Healing* is a masterpiece, which reconciles rational philosophy and Islamic theology through science and logic.

Avicenna, *Proof of the Truthful*

Written by Islamic philosopher Avicenna, *Proof of the Truthful* is a philosophical argument on the existence of God. The author argues that there must be a "necessary entity," one that cannot *not* exist. Avicenna further asserts that the qualities of God described in Islam (unity, intellect, power, generosity, immateriality, and goodness) depict the nature of God's existence. He goes further to differentiate between things that need an external cause to exist and a thing that exists by its essence or intricate nature, namely God. In *Proof of the Truthful*, the philosopher argues that the necessary existent must be unique and that there cannot be more than one of such entities. He derives other attributes of the Supreme Being as described by other religious texts to justify the comparison of the Islamic God to the necessary existent. Overall, Avicenna provides a philosophical justification from the Islamic doctrine of the oneness of God by explaining the uniqueness and simplicity of the necessary existent.

Moses Maimonides, *Guide for the Perplexed*

Guide for the Perplexed is a theological work by the Jewish scholar and philosopher Moses Maimonides, written to reconcile Aristotelian ideas with Jewish theology. Published in 1190, the treatise begins with a criticism of anthropomorphism in the Bible. Maimonides regards as heresy the use of expressions that refer to God in human terms. He also insists that God is completely incorporeal and can only be described using negation. To explain his argument, the philosopher dedicates over twenty chapters of the first part of the text to the Hebrew terms used to refer to the Divine. In addition to defining the meaning of each term, the philosopher identifies each with some metaphysical expression. The second part of the book discusses the physical structure of the universe. While Maimonides recognizes Aristotle's worldview—a spherical earth surrounded by concentric Heavenly Spheres—he rejects the idea that the universe is eternal. The treatise reaches its climax in the third book, a section in which Maimonides explores the mystical passage of the chariot described in the Book of Ezekiel and analyzes the moral aspects of the universe. The work concludes that the correct worship of God is essential to a perfect and harmonious life.

Moses Maimonides, *Mishneh Torah*

Published in the twelfth century by Jewish philosopher and rabbinical authority Maimonides, the *Mishneh Torah* is a guide to the entire system of Jewish traditions and laws. The work is divided into fourteen volumes, each analyzing a different aspect of Rabbinic Judaism. The author discusses such topics as marriage, divorce, ethics, civil law, and helping the needy. Using the Talmud as its basis, the text offers instruction in such secular subjects as psychology, astronomy, physics, and dietetics. The author also incorporates the neglected theoretical branches of the Oral Torah to inspire renewed interest in them. In addition, he includes entire realms of the *halakha*, which contains laws that are not applicable in the post-Temple era. Maimonides states the final decision on the law that Jews should follow in each situation. Overall, he uses an unconventional approach to simplify the Talmud and make Jewish laws accessible to non-scholars.

Saadia Gaon, *Emunoth ve-Deoth*

Published in 933, *Emunoth ve-Deoth* is a philosophical treatise written by Saadia Gaon. The rabbi begins the book by decrying the doubts and confusion plaguing followers of Judaism. Part of his mission in life, he writes, is to strengthen their beliefs and remove their doubts. Gaon rejects the concept of the trinity, arguing that God is one. He also proves that the Torah was divinely inspired, that the universe was created by a supreme being, that man has an indestructible soul, and that the creator is not a trinity. He goes further to assert that the creator has given man free will and that man will receive the appropriate rewards according to his choices. Most importantly, Gaon insists that one can believe in Scripture and still search for knowledge outside of it. In sum, the aim of the author in this treatise is to correct all the misinterpretation and misconception of Judaism.

Al-Ghazali, *The Incoherence of the Philosophers*

Written in the eleventh century by the Persian philosopher Al-Ghazali, *The Incoherence of the Philosophers* is a masterpiece that refutes the superiority of science to divine revelation. Consisting of twenty discussions, the treatise criticizes philosophers who do not believe in the teachings of Islam. The Persian philosopher begins this treatise by complaining of the heresy and blasphemy committed by philosophers and their followers. He discusses the main teachings of philosophy and argues that none of them can be sufficiently proven. Al-Ghazali argues that followers of philosophers blindly emulate the teachings of such founders as Aristotle and Plato without evaluating their credibility. Furthermore, he claims that philosophers propagate irrational beliefs, which cannot be demonstratively proven. For this reason, Al-Ghazali regards philosophy as a pseudo-religion that is at odds with Islam. Al-Ghazali concludes his book by suggesting several strategies that can be used to integrate philosophy into Islam.

Averroes, *The Incoherence of the Incoherence*

The Incoherence of the Incoherence is a philosophical text written in the eleventh century by the Islamic scholar Averroes. The treatise refutes the ideas of Al-Ghazali (*The Incoherence of Philosophers*), who claims that the teachings of philosophers are nothing but false. The writer argues that philosophy has a place in Islam. He supports his argument by using Quranic verses to portray philosophy as the best path one can take to arrive at religious truths. More specifically, Averroes asserts that, given that Islam is the ultimate truth, one can use philosophy to discover its hidden revelations.

Furthermore, he demonstrates that deeper meanings of Islamic truth can be lost if one fails to engage philosophically and critically with the religion. He also thinks that such an omission can lead to one having an incorrect understanding of divinity. Averroes further challenges the concepts of God's actions and attributes. In the end, the writer concludes that philosophy is compatible with the teachings of Islam.

Anselm, *Proslogion*

Written in 1078, *Proslogion* is a treatise written by Italian theologian Anselm with the aim of proving the existence of God with ontological reasons. Anselm begins the work by proposing his famous ontological argument, arguing that merely having the idea that a supreme being exists is sufficient proof of God's existence. According to Anselm, if God exists in an idea, then he must also be real, for it is better for the Supreme Being to exist in reality than to be just an idea. Nonetheless, Anselm notes that if such a being does not exist, then one should conceive a much greater being. In the end, the theologian points out that even an unbeliever will come to the same conclusion that God exists.

St. Thomas Aquinas, *Summa Contra Gentiles*

Summa Contra Gentiles is a philosophical treatise written between 1259 and 1265 by St. Thomas Aquinas, a Dominican priest, philosopher, and theologian. The text is divided into four numbered books, in which Aquinas refutes certain heretical beliefs in Islam and Judaism and addresses the core tenets of Christianity. He also examines the nature and existence of a monotheistic God. In Book I, Aquinas talks about the concept of truth and reasoning. He dedicates Book II to the creation of the universe. In Book III, Aquinas investigates the human condition, fate, intellect, and good and evil. He also examines divine intervention in the lives of people and the relation between the creator and his creation. The fourth book discusses the teachings of Christian doctrine such as Incarnation, Trinity, and Sacraments. Here, the philosopher distinguishes Christianity and the Catholic faith from other monotheistic religions. In sum, in *Summa Contra Gentiles,* Aquinas provides a detailed explanation of the Christina faith and defends it against nonconforming doctrines in Islam and Judaism.

St. Thomas Aquinas, *Summa Theologica*

Written during 1265-1274 by the Dominican priest and philosopher St. Thomas Aquinas, *Summa Theologica* is a theological summary that explores the relationship between God and man. The book focuses on several aspects of religion and the core tenets of the Catholic faith. After explaining how Christ makes possible the reconciliation of man with the Divine, Aquinas examines the nature of God by answering 119 questions concerning creation, the nature of man, divine government, and the existence of God and angels. He then focuses on questions concerning man, virtue, justice, temperance, and law. From here, Aquinas proceeds to explore the difference between a religious and a secular life. He goes further, elucidating other questions regarding Christ, such as incarnation, sacraments, and resurrection. The text includes 99 more questions concerning other aspects of theology, such as confession, marriage, purgatory, and the union of body and soul. In sum, Aquinas offers an instructional guide to theology students just learning the teachings of Christianity.

John Duns, *Ordinatio*

Ordinatio is a philosophical treatise written in the thirteenth century by the Scottish philosopher John Duns, popularly known as Duns Scotus. In the book, Scotus focuses on mind and knowledge, commenting on the *Four Books of Sentences*, which was written by theologian Peter Lombard. Scotus's powerful views are very different from the Augustinian doctrine, which is grounded in the belief that humans have a tendency to understand and love the Divinity Trinity. Unlike Aquinas, Scotus believes that humans can discover truths (including God) without divine revelation, that thoughts are a function of one's experience or mental representations, and that being is an embodiment of one's intellect. Scotus goes further to explore the challenge of individuation, adding that angels may be difficult to distinguish as they are not corporeal beings. In summary, this book contains Scotus's arguments for univocal predication, which Aquinas had declared "impossible."

William Ockham, *Summa Logicae*

The *Summa Logicae* was written between 1323 and 1326 by the English philosopher, theologian, and logician William Ockham. Even though the author presents the treatise as a logic textbook, he uses it as a venue for defending his reductionist ontology. This masterpiece also promotes the Ockham's nominalist views in the context of developing a systemic account of logic and language. According to the author, only concrete individuals exist, and other purported entities are only names. Like other medieval works of logic, the content of the *Summa Logicae* is organized according to Aristotle's three functions of the understanding: concepts and terms that signify them, propositions formed when the terms are combined, and argumentation. He also attributes an individual quality to an individual substance. Ockham then explores the truth conditions of propositions and truth preservation of arguments. Overall, the author proposes in the *Summa Logicae* that the correct logical analysis of language is essential to solving philosophical and theological problems.

Early Modern Philosophy

Desiderius Erasmus, *The Praise of Folly*

Published in June 1511, *The Praise of Folly* is a satirical essay written by Dutch Renaissance humanist Desiderius Erasmus of Rotterdam. Based on the previous works of the Italian humanist Faustino Perisuali, the text mocks the traditions of the Renaissance period and depicts Erasmus' disappointment with the Roman Empire's use of fictitious characters. In the essay, fictional character Folly is a goddess. Her parents are Plutus, god of wealth, and Freshness, a nymph. Nursed by the gods Ignorance and Drunkenness and her friends Flattery, Laziness, and Self-Love, Folly lives a life of indulgence and privilege. She praises herself endlessly and feels that life would be boring and unpleasant without her. The text takes a darker tone as Folly praises self-deception and madness and proceeds to examine the corrupt practices in Rome and the superstitious abuses of Catholic doctrine. Erasmus concludes with a Christian anecdote supporting the contention that no man is wise at all times or without fault.

Niccolò Machiavelli, *The Prince*

The Prince is a sixteenth-century philosophical masterpiece by Niccolò Machiavelli, an Italian diplomat and politician. The book focuses on how to conquer, rule, govern, and control a state. It also talks about politics, goodwill, alliances, power, and the art of war. Machiavelli starts the book by describing princedoms or autocratic regimes in detail. He then goes on to explain the nature and types of states and how to keep and control them. The writer then provides practical pieces of advice on how to build a strong military, acquire and keep new provinces, deal with internal rebellion, and form alliances. As part of his advice, he warns that a prince should choose to be feared rather than to be loved by his subjects. In his view, the ends justify the means. In addition to explaining the pros and cons of the diverse routes to power, Machiavelli discusses the qualities of a ruler and insists that virtuousness is a hindrance to governance. In sum, *The Prince* is a practical guide on how to acquire and hold on to political power.

Niccolò Machiavelli, *Discourses on Livy*

Published in 1517, *Discourses on Livy* compares the political systems of ancient Rome with the government of Machiavelli's time. The texts consist of three books, all of which are a compilation of the author's views on politics, affairs of the state, and war. In Book I, Machiavelli describes the internal politics of Rome under open counsel. In Book II, he discusses the strategy used by the Romans to maintain and expand their empire. In Book III, the Italian diplomat addresses how the exploits of such great men as Quintus Maximus catapulted Rome to greatness. The three books also explore how Rome was founded and governed. Machiavelli reveals how values, culture, and religion can corrupt governments and its citizenry. After pointing out that a country can be devastated by occupation and war, he suggests several ways to manage and govern a state and concludes by explaining how to assimilate citizens of a conquered nation into a new republic.

Michel de Montaigne, *Essays*

Essays by Michel de Montaigne chronicles the author's observations and opinions of French Renaissance society. Published in 1580, the compilation deals with diverse topics, including happiness, the human body, emotions, education, conscience, politics, death, solitude, and love. The French philosopher first explains that the aim of his work is to understand his true self and, through it, the human condition. He goes further to state that he is skeptical of human motives and experience. According to him, humans should not trust their reasoning because they cannot control their thoughts. Montaigne focuses especially on man's understanding of truth. In his opinion, man's finite nature prevents him from understanding an infinite reality. Nevertheless, Montaigne believes that a divine revelation can help man discover the absolute truth. The author, therefore, urges people to push themselves beyond their limits to achieve divine qualities. In conclusion, Montaigne's *Essays* aims to educate readers on perceived ills in the society.

Francis Bacon, *Novum Organum*

In 1620, Sir Francis Bacon wrote *Novum Organum* as a template to facilitate the discovery of the truth about nature and the world. The philosophical treatise is divided into two books. In Book I, the philosopher criticizes the use of logic-based arguments or pure *a priori* deduction to discover scientific laws. In Book II, he presents a new method of inductive reasoning, which he believes superior to the traditional system. The English author begins his argument by stating that the human mind is untrustworthy because it perceives things with a bias. Elaborating further, he proposes the four idols that prevent objective reasoning: idols of the tribe, market, cave, and theater. As Bacon puts it, depending on the human mind to make accurate judgments will only lead to errors in research. The philosopher then explains that his new method involves collating and studying data from observations and experiments. In conclusion, this text introduces an empirical, scientific approach to obtaining accurate data and true knowledge.

Hugo Grotius, *De Jure Belli Ac Pacis*

De Jure Belli Ac Pacis (*On the Law of War and Peace*) is a 1625 philosophical work by Dutch writer Hugo Grotius. Grotius discusses the nature of war, who should wage war, how to wage war, how to prevent war, how to treat prisoners of war, and other war-related issues. He points out the flaws in the customs used by leaders to wage war. The philosopher believes that God has no direct influence in the affairs of humans. Hence, he reasons that wars should be guided mainly by natural laws, not divine laws. He admits, however, that some laws in the Old Testament or New Testament can be used by political leaders to prevent war. States should only wage wars, Grotius contends, for causes that are just or good in themselves. Overall, the author's aim in this book is to regulate warfare and, most importantly, reduce human casualty during wars.

René Descartes, *Rules for the Direction of the Mind*

Rules for the Direction of the Mind is a 1628 philosophical work by Franco-Dutch philosopher René Descartes. In this work, he proposes twenty-one rules not only to guide human thought but also to investigate truths. The rules can be classified into four groups: (1) the purpose of any research is to unravel the truth, (2) only issues that can be verified with experiments or known for certainty should be investigated, (3) the result of scientific inquiries must be rational, not vague, and not based on luck, and (4) the result of any research should not be compromised, regardless of whether the outcome is favorable or not.

René Descartes, *Meditations on First Philosophy*

Franco-Dutch philosopher René Descartes' 1641 treatise *Meditations on First Philosophy* comprises six meditations in which the author first doubts and then works to discover what he can know for certain. In the first meditation, Descartes questions all his beliefs and begins to doubt them. In the second meditation, he talks about the nature of the human mind, concluding that he exists because he has the capacity to think. He later rejects the notion that the idea of God is artificially created by humans to control others. After a series of arguments, he concludes in the third meditation that the idea of God is embedded in the human mind by God. If God is naturally benevolent and good, how can falsehood exist in the world? Descartes explores this question in the fourth meditation. His response to the source of human error is that humans have free will and understanding. The latter (understanding), according to him, can be obtained only in an incomplete form, meaning human understanding is susceptible to errors. That humans can think about God is sufficient proof that God exists, Descartes explains in the fifth meditation. In the sixth meditation, he explores the existence of materials outside the self and then concludes that the body and the mind are different.

René Descartes, *Discourse on the Method*

Originally published in 1637, *Discourse on the Method* is a philosophical treatise by René Descartes, a Franco-Dutch writer, philosopher, mathematician, and scientist. Consisting of six parts, the work explores the nature of skepticism and its challenge to intellectual discourse. In Part I, Descartes emphasizes the importance of acquiring and applying knowledge in the right way. In Part II, he abandons old scientific methodology and explores new ways of finding knowledge. In Part III, he adopts three rules for investigating the ways of finding knowledge. The first rule is to follow the laws and customs of his country. The second is to be resolute in his actions and decisions. The last is to always remain flexible and receptive to new ways of doing things. In Part IV, Descartes proves the existence of God with the maxim "I think, therefore I am." The writer delineates the nature and laws of the universe in Part V, and, in Part VI, concludes the book by further examining the conditions that must be satisfied to investigate the nature and laws of the universe.

René Descartes, *Principles of Philosophy*

Published in 1644, *Principles of Philosophy* was written by the Franco-Dutch philosopher René Descartes. The treatise is a synthesis of two prior works by Descartes: *Discourse on Method* and *Meditations on First Philosophy.* More specifically, the book introduces the laws of nature (physics) and introduces philosophy, defining it as the study of wisdom. The writer goes on to explain why only God is perfectly wise. In his view, a man is wise only in proportion to his knowledge of important truths obtained from God. Apart from presenting the scientific principles that govern the universe, the book discusses the nature and forms of knowledge, certainty, doubt, higher wisdom, the tree of philosophy, and meditations. In summary, *Principles of Philosophy* amalgamates the basics of physics with the basics of philosophy.

Baruch Spinoza, *Ethics*

Ethics is a philosophical treatise written between 1661 and 1675 by the Dutch philosopher Baruch Spinoza. Consisting of five parts, the book explains what it means to live an ethical life. It touches on such topics as the nature of God, nature, emotions, and free will. In Part I of the treatise, Spinoza discusses the relationship between the universe and God. God is the main constituent of the universe, the philosopher argues. This means everything in the universe depends on God. Criticizing Descartes' view that the body and mind are distinct but dependent on each other, Spinoza contends in Part II that the body and mind are one. In Part III of *Ethics*, the philosopher points out that human emotions (sadness, love, hate, happiness, etc.) can last as long as the mind is active. He goes further in Part IV to emphasize the human tendency to avoid pain and seek pleasure. The last part of the book, Part IV, talks about the superiority of reason over emotion in living a good life.

Gottfried Leibniz, *Discourse on Metaphysics*

Written in 1686 by German logician and mathematician Gottfried Leibniz, *Discourse on Metaphysics* is a short treatise on fundamental philosophical issues. Leibniz explores such philosophical topics as theology, logic, philosophy, and physics. The text begins with a reflection on the perfection of God and His role in the universe. The mathematician goes further to discuss the relationship between mind and matter, contending that the soul is the fundamental substance of nature. Concluding that the world that we perceive is composed of ideas rather than matter, Leibniz categorizes souls into two groups: (1) simple souls such as insects and plants, and (2) intelligent souls, such as humans. Concerning fate and freedom, Leibniz reasons that if God knows in advance what will happen to every person, people cannot make their own decisions. He suggests, therefore, that God allows free will, even though He knows in advance what decision people will take, including the evil occurrences required to create a balance in the world. The text concludes with a short discussion on the immortality of souls and the afterlife. In sum, the *Discourse on Metaphysics* seeks to establish that God is perfect and that goodness exists independently of God.

Gottfired Leibniz, *Monadology*

Written in 1714, *Monadology* is a book by Gottfried Leibniz that introduces the concept of monads. In the text, the German polymath discusses the principles governing reasoning and truth, the nature of the monadic consciousness and perception, and the relationship between God and the monadic universe. Leibniz starts his book by defining monads as unique, indivisible, self-propelled substances created by God. He goes further to describe the three types of monads: perceiving monads, created monads, and rational monads. According to Leibniz, humans are rational monads because they possess both reasoning and memory. Apart from depicting God as a being without limits, Leibniz further claims that God permits rational monads to perceive and interact with one another. The philosopher later reveals that even though many universes exist, the universe created by God is supreme. He ends his book with an illustration of an imaginary city ruled by God, in which all monads are moral and perfect.

Gottfired Leibniz, *New Essays on Human Understanding*
New Essays on Human Understanding is a philosophical dialogue written by German philosopher Gottfried Leibniz in 1704. Written as a rebuttal of John Locke's *An Essay Concerning Human Understanding*, it is a dialogue between Leibniz and Locke. In the text, the author refutes all the ideas and claims in Locke's book, the major theme of the rebuttal being that all the actions and thoughts of the soul are innate. According to Leibniz, all humans are born with human inclinations. After disproving Locke's proof of God's existence, the writer contends that an object's identity is based on all visible and discernible characteristics of the object. Leibniz also offers arguments concerning free will, morality, necessary truth, personal identity, mind-body dualism, language, and other theories presented in *An Essay Concerning Human Understanding*.

John Locke, *Two Treatises of Government*
Authored anonymously in 1689 by English philosopher and physician John Locke, *Two Treatises of Government* is a masterpiece on politics. The text is a response to Charles II's savage purge of the Whig movement and the resulting political upheaval in England. In the *First Treatise*, Locke criticizes Robert Filmer's support of Patriarchalism in his *Patriarcha*. The philosopher contends that every man can virtuously govern himself according to God's law. The *Second Treatise* lays the groundwork for modern liberalism. In this section, Locke proposes solutions for a more civilized society based on natural rights and social contracts. He defines political power as the right to make the laws that protect the public. The philosopher further contends that people accept these laws because it is for their good. In his

view, political societies exist to defend the lives and properties and liberties of their citizens, and the authority of the government resides in its political legitimacy. In *Two Treatises of Government*, Locke concludes that people have the right to revolt against their government when their rulers become tyrants.

John Locke, *An Essay Concerning Human Understanding*

An Essay Concerning Human Understanding is authored by English philosopher and physician John Locke. The book is the author's attempt to explain the foundation of human knowledge and understanding. According to Locke, the human mind is blank at birth and is filled through life experiences. In Book I, Locke refutes the rationalist notion of innate ideas, explaining that while some ideas are in mind from an early age, newborn children do not come into the world with ideas. For this reason, he believes that there is no universally accepted truth. Book II establishes Locke's theory of ideas. In this section, he points out his distinction between such passively acquired ideas as taste, color, and shape. He also investigates complex ideas, such as causes, effects, numbers, identity, and other abstract ideas. Book III explores language, while Book IV discusses knowledge, which includes mathematics, faith, opinion, and natural philosophy. In *Concerning Human Understanding,* Locke's overall aims are to discover the sources of ideas, question the implication of having ideas, and examine the issues of faith and opinion.

Jean-Jacques Rousseau, *Discourse on the Arts and Sciences*

Discourse on the Arts and Sciences is a philosophical masterpiece by Jean-Jacques Rousseau. Published in 1750, the book comprises two main sections. The first reviews ancient civilizations that were destroyed by arts and sciences. The second examines the fields of art and sciences and the perils associated with them. The Genevan philosopher argues that the arts and sciences are created from human vices and that their progress has corrupted human morality and virtue. He argues that science does not aid morality but distracts people from such important activities as cultivating relationships. Rousseau goes on to claim that artists produce arts only so they can earn special recognition. Furthermore, he asserts that a society's emphasis on both arts and sciences usually results in a decline of military prowess, which could jeopardize a people's defense. Rousseau ends his book by urging humans to concentrate on building their character rather than dabbling in the arts and sciences.

David Hume, *An Enquiry Concerning the Principles of Morals*

Written in 1751, *An Enquiry Concerning the Principles of Morals* explores how reason and moral sense contribute to human moral judgment. Hume begins his treatise by rejecting the theory that people base their decisions solely on reason. Instead, the Scottish philosopher posits that feelings play a significant role in moral judgments. Elaborating further, he contends that humans make moral evaluations because of their emotional *and* reasoning capacities. He further suggests that the human ability to share and empathize with one another significantly influences moral judgments. With this claim, Hume creates an unmistakable connection between human sociability and morality. Hume also discusses the different types of virtues and how they manifest in society, and he examines the role of benevolence in moral judgments. In sum, Hume proposes a theory that bases morality on human nature rather than religion or a supernatural being.

Jean-Jacques Rousseau, *Discourse on the Origin and Basis of Inequality Among Men*

Written in 1755, *Discourse on the Origin and Basis of Inequality Among Men* discusses how human society was founded. It is divided into two parts, the first of which explores the natural human state before the advent of socialization and civilization. The second part describes how humans evolved to form society. Rousseau argues that primitive man was happy alone and had no need for socialization. He explains that socialization caused man to begin making unhealthy comparisons to other humans. Thus, to remain happy, man had to dominate his fellow humans. Rousseau asserts that man invented property as a tool for exploitation and domination. The author then goes ahead to predict that if wealth and property ownership becomes the standard by which people compare themselves to one another, society will devolve into despotism. In conclusion, Rousseau holds that private property is the source of inequality in society.

Adam Smith, *The Theory of Moral Sentiments*

The Theory of Moral Sentiments was published in 1759 by Adam Smith, a Scottish philosopher. Divided into seven parts, the text explores the origins of morality, how humans make moral judgments, and the components of virtue. Smith begins with a description of sympathy and details how it influences moral ideals and norms. Next, he distinguishes between moral rules and virtues. Rules are important in a society, according to Smith, because they help non-virtuous people act in a socially acceptable manner. Based on this assertion, he advocates that humans should readily embrace and submit to rules. Adhering to rules, the philosopher believes, is not difficult because an omniscient God designed humans to be intrinsically moral. He nevertheless warns of outside influences that could corrupt morals. Smith concludes his book by offering his readers pragmatic rules of morality.

George Berkeley, *A Treatise Concerning the Principles of Human Knowledge*

A Treatise Concerning the Principles of Human Knowledge was written in 1710 by the Irish philosopher George Berkeley as a rebuttal to John Locke's theories on the nature of human perception. The central point of the treatise is that the external world, which depicts the ideas in a man's mind, is made up solely of ideas. According to the author, ideas can only look like the ideas of others, meaning the human mind is incapable of conceiving abstract ideas. Furthermore, Berkeley points out that the external world consists of ideas, not physical forms. Because God gives the world regularity and logic, Berkeley believed that names are not abstract and that all names come from general ideas. He argues further that numbers are relative; they exist only in the mind. In summary, *A Treatise Concerning the Principles of Human Knowledge* rebuts John Locke's philosophical views by presenting the concept of subjective realism.

Gottfired Leibniz, *Théodicée*

Written in 1710 by German philosopher Gottfried Leibniz, *Théodicée* explains why a good God permits the existence of evil. Responding to arguments posed by the French philosopher Pierre Bayle, *Théodicée* does not defend the nature God, but presents a logical, philosophical framework in which God and evil are portrayed as not mutually exclusive in the universe. Leibniz argues that God is a perfect being who created a perfect world. In addition to pointing out that achieves a unique balance of good over evil, he classifies evil into three categories: physical, metaphysical, and moral. Metaphysical evil is unavoidable because the universe must fall short of God's perfection. Leibniz goes on to argue that moral evil is sin and that physical evil is pain, concluding the book by stating that God has complete freedom, and human free will is consistent with God's foreknowledge.

David Hume, *A Treatise of Human Nature*

Scottish writer David Hume's 1739 book *A Treatise of Human Nature* touches on naturalism, skepticism, and empiricism. The work consists of three books. In Book I ("Of the Understanding"), Hume argues that all human knowledge stems from experience. For this reason, all human knowledge is based on empirical investigation. Hume's aim in this section is to unravel the "extent and force of human understanding." In Book II ("Of the Passions"), the philosopher focuses on passions, contending that human behavior is influences mainly by emotions, not reasons. He goes further to show the problem of induction and asks if inductive reasoning can spawn philosophical knowledge. Inductive reasoning and human belief in cause and effect, according to Hume, cannot be justified by reason but only by faith. In Book III ("Of Morals"), the philosopher concludes that ethics is subjective and is based more on sentiments than on reasons.

David Hume, *An Enquiry Concerning Human Understanding*
An Enquiry Concerning Human Understanding is a philosophical masterpiece by David Hume, a philosopher best known for championing empiricism. The book explains the nature of knowledge, ideas, and beliefs. Hume begins with an introduction to the different branches of philosophy. He then explains the difference between impressions and ideas. In his view, impressions are what one thinks about an object, while ideas are the memories one has about the object. After explaining these two terms, Hume contends that ideas are the product of impressions and that they are associated with one another in the form of trains of thought. The philosopher concludes by arguing that humans and animals are analogous and that all ideas are derived from experience.

Charles de Secondat, Baron de Montesquieu, *The Spirit of the Laws*
The Spirit of the Laws is a philosophical masterpiece by French thinker Charles de Secondat, Baron de Montesquieu. Published in 1748, the treatise consists of 31 books, which discuss political systems around the world, showing how geography, climate, and culture influence the nature of political systems. Montesquieu begins the book by explaining three different forms of government: republican, monarchical, and despotic. He presents the advantages and disadvantages of each. The philosopher then points out that the principle of a democratic republic is the love of virtue, that of monarchies is the love of honor, and that of despotism is the fear of the ruler. Without the principle suffused in a state, Montesquieu reasons that political leaders will find it increasingly challenging to govern their peoples. Furthermore, the work explains the meaning of political liberty

and how best to preserve it. Political liberty, as Montesquieu puts it, is almost impossible in a despotic political system but possible in both democratic and monarchical political systems. For political liberty to exist in a state, the writer argues, there must be a separation of powers and obedience to the rule of law. He concludes by calling for an end to slavery, the preservation of liberty, obedience to the rule of law, and the separation of powers.

Jean-Jacques Rousseau, *Emile, or On Education*

Emile, or *On Education* is a philosophical treatise authored in 1762 by Genevan philosopher Jean-Jacques Rousseau. The work, which consists of five books, talks about the nature of education and man. It also discusses how man and society can improve their relationship. In Book I, the author points out that man needs to suppress a child's natural instincts so that the child can live successfully in society. He advises parents (in Book II, Book III, and Book IV) to allow their children to learn from the world (experience), not from books. Rousseau reasons that this form of education will help the child to learn practicable skills, draw inferences, and make informed decisions. He goes further in Book V to discuss female education, arguing that men and women are never equal. The writer implies in the book that women are the weaker sex, that women need less education, and that men should protect them.

Jean-Jacques Rousseau, *The Social Contract*

Published in 1762, *The Social Contract* sets out to explain how to create a just society. Rousseau laments the current political system, in which man is born free but subsequently oppressed and constrained by unjust laws crafted by society. In his view, laws in society are only useful and legal if and only if they are acknowledged by the majority. He goes further to paint what an ideal society should look like. According to the writer, an ideal state should respect the free will of the people. It should also allow freedom of speech, fight for the common good, and ensure liberty and equality. After examining the various forms of political systems, Rousseau recommends the separation of powers in an ideal society to prevent the state from sliding into tyranny.

Voltaire, *Treatise on Tolerance*

Published in 1763, *Treatise on Tolerance* is a philosophical work by the French philosopher Voltaire. As the title implies, the treatise deliberates on religious fanaticism and urges citizens to be religiously tolerant. The book examines the rationale behind violent conflict over religious dogma. Dispute over another's religion is not just reason for mistreating or killing the "unbeliever," Voltaire contends. He cites an incident in Paris in which a Protestant man, accused of killing his son (for having converted to Catholicism) was unjustly killed by a Catholic mob. In the end, Voltaire argues that people should love each other regardless of their religious affiliations.

Immanuel Kant, *Critique of Practical Reason*

Critique of Practical Reason is a philosophical masterpiece by German philosopher Immanuel Kant. Published in 1788, the book deals with ethics and moral philosophy. Kant begins by comparing theoretical (speculative) reason and practical reason. Theoretical reason informs which theory one should follow, the writer explains, adding that practical reason is like a plan of action. It determines one's will. That is, it informs how one should act in a particular situation. Kant believes that, unlike theoretical reason, practical reason can be used to obtain metaphysical truth. He advises people to seek good, not pleasure. According to him, being good is the object of practical law. He contends that while good always produces pleasure, pleasure does not guarantee good. To be morally good, Kant believes that one's actions and motivations must be categorically imperative. The writer concludes by discussing the importance of communication and the public use of reasons.

Immanuel Kant, *Critique of Pure Reason*

Published in 1781, *The Critique of Pure Reason* is a philosophical treatise by German philosopher Immanuel Kant. Divided into two books, the work highlights the limitations of metaphysics. The author starts by conceptualizing transcendental idealism, positing that subjects recognize objects based on their appearance under the conditions of the subject's sensibilities. In his view, human sensibilities are affected by space, causality, and time. Kant next divides knowledge into two categories: *a posteriori* knowledge (knowledge gained with experience), and *a priori* knowledge (knowledge gained without experience). The philosopher then distinguishes synthetic judgment from analytic judgment. Kant asserts that mathematics and science are both synthetic and *a priori* because they are universally applicable. In sum, *The Critique of Pure Reason* is a treatise on the nature of human reasoning and the origin of knowledge.

Thomas Reid, *Inquiry into the Human Mind on the Principles of Common Sense*

Published in 1764 by the Scottish Philosopher Thomas Reid, *An Inquiry into the Human Mind on the Principles of Common Sense* is a work on the philosophy of the mind. The author begins by asserting that the mind is the greatest and noblest part of the body. He calls the mind the "engine room" or the "root fabric" of the body, from which all artisans, engineers, philosophers, and people from all professions draw their inspiration. Apart from distinguishing between perception and sensation, the philosopher argues that common sense is the foundation of all philosophical inquiry. Reid emphasizes that the external world is not an extension of the human mind but exists on its own. Man must reason like a child to overcome the artificial illusions of the adult mind, Reid argues. In sum, *An Inquiry into the Human Mind on the Principles of Common Sense* critically studies the human mind and proposes new ways of reasoning and perception.

Adam Smith, *The Wealth of Nations*

Published in 1776, *The Wealth of Nations* is a philosophical masterpiece by Adam Smith, the Scottish economist and philosopher. The work is an inquiry into the factors that build a nation's wealth. In the book, the author covers division of labor, productivity, free market, the origin and use of money, theories of demand and supply, factors of production, taxation, and several other economic concepts. Smith studies the economic systems of various countries and compares them to one another before revealing each system's failures and successes. Apart from warning against government interference in an economy, the writer asserts that a high level of literacy will make a nation prosperous. The economist also insists on fair compensation for all workers, along with freedom of production. *The Wealth of Nations* is a classical economic treatise that reveals the elements that make a nation wealthy or poor.

Jeremy Bentham, *An Introduction to the Principles of Morals and Legislation*

An Introduction to the Principles of Morals and Legislation was published in 1789 by Jeremy Bentham, an English philosopher and legal theorist. Bentham first develops the theory of utilitarianism, which states that what is morally right or good is that which will maximize the happiness of the majority. The outcome of an action, Bentham insists, determines its rightness or wrongness. He begins his treatise by asserting that pleasure or happiness is the only thing that is intrinsically good. The philosopher then goes further, suggesting that humans should maximize ethical pleasure because it is a motivator. As he puts it, if pleasure is carefully studied, humans can use the knowledge to enact sensible laws. Bentham also discusses the nature, origins, and types of pleasure and pain. Moreover, he proposes the "hedonic calculus," a method of calculating which future action will promote the highest amount of pleasure in relation to pain. In sum, Bentham explores the idea of a society governed by laws that cater to human pleasures.

Edmund Burke, *Reflections on the Revolution in France*
Written by Edmund Burke in 1790, *Reflections on the Revolution in France* criticizes the French Revolution and predicts that France will come to a disastrous end. Burke's reason for the prediction is the complex nature of humans and their societies. According to Burke, a gradual reform of the constitution is preferable to revolution. Next, the Irish statesman emphasizes that a political ideology should be founded on such abstract ideals as liberty to prevent abuse of power. In addition, Burke rejects the idea that citizens have no right to overthrow a tyrannical government. Apart from advocating for a government with a "heart," the philosopher calls for the enactment of laws to protect citizens against government oppression. Burke concludes his book with the assertion that reform is the only way to bring about changes in a country, not revolution.

Julien Offray de La Mettrie, *Man a Machine*
Published in the eighteenth century, *Man a Machine* is a philosophical masterpiece by French philosopher Julien Offray de La Mettrie. The work discusses spiritualism and materialism and focuses on man's soul. La Mettrie argues that soul and matter are one, meaning that there is no separate distinction to be made between dead matter and living matter. His views on animals are, in part, similar to those of Descartes. The philosopher argues that animals are nothing but tools or machines to humans. Humans use animals to achieve their instrumental and end goals. Yet he believes that humans and animals have many things in common. They both die, eat, and cherish life. Even though man is both an emotional and a rational being, La Mettrie concludes that man, like animals, is a machine.

Immanuel Kant, *Critique of Judgment*
Critique of Judgment was written in 1790 by the German philosopher Immanuel Kant. The work is divided into two sections. The first section

discusses aesthetic judgments, while the second analyzes the purpose of teleology in understanding science and nature. In the text, Kant proposes the deductive principles that shape human judgment. He starts his book by claiming that humans judge an object's aesthetics based on their feelings. He then enumerates four aesthetic judgments common to humans: the good, the beautiful, the sublime, and the agreeable. Kant goes on to opine that man's morality and practicality make him the highest teleological end. As he puts it, other species in nature directly or indirectly exist because of man. After pointing out that human judgment is influenced by the mind's inclination to see order and purpose in nature, he nonetheless argues that this does not prove the existence of God. In the end, Kant believes that a genuine aesthetic experience does not consider the purpose of an object.

René Descartes, *Passions of the Soul*

Passions of the Soul by René Descartes was published in 1649 and is a philosophical dialogue on the passions (emotions), which is divided into three sections. Book I is focused on human physiology as well as the nature of emotions and soul. In Book II, the philosopher analyzes emotions in general. In Book III, he examines specific emotions, such as generosity. In *Passions of the Soul*, Descartes uses natural philosophy, instead of rhetoric or moral philosophy, to explain passions. The body and mind are separate from one another, he argues. Thus, he suggests that emotions are generated by the mind or body interacting with itself. Descartes goes further, examining and explaining the six primary human emotions: love, sadness, wonder, hatred, joy, and desire. He also investigates the influence and psychological effects of these emotions on human behaviors. In the end, Descartes concludes that emotions are good for the soul, provided they are restrained by morals and freewill

Thomas Hobbes, *Leviathan*

Published in 1651, *Leviathan* is a masterpiece by Thomas Hobbes, an English philosopher. It consists of four books, which discuss governmental and societal structures. "Leviathan" is a sea serpent mentioned in the Book of Job. Hobbes uses it to represent the power of government. In Book I, Hobbes sets the philosophical groundwork for the treatise. Book II discusses the rights of rulers and their subjects, how to select a "Leviathan"—the kind of government best for your commonwealth. The three types are monarchy, aristocracy, and democracy. In Book III, the philosopher examines the characteristics of a Christian commonwealth. He next argues, in

Book IV, about the necessity of the Leviathan (government) in a Christian commonwealth and debunks false religious teachings. Hobbes advocates for social contract and a strong commonwealth governed as a monarchy by an absolute ruler. He further proposes that this strong Leviathan can promote peace and unity in the commonwealth. In concluding his book, Hobbes analyzes how erroneous religious doctrines benefits only the churches and its members.

Blaise Pascal, *Pensées*

Pensées by Blaise Pascal is a collection of fragments, notes, and short essays that examine the contradictory nature of humans. Published in 1670, the text explores varied subjects, including death, eternity, the meaning of life, God's love for mankind, the limits of human reasoning, human fallibility, and the nature of the universe. In *Pensées*, Pascal introduces his famous wager concerning belief in God, concluding that it is better to believe God exists because such belief costs nothing. As Pascal puts it, a life without God is generally filled with anxiety, ennui, loneliness, misery, and alienation. The author goes further, encouraging people to actively seek God, arguing that it is the only way to gain peace. *Pensées*, then, is the French philosopher's defense of Christianity against paganism, deism, atheism, and libertinism.

Baruch Spinoza, *Tractatus Theologico-Politicus*

Tractatus Theologico-Politicus is a philosophical masterpiece on theology and politics published anonymously in 1670 by Dutch philosopher Baruch Spinoza. The text explores the relationship between Western philosophy and religion, critically analyzing contemporary Jewish and Christian religion. Here, Spinoza contends that Biblical literature should be treated like other historical documents. He also notes that as the Torah is a political institution of the ancient state of Israel, it is no longer valid in the affairs of government. The philosopher further argues that the state must be a sovereign authority and that citizens must obey constituted laws for society to remain in good order. However, he thinks that a wise government should secure the goodwill and cooperation of its citizens to ensure peace. Spinoza highlights the major types of government (Monarchy, Aristocracy, and Democracy) and the features of each system. In sum, *Tractatus Theologico-Politicus* advocates a government that guarantees freedom of speech and religion for its citizens and proposes that religious leaders should not meddle in politics.

Immanuel Kant, *Groundwork of the Metaphysic of Morals*

Groundwork of the Metaphysic of Morals is a work on moral philosophy published in 1785 by Immanuel Kant. In this work, Kant explains what morality is and how it influences people. He begins by dividing philosophy into ethics, physics, and logic and then delves into the metaphysics of morals. Moral laws, according to him, are liable to corruption because there is no specific guide to rationalize them. Kant goes further to explain the concept of the *categorical imperative*, which states that humans should act according to the universal laws they wish others to follow. While he admits that what is moral to one man may be immoral to another, he urges people to treat the persuasion of others as an end goal rather than as an instrumental goal. In summary, *Groundwork of the Metaphysic of Morals* explains the nature of morality and distinguishes what is morally right from what is morally wrong.

Marquis de Condorcet, *Sketch for a Historical Picture of the Progress of the Human Mind*

Written by Condorcet in 1795, *Sketch for a Historical Picture of the Progress of the Human Mind* discusses how science has aided the evolution of humankind. This includes the connection between progress in human rights and scientific progress, and it lays out the characteristics of a future society wholly influenced by science. The French philosopher claims that humans can understand the natural world only through collating and sharing information with each other. According to his argument, this expansion of knowledge in the sciences would result in a world of greater affluence, freedom, and compassion. Condorcet goes on to explore the evolution of humans with the aid of science. He contends that no one can define the perfection of human existence. For this reason, he believes that humanity will continue to progress toward a utopian society for as long as the earth exists. The book concludes that this ideal utopia can only come about if humans unite, irrespective of race, culture, gender, and religion.

Sophie de Condorcet, *Letters on Sympathy*

Letters on Sympathy was written in 1798 by French philosopher Sophie de Condorcet, wife (and subsequently widow) of the Marquis de Condorcet. Comprising eight letters, the work is a commentary on Adam Smith's *The Theory of Moral Sentiments*. Condorcet begins the work by explaining the nature of sympathy, including its root causes. In her view, people are likely to sympathize with those with whom they were familiar during childhood.

After talking about sympathy and explaining her disagreements with Smith's views, the writer shifts her focus to the nature of justice and injustice, including why people act justly or unjustly. She believes that social injustice is fueled by social inequality. According to her, social inequality limits people's ability to sympathize with one another. The writer further explains the relationship between sympathy and penal law, thereby concluding that sympathy is a necessary good for the well-being of society.

Thomas Paine, *Rights of Man*

Rights of Man is a political work on republicanism by English-born American philosopher and political activist Thomas Paine. Published in 1791, the book is first and foremost a defense of the French Revolution. Paine begins with an analysis of the underlying reasons for the discontent in European society, including illiteracy, poverty, war, and unemployment. After emphasizing that political revolt is unavoidable when a government fails to protect the natural and civil rights of its citizens, he lists the values of revolution as liberty, equality, and brotherhood. The author goes further to criticize the fact that only a fraction of the people who pay taxes in France are allowed to vote. To solve the problem, he outlines a tax system that could provide social welfare in the form of education, pensions, child benefit, and relief for the poor. In sum, the *Rights of Man* advocates for republicanism as against monarchy and proposes income tax as a viable solution to providing adequate welfare for the people.

Mary Wollstonecraft, *A Vindication of the Rights of Women*

Mary Wollstonecraft, a British feminist and philosopher, published *A Vindication of The Rights of Women* in 1792. An early work of feminist philosophy, the text advocates for women's rights. The author counters those who believe that women should be educated or receive the same rights as men. Wollstonecraft argues that women are not ornaments or properties belonging to men. She argues further that women must be treated with respect as companions to their husbands and that there must be equality between men and women in various areas of life. She writes that women deserve to be educated because, despite arguments to the contrary, they are capable of abstract or rational thought. Wollstonecraft argues that women can become successful in any career they choose. As a feminist, the writer reasons that women are the primary educators of children and that educated women can contribute considerably to a more educated society. *A Vindication of The Rights of Women* encapsulates Wollstonecraft's 18th-century feminist philosophy.

Johan Gottlieb Fichte, *Foundations of the Science of Knowledge*
Written in 1794, *Foundations of the Science of Knowledge* is an epistemological work by German philosopher Johann Gottlieb Fichte, who here asserts that philosophy is a science. He argues that philosophy is a systematic method of unraveling the truth and is the foundational discipline from which all practical and theoretical knowledge is derived. The author coins the phrase "I am I" to explain why philosophy or "I" is the root of all knowledge. Furthermore, he insists that consciousness is self-determining. He goes on to reason that an individual must be aware that he is experiencing something before he can notice the thing. After that, he conceptualizes the absolutely unconditioned principle of experience, which states that "the I posits itself." In this masterpiece, Fiche introduces two approaches to philosophy: dogmatic realism and idealism. In sum, *Foundations of the Science of Knowledge* discusses the epistemology of philosophy.

Nineteenth-Century Philosophy

Georg Wilhelm Friedrich Hegel, *Phenomenology of Spirit*

Published in 1807, *The Phenomenology of Spirit* is a philosophical masterpiece by Georg Wilhelm Friedrich Hegel, which takes as its subject the origin of knowledge. The work develops the theory that knowledge originates from *Geist*, or spirit. This requires Hegel to develop theories on epistemology, ethics, politics, metaphysics, physics, perception, religion, history, and consciousness as he argues that humans underwent a spiritual evolution through which they evolved from objects to creatures to human beings. He reasons that consciousness must go through various steps before it can become fully adequate as a vehicle of knowledge. Hegel further contends that the conscious self is alienated from the absolute self and that both of them can only get acquainted with each other through the unfolding of the spirit. In addition to equating form with content, Hegel argues that people can have morals without attending church.

Georg Wilhelm Friedrich Hegel, *Science of Logic*

Published in 1812, *The Science of Logic* presents the author's conception of logic as the science of both human thought and the thought of God. According to the author, thought and being (reality) make up a single, active unity. He goes on to argue that reality is not only identical to thought but also thoroughly shaped by thought. Hegel posits that the structure of subjects, objects, thoughts, and beings are identical and that logic is not about argument or reasoning alone, but is the foundation of reality and all the dimensions of reality. Hegel critically examines method, being, existence, reality, reflection, nothingness, becoming, concept, and essence to lay out his conception of logic and its principles.

The Philosophy of Right

The Philosophy of Right is a masterpiece by Georg Wilhelm Friedrich Hegel in 1820. The book begins with Hegel's discussing key concepts like freewill and right. Freewill, according to the German philosopher, can only be attained in the context of family life, the legal system, property rights, moral commitments, the polity, and the economy. In addition, Hegel argues that humans will be free only when they fully participate in the various stages of the life of a state. He notes, however, that the state is itself included in history, which reveals a a familiar pattern of states rising only to fall. Nonetheless, he acknowledges that this erratic pattern helps correct the mistakes of previous regimes and shifts emerging states toward perfection. The author dedicates a large portion of the book to explaining his three versions, or "spheres," of right: abstract rights, morality, and ethical life. In sum, *The Philosophy of Right* contains Hegel's thought about modernity.

Georg Wilhelm Friedrich Hegel, *The Philosophy of History*

Written by the German philosopher Georg Wilhelm Friedrich Hegel, *The Philosophy of History* was published posthumously in 1837. The work is a compilation of lectures Hegel delivered from 1822 to 1830. The main point of history, Hegel argues, is the unraveling of the Spirit (*Geist*), or God. The author begins the book by pointing out three methods of observing history: original history, reflective history, and philosophical history. He goes on to evaluate human history, starting from the origin of man until the nineteenth century. Next, the scholar criticizes famous historians of his time and argues that history should be based on empirical facts. History allows man to evaluate his situation and ultimately gain an understanding of God, Hegel reasons. According to him, the understanding of history leads to freedom. In sum, *The Philosophy of History* explains the foundation and purpose of history.

Arthur Schopenhauer, *The World as Will and Representation*

In 1818, Arthur Schopenhauer published *The World as Will and Representation*. In four sections, the philosopher discusses epistemology, ontology, aesthetics, and ethics. He begins with a discussion of how humans perceive the world and argues that an aesthetic object studied by humans becomes their object of perception. Schopenhauer further claims that the world exists as an idea as long as the human mind perceives it as an object. Next, he argues that all phenomena and objects are based on the essence of the will. He further clarifies that art is the direct objectivity of the will because it sees things independent of reason. The philosopher then goes on to identify the two behaviors that make up the essence of humans: (1) denial of the will to live and (2) affirmation. In his opinion, the will is inherently selfish because it is chiefly concerned with its own satisfaction. Thus, Schopenhauer advocates for moral asceticism as it helps reduce one's destructive willpower. He concludes, however, that, because the will is inherent in itself, it can never be destroyed.

Auguste Comte, *Course of Positive Philosophy*

Course of Positive Philosophy is a philosophical dialogue written by Auguste Comte, a French philosopher. Published in 1830, the book is divided into six sections. The first three examine the primary sciences of the era, mathematics, physics, astronomy, biology, and chemistry. The remaining three sections discuss social sciences. Comte proffers the Law of Three Stages to explain the evolution of human thought. According to him, these stages include the theological, the metaphysical, and positive stages. The philosopher insists that primary sciences precede social sciences. As he puts it, social sciences, especially sociology, are the culmination of the other sciences. The author ends the book by arguing that sociology is the only universal science that can depict human thoughts adequately.

Søren Kierkegaard, *Either/Or: A Fragment of Life*

Written by Danish philosopher Søren Kierkegaard, *Either / Or: A Fragment of Life* is an 1843 masterpiece of duality, the conflict between the ethical life and the aesthetic life. In the two-volume book, Kierkegaard uses the voices of two characters to present two contrasting views of life. One view is dominated by ethics and the other view by aesthetics. In the ethical life view, Kierkegaard talks about marriage, responsibility, and critical reflection. In the aesthetic life view, he discusses issues related to pleasure, beauty, drama, music, and seduction. The ethical world, Kierkegaard notes, is the domain in which one's actions and intentions are objectively judged and regulated. The aesthetic world, in contrast, permits individuals to explore all forms of pleasure for their own sake. Kierkegaard goes on to note that, while each of these two worlds has its intrinsic advantages, individuals can lose their self-identity if they go too deeply into either of these realms. The author concludes by arguing that only faith can rescue individuals from both the *either* and the *or*.

Søren Kierkegaard, *Fear and Trembling*

Published in 1843, *Fear and Trembling* is a classic study of anxiety. Drawing inspiration from the Bible, the philosopher studies the various reasons why humans experience anxiety and fear. He critically examines the terror felt by Abraham when he was about to sacrifice Isaac, his son. His examination of this story reveals that fear can result in two types of hope: hope for happiness and hope from things in themselves. Kierkegaard goes on to define infinite resignation as the willingness to dispose of everything one loves in service and obedience to God. In his opinion, a man must have infinite resignation before he can have faith. Infinite resignation paves the way for eternal validity. After explaining the difference between the inner spirit world and the outer world of ethics, the philosopher concludes that to overcome fear, one must have faith and that to have faith, one must have passion. In sum, *Fear and Trembling* is a philosophical work that uses theological principles to explain the principles behind fear, anxiety, and faith in humans.

Søren Kierkegaard, *Concluding Unscientific Postscript to Philosophical Fragments*

Published in 1846, *Concluding Unscientific Postscript to Philosophical Fragments* is a philosophical masterpiece by Søren Kierkegaard, the Danish philosopher. The work is a criticism of *Science of Logic* and other works by Georg Wilhelm Friedrich Hegel. Kierkegaard decries Hegelianism and other philosophical principles Hegel espouses. Unlike Hegel, who argues that truth is objective, Kierkegaard believe that it is profoundly subjective. He also refutes the idea that only the rational is real. Truth cannot be possessed, according to the philosopher, because it is pursued and desired in a lifelong search. He reasons that objective truth exists only in the world of science, and not in the realm of human activity or religion. Kierkegaard concludes his argument by stating that God is the absolute truth. In sum, *Concluding Unscientific Postscript to Philosophical Fragments* is the antithesis of the philosophy of Georg Wilhelm Friedrich Hegel.

Søren Kierkegaard, *The Concept of Anxiety*

Published in 1844, *The Concept of Anxiety* is Søren Kierkegaard's attempt to explain the nature of anxiety through the lens of Christian dogma. The Danish philosopher opens the text with a reconstruction of Adam's emotional state after he ate the forbidden fruit in the Garden of Eden. Anxiety, as Kierkegaard defines it, is an ambivalent structure that both attracts people to and repels them from freedom. He believes that anxiety is the symbol of human freedom. To exercise this freedom, Kierkegaard reasons that one needs to self-alienate and depend solely on God. He, warns, however, that this route could lead one into the trap of demons. Nonetheless, Kierkegaard thinks that anxiety can save humanity because it helps individuals discover their self-awareness, personal responsibilities, choices, and potential. In short, while anxiety breeds vices, it helps uncover one's true freedom and identity.

Max Stirner, *The Ego and Its Own*

Published in 1844, *The Ego and Its Own* is a philosophical book by Max Stirner, a German philosopher. The book advocates for egoism but criticizes socialism, liberalism, utilitarianism, Christianity, humanism, and other philosophical ideas. The writer argues that egoism is the ultimate stage of human development, in which an adult is free from all constraints, thus attaining self-ownership. To clarify his views further, Stirner states that every human starts life as a child who is restricted by external forces. He adds that when children become youths, they begin to learn how to overcome the restrictions imposed on them by society. Modern man is not as free as his ancestors, Stirner points out. In his view religion, the political state, and other modern institutions are created to enslave man. Ownness, or egoism, according to Stirner, gives individuals the power and autonomy they need in society.

Karl Marx and Friedrich Engels, *The Communist Manifesto*

Published in 1848, *The Communist Manifesto* is a political treatise by two German philosophers, Karl Marx and Friedrich Engels, who present the class struggle between the proletariat and the bourgeoise, exposing the disadvantages of capitalism in society. The philosophers begin by chronicling the age of feudalism down to the era of capitalism. Their analysis reveals that all historical developments are driven by class struggle, and they explain how the rich (bourgeoise) control the means of production, enrich themselves, and make workers (the proletariat) poorer. Marx and Engels argue that communism is better than capitalism because it champions the rights of the working class. Marx and Engels predict that communism will inevitably replace capitalism in the future. After conceptually defending communism, Marx and Engels call for such short-term reforms as the eradication of slavery, the abolishment of child labor, the termination of inheritance and private property, and the provision of free education. In the final part of the book, the philosophers advocate for a world revolution, which will upend the current political system and replace capitalism with communism.

Karl Marx, *Das Kapital* (*Capital*)

One of the most influential works of philosophy ever written, *Das Kapital* (*Capital*) was written in 1867 by German philosopher Karl Marx. In its final, posthumously published version, *Das Kapital* consists of four volumes. The purpose of this mammoth work is to refute classical economic theory and provide a theoretical foundation for the replacement of capitalism with communism. The philosopher notes that capitalism is exploitative in nature: it robs the poor (proletariat) to provide wealth for the rich (bourgeoise).

Apart from breeding a large army of underpaid workers, capitalism creates false consciousness and an illusion of power among the proletariat. The reality, Marx argues, is that, in a capitalist society, all the economic institutions are controlled by the rich. After explaining the dynamics of capitalism and pointing out its flaws, the philosopher concludes by calling for the overthrow of this economic system in societies.

John Stuart Mill, *On Liberty*

Published in 1859, *On Liberty* is perhaps the most widely read work of English philosopher John Stuart Mill. In this work, Mill uses the principles of utilitarianism to explain how best to govern a state and how best to enforce authority without restricting people's liberty. He opens the book with an explanation of the dynamic struggle between liberty and authority. Mill argues that what is morally right is that which will produce the greatest utility for the majority. Nevertheless, he admits that utilitarianism can result in the tyranny of the majority, a situation in which the majority takes actions or makes decisions to oppress and marginalize the minority. He further enumerates the ways in which society limits the freedom of individuals. In his view, governments should never interfere in the affairs of people unless their personal freedom of action will harm others. Mill emphasizes that the interest and liberty of individuals should be respected at all times, provided that their actions cause no harm to others.

John Stuart Mill, *Utilitarianism*

John Stuart Mill's 1863 masterpiece *Utilitarianism* is an intellectual defense of Jeremy Bentham's concept of utilitarianism. Mill begins by explaining what utilitarianism is and why utilitarianism is better than other ethical principles. Like Bentham before him, Mill believes that people naturally avoid pain and seek happiness. This means that happiness should be the goal of ethics; however, unlike Bentham, who measures the worth of any political idea by the quantity of pleasure it will afford, Mill recognizes both the quantity and quality of pleasure. According to him, higher (intellectual) pleasures are intrinsically superior to and more valuable than lower (bodily) pleasures. Given that everyone desires happiness, Mill argues that the general happiness of society is the aggregate happiness of all individuals. Mill concedes in the last section of the book that the only problem with utilitarianism is that it may sometimes result in the tyranny of the majority, a situation in which the majority takes actions or makes decisions to oppress and marginalize the minority.

John Stuart Mill, *The Subjection of Women*

John Stuart Mill wrote *The Subjection of Women* in 1869 to argue for the equality between men and women. He begins by lamenting the unfair laws favoring physical strength, which gave men an undue advantage in society. He canvasses for a fair societal system to ensure both males and females thrive in society. In response to the argument that women are naturally weak, emotional, docile, and passive, Mill contends that society nurtured them that way. Arguing further, he insists that the full capabilities of women will never be known until society considers them equal to men. Equality, he argues, will liberate both women and the society in general. Apart from calling for marriage legislation reforms, the English philosopher also suggests that marriage should be treated as a business arrangement with no restrictions on either party. In addition, he reasons that women should have the right to vote for whom they believe will represent their best interest. The author ends the text with examples of women who have excelled when given the opportunity.

Herbert Spencer, *System of Synthetic Philosophy*

System of Synthetic Philosophy is an 1882 philosophical text by British philosopher Herbert Spencer. The book focuses on the nature of synthetic philosophy, a form of philosophy that draws knowledge from diverse areas of science to explain complex systems. Central to Spencer's claims is that it is possible to believe in human perfection. Rather than relying on religion, the author supports his claim by drawing on such complex science as the Theory of Evolution and the laws of thermodynamics. Spencer discusses such topics as the relation between religion and science, the relativity of all knowledge, the direction of motion, the indestructibility of matter, space, time, matter, and force.

Henry Sidgwick, *The Methods of Ethics*

Henry Sidgwick's *The Methods of Ethics* was published in 1874. In it, the English philosopher proposes that all discussions of ethics should start with commonsense, or ordinary, morality. This conception of morality, according to Sidgwick, deals with the way ordinary people consider moral behavior. From here, Sidgwick proceeds to point out the problems affecting ordinary morality and proposed ways to these problems. He reveals three methods commonly used in commonsense morality to make value choices: egoism hedonism, utilitarianism, and intuitionism. He also identifies the problems inherent in each method and proffers solutions to them. Equally important in the book is the utilitarian theory Sidgwick develops to evaluate conventional morality and other ethical hypotheses. Sidgwick concludes that utilitarianism is compatible with ordinary morality.

Friedrich Nietzsche, *On the Genealogy of Morals*

On the Genealogy of Morals was written in 1887 by Friedrich Nietzsche, a German philosopher. In three essays, the author traces the evolution of human morality and critiques moral values. In the first essay, Nietzsche examines various origins of the concept of good, evil, and bad. He also defines and compares the slave morality and the master morality. The second treatise explores how guilt, punishment, and bad conscience came into human consciousness. Nietzsche hypothesizes that these concepts did not originally refer to moral transgressions. Guilt, for instance, meant that one was a debtor and punishment was a means to ensure the debt was paid. According to Nietzsche, the propagation of slave morality led to the present "moral" definitions of the terms. The author criticizes asceticism in the third essay, deeming it the manifestation of a sick and weak will. Nietzsche observes that people who live an ascetic life will always struggle with their true animal nature and concludes that one needs to criticize the value of truth instead of the will of truth as propagated by asceticism.

Friedrich Nietzsche, *Beyond Good and Evil*

Written in 1886 by Friedrich Nietzsche, *Beyond Good and Evil* begins with a criticism of previous philosophers who blindly accept ideological theses on morality without scrutinizing them. Nietzsche expresses the hope that future philosophers will possess the free spirit to investigate any hypothesis before accepting it. Nietzsche also criticizes "herd morality" because it only encourages societal mediocrity, and he asserts that it is absurd to apply the same moral code to everyone because society already ranks every individual's spiritual strengths and weaknesses. *Beyond Good and Evil* concludes with a short poem celebrating nobility and friendship.

Henri Bergson, *Time and Free Will*

Published in 1889, *Time and Free Will* refutes the principal arguments against free will by introducing a new conception of time. Bergson observes that scientists commonly assume time and space are measurable variables and conflate their representation of these thing in accordance with their conception of reality. Bergson counters that we perceive and measure time qualitatively instead of quantitatively. He admits that there is no consensus definition of either time or freedom, yet he believes that both endure in reality. Because human actions cannot be predicted accurately, the French philosopher believes that humans have free will. He goes on to argue that intuition is superior to intellect as a means of understanding time and therefore also understanding both free will and freedom. Thus, *Time and Free Will* deals with the problem of time and free will by rejecting the traditional abstract and conceptual methods used to solve these and other metaphysical problems.

Henri Bergson, *Matter and Memory*

French philosopher Henri Bergson's 1896 book *Matter and Memory* deals with the spirituality of memory. Bergson begins with a description of both the brain and memory. He categorizes memory into two types: hand memory and pure memory. Hand memory helps one to repeat or replay past actions, while pure memory enables one to store the past in the form of images. After investigating the nature of the brain, Bergson asserts that memory is spiritual, not material, in nature. He goes further, establishing the difference between spirit and body. Unlike In contrast to such philosophers as René Descartes, Bergson believes that the spirit represents the past, and the body depicts the present. He adds that the more one spirit-journeys to the past, the more one becomes more conscious. However, Bergson believes thinks that the more one carries out a task automatically, the more one exists in the present in the body. The philosopher argues that one needs both the body and the spirit to achieve true awareness and to function properly in the world. Overall, *Matter and Memory* captures Bergson's views on dualism—the classic mind-body problem—and echoes his opposition to the idea that memory is material in nature.

Phenomenology and Existentialism

Edmund Husserl, *Logical Investigations*

Published in 1900, *Logical Investigations* is a philosophical work by Edmund Husserl. In the book, Husserl focuses on the philosophy of logic and decries logical psychologism, the belief that logic originates from psychology. Husserl begins the two-volume work by revealing the logical shortcomings inherent in pure mathematics. He next investigates logic in philosophy, revealing existing defects that prove that philosophical logic cannot originate from psychology, including the fact that logic uses relevancy in validating empirical sciences. Next, Husserl criticizes several philosophers who champion empiricism and psychologism in logic and instead evaluates the importance of linguistic analysis in logic before conducting epistemological investigations on universals, mereology, cognition, intentionality, meaning, intuition, and truth. In sum, *Logical Investigations* investigates the philosophy behind logic and argues most vigorously against psychologism.

Max Scheler, *Formalism in Ethics and Non-Formal Ethics of Values*

Written in 1913 by the German philosopher Max Scheler, *Formalism in Ethics and Non-Formal Ethics of Values* critiques Kant's apriorism and the imperative nature of Kantian ethics. Scheler argues that Kant's ethics is too formal and obstructive in that it limits the path to the discovery of an individual theory of morality and restricts the understanding of the moral values of humans within their social world. He also rejects Kant's ethics of good because it ignores the perception and subjective experiences of individuals. What one person may consider good or evil may not be what another person considers good or evil, he argues. Unlike Kant, Scheler does not believe that purposes should be justifiable only when one's intention (will) is good. In sum, Scheler argues that values are inherently subjective and that ethics, therefore, should not be too formal in distinguishing between good and evil values.

Martin Buber, *I and Thou*

I and Thou was published in 1923 by the Austrian-Israeli philosopher Martin Buber. Its fundamental concept is that relationships bring meaning to human life. Buber proposes that existence can be addressed either using the mindset or attitude of "I" toward "It" or of "I" toward "Thou." Whatever choice is made, Buber argues all relationships exist to bring man into a relationship with God, the Eternal Thou. I-It and I-thou relationships thus define humans. "It," Buber explains, refers to the world as humans experience it through sensation and experience, whereas "I" and "Thou" are human. People should develop as many I-It and I-Thou relationships as possible, but it is the I-Thou relationships that sustain and are sustained through the spirit and the mind of the "I." *I and Thou* is thus ultimately a book about finding meaning, happiness, and a relationship to God in life through human relationships.

Martin Heidegger, *Being and Time*

Being and Time is a philosophical masterpiece published in 1927 by the German philosopher Martin Heidegger. An ontological study of *being*, the work draws inspiration from Edmund Husserl's *Logical Investigations*. Heidegger questions the sense of being. Apart from arguing that "being" is different from "a being," the philosopher asserts that being is also different from beings. He argues that being precedes *sense* of being and must be understood before the sense of being can be understood. A hermeneutic circle must be used to understand being, the philosopher reasons, and then introduces the concept of *Dasein* ("being there" or "presence"), which is about being in the world, in effect caring for the immediate world in which one lives. The philosopher also explains that time may or may not be the horizon of being, arguing that, for this reason, being, like time, does not show its presence.

Edmund Husserl, *Cartesian Meditations*

Published in 1931, *Cartesian Meditations* is an exposition of phenomenology through the concepts of transcendental reduction, genetic phenomenology, eidetic phenomenology, eidetic reduction, and other ideas. In this book, Husserl uses phenomenology to explain the fundamental processes of rationality and consciousness. Inspired by René Descartes' *Meditations on First Philosophy*, the work is divided into five meditations. In the first meditation, the philosopher reviews the transcendental ego, emphasizing that the world exists because of ego. The second meditation focuses on the transcendental experience. Here, Husserl argues that consciousness is always directed at something. He then evaluates constitutional problems in the third meditation, going on to explore the constitutional problems of the transcendental ego in the fourth. In fifth and final meditation, Husserl discusses the transcendental being, arguing that it has the power of intersubjectivity. *Cartesian Meditations* is an introduction to the modern principles and concepts of phenomenology, which Husserl sought to elevate to the status of an independent science.

Alfred Schutz, *The Phenomenology of the Social World*

Originally published in 1932, *The Phenomenology of the Social World* is a book by the Austrian philosopher Alfred Schutz. Schutz explores social phenomenology and provides a philosophical explanation to Max Weber's sociology, which focuses on understanding human actions and experiences by focusing on subjective views. The author opens the book by commending Weber for his contribution to the social sciences but points out that Weberian sociology is imperfect in that it ignores the fundamental, philosophical problems of the social sciences, such as how individuals assign meanings to their actions, the knowledge of other selves, and the psychological relation between people. Schutz seeks to address the weaknesses in Weberian sociology by using the phenomenological ideas of German philosopher Edmund Husserl to investigate the nature of human actions to tease out how social science can be used to understand human beings. Schutz acknowledges the difficulty of interpreting the experiences or consciousness of others from their subjective views. yet he argues that, failing to meet this challenge, would make human society all but impossible. The philosopher goes on to argue that one can indirectly interpret the experiences of others through logical constructs, which are obtained from the past experiences with others. This mode of interpretation is nevertheless prone to errors and misconceptions. Schutz ends by insisting that the success of the social sciences depends on understanding the subjective experience of individuals within their social worlds.

Albert Camus, *Myth of Sisyphus*

Published in 1942, *Myth of Sisyphus* is a philosophical essay by Albert Camus. In the essay, Camus introduces the principle of the absurd, a life situation in which people continue to desire something (such as meaning, values, reasons, and so on) in the universe that the universe is incapable of providing. People naturally seek what they cannot have, Camus observes. To illustrate what absurdity means, the philosopher uses the story of Sisyphus, the Greek king who was punished by the gods for self-aggrandizing craftiness by being required to perpetually push a heavy boulder up a hill. Each time he neared the top, the giant rock would fall back. By acknowledging absurdity with reasons, the philosopher argues that one can pursue pure passions, accept reality, and enjoy true freedom. Camus introduces the example of Don Juan, the Spanish serial seducer who knows that love is fleeting and nothing lasts forever, to explain what it means to completely acknowledge absurdity. In summary, *Myth of Sisyphus* explains the conflict between human reality and humanity's phantom desires.

Jean-Paul Sartre, *Being and Nothingness*

Being and Nothingness is a seminal 1943 ontological essay by French philosopher Jean-Paul Sartre. In three parts, the work lays out the writer's views on such existential issues as being, free will, psychoanalysis, nothingness, perception, and consciousness. In Part I (Origin of Negation), Sartre develops a theory of nothingness and contends that nothingness is an objective, experienced reality. In Part II (Bad Faith), he points out two forms of deception people use to deny their reality. One is believing in attributes one does not have; the other is perceiving oneself as an object without freedom. Sartre argues that existence precedes essence, meaning that one needs to exist first before one can understand the essence of things. In his view, "bad faith" occurs when one refuses to acknowledge reality or facts. Sartre explains the recognition of subjectivity in others in Part III (The Look). People go into relationships not because of how beautiful their partners are but because of how their partners make them feel, he observes. The writer points out that people who fail to acknowledge their subjectivity toward others may experience emotional alienation. In the last part of the book, Sartre criticizes Sigmund Freud's view that consciousness is essentially a heightened state of awareness.

Maurice Merleau-Ponty, *Phenomenology of Perception*

Published in 1945 by French philosopher Maurice Merleau-Ponty, *Phenomenology of Perception* deals with the nature of perception, beginning by identifying the contradiction in the definition of phenomenology. Merleau-Ponty notes that some people consider phenomenology a philosophy embedded within rationalism, while others define it through the lens of empiricism. These two contrasting views, according to the philosopher, have failed to address the true nature of phenomenology. After repudiating traditional metaphysical philosophy, Merleau-Ponty points out the structures of perception: experience or consciousness. He goes further to state that what people regard as sensations are based not on what people feel but on people's prejudices. The body, according to the philosopher, is the platform on which perception rests. He adds that, without the body, there cannot be existence, awareness, or consciousness. In addition to emphasizing the significance of the body in relation to the self, Merleau-Ponty concludes by defining freedom as a form of consciousness, in which one can make decisions or show commitments within a sphere of possibility.

Jacques Maritain, *Existence and the Existent*

Published in 1947, Jacques Maritain's *Existence and the Existent* explores the writer's views on existence. The author defends Catholic orthodoxy and establishes Christianity as a human-oriented religion. Maritain devotes much of the book to defending the philosophy of Thomas Aquinas. He believes that metaphysics is the study of being, that being can be understood only through intuition, and that one can verify the existence of God through intuition or by using Aquinas's five proofs. The writer agrees with several Thomistic views, including being curious and inquisitive about the universe. Maritain further rejects atheistic existentialism, calling it a false doctrine. According to the philosopher, Christianity is the sure path to living a good life. He goes on to argue that evil does not exist and points out the importance of distinguishing what a thing is (essence) from the existence of that thing (existent). He adds that existence precedes essence, that one must first exist before understanding the essence of things. In sum, *Existence and the Existent* captures Maritain's thoughts on Thomistic metaphysics and its relation to philosophy and modern science.

Simone de Beauvoir, *The Second Sex*

French writer Simone de Beauvoir's 1949 book *The Second Sex* analyzes the abuse, oppression, and subordination of women throughout history. She opens by describing what a woman is and goes on to explain how men have treated women by default as the weaker sex. She traces women's subordination to an era of slavery, in which women were forced to give birth to future soldiers. Beauvoir also believes men's domination over women started when men desired to perpetuate the family. Women's historical insignificance, according to the author, contributed largely to women's inferiority, not the other way round. Furthermore, she points out how society has indoctrinated women from a young age to be subservient to men and how society has employed religion to further subordinate them, restricting their freedom and individuality. In her conclusion, Beauvoir advocates for a society in which women are accorded the same rights as men.

Emmanuel Levinas, *Totality and Infinity*

Totality and Infinity is a 1961 philosophical masterpiece on ethics by Emmanuel Levinas, a French philosopher. Here he explores the distinction between totality and infinity, arguing that all ethics comes from an interaction between the self and the other. According to him, the interaction with the other brings awareness to the self and helps it to understand the idea of infinity. Levinas clarifies the subjective nature of infinity, pointing out that the idea of infinity is produced when one person interacts with the other. Humans can only truly connect with infinity by a physical or face-to-face meeting, Levinas writes. After explaining the meaning of infinity, he goes further to explain what totality means. The idea of totality, he argues, integrates the self and the other as one. In contrast to the idea of totality, infinity reveals the difference between the self and the other. Levinas also points out that the idea of infinity is moral but that the idea of totality is theoretical. *Totality and Infinity* focuses on the nature of being in relation to others.

Emmanuel Levinas, *Otherwise than Being*

French philosopher Emmanuel Levinas's 1974 book *Otherwise than Being* is a sequel to his previous work, *Totality and Infinity*. In the second work, Levinas elucidates his view of ethical metaphysics, beginning by explaining the meaning of the "other." The philosopher defines the limitations of totality and writes that exteriority must maintain a relationship with interiority. He argues that ethics is never secure, so that it is impossible to derive every moral theory from ethics. He also posits that humans have a responsibility to listen to the demands of the other. These demands fuel the search for ethics and makes ethics necessary. Furthermore, the author argues that the ethical proximity of one human to another ensures that the responsibility of justice lies with all humans. From this viewpoint, he justifies the importance of "the I" in relation to the objects with which "the I" relates. The other, he writes, disrupts the interaction of the I with the objects it uses and enjoys. In summary, *Otherwise than Being* argues against an abstract and absolute ethics and explains the role humanity plays in creating a viable ethics.

Jean-Luc Marion, *Being Given: Toward a Phenomenology of Givenness*

Published in 1997, *Being Given: Toward a Phenomenology of Givenness* opens with Edmund Husserl's phenomenological ideas (mainly, "reduction to consciousness") and Martin Heidegger's phenomenological ideas (the concept of *Dasein*), rejecting their views and pointing out the reasons why philosophers have not achieved the objective of phenomenology, an understanding of the actions and experiences of human beings based on their subjective views. To meet the challenges of phenomenology and extend it to its limits, Marion introduces the concept of givenness, which is the ability to accept phenomena just as they present themselves. In his view, givenness must occur before phenomena can enter the realm of consciousness. The writer also introduces such concepts as the nature of saturated phenomena and the "gifted" (the receiver who is free from all subjectivity). After providing and explaining the structures of phenomenology through the lens of givenness, Marion concludes by inferring that the only way to achieve the ideals of phenomenology is through divine theology, an approach to God.

Thomas Nagel, *The View from Nowhere*

The View from Nowhere, a 1986 book by the American philosopher Thomas Nagel, postulates that humans are capable of adopting both subjective and objective (scientific) perspectives. He also explains how these opposing views interfere with the everyday life and thinking patterns. Nagel begins by defining the subjective perspective as the view of the world from the inside and through the private window of the individual. Next, he defines the objective perspective as the impersonal or centerless view obtained by an individual when viewing the world from the outside. Nagel calls this objective perspective "the view from nowhere." Following this, Nagel points out how both perspectives/standpoints collide in such philosophical topics as ethics, mind-body problem, free will, death, the meaning of life, personal identity, skepticism, and more. At the end of the book, he concludes that both perspectives are reconcilable, although it may not always be possible to do so.

Roger Penrose, *The Emperor's New Mind*

Published in 1989, *The Emperor's New Mind* is a book on human consciousness and artificial intelligence by the English physicist Roger Penrose. The author argues that the human mind, thinking, and consciousness can never be fully modeled or replicated by a digital computer due to the mind's non-algorithmic nature. Penrose starts the book by providing a lay interpretation of such scientific concepts as complex numbers, Turing machines, relativity, quantum physics, black holes, Hawking radiation, phase spaces, time, and Gödel's incompleteness theorem. After introducing each concept, he explains how it is related to his arguments. Although Penrose agrees that quantum mechanics is essential for understanding human consciousness, he argues that classical mechanics is more relevant for computing than quantum mechanics because it is more practical. By comparing the ridiculousness of "the Emperor's new clothes" in the children's fairytale to the "computer-driven new mind," Penrose asserts that complete artificial intelligence is impossible and that computers will never replace the human mind because they will eventually run out of relevant algorithms. In short, *The Emperor's New Mind* is a treatise on the superiority of the human mind to digital computers.

Daniel Dennett, *Consciousness Explained*

Written in 1991 by American philosopher Daniel Dennett, *Consciousness Explained* explores the nature and development of human consciousness. Dennett proposes that consciousness does not occur in a central place in the brain but is based in several places in the brain at various times. This phenomenon is responsible for the brain's multitasking abilities, he argues. Furthermore, the reason humans can function at all is because the brain stores only a few key details about the world to conserve computing power. The consequence of this system is that the brain tends to miss some details in a given situation because it merely records the change and assumes the rest is still the same. Dennett concludes by positing that consciousness can be explained only through a hypothesis that uses unconscious events to analyze conscious events.

David Chalmers, *The Conscious Mind*

Written in 1996 by Australian philosopher David Chalmers, *The Conscious Mind* focuses mainly on the problem of consciousness. In section I, the philosopher addresses the difficulty of trying to account for consciousness. To explain his thesis, he points identifies two types of consciousness: psychological consciousness and phenomenal consciousness. The former addresses the nature of consciousness, while the latter focuses on the structures of consciousness. From here, Chalmers goes on to investigate the dependency of consciousness on the natural order of things. In section II, Chalmers argues that the standard explanation of reduction cannot explain the theory of consciousness, that materialism is false, and that the form of dualism is true. In section III, he explores in detail the "remarkable coherence" between conscious experience and cognitive structure. Section IV considers such applications as Artificial Intelligence, machine consciousness, and the framework of quantum mechanics in relation to perception. In summary, *The Conscious Mind* identifies the problem of consciousness, suggests the impossibility of using reduction to explain consciousness, and argues for a form of dualism.

Hermeneutics and Deconstruction

Hans-Georg Gadamer, *Truth and Method*
Published in 1960, *Truth and Method,* by the German philosopher Hans-Georg Gadamer, develops the concept of philosophical hermeneutics, a branch of philosophy introduced in *Being and Time* by Martin Heidegger. Gadamer argues that objectivity is unachievable and that meaning is found in intersubjective communication. After reasoning that human consciousness is affected by history and culture, he warns against the use of scientific methods in philosophy and the humanities. Subjectivism should be employed to gain insight into the human sciences, as any form of understanding is self-understanding. In addition to explaining the nature of human understanding, Gadamer argues that truth and method work against each other. He goes on to explain that aesthetic differentiation is a part of aesthetic consciousness.

Hans-Georg Gadamer, *Philosophical Hermeneutics*
Published in 1976, *Philosophical Hermeneutics,* by Hans-Georg Gadamer, applies the phenomenological ideas of Husserl and Heidegger to analyze hermeneutics in an exploration of the nature of human understanding. He rejects the objective approaches of the natural sciences in analyzing texts and works of art and instead argues for the use of subjective approaches to gain insight into the writer's or artist's thought and intention. Gadamer asserts that one of the goals of hermeneutics is to understand the human thought process from a subjective vantage point. Central to this "philosophical hermeneutics" are four key concepts: horizon, authority, tradition, and prejudice. He argues that one needs to understand the prejudice, tradition, authority, and horizon of an author to interpret his text properly. He also encourages the use of "the give-and-take of question and answer" in such interpretation.

Paul Ricœur, *Freud and Philosophy: An Essay on Interpretation*
Published in 1965, *Freud and Philosophy: An Essay on Interpretation,* by the French philosopher Paul Ricœur, focuses on Sigmund Freud and his work on psychoanalysis in the framework of philosophy. Ricœur begins with an introduction to psychoanalysis and interprets key terms in Freud's work. He explains the nature of psychoanalysis, especially how it can help to understand the psychological architecture of human nature. Besides making comparing and contrasting psychoanalysis and phenomenology,

Ricœur compares Freud's work with that of various philosophers. He also examines Freud's theories on religion, language, history, and symbolism. Ricœur concludes that psychoanalysis is not an observational science but an interpretation of historical occurrences and culture. This leads him to emphasize that psychoanalysis gravitates more toward philosophy and history than toward psychology. He concludes that psychoanalysis is more concerned with motives than with causes.

Jacques Derrida, *Of Grammatology*

Published in 1967, *Of Grammatology* is a book about linguistics and grammar by Jacques Derrida, a French philosopher. In the first half of the work, Derrida advocates for the adoption of a new linguistic structure based on concepts from grammatology, the scientific study of wtiting systems or scripts. Derrida begins by reviewing the linguistic structuralism of Ferdinand de Saussure. With reference to sign language, Derrida argues that language and writing are unique and separate from one another. He also argues that a written text should never be considered a derivative of speech. From here, the philosopher calls for an independent study of writing that is free from the influence of speech. In the second half of the text, Derrida reviews *Essay on the Origin of Languages* by Jean-Jacques Rousseau and introduces the logic of supplementarity, which states that the copies of an idea (language) always contaminate the original idea (language). These copies, or supplements, can be in the form of accents, writing, and articulation among other things, Derrida writes. Nevertheless, he reasons that supplementation is unavoidable in language because it is the very order of language. *Of Grammatology* introduces into philosophy the key concepts of grammatology and advocates for its adoption in the field of linguistics.

Structuralism and Post-Structuralism

Georges Bataille, *The Accursed Share*

Published in three volumes in 1949, *The Accursed Share,* by the French philosopher Georges Bataille, begins by illustrating man's economic history from prehistoric times to the present. From here, the work conceptualizes an economic theory, which Battaille calls the "general economy." In the general economy, organisms are motivated by excess energy, a view that contrasts with classical economy, in which organisms (including humans) are motivated by scarcity. Excess energy can be used either to grow an organism or it can be wasted. When excess energy is wasted, Battaille explains, it becomes the accursed share—energy often destructively squandered on random sex, unnecessary warfare, vain luxuries, and white-elephant projects. Bataille concludes by calling for excesses to be invested in improving standards of living rather than prodigally spent on wasteful ventures.

Michel Foucault, *The Order of Things*

Written in 1966 by French philosopher Michel Foucault, *The Order of Things* is a work of epistemology that investigates the origins and history of linguistics, economics, and biology. Foucault postulates that at every point in history there were always new epistemes and theories that enshrouded or confined all acceptable beliefs. Knowledge is restricted by the limits of these epistemes, Foucault argues. He goes on to examine the renaissance episteme, the classical episteme, and the modern episteme. After defining each, he points out the various changes in consciousness that humans underwent during these historical epochs. Foucault argues that current scientific truths are grounded in archaic thinking patterns and urges philosophers to critically analyze theories with an understanding of the epistemes of the era in which they were developed.

Gilles Deleuze, *Difference and Repetition*

Published in 1968, *Difference and Repetition,* by Gilles Deleuze, a French philosopher, critically examines difference and repetition as mutually exclusive concepts. He describes repetition as a difference without a concept or as a shared value of a disparate trio. According to him, repetition relies on difference and can only define a unique set of events or things. Citing Leibniz, Deleuze goes on to define difference using formulas of differential calculus. Following this, he examines repetition and difference in the framework of time and thought. Everything is a multiplicity, he concludes. Deleuze asserts that thinking occurs as a result of new experiences, not because of recognition. A work of metaphysics, *Difference and Repetition* is a fresh philosophical examination of the basic concepts of difference and repetition.

Gilles Deleuze, *The Logic of Sense*

The Logic of Sense, written in 1969 by Gilles Deleuze is metaphysical inquiry into the concepts of meaning, meaninglessness, sense, and nonsense. Drawing lessons from Lewis Caroll's *Alice in Wonderland* and its sequel, *Through the Looking Glass,* the writer classifies nonsense into two categories: (1) surface-level, innocent nonsense and (2) inner space, strongly opinionated, contradictory nonsense. Following from this, he examines pure becoming, paradox, depths, and surfaces. By way of conclusion, Deleuze introduces the philosophical concepts of the body without organs, the plane of immanence, games structure, and the mythic conceptions of time and then plunges into the logic of psychoanalysis.

Felix Guattari and Gilles Deleuze, *Capitalism and Schizophrenia*

Published in 1972, *Capitalism and Schizophrenia* is a two-volume work by the French philosophers Felix Guattari and Gilles Deleuze. In the first volume, titled *Anti-Oedipus,* the authors examine the relationship between reality and desire through the frameworks of psychology, psychiatry, politics, economics, art, literature, and philosophy. They argue that libido, or sexuality, can be found the working process of any industry. They demonstrate this by using "schizoanalysis," a psychoanalytical method the authors developed to address perceived drawbacks of classical psychoanalysis. After criticizing several psychoanalysts, the writers conclude that desire produces reality and that desire is a core foundation of production in a society. The second volume, titled *A Thousand Plateaus,* is a work of what the authors call rhizomatic philosophy—the rhizome being an "image of thought" (based on the botanical rhizome) that apprehends multiplicities. Guattari and Deleuze explain abstract machines, language structures, body without organs, faciality, stratification, and other philosophical concepts in relation to psychoanalysis. They also carry out a psychoanalytic literary criticism of several philosophers, psychoanalysts, composers, historians, and linguists with the objective of studying psychoanalysis and its practicality in the context of modern capitalist society.

Jean Baudrillard, *The Mirror of Production*

French philosopher Jean Baudrillard's 1973 book, *The Mirror of Production,* is a philosophical critique of Marxism, in which the author argues that Marxism is too theoretical and impractical. Baudrillard starts by examining the lessons of Marxism, pointing out various ideological errors, chief among which is the Marxist theory that labor will become emancipated and unrestricted once a communist regime takes over. Baudrillard argues that ending capitalism will leave a void in society. To fill the void, labor will still be needed because, Baudrillard argues, labor is more than just a tool of production. It is a form of human expression, creativity, and dignity. Baudrillard also argues that the Marxist logic is restrictive and hypocritical. He compares Marxist logic to a mirror in which everything is reflected in reverse. That is, almost everything Marxism promises to end comes back in another way. Baudrillard concludes by calling for humans to break the mirror of production.

Michel Foucault, *Discipline and Punish*

Published in 1975, *Discipline and Punish,* by Michel Foucault, examines the social and historical factors that have led to changes in the prison system and legal punishments. He begins the work by explaining that torture was an ancient method used sow people's minds with fear. When it proved ineffective, torture then gave way to public chain gangs, the product of new technologies and new ideologies that called for less aggressive means of punishment. The individuality of bodies and emerging sociopolitical organization of the early modern era gave rise to discipline as a form of punishment, Foucault writes. He argues that the modification of various discipline schemes gave rise to the popularity of the prison system. In the concluding section of the book, Foucault examines the modern prison system, its function, and its problems, recommending various prison reforms.

Jean Baudrillard, *Simulacra and Simulation*

Published in 1981, *Simulacra and Simulation,* by French philosopher Jean Baudrillard, examines how symbols and signs are related to reality and society. The author begins by defining *simulacra* as copies that do not have an original, while he describes *simulation* as an imitation of a real-world system or process. Human lives have become saturated with meaningless societal constructs and simulacra, the writer reasons. In addition to asserting that television, film, print, and other media have blurred the lines between reality and simulation, Baudrillard points out the destructive effects of capitalism, fiat currency, and urbanization. He argues that simulation has overridden reality, thereby posing a threat to human existence. In summary, *Simulacra and Simulation* is a treatise on how symbolism and simulation have replaced reality in modern culture.

Critical Theory and Marxism

Gyorgy Lukacs, *History and Class Consciousness*

Published in 1923, *History and Class Consciousness* is a collection of essays by Gyorgy Lukacs on such topics as class consciousness, orthodox Marxism, and the ever-shifting dynamics of historic materialism. The Hungarian philosopher begins by arguing that methodology distinguishes Marxism from other ideologies. He also argues in favor of dialectics over historic materialism. Marx's usage of dialectic, Lukacs writes, can help capitalist societies become reified and can enable the proletariat to become saviors of humanity. To this end, Lukacs proposes that humans view truth in relation to the historical mission of the proletariat. He suggests that the concept of totality be treated as an utmost priority. Lukacs uses concepts like reification and alienation to develop the central themes of his theory about class consciousness.

Herbert Marcuse, *Reason and Revolution*

Written in 1941, *Reason and Revolution*, by Herbert Marcuse, begins with a discussion of the decline of dialectical thinking in society. The German-American philosopher proposes to put an end to the obliteration of this form of thinking, which, he writes, uses revolutionary actions to expose and overcome capitalist contradictions. Furthermore, Marcuse argues that the fundamental concepts of Hegel's philosophy are unfavorable to the practice and theory of fascism. He specifically disapproves of the hypothesis that Hegelian philosophy laid the groundwork for authoritarianism in Germany. According to Marcuse, the only contribution of Hegel's philosophy at the time was authoritarianism's postwar resurgence in France. *Reason and Revolution* illuminates Hegelian philosophy and its influence on European thought evolution.

Theodor Adorno and Max Horkheimer, *Dialectic of Enlightenment*

Adorno and Horkheimer's 1944 *Dialectic of Enlightenment* is an extensive critique of society. It begins with an analysis of history and sets out to discover the reason for humanity's moral regression despite technological advancements. After several historical analyses, the authors blame the development of destructive enlightenment in the West for the regression. They also accuse the ancient Greek philosophers and the Hebrew Scriptures of contributing to man's decline. It is difficult to separate the Enlightenment pursuit of culture from the social pursuit of freedom, Adorno and Horkheimer reason. The lack of separation, they argue, led to little or no freedom in society. The authors attribute humanity's decline to humanity's triple domination of nature, natural human instincts, and man's domination of his fellow beings. The absurd fear of the unknown motivates this triple domination, and the fear, in turn, is driven by a capitalist economy that wants to uncover all mysteries in nature and society.

Herbert Marcuse, Eros and Civilization

Eros and Civilization, was written in 1955 by the German-American philosopher Herbert Marcuse. He employs Freudian and Marxist ideologies to highlight the social ramifications of subjugating human instincts and restricting human freedom. Unlike Sigmund Freud, Marcuse holds that the human tendency to repress sensuality is a result of capitalist domination. He observes that such repression, common in capitalist society, rewards the rich at the expense of the poor. Contrary to Freud's claim that human instincts are fixed, or biological, Marcuse argues that they can also be malleable and social. He reasons that when capitalism is overthrown, humans will be able to live in a natural state of self-gratification and freedom. In the last part of the work, Marcuse shifts his focus to his utopian dream. Unsatisfied with the fact that modern capitalism restricts human freedom, he proposes a non-repressive society in which work will be pleasurable and civil disobedience will therefore be nonexistent. Recognizing the importance of *Eros* (desire) in human development, the writer concludes by rejecting the subjugation of *Logos* (reason) and the social restoration of *Eros*.

Jean-Paul Sartre, *Critique of Dialectical Reason*

Critique of Dialectical Reason is a 1960 philosophical treatise by the French novelist and philosopher Jean-Paul Sartre. Sartre revises existentialist and Marxist theory, simultaneously depicting Marxism as a philosophy for modern times. Apart from analyzing the individualism inherent in imperialist and capitalist societies, Sartre explores the tyrannical institutions upholding the socio-political structures of capitalism and advocates for the abolition of personal property. The philosopher favors a society devoid of rank and class, in which man and the universe are clearly intertwined. Dialectical reason, Sartre argues, shows that man is shaped by the political, economic, and social forces around him. Yet he disagrees with the dialectical theory that man's future is pre-determined by his history. He counters that man has the capacity to be free in that he can relate freely with others and the external world. Sartre concludes by advocating for the adoption of communism.

Herbert Marcuse, *One-Dimensional Man*

German-American philosopher Herbert Marcuse's 1964 masterpiece *One-Dimensional Man* critiques modern capitalism by dissecting the state of capitalist society. Capitalism, he argues, softly enslaves humans by providing them comfortable lures and temptations and producing a one-dimensional man. This is a person controlled by totalitarianism disguised as technological and consumerist capitalism. Marcuse explains that mass media and consumerism are tools rulers use to prevent resistance and promote conformity among their subjects. The problem with capitalism, he argues, is that it conceals conflicts in a manner that prevents change. As conflicts make men multidimensional and therefore capable of change, Marcuse reasons, capitalism turns men into one-dimensional beings, capable only of obedience. Liberal Western capitalism is no better than dictatorial rule, he concludes, ending the book by promoting an anti-consumerism culture as an antidote to a consumerist society.

Louis Althusser, *Reading* Capital

Published in 1965, Louis Althusser's, *Reading* Capital analyzes the theory of Marxism. The treatise begins by reflecting on the status of Marxism ideology in a discussion of Western Marxism from its inception to its present state. Marxism, according to the writer, has been stripped of its revolutionary and scientific novelty by the influence of Hegelianism, humanism, historicism, and idealism. He goes on to urge that these outside influences be purged from Marxism for the good of society. Furthermore, the author suggests how to make the primary idea of Marxism clearer and more explicit. Althusser goes on to discuss the labor theory of value, historical materialism, and dialectical materialism what amounts to a philosophical attempt to rescue Marxism from a variety of ideological threats attacking its core tenets.

Theodor Adorno, *Negative Dialectics*

Theodor Adorno's *Negative Dialectics* was published in 1966 and aims to strip away putative traits falsely attributed to dialectics. Adorno seeks to update dialectics to create a version that conforms to modern times. He begins by disputing Hegelian positive dialectics ideology, which holds that the whole is always greater than the sum of parts preceding it. Dialectics, in Adorno's view, produces a whole that is essentially negative. As he puts it, human thought has ignored or suppressed diversity and differences in objects to achieve unity and identity. Thus, he advocates that objects should be given priority in philosophy. In his opinion, this preferential treatment can only happen dialectically. He goes on to describe dialectics as an attempt to identify the nonidentity between the object and thought while carrying out a project of conceptual identification. Adorno effectively urges his readers to reject the positive outcome of dialectics without abandoning its explanatory model.

G. A. Cohen, *Karl Marx's Theory of History*

Published in 1978, *Karl Marx's Theory of History* is a landmark in the philosophy of history by G. A. Cohen, a Canadian philosopher. Cohen analyzes and elucidates Karl Marx's theory of historical materialism. Using analytic philosophy, he elucidates Marx's views on history, politics, and economics, using Marx's primary thesis and developmental thesis to argue that the German philosopher's technological determinism is correct. Cohen argues, however, that human intelligence brings about innovations that reduce scarcity, adding that such innovations are adopted from motives of human rationality. In addition to positing that the historical situation of man is scarcity and that scarcity breeds innovation to ensure humanity's survival, Cohen contends that human beings are rational and that they possess the intelligence necessary to improve their situation. He concludes that a society's economic structure is determined by the level of development of the society's productive forces.

Jürgen Habermas, *The Theory of Communicative Action*

The Theory of Communicative Action is a 1981 masterpiece by German philosopher Jürgen Habermas. In it, Habermas defines communicative action as cooperative action taken by individuals after mutual arguments and discussions. He then defines language as the fundamental component of society and a suitable tool of guidance toward modernity. Habermas goes on to explain that humans are rational, meaning they are capable of communicative action, and that human understanding and actions possess a linguistic communication structure that can be used to create a better understanding of the underlying society. Communicative action can help advance society and adapt it to a rapidly changing world. The philosopher ends the book by warning against the danger such media as money and power pose, which is that they may be used to bypass socially oriented communication.

Marshall Berman, *All That Is Solid Melts into Air*

All That is Solid Melts into Air by Marshall Berman, the American philosopher, was published in 1982. It draws inspiration from numerous literary and philosophical texts to explain economic and social modernization in relation to modernism. The author argues that modernization is self-destructive. He shows how communities are destroyed as cities are built in an unending quest for modernity and criticizes the depiction of modernity in ancient literature, art and philosophy. From here, Berman argues against creative destruction, pointing out how New York was torn down and rebuilt to accommodate modern architecture and highways for modern cars. Berman illustrates how modernity empowers destructive capitalism and how it causes people to lose their jobs. *All That Is Solid Melts into Air* is a unique philosophical treatise arguing against modernism.

Epistemology

Bertrand Russell, *The Problems of Philosophy*

The Problems of Philosophy was published in 1912, the work of the English philosopher Bertrand Russell. He discusses problems of philosophy related to epistemology (knowledge), including the nature of matter and the world of universals. Russell begins by enumerating popular philosophical theories and then asking relevant questions of them. He wonders if any knowledge immune to doubt exists in the universe. Regarding the nature of matter, he questions if anything exists independent of man's knowledge or perception. He also asks, if philosophy says that external objects do not exist, how is that humans know them? He points out certain weaknesses in previous philosophical works and lays a framework for further analysis and criticism. Philosophy, according to Russell, is to be studied continuously, as answers in philosophy are never definitive. To distinguish truths from falsehoods, he writes, people must continue to question philosophical theories and principles in the quest for clarity and the best products of intellectual imagination.

George Edward Moore, *A Defense of Common Sense*

Published in 1925, *A Defense of Common Sense* is an essay in epistemology by George Edward Moore, who argues against skepticism by demonstrating that common sense beliefs have validity. Furthermore, the British philosopher asserts the certainty of some universally accepted facts and beliefs. He begins by pointing out several truisms or claims so obvious that their veracity cannot be denied. After that, he distinguishes between physical facts and mental facts. He goes on to state that physical facts are not necessarily dependent on mental facts. Next, he reveals his non-belief in God and the afterlife, based on commonsense reasoning. He goes on to discuss methods for analyzing commonsense propositions and concludes by examining "the problem of other minds," contending that other selves do exist. *A Defense of Common Sense* thus posits that common sense exists and argues against absolute skepticism.

Jacques Maritain, *The Degrees of Knowledge*

Published in 1932, Jacques Maritain's *The Degrees of Knowledge* presents the French philosopher's views on epistemology in relation to critical realism, the belief that what man knows is identical to what exists. Maritain uses critical realism to explain the degrees of knowledge in philosophy, as well as in science, mysticism, and religion. He argues that there are various degrees of knowledge and that they vary, depending on their degree of abstraction. The philosopher states that, while knowledge is synonymous with being, it is not an activity. Defining wisdom as a supreme form of knowledge, he asserts that the three forms of wisdom are theology, metaphysical knowledge, and knowledge by analogy. He goes on to clarify the differences between communicable and incommunicable knowledge in a book that endeavors to explain the nature of knowledge in various fields.

Richard Rorty, *Philosophy and the Mirror of Nature*

Written in 1979 by the American philosopher Richard Rorty, *Philosophy and the Mirror of Nature* dismantles a number of familiar philosophical problems, branding them the pseudo-problems of epistemology. Rorty explains how philosophy relies on objective and subjective perceptions and truths to observe or examine reality. After analyzing the nature of the mind, he reveals how philosophers erroneously compare the mind to a mirror that reflects reality. This, he argues, prevents them from understanding the theory of knowledge. Rorty shies away from conventional philosophical dialogue, decrying analytic philosophy, and he relies instead on layman/communal thinking patterns. According to the author, philosophical metaphors, vocabularies, and paradigms change periodically, and certain unnecessary philosophical problems arise due to these conventional changes. Rorty concludes by advising that philosophers break the mirror of philosophy, move beyond pseudo-problems, and become productive thinkers.

Olaf Helmer and Nicholas Rescher, *On the Epistemology of the Inexact Sciences*

Published in 1959, *On the Epistemology of the Inexact Sciences* was written by two German-American philosophers, Olaf Helmer and Nicholas Rescher. They open the book with an explanation of two categories of science: exact sciences and inexact sciences. According to them, exact sciences rely on formal reasoning whereas inexact sciences depend on informal reasoning. Another difference between exact and inexact sciences is that the former use well-defined terms and mathematical notations to explain observations, whereas the latter make use of terminologies that are inherently vague or subjective. After explaining the difference between the exact and inexact sciences, the philosophers argue that some branches of the social sciences (such as demography) are considered exact sciences but have characteristics that push them into the category of inexact sciences and that some physical sciences (such as engineering) include features very similar to the social sciences. In the end, Helmer and Rescher propose relying on expert judgment and pseudo-experimentation in inexact sciences like social sciences.

Edmund Gettier, *Is Justified True Belief Knowledge?*

Authored in 1963 by American philosopher Edmund Gettier, *Is Justified True Belief Knowledge?* is a three-page treatise on what constitute knowledge. The author challenges the long-held view that having a justified, true belief about a claim is equivalent to having knowledge about it. With two examples, Gettier demonstrates shows that this notion is not true. Sometimes, one can have a justified, true belief in a claim without having any knowledge about that claim, Gettier argues. *Is Justified True Belief Knowledge?* posits that knowing the definition of something does not imply having knowledge about that very thing.

Roderick Chisholm, *Theory of Knowledge*

Theory of Knowledge, published in 1989 by American philosopher Roderick Chisholm, addresses the nature of knowledge, skepticism, perception, reason, truth, and evidence. Chisholm begins with what he calls the skeptic's challenge, which is how to know something with certainty. According to the philosopher, being skeptical is inevitable and also helps one to separate justified knowledge from quasi-knowledge. He also talks about the nature of epistemic justification, pointing out that people believe in a claim because they have knowledge about that claim. He goes on to maintain that a proposition should be evident to know a proposition. Even though the philosopher writes that it is more reasonable to trust the senses than to doubt them in finding out the truth about the external world, he admits that one can be knowledgeable about a claim without relying on the senses. Having knowledge about a claim is more than just believing in the claim, Chisholm contends, and concludes by providing three conditions that must be satisfied for one to be certain of possessing justified, true knowledge about a proposition: One, the proposition must be true. Two, the person must believe in the proposition. Third, the proposition should be evident to the person.

Willard Van Orman Quine, *Epistemology Naturalized*

Epistemology Naturalized is a 1969 epistemology essay written by American philosopher Willard Van Orman Quine. Quine advocates for the replacement of traditional epistemological methods with natural scientific methods. He criticizes traditional epistemological methods for not focusing on epistemological phenomena, not investigating how knowledge is generated and developed, and not achieving the Cartesian quest for certainty. Using logic and set theory, he begins the work by reducing mathematics, as well as natural knowledge, to conceptual and doctrinal components. After several analyses, the philosopher realizes that the Cartesian project of acquiring knowledge with certainty is a lost cause. He therefore advises those seeking to understand knowledge to shift their focus to understanding how knowledge is acquired rather than studying what constitutes knowledge logically. Quine ends by inferring that psychology can and should be able to replace epistemology.

Peter Unger, *Ignorance: A Case for Skepticism*

Written by American philosopher Peter Unger, *Ignorance: A Case for Skepticism* is a 1975 philosophical treatise on skepticism, the view that no one can know anything with certainty. The philosopher takes traditional skepticism to the extreme, arguing that no reasons or actions can be justifiable and that no one can be justified in believing in anything. In his view, one can never be sure about their reasons, ideas, emotions, or intuitions. Unger supports his thesis with classical Cartesian skepticism arguments, including other classical forms of arguments with normative premises. He admits, however, that his thesis is contradictory in nature in that it presupposes that which it aims to reject. Unger concludes the paper by pointing out the benefits of skepticism in philosophy, such as improving the understanding of human knowledge and spurring innovative thinking.

Alvin Goldman, *What Is Justified Belief?*

American philosopher Alvin Goldman's book *What is Justified Belief?* proposes a set of theories for determining whether a belief in a proposition is justifiable. He begins with an explanation of what a justified belief is. According to the philosopher, a justified belief is a compelling argument given to support the belief. Goldman, however, admits that what may be a justified belief to one may not be a justified belief to others. After explaining the meaning of justified belief, he shifts his attention to what the theories of justifiable belief should look like. Theories of justification, in his view, should specify conditions for justifying a belief without invoking the concept mentioned to avoid the problem of circularity. Theories of justifiable belief should be able to specify what concepts are permissible and what concepts are not admissible, Goldman adds. To know whether a particular belief is justified, one needs to study the causal relation of the proposition and the reliability (truth ratio) of the process that produces the belief. He also explains the reliable process theory of knowledge, which states that a person knows a proposition if and only if he believes in the proposition and if and only if the proposition is true. Goldman concludes by pointing out the inherent weaknesses in his truth-conduciveness theories.

Laurence Bonjour, *The Structure of Empirical Knowledge*
Published in 1985, *The Structure of Empirical Knowledge*, by American philosopher Laurence Bonjour, challenges the traditional method of obtaining knowledge, which relies on developing knowledge from previous knowledge. Bonjour proposes instead an empirical-based method of acquiring knowledge. More specifically, he criticizes foundationalists (such as Descartes), who hold that every justifiable belief must be well-grounded in the foundation of non-inferential knowledge. Bonjour explains the flaws in foundationalism, arguing that it does not consider empirical observation in determining whether a belief is justifiable. Bonjour goes on to introduce the coherence theory of empirical justification, which states a belief is valid so long as it belongs to a coherent group of beliefs. The philosopher argues that the coherence theory of empirical justification is superior to the foundationalist theories of empirical justification because it acknowledges a priori knowledge and takes into account the use of observations in justifying empirical beliefs. In his view, what justifies a belief is not by how logical the belief is in relation to other beliefs (premises) but by how coherent the belief is with other sets of beliefs shared by others. Bonjour also uses the coherence theory of empirical justification to respond to the skeptic challenge without falling into the trap of vicious circularity.

John Hardwig, Epistemic Dependence
American philosopher John Hardwig's 1985 *Epistemic Dependence* is a treatise on acquiring knowledge from intellectual authority. It begins with the observation that the author has no evidence for most of the things in which he believes. Even though Hardwig points out that he could collect evidence to justify some of the things he believes in, he admits that time constraints and unforeseen obstacles will prevent him from gathering all that is required to justify all his beliefs. He then goes on to define epistemic dependence, which is a practice in which people draw the justification for their beliefs from the beliefs of others. He contends that one can believe in a proposition so long

as one has good reasons to believe that others believe in the same proposition. Epistemic dependence on experts, Hardwig argues, is a smart choice for average individuals who do not have the luxury of time and energy to justify their beliefs. Put simply, Hardwig implies that, sometimes, one does not need much thinking or any evidence to make rational decisions. The philosopher concludes that the relationship between an average person and an expert is crucial to the scholarly acquisition of knowledge in society.

Alvin Goldman, *Epistemology and Cognition*

American philosopher Alvin Goldman's 1986 book, *Epistemology and Cognition,* discusses the nature of acquiring and justifying knowledge. Goldman begins with an explanation of such epistemological topics as truth, belief, justification, realism, and skepticism. He comments on reliabilism, especially its epistemic justification of beliefs. After that, he argues that all knowledge is derived from one's natural cognitive capacities. Goldman supports his argument by analyzing the human mental processes, including the nature of the mind, brain, perception, memory, and representational constraints. He rejects the view that skepticism, logic, linguistic analysis, and probability theory can assist individuals in justifying their beliefs and concludes with a theoretical framework to explain the link between cognitive science and epistemology.

John McDowell, *Mind and World*

Published in 1994, *Mind and World* is an epistemological treatise by South African philosopher John McDowell. It consists of six lectures, all of which revolve around the nature of knowledge. In Lectures I and II, the author points out the challenge of modern philosophy, which is the continuous reliance on dualism in understanding reality and acquiring knowledge. In Lecture III, McDowell enumerates the pitfalls of assuming that empiricism is rationality grounded in one's observation, citing the works of philosophers like Donald Davidson and Wilfrid Sellars, which he analyzes. These pitfalls, according to the writer, expose the inability of philosophers to integrate reasons into the world. In Lectures IV, V, and VI, McDowell proposes a theory of experience that not only considers independent reality but also connects empirical thinking to the natural world.

David K. Lewis, *Elusive Knowledge*

Elusive Knowledge, a 1996 work by American philosopher David K. Lewis, addresses the subjects of skepticism, infallible knowledge, justified belief, and the rules of his own "Lewisian relevant alternatives" theory. Working form the thesis that "knowledge does not imply belief," Lewis begins by questioning whether it is possible to acquire infallible knowledge. He notes that the validity of knowledge ascriptions is based on their contexts. That is, *s* knows *p* if and only if *s* eliminates all the possibilities that *p* is not. He criticizes this context-dependence theory of knowledge in that it avoids both fallibilism and skepticism. To reconcile fallibilism and skepticism, the philosopher proposes his Lewisian relevant alternatives theory, according to which *s* knows *p* if and only if *s* presents evidence that eliminates all relevant alternatives to *p*. Lewis goes on to enumerate seven rules that can help determine the relevance of a possibility at a context: (1) Rule of Actuality, (2) Rule of Belief, (3), Rule of Resemblance, (4) Rule of Reliability, (5) Rule of Method, (6) Rule of Conservatism, and (7) Rule of Attention. After explaining Lewisian contextualism, he concludes with different kinds of a possibility and what could prevent a possibility from becoming relevant.

Alvin Goldman, *Knowledge in a Social World*

Knowledge in a Social World was written in 1999 by Alvin Goldman, an American philosopher and investigates the nature of knowledge in the social world. Goldman begins by pointing out how the evolution of technology and the wave of modern civilization and social constructionism have altered how people acquire and understand knowledge in communities. He observes how opinions and beliefs are profoundly shaped by their culture and community and, therefore, reasons that more effort must be invested in understanding the social dimension of knowledge. To elaborate on this, Goldman proposes veritistic social epistemology, a discipline that uses social processes to understand how people acquire and understand knowledge. While information technology, the media, and other cyberspace technologies help improve human communication, the writer warns society to promote the quality of content published on the Internet. After presenting and criticizing the existing theories of truth, he encourages people to pursue the integrity of truth and explains how to promote virtue and knowledge through social interactions. More specifically, he urges social and public institutions to champion the acquisition and spread of knowledge in the environment. *Knowledge in a Social World* applies epistemology to a social world and offers a social theory of knowledge.

Jürgen Habermas, *Truth and Justification*
Published in 1999, *Truth and Justification* is a collection of philosophical essays by German thinker Jürgen Habermas. It covers such topics as moral and epistemological cognitivism, legal theory, cultural relativism, practical reasoning, and human reason. Habermas answers two critical questions in the work. The first is the question of how the evolution and emergence of human lives can be reconciled with their ability to interact in a linguistically structured world. The second is how humans can reconcile their inability to recognize reality with their assumption that the world exists independently of their existence. Apart from explaining his views on objectivity, reality, and truth, Habermas answers these questions using a weak version of naturalism and epistemological realism. He later defends Kantian pragmatism and develops a pragmatic theory that relies on communicative actions and speech acts. The author concludes by addressing the limits of philosophy and reviewing the relationship between practice and theory from a "post-Marxist" perspective.

Timothy Williamson, *Knowledge and its Limits*
Published in 2000, *Knowledge and its Limits*, by British philosopher Timothy Williamson, explores the limit of knowledge and examines skepticism, realism, anti-realism, assertion, probability, evidence, externalism, transparency, luminosity, and other concepts. The philosopher begins by defining knowledge as a mental state and continues by arguing that knowledge is a concept or entity of its own and that it cannot be broken down into other concepts. Next, Williamson illustrates that even though knowledge requires truth, belief, and justification, it is not factual or accurate to define knowledge as justified true belief. In addition to asserting that knowledge is evidence and evidence is knowledge, the writer argues for externalism and emphasizes that humans do not know as much as they think they do. In sum, *Knowledge and its Limits* is an epistemological work that points out ways of analyzing knowledge within its limits.

Donald Davidson, *Subjective, Intersubjective, Objective*
Published in 2001, *Subjective, Intersubjective, Objective* is a collection of essays on epistemology by Donald Davidson, an American philosopher. Davidson explores the knowledge of one's self (subjective knowledge), knowledge of other minds (intersubjective knowledge), and knowledge of the external world (objective knowledge), including the relationship

between them. He also writes about the emergence of thought, discusses the relation of epistemology to truth, and criticizes epistemic skepticism. Davidson focuses not only on the nature of truth, reality, and human rationality but also on the relations among the world, thought, and language, concluding by arguing that truth of the subjective, intersubjective, and objective assertions is independent of whether one believes them to be true or not. He further concludes that the three varieties of knowledge (subjective, intersubjective, and objective knowledge) are not reducible to one or both of the others, but that they are connected like a tripod, meaning no form of knowledge can stand on its own.

Hilary Kornblith, *Knowledge and its Place in Nature*

Published in 2002, *Knowledge and its Place in Nature* is a book by American philosopher Hilary Kornblith that focuses on the nature of knowledge and its relation to the external world. Kornblith begins by discussing what knowledge is and the methods used in acquiring knowledge. From here, most of the rest of the book is devoted to defending and advocating for the use of a natural method in exploring knowledge. Given that knowledge is acquired mainly from the natural world, the author reasons that scientific methods should be used to investigate knowledge. He defends this notion against the views of many philosophers and explains his argument further by providing a scientific explanation of animal behaviors. Kornblith also discusses how a naturalistic method can deal with epistemic normativity. In his final chapter, he distinguishes philosophy from special sciences used in responding to philosophical questions and sums up that conceptual analysis should be replaced with a natural approach in epistemological research.

Jonathan Kvanvig, *The Value of Knowledge and the Pursuit of Understanding*

The Value of Knowledge and the Pursuit of Understanding, by American philosopher Jonathan Kvanvig, was published in 2003. It begins with a discussion of the value of knowledge, the value of belief, and the value of knowledge justification. The writer explores two main questions: How much knowledge humans can acquire? and How much knowledge exists in the universe? After several analyses, he finds that it is nearly impossible to account for the nature of knowledge in that knowledge acquisition is subjective in nature. One cannot talk about understanding knowledge without considering that knowledge acquisition is strongly influenced by intuitions, he argues. He goes on to consider normativity, reliabilism, and the special promise of epistemology and then comments on the Gettier problem. Kvanvig admits that while certain subcomponents of knowledge are valuable, they cannot solve the Meno problem, which is the question of why knowledge is more valuable than true belief. He devotes the last chapter of the work to arguing that understanding (grasping connections in a body of information) has a unique value different from knowledge, and that understanding has the potential to resolve the Meno problem.

Keith DeRose, *The Case for Contextualism: Knowledge, Skepticism, and Context*

Published in 2009, *The Case for Contextualism: Knowledge, Skepticism, and Context,* by American philosopher Keith DeRose, makes a case for contextualism, arguing that contextualism is true and is superior to all forms of invariantism, such as classical invariantism and subject-sensitive invariantism. The philosopher also points out that, unlike invariantism, contextualism respects intellectualism and considers the subjective views of individuals. DeRose supports his arguments further with the knowledge account of assertion and provides various ways context-sensitive terms can be handled semantically when disagreements exist among speakers. In the concluding portion of the work, DeRose defends criticism of contextualism and concludes that compared to subject-sensitive invariantism, contextualism handles the connection between knowledge and actions properly.

Miranda Fricker, *Epistemic Injustice: Power and the Ethics of Knowing*

Miranda Fricker's 2007 *Epistemic Injustice: Power and the Ethics of Knowing* explores the nature of epistemic injustice, which the British philosopher describes as the unjustness associated with knowledge. She argues that there are two types of epistemic injustice: testimonial injustice and hermeneutical injustice. The first is unfairness caused by placing or not placing trust in someone's word, while the second is unjustness due to the misinterpretation or misconception of one's lives or other people's lives. The author's principal argument is that epistemic injustice exists in society and is shaped and fueled by prejudices, biases, stereotypical views, and all forms of discrimination. Fricker goes on to outline two hybrid ethical virtues of epistemic justice that can reduce or eliminate epistemic injustice.

Jason Stanley, *Knowledge and Practical Interests*

Knowledge and Practical Interests, by American philosopher Jason Stanley, was published in 2005 and explores the relationship between knowledge and practical interests. Stanley's main thesis centers on interest-relative invariantism, which states that acquired knowledge acquired by people is a function of their practical interests or how much is at stake in acquiring the knowledge. Stating this another way, the writer advises philosophers to write not only for experts but for all interested readers. He defends interest-relative invariantism, arguing that the truth of a knowledge claim is directly linked to the person making the knowledge claim. He goes on to show that the defense of interest-relative invariantism stems from the unique nature of epistemological properties, not from epistemological applications. Stanley concludes by proposing ways of combating skepticism and other philosophical paradoxes.

Metaphysics

Henri Bergson, *Introduction to Metaphysics*

Bergson's 1903 *Introduction to Metaphysics* discusses intuition as well as how humans approach rational objects. In the opening pages, the French philosopher argues that reductionistic analysis cannot adequately explain reality. He proposes intuition as the solution to this problem. Equating intuition with sympathy, Bergson maintains that sympathy itself requires put oneself in another's place. In his view, intuition requires that one enter an object rather than moving around it. Entering an object, Bergson argues, enables one to gain complete knowledge of reality. Nevertheless, the philosopher reveals that no two attempts to enter an object will be the same because each new entrance builds on the earlier entrance. Bergson concludes by expounding on nine propositions that form the core tenets of his argument.

George Edward Moore, *The Refutation of Idealism*

Published in 1903, *The Refutation of Idealism*, by English philosopher George Edward Moore, begins with a criticism of the idealist view that reality is spiritual. Moore observes that idealist arguments rest on a single pillar: "*esse is percipi*" ("to be is to be perceived"). The philosopher reasons that by refuting the arguments for *esse is percipi*, he can dismantle the idealists' claim that reality is spiritual. Moore defines "*percipi*" as anything that includes thoughts and sensations and goes further to explain the three senses of "esse is percipi": synonym, analytical containment, and synthetic necessity. After several analyses, he arrives at the conclusion that *esse is percipi* is false in that it is not *a posteriori* and cannot be proved by the law of non-contradiction alone. In short, the views of idealism concerning reality lead to contradictions.

Henri Bergson, *Creative Evolution*

Creative Evolution, by Henri Bergson and published in 1934, proposes a directed, orthogenetic version of evolution to replace Charles Darwin's random evolutionary mechanism. This version believes that evolution is stimulated by a life force or élan vital, which can also be interpreted as man's inherent impulse of creativity. In the beginning of the book, the author reveals how to reconcile the two senses of life. This process, in his opinion, entails analyzing real life, how evolution happens to species, and the reflective causes. He later criticizes mechanism as it pertains to the concepts of evolution and life. As he puts it, creation must be equated to life because creativity can be solely used to explain both the cohesion of life and the disruption of evolutionary products. Bergson further suggests that intuition is the best method for one to understand time as duration. In conclusion, *Creative Evolution* is Bergson's attempt to resolve some of the main problems of Darwin's evolution theory.

William James, *Pragmatism: A New Name for Some Old Ways of Thinking*

Pragmatism: A New Name for Some Old Ways of Thinking is a 1907 collection of eight lectures on metaphysics by William James. Here, the American philosopher makes a strong case for Pragmatism. In Lecture I, he points out the strengths and weaknesses of rationalism versus empiricism. He calls the rationalist "tender-minded" and the empiricist "tough-minded" and advocates for Pragmatism, a philosophical system that synthesizes rationalism and empiricism. In Lecture II, James defines Pragmatism as a philosophical method that relies on practical actions. He goes on in Lectures III, IV, and V to explain how to apply Pragmatism to specific problems and argues that all human thought is derived from proto-human ancestors. In Lecture VI, James addresses the Pragmatic concept of truth, arguing that the truth of an idea is dynamic rather than static. He concludes by discussing the relationship between pragmatism and religion, positing that any religion is good as long its consequences are beneficial to society.

John Dewey, *Experience and Nature*

Authored in 1925 by American philosopher John Dewey, *Experience and Nature* is a metaphysical work that considers theories of nature and experience as well as their respective difficulties. Dewey also examines the relationship between nature and experience, the role of societal factors and language in knowledge, the effect of law, and the interrelationship between mind and matter. He explores concepts of mind, knowledge, and the external world. His chief aim in this work is to replace prevailing theories that separate nature from experience with the idea of continuity and, in this vein, to apply pragmatic methods (empirical naturalism) to specific issues of metaphysics and ethics.

Alfred North Whitehead, *Process and Reality*

Published in 1929, *Process and Reality,* by the English mathematician and philosopher Alfred North Whitehead, seeks to replace the conventional philosophy of substance or material with a philosophy of organism, with the objective of better understanding the universe. Whitehead proposes a structure of speculative philosophy founded on a scheme of categorical investigation designed to clarify how existing parts of human experience may promote the understanding of reality. He analyzes how humans can define reality as a system not of being but of becoming. As he sees it, the final realities of the world are made up of actual entities. These entities, in turn, are the solid facts on which human feelings and thoughts are based. *Process and Reality* explains "process philosophy," in which the constituents of reality seen in a "becoming" relation to one another.

Robin George Collingwood, *An Essay on Metaphysics*

English philosopher Robin George Collingwood's 1940 *An Essay on Metaphysics* begins with an introduction to the history of metaphysics and goes on to argue that metaphysics should not start with "propositions" but with "absolute presuppositions." The reason, Collingwood argues, is that absolute presuppositions proceed from claims that are neither true nor false, while propositions can be verified as true or false. Collingwood also contends that the aim of metaphysics is to provide a solid foundation upon which science can succeed in the quest for knowledge. Toward the conclusion of the book, the writer shifts attention to the history of psychology and attempts to distinguish metaphysics from that discipline. He ends with a discussion of such metaphysical issues as the existence of God, the concept of causation, and the work of Kant.

Willard Van Orman Quine, *On What There Is*

Published in 1948, Willard Van Orman Quine's *On What There Is* focuses on the problems of ontology. The American philosopher begins by noting the disagreements among philosophers over the ontological question of "What is there?" He reasons that anyone who claims that "nothing is there" is also saying indirectly that "something exists that does not exist." He calls this paradox *Plato's beard*. Quine further applies Bertrand Russell's Theory of Descriptions (RTD) to *Plato's beard* and concludes that, unlike negative existential statements, positive existential statements commit one to ontology. In another attempt to resolve *Plato's beard*, Quine notices that it is wrong to confuse meaning and naming in addressing the existence of universals. According to him, the slogan "to be is to be the value of a variable" does not stipulate "what there is"; rather, it states only what a proposition says "there is." After proposing that parsimony can be used to determine ontology, Quine admits that his application of RDT to *Plato's beard* eliminates some ontological reasoning, such as the treatment of "abstract noun" as a name for an entity. He concludes that, on the subject of "what is there," it is wrong to address the existence of abstract entities using *Plato's beard*.

Rudolf Carnap, *Empiricism, Semantics, and Ontology*

Empiricism, Semantics, and Ontology is a 1950 work of metaphysics by the German-American philosopher Rudolf Carnap. His principal argument is that the existence of abstract entities (i.e., properties, classes, and numbers) can be accepted using pragmatic linguistic frameworks rather than resorting to a Platonic ontology theory that posits a system of entities existing independently. Carnap writes about the problems of abstract entities in the context of semantics, pointing out that, without resolving these problems, empiricists will find it challenging to justify their scientific claims to knowledge. As a resolution, Carnap proposes several linguistic frameworks to clarify internal questions (questions related to the existence of entities) and external questions (questions related to the reality of the whole entities) and to address Plato's problems of universals. According to him, a good linguistic framework must contain such relevant features as fruitfulness, simplicity, efficiency, and one's experiences. Carnap goes on to distinguish internal questions from external questions and argues that anyone who fails to accept his linguistic frameworks will be unable to distinguish between external and internal questions, as was the case with such philosophers as Plato, who simply assert the reality of abstract entities. The author concludes by noting that the acceptance of abstract linguistic forms would be influenced by their efficiency and effectiveness.

Willard Van Orman Quine, *Two Dogmas of Empiricism*

Published in 1951, W. V. O. Quine's *Two Dogmas of Empiricism* criticizes the two major tenets of logical positivism. The book is divided into six parts, each of which considers the analytic/synthetic difference and reductionism. In the first four parts, Quine posits that there is no reasonable justification for analyticity because all its many explanations are circular. In the concluding two parts, he argues that reductionism is simply another ethereal object of faith because it is unproven. According to Quine, abandoning reductionist belief would blur the alleged boundary between natural science and metaphysics. He also predicts that this abandonment will lead to a shift toward Pragmatism. Thus, the author proposes that the entire field of science should be verified, in contrast to the reductionist process, which only accredits individual statements. Quine concludes with a synopsis of a new philosophy, which maintains the ideology of logical positivism while discarding its elemental issues.

David Malet, *Universals and Scientific Realism*

Universals and Scientific Realism is a 1978 metaphysical book by David Malet Armstrong, a sequel to his *Nominalism and Realism: Volume 1.* In the 1978 book, Malet explores the problem of universals, arguing that universals exist and that their existence can only be proved by the physical sciences. The writer criticizes previous approaches used to address the problem of universals. He rejects the nominalist account of properties, the use of linguistic frameworks to address universals, and Plato's realism, which posits a system of entities that exist independently. Armstrong proposes an objective theory of universals, one that does not rely on linguistic frameworks but on natural science to explain the relation between natural laws and universals. He concludes with observation that the relation between universals provides insights into physical laws.

Willard Van Orman Quine, *Theories and Things*

Published in 1981, *Theories and Things* consists of four lectures by the American mathematician and philosopher Willard Van Orman Quine. In these lectures, he presents his views on nominalism and the nature of existence. He argues that the notion of universals has been a source of disagreement among nominalists and realists and observes that nominalists deny the use of abstract objects and universals yet acknowledge the existence of abstract terms. From here, he compares what the nominalist and realist think about the notion of universals.

Timothy Williamson, *Modal Logic as Metaphysics*

Published in 2013, *Modal Logic as Metaphysics*, by British philosopher Timothy Williamson, explores the nature of necessitism, the nature of being and its relations with change, and contingency. Williamson proposes the use of higher-order modal logic to resolve metaphysical problems. He argues that anything that exists in the logical space also exists in other space. Using the technical resources of modal logic, he points out the structural features of metaphysical theories and explains how to answer metaphysical questions. He also addresses several individual metaphysical topics, including the relation between metaphysics and logic, the nature of possible worlds, and problems for truthmaker theory. Williamson seeks here to establish the formal logic of modality as a science.

David Chalmers, *Constructing the World*

David Chalmers's *Constructing the World*, published in 2012, covers a wide range of philosophical topics, including metaphysics, epistemology, skepticism, the philosophy of mind, and the philosophy of language. Chalmers analyzes the nature of reality and argues that all truths can be derived from a small category of truths. To understand reality and paint a picture of the world, he uses Rudolf Carnap's scrutability theory, which states that all truths of the world can be derived from a limited class of truths. His defense of this theory results in his development of a philosophical (metaphysical epistemology) framework for a global picture of the world. From within this framework, Chalmers rejects Willard Van Orman Quine's claims that *a priori* truths do not exist, defends conceptual metaphysics and the unity of science, and advocates for an internalist method as a means of assessing the nature of thoughts.

Theodore Sider, *Writing the Book of the World*

Writing the Book of the World, a 2011 metaphysical book by Theodore Sider, an American philosopher, contends that describing the world through the lens of metaphysics presents an insufficient picture. Instead, he argues, one must use the proper methods and tools to adequately describe the world. He begins with a description of the nature of metaphysics. After discussing metaphysics fundamentality, he explores several ontological problems and philosophical topics, such as truths, causal relations, modal structures, quantifiers, time, and modality with the objective of providing a systemic clarity of the philosophical architectures, structures, and features through which the world may be interpreted.

Stephen Mumford, *Dispositions*

Published in 1998, *Dispositions*, by British philosopher Stephen Mumford, puts forward a theory of dispositions—the metaphysical term used to indicate a property, state, or condition that possesses some causal power—to clarify what it means to say an object or idea has certain properties. He investigates the relation between dispositions and metaphysics and argues that one needs to understand the nature of disposition to understand scientific laws, causation, truth, and properties. Mumford also discusses the relationship between conditional ascriptions and dispositional ascriptions, arguing that just because one can distinguish between categorical and dispositional ascriptions does not mean one can distinguish between categorical properties and dispositional ascriptions. The philosopher concludes by supporting the thesis of dispositional essentialism, a view that replaces the laws of nature with disposition, and by also proposing a "revised contingency thesis" to avoid the necessity of including physical laws in his claims.

Derek Parfit, *Reasons and Persons*

Reasons and Persons, is a 1984 book by British philosopher Derek Parfit. Divided into four sections, it begins by arguing that such ethical theories as commonsense morality and ethical egoism are self-defeating. After detailing the problems of these theories, Parfit endorses the adoption of impersonal ethics. In the second section of the work, Parfit expands his criticism of the self-interest theory. The self, he writes, is a fabrication founded on false ideology in Cartesian dualism. The third section contains the argument for a reductive description of personal identity. Connectedness and mental continuity should matter more than personal identity in human society, Parfit argues. In the final section, the philosopher tackles population ethics and questions humanity's obligations to future generations. The unifying thesis of Parfit's book is that people should abandon belief in the permanence of their identity and nature because no one remains the same throughout their lifetime.

David K. Lewis, *On the Plurality of Worlds*

Written by the American philosopher David K. Lewis in 1986, *On the Plurality of Worlds* is a four-chapter treatise that defends the theory of modal realism. It begins with an explanation of modal realism. As Lewis presents it, there is a plurality of worlds (for instance, earth) that are real but disconnected from each other. Modal realism can help us to understand counterfactual conditions implied by the existence of this plurality. The hypothetical function of modal realism confirms its validity, he asserts. After countering several criticisms of modal realism, Lewis focuses on ersatz modal realism. This concept, he argues, is merely an attempt to define the plurality of worlds without committing ontologically to an infinity of possible worlds. In the last chapter of the book, Lewis develops the counterpart theory, which states that every actual object exists only in the real world. However, he concludes, each object has duplicates existing in an endless plurality of worlds and, even though the duplicates are not identical to the main object, they still resemble it in important aspects.

Nicholas Malebranche, *Dialogues on Metaphysics*

Originally published in 1688 and authored by Nicolas Malebranche, *Dialogues on Metaphysics* presents Malebranche's philosophy in fourteen dialogues between Aristes and Theodore. Each addresses the nature and existence of God, the soul, the mind, the body, and the external world. Most of the dialogues conclude that the human senses are unreliable. That one can see something does not mean one can accurately explain it, Malebranche argues. To illustrate this, he points to Descartes' Laws of Motion, which states that the energy conserved in an object is equal to the net sum of the product of the mass of the body and the velocity of the body. While the author agrees with this law, he disagrees with Descartes' assertion that a force is needed for a body to be in a state of inertia. He ends by pointing out the folly of criticizing providence or the laws created by God to govern the world.

Anne Conway, *The Principles of the Most Ancient and Modern Philosophy*

Published posthumously in 1690, *The Principles of the Most Ancient and Modern Philosophy* is a masterpiece written anonymously by English philosopher Anne Conway. The book develops the author's views on monism. It begins by explaining the nature and attributes of God. According to Conway, God is the "most supreme being," followed by Jesus Christ (the mediator) and, third in line, human beings. Conway argues that no humans can possess God's attributes, meaning that man cannot be omnipresent, omniscient, infinite, and eternal. In addition to pointing out that no man can be like Jesus Christ, she notes that it is not uncommon for humans, especially philosophers, to make erroneous statements about the nature of God. Conway ends with the claim that all creatures are made of two things: the body and the spirit.

Francis Hutcheson, *An Inquiry into the Original of our Ideas of Beauty and Virtue*

An Inquiry into the Original of our Ideas of Beauty and Virtue is a philosophical work by the Scottish thinker Francis Hutcheson and published in 1725. The book comprises two treatises. In the first, Hutcheson argues that all human ideas are a function of experiences and perception, which are directly influenced by the senses. He explains further that one's ethical and aesthetical preferences are also directly linked to one's perception. This means that two different persons are likely to have different views about beauty, he asserts. In the second treatise, Hutcheson analyzes the nature of love and benevolence, contending that people inherently have moral principles. His views on humanity's natural ability to be morally upright are coherent with the ideas of Lord Shaftesbury (Anthony Ashley Cooper, 3rd Earl of Shaftesbury). Responding to Bernard Mandeville's *Fable of the Bees* (1714), Hutcheson rejects the view that moral principles are invented by the state for self-serving reasons. He concludes by arguing that the best moral principles are those that maximize the happiness of the majority.

Philosophy of Mind

Gilbert Ryle, *The Concept of the Mind*

Published in 1949, Gilbert Ryle's *The Concept of the Mind* criticizes the belief that the mind is separate from the body. The English philosopher begins by rejecting Descartes' theory of mind-body dualism because it isolates the mental processes of the body from its physical processes. Mental processes are merely a way to explain how the body works, the author argues. Thus, he asserts that the actions of the body cannot be separated from the workings of its mind. Ryle also condemns the conjecture that the mind is the site in which mental images are perceived, created, remembered, and understood. As he puts it, the mind is not a space where these dispositions are located or situated, but these dispositions belong to a world where there is no distinction between the mental and physical states. Ryle ends by maintaining that the behaviorist and Cartesian theories are too mechanistic and rigid to help one thoroughly understand the concept of the mind.

Wilfrid Sellars, *Empiricism and the Philosophy of Mind*

Empiricism and the Philosophy of Mind is a 1956 book by American philosopher Wilfrid Sellars. It presents a critique of the framework of *given*, by which what is seen is actually what is being seen. Sellers begins with a discussion of the ambiguities in sense-datum theories. As the writer puts it, these theories posit that phenomenal qualities are characterized by a state of awareness and are derived from sense data. He notes that many (not all) sense-datum theorists are confused. They are not sure whether sensing is a form of knowing, whether givenness precedes learning, or whether experiences are veridical. According to the philosopher, the purpose of pointing out these confusions is to argue that a red-triangle sensation is the paradigm of empiricism. Sellers finds through his analysis of another language that the vocabulary of sense data does not change the description of discourses. After analyzing the logic of looks, the author reasons that the looks of an object are subjective and are based on one's perceptual experience. He goes on to discuss impressions and ideas, including how they affect one's immediate experience. In addition to commenting on the abstract ideas of Locke, Berkeley, and Hume, Sellars contends that the Myth of the Given has contributed to flawed ways of "thinking in absence" rather than "thinking in presence." Having reached this conclusion, the philosopher concludes by considering the nature of empirical knowledge, the methodological thesis of behaviorism, and the debate of whether impressions can be regarded as theoretical entities.

Herbert Feigl, *The "Mental" and the "Physical"*

Herbert Feigl's 1958 *The "Mental" and the "Physical"* argues that sentience (raw feels) can be identified with neural events. To support his argument, he proposes the identity theory, which holds that the direct conscious experience of humans and some other higher animals are identical in terms of their neural processes. Questions Feigl answers in this treatise include whether a difference exists between identity theory and psychophysiological parallelism, whether the identity theory can identify the relationship between sentience and neural events, and whether it can be defended against interactionistic dualism. The philosopher rejects philosophical arguments that support dualism, including Spinoza's double-aspect theory, which assumes that an unknown third of mental and physical aspects exist. Feigl concludes by justifying the identity theory with several scientific findings in the literature.

David K. Lewis, *An Argument for the Identity Theory*

David K. Lewis's *An Argument for the Identity Theory* is a 1966 essay on the identity theory of mind. The theory holds that mental states (experiences) are physical, and to support it, Lewis provides two premises. The first is that all experiences have causal roles. The second is that physics is sufficient to explain all physical phenomena. According to Lewis, all experiences have causal roles, as do physical states (for instance, pain). From these two premises, Lewis reasons that all experiences are identical with some physical states. He concludes by defending the identity theory against several objections, including the assumption that the physical state is the object of the mental state, the premise that mental states are unlocated, the confusion between the neural-state ascription, and the mental state ascription.

Jerry Fodor, *The Language of Thought*

The Language of Thought, a 1975 book by American philosopher Jerry Fodor, is focused on how the mind works. It begins with a critique of speculative, cognitive psychology theories of mind, pointing out that these theories have failed to sketch a true picture of human mental processes. He proposes the language of thought hypothesis, which posits that humans process their thoughts in a manner similar to the way they structure their languages. Fodor hypothesizes that one's mental representations are "language-like," meaning that, like one's language, one's thought has syntax or a semantic structure. Relying on functionalist materialism, the American writer argues that mental representations are not only transferable but also characterized by different forms. Fodor supports his hypothesis with empirical evidence drawn from cognitive science and linguistics and concludes that the only psychological models that can accurately depict the structures of the mind are those that assume that the mind is linguistically structured.

Hilary Putnam, *The Meaning of "Meaning"*

The Meaning of "Meaning" is a 1975 work by the American philosopher Hilary Putnam, who focuses on the nature of meanings, maintaining that the meaning of something (an idea or object) is a psychological state. This undermines the view that the meaning of a word (intension) can determine the reference of a word (extension). To support his thesis, Putnam rejects descriptivism, a notion that the meaning of a word is shaped by how it is written, spoken, or described by a speaker. The philosopher begins with a description of three semantic components of a word: its reference, its meaning, and the psychological state of the speaker. According to Putnam, the meaning of a word is its epistemological component, and the reference is the context the speaker uses to describe a word. Putnam's principal interest is the psychological state of the speaker, how the meaning of a word is shaped by the mental content of an individual. Putnam believes that descriptivism (semantic internalism) is an imperfect approach to the meaning of a word because it creates confusion or ambiguity, especially when one is describing natural terms (water, gold, protein, etc.) or different words with similar meanings. To support semantic externalism and show that the internal state of a person cannot alter the meaning of a word, Putnam carries out a Twin-Earth experiment. This thought experiment requires one to imagine a planet similar to Earth, except that, on the imaginary planet, water is not called H_20 but XYZ. He argues that a layperson on Earth and the imaginary planet will not be able to distinguish XYZ from H_20. Natural kinds, according to him, exist independently of individual's ability to recognize them. He adds that the description of natural kinds is usually accompanied with a form of ostentation. Overall, Putnam argues that an individual's psychological state cannot determine the meaning of natural kinds.

Tyler Burge, *Individualism and the Mental*

American philosopher Tyler Burge's 1979 book *Individualism and the Mental* is an argument for anti-individualism. According to Burge, anti-individualism posits that the meaning of a word (intension) is to some extent dependent on factors outside an individual. Using a three-step thought experiment, Burge reasons that things like human reasoning, moral values, and self-knowledge are determined by the social environment. Burge also rejects the views of Hilary Putnam, in *The Meaning of "Meaning,"* and instead argues that the attribution of the meaning of natural kinds is dependent on the nature of the physical environments. The philosopher devotes a significant portion of his book to defending his argument in support of the three-step thought experiment. He ends by considering the application of anti-individualism to such philosophical fields as metaphysics, epistemology, phenomenology, and linguistics.

Jerry Fodor, *The Modularity of Mind: An Essay on Faculty Psychology*
The Modularity of Mind: An Essay on Faculty Psychology, by Jerry Fodor, an American philosopher, is a 1983 book on the psychology of cognitive processes. Fodor explains the concept of modularity in the context of cognitive systems. Fodor's modularity theory holds that modular systems are computational mechanisms with specific purposes. Fodor posits that the human mind is a modular system, meaning that it is compartmentalized in modules and is limited in carrying out certain cognitive functions. He further reasons that a module lies somewhere between the cognitive and behavioral scientific views of lower-level cognitive processes (perception and language). He goes on to argue that any cognitive system is modular if it has certain features, such as being domain-specific, being fast, having shallow outputs, limited accessibility, and possessing a fixed neural architecture. However, the philosopher maintains that higher-level cognitive processes (involved in practical reasoning and belief fixation) are not modular in nature due to their dissimilar properties. After discussing the application of modularity theory to methodological and epistemological issues, Fodor concludes that the mind is epistemically bounded, constrained to carry out certain cognitive functions only.

John Searle, *Intentionality: An Essay in the Philosophy of Mind*
Published in 1983, John Searles' *Intentionality: An Essay in the Philosophy of Mind* focuses on the relation between mind and language. Central to the work is the nature of intentionality, the view that the mind can depict the nature, status, features, and properties of affairs. Searle begins with an explanation of intentionality, enumerating the three factors that determine the intentionality of a mental state: the nature of the mental state, the

subject's network, and the subject's background. He goes on to apply the knowledge of intentionality to several topics, including reference, meanings, causality, intentions, perceptions, and beliefs. According to Searle, a mental state has the property of intentionality, and the property of a mental state is not dependent on the reality of the environment and the relationship of the mind with extra-mental reality. He believes that speech acts depict the capacity of the mind to connect humans to the outside world and goes on to argue that speech acts and mental states are similar in terms of intentionality. Searle defends his views against proponents of causal theory, who assert that linguistic reference cannot be determined by intentionality.

Stephen Stich, *From Folk Psychology to Cognitive Science: The Case Against Belief*

American scholar Stephen Stich's 1983 book, *From Folk Psychology to Cognitive Science: The Case Against Belief*, addresses the relationship between folk psychology and cognitive science. Stich's thesis is that cognitive science and folk psychology are incompatible. The book is divided into two parts. In Part I, Stich explores the folk psychology theory of belief, pointing out its flaws. He then proposes the theory of content-ascription to claim that the folk psychology theory of belief has no significant benefits for scientific purposes. In Part II, he defends his arguments against all proponents of representational theories of the mind, who hold that folk psychology and cognitive science can be reconciled or made compatible.

Ruth Garrett Millikan, *Language, Thought, and Other Biological Categories: New Foundations for Realism*

Language, Thought, and Other Biological Categories: New Foundations for Realism is a 1984 work by American philosopher Ruth Garrett Millikan. She refutes meaning rationalism, a principle that reason (not experience) is the only way to acquire knowledge. She argues that reason alone cannot help one to know anything with certainty, and she contends that one can understand the intention of the language used by a speaker without understanding the intention of the speaker. The content of thoughts and the meaning of words are dependent on their "natural history," she argues. Millikan suggests that "language devices" and biological organs (for instance, hearts) are similar. They are used in standard ways, and their functions can be explained through causal connections. The philosopher spends devotes the concluding portion of her work to defending her arguments and explaining the relation between intentionality and language.

Patricia Churchland, *Neurophilosophy: Toward a Unified Science of the Mind-Brain*

Neurophilosophy: Toward a Unified Science of the Mind-Brain, by Canadian-American philosopher Patricia Churchland, was published in 1986 and explores the relation between the mind and the brain, making the argument that the mind is the brain. Churchland begins with an introduction to neuropsychology, neuroanatomy, and neurophysiology. She next discusses recent trends in the philosophy of science and focuses on how they have shaped the understanding of the mind and the brain, but she rejects the arguments that distinguish between mind and brain. The author argues that mental states are reducible to brain states, supporting this thesis with a general account of intertheoretic reduction and a reduction strategy. In the concluding portion of the book, Churchland discusses what she calls a neurophilosophical perspective and ends by providing insights into recent neurobiological theories and the implication of contemporary functional-neurobiology developments on psychology and neuroscience.

Mark Johnson, *The Body in the Mind: The Bodily Basis of Meaning, Imagination, and Reason*

Published in 1987, *The Body in the Mind: The Bodily Basis of Meaning, Imagination, and Reason,* by the American philosopher Mark Johnson, posits that all thoughts (reasoning, meaning, and understanding) are shaped by and derived from bodily experience. In eight chapters, Johnson investigates the role of imagination in reasoning, meaning, and understanding. He devotes the first three chapters to a general account of meaning and reasoning and their roles in image schemata (pictures in the mind). He suggests that image schemata are abstract images that depict one's experience and understanding and that gestalt structure limits the understanding of meaning. He argues that image schemata occur when the body interacts with the world through experience and that they are generated from recurring patterns of experience. The writer goes on to explain the schematic constraints on reasoning, meaning, and understanding. In Johnson's view, four mental-process factors are needed to explain a concept. They include a concept, a schema, an image of the object, and an object perceived. One needs to have insights into these four factors to understand the meaning of something. Johnson nevertheless admits how difficult it is to interpret and comprehend complex image-schematic structures, let alone share the meanings of such experiences with others. Following this, he points out the flaws in Kant's mathematical reasoning regarding the question of how imagination works. In his final chapter, Johnson argues that the background for the construction of image schemata is an essential component for understanding meaning.

Francisco J. Varela, Evan Thompson, and Eleanor Rosch, *The Embodied Mind: Cognitive Science and Human Experience*

The Embodied Mind: Cognitive Science and Human Experience, a 1991 work authored by Francisco J. Varela, Evan Thompson, and Eleanor Rosch, proposes that only a cross-fertilization of ideas obtained from mind in experience and mind in science can fully explain how human cognition works. The authors employ both Buddhist meditative psychology and cognitive science to understand human experience and reinvigorate phenomenology and psychoanalysis. They also propose the "enactive approach," a method grounded in the belief that the body can be used to understand the mind and explain the nature of human cognition.

Andy Clark, *Being There: Putting Brain, Body and World Together Again*

Andy Clark's 1997 *Being There: Putting Brain, Body and World Together Again* shows the relation of the mind with the brain, the body, and the world. Using the ideas of artificial intelligence, robotics, neuroscience, and psychology, the British philosopher addresses several adaptive behaviors, including the use of linguistic devices in higher-level reasoning, the movement and neural processes of a cockroach, and the visual capacity of primates. The writer makes two central claims. One is that an essential feature of consciousness is having a sense of being in the world. The other is that the brain acts as a controller of embodied activities.

Shaun Gallagher, *How the Body Shapes the Mind*

Published in 2005, *How the Body Shapes the Mind,* by the American philosopher Shaun Gallagher, answers philosophical questions about the relation between the body and the mind. Gallagher argues that embodiment plays a key role in cognition, including shaping how the mind works. The writer responds to two key groups of questions. The first group is related to the phenomenal field of consciousness, most especially how conscious experience shapes the body. To respond to these questions, Gallagher reasons that the body can be depicted from many perspectives. He then compares and contrasts body schema and body image. In his view, the former functions without being conscious of perceptual monitoring, while the latter includes beliefs, perceptions, and attitudes that are available to consciousness. The author nonetheless notes that both body schema and body image are multimodal. The second group of questions is associated with the structure of experiences that are hidden from one's direct observations. Stated another way, in the second sets of questions, Gallagher responds to how perception, judgment, belief, memory, and other cognitive processes are embodied. To answer these questions and describe body awareness, he develops a theory of embodied cognition, which assumes that the body schema shape perception, which in turn shapes cognition. According to Gallagher, just as the world, the self, and others can perceive and interact with environmental structures, so, too, can the body. In short, *How the Body Shapes the Mind* explains the influence of the body on the mind.

Andy Clark, *Supersizing the Mind: Embodiment, Action, and Cognitive Extension*

The 2008 *Supersizing the Mind: Embodiment, Action, and Cognitive Extension,* by British philosopher Andy Clark, is a defense of Clark's own embodied theory, the principle that the body can shape the mind. The main argument of the work is that certain forms of human cognition (such as thinking) do not happen in the head alone but occur through the dynamic intermingling of the body, brain, and the world. Drawing upon recent work in artificial intelligence, robotics, neuroscience, and psychology, the writer defends his thesis against proponents of Cartesianism, who believe that the mind is separate from and superior to the body and that the mind is thereby separated from the world. Clark goes on to discuss the location of the mind. In his view, the mind is not in the head but emerges through the world, the brain, and the body. The author devotes the final section of the book defending his thesis against those who have extended the embodied theory beyond its scope or limits.

David Chalmers, *The Character of Consciousness*

The Character of Consciousness is a 2010 philosophical book by Australian philosopher David Chalmers. Chalmers discusses the meaning, science, metaphysics, contents, problems, and unity of consciousness. More specifically, he addresses such complex issues as the challenge of phenomenal consciousness to standard materialism, the difference between positive and negative conceivability, and the difference between Russellian and Fregean contents. He also replies to those who criticize his earlier book *The Conscious Mind.* Chalmers adopts an acquaintance model in the latter part of the work to explain how one can have epistemic access to phenomenal states. The book contains several controversial ideas—such as the consciousness meter and the Matrix of consciousness—the writer uses to explain the nature of consciousness. He ends by addressing the problems of the unity of conscious experience.

Evan Thompson, *Mind in Life*

Published in 2010, *Mind in Life,* by American scholar Evan Thompson, explores the relation between life and mind and attempts to close the gap between phenomenology (consciousness) and biology (nature). Thompson opens by discussing traditional views in cognitive science. After rejecting these, pointing out that they are ineffective in addressing recent phenomenological issues, he draws upon several sources in the literature (including Husserl, Clark, and Merleau-Ponty) to argue that life and mind have much in common in terms of self-organization. He argues for the enactive approach, which is grounded in the view that adaptivity and autopoiesis are individually and jointly essential to life. Thompson captures his thoughts eloquently with the statements "where is life, there is mind." Toward the end of his book, Thompson discusses boundary issues of cognitive systems, such as externalism vs. internalism and concludes with the problem of consciousness.

Andy Clark, *Surfing Uncertainty: Prediction, Action, and the Embodied Mind*

Surfing Uncertainty: Prediction, Action, and the Embodied Mind, a 2015 book by British cognitive scientist Andy Clark, draws on robotics, artificial intelligence, psychology, and neuroscience to explore how material mental states (the brain and mind) produce non-material mental states such as perception and consciousness. He proposes the Hierarchical Action-Oriented Predictive Processing (PP) models, which assume that cognitive systems are arranged in hierarchical levels, to understand mental phenomena. He contends that mental states are predictive machines, which can predict streams of non-mental states even before they form. Stated another way, Clark reasons that the brain uses prior information to predict sensory inputs and minimize sensor errors. He admits that PP models are not bulletproof. There are some sensory errors PP models cannot explain. Clark also considers the views of nativists and empiricists regarding cognitive architecture, including the nature of such neuropathologies as depersonalization disorder, autism, and schizophrenia. *Surfing Uncertainty: Prediction,*

Action, and the Embodied Mind is an attempt to provide a framework capable of unifying cognitive phenomena and the nervous system.

Thomas Nagel, *What Is It Like to Be a Bat?*

Published in 1974, *What Is It Like to Be a Bat?* is a philosophical treatise by American philosopher Thomas Nagel. It argues that even if humans can imagine what it is like to be a bat by taking the bat's point of view, they cannot know what it is like for a bat to be a bat. Nagel raises several ideas on consciousness by using bats to differentiate between objective and subjective concepts. According to the philosopher, an organism has conscious mental states only if there is something that it is like to be that organism. Furthermore, he asserts that consciousness is not exclusive to humans because many organisms share it. In his view, subjectivity and not objectivity is feasible in humans because their mental activity is the only undeniable fact of their experience. The philosopher ends by contending that objective and subjective experiences must be characterized before physicalism can be comprehended.

Thomas Nagel, *The View from Nowhere*

Published in 1986, *The View from Nowhere,* by American philosopher Thomas Nagel, aims to contrast the active and passive standpoints through which humans interact with the world. In the first chapter, Nagel discusses the nature of the human mind and reveals the two perspectives through which humans view the world: objective standpoint and subjective standpoint. Unlike the objective standpoint, which Nagel describes as an impersonal perspective, the subjective standpoint is a person's private window to the world. With this definition in mind, Nagel postulates that the tension between both standpoints is responsible for many musings in philosophy. The philosopher then analyzes how the two standpoints affect such philosophical issues as human freedom and value, the mind and self, and the nature of reality and humans' ability to recognize reality. He argues that the two opposing standpoints influence how humans view each issue and are responsible for conflicts in society. He nevertheless concludes that these conflicts play an essential role by helping humans have a concept of themselves and the world in general.

Roger Penrose, *The Emperor's New Mind*

Published in 1989, *The Emperor's New Mind* is a book on human consciousness and artificial intelligence by the English physicist Roger Penrose. The author argues that the human mind, thinking, and consciousness can never be fully modeled or replicated by a digital computer due to the mind's non-algorithmic nature. Penrose starts the book by providing a lay interpretation of such scientific concepts as complex numbers, Turing machines, relativity, quantum physics, black holes, Hawking radiation, phase spaces, time, and Gödel's incompleteness theorem. After introducing each concept, he explains how it is related to his arguments. Although Penrose agrees that quantum mechanics is essential for understanding human consciousness, he argues that classical mechanics is more relevant for computing than quantum mechanics because it is more practical. By comparing the ridiculousness of "the Emperor's new clothes" in the children's fairytale to the "computer-driven new mind," Penrose asserts that complete artificial intelligence is impossible and that computers will never replace the human mind because they will eventually run out of relevant algorithms. In short, *The Emperor's New Mind* is a treatise on the superiority of the human mind to digital computers.

William James, *Pragmatism: A New Name for Some Old Ways of Thinking*

Pragmatism: A New Name for Some Old Ways of Thinking is a 1907 collection of eight lectures on metaphysics by William James. Here, the American philosopher makes a strong case for Pragmatism. In Lecture I, he points out the strengths and weaknesses of rationalism versus empiricism. He calls the rationalist "tender-minded" and the empiricist "tough-minded" and advocates for Pragmatism, a philosophical system that synthesizes rationalism and empiricism. In Lecture II, James defines Pragmatism as a philosophical method that relies on practical actions. He goes on in Lectures III, IV, and V to explain how to apply Pragmatism to specific problems and argues that all human thought is derived from proto-human ancestors. In Lecture VI, James addresses the Pragmatic concept of truth, arguing that the truth of an idea is dynamic rather than static. He concludes by discussing the relationship between pragmatism and religion, positing that any religion is good as long its consequences are beneficial to society.

Cordelia Fine, *Delusions of Gender: How Our Minds, Society, and Neurosexism Create Difference*

Delusions of Gender: How Our Minds, Society, and Neurosexism Create Difference is a 2010 book on gender by Canadian-born British philosopher Cordelia Fine. The text examines the nature versus nurture debate:

whether one's biological sex or social environment determines gender. Fine echoes the flaws in popular scientific belief, pointing out that gender differences are evident in variations of male and female brain structure. In the first part of the book, Fine draws on the work of fellow cultural and social psychologists to illustrate that social and environmental factors influence the mind, not the brain. Humans, according to the author, learn and observe gendered behaviors and rules and subsequently change self-perception, choose interests, and become sexist. The second and third sections explore the gaps, assumptions, inconsistencies, and methodologies used by researchers in neuroscience. The author adds that "neurosexism" sets rules and limits of gender differences and inculcates generations of children into a society organized along a gender divide. In sum, *Delusions of Gender* explores how binaries of gender difference frame development and shape experiences of families, play groups, sports, and schooling.

Philosophy of Religion

William James, *The Will to Believe*

Written in 1896 by American philosopher and psychologist William James, *The Will to Believe* is a lecture on the rationality of religious faith. In the introduction, James comments on the situation in his university, Harvard, in which freethinkers consider religious beliefs irrational because of the absence of evidence. James counters with the argument that religious faith is rational as long as it flows from one's free will. He further states that genuine religious choices must be lived, forced, and momentous. According to the philosopher, a live hypothesis is that which appeals to whom it is proposed as a real possibility. The author explores the idea that humans look up to leaders and authority figures and model their beliefs after theirs without questioning their faith in these role models. James also notes that, when presented with a genuine option, one cannot decide solely on intellectual grounds. Instead, one must consult one's passion—the will or right to believe. James further implies that, unlike empiricists, absolutists know when they have found the truth. One should continually search for the truth to overcome the weakness of absolutism, he adds, observing that a genuine option offers more gain than loss and that the will plays an essential part in how people form opinions. In addition to arguing that people base their moral opinions on a personal proof of what one wants to believe, James supports an individual's right to choose religious hypothesis, arguing that skepticism is not an avoidance of an option but a particular kind of option. He concludes that whether one chooses to believe or not, each of us is responsible for our own fate.

William James, *Varieties of Religious Experience*

The *Varieties of Religious Experience* is a compilation of edited lectures on natural theology delivered at the University of Edinburgh between 1901 and 1902 by Harvard psychologist and philosopher William James. In these lectures, James cites first-person accounts of religious experiences to examine the spiritual constitution of humans. He posits that individual religious experiences, not the dogma of organized religion, form the backbone of religious life. For this reason, the author uses people's autobiographies to describe the variety of religious experience. He contends that the visible world belongs to an unseen spiritual world and that the purpose of life is to unite with divinity. He goes on to differentiate between healthy-minded religion (which inspires a life of goodness) and the religious conviction of the sick soul (which cannot overcome the radical sense of evil in the world). In addition to stating that prayer is the conduit of spiritual energy, the author implies that religious experiences add meaning to life and increase feelings of both security and love. He adds that, even though religious experience can be irrational, it has an enduring, positive impact on individuals. Regarding mysticism, the philosopher asserts that mystical experiences are central to faith. These experiences include the ineffable, noetic, transient, and passive. James concludes that people will continue to rely on religion despite technological advancements.

Aldous Huxley, *The Perennial Philosophy*

The Perennial Philosophy is a 1945 book on the philosophy of religion by English scholar and novelist Aldous Huxley. The book is based on perennialism, a doctrine grounded in the belief that all religions originate from the same metaphysical source. The author argues that all religions are strengthened by universal beliefs. Employing Western and Eastern mysticism, Huxley cites many religious doctrines in the West (Christianity) and East (Taoism, Hinduism, Zen Buddhism, and Islamism) to examine what they all have in common. Topics discussed include truth, self-knowledge, faith, suffering, immortality, silence, perseverance, salvation, time, eternity, prayer, good and evil.

Frithjof Schuon, *The Transcendent Unity of Religions*

Published in 1948, *The Transcendent Unity of Religions* is a philosophical masterpiece on religion by the Swiss-born Frithjof Schuon. Based in perennialism, the work includes two important arguments. One is that only through spiritual oneness can religious differences be transcended. The other is that all religions point toward the same purpose, even though they may be superficially contradictory. Schuon compares many religions around the world, pointing out the similarity of transcendent experiences in all. More specifically, the author discusses the inter-relationship between Eastern religions (Islam, Buddhism, etc.) and Western religions (Christianity). He acknowledges the spiritual doctrines of diverse religions but points out what they all have in common.

Alvin Plantinga, *God and Other Minds: A Study of the Rational Justification of Belief in God*

God and Other Minds: A Study of the Rational Justification of Belief in God is a 1967 work of religious philosophy by the American scholar Alvin

Plantinga. He argues throughout that belief in God is rational, meaning a rational mind should have no problem believing in the existence of God. Plantinga explores the rationality of God's existence by reviewing traditional debates over the existence of God. While the author admits that a chronic skeptic may not accept his view, he rejects some contentions against God's existence, such as the paradox of omnipotence, the problem of free will, the problem of evil, and verificationism. In the closing section of the book, Plantinga reasons that there is no difference between belief in God and belief in other minds. According to him, if the belief in other minds is rational, the belief in God's existence is also rational. He thus uses the rationality of other minds to justify the rationality of God's existence.

Dewi Zephaniah Phillips, *Religion Without Explanation*

Published in 1976, *Religion Without Explanation,* by Welsh philosopher Dewi Zephaniah Phillips, contends that the philosophy of religion should not be concerned about whether God exists but should study the notions of reality involved in religion. In his view, trying to justify the rationality of God's existence is absurd. He argues in favor of exploring the non-rational basis for religious beliefs.

Richard Swinburne, *The Existence of God*

The Existence of God is a 1979 book by English philosopher Richard Swinburne. Does God exist? This is the question Swinburne seeks to answer. After examining the laws of nature, the occurrence of human consciousness, religious miracles, and the nature of the universe, the author reasons that it is more probable that God exists. He admits that arguments in favor of these examinations are not valid deductively, yet he argues that they are valid inductively. Swinburne's main argument is that the existence of human evolution, religious miracles, and natural laws are sufficient to justify the belief in the existence of God.

William Lane Craig, *The Kalam Cosmological Argument*

The Kalam Cosmological Argument is a 1979 book by British scholar William Lane Craig that offers a cosmological argument for the existence of God. Craig infers that the existence of causation or the events in the universe is sufficient to justify the existence of God. Central to his argument is the assumption that there is always something rather than nothing and that there must be God to explain causation and the events in the universe. His argument goes like this: (1) Everything that exists is caused by something; (2) the universe exists; (3) therefore, the universe is caused by something. Craig reasons that this cause can be used to infer the existence of God.

Alvin Plantinga, *Is Belief in God Properly Basic?*

Is Belief in God Properly Basic? is a 1981 book by American scholar Alvin Plantinga. He counters the arguments against the rationality of religious doctrines, arguing that God's existence can be justified without the use of any external evidence. More specifically, the author rejects evidentialism, the view that theistic belief is rationally acceptable as long as there is compelling evidence for it. There is no way, Plantinga contends, critics can justify the defectiveness of religion epistemologically. After exploring evidentialist objections and the criteria for proper basicality, Plantinga concludes that one does not even need to rely on the senses to conclude that the belief in God is properly basic. This philosophical work offers an alternative to the view that religious beliefs must be supported by evidence.

Jean-Luc Marion, *God Without Being*

Published in 1982, *God Without Being,* by French philosopher Jean-Luc Marion, argues against the premises of traditional metaphysics, which assume that God predates all things. To be more specific, Marion argues that God does not exist before everything else. The author asks his readers to view God as love. According to him, if God is love, that means that God perceived love before he became love. Overall, Marion reasons that to understand God, one should think of God outside the realm of "Being."

John Leslie Mackie, *The Miracle of Theism: Arguments for and against the Existence of God*

The Miracle of Theism: Arguments for and against the Existence of God is a 1982 work on the philosophy of religion by John Leslie Mackie. Mackie presents, from a rational perspective, the arguments against and for God's existence. On the one hand, he thinks that arguments for the existence or non-existence of God cannot be justified deductively. On the other hand, the author believes that God's existence can be inductively proved to be more probable. Topics discussed include Descartes' idea of God, Berkeley's God, cosmological and moral arguments for God's existence, and the replacement of God.

John Hick, *An Interpretation of Religion: Human Responses to the Transcendent*

Published in 1989, *An Interpretation of Religion: Human Responses to the Transcendent,* by British-born philosopher John Hick, begins by explaining the nature of religion and how diverse religions can be understood from different perspectives. In addition to pointing out the similarities and differences between major religions around the world, the author contends that the ambiguity of the universe can be understood through the lens of religion. This book explores religious pluralism.

William Alston, *Perceiving God*

Authored in 1991 by philosopher William Alston, *Perceiving God* is a masterpiece in the philosophy of religion. The central theme is an argument that non-sensory experiences of God are essential to justifying religious beliefs. Alston begins by suggesting that the perception of God is a real possibility. He calls this mode of perception "mystical perception," a presentation or appearance of something that the person identifies as God. After explaining what the perception of God means, the writer explores several claims of direct awareness of God as a basis for genuine experiential cognition of God. The philosopher then explores whether mystical perception is a reliable source of beliefs about divine manifestations. Alston further examines the reliability of sense perception compared to mystical perception. He later discusses the Christian Mystical Perceptual Doxastic practice (CMP), a belief based on perceptual experience. In the last part of the book, Alston addresses the issue of religious diversity and non-Christian views on mystical perception and sense perception, as well as indicating how mystical perception is related to the direct perceptions of God. The treatise is an epistemological account of religious experience.

John L. Schellenberg, *Divine Hiddenness and Human Reason*

Divine Hiddenness and Human Reason is a 1993 philosophical text by John L. Schellenberg. Why is the existence of God not obvious to non-believers if truly God exists? This is the question Schellenberg attempts to answer in this book. The author believes that the argument for atheism is compelling because God's moral character is questionable. Schellenberg observes that theists are fond of saying that the proof of God's existence is weak because God is hidden. Yet he reasons that if God's moral character were as pure as claimed by theists, God should not have obscured the fact of his existence from humans. Schellenberg defends his views against such theists as Hick, Kierkegaard, Butler, and Pascal.

William Leonard Rowe, *The Evidential Argument from Evil: A Second Look*

The Evidential Argument from Evil: A Second Look is a 1996 book on the philosophy of religion by William Leonard Rowe, an American philosopher. The book explores the evidential argument from evil, which is grounded in the belief that the presence or absence of evil can be inductively used to prove or disprove God's existence. Rowe addresses the argument that if God truly exists, He should not have permitted evil to exist. He also addresses the contention that the biological role of pain and pleasure can be better explained with hypotheses unaffiliated with theism.

Jay Lazar Garfield, *Empty Words: Buddhist Philosophy and Cross-Cultural Interpretation*

Published in 2001, *Empty Words: Buddhist Philosophy and Cross-Cultural Interpretation* comprises fourteen essays on Buddhist philosophy by Jay Lazar Garfield. He interprets Madhyamaka and its connections with Yogācāra from several perspectives, such as causality and skepticism. In addition, he explores the work of other philosophers on Buddhism. Garfield's main argument is two-fold. First, that Sthiramati and Vasubandhu are idealists and, second, that Madhyamaka and Yogācāra are not the same philosophical systems.

Keith Yandell, *Philosophy of Religion: A Contemporary Introduction*

Philosophy of Religion: A Contemporary Introduction is a 2002 philosophical text on religion by Keith Yandell. The work endeavors to explain the meaning of philosophy and religion, the connection between religion and philosophy, the importance of religious doctrines and traditions, and arguments concerning monotheistic conceptions. Yandell points out several central and emerging issues in the philosophy of religion. These include religious pluralism, the problem of evil, evidentialist moral theism, the nature of faith and reasons, and ontological and cosmological arguments. The author provides guidance on analyzing key viewpoints in Islam, Christianity, Buddhism, Hinduisms, Judaism, and Jainism.

Philosophy of Science

William Whewell, *The Philosophy of the Inductive Sciences: Founded upon their History*

Published in two volumes in 1840, *The Philosophy of the Inductive Sciences: Founded upon their History* by the English mathematician William Whewell covers topics including mechanical sciences, classificatory sciences, and pure sciences. Volume 2 focuses on the nature of knowledge and how to obtain it. According to the English mathematician, knowledge has three main dimensions: ideal dimension, objective dimension, and subjective dimension. He further reasons that knowledge consists of two opposed forms: ideas and perceptions. In the second volume, the writer criticizes several philosophers (Immanuel Kant, John Locke, and other German idealists) for their exclusive focus on a few dimensions of knowledge. Whewell goes on to discuss his inductive theory and how it can be used to discover causal, natural, and phenomenal laws.

William Stanley Jevons, *The Principles of Science: A Treatise on Logic and Scientific Method*

Published in 1984, *The Principles of Science: A Treatise on Logic and Scientific Method,* by the English scholar William Stanley Jevons, is devoted to the methods of science and discusses the nature and application of inductive and deductive investigations. Jevons covers several such topics as logic, propositions, deductive reasoning, inferences, hypotheses, units and standards, the phenomena of nature, and the theory of probability. He also discusses the Fundamental Laws of Thought, the Principle of Substitution, and the Inverse Method of Probabilities. Using the theory of probability and formal logic, Jevons reasons that no inductive method is distinct or perfect and that the science of numbers originates from the science of logic. An important part of inductive inquiries is the hypothetical anticipation of nature, Jevons asserts. He goes on to address misconceptions about logic and argues that the theory of probability is crucial to logical development.

Charles Sanders Peirce, *Illustrations of the Logic of Science*

Published in 1877, *Illustrations of the Logic of Science*, by American mathematician and philosopher Charles Sanders Peirce, consists of two parts. The title of the first part is "The Fixation of Belief," while the title of the second part is "How to Make Our Ideas Clear."

In the first part, Peirce argues that scientific methods are superior to other methods of seeking knowledge. In the second, he contends that concepts of ideas should be pragmatically clear in fixing belief. Peirce argues that logic derives its theories and principles from mathematics, ethics, and phenomenology and that epistemology and metaphysics draw their principles from logic. A good scientific method, according to him, should not only be effective but also efficient. Overall, *Illustrations of the Logic of Science* presents Peirce's notion of how science should be investigated.

Henri Poincaré, *Science and Hypothesis*
Science and Hypothesis, published in 1902, focuses on nature, physics, space, and mathematics. Its thesis is that absolute scientific truth is impossible to attain. The French mathematician argues that most scientists stick to certain theories not because the theories are the best, but because they are the most convenient options available. He defends his argument by describing questions related to Brownian motion, the photoelectric effect, and the relativity of physical laws in space. Topics covered include thermodynamics, probabilities, electricity, space, geometry, space, numbers, magnitude, and their relationships with other scientific variables.

Hermann Weyl, *Philosophy of Mathematics and Natural Science*
Published in 1949, *Philosophy of Mathematics and Natural Science,* by the German mathematician Hermann Weyl, is divided into two sections, the first section focusing on topics in mathematics, such as logic, numbers, and geometry, the second devoted to issues in physical science, such as space and time, methodology, and the physical picture of the world. Weyl draws on the ideas of previous philosophers (such as Newton, Leibniz, Hume, Galileo, and Kant) to point out the relevance of scientific discoveries, to highlight the challenges of science, and to provide a general account of science through a philosophical lens.

Otto Neurath, *Physicalism: The Philosophy of the Viennese Circle*
Published in 1931, *Physicalism: The Philosophy of the Viennese Circle,* by Austrian scholar Otto Neurath, contends that no science can be exact without being tested. By testing and criticizing scientific methods, Neurath reasons, science progresses and generates more knowledge. Neurath argues that human knowledge is influenced by the senses. He further posits that an independent system of fixed doctrines can no longer be used to explore philosophy. According to Neurath, no scientific theory is perfect. Better

new theories have continued (and will continue) to replace weak existing theories. After commending members of the Viennese Circle for seeking scientific truth, Neurath concludes that philosophical speculations or any methods "devoid of sense" should be eliminated from scientific inquiries.

John Dewey, *Logic: The Theory of Inquiry*

Logic: The Theory of Inquiry was written in 1938 by American thinker John Dewey. It presents a general account of logic and the nature of the logic theory as developed in Dewey's earlier *Studies in Logical Theory*. The author analyzes the process of inquiry and how to use inquiry in making decisions. He also draws attention to the continuum of inquiry, the theory of propositions, the construction of judgments, the logic of scientific method, universal propositions, and its connection with generalization. In the book, there are chapters on sociology, biology, mathematics, and culture. *Logic: The Theory of Inquiry,* in short, covers the pragmatic use of logic.

Steven Shapin and Simon Schaffer, *Leviathan and the Air-Pump: Hobbes, Boyle, and the Experimental Life*

Published in 1985, *Leviathan and the Air-Pump: Hobbes, Boyle, and the Experimental Life* is a book by American professors Steven Shapin and Simon Schaffer that critically analyzes the debates between Thomas Hobbes and Robert Boyle. Boyle believed that experiments and observation are the best methods for science, politics, and natural philosophy, and he clarified his assertions with the air-pump experiments. Hobbes, however, argues that deduction and other forms of reasons are more valid than observation. In his view, observation excludes metaphysics and cannot account for several philosophical theories. Shapin and Schaffer go on to examine Hobbes's philosophical critique of Boyle and other scientists. They also scrutinize Boyle's rebuttal to Hobbes's criticism, pointing out the connection between the history of scientific thought and the history of political thought. The authors conclude that politics and science are, in fact, inseparable.

Edward Osborne Wilson, *Consilience: The Unity of Knowledge*

Published in 1998, *Consilience: The Unity of Knowledge,* by Edward Osborne Wilson, an American biologist, examines possible methods that may be used to reconcile the sciences and the humanities. Wilson defines consilience as the synthesis of knowledge from various specialized fields to form a common explanatory framework. He analyzes how sciences and humanities deviate from each other. The writer emphasizes that sciences, arts, and humanities all share the same common goal. Wilson believes that this common goal should be to solidify the theory that humans live in an orderly world that can be explained through natural laws. The scholar asserts that evolution and human nature affect culture, thereby building up a sociobiological effect. Wilson also points out various examples of consilience that merge science and the humanities. *Consilience: The Unity of Knowledge* endeavors to unify knowledge by reconciling knowledge derived from the sciences with knowledge from the humanities.

Roland Omnès, *Quantum Philosophy: Understanding and Interpreting Contemporary Science*

Published in 2002, *Quantum Philosophy: Understanding and Interpreting Contemporary Science*, by the American scientist Roland Omnès, explains how developments in quantum mechanics have altered humanity's commonsense view of the world. In the author's estimation, modern science has strayed far away from common sense in pursuit of mirroring the physical world. The scholar argues for practicality in reconciling contemporary science with human commonsense needs. He starts the four-section book by reviewing the history of epistemology, science, and mathematics up to the present. In the second section, he studies the adoption of formalism in mathematics and physical science. The third section is devoted to how humans can recover common sense from developmental theories in quantum mechanics. In the final section, Omnès concludes by reflecting on what the future of science holds for humans.

Karl Pearson, *The Grammar of Science*

Published in 1892, t*he Grammar of Science* was written by American mathematician Karl Pearson, who covers such scientific concepts as antimatter, the ether, physics, energy, the relativity of motion, and more. The scientist argues that science can verify truth in every field of knowledge. He asserts that science and philosophy are inseparable. Pearson evaluates the features of the scientific process and methods. The writer also appraises the facts of science, the scientific law, civil law, cause and effect probability, correlation and contingency causation, space and time, the geometry of motion, the laws of motion, matter, and modern physical ideas. In the latter part of the book, Pearson discusses the future of science and its application to philosophy. *The Grammar of Science* covers the foundational principles of science and its relevance to philosophy.

Henri Poincaré, *The Value of Science*

Authored in 1905 by French philosopher Henri Poincaré, *The Value of Science* is a philosophical treatise that discusses issues in the philosophy of science. The book is comprised of two sections. The first considers the mathematical sciences, especially the mathematical relationship between logic and intuition. The author proposes that there is a primary relationship between the sciences of analysis and geometry. He argues that intuition allows one to choose between both sciences in search of truth and to understand logical developments. He then goes on to distinguish between the three types of intuition: generalization by induction, intuition of pure number, and an appeal to sense and imagination. In the second section, Poincaré analyzes the links between mathematics and physics. He explains further in this section that the disciplines are interdependent because they are of the same aesthetic and because they share a common goal. In addition, the writer believes that mathematics and physics can liberate humans from their ordinary existence. Poincaré concludes by proposing that science focus mainly on the development of a mathematical language, which can offer useful predictions.

Rudolf Carnap, *Logical Foundations of Probability*

Logical Foundations of Probability is a 1950 book by German-American scholar Rudolf Carnap, which focuses on problems related to the nature of probability and inductive reasoning. Carnap begins the first volume of the work with an explanation of the challenge of explication and the nature of deductive logic. After that, he explains the logical concept of induction and probability in detail. More specifically, Carnap explains the fundamentals of inductive logic as well as binomial law and the theorem of Bayes and Bernoulli. In the second volume of the book, the writer presents a new technique for approaching the challenges of induction and probability. The technique relies on four key assumptions. The first assumption is that all inductive reasoning is the same thing as reasoning in terms of probability. The second assumption is that inductive logic is the same thing as probability logic. The third assumption is that probability concepts based on inductive logic refer to the logic relation between two propositions or premises. The fourth assumption is that all theories of logic are analytical in nature. The goal of this technique, according to Carnap, is to construct a system of inductive logic that can prove several theorems related to qualitative concepts of relevance, confirmation, and irrelevance. At the end of the book, Carnap offers some solutions to the problems of inductive logic.

Hans Reichenbach, *The Rise of Scientific Philosophy*

The Rise of Scientific Philosophy is a 1951 book by German scholar Hans Reichenbach devoted to a new approach to philosophy. The author compares speculative philosophy and scientific philosophy. He rejects the former and contends that philosophy should be treated not as a collection of speculation but as an investigation of problems. According to him, philosophy should be science-based or evidence-based, and it should help provide irrefutable answers to problems. Reichenbach further explores the causes of what he counts as the failure of philosophy. His analysis reveals that this failure can be traced to psychological causes. In his view, many speculative philosophers resorted to pseudo-science provided false answers to philosophical problems before scholars like Kant, Descartes, and Plato revealed how to acquire knowledge. Reichenbach provides answers to the problems of time, space, life, and causality. He supports his new approach to philosophy, which relies on scientific methodology, with natural laws, atomic theory, inductive inference, symbolic logic, and geometry in what is an attempt to explain the flaws of speculative philosophy and the benefits of scientific philosophy.

Stephen Toulmin, *The Philosophy of Science: An Introduction*

Published in 1953, *The Philosophy of Science: An Introduction*, by British scholar Stephen Toulmin, provides a layperson's explanation of the philosophy of science. Toulmin clarifies the nature, meaning, and logical basis of scientific theory. He specifically focuses on the theories of physics and the nature of logic as well as their relevance to modern science. Toulmin also draws attention to questions, arguments, and problems left unaddressed by philosophers. Topics include Laws of Nature, Uniformity and Determinism, Theories and Maps, and Induction. *The Philosophy of Science: An Introduction* covers the fundamentals of the philosophy of science.

Nelson Goodman, *Fact, Fiction, and Forecast*

Published in 1955, *Fact, Fiction, and Forecast* is a philosophical masterpiece by American philosopher by Nelson Goodman. The author examines problems with induction, counterfactual conditionals, and some scientific laws. After examining David Hume's problem of induction, Goodman introduces the New Riddle of Induction, which postulates that predicates are unusual as their application is time-dependent. He conceptualizes the time-dependent "grue" and "bleen" to illustrate the difference between hypotheses that apply to only one thing, and hypotheses that apply to everything in a class.

Following this, the writer argues that "anything can confirm anything." Goodman also distinguishes between warranted generalizations and unwarranted generalizations. He concludes that ordinary learning and scientific induction cannot take place without a priori ordering of a hypothesis. *Fact, Fiction, and Forecast* explains the theories of induction in details.

Michael Polanyi, *Personal Knowledge: Towards a Post-critical Philosophy*

Personal Knowledge: Towards a Post-critical Philosophy is a 1958 treatise on the philosophy of science by Hungarian-British philosopher Michael Polanyi, who explores the nature of knowledge and the justification of scientific knowledge. The work is divided into four sections. In the first, Polanyi discusses the human ability to acquire knowledge. He uses the Copernican revolution, the stories of several scholars—Pythagoras, Galileo, and Kepler—and Einstein's theories of relativity to explain the development of scientific theories. In the second section, Polanyi focuses on the tacit components of personal knowledge. He specifically focuses on the role of articulation, intellectual passions, and conviviality in knowledge acquisition. In the third section, Polanyi seeks to justify knowledge using the logic of affirmation, the critique of doubt, and the nature of commitment. The last section is devoted to knowing and being. Topics covered include the logic of human achievement, the act of knowing the meaning of life, and the rise of man. Polanyi ends the book with a discussion of first causes and ultimate ends.

Karl Popper, *The Logic of Scientific Discovery*

Published in 1959, *The Logic of Scientific Discovery,* by Karl Popper, the German philosopher, argues that scientific methodologies should focus on falsifiability because experiments are insufficient proof of the validity of a scientific theory. Observations and experiments are sufficient to disprove a scientific theory, Popper contends. Furthermore, he calls for a balance between falsifiability and verifiability, adding that only the logical form of universal statements can obtain this balance. The philosopher then asserts that, while scientific theories can be contradicted by singular statements, they cannot be derived from singular statements. Popper goes on to reject inductive logic, condemns logical positivism, and emphasizes that positivist conceptions destroy science with their unreasonable verification principle. In his view, a few vague statements refuting a scientific theory are insufficient to disprove the theory. *The Logic of Scientific Discovery* advocates for the revalidation of scientific theories using falsifiability.

Mario Bunge, *Treatise on Basic Philosophy*

Treatise on Basic Philosophy is an eight-volume collection of books by Argentine scholar Mario Bunge published between 1974 and 1989. The first two volumes focus on semantics, while the third and the fourth cover topics on ontology. The fifth, sixth, and seventh volumes are mainly concerned with issues on epistemology. In the eighth and final volume, Bunge discusses ethical topics such as metatheory, morality and action, truth, and value.

Michael Friedman, *Explanation and Scientific Understanding*

Explanation and Scientific Understanding is a 1974 book by American philosopher Michael Friedman that delivers the author's views on scientific explanation. Friedman explains the relation between phenomena and the unification of phenomena. According to him, a good scientific explanation should not only be objective but also easy to understand. He rejects the notion that science is incapable of explaining certain things, arguing instead that the concepts used by science to explain the apparently inexplicable are simply improperly understood. Central to this argument is that the unification of diverse phenomena is essential to understanding science. In his view, law X can explain laws Y_1, Y_2, and Y_n if law X can unify all the laws of Y. Friedman draws on philosophical literature to defend the unifying effect of scientific theories. He goes on to argue for his concept of independent acceptability, arguing that, even though a sentence is equal to other groups of independent n sentences, one sentence can be acceptable independently of other sentences. He concludes by asserting that scientific explanation is a global affair, meaning science can only be explained with a more comprehensive explanation of phenomena.

Rudolf Carnap, *Meaning and Necessity: A Study in Semantics and Modal Logic*

Published in 1947, *Meaning and Necessity: A Study in Semantics and Modal Logic* is a book by German-American philosopher Rudolf Carnap. Carnap's book focuses on the nature of expressions in linguistics as he aims to develop a new system for the semantic examination of meaning. This system, which he calls the method of extension and intension, is based on the extension and modification of such concepts as property and class. Apart from analyzing the concept of meaning, the philosopher also expounds on modal logic. Subsequently, he coins the term "state-description" to refer to a set of atomic sentences and their negations.

John Stuart Mill, *A System of Logic*

A System of Logic, published in 1843, is a philosophical masterpiece by English philosopher John Stuart Mill. Divided into books, the work covers the principles of inductive arguments and how they can be applied to political and moral philosophies. In Book I, Mill defines logic as a system or method of proof that involves an assertion that must be verified. The author then proceeds to analyze concepts such as the nature of predicates, action and volition, body, relation, attribute and substance, states of consciousness, attributes of mind, quality, resemblance, and mind. Book II examines the role of logic in the field of knowledge. In this section, Mills does not restrict logic to a particular structure. Rather, he includes logic with different fields of knowledge and science. Book III covers the introduction of Mill's inductive method. An inductive inquiry, in his view, starts with analyzing objects according to their elements. The writer also distinguishes between compound and complex effects in this section. In Book IV, Mill calls for a philosophical language that could enable one to correctly survey, document, and communicate their findings. In Book V, the writer discusses numerous logical fallacies and provides ways of resolving them. Overall, the treatise examines the formulation of a type of logic that draws its principles from natural sciences.

Ernest Nagel, *The Structure of Science*

Authored by Ernest Nagel, *The Structure of Science* is a philosophical treatise published in 1961. Nagel analyzes the function of reduction in scientific hypotheses, the nature of explanation, the rational structure of the arrangement of scientific knowledge, and the logic of scientific inquiry. He also discusses the various branches of social sciences and natural sciences and how they affect scientific inquiry. In addition to studying the links between wholes and their parts, the author further evaluates the ideologies of philosophers of science such as Isaiah Berlin and Henri Poincaré. In sum, the book examines the nature of scientific inquiry using both the social sciences and the natural sciences as references.

Thomas Kuhn, *The Structure of Scientific Revolutions*

The Structure of Scientific Revolutions is a masterpiece published in 1962 by American philosopher Thomas Kuhn. The text is devoted to the history of science and the philosophy of scientific knowledge. According to Kuhn, scientific innovations do not always come from accumulated knowledge. The breakthroughs, Kuhn argues, create scientific revolutions that disrupt the status quo and challenge popularly held scientific theories, facts, and models. In his view, periods of revolutionary science disrupt periods of regular or normal science. Kuhn analyzes such revolutionary scientific concepts and innovations as John Dalton's atomic theory, Galileo's law of gravity, Kepler's laws of planetary motion, and the Copernican Revolution. Following his analysis of scientific history, the author coins the term "paradigm shift," which refers to a scientific revolution or radical change in the practices and concepts of a scientific field. *The Structure of Scientific Revolutions* conceptualizes the development of radical shifts, differentiating these from the incremental increase of knowledge that is the scientific norm.

Carl Gustav Hempel, *Aspects of Scientific Explanation*

Published in 1965, *Aspects of Scientific Explanation* is a philosophical book by German scholar Carl Gustav Hempel, who argues that the logic of explanation in the natural sciences and the logic of explanation in the arts are the same. Hempel defines the scientific explanation of a fact as a deduction of an explanandum, a statement that describes the fact being explained. He names the premises to a fact "explanans" and asserts that the explanans of a fact must be true for the explanation to be acceptable. After that, Hempel derives the deductive-nomological model, according to which the explanation of a fact depends on the logical relationship between statements. The philosopher goes on to argue that fundamental theories in science are true statements with unremovable quantifiers. Furthermore, he contends that generalized statements that result from fundamental theories are derived theories. In sum, *Aspects of Scientific Explanation* analyzes explanations, statements, facts, and theories in science.

Bas C. Van Fraassen, *The Scientific Image*

Published in 1980, *The Scientific Image,* by Dutch scientist Bas C. Van Fraassen, posits that the language of science is literal, not metaphoric. The author calls for an alternative to scientific realism and logical positivism and further argues for an agnostic view on the reality of unobservable entities. Van Frassen reasons that philosophers could be scientific empiricists without becoming logical positivists. He rejects metaphysical interference in science, yet he believes that science should do away with findings that are based excessively on theories. In his view, science should not aim at mirroring the physical world. Rather, it should focus on empirically adequate theories. *The Scientific Image* calls for a balance between logical positivism and scientific realism in science.

Roy Bhaskar, *A Realist Theory of Science*

A Realist Theory of Science, a 1975 book by English philosopher Roy Bhaskar, consists of four chapters devoted to what Bhaskar calls critical realism, a new alternative to positivism. The writer begins by rejecting positivism, calling it obsolete, inefficient and ineffective in addressing the problems of philosophy. According to him, the positivist conception should never be allowed to return to science. Bhaskar proposes critical realism not only to provide a new systematic account of science but also to explain how scientific laws should be developed. Central to this argument is that without a realist philosophy of science, one cannot make sense of science. To support his argument further, Bhaskar explores such philosophical topics as the two sides of knowledge, the nature of perception, the concept of closure, the problem of universals, the problem of induction, and the logic of scientific discovery.

Larry Laudan, *Progress and its Problems: Towards a Theory of Scientific Growth*

Published in 1978, *Progress and its Problems: Towards a Theory of Scientific Growth,* by American scholar Larry Laudan, is a critical review of the history and development of scientific theories. Laudan observes that science is a unique problem activity, in which new problems are generated in the effort to solve existing problems. Using historical counterexamples, the American philosopher rejects traditional research views. He calls for the replacement of traditional research methods with a scientific model that draws its strength from rationality and pragmatic progress. Laudan criticizes the shift of scientific theories toward relativism and investigates the problems of scientific-theory evaluation. In his view, a good scientific theory should be not only effective but also efficient. The concludes with a defense of rationality in scientific growth.

David Kellogg Lewis, *How to Define Theoretical Terms*

How to Define Theoretical Terms is a 1979 philosophical book on science by American scholar David Kellogg Lewis. As suggested by its title, the work explores the nature of defining terms. More specifically, Lewis argues that there is a general technique for defining newly introduced terms in a definition. He rejects the independent use of bridge laws in reducing one scientific theory to another. He also analyzes F. K. Ramsey's proposal (The sentence of a theory [T] says a theory [T] is realized) and Rudolf Carnap's proposal (if a theory [T] is realized, then a theory [T] is true), pointing out the flaws and strengths of their arguments. In his opinion, neither proposal is attractive, and he proposes a new model that eliminates theoretical terms and combines Ramsey's and Carnap's proposals.

Mark W. Wartofsky, *Models: Representation and the Scientific Understanding*

Published in 1979, *Models: Representation and the Scientific Understanding,* by American philosopher Marx W. Wartofsky, offers a confluence of ideas on several topics on the philosophy of science. Some of the issues covered include metaphysics as a heuristic for science, reduction and ontology, the nature of scientific realism, and the vagaries of empiricism.

Carolyn Merchant, *The Death of Nature: Women, Ecology, and the Scientific Revolution*

The Death of Nature: Women, Ecology, and the Scientific Revolution is a 1980 book by American philosopher Carolyn Merchant. In it, she explores the emergence of modern science from the perspective of ecology and feminism, arguing that women have been unjustly dominated and exploited by men since the seventeenth century, when men started using scientific knowledge to plunder the resources of the earth. She also contends that the ecological crises in the world today can be traced to the blatant plundering of natural resources by men throughout history. Merchant also responds to some philosophers' arguments, especially the views of Francis Bacon, who argues in *The Death of Nature* that nature should be tamed, controlled, and exploited. In sum, Merchant concludes that animal torture is wrong and unethical and that even Bacon (if alive today) would reject his own simple but far-reaching rhetoric, which allows animals to be tortured when performing experiments.

Wesley Charles Salmon, *Scientific Explanation and the Causal Structure of the World*

Published in 1984, *Scientific Explanation and the Causal Structure of the World* is a book on the philosophy of science by American scholar Wesley Charles Salmon. In proposing a new method of addressing causal relations, Salmon provides three concepts of scientific explanations: ontic, modal, and epistemic. The author supports the reality of things that cannot be observed, contending that the existing concept of epistemology is obsolete, ineffective, and inefficient. He goes on to discuss statistical relevance relations, defending a causal theory of conception and offering a new account of physical randomness. In his view, a scientific concept can be better explained by fitting it into the causal nexus of the world. Salmon also emphasizes the nature and benefit of "interventionist counterfactuals" in distinguishing causal relations from non-causal relations. *Scientific Explanation and the Causal Structure of the World* elaborates on an ontic perspective regarding causal explanations.

Ronald Giere, *Explaining Science: A Cognitive Approach*

Published in 1988, *Explaining Science: A Cognitive Approach,* by American scholar Ronald Giere, concerns what a unified cognitive theory of science should be. Giere's aim here is to provide a cognitive approach to scientific inquiry by exploring theories of science, scientific judgment, constructive realism, and the revolution in geology. According to him, the existing accounts of science have some shortcomings that need to be fixed. The writer argues that the development of science should be considered as a "natural evolutionary process" based on the mechanisms of judgment and representation. He challenges some traditional philosophical views on sociology and science and criticizes the scientific realism inherent in sociology. Giere outlines his objections to the universal generalizations of scientific theories based on intuited principles of rationality and proposes a scientific framework to explain how scientists can use their cognitive capacities to acquire knowledge. In concluding the book, Giere recommends that all scientific theories be based on the cognitive preferences of their authors, not on Enlightenment ideals of rationality and empiricism.

David Hull, *Science as a Process: An Evolutionary Account of the Social and Conceptual Development of Science*

Authored by American philosopher David Hull, *Science as a Process: An Evolutionary Account of the Social and Conceptual Development of Science* attempts to provide an account of and an evolutionary framework for both conceptual change and social change. Hull asserts that a theory of selection processes can explain not only biological evolution but also the growth and development of scientific ideas. He begins with a historical account of systematics and then explains how interactions among scientists engender conceptual change. He reasons that science is a force of progress and that scientific theories must compete with one another to gain public recognition or public acceptance or both.

Paul Thagard, *Computational Philosophy of Science*

Written by Canadian philosopher Paul Thagard in 1988, *Computational Philosophy of Science* discusses the application of computational models of scientific thinking to the challenges of philosophy. More specifically, Thagard applies AI (artificial intelligence) and cognitive psychology to philosophical problems in science. He also discusses how scientific thinking is applied in science and how it ought to be applied to scientific problems. Using computational knowledge to draw insights into the development of scientific theories, Thagard provides a rich and interesting alternative to scientific reasoning based on formal logic. He also expatiates on the theory of justification, the progress of inquiry, theory evaluation, analogy, hypothesis formation, and the nature of concepts. In the last few chapters of the book, Thagard applies his knowledge of scientific reasoning to particular fields of AI and psychology.

Helen Longino, *Science as Social Knowledge: Values and Objectivity in Scientific Inquiry*

Science as Social Knowledge: Values and Objectivity in Scientific Inquiry is a 1990 work by American scholar Helen Longino, which addresses the objectivity and subjectivity of scientific research. Longino reasons that being objective or non-biased cannot alone account for scientific methodology. In her view, social and cultural influences shape the outcome of scientific inquiries. The author develops a framework called "conceptual empiricism" to analyze the views of social and methodologist critics of science. She also examines theories of prenatal hormonal determination and human evolution to prove that assumptions influenced by social values affect the outcome of scientific research. Drawing on the works of other philosophers, Longino concludes by discussing the relations among science, ideology, and values.

Peter Achinstein, *Particles and Waves: Historical Essays in the Philosophy of Science*

Published in 1991, *Particles and Waves: Historical Essays in the Philosophy of Science* is a collection of essays by American scholar Peter Achinstein concerning the nature of philosophical problems related to such non-observable entities as particles, electrons, molecules and light waves. Achinstein's aim is to explore how to verify scientific hypotheses of non-observable entities. Drawing on the works of such prominent scientists in the eighteenth and nineteenth centuries, including Isaac Newton, James Clerk Maxwell, and J.J. Thompson, he analyzes various scientific methodologies used in studying non-observable entities, such as inductivism, hypothetico-deductivism, and a method that combines the features of both. The author later proposes his scientific solution for observing unobservable entities and devotes the remainder of the book to defending it.

Lorraine Code, *What Can She Know? Feminist Theory and the Construction of Knowledge*

Written by Canadian scholar Lorraine Code, *What Can She Know? Feminist Theory and the Construction of Knowledge* is a 1991 book on the philosophy of science. Code seeks to answer the question of whether the sex of a person is epistemologically significant. She first reviews several previous works on epistemology, pointing out assumptions and flaws in the epistemological literature. From here, the writer discusses the relation among autonomy, objectivity, and subjectivity in scientific inquiry. She also highlights the relevance and characteristics of individuals involved in knowing, including their social status and their way of life. Code goes on to examine how knowing (knowledge) can shape the minds of the knower and the known, and she assess the function of knowledge in influencing institutions in society with an eye toward distinguishing what counts as knowledge and what does not. Overall, the book explores the nature of knowledge in relation to the gender of the knower.

Sandra Harding, *Whose Science? Whose Knowledge? Thinking from Women's Lives*

Whose Science? Whose Knowledge? Thinking from Women's Lives, by Sandra Harding, an American philosopher, offers a compelling analysis of feminist theories on epistemological problems. In Part I, Harding talks about the social bases of the philosophy of science. In Part II, she analyzes many philosophical issues relating to feminism pointed out by feminist philosophers, such as masculine biases, the domination of women, and the abuse of women's rights. After examining, in Part III, how feminists, lesbians, gays, people of color, and other minority groups in society are affected by straight men's accounts of what knowledge should be, Harding concludes by suggesting that the perspective of the dominant groups should not be the only version that determines the direction, exploration, and application of knowledge.

Paul Thagard, *Conceptual Revolutions*

Written in 1992 by Canadian philosopher Paul Thagard, *Conceptual Revolutions* explores the nature, dynamics, and evolution of conceptual change. Thagard explains what concepts are, their purpose, conceptual hierarchies, and theories of conceptual revolutions. The philosopher contends that conceptual change is not just about the revision of beliefs, and he argues that questions central to cognitive psychology are also invaluable in epistemology. He summarizes the psychological roles of conceptual changes and analyses contemporary ideas of what constitutes concepts. Thagard proposes a framework of concept as computational structures. This proposal reveals that conceptual changes can occur in many different forms, some of which may require the reorganization of the concepts. Other topics in the book include conceptual changes in children and scientists, dynamic relations of theories and revolutions in psychology, physics, geology, and biology. This book is an exploration of the fundamental aspects of conceptual change.

John Dupré, *The Disorder of Things: Metaphysical Foundations of the Disunity of Science*

Published in 1993, *The Disorder of Things: Metaphysical Foundations of the Disunity of Science* is a book by British scholar John Dupré. At its core is the writer's disbelief in the notion of a general scientific formula, method, attitude, or process. Dupré points out three major components of the mechanistic ideas of modern science: materialistic reductionism, causal determinism, and essentialism. He criticizes the mechanistic ideals of modern science, arguing that the assumptions of these ideals is incompatible with the conclusions of science. Dupré goes on to provide a metaphysical explanation of science in relation to the world, pointing out that the more science is fragmented and diversified, the more knowledge will be united. He believes that the world is far more complex than we believe, meaning it is impossible to unite science. The book analyzes the disunity of science and offers several arguments against the notion that science can be united.

Deborah Mayo, *Error and the Growth of Experimental Knowledge*

Error and the Growth of Experimental Knowledge is a 1996 book by American philosopher Deborah Mayo. It explores the nature and development of experimental knowledge, focusing on Bayesian and Neyman-Pearson views of statistical inference. Mayo begins by asserting that, while part of the purpose of experimental knowledge is to learn from mistakes, humans have not learned enough from their blunders. She talks about several models of experimental inquiry and the experimental bases to test hypotheses. She points out the flaws in Bayesian inference, explains why one cannot be more Bayesian, and discusses her reformulation of Neyman-Pearson statistics as a formidable alternative to Bayesian methodologies. The author calls the reinterpretation approach the "error statistical account."

John Ziman, *Real Science: What it Is, and What it Means*

Real Science: What it Is, and What it Means was written in 2000 by John Ziman, a British scholar. It describes how experimental studies are carried out and how experimental outcomes are obtained. Ziman covers several topics on the philosophy of science, such as universalism and unification, disinterestedness and objectivity, originality and novelty, skepticism and the growth of knowledge, and realism.

Patrick Suppes, *Representation and Invariance of Scientific Structures*

Published in 2002, *Representation and Invariance of Scientific Structures,* by American philosopher Patrick Suppes, explains how a set-theoretical approaches can be used to represent a variety of science topics such as probability, representation, invariance, and mechanics. More specifically, Suppes demonstrates the representation and invariance of scientific structures using representation theories for scientific structures. Topics covered include representation, invariance, probability, representations of space and time, mechanics, language, axiomatic definition of theories, and theory of isomorphic representation.

Hasok Chang, *Inventing Temperature: Measurement and Scientific Progress*

Inventing Temperature: Measurement and Scientific Progress is a 2004 book by Korean-born American Hasok Chang. In six chapters, Chang uses temperature as an example to explain how scientific concepts are measured. He devotes four chapters to how the measurement of temperature (namely, the boiling and freezing points of water) was developed and achieved. In Chapter 5, he turns to measurement, justification, and scientific progress and specifically analyzes William Thompson work's on absolute temperature, developing his own philosophical views on measurements based on the principle of iteration. In Chapter 6, Chang argues that modern science makes several assumptions that are confusing at worst and dubious at best. He disagrees with the fixity of the boiling point of water and calls for further laboratory investigation to confirm it. This book explores some of the scientific achievements taken for granted today.

William C. Wimsatt, *Re-Engineering Philosophy for Limited Beings: Piecewise Approximations to Reality*

Re-Engineering Philosophy for Limited Beings: Piecewise Approximations to Reality was written in 2007 by American scholar William C. Wimsatt. Wimsatt argues that reductionism is only used by scientists when absolutely necessary in trying to understand how events, entities, and phenomena are structured at different levels. Wimsatt emphasizes natural complexity and human limitation throughout the book. According to him, the world is too complex understand. He reasons that humans are limited beings, who can only overcome their limitations with reasoning strategies. Besides providing a method for error-prone individuals who want to understand complex systems in the real world, Wimsatt also recommends that heuristic and pragmatic models be the foundation of philosophy in society. After analyzing the weaknesses and strengths and recalibrating analytic and reductionistic methodologies, Wimsatt concludes that his recommendation is feasible.

Nancy J. Nersessian, *Creating Scientific Concepts*

Published in 2008, *Creating Scientific Concepts,* by American philosopher Nancy J. Nersessian, aims not only to shed light on the nature of novel concepts in science but also to develop a framework for understanding conceptual innovation. She argues that, contrary to contemporary beliefs regarding novel concepts, these stem from the need to solve specific problems, the need to use scientific tools to analyze specific problems, and the need to adopt certain reasons to understand specific problems. Nersessian provides detailed explanations regarding the type of scientific reasoning that supports conceptual innovation. She also focuses on the cognitive implications of two examples of conceptual innovation: James Clerk Maxwell's conception of electric and magnetic fields, and a person confronted with the problem of a coiled spring under tension.

Heather Douglas, *Science, Policy, and the Value-Free Ideal*

Science, Policy, and the Value-Free Ideal is a 2009 philosophical book on science by American scholar Heather Douglas. It is based on Douglas's argument against the view that science should be value-free, which, she argues is neither desirable nor adequate for science. As Douglas explains, a value-free ideal supports the uninterrupted pursuit of knowledge about the natural world regardless of whether or not the knowledge is good for society. The author rejects this ideal, contending that values should be integral to the pursuit of scientific inquiries. According to her, scientists have the moral responsibility to consider the ethical implications of their work. Douglas explains the benefits of introducing values to reasoning and discusses how seven senses of objectivity can be applied in determining the validity and reliability of scientific outcomes. Apart from distinguishing junk science from sound science, the writer proposes a new ethics-based ideal that may not only help scientists consider values in their pursuit of science but also aid policymakers in creating value-oriented laws.

Peter Godfrey-Smith, *Theory and Reality: An Introduction to the Philosophy of Science*

Theory and Reality: An Introduction to the Philosophy of Science, a 2009 book by Australian philosopher Peter Godfrey-Smith, concerns the nature, theory, and reality of science, with particular focus on how science works. Godfrey-Smith explores the philosophy of science and discusses the scientific views of many philosophers, including Thomas Kuhn, Karl Popper, Larry Laudan, Paul Feyerabend, and Imre Lakatos. He also points out some theories that have yet to provide perfect solutions to the problems of science, such as the theory-ladeness of observation, scientific realism, logical empiricism, naturalism, and Bayesianism. The book links science to many branches of philosophy, especially epistemology and metaphysics.

William Bechtel and Robert C. Richardson, *Discovering Complexity: Decomposition and Localization as Strategies in Scientific Research*

Published in 2020, *Discovering Complexity: Decomposition and Localization as Strategies in Scientific Research* was written by two philosophers, William Bechtel and Robert C. Richardson. They use historical examples on genetics, cognitive neuroscience, to analyze two heuristic approaches to developing mechanistic models. Besides examining the benefits of these approaches, the authors also distinguish the difference between structural and functional components of a system. They articulate the reasons for the divergence in explanatory models proposed by scientists. In sum, drawing on several examples in different branches of science, the book demonstrates the complexity of scientific research.

Paul Feyerabend, *Against Method*

Against Method, by Austrian philosopher Paul Feyerabend, argues that science is an anarchic field. Feyerabend contends that methodological rules should not govern the growth of scientific knowledge. Using various case studies, he emphasizes that science thrives in epistemological anarchism and that it is ridiculous to believe that science needs specific, fixed, universal rules to thrive. Feyerabend further refutes the idea that science is a nomic field, arguing that to believe otherwise would be detrimental to science. After analyzing the work of such radical scientists as Galileo Galilei, Isaac Newton, and Albert Einstein, the writer points out that all scientific revolutions come from epistemological anarchism, not from fixed scientific methods. In summary, *Against Method* argues against the practice of following specific methodologies and fixed rules in science.

Philosophy of Biology

Edwin Schrödinger, *What Is Life? The Physical Aspect of the Living Cell*

What is Life? The Physical Aspect of the Living Cell is a 1944 philosophical masterpiece by Austrian-Irish scientist Erwin Schrödinger. Based on a public lecture delivered by Schrödinger in Dublin, the book applies the laws of chemistry and physics to biological events that take place within living organisms. Schrödinger argues in favor of "order-from-disorder," a principle in which large-scale events in the universe are a result of the accumulation of chaos on a small scale. He uses the Second Law of Thermodynamics as well as the concept of diffusion to explain this principle. From here, the author discusses the role of mutations in biological evolution and the role of molecules in carrying genetic information. Schrödinger ends by sharing his ideas on free will, determinism, and the nature of human consciousness. This book is a bold attempt to reconcile the fields of biology, physics, and chemistry.

Stephen J. Gould and Richard Lewontin, *The Spandrels of San Marco and the Panglossian Paradigm: A Critique of the Adaptationist Program*

The Spandrels of San Marco and the Panglossian Paradigm: A Critique of the Adaptationist Program is a 1979 philosophical text on biology by Stephen Jay Gould and Richard Lewontin. It is a critique of adaptationism, the view that psychological and physical traits are evolved adaptations. According to the authors, constraints on the development of organisms are what influence how they evolve certain traits. Gould and Lewontin devote most of the book to defending their arguments using analogies to architectural structures (spandrels) and some parts of organisms.

Stephen J. Gould, *The Mismeasure of Man*

The Mismeasure of Man is a 1981 philosophical book on biology by American scientist Stephen Jay Gould, who criticizes the assumptions and statistical methods underlying biological determinism, the principle that one's socioeconomic status is influenced by one's biological inheritance (for instance, IQ). He goes on to point out the flaws in two methods used in biological determinism, such as psychological testing and craniometry. The methods, Gould reasons, contain two fallacies: the fallacy of reification and the fallacy of "ranking." The first treats abstract ideas as concrete entities, while the second organizes complex variation in ascending order. In summary, this book provides a critical analysis of scientific racism and illustrates the social biases of researchers in favor of racial supremacy.

David Lee Hull, *Philosophy of Biological Science*

Published in 1974, *Philosophy of Biological Science,* by American philosopher David Lee Hull, addresses the history of biology, applying philosophy to biological science. Hull provides philosophical insights into the classification of biology and the relation between evolutionary and classification theory. Rejecting the application of essentialism to biological classification, Hull analyzes evolutionary processes, with emphasis on the theories of prominent scientists who contributed to the progress of the field.

Elliott Sober, *The Nature of Selection: Evolutionary Theory in Philosophical Focus*

The Nature of Selection: Evolutionary Theory in Philosophical Focus is a 1984 work on the philosophy of biology by American scientist Elliott Sober. The author provides an introduction to the philosophy of biology and the nature of selection. He discusses the concepts of fitness, adaptation, and selection and analyzes the evolutionary theory, arguing that evolution is a theory of forces. Sober points out several biological problems in the theory of evolution, such as those of causality and tautology. He also investigates how natural selection operates and what factors influence it. After expatiating on such biological issues as group selection, Darwinian fitness, and altruism, the author concludes that even though no evolutionary theory is perfect, they do explain why one living creature is more likely to adapt, survive, and reproduce than others.

Michael Ruse, *Taking Darwin Seriously: A Naturalistic Approach to Philosophy*

Published in 1986, *Taking Darwin Seriously: A Naturalistic Approach to Philosophy,* by British-born Canadian scholar Michael Ruse, centers on naturalism. Ruse explains the theory of evolution, supports Darwinian views, and discusses the relation between evolution and such branches of philosophy as ethics, metaphysics, and epistemology. He argues that the problems of philosophy can only be properly addressed by the notion that humans are the end product of evolution. The writer further reasons that the atheistic, secular views propagated by some evolutionists only compound the problems of philosophy. The author supports the arguments of

Darwin and applies naturalism to ethics, commonsense realism, epistemology, metaphysics skepticism. In summary, this book covers the application of the theory of evolution to philosophical issues.

Kristin Shrader-Frechette and Earl D. McCoy, *Method in Ecology: Strategies for Conservation*
Method in Ecology: Strategies for Conservation, a 1993 philosophical book on biology by Kristin Shrader-Frechette and Earl D. McCoy, explains the nature of ecology, pointing out its contributions to society. Shrader-Frechette and McCoy first lay out the conceptual problems limiting the development of biological and ecological theories. After this, they discuss the application of ecology to solving challenging social problems. Also discussed is rationality in ecology and policy aspects of the Florida panther case.

Elliott Sober, *Philosophy of Biology*
Philosophy of Biology is a 1993 philosophical text by Elliott Sober, an American philosopher. Sober points out recent developments in evolutionary theory and discusses controversial issues in biology, such as the debates on teleology, sociobiology, creationism, and nature vs. nurture. The author begins by explaining the meaning of evolution and then moves on to the problems of creationism and tautology. After pointing out the evidence for evolution, Sober focuses on the problems of natural selection and the nature of adaptationism. He concludes with a discussion of sociobiology and the application of evolutionary theory to ethics and sociology.

Martin Mahner and Mario Bunge, *Foundations of Biophilosophy*
Published in 1997, *Foundations of Biophilosophy* is a book on the philosophy of biology by Martin Mahner and Mario Bunge, who provide a systematic account of biology and the life sciences through the lens of realism and naturalism. In addition to defining and clarifying key concepts in biology, they also address some of the issues related to the philosophy of biology. Topics include ontological fundamentals, semantical and logical fundamentals, epistemological fundamentals, psychobiology, systematics, developmental biology, and evolutionary theory.

Kim Sterelny and Paul E. Griffiths, *Sex and Death: An Introduction to Philosophy of Biology*
Sex and Death: An Introduction to Philosophy of Biology is a 1999 philosophical book on biology by Kim Sterelny and Paul E. Griffiths, who bridge

the gap between biology and philosophy to answer controversial questions shaping how we view life. The authors begin by asking several key bio-social questions, such as Are humans programmed by their genes? What should conservationists conserve? and Does life exist by accident?. After using the theory of evolution to explain the diversity of life and exploring other issues pertaining to the philosophical problems raised by evolutionary theory, Sterelny and Griffiths turn their attention to the nature of genes, molecules, and organisms. They conclude with evolutionary explanations for adaptations, ecology, emotions, mass extinction, disparity, and life on Earth. The book provides a valuable perspective on philosophical issues implied by evolutionary theory.

Sandra Mitchell, *Biological Complexity and Integrative Pluralism*

Published in 2003, *Biological Complexity and Integrative Pluralism* is a collection of essays by American philosopher Sandra Mitchell. The thesis of the book is that biological complexity can be best explained using integrative pluralism rather than reductionism. Mitchell contends that reductionism cannot properly address problems in biological sciences. She first describes what constitutes complexity, listing three forms of complexity: constitutive complexity, dynamical complexity, and evolved complexity. She goes on to explain what integrative pluralism means and opens up the complexity of evolution. According to her, integrative pluralism is the use of multiple theories or models to explain biological sciences. Mitchell rejects reductionism and the notion that the sciences can be unified. She devotes the rest of the book to a defense of integrative pluralism and discusses how it can provide evolutionary explanations to biological issues.

Daniel C. Dennett, *Darwin's Dangerous Idea: Evolution and the Meanings of Life*

Darwin's Dangerous Idea: Evolution and the Meanings of Life is a 1995 book by Daniel C. Dennett. Its three sections support Darwin's theory of evolution and aim to show the consequences of the theory. The first section discusses why Darwin's theory is "dangerous" and revolutionary. According to the American philosopher, Darwin's natural selection theory overturned and demolished the traditional belief that a divine designer created the world of nature. The second section discusses the criticisms of Darwinism and how the theory has been applied in the biological sciences. Dennett argues that Darwin showed how a random shuffle in a previously chaotic world led to the orderly planet that humans currently inhabit. In the third section, Dennett examines how such fields as philosophy, ethics, and linguistics have resisted Darwinism. He emphasizes that memes will play a major role in the cultural evolution of Darwinism, and he concludes that Darwinism is a beautiful idea that infuses diversity with value.

Denis Noble, *The Music of Life: Biology Beyond the Genome*
The Music of Life: Biology Beyond the Genome is a 2006 philosophical book on biology by British philosopher Denis Noble. Noble argues that understanding life requires looking beyond the genome and toward various life dimensions. To him, life is a form of music in which many factors (tissues, cells, organs, genes, the environment, and so on) "sound" together to achieve a specific function or purpose. Noble discusses the nature of genomes and explains how the body and the organs work hand-in-hand to create a symphony of functions. Noble talks not only about human evolution but also demonstrates how humans perceive the world through the lens of philosophy. He ends with a discussion of the self and its role in cultures.

Samir Okasha, *Evolution and the Levels of Selection*
Evolution and the Levels of Selection, a 2006 book by Samir Okasha, explores the nature of evolution as well as the role of natural selection in the dynamics of evolution. Okasha argues that natural selection operates at multiple levels and provides insights into fundamental, philosophical questions of evolution. The author begins with a systematic model of how natural selection acts on such multiple variables as genes, groups, and individual organisms. With this model, Okasha answers foundational questions related to natural selection and responds to the causality problems in which natural selection at one level can affect other levels. Apart from pointing out the nature of hierarchical organizations and major evolutionary transitions, he also reviews both past and recent works in the literature on evolutionary theory, discussing evolutionary game theory, the evolution of individuality, Price's equation, reductionism and holism, realism and pluralism, and the gene's eye view.

Elliott Sober, *Evidence and Evolution: The Logic Behind the Science*
Evidence and Evolution: The Logic Behind the Science was written in 2008 by the American philosopher Elliott Sober. As the title suggests, the focuses on the nature and concept of evolution through a statistical lens. Sober writes about the concept of evidence and uses a few examples to analyze whether certain claims and hypotheses about natural selection and evolution can

be tested. He then provides answers to questions on probability and later applies his solutions to evolutionary problems. Even though Sober admits that creationism cannot be analyzed with his statistical framework, he explains how one can test whether a hypothesis on natural selection is valid or not. The author concludes the book with an analysis of the common ancestry hypothesis and a discussion of asexual species, the species concept, single ancestral organisms, and the last universal common ancestor.

Michael Ruse, *The Philosophy of Human Evolution*

Published in 2010, *The Philosophy of Human Evolution,* by Anglo-Canadian scholar Michael Ruse, provides a detailed account of human evolution from the vantage point of philosophy. He highlights and analyzes the morality problems precipitated by natural selection and evolutionary theories. Other topics discussed include the nature of scientific theories, sex, race, eugenics, and the problem of progress and the relationships between culture and biology.

Philosophy of Physics

Pierre Duhem, *The Aim and Structure of Physical Theory*

Published in 1906, *The Aim and Structure of Physical Theory,* by French philosopher Pierre Duhem, investigates the nature of physical science and the scientific method. In Part I, Duhem analyzes the history of physical theories, explains the benefit of physical theories, and offers insight into the value of physical theories applied to metaphysics. Duhem argues that physics should be separated from metaphysics. He also discusses the role of natural classification in the evolution of physical theories and the two types of mind: ample mind and deep mind. In Part II, the philosopher turns his attention to the structure of physical theories. Some of the topics discussed include the quantity and quality of measurement, the mathematics of approximation, the nature of experiments in physics, and the choice of hypothesis.

Albert Einstein, *The Meaning of Relativity*

Published in 1922, *The Meaning of Relativity* is a scientific masterpiece by German-born scientist Albert Einstein. It explicates Einstein's famous theories of time and space and begins with a look back at previous theories. Part of Einstein's aim is to answer the question of how the human understanding of space and time is influenced by experience. Einstein points to his general theory of relativity, according to which all laws of physics are identical to an observer in a fixed location, and the motion of an observer does not alter the speed of light in a vacuum. Overall, the book is a general guide to interpreting space and time in the universe.

Hans Reichenbach, *The Philosophy of Space and Time*

The Philosophy of Space and Time is a 1927 book on the philosophy of physics by German scholar Hans Reichenbach. It clarifies problems inadequately addressed or left unaddressed by major physical theories. These include the problem of rotation, the relativity of geometry, and the limitations of visualization. The author provides an account of Einstein's general theory of relativity and several other theories of space and time. More specifically, he analyzes the nature and problems of physical geometry, explains the difference between space and time, and evaluates Einstein's concept of gravitation as well as the reality of space and time.

Arthur Eddington, *Philosophy of Physical Science*

Philosophy of Physical Science is a 1939 book by Arthur Eddington. The British physicist argues in favor of "a priori knowledge" and champions a philosophical view he calls "selective subjectivism," a philosophical doctrine grounded in the belief that all knowledge is based on one's subjective experience. According to Eddington, most philosophies are not philosophies of science but of some scientists. He points out several physical science theories to defend this thesis and goes on to reason that the continual modification of theories of the philosophy of physical science will ultimately draw science to the truth of knowledge. Topics discussed include the concept of structure and existence, quantum theory, relativity theory, and the scope of epistemological methods.

Werner Heisenberg, *Physics and Philosophy: The Revolution in Modern Science*

Published in 1958, *Physics and Philosophy: The Revolution in Modern Science,* by German physicist Werner Heisenberg, explores the revolutions in modern science, with emphasis on the fundamental transformation that shaped the understanding of physics. Heisenberg discusses the nature and history of quantum theory and contrasts philosophical ideas during the time of Descartes with new ideas in quantum theory. He also points out how Albert Einstein's theory of relativity and Max Planck's theory of electromagnetic radiation have changed the world for the good. In the last part of the book, Heisenberg discusses the role of quantum physics in the formation of human thinking. Central to his exposition is the proposition that most of what people take granted are no longer true when scientists analyze the universe through the lens of quantum physics.

John Stewart Bell, *On the Einstein–Podolsky–Rosen Paradox*

On the Einstein–Podolsky–Rosen Paradox is a short book on the philosophy of physics by Irish scientist John Stewart Bell. Bell observes that including additional variables to Albert Einstein's theory of relativity with the aim of restoring theory causality and locality would produce results incompatible with quantum mechanics. He calls this logically contradictory situation the Einstein–Podolsky–Rosen Paradox. The author also notes that fault lines in the explanations provided by scientists to show that the measurement of a system in the present is unaffected by the operations of a system elsewhere appear after the addition of new parameters to the theory of relativity. This book explores the paradox of adding more parameters to the theory of relativity without changing statistical predictions and without being incompatible with quantum mechanics.

Lawrence Sklar, *Space, Time, and Spacetime*

Space, Time, and Spacetime is a 1987 philosophical text by American scholar Lawrence Sklar, which explores the nature of space and time. Sklar points out the interdependence of philosophy and science by observing problems related to the nature of time and space. The author begins with a historical account of geometry, covering such topics as the rise of non-Euclidean geometry and epistemological views about geometry. In the middle of the book, he reviews the major issues in philosophy, summarizing traditional ontological disputes, the theory of relativity, and the problem of substantive space. In the last chapter of the text, Sklar focuses on the nature of time, the universe, statistical physics, and time asymmetry.

Nancy Cartwright, *How the Laws of Physics Lie*

How the Laws of Physics Lie is a 1983 book on the philosophy of physics by Nancy Cartwright, an American scientist. Cartwright argues for the creation of new scientific theories or laws that account for the reality of situations in the universe. The author observes that most of the scientific theories are idealistic and inadequate to describe reality. To account for the realities that exist in nature, Cartwright advocates for a simulacrum view of science instead of a traditional view of science, describes idealized systems in models. She cites many examples to defend her thesis that it is possible to create scientific models to explain the regularities that exist in the universe. In sum, this book is a critical evaluation of the reality of scientific laws.

Michael Friedman, *Foundations of Space-Time Theories: Relativistic Physics and the Philosophy of Science*

Foundations of Space-Time Theories: Relativistic Physics and the Philosophy of Science is a 1983 book by American philosopher Michael Friedman. Here, Friedman leaves almost nothing untouched concerning the conceptual foundations of the theories. He begins with an examination of Newtonian physics, pointing out the strengths and weakness of gravitational theory and the laws of motion. Following that, the philosopher shifts his focus to the concept of kinematics, electrodynamics, and simultaneity relations. Friedman analyzes the concept of general relativity as well as the philosophical, physical, and mathematical implications of relativity theory. Overall, the book illustrates how Einstein's theory of relativity has shaped the modern understanding of the universe.

John Stewart Bell, *Speakable and Unspeakable in Quantum Mechanics: Collected Papers on Quantum Philosophy*

Speakable and Unspeakable in Quantum Mechanics: Collected Papers on Quantum Philosophy is a 1987 text on the philosophy of physics by Irish scientist John Stewart Bell. The book contains all of Bell's work on quantum mechanics. He considers the Einstein–Podolsky–Rosen Paradox, the problem of hidden variables in quantum mechanics, the theory of local beables (that is, anything that could possibly be), locality in quantum mechanics, and de Broglie-Bohm experiment. Other topics include the nature of reality, local causality, and the nature of measurement.

Lawrence Sklar, *Philosophy of Physics*

Published in 1992, *Philosophy of Physics,* by Lawrence Sklar, an American philosopher, attempts to bridge the gap between physics and philosophy. Sklar argues that scientific discoveries in the last two centuries have blurred the fault lines separating the two fields, bringing both together. The author discusses what the philosophy of physics means and goes on to analyze contemporary problems facing the discipline.

Lawrence Sklar, *Physics and Chance: Philosophical Issues in the Foundations of Statistical Mechanics*

Physics and Chance: Philosophical Issues in the Foundations of Statistical Mechanics is a 1993 book by the American scholar Lawrence Sklar. It introduces the fundamentals of statistical mechanics, covering a wide range of topics on the subject, including thermodynamics, kinetic theory, Boltzmannian theory, equilibrium and non-equilibrium theories, probability, Gibb's statistical mechanics, and the role of cosmology.

Jeffrey Bub, *Interpreting the Quantum World*

Interpreting the Quantum World, a 1997 philosophical work on physics by American scientist Jeffrey Bub, not only interprets quantum mechanics but resolves the measurement problem that bedeviled Werner Heisenberg. Bub explores the history of the quantum world, from classical mechanics to quantum mechanics, addressing such problems as the Einstein–Podolsky–Rosen Paradox, the problem of interpretation, the coloring problem,

Schütte's tautology, and the modal interpretation. Bub discusses the new orthodoxy and formal constructions of the quantum world.

Roberto Torretti, *Philosophy of Physics*
Published in 1999, *The Philosophy of Physics* is a philosophical text on physical science by Chilean scholar Roberto Torretti. The author presents key philosophical issues in physics, providing a historical account of natural philosophy from the seventeenth century to the nineteenth century. After providing an account of the conceptual development of physics, Torretti discusses Newtonian physics and Kant's philosophy concerning space, geometry and quantity. In the last three chapters, he focuses on quantum mechanics, examining both old theories and new developments. Included are Einstein's relativity theory and Heisenberg's indeterminacy relations. The author ends the book by analyzing the interaction between physics and philosophy and presenting his views on contemporary methodological issues in physics.

Craig Callender and Nick Huggett, *Physics Meets Philosophy at the Planck Scale: Contemporary Theories in Quantum Gravity*
Physics Meets Philosophy at the Planck Scale: Contemporary Theories in Quantum Gravity is a 2001 book on the philosophy of physics by Craig Callender and Nick Huggett. The authors argue in favor of theories of quantum gravity, as they believe such theories can reconcile quantum mechanics and the relativity theory. With quantum gravity theories, they reason that the gravitational theory may be quantized. To prove this, the authors thoroughly examine the quantum gravity field, pointing out the challenge of quantum gravity theories and how quantum gravity theories can be used to interpret general relativity theory and quantum mechanics. The book thus provides a new way of understanding the notions of time, space, and matter.

Harvey Brown, *Physical Relativity: Space-time Structure from a Dynamical Perspective*
Physical Relativity: Space-time Structure from a Dynamical Perspective is a 2005 book on the philosophy of physics by British scientist Harvey Brown. It focuses on Einstein's relativity theory. Brown begins with an account of those who believe in space-time theories and those who do not. Conceding both space-time theories and non-space-time theories have their strengths and weaknesses, Brown argues for Einstein's relativity theory and defends

it against the other theories. The main question he addresses is this: What roles does the geometry of space-time play? He rejects the view that the geometry of space-time explains the movement of free bodies on geodesics, but enumerates the benefits of the general theory of relativity in space-time problems.

Laura Ruetsche, *Interpreting Quantum Theories: The Art of the Possible*

Interpreting Quantum Theories: The Art of the Possible is a 2011 book by American philosopher Laura Ruetsche. As the title suggests, the text focuses on the philosophy of quantum mechanics, especially such complicated systems as quantum fields at the thermodynamic limit of quantum statistical mechanics. Ruetsche's goal is to provide a conceptual analysis of quantum mechanics infinity and to respond to the ontological nature of a particle through the lens of quantum theories. To achieve this objective, she interprets several physical theories and presents notions of phenomenological particles.

Ethics and Value Theory

George Edward Moore, *Principia Ethica*

Written by English philosopher G.E. Moore, *Principia Ethica* is a 1903 philosophical masterpiece on ethics. The book centers on the idea that good cannot be defined. Moore argues that it would be a fallacy to define what is good in terms of desirability, pleasantness, and other natural properties. The writer calls this the "naturalistic fallacy." He goes on to assert that good is indescribable in terms of intrinsic value. Furthermore, he criticizes and refutes hedonism, metaphysical ethics, evolutionary ethics, social Darwinism, utilitarianism, and naturalistic ethics. While Moore admits that man cannot always know the consequences in every situation, he opines that there are some general situations in which the likelihood of consequences can be learned. The writer also contends for the multiplicity and objectivity of values, pointing out that the knowledge of values cannot be derived from the knowledge of facts. In summary, *Principia Ethica* argues against generally accepted theories of ethics on the grounds that good is indefinable.

Gertrude Elizabeth Margaret Anscombe, *Modern Moral Philosophy*

Modern Moral Philosophy was published in 1958 by British philosopher Gertrude Elizabeth Margaret Anscombe. Anscombe argues that moral philosophy should be effectively suspended until philosophers can develop a practical philosophy of psychology. Philosophers, according to her argument, cannot provide moral guidance until they are clear about the meaning of such terms as virtue, intention, and wanting. Next, she criticizes the secular moral theories of Kantian ethics, social contract, and utilitarianism as lacking proper foundation because they have abandoned the concept of divine law. Anscombe contends that in the absence of a divine overseer, moral arguments are attractive only to societal and personal dispositions, retaining a baseless undertone of special importance because of the absence of the divine. The writer subsequently proposes the term "consequentialism" to describe a moral philosophy holding that it is impossible to prohibit any line of action as a means to a particular end. *Modern Moral Philosophy* concludes that moral theory must be based on religion.

Conrad Hal Waddington, *The Ethical Animal*

The Ethical Animal, published in 1960 by British philosopher Conrad Hal Waddington, explores man's nature as an ethical animal and how human actions affect the biological world. Waddington critiques classism, social mobility, and societal upheaval. He examines how philosophical thinking changes in history and reasons that humans undergo an evolution different from biological evolution. This alternate evolution is a result of man's learning and teaching capability. He also argues that humanity is capable of ethical ideas, a capability that aids in the propagation of new forms of evolution. Waddington concludes by examining the most relevant ethical problems humanity faces and provides possible solutions to them.

Peter Singer, *Famine, Affluence, and Morality*

Famine, Affluence, and Morality is a 1972 book by Australian philosopher Peter Singer. In it, he argues that affluent countries have a moral obligation to contribute more to humanitarian causes. He cites the example of a drowning child to illustrate the immorality of refusing to help others when one has the power to do so. He argues that taking action to help others is virtuous and that refraining from taking action to assist the poor is wrong. After considering instances where populations suffer and die due to lack of food, shelter, and medical care, he states that proximity is not an essential factor in offering aid. Western countries like the United States must give more than they consider normal, he insists. To support his argument, the author proposes some ethical principles using an implicit premise. He posits that helping the needy is a duty. The moral compass of charity, in his view, does not make a distinction between being the only person that can help or being one of millions. Singer further states that one can prevent people from dying of starvation by donating more than what is considered normal. In *Famine, Affluence, and Morality,* Singer encourages people to do what is morally right.

J. L. Mackie, *Ethics: Inventing Right and Wrong*

Written in 1977 by Australian-born Oxford philosopher J. L. Mackie, *Ethics: Inventing Right and Wrong* is a treatise on moral skepticism. The philosopher employs the subjectivism method, an "error" theory of the apparent objectivity of values, and rejects the moral universalism of ethics. Mackie begins by stating, "There are no objective values." This means that everyday moral codes are based on moral facts that do not exist. The philosopher proposes a practical moral system and supports his ideology with two arguments: Argument from Disagreement and Argument from Queerness. In his view, right and wrong are not objective truths; people invent them. The author further explains that if objective ethical values existed, they would be strange. He goes on to examine the content of ethics. Morality, he writes, is a functional device that changes according to the human condition. Mackie concludes by exploring the frontiers of moral principles, psychology, metaphysics, theology, law, and politics.

Sissela Bok, *Lying: Moral Choice in Public and Private Life*
Lying: Moral Choice in Public and Private Life was published in 1978 and written by Sissela Bok, a Swedish-born American philosopher. She begins by expounding on the nature of lying, the basic philosophical and religious approaches to assessing lies, and the effects of lying on human choices. According to her, all people resort to lying in certain scenarios despite society's cpndemnation of the practice. After examining the numerous justifications people use to rationalize lies, Bok acknowledges that, while some of the reasons are valid, most of them are not. To corroborate her claim, she uses examples in politics and television evangelism to expound on the ramifications caused by lying. Bok also posits that lying erodes public confidence, victimizes people, and serves humanity poorly. In addition to examining the alternatives to lying, she outlines the many risks associated with the practice. Bok concludes by offering suggestions on how society can stop lying, and she enumerates the likely inducements for doing so.

Alan Gewirth, *Reason and Morality*
Reason and Morality was written in 1978 by American philosopher Alan Gewirth. In the book, he attempts to solve the philosophical problem of justifying moral claims. By way of context, Gewirth constructs a deduction of moral obligation based on Kantian principles. The first section explores the problem of justification. After discussing the conflicts that can arise from challenging ethical rules, the author identifies the main issues of moral philosophy. These include the necessity of morals, the factors one should consider in decision-making, and the other interests that are good enough to affect one's decisions. Gewirth goes on to an analysis of each of the issues, outlining objections that critics may raise regarding his solutions. A moral system, the philosopher asserts, is necessary to provide some consistency in people's lives. He also adds that neither deductive nor inductive methods can help in justifying moral principles. Gewirth concludes by inferring that the ultimate solution is the application of reasons to actions.

Peter Singer, *Practical Ethics*
Practical Ethics is a book on applied ethics published in 1979 by English philosopher Peter Singer. Singer applies utilitarian ethics to such issues as

abortion, overseas aid, euthanasia, job recruitment, racial discrimination, infanticide, equality, civil disobedience, political violence, embryo experimentation, disability, climate change, and more. He asks relevant, probing questions about a number of ethical issues and makes sound arguments to support his claims. According to him, a being's interest should be weighed on the being's concrete property, not on its abstract properties. He opposes Marxism, which states that morality is tuned relative to the ruling upper class. Singer counters that the masses can change the ethics of the ruling class by changing their habits. *Practical Ethics* applies ethics to practical everyday issues and debates.

Alasdair MacIntyre, *After Virtue*

Published in 1981, *After Virtue,* by the Scottish philosopher Alasdair MacIntyre, examines the roots of virtue and the reasons for the disappearance of virtue in modern life; he makes suggestions for the recovery of virtue. The author begins with a reimagining of Walter M. Miller Jr.'s science-fiction novel, *A Canticle for Leibowitz.* He illustrates an imaginary world in which all sciences have been hastily reassembled after a catastrophe has dismantled them. In his view, such new sciences will only be superficial as they won't have actual scientific depth and content. He infers that precisely such an occurrence could happen to morality. According to MacIntyre, moral structures derived from historical times are faulty as they were assembled from a faulty, incoherent language of morality, citing issues with the Aristotelian approach to morality among others. MacIntyre concludes by suggesting modern approaches to morality and virtue.

Samuel Scheffler, *The Rejection of Consequentialism*

Published in 1925, *The Rejection of Consequentialism,* by American philosopher Samuel Scheffler, studies the rejection of consequentialism by several philosophers. Scheffler analyzes deontological moral theories and consequential moral theories and derives the morals behind both schools of thought. The philosopher agrees with consequentialist view of classical utilitarianism but reasons that consequentialism itself is not plausible. He asserts that agents do not always produce the best outcome and argues instead for reviving a neglected view of moral conception in which agents are permitted but not necessarily required to produce the best outcomes. Scheffler further argues that an agent-centered prerogative should qualify consequentialism. He proposes a hybrid theory that avoids distributive justice and the integrity of agents. The philosopher explains that this hybrid theory will always permit agents, but it will not always require them to produce the best outcomes. In sum, *The Rejection of Consequentialism* studies consequentialism and suggests viable alternatives to it.

Derek Parfit, *Reasons and Persons*

Reasons and Persons is a 1984 book by British philosopher Derek Parfit. Divided into four parts, the book examines personal identity and rationality. Parfit argues in the first part of the book that people have self-defeating moral views and ethical theories that work against their interests. He further contends that current self-interest can conflict with future/long-term self-interests. In the second part, Parfit considers the relationship between rationality and time, pointing out several flaws in self-interest theory. Claiming that personal interest does not matter as much as mental continuity and connectedness, Parfit reasons in the third section of the book that people should lessen their personal interest in service to their fellow humans. In the final section, Parfit examines population ethics and questions the morality of procreation and its environmental impact. *Reasons and Persons* analyzes individuals' personal identity, the rationality of their actions, and their responsibility toward society and future generations.

Ethics and the Limits of Philosophy

Ethics and the Limits of Philosophy, a 1985 philosophical book by Bernard Williams, discusses problems with moral theory in modern civilization and proffers an alternative way of addressing morality. In the opening pages, the English philosopher criticizes modern moral philosophers for favoring systems over individuals in the contemporary social context. Modern theories, he writes, condense ethics into a code or system of moral theories that are unsuitable to explain human motivation. In addition to singling out Kantianism and Utilitarianism as the major propagators of these modern theories, Williams contends that they are harmful and invasive in contemporary society. He proposes that one should instead study the ethical works of Aristotle and Plato to understand an ethical life. Nevertheless, the author claims to understand the demands that modern society imposes on ethical thought.

David Gauthier, *Morals by Agreement*

Morals by Agreement, published in 1986, is an epistemological masterpiece by Canadian-American philosopher David Gauthier. Gauthier deems the original formulation of morality to be a fair and rational constraint on the human pursuit of benefits or interests. He opens by arguing that moral principles are ideologies of rational choice. After this, he points out two methods for developing a connection between morality and rationality: the social science approach and the Kantian approach. Gauthier goes further to propose a theory in which humans make choices based on mutual cooperation rather than on individual interests. Apart from claiming that his theory will lead to fairness, Gauthier adds that it will encourage humans to adhere to morality because of its inherent benefits. Thus, the philosopher bases morals on the groundwork of reason. He concludes *Morals by Agreement* by viewing individuality and society through the lens of his personal conception of morality and rationality.

Peter Railton, *Moral Realism*

Published in 1986, *Moral Realism,* by American philosopher Peter Railton, argues for the existence of moral facts. Railton defines moral facts as natural facts that make moral statements. In addition, he endorses naturalistic cognitivism by insisting that a complicated set of natural facts constitute moral facts. Afterward, Railton proves that moral facts are both normative and explanatory in nature, and he argues that some moral propositions can be true or false. He also emphasizes that moral properties and facts are natural properties and facts. Railton points out that facts and values do not have any epistemic distinction. Based on this, he reasons that some beliefs are independent of our desires. The philosopher then points out the relevance of epistemic relativism. Railton concludes by calling for adopting a moral realism, in which moral judgments are both objective and relational with a cognitive truth value.

Martha Nussbaum, *The Fragility of Goodness*

Published in 1986, *The Fragility of Goodness,* by Martha Nussbaum, an American philosopher, examines the reasons why good humans are morally susceptible to luck and chance, external factors outside of their control. Nussbaum uses Aristotelian methodology to study ancient Greek tragedies and ethical philosophy. She prefers to use tragedies because they explore such themes as human suffering, external circumstances, and goodness. After several analyses, she concludes that there is a continuity between Greek philosophical treatises and tragedies. Using Plato as an example, Nussbaum maintains that the ancient Greek philosopher's search for a good life shares many concerns with what is seen in the tragedies. *The Fragility of Goodness* seeks to discover the influence of luck and chance on human goodness through ancient Greek texts.

Paul W. Taylor, *Respect for Nature: A Theory of Environmental Ethics*

Respect for Nature: A Theory of Environmental Ethics is a 1986 book by American philosopher Paul W. Taylor, who advocates for a biocentric approach to nature and introduces his theory of biological egalitarianism. According to the theory, all living things have intrinsic and instrumental value; hence, they deserve equal moral consideration and concern. The author also expounds on how the earth works in relation to its biosphere. Furthermore, he argues that humans are not superior to other living things because all living things have equal moral worth and inherent value. The philosopher agrees that human interest will conflict with the interest of other living things and offers principles for resolving these conflicts. *Respect for Nature: A Theory of Environmental Ethics* expounds on biological egalitarianism and human respect for all biological creatures.

Holmes Rolston III, *Environmental Ethics: Duties to and Values in the Natural World*

Environmental Ethics: Duties to and Values in the Natural World was written in 1988 by American philosopher Holmes Rolston III. The book examines the values and duties of man relating to plants and animals. Rolston argues that people have a moral duty to protect and conserve the biodiverse ecosystem. According to Rolston, the conservation of the ecosystem is for the ultimate good of man and all other forms of life. The philosopher explores the interconnectivity of all life and how every life on earth depends on a balanced ecosystem. Finally, he illustrates several examples of how individual actions on the ecosystem impact science, culture, religion, economics, and other aspects of human life.

Susan Hurley, *Natural Reasons: Personality and Polity*

Published in 1989, *Natural Reasons: Personality and Polity* is a philosophical book on rationality. In the work, Susan Hurley examines the rationality behind actions and decisions. She draws analogies between the structure of society and the structure of personality and analyzes rationality within the two structures. She also examines Wittgenstein's theory of interpretation and compares it to Dworkin's theory of adjudication. The addresses the philosophy of mind, ethics, social choice theory, decision theory, subjectivism, cognitivism, coherence, commensurability, and skepticism to study the rationality behind decision-making in relation to values and ethics.

Shelly Kagan, *The Limits of Morality*

The Limits of Morality, published in 1989 by American philosopher Shelly Kagan, discusses the nature of moral acts that are within or off limits. The author begins by defining ordinary morality as basic views accepted by the majority. According to Kagan, ordinary morality is a system founded on constraints. The writer points out two types of morality limits: one that limits human actions and one that limits the demands of morality. Central to the argument is that neither of these two constraints on morality can be defended, and the book aims to prove that philosophers cannot adequately defend the concept of ordinary morality despite its intuitive appeal.

Allan Gibbard, *Wise Choices, Apt Feelings: A Theory of Normative Judgment*

Wise Choices, Apt Feelings: A Theory of Normative Judgment was written in 1990 by Allan Gibbard, an American philosopher. It discusses such topics as morality, human conduct, and rational thought in the context of Gibbard's proposed universal theory of moral judgment. He calls the theory a "norm-expressivistic analysis of rationality" and develops it based on experimental psychology, evolutionary theory, and traditional political and moral philosophy. Gibbard contends that when humans regard each other's feelings, actions or beliefs as rational, they show their approval of a structure of norms. The author thus concludes that morality is principally about norms related to the appropriateness of moral feelings.

Joan Tronto, *Moral Boundaries: A Political Argument for an Ethic of Care*

Published in 1993, *Moral Boundaries: A Political Argument for an Ethic of Care,* by American philosopher Joan Tronto, criticizes the social imposition of care on women as politically unwise and argues that the link between care and woman is not accurate historically. Tronto further reveals how social and political institutions have excluded women from power and marginalized them in society. In the interest of gender equality, Tronto argues that the boundaries between women's public life and private life need to be eliminated. She proposes four caring practices that to accomplish this: care-receiving, taking care, caring about, and care-giving. In addition to claiming that caring is not merely restricted to individuals, Tronto insists that institutions can use the ethic of care to guide their practices. She argues that society currently degrades the act of caring to maintain its patriarchal power hierarchy. Caring positions, in her view, are disproportionately held by marginalized persons such as minorities and women. Tronto, therefore, concludes that an equal societal distribution of care work will happen when there is a re-examination of socio-political values.

Annette Baier, *Moral Prejudices: Essays on Ethics*

Published in 1994, by New Zealand philosopher Annette Baier, *Moral Prejudices: Essays on Ethics* begins by acknowledging the difference between the way women and men interact with the world. According to Baier, women focus on love, relationships, nurturing, and caring, while men are chiefly concerned with protecting their loved ones. She further adds that the history of philosophy cannot adequately account for this difference because it is written almost exclusively by men. To bridge the gap between men and women, Baier develops a moral theory whose main concept is based on trust. Trust, she writes, can bring both genders together. Apart from discussing the consequences of trust between the genders, Baier examines the role trust plays in relations of equals and non-equals.

Michael A. Smith, *The Moral Problem*

Published in 1995, *The Moral Problem*, by Australian philosopher Michael A. Smith, examines the incompatibility between the practicality and objectivity of moral judgments. In the opening pages of the text, the philosopher discusses the contrast between meta-ethics and normative ethics. He then goes on to argue against the three meta-ethics theories concerning moral judgments: externalism, expressivism, and anti-humean. These theories contradict each other and are not convincing, the author argues. Smith offers his own normative theories in the final two chapters of the book. Normative moral actions originate in rationality. Smith argues that rational individuals will take normative reasons as advice and modify their behavior accordingly. He concedes, however, that his definition of normative reasons is abstract and that the existence of such reasons cannot be proved.

Christine Korsgaard, *The Sources of Normativity*

The Sources of Normativity was published in 1996 by Christine Korsgaard, an American philosopher. The book aims to explain and justify one's moral obligations to others. The philosopher begins by examining the four versions of the source of normativity that are proposed by contemporary moral philosophers: realism, the appeal to autonomy, reflective endorsement, and voluntarism. Following this examination, she traces the origin of each account and compares each to the modern theories. Korsgaard points out that the appeal to autonomy version espoused by Kantian philosophers is a fusion of the other three accounts. The philosopher proposes her own version of the autonomy theory. Autonomy, she argues, is the source of all human obligations. According to Korsgaard, humans must value their practical identities or risk losing their identity and integrity. She reasons that valuing practical identities is tantamount to valuing humanity. Korsgaard concludes that it is in the self that the source of normativity is to be found.

Peter Unger, *Living High and Letting Die*

Written by Peter Unger, *Living High and Letting Die* is a 1996 treatise that discusses the obligations of privileged people with respect to the less-privileged. The writer begins by claiming that it is costly to live a morally decent life. According to the American philosopher, people in the developed world are morally obligated to help alleviate premature death and human suffering in Third World countries. Most people, in Unger's opinion, have an inconsistent and untrustworthy moral judgment concerning various moral scenarios. He further argues that psychological factors prevalent in society are mostly to blame for obscuring the moral questions. He, therefore, reasons that human moral intuitions about issues provide an incorrect view of one's true values. Unger proposes his own "liberation hypothesis" as a solution. According to the hypothesis, it is morally right and acceptable for persons to steal, lie, cheat, and even harm others to mitigate suffering among the less privileged.

Thomas M. Scanlon, *What We Owe to Each Other*

Published in 1998, *What We Owe to Each Other* is a work of moral philosophy by American philosopher Thomas M. Scanlon. Scanlon argues that central to morality is the concept of what we owe to one another. He calls this idea contractualism and argues that thoughts about right and wrong are borne out of a sense of having to justify our actions to others. Judgments about right and wrong, according to Scanlon, are practical claims about what humans must do. He argues that contractualism, not state of mind, desires, or well-being, is responsible for most moral values. He asserts that when plurality of moral and immoral values is considered, contractualism allows for variability in moral requirements. *What We Owe to Each Other* is an introduction to the nature of contractualism.

Rosalind Hursthouse, *On Virtue Ethics*

On Virtue Ethics, published in 1999, is a philosophical treatise by New Zealander Rosalind Hursthouse. The first of the book's three sections examines the ways in which virtue ethics can provide guidance and assessment of human actions. In the second section, the author discusses the role of emotions in vice and virtue, using the indoctrination of racism as a reference. The third section studies the relationship between virtue ethics and the rationality of morality. It also seeks to understand if there is any unbiased criterion for a specific character trait to be classified as a virtue. In conclusion, *On Virtue Ethics* clarifies and defends Hursthouse's neo-Aristotelian virtue ethics.

Phillipa Foot, *Natural Goodness*

Natural Goodness is a 2001 masterpiece by English philosopher Phillipa Foot. She begins by critically examining the non-cognitivism and subjectivism pervading modern analytical moral philosophy. She proposes a naturalistic theory of ethics as an alternative to these traditional theories. The naturalistic approach, she argues, involves a special type of assessment found in moral judgments. The philosopher further asserts that moral evaluations share a conceptual framework with assessments of the operations and characteristics of living things. Thus, the author reveals that virtue is a goodness of will while vice is a natural flaw. Foot concludes that psychological terms cannot be used to understand propositions that have to do with human ethics.

Derek Parfit, *On What Matters*

Published in 2011, *On What Matter* is a three-volume philosophical work by Derek Parfit, the British philosopher, and is a sequel to his *Reasons and Persons*. The author argues for objective ethical theories, claiming that subjective ethical theories cannot account for some human actions. He notes that facts can give individuals reasons to act, desire, and believe things. The philosopher unifies the three ethical theories of contractarianism, consequentialism, and Kantian deontology and proposes the Triple Theory. According to this theory, an act is wrong only if it is disallowed by one of the following principles: (1) a principle that no one can reject on reasonable grounds, (2) a universal principle agreeable to everyone, (3) a universal principle that works for the best of everyone. Additionally, Parfit discusses consent, responsibility, and free will. *On What Matter* promotes objective ethical thinking.

Allan Gibbard, *Thinking How to Live*

Thinking How to Live was published in 2003 by Allan Gibbard, an American philosopher. It endeavors to broaden Gibbard's expressivism theory, which he introduced in his earlier *Wise Choices, Apt Feelings: A Theory of Normative Judgment*. Gibbard *Thinking How to Live* by discussing normativity. Normative questions, he argues, are principally questions of what to believe, how to feel, and what kind of actions to take. Thus, he suggests that planning ways to bring a plan to fruition is a need common to human beings. In addition to drafting plans for random situations, the philosopher points out that we need to consider the perspectives of different people before taking action. Humans acquire a quasi-belief, he argues, when they finally decide to act. *Thinking How to Live* explores the role of normative patterns in decisions and beliefs.

Michael Huemer, *Ethical Intuitionism*

Ethical Intuitionism was written in 2005 by American philosopher Michael Huemer, who argues for and defends ethical intuitionism. He posits that objective moral truths exist and that these truths are known through intuition or innate intellectual awareness. The author goes on to explain that understanding these moral truths gives human beings the rationale to behave independently of their desires. In his view, nothing is good or bad and individuals do not have any moral reason to do or ignore anything. He argues that moral views are passed on from one generation to another through evolution. After comparing morals to mathematical formulas and scientific facts, Huemer postulates that morals are as visible and obvious as everyday objects. He classifies the moral intuitions of humans as a priori knowledge, arguing that they include inherited knowledge, knowledge received via the senses, and knowledge observed directly from others.

Virginia Held, *The Ethics of Care: Personal, Political, and Global*

The Ethics of Care: Personal, Political, and Global was published in 2005 by American philosopher Virginia Held. Consisting of two sections, the book advocates that the ethics of care theory replace other moral theories. The first section of the book traces the origin of this theory and its association with such traditional moral theories as utilitarianism and liberalism. Held argues that the ethics of care should be regarded as a feminist moral theory because it originated from the caring experiences of women. She further states that, with the ethics of care theory, the patriarchal origins of the more popular moral theories will be exposed. In the second section of the book, Held discusses how the ethics of care theory can be applied to society. She goes on to argue that, unlike other moral theories, ethics of care can ensure that markets operate with values rather than from unalloyed commercial greed.

Logic and Philosophy of Logic

Charles Sanders Peirce, *How to Make Our Ideas Clear*

Published in 1878, *How to Make Our Ideas Clear* is a treatise on pragmatism by American philosopher Charles Sanders Peirce. According to Peirce, most people are intellectually impoverished because of deficient reasoning abilities. Poor reasoning also causes bad decision making, poor problem-solving skills, and mediocrity, the philosopher writes. To solve flawed reasoning, Peirce introduced pragmatism as a viable school of thought. In his view, pragmatism can educate humans on how to reason. Rejecting the idea that thought and words are for describing and representing reality, Pierce argues instead that thought and words are tools for problem-solving and action-taking. The author reasons that the brain is a mental tool that can be sharpened like any other tool. He points out various scientific theories on reasoning, time management, and resource management and illustrates practical steps for making one's ideas clearer and smarter in order to reason more effectively. *How to Make Our Ideas Clear* is a treatise on the tenets of pragmatism.

Gottlob Frege, *Begriffsschrift*

Published in 1879, *Begriffsschrift* is a book on logic by German philosopher Gottlob Frege. Here, Frege introduces the logical calculus notation system for logic and his ideas on logic. He starts by defining the negation, the conditional, the universal quantifier, identity of content, quantified variables, and other basic logical ideas. Next, he illustrates quantified variables as bivalent second-order logic with an identity. In the second chapter of the book, Frege presents nine axiomatic propositions of logic and argues for the validity of these propositions by reasoning that they connote self-evident truths. Next, the philosopher asserts that identity is a reflexive relation. In the third and final chapter, Frege introduces the ancestral of relation R (aR*b). In sum, *Begriffsschrift* reveals Frege's modern logic notation and his ideas on philosophical logic.

Kurt Gödel, *On Formally Undecidable Propositions of Principia Mathematica and Related Systems*

On Formally Undecidable Propositions of Principia Mathematica and Related Systems, published in 1931 by Kurt Gödel, the German philosopher, set out the author's "incompleteness theorems" and their proofs. According to the theorems, all formal axiomatic systems that model basic arithmetic are limited. Gödel uses the theorems to prove the impossibility of Hilbert's program and to find a consistent and complete set of axioms for all mathematics. Gödel also unveils the Gödel numbering method, which assigns a distinct natural number to all formal proofs and sentences in mathematical logic. Following this, the mathematician creates self-referential sentences to prove that classical paradoxes can be rewritten in arithmetic form. Gödel concludes by asserting that type theory can be linked to consistency proofs.

Frank P. Ramsey, *Foundations of Mathematics and other Logical Essays*

Published in 1931, *Foundations of Mathematics and other Logical Essays* is a collection of essays by British philosopher and mathematician Frank P. Ramsey. In his work, Ramsey reveals his ideas on mathematical logic, formal logic, facts, propositions, universals, truth, and probability. He also reviews Ludwig Wittgenstein's *Tractatus Logico-Philosophicus* and the work of other philosophers and mathematicians. He begins by reviewing the basic mathematical logic of 2 + 2 = 4 and exposing the philosophical thought behind this equation. He goes on to define the class of universals as an addition of the class of relations and the class of predicates. Lastly, he clarifies the distinction between perceptions and judgments.

Alfred Tarski, *The Concept of Truth in Formalized Languages*

The Concept of Truth in Formalized Languages is a 1933 book on logic by Polish philosopher Alfred Tarski, which proves that the concept of truth can be clearly defined for classical, formal, logical languages. Tarski also presents a method for constructing truth definitions for classical languages. He argues that a language is fully interpreted if all its sentences have meanings that are either true or false. Furthermore, the philosopher illustrates that the defined notion of truth can provide explicit semantic definitions for denotation and definability. Tarski then introduces the theory of types to solve the paradoxes of naïve set theory.

Alfred Tarski, *Introduction to Logic and to the Methodology of the Deductive Sciences*

Written in 1936, by the Polish philosopher Alfred Tarski, *Introduction to Logic and to the Methodology of the Deductive Sciences* is in two parts. In the first, devoted to the deductive method, the author introduces basic concepts of logic and its applications. He covers such topics as truth tables, proofs, sentential calculus, the theory of classes, the theory of relations, the theory of identity, and logical statements. The second part of the book focuses on the application of logic to the construction of mathematical theories. Here, Tarski covers the theory of real numbers, the laws of addition, and the laws of subtraction. He also provides examples of logical applications and points out the inherent logical principles at work. *Introduction to Logic and to the Methodology of the Deductive Sciences* presents the basics of logic and its practical applications.

Wilfrid Sellars, *Inference and Meaning*

Inference and Meaning is a 1953 book by American philosopher Wilfrid Sellars in which he distinguishes logical inferences from material inferences. The author defines formal inferences as those that depend on syntactic rules. He defines material inferences as those that do not depend on syntactic structure. Unlike reference, meaning is not extensional, nor is it a relation, the philosopher explains. Sellars analyzes meaning statements and points out how they clarify certain words. He goes on to examine reference statements and illustrates how they quantify implicitly over senses. Following these discussions, Sellars rejects the idea that meaning and reference are relations. He concludes by conceptualizing a theory on material rules of inference to solve the connecting problem between the semantic and syntactic rules of the human relation to the world. *Inference and Meaning* is a text on meaning, inference, and their linguistic importance.

William Kneale and Martha Kneale, *The Development of Logic*

The Development of Logic is a 1962 book on logic by American philosophers William and Martha Kneale. The authors review the history of logic in philosophy, reviewing the works of logic by Aristotle, Plato, Zeno, and other philosophers. They emphasize groundbreaking and revolutionary theories in logic, identifying milestones in the history of logic, such as Aristotle's Organon, the Stoics, Roman logic, Medieval logic, logic during and after the Renaissance, mathematical abstraction, sets and series, Frege's general logic, the philosophy of mathematics, the theory of deductive systems, and so on. *The Development of Logic* uncovers the origins and history of logic from ancient times to modern times.

Saul Kripke, *Semantical Considerations on Modal Logic*

Published in 1963, *Semantical Considerations on Modal Logic,* by American philosopher Saul Kripke, develops statements that can be used to represent possibility and necessity. Kripke assigns truth values to formulas and argues that the truth value of a formula in a possible world can depend on the truth value of other formulas in other possible worlds with accessibility relations. Kripke then develops relational or frame semantics <W, R> for modal logics and other non-classical logic systems. Possibility depends on accessibility relation R, the philosopher illustrates. He then asserts that the accessibility relation R makes room for expressing the relative nature of possibility. Additionally, Kripke points out the five frame conditions for defining modal logic: (1) Euclidean, (2) symmetric, (3) transitive, (4) serial, and (5) reflexive. *Semantical Considerations on Modal Logic* introduces Kripke's seminal concepts in modal logic.

Donald Davidson, *Truth and Meaning*

Truth and Meaning, a 1967 book by American philosopher Donald Davidson, addresses communication, belief, reference, and the relation between theories of meaning and theories of truth. Davidson argues that truth is a less opaque concept than meaning. He reviews Tarski's theory of truth and calls it a theory of meaning for language. Davidson then introduces a truth theory to convey his ideas on the compositional meaning theory. Following this, he argues that meanings are satisfactory conditions. In his view, a language with limitless expressive capacity can be learned with limited means using familiar combinatorics and the finite base of a Tarskian theory.

Willard Van Orman Quine, *Philosophy of Logic*

Philosophy of Logic is a 1970 masterpiece on logic by Willard Van Orman Quine, the American philosopher. He argues here that logic is the product of grammar and truth and rejects the argument that logic is all about words. Quine refutes the concept that logical truths are true because of language or grammar. The philosopher defines a logical truth as true sentences that essentially consist of logical words. He defines a logical true or false sentence as a sentence whose falsity or truth is verifiable by its logical structure. Lastly, Quine asserts that a sentence is logically true if all sentences that share its logical structure are true, and if it stays true regardless of any change in its predicates.

David K. Lewis, *Counterfactuals*

Published in 1973, *Counterfactuals*, by American philosopher David K. Lewis, presents the writer's ideas on counterfactual conditionals. Topics include strict conditionals, limit assumption, outer modalities, potentialities, reformulations, propositional quantifiers, comparative similarity, comparative possibility, cotenability, selection functions, selection operator, metalinguistic theory, analogies, conditional obligation, decidability results, completeness results, and derived modal logics. Lewis defends realism about possible worlds and posits that counterfactuals reflect the real truth about propositions. In addition, the philosopher introduces the Stalnaker-Lewis theory for analyzing counterfactual conditionals. *Counterfactuals* addresses counterfactual conditionals and their relevance to other philosophical fields.

Susan Haack, *Philosophy of Logics*

Philosophy of Logics is a 1978 book by British philosopher Susan Haack. Focusing on the basics and fundamentals of the philosophy of logic, she covers topics that include the purpose of logic, the scope of logic, tense logic, fuzzy logic, non-classical logic, modal logic, tense logic, relevance logic, truth, modality, set theory, validity, truth functions, semantic paradoxes, many-valued logic, names, description, ontology, sentence connectives, 2-value propositional, predicates, quantifiers, singular terms, and quantification. Haack reviews concepts and theories of logic from philosophers such as Frege, Wittgenstein, Gödel, Kripke, Tarski, Davidson, Russell, Quine, and Ramsey and concludes by answering metaphysical and epistemological questions about logic.

Peter Spirtes, Clark Glymour, and Richard Scheines, *Causation, Prediction, and Search*

The 1993 *Causation, Prediction, and Search,* writted by American scholars Peter Spirtes, Clark Glymour, and Richard Scheines, discusses causal knowledge and its applications. The authors use the formalized Bayesian networks to answer questions relating to causal knowledge, and they also discuss such topics as the theory of manipulation, causal structures, causal models, categorical data, probabilistic independence, theoretical statistics, inferential statistics, axioms, Markov equivalence, correlation chains, and partial identification. Spirtes, Glymour, and Scheines present methods for developing observations into causal knowledge, and they point out how causal knowledge is useful for creating prediction and planning models to influence the social, physical, and behavioral environment. The authors also examine the relationship between probability and causality and its application to statistics. *Causation, Prediction, and Search* is a book on causal models, prediction analysis, and their practical applications.

Robert Brandom, *Articulating Reasons: An Introduction to Inferentialism*

Articulating Reasons: An Introduction to Inferentialism is a 2000 philosophical book on the philosophy of language by American philosopher Robert Brandom, in which the author introduces his ideas on inferentialism. He defines *inferentialism* as the theory of meaning. In his view, the norms governing inferences to a sentence and from the sentence determine the semantic content of the sentence. Brandom also postulates that the major function of logical vocabularies is to clarify tacit inferential commitments. He highlights the relationship between semantic inferentialism and logical expressivism and writes about singular terms, reliabilism, objectivity, intentionality, normativity, justification, practical reason, and linguistic rationalism. In addition to supporting the use of inference over reference, the philosopher advocates for a shift from representationalism to inferentialism.

Philosophy of Language

Gottlob Frege, *On Sense and Reference*

Published in 1892, *On Sense and Reference,* by German philosopher Gottlob Frege, explains how the sense of a sign or term is related to the sign's expressed meaning. Frege theorizes that the meaning of a complete sentence depends on its being true or false. Following from this, he defines the reference of a proper name as the object that the name indicates or means. The author describes the sense of a name as what the name expresses. According to Frege, the reference of a sentence is the truth value of the sentence, and the sense of a sentence is the thought expressed by the sentence. The philosopher argues that the sense of different names is different even when they have the same reference. Furthermore, Frege argues that a name possesses sense, whether or not it has a reference.

Bertrand Russell, *On Denoting*

On Denoting, published in 1905 by the British philosopher Bertrand Russell, presents his theory on denoting phrases. He defines a *denoting phrase* as a complex expression that can serve as the grammatical subject of a sentence. He also asserts that denoting phrases do not have any meaning in themselves and do not need to have a denotation. Russell reveals two modes of knowledge: (1) knowledge by acquaintance (2) knowledge by description. Following from this, he introduces the descriptivist theory of names, which holds that proper names are abbreviated or disguised definite descriptions. After criticizing Alexius Meinong's theory of objectives, Russell resolves the problem of negative existentials. In summary, *On Denoting* explains denoting phrases and their applications to the fields of linguistics and philosophy.

Ludwig Wittgenstein, *Tractatus Logico-Philosophicus*

Published in 1921, *Tractatus Logico-Philosophicus,* by the Austrian philosopher Ludwig Wittgenstein, is one the most influential philosophical works of the twentieth century. In a series of propositions, beginning with "The world is everything that is the case," the philosopher argues that a logical picture of a fact is a thought. He goes on to explain how language depicts the world accurately and how the forms of language reflect various objective parts of reality. From here, he contends that the laws of science are not logical because they cannot explain the world. He goes on to propose the logical atomism theory, which states that the world consists of ultimate logical atoms or facts that cannot be broken down or understood independently from other facts.

Alfred Jules Ayer, *Language, Truth, and Logic*
Published in 1936, *Language, Truth, and Logic,* by the British philosopher Alfred Jules Ayer, introduces logical principles and theories on statements, tautology, propositions, meaning, verification, and verifiability. The philosopher rejects metaphysics by refuting various metaphysical arguments and argues that metaphysics cannot be verified empirically. In his view, logical certainty is more relevant to philosophy than are metaphysics and rationalism. Ayer defines truth, extolls logical positivism, and introduces the theory of emotivism, which states that ethical sentences express only emotional attitudes and not propositions. The author asserts that mathematics can be reduced to logical propositions.

Ludwig Wittgenstein, *Philosophical Investigations*
Published posthumously in 1953, *Philosophical Investigations* is an epistemological masterpiece by Ludwig Wittgenstein. The book is divided into two sections. In the first part, the Austrian-born philosopher explores the role of philosophy in understanding the nature of language. He begins by rejecting the Saint Augustine's belief that the purpose of language is to identify objects in nature. In contrast to Augustine, Wittgenstein argues that the meaning of a word lies in how it is used in a language. Language is an activity that makes the form of life evident, the writer argues. In the second section of the book, Wittgenstein discusses how language usage is the cause of many philosophical problems in such fields as logic, philosophy of mind, semantics, philosophy of psychology, philosophy of mind, and philosophy of action. He concludes that philosophers should only describe language, not attempt to explain it.

Stanley Cavell, *Must We Mean What We Say? A Book of Essays*
Must We Mean What We Say? A Book of Essays, by the American philosopher Stanley Cavell and published in 1959, endeavors to show that a combination of practicality and instincts can enable one to arrive at balanced conclusions. Cavell uses ordinary-language philosophy to discuss subjects that include skepticism, language usage, literary interpretation, metaphor, sarcasm, and tragedy. He argues against the belief that words have a specific meaning. Beliefs, he writes, do not really influence the meaning of a word. Instead, the socio-cultural conditions of society determine the

meaning that is being expressed. In addition to analyzing the relationship between linguistic theory and art theory, Cavell asserts that both theories are used to express meaning. Cavell asserts that external conditions impact the meaning of expressed words.

Willard Van Orman Quine, *Word and Object*

Published by the American philosopher Willard Van Orman Quine in 1960, *Word and Object* examines how linguistic analysis can be used to solve philosophical issues. Quine opens by discussing the role of stimulus-response mechanisms in language acquisition. According to his argument, language acquisition is a process that regulates the performance of verbal conduct. He contends that one can infer the meaning of a sentence from the type of response it elicits in a listener or reader. Following this, the philosopher distinguishes between two types of sentences: standing sentences and occasion sentences. Not only does Quine analyze how both sentence types respond to spontaneous stimulation, he also offers his indeterminacy of translation theory to describe what happens when a linguist comes into contact with an alien culture. According to the theory, it is possible to devise two compatible but dissimilar systems of translating one language into another. *Word and Object* attempts to demonstrate that the reference of terms is unreadable and that the significance of theoretical sentences cannot be determined.

John Langshaw Austin, *How to Do Things with Words*

John Langshaw Austin's *How to Do Things with Words* is a 1962 book that explores how certain uses of language seem to create an act. The British philosopher begins by claiming that there is no distinction between constatives and performatives. He argues that every act concerning an utterance falls under any of the following types: periocutionary act, locutionary act, and illocutionary act. The author goes on to reveal that performatives are simply verbs that clearly describe an action. In addition, he discusses the five performative categories: verdictives, commissives, exercitives, expositive, and behabitives. Austin also argues that almost every human utterance is a speech act. Within this framework, Austin concludes that one should focus on human actions rather than trying to decipher semantics and the meaning of words.

John Langshaw Austin, *A Plea for Excuses*

A Plea for Excuses, published in 1957 by British philosopher J. L. Austin, analyzes the issues language encounters when it discusses such actions as excuses. Austin begins by examining the subtleties common to the word "excuse" itself. He also studies the diverse ways people attempt to escape from unpleasant conditions. Based on several analyses, the author coins the term "clarification of use" to describe what it means to perform an action. He further mentions that one can categorize the different stages of action by analyzing the modifying expressions common to excuses. At this point, Austin enumerates the five stages of action: intelligence, appreciation, planning, decision, and execution. Breaking down actions into these stages enables one to precisely determine the validity of an excuse, he argues. He concludes by advocating for the importance of accurately determining and delimiting the action behind an excuse.

John Searle, *Speech Acts: An Essay in the Philosophy of Language*

Published in 1969, *Speech Acts: An Essay in the Philosophy of Language*, by John Searle, sets out to prove that language is a form of activity governed by rules. In the opening pages, the American philosopher distinguishes between constitutive and regulative rules. Constitutive rules, he explains, are activities that logically depend on rules while regulative rules are independent of rules. Thus, he argues that the semantics of language is a sequence of systems composed of constitutive rules, which guide the performance of illocutionary acts. After claiming that illocutionary acts are the most important element of linguistic communication, Searle explains that proposition gives illocutionary acts its content. On this basis, he concludes that natural language semantics should set propositions and forces as its main interest.

Donald Davidson, *Radical Interpretation*

Radical Interpretation, a 1973 book by American philosopher Donald Davidson, defines radical interpretation as the interpretation of a speaker without any dictionary, translator, reference point, or prior knowledge of their mental state while attributing specific desires, beliefs, and meanings to their words. Davidson argues that it is possible to translate a speaker's language without any prior knowledge by merely observing how the speaker uses the language. According to the philosopher, the knowledge required for interpretation is different from that required for translation. He explains that interpretation is more comprehensive than translation because individuals can interpret a sentence that cannot be translated. Referencing Quine's radical translation and Alfred Tarski's theory of truth, Davidson asserts that radical interpretation is the fundamental viewpoint from which to resolve facts about meaning. What is more, the scholar contends that mutual interpretation cannot be successful unless both parties make complete, true assumptions about one another. In his view, entirely true assumptions are, however, impossible for any interpretation.

Donald Davidson, *On the Very Idea of a Conceptual Scheme*

Published in 1973, *On the Very Idea of a Conceptual Scheme,* by American philosopher Donald Davidson, defines conceptual schemes as methods of organizing, rendering, and ordering that allow individuals to break down empirical reality and give rise to sensation. From here, the author uses the conceptual relativism thesis to reject the idea of an untranslatable language. He examines Quine's conceptual relativity and ontological relativity and points out why they are not valid. He goes on to scrutinize scheme-content dualism and proves that incommensurability is an incoherent idea. In the end, the philosopher rejects the "very idea" of a conceptual scheme along with any form of conceptual relativism.

Michael Dummett, *Frege: Philosophy of Language*

Frege: Philosophy of Language, by Michael Dummett and published in 1973, analyzes the philosophical contributions of German analytical philosopher Gottlob Frege. Dummett begins by commending the intellectual efforts of Frege and explains why he titled his book "philosophy of language" instead of using "logic" or "philosophy of thought." Frege's ideology, Dummett argues, makes it easy to become an analytical philosopher. He next proposes what the ideal Fregean model of language is composed of and how one can understand the place of Frege in analytical history. He also shows how various problems in logicism can be resolved using Frege's theses. In sum, *Frege: Philosophy of Language* is Dummett's attempt to systematically interpret the ideology of Frege.

Herbert Paul Grice, *Logic and Conversation*

Logic and Conversation, published in 1975 by Herbert Paul Grice, a British philosopher, begins by distinguishing between the opposing roles of formal language and natural languages. Grice argues that there is no difference or conflict between these languages, despite philosophers' common belief. The implied conflict, in his view, is traceable to the lack of attention given to understanding the conditions influencing conversations. Grice proposes the cooperative principle as an essential element to which all successful conversations must adhere. As he puts it, the cooperative principle enables one to achieve the purpose of a conversation because it allows only the communication of what is necessary for the conversation. He further suggests four maxims to support the cooperative principle: quantity, manner, quality, and relation. After asserting that rationality is built into a successful conversation, the author delves into how one can infer different meanings from what is being communicated. In short, *Logic and Conversation* philosophically explores the art of having good communications.

Saul Kripke, *Naming and Necessity*

Naming and Necessity, written in 1980 by American philosopher Saul Kripke, comprises three lectures that criticize the philosophy of the descriptivist theory of proper names. Kripke begins by categorizing proper names as rigid designators, a definition at variance with that of descriptivist theory. According to the author, while the descriptivist theory assigns varied objects to diverse possible worlds, a proper name defines a named object in all the possible worlds in which the object exists. Kripke therefore proposes a casual theory of reference, in which a name is assigned only to an object because of its causal link to the object. He points out two types of truths: conditional *a priori* truth and essential *a posterior* truth. The main distinction is that the latter relies on experience evidence, while the former does not. Kripke concludes by arguing against identity materialism's belief that mental and physical facts are identical. In his view, one can only use *a posteriori* identity to defend this belief, even though doing so may not be essential.

Cora Diamond, *The Realistic Spirit: Wittgenstein, Philosophy, and the Mind*

Published in 1991, *The Realistic Spirit: Wittgenstein, Philosophy, and the Mind* consists of fifteen papers by American philosopher Cora Diamond. In this collection, the author critically reviews the work of Ludwig Wittgenstein and Gottlob Frege. She also reveals her thoughts on ethics, the mind, religion, and literature. The first five papers address Wittgenstein's and Frege's ideas on sense and nonsense. In the next five essays, Diamond discusses Wittgenstein's *Tractatus Logico-Philosophicus*, other scholars' interpretations of Wittgenstein, as well as the issue of secondary sense. In the final five chapters, she shifts her focus to Anselm's ontological argument for God's existence, the philosophical ethics of animal experimentation and meat eating, and the intersection of philosophy with literature.

Robert Brandom, *Making It Explicit: Reasoning, Representing, and Discursive Commitment*

Published in 1994, *Making It Explicit: Reasoning, Representing, and Discursive Commitment,* by Robert Brandom, investigates how the use of an expression offers insights into its linguistic meanings. The American philosopher proposes an abstract theory, which he calls normative inferentialism. It is based on the premise that an expression gets its meaning from being among a set of social practices governed normatively by inferential rules. Brandom gives the three core elements that make up this theory: inferential semantics, normative pragmatics, and rational expressivism. With these three variables, he explains such important semantic concepts as singular terms or reference. Brandom uses normative pragmatics to argue that inferences determine the meaning of an expression.

Michael Devitt and Kim Sterelny, *Language and Reality: An Introduction to the Philosophy of Language*

Language and Reality: An Introduction to the Philosophy of Language, published in 1999 by Australian philosophers Michael Devitt and Kim Sterelny, addresses such topics as the origin of language, the influence of language, the problems of linguistic competence, the theory of meaning, the theory of transformational grammar, and the relation of language to the mind and the world. The philosophers argue in favor of an empirical, philosophical theory of language. Humans, they write, are intricate parts of a physical world. In their view, the study of language is not particularly relevant to the philosophy of language, and they adopt a functionalist approach to explore the nature of the mind.

Philosophy of Mathematics

Gottlob Frege, *The Foundations of Arithmetic*

Published in 1884, *The Foundations of Arithmetic*, by German philosopher Gottlob Frege, explores the philosophical basis of arithmetic. Frege devotes the first half of the book to criticizing the theories of numbers advocated in Kantianism, psychologism, and empiricism. These theories, he writes, are the results of an erroneous understanding of the meaning of numbers. He therefore proposes his context principle, according to which one should ask only for the meaning of a number term in the context of a proposition and should never ask for it in isolation. After arguing that numbers are objects, the author defines numbers as the extensions of concepts. Frege examines how numbers function like adjectives in natural language. He argues that number statements composed of number words appearing adjectivally can be converted into number statements in which the number terms are seen as singular terms. Frege concludes that statements about number terms are also statements on concepts.

Alfred North Whitehead and Bertrand Russell, *Principia Mathematica*

Published in three volumes (1910, 1912, and 1913), with a revised second edition appearing in 1925-1927, *Principia Mathematica,* by British philosophers Alfred North Whitehead and Bertrand Russell, is a magisterial three-volume masterpiece that treats the logical and philosophical foundations of mathematics. The authors set out to create a set of inference rules and axioms in symbolic logic that may be used to prove all mathematical truths. In their view, mathematics can be solely based on pure logic. Whitehead and Russell begin by introducing their concept of numbers and the theory of types. They develop the ramified theory of types to solve Russell's paradox and other paradoxes in set theory and logic. Whitehead and Russell also address ordinals, series, vectors, propositions, classes, relations, truth functions, the deduction theory, unit classes, variables, and identity.

Eugene Wigner, *The Unreasonable Effectiveness of Mathematics in the Natural Sciences*

The Unreasonable Effectiveness of Mathematics in the Natural Sciences was published in 1960, the work of Eugene Wigner, a Hungarian-American theoretical physicist. Wigner argues that the mathematical composition of a physical theory usually leads to the development of that theory and produces heuristic predictions. He begins by stating that there is no rational explanation for the usefulness of mathematics in sciences and goes on to assert that mathematical concepts can be applied in areas far beyond their original purpose. Elaborating, he uses the law of gravitation and James Clerk Maxwell's equations as examples of this principle. Maxwell's equations, he points out, were originally used to model magnetic and electrical phenomena but were later used to depict radio waves. In addition to speculating on the relationship between the foundations of mathematics and the philosophy of science, Wigner analyzes the challenges involved in unifying the sciences. The physicist ends by arguing that humans should be grateful for the gift of mathematics and that they should hope it continues to remain applicable in future research.

Ian Hacking, *The Emergence of Probability*

Published in 1975, *The Emergence of Probability: A Philosophical Study of Early Ideas about Probability, Induction and Statistical Inference* is a book by Canadian scholar Ian Hacking. It is an epistemological discussion of statistical inference, probability, induction, and other early ideas in philosophy. The Canadian philosopher develops a model to understand the theories of probability. In the process, he points out the flaws in these theories and then uses Michel Foucault's "archaeology of knowledge" concept to analyze alternative ideas of probability. The author suggests that a philosophical split, which involves two dissimilar models of chance and uncertainty, led to the emergence of the modern division between the long-run frequency deduction and personalistic, or subjective, probability.

Imre Lakatos, *Proofs and Refutations*

Written in 1976 by Hungarian philosopher Imre Lakatos, *Proofs and Refutations* is a philosophical dialogue that discusses the nature and development of mathematics. The Hungarian scholar explores several logical ideas. He argues that informal mathematics has no perfect or final theorem and believes that rather than accepting a theorem as the ultimate truth, one should assume that the theorem is yet to be disproved. Lakatos warns that one should adjust the existing theorem once a counterexample emerges to challenge the validity of the current theorem. The writer further argues that knowledge continuously accumulates through the process of proofs and refutations. He suggests that mathematical knowledge should be based on heuristics and offers examples of how the heuristic process can be applied to mathematical discovery. In addition to comparing the heuristic process to the deductivist approach, he also uses heuristics to analyze such concepts as bounded variation, Carathéodory definition, and uniform convergence. Lakatos concludes by rejecting the formalist ideology of proof prevalent in logicism.

Mark Colyvan, *The Indispensability of Mathematics*

Published in 2001, *The Indispensability of Mathematics,* by Australian scholar Mark Colyvan, addresses the Quine-Putnam indispensability argument in the philosophy of mathematics. According to the argument, one should place both mathematical and other hypothetical entities that are essential to the formulation of scientific theories on equal ontological footing. Using applications of mathematics as illustrations, the Australian philosopher supports the indispensability argument. Unlike Quine, however, who supports the indispensability argument with semantic holism, Colyvan reasons that a supporting argument requires only conformational holism to make it valid. The author concedes, however, that there will be continuous debates over what standard requirements are needed to make the indispensability argument a good scientific theory. Colyvan concludes that such disputes over validity will need to be addressed and resolved outside of the issues surrounding the indispensability argument.

Synopses of Classic Philosophical Fiction

Philosophical fiction refers to any work of fiction suffused with philosophical ideas. These scholarly ideas include debates on ethics, virtues, metaphysics, free will, rationality, and fatalism, among others. In philosophical fiction, it is not unusual for authors to use literary techniques to point out the argument for or against views commonly discussed in philosophy. Yet not all philosophical fiction works are the same. Some are written in the form of essays or novels, while others are composed in the form of plays. Following are synopses of classic philosophical fiction works written by prominent philosophers.

Saint Augustine, *De Magistro*

The *De Magistro* (*Concerning the Teacher*) was written in the fourth century by Saint Augustine, a theologian and philosopher who spent most of his life in the Roman Empire. This philosophical fiction is a dialogue between Augustine and his son Adeodatus. Although the work focuses on Augustine's philosophy of language, the central theme of this fiction is the acquisition of knowledge. In *De Magistro*, Augustine is concerned with two things: how words (signs) convey meaning and how teachers impart knowledge.

Augustine notes that words (signs) have a specific meaning and that they encapsulate thoughts, yet he argues that signs are inferior to knowledge. Without signs, he argues, the knowledge of something can exist. But without knowledge, signs are practically useless. Even though Augustine admits that learning (teaching) cannot be achieved without the use of signs, he adds that the acquisition of knowledge through signs cannot be achieved without understanding the objects, which the signs represent.

In conclusion, Augustine points out in *De Magistro* that the acquisition of knowledge from signs or words is possible only if the knowledge of the things represented by the signs is properly understood. A person who does not understand the meaning of a word cannot derive any sense from the word. So, to learn about something, the author believes that one needs to understand what the word signifies before using it. He also concludes that the truth "dwells in the internal man," meaning true knowledge can only be obtained from God or Jesus Christ.

Peter Abelard, *Dialogue of a Philosopher with a Jew and a Christian*
The Dialogue of a Philosopher with a Jew and a Christian is one of the philosophical masterpieces of erudite scholar Peter Abelard. This philosophical fiction published in the twelfth century contains two debates over the essentials of moral life, including the nature of happiness and supreme good. In the first debate, a philosopher uses natural reasons to contend with a Jew about the pertinence and relevance of adding the Old Law to the preexisting law of nature. In the second debate, the same philosopher discourses with a Christian on whether the religion can rationally achieve supreme good and avoid ultimate evil. The philosopher, in the end, provides rational grounds for the moral superiority of Christianity. Overall, the philosophical goal of Abelard in *Dialogue of a Philosopher with a Jew and a Christian* is to use reason to analyze matters of faith.

Ibn Tufail, *Hayy ibn Yaqdhan*
Hayy ibn Yaqdhan (*Alive, Son of Awake*) is a philosophical tale grounded in the teachings of Sufism, Kalam, and Avicennism. The philosophical relevance of this novel, which was published by Ibn Tufail in the twelfth century, is threefold. First: humans can train themselves to reach the perfection level of Prophet Muhammed. Second: Anybody can obtain absolute information about the universe. Third: The truth obtained from science can never contradict the truth derived from religion, meaning that reason and faith are complementary and compatible.

According to *Hayy ibn Yaqdhan*, a little boy named Hayy ibn Yaqdhan is found helpless on an island populated by gazelles. One of them raises him as its own until he can fend for himself. Curious about his surroundings, Hayy experiments with many things. He studies celestial objects, learns the languages of different animals, and eventually becomes a scholar in religion, philosophy, and science. His intellectual findings over the years motivate him to conclude that everything in the universe is created by God. He spends most of his time, teaching people around him the truths of things. To his mortification, many people are uninterested in following the tenets of his teachings. Instead, they are motivated by greed, avarice, and selfish desires. Hayy, therefore, concludes that people need the guidance of religion to make good and intelligent decisions.

Judah Halevi, *Kuzari*

Written in the 12th century by Jewish philosopher Judah Halevi, the *Kuzar* is philosophical fiction subtitled *Book of Refutation and Proof on Behalf of the Despised Religion*. The book, which takes the form of a dialogue, is divided into five parts, all of which focus on the discussion between the Rabbi and the pagan, the King of the Khazars. According to this philosophical masterpiece, God appears in the dream of the King of the Khazars, informing him that his intentions are pleasing but his actions are displeasing. Keen on becoming a virtuous leader, the king invites a rabbi to interpret the dream. The Jewish sage later explains the dream and, in the process, converts the king to Judaism after responding to the ruler's doubts and questions. In *Kuzar*, Halevi aims not only to defend Judaism against the polemics of theologians and philosophers but also to use reason to establish the superiority of Judaism over other Abrahamic-related religions such as Islam and Christianity.

Thomas More, *Utopia*

Utopia is a work of fiction published in 1516 by English lawyer and social philosopher Thomas More. The philosophical fiction is divided into Book 1 (*Dialogue of Counsel*) and Book 2 (*Discourse on Utopia*). In Book 1, English ambassador Thomas More travels on official business to Antwerp to meet the town clerk Peter Gills. Gills introduces More to his friend Raphael Hythlodaeus, a philosopher. The three men discourse on several social ills plaguing the future of Europe, including how kings execute citizens unjustly and how they embark on unnecessary, costly wars and make decisions based on whims. In their dialogues, Hythlodaeus criticizes the king's use of capital punishment against thieves, arguing that severe punishments encourage criminals to kill witnesses who may testify against them in the court of law. Impressed by Raphael's arguments, More suggests that Hythlodaeus would be a good advisor to the king.

In Book 2, Hythlodaeus talks about an ideal city named Utopia. According to him, in Utopia, there are is no capital punishment for thieves, no arbitrary or unjust laws, no selection of incompetent leaders, no kings, and no religious intolerance. Everyone is treated equally, and anyone is given an opportunity to succeed, regardless of their background. More comments that the Utopian society Hythlodaeus describes is ridiculous, yet he admits that he would like some of the laws of Utopia implemented in England and other European states.

Voltaire, *Zadig*

Zadig (The Book of Fate) is a 1747 novella by Voltaire, a French philosopher whose given name was François-Marie Arouet. The book narrates the story of a Babylonian philosopher named Zadig, who learns from brutal experience that everything in life happens for a reason. He loses his girlfriend to another man and later becomes an outcast in Babylon. In exile, his wisdom sometimes helps him to court favors from others. At times, his sagacity puts him in trouble. Despite suffering from many injustices at the hands of his superiors, Zadig returns to Babylon to challenge his enemies. In the end, he marries his love and becomes the king of Babylon.

Voltaire, *Candide*

Candide is another of Voltaire's philosophical fictions, published in 1759. The novel tells the story of Candide, who imbibes Leibnizian optimism from his tutor, Professor Pangloss. It is grounded in the faith that this world is "the best of all worlds." One fateful day, Pangloss finds Candide and his daughter intimate with one another. Pangloss responds by exiling his student, and Candide wanders far and wide in a journey fraught with hardship, betrayal, cannibalism, slavery, and war. These harsh experiences compel Candide to abandon Leibnizian optimism and adopt a practical philosophy that eschews excess idealism. He and his companions end up retiring, working a small farm, where they find peace, joy, happiness, and rest of mind.

Jean-Jacques Rousseau, *Julie, or The New Heloise*

Julie, also known as *The New Heloise,* is a philosophical novel published in 1761 and authored by Jean-Jacques Rousseau. Madame d'Étange hires a young Swiss man named Saint-Preux to teach her daughter Julie and Julie's cousin Claire. The teacher and Julie fall in love and desire to marry each other. Julie's father, however, disapproves of the marriage. Disappointed, Saint-Preux travels to Paris, from which he sends Julie a series of letters about his horrific experiences in the capital. Madame d'Étange discovers the correspondence, which makes her sad about her daughter's persistence in wanting to marry Saint-Preux. Julie's mother soon dies due to illness, an event that prompts Julie to marry another man, a M. de Wolmar. After a few years of marriage, Julie becomes increasingly religious and lives a life of virtue. She has two children with Wolmar, yet still has a soft spot for Saint-Preux. That Wolmar is a good man yet an atheist makes her miserable, and she sometimes falls into despair. Saint-Preux later marries Claire and becomes the tutor of Julie's children. The story ends with Julie's death—she drowns while trying to rescue one of her children. The philosophical dimension of this novel, according to the author, is that inauthentic actions usually lead to self-destruction.

James Hogg, *The Private Memoirs and Confessions of a Justified Sinner*

Published in 1824, *The Private Memoirs and Confessions of a Justified Sinner,* by Scottish writer James Hogg, depicts the absurdity of Calvinism, whose adherents believe that God has predestined some people to heaven and others to hell, regardless of their behavior in life. The story begins with the Editor's Narrative, which tells how Robert Wringhim meets Gil-Martin, who indoctrinates him into Calvinism. Convinced by Gil-Martin to destroy sinners who disobey God, Wringhim torments his brother many times before murdering him. Wringhim goes into hiding to evade the law. In his hiding place, he recollects all his previous malevolent actions and regrets all the cruel decisions made in the past. Wringhim subsequently decides to publish his memoirs before he ends his life in solitude. The novel concludes with how the "Editor" discovered Wringhim's memoir in his grave.

Walter Pater, *Marius the Epicurean: His Sensations and Ideas*

Marius the Epicurean: His Sensations and Ideas is a philosophical fiction by the Victorian English writer Walter Pater. Set in Rome during 161-177, the philosophical novel, which was published in March 1885, begins with the story of a young boy named Marius, who finds great joy in worshiping local gods. He later becomes skeptical about paganism when the household gods fail to cure his mother's illness. Marius subsequently abandons the religion altogether when he meets Flavian, a schoolmate, who teaches him about philosophy and literature. His friendship is cut short, however, when Flavian fall ill and dies. Depressed, Marius leaves his village for Rome, where he learns the teachings of Epicurus, Aristippus, Marcus Aurelius, Heraclitus, and Christianity. He eventually finds satisfaction in Christianity and sacrifices his life to save a Christian friend.

Thomas Carlyle, *Sartor Resartus*

Sartor Resartus (*The Tailor Re-Tailored*) is an 1833 philosophical novel by the English essayist and historian Thomas Carlyle. The novel is divided into three books. In Book 1, the "Editor" laments that the scientific community has yet to create philosophies of clothes despite the fact that humans are by nature naked animals. To correct this deficiency, the Editor translates the writings of Diogenes Teufelsdröckh (literally, "Devil's Dung") from German to English to share the writer's philosophy of clothes with English readers. In Book 2, Teufelsdröckh explains why he focuses only on the philosophy of clothes. He suggests that all language is a type of naming and that one's name influences one's future actions. In Book 3, Teufelsdröckh discusses the different clothing styles, including the ideology of many clothes wearers. The book ends with the Editor's comments, in which he commends the services of tailors and men like Teufelsdröckh, who devote so much effort to clothes.

Johann Wolfgang von Goethe, *Wilhelm Meister's Apprenticeship*

Wilhelm Meister's Apprenticeship is a 1795 novel by Johann Wolfgang von Goethe, the great German writer and polymath. Wilhelm Meister is a young man who attempts to disentangle himself from his bourgeois background. His father wants him to become a businessman, but Meister wants to become an artist. The young man falls in love with Marianne while pursuing his career as a playwright and actor. She cheats on him with wealthy man, leaving Meister distraught and hopeless. He then heeds his father's advice to be a merchant and, on his father's behalf, embarks on a business trip with Werner, his best friend. On their journey, the two men meet a troupe of actors, which inspires Meister to rekindle his career as an actor. He travels with the actors from one town to the other. One day, during a picnic, the troupe is attacked by bandits. Meister fights them and is injured. After recovering, he quits acting and resolves to be a businessman once again. He eventually surrenders to a simple but happy life with his family.

Fyodor Michailovich Dostoevsky, *Crime and Punishment*

Crime and Punishment is a dark masterpiece of Russian fiction written by Fyodor Mikhailovich Dostoevsky. Published in 1866, the novel centers on a proud but intelligent man named Raskolnikov, who believes that "superior" (intelligent) people have the right to kill "lesser" or despised members of society. Motivated by this radical idea, Raskolnikov murders an elderly pawnbroker named Alyona Ivanovna. He also assassinates Alyona's sister, Lizaveta, to cover up the murder. After committing the crimes, Raskolnikov disintegrates emotionally, alienating himself from everyone who cares about him, including his mother, sister (Dunya), and friends (Marmeladov and Razumikhin). He is eventually brought to justice and is imprisoned for eight years. During his incarceration, he repents of all his cruel decisions and realizes his love for Sonya, Marmeladov's daughter.

Leo Tolstoy, War and Peace

One of the world's greatest novels, *War and Peace* was published in 1867 by Russian writer Leo Tolstoy. It focuses on three influential (fictional) Russian families: the Bezukhovs, Bolkonskys, and Rostovs. The ongoing Napoleonic Wars threaten to destroy the way of life of the families. Pierre, who belongs to the Bezukhovs, marries Helen Kuragina, who later commits adultery. Disappointed over Helen's infidelity, Pierre leaves St. Petersburg to join the Freemasons. Andrei Bolkonsky in the meantime falls in love with Natasha Rostov, whose family is on the brink of financial ruin.

Andrei desires to marry her, but his father balks at the decision and advises his son to postpone the wedding for one year. He agrees with his father's advice and joins the military. During Andrei's absence, Natasha meets another wealthy man whom she wants to marry. Andrei finds out about Natasha's unfaithfulness and then cancels their marriage plans. Heartbroken, Natasha falls ill due to Andrei's decisions to discontinue the relationship. Pierre comes to Natasha's rescue, providing her succor and restoring her health. In the process, Pierre falls in love with Natasha and weds her. All takes place against the backdrop of war and other profoundly existential issues.

Giacomo Leopardi, *Operette Morali*

The *Operette Morali* is a collection of twenty-four works by the nineteenth-century Italian writer Giacomo Leopardi. Mainly short stories and dialogues, these works explore themes of natural forces, boredom, glory, illusions, and power; comparison between the ideas of the past and those of the present; and the relationship of man with nature and history. The dialogues and stories follow a general pattern: arguments, ideas, and messages create a sense of despair followed by a feeling of happiness. That is, the author often instills fear in the mind of the reader at the beginning of a piece and then provides a beacon of hope.

Robert Musil, *The Man Without Qualities*

Published in 1930, *The Man Without Qualities* is a novel by the Austrian philosophical writer Robert Musil. Part 1 (*A Sort of Introduction*) revolves around Ulrich, a scientist, ex-soldier, skeptic, and seducer who is indecisive about his values. Ulrich is a chronic thinker, too. He spends most of his time, ruminating about the ills of Austrian society. He seeks neither to offer a solution to Austrian social problems nor to promote the status quo. Ulrich eventually realizes his hypocrisy, for he engages in the very vices he complains about. The latter part of Part I focuses on Moosbrugge, a notorious man who commits all sorts of crimes. This man is found guilty of killing a prostitute and is then sentenced to life imprisonment. While incarcerated, he ponders about his past actions and the nature of reality.

In Part II (*Pseudoreality Prevails*), the novel considers Kakanian (Austrian) society as well as the implications of the looming World War I on Austria. Many Austrians prepare for the war. Unsure of what the future holds, they become fanatically patriotic and fantasize about making Austria great and even superior to Germany. Part III (*Into the Millennium*) centers on Agathe, Ulrich's sister. Ulrich meets her for the first time after their father's demise. Both share the same romantic feelings for each other and call themselves soulmates. The book ends with drafts and unfinished notes, indicating that Musil did not complete the masterpiece before his death.

Milan Kundera, *The Unbearable Lightness of Being*

The Unbearable Lightness of Being is a 1984 masterpiece by Czech writer Milan Kundera. It begins with the evaluation of Friedrich Nietzsche's concept of eternal return and Parmenides' understanding of life as light. The author explains the theory of Nietzsche, which states that all human experiences happen an infinite number of times. These experiences, according to Kundera, make individuals light or to experience "the unbearable lightness of being." After that, he argues, any human experience that happens only once is insignificant, meaningless, and "heavy." Kundera then ponders whether lightness is better than heaviness.

Next, the novel narrates the story of Tomas, a Czech surgeon who chooses to love his wife Teraza but nevertheless has an affair with a free-spirited photographer named Sabina. Teraza later finds out about Tomas's adulterous way of life and accepts it. Meanwhile, the Czech Communists want Tomas to join their government, but he refuses to acquiesce to their demands. Even Simon, Tomas's estranged son from an earlier marriage, tries to persuade him to work with the government. And yet he demurs. Both Tomas and Teraza eventually die in a car accident. In the meantime, Sabina meets another man, Franz, who loves her so much that he abandons his wife to be with her. Sabina later finds out about the death of Tomas and Teraza and relocates to the United States to start a new life. Distraught by Sabina's decision, Franz finds it impossible to forget her, even onto the day of his death.

Aldous Huxley, *After Many a Summer*

After Many a Summer is a 1939 philosophical novel by Aldous Huxley. It portrays Stoyte, an old Hollywood millionaire, who, seeking to prolong his life indefinitely, hires Obispo, an English doctor, to provide him longevity treatments. Obispo takes advantage of his patient, sedating him and raping Virginia, Stoyte's mistress. Suspicious that Virginia's admirer Pete is in a romantic relationship with her, Stoyte accidentally kills him with his pistol. Obispo believes Stoyte intended to murder him instead of Peter but nevertheless covers up the crime and continues to work for the millionaire to get money for his research. Stoyte, Obispo, and Virginia later relocate to a dungeon, where they find a 201-year old man named Fifth Earl. Despite Earl's ape-like appearance, Stoyte decides to extend his life with Obispo's treatment.

Aldous Huxley, *Island*

Island is a 1962 novel by Aldous Huxley, which narrates the story of Faranby, who, at the behest of a powerful oil baron, travels to the Kingdom of Pala (a utopian Island in the Pacific Ocean) to plunder its natural resources. He later discovers that other malicious foreign actors living on the island also intend to steal the island's wealth; however, the Utopian values and culture of Palanese islanders intrigue him and encourage him to change his plans to exploit the kingdom. In the end, a group of invading troops takes control of Pala.

C.S. Lewis, *The Space Trilogy*

The Space Trilogy is a group of three related science fiction novels authored in 1938-1945 by English writer C. S. Lewis. The trilogy consists of *Out of the Silent Planet* (1938), *Perelandra* (1943), and *That Hideous Strength* (1945). In *Out of the Silent Planet*, two malevolent scientists, Dr. Weston and Dick Devine, kidnap Elwin Ransom and set out on a voyage to Malacandra (Mars), where they intend to sell him to the sorns, horrible monsters. Ransom escapes from his captors and runs away, encountering the tribes of Malacandra. He learns their language and culture and is later instructed by the Oyarsa (ruler of Malacandra) to find Weston and Devine and banish them.

In *Perelandra*, Ransom journeys from Malacandra to a planet called Perelandra (Venus). There, he notices that the Queen and King of Perelandra are the only intelligent individuals on the planet. While the King is away, Ransom protects the Queen and the planet from being destroyed by Weston, whose identity is controlled by dark forces. In *That*

Hideous Strength, a scientific organization called the National Institute of Co-ordinated Experiments (NICE) plans to corrupt and destroy planet Earth. Ransom, in partnership with some strange friends, discovers their evil plans, battles with their troops, defeats the enemies, and eventually rescues Earth from imminent destruction.

Søren Kierkegaard, *The Seducer's Diary*

The Seducer's Diary is an 1843 novel written by Danish philosopher Søren Kierkegaard under the pseudonym of Johannes the Seducer. This book echoes Johannes's philosophical views on childbearing, marriage, and freedom. The novel depicts Johannes as a libertine/libertarian who derives satisfaction in seduction but resists marriage or anything that stifles his freedom. Johannes orchestrates a meticulous plan to seduce Cordelia, who is ten years younger. He succeeds, the young woman accepts his proposal, and they marry, whereupon Johannes subsequently manipulates her into questioning the union, which ends in divorce. Johannes later regrets his rash action after Cordelia, his truest love, marries another man just one year after the dissolution of the marriage.

Friedrich Nietzsche Thus Spoke Zarathustra: *A Book for All and None*

Thus Spoke Zarathustra: A Book for All and None is Friedrich Nietzsche's 1883 novel. This popular masterpiece chronicles the humanitarian efforts of Zarathustra (Zoroaster), a sage and prophet who desires to elevate people to "Superman" (or "Overman") status. Zarathustra abandons the solitude of his cave and preaches to anyone who cares to listen that God is dead. He goes further to lambaste the beliefs of Christians, as well as the precepts of nationalism, calling both insane and barbaric. The sage advises people to abandon religion and embrace the ways of the Superman.

When almost everyone rejects his teachings, Zarathustra changes his proselytizing tactics, which helps him to find a handful of disciples. He teaches these followers the values of the Superman, which include being happy, courageous, and resilient in the face of oppression. His efforts nonetheless fail to produce the desired result, as most of his disciples dilute and distort his teachings. Feeling that no one understands him, he returns to his cave. There, he realizes the idea of eternal recurrence, which means that all human experiences occur an infinite number of times. He eventually leaves the cave again to spread these newly augmented teachings to those who value them.

Leo Tolstoy, *Resurrection*
Resurrection is the final masterpiece of Leo Tolstoy. Published in 1899, the novel centers on Dmitri Ivanovich Nekhlyudov and Katerina Mikhaelovna Maslova. During their adolescent years, Dmitri impregnates Katerina and relocates to another city. She loses the baby and becomes a prostitute to make ends meet. Years later, Katerina is accused of being complicit in the murder of a Siberian merchant and is to be tried in court. Dmitri appears as one of the jurors. Katerina does not recognize him, but Dmitri recognizes her, and he feels partial responsibility for her predicament. Although he is unable to save her from a prison sentence, he later consults a lawyer to discuss how he can manage Katerina's release. Dmitri visits her in prison and reveals his true identity, thinking she will still love him. To his mortification, Katerina resents him. His visits to the prison nevertheless expose him to the horrors of the prison, and he later helps Katerina gain release. He proposes, but Katerina rejects the proposal and marries another man. In the end, Dmitri reconciles himself both to her decision and to a life without her.

Samuel Beckett, *Waiting for Godot*
Waiting for Godot is a 1952 play by the Irish dramatist Samuel Beckett. It opens with two men, Vladimir and Estragon, waiting near a leafless tree for a mysterious figure named Godot. While waiting for Godot, they discuss both trivial issues and the purpose and meaning of their existence. Pozzo and his servant Lucky meet them as they banter and join the conversation. After a while, Pozzo and Lucky leave the two men, and Godot's messenger arrives and notifies Vladimir and Estragon that Godot will not be able to come today but will come tomorrow. The messenger departs, and the men wait near the leafless tree for Godot to arrive the next day. The same pattern of events unfolds the following day. Vladimir and Estragon wait for Godot's arrival. While they wait, Pozzo (now blind) and Lucky (now deaf) meet the gentlemen as they have a conversation. As before, the pair participates in the discussion and then departs. Godot's messenger reappears, informing Vladimir and Estragon that Godot will not be coming on that day. When questioned, the messenger claims he did not communicate with them the previous day. In the end, Vladimir and Estragon decide to leave.

Louis-Ferdinand Céline, *Journey to the End of the Night*
Journey to the End of the Night is a 1932 novel by Louis-Ferdinand Céline. According to the story, a young man named Ferdinand Bardamu enlists in the French army to fight against German troops during World War I.

After experiencing the horrors and brutality of the war, his enthusiasm for killing Germans wanes. Bardamu is sent on a reconnaissance mission, where he meets Robinson, a fellow soldier who wants to leave the army. Bardamu tries to escape with Robinson, but their plans fail. Wounded, Bardamu is dispatched to Paris for medical treatment. There, he meets two women, Lola and Musyne, who later abandon him for his cowardice. Heartbroken, Bardamu relocates to Africa, then travels to America, and then moves back to France to become a doctor. Tired of his new profession, he joins a troupe of musicians and later meets Robinson and his fiancée Madelon. Madelon ends up killing Robinson for his disloyalty, leaving Bardamu to ponder the meaning and purpose of life.

Marcel Proust, *In Search of Lost Time*

Also translated as *Remembrance of Things Past*, *In Search of Lost Time* is a seven-volume novel authored between 1913 and 1927 by Marcel Proust. The volumes include *Swann's Way* (Volume 1), *In the Shadow of Young Girls in Flower* (Volume 2, also translated as *Within a Budding Grove*), *The Guermantes Way* (Volume 3), *Sodom and Gomorrah* (Volume 4, also translated as *Cities of the Plain*), *The Prisoner* (Volume 5, also translated as *The Captive*), *The Fugitive* (Volume 6, also translated as *The Sweet Cheat Gone*), and *Finding Time Again* (Volume 7, also translated as *Time Regained* and *The Past Recaptured*). Overall, the story recounts in exquisite detail the experience of a man named Marcel, who grows up learning art, studying high-class society, and falling in love. The detail of experience in this vast novel has prompted some to consider it a work of phenomenological fiction.

Antoine de Saint-Exupéry (Antoine Marie Jean-Baptiste Roger, comte de Saint-Exupéry), *The Little Prince*

The Little Prince is a 1943 novella by Antoine Marie Jean-Baptiste Roger, who wrote under the name Antoine de Saint-Exupéry. A little prince with golden hair meets a pilot stranded in the Sahara Desert. The prince implores the pilot to draw an elephant for him. The pilot obliges, sketching a big snake with a mammoth in its stomach. Upon seeing the image, the prince concludes that humans cannot comprehend anything with simple explanations. The pilot and the prince become friends and learn about each other in the desert. The pilot explains how the engine of the plane malfunctioned and forced him to land in the desert. In turn, the prince tells the pilot that he comes from an asteroid. While the pilot is fixing the plane, the little prince narrates his weird experience journeying from one asteroid to another. Both later become so hungry and thirsty that they can barely move. Lucky for them, they find water in a well. The prince decides to return home, to the mortification of the pilot. He promises the pilot, however, that he will never forget him when he gets home. The pilot completes the repair of his plane, leaves the desert, and narrates his experience.

André Malraux, *Man's Fate*

Published in 1933, *Man's Fate* is a novel by French writer André Malraux. It narrates the fate of four revolutionists—Chen Ta Erh, Kyo Gisors, Katow, and Baron Clappique—who collaborate to take over Shanghai against the will of the government. Chen Ta Erh is sent to assassinate an authority. He succeeds, but the deaths of the people he killed haunt him, leaving him with suicidal thoughts. His life comes to an end in a failed suicidal attempt to kill the Chinese leader Chiang Kai-shek. Kyo Gisors, a leader of the revolt, desires a world in which people will be free and not controlled by governments. He is later captured but chooses to end his own life. After Katow learns of Kyo's death, he attempts to take his own life by swallowing poison. However, discovering there is not enough poison for all the conspirators, he gives his comrades the poison and faces the horror of being thrown alive into the boiler of a steam locomotive. Among the four revolutionists, only Baron Clappique escapes the cold hands of death.

Thomas Mann, *The Magic Mountain*

The Magic Mountain is an epic 1924 novel by Thomas Mann. A young German engineer, Hans Castorp, journeys from Hamburg, Germany, to Davos, Switzerland, to visit his tubercular cousin Joachim Ziemssem in a tuberculosis sanatorium. Castorp intends to spend a few weeks in the sanatorium with Ziemssem but it is discovered that he, too, has TB and is therefore compelled to stay in the sanitorium. During his long time in the clinic, Castorp becomes a philosopher. He meets several people with different philosophical views. They discuss free will, religion, civilization, humanity, and other contentious topics concerning human society. After spending seven years in the sanatorium, Castorp returns to Germany and volunteers to serve in World War I. The novel ends with the hint that the war will lead to his untimely death.

Franz Kafka, *The Trial*

The Trial is a philosophical fiction written in 1925 by German writer Franz Kafka but not published until some years after his death. A pair of guards visit a bank official, Joseph. K., on his thirtieth birthday, They arrest him. Joseph is furious over his arrest because he believes he has not violated any law or, indeed, done anything wrong. Not only are his protestations of innocence used against him, he is subjected to several interrogations without knowing why he has been arrested and charged. Tired and frustrated, Joseph tries to understand the vague law or the nature of his crime, so that he may prove his innocence. All his efforts to save himself from the arbitrary law of the land end in vain. On his thirty-first birthday, another two men arrest him in his house and notify him that he has broken another law. Again, they decline to explain his crimes. Unlike before, they take him this time to an abandoned site and stab him to death.

George Orwell, *Animal Farm*

Animal Farm, a novella by George Orwell published in 1945, tells the tale of a collection of animals who rebel against their farmer-owner Mr. Jones with the aim of creating a farm in which all animals will be happy, free, and treated as equals. The animals, led by two intelligent pigs, Napoleon and Snowball, succeed in their rebellion. They take over the farm, chase Mr. Jones away, and rename the property Animal Farm. Mr. Jones reappears to retake his farm by force, but the animals defeat him again. Animal Farm prospers for a brief period.

Trouble begins when the two pig-leaders contend for the top leadership position. Napoleon eventually defeats his rival, chasing Snowball away from the farm and humiliating or killing any animal who challenges his authority. After becoming the leader of the farm, Napoleon becomes a totalitarian tyrant. He and his team abuse other animals, treat them like second-class beings, and force them to do hard labor while they themselves enjoy the largest share of their harvests. The novel ends with Napoleon and his friends walking, dressing, and behaving exactly like the human beings—Mr. Jones—the animals had struggled so hard to remove from power.

B.F. Skinner, *Walden Two*

Walden Two is a 1948 philosophical novel by American behavioral psychologist B. F. Skinner. The book begins with how two men, Rogers and Steve, just returned from World War II, visit their old Professor, Burris (Skinner's first name is Burris), and discuss a utopian community. During their discussion, the three men remember that T. E. Frazier, one of Burris's students, is an advocate of utopianism. Burris contacts Frazier and discovers that his former student lives in a utopian community named Walden Two.

Six people journey to Walden Two to learn about the utopian city, including Burris and his friend Castle; Rogers and his girlfriend Barbara; Steve and his girlfriend, Mary.

Frazier welcomes the six guests to the utopian city and introduces them to the utopianism of Walden Two. In Walden Two, people live a communal life, with all property belonging to the community. Everyone, including children and adults, attends the same school and eats in the same restaurant. They also discover that citizens of Walden Two are conditioned from a young age to be happy, diligent, and productive. Steve, Rogers, and Mary are willing to live in Walden Two, whereas Barbara does not like the lifestyle she sees there. Castle and Burris are skeptical about the feasibility of Walden Two, so they decide not to stay. As he attempts to board a train home, Burris changes his mind and returns to Walden Two, intending to spend the rest of his life there.

George Orwell, *Nineteen Eighty-Four (1984)*

Nineteen Eighty-Four is a George Orwell's dystopian masterpiece, published in 1949. Winston Smith lives in Oceania, a city controlled by a mysterious totalitarian government ruled by Big Brother. No one is permitted to question or criticize the government or to express thoughts or speak languages not approved by the government. In Oceania, everyone is under surveillance. Big Bother monitors the activities of all citizens with cameras and listening devices.

Employed by Big Brother's government to falsify historical records, Smith hates the government's suppression of truth and writes down his rebellious thoughts in a secret diary. He later falls in love with a woman named Julia and tells her about his vision and dream of working against the government. Both meet a rebel named O'Brien and agree to work against the government. Unknown to Smith and Julia, O'Brien is an undercover agent of Big Brother. Winston and Julia are arrested, incarcerated, humiliated, and tortured until Smith is fully brainwashed, renounces both Julia and rebellion, is released, and confesses his love, not for Julia, but for Big Brother.

Anthony Burgess, *A Clockwork Orange*

A Clockwork Orange is a 1962 masterpiece by English writer Anthony Burgess. The novel tells the story of Alex, a gang leader in a totalitarian country. With fellow gang members Dim, Pete, and Georgie, he spends his time committing robbery, assault, robbing and rape. Apprehended, Alex is sentenced to fourteen years in prison. In jail, he meets a prison chaplain who teaches him how to read the Bible and follow the teachings of Christianity. His life, however, transitions from bad to worse when he fights with and murders a cellmate.

Alex is taken to another cell, where he is subjected to Ludovico's Technique, a form of brainwashing that eliminates free will. He is injected with a substance that causes extreme fatigue and then subjected to violent films. He loses his mind and learns to hate anything violent as well as music, which had been his favorite hobby. A political dissident named F. Alexander hears about Alex's story and is willing to use it not only to expose government oppression but also to incite public outrage. To thwart Alexander, the government intervenes and restores Alex's free will. Alex returns to his old ways of crime. In the end, however, he tires of his violent lifestyle, decides to be a better man, and intends to start a family.

Philip K. Dick, *Do Androids Dream of Electric Sheep?*

Do Androids Dream of Electric Sheep? is a science fiction novel written in 1968 by Philip K. Dick. San Francisco Police bounty hunter Rick Deckard is hired to destroy six highly intelligent androids who escaped from Mars to Earth after rebelling against and killing their masters. These androids are nearly identical to human beings, so only a scientific test can reveal their true identity. Some of the androids try to befriend Deckard and deceive him into believing they are human, while others confront the bounty hunter. Deckard eventually kills all six androids and reflects on the morality of his actions.

Philip K. Dick, *A Scanner Darkly*

A Scanner Darkly is a 1977 science fiction masterpiece by American writer Philip K. Dick. An undercover cop, Bob Arctor, whose code name is Fred, is sent to disrupt the drug supply chain in America. He becomes involved with a dangerous psychoactive drug called "Substance D" and begins to lose his own identity. Because of his addiction, he cannot figure out whether he is Arctor or Fred, whether he is working for law enforcement or the drug household. He falls in love with a low-level dealer named Donna, who takes him to New-Path, a rehabilitation clinic, to overcome his addiction. Unknown to Arctor, Donna is an undercover agent sent to use him to infiltrate New-Path and discover the funding source of the rehabilitation center. While withdrawing from Substance D addiction, Arctor discovers the mysterious source of the drug and discloses it to undercover police agents.

Philip K. Dick, *Valis*

Valis (*Vast Active Living Intelligence System*) is a three-part science fiction novel by American writer Philip K. Dick. The *Valis* trilogy includes *The Divine Invasion* (1981), *The Owl in Daylight* (1982), and *Radio Free Albemuth* (1985). The hero of the three books is a paranoid named Horselover Fat, who discovers the hidden mysteries of Gnostic Christianity through a revelation from VALIS, an intelligent satellite that beams pink light. Fat believes that the purpose of this "theophany" is to lead him to a messiah named Sophia. Fat and his friend eventually meet her—she is a two-year-old girl—who tells them that all their convictions about VALIS are true. Sophia later dies in an accident. Disappointed, Fat goes on a global search to find her next incarnation.

Jean-Paul Sartre, *Nausea*

Nausea is a philosophical novel by Jean-Paul Sartre. Written in 1938, the work recounts the story of a restless historian named Antoine Roquentin, who travels out of Paris to research the life of a French aristocrat named Marquis de Rollebon for a biography. During his research, Roquentin becomes aware that he worries about everything around him. Apart from using the term "nausea" to describe his restless behavior, he tries to understand the feeling or to escape it altogether. His efforts, however, are met with failure.

His nausea infects his research. He becomes uninterested in writing the biography of Marquis de Rollebon, arguing that there is no point in trying to understand the past of a dead man. He later figures out that his nausea is trying to reveal to him the idea that existence precedes essence, a cornerstone of Existentialism. Roquentin travels to Paris to share this new-found knowledge with his ex-girlfriend, Anny, but notices that she struggles to comprehend him. He then relocates to another town, where he meets an acquittance nicknamed Self-Taught Man. Roquentin explains his ideas to this stranger, but Self-Taught Man does not embrace his philosophical ideas. Frustrated, Roquentin finally relocates to Paris to write a novel.

Ralph Ellison, *Invisible Man*

Published in 1952, Ralph Ellison's *Invisible Man* chronicles the journey of an unnamed black narrator who finds himself locked in a cellar, forced to live an underground existence. The narrator recounts his teenage years in a small town, where he learns from his grandfather always to be subservient to the white folks, even though such behavior is treacherous. Not long after his grandfather's death, the narrator delivers a graduation speech, encouraging black people to be subservient to the whites. A group of prominent white men, impressed by this message, give him a scholarship to a prestigious black college. For exposing a white man to an idealized version of a black person, the narrator is expelled from school and given a bunch of sealed recommendation letters to help him find work in New York City. No company hires him. He later discovers that the letters condemned him.

After bouncing from one menial job to the other, the narrator is eventually employed as an orator by a black political organization named the Brotherhood. The organization indoctrinates him, helps him to forget his past, and assigns him to a branch in Harlem, New York. Everyone loves the narrator for his rhetorical skills. Suspicious that he is using the organization for his selfish aims, the Brotherhood assigns him to another job in which his primary duty is to advocate for women's rights. The narrator comes to believe that the Brotherhood is being controlled indirectly by whites for whites, so he rejects all the ideals of the Brotherhood and seeks to destroy it from inside. While trying to run away from brutal race riots across Harlem, the narrator is chased by a group of policemen. They continue to run after the narrator until he falls into an open manhole. The police cover the manhole. He stays in this dungeon for fifteen days writes his story.

Simone de Beauvoir, *She Came to Stay*

She Came to Stay is a 1943 novel by French writer Simone de Beauvoir. Françoise engages in an open relationship with Pierre. Both are Existentialists. After some time, Pierre meets another young woman, Xaviere, and teaches her about freedom and free will. The three form a ménage à trois, a relationship that is met with challenges as each wants to possess the other person's sole desire. Xaviere tries to drive a wedge between Pierre and Françoise to acquire one of them for herself.

Simone de Beauvoir, *All Men Are Mortal*

All Men Are Mortal is a 1946 novel by French writer Simone de Beauvoir. Ambitious actress Regina meets a mysterious immortal man, Raimon Fosca. Fascinated by his immortality, Regina seeks to understand why Fosca has lost hope in the world. Fosca recounts the story of his immortal existence to her, a narrative filled with significant moments in history and the greedy nature of humans. She eventually comprehends why the immortal man is indifferent to the very things she considers unique and significant.

Osamu Dazai, *No Longer Human*

Osamu Dazai's 1948 novel *No Longer Human* tells the story of Ōba Yōzō, a troubled man who is incapable of revealing his identity to others. Realizing at a young age that people are hypocritical and egotistical, Yōzō rejects his own personality and becomes a kind of clown to establish interpersonal relationships with others. He meets Takeichi who introduces him to the art world. He later finds himself entangled in such vices as smoking, drinking, and sleeping with a married woman. His life becomes more complicated when he is expelled from school. While trying to start his life afresh, Yōzō meets a single mother and tries to be part of her family. His effort ends in futility, however. He continues to change his behavior (from good to bad) and to bounce from one woman to another until he is put in a correctional facility. After his release from the facility, Yōzō isolates himself.

Walker Percy, *The Moviegoer*

Walker Percy's 1961 philosophical fiction *The Moviegoer* narrates the story of young stockbroker Binx Bolling, who searches for the meaning of life after returning from the Korean War. Bolling finds everything around him boring and empty except watching movies and television. In search of greater meaning in life, he frequently visits his aunt Aunty Emily, who lectures him on how to be a good man. One day, Aunt Emily implores Bolling to help her watch over Kate Cutrer, his aunt's stepdaughter. He obliges but flirts with Kate. Both Kate and Bolling believe they understand each other. Their relationship remains platonic. Finally, as Bolling's instability becomes more telling, Kate plans to marry a man named Walter Wade. When she calls off the marriage, Bolling proposes marriage, and she eventually accepts.

Yukio Mishima, *The Sailor Who Fell from Grace with the Sea*

First published in 1963, Yukio Mishima's *The Sailor Who Fell from Grace with the Sea* tells the story of thirteen-year-old Noboru, who belongs to a gang. Noboru's mother, Fuskao, falls in love with Ryuji Tsukazaki, an ambitious sailor who desires nothing but glory. Noboru admires Tsukazaki for his masculine traits, calling the sailor his hero. They become close friends, but their friendship is cut short when the young boy loses respect for him the day he sees the sailor drench himself in a fountain, behavior Noboru believes is "childish" and thus dishonorable. While Tsukazaki is planning to marry Fuskao, Noboru reveals the incident to his gang, which orchestrates a plan to poison the sailor. The novel ends when Tsukazaki unwittingly drinks the poison and becomes lost in his thoughts and he passes away.

José Lezama Lima, *Paradiso*

José Lezama Lima's 1966 novel *Paradiso* tells the story of Cemí, a young man suffering from a mysterious illness. Losing his father at a young age, he searched for an identity and, in the process, is exposed to the allure of sex but survives the dangers of this phase. He later falls in love with art and poetry at the university while working as an apprentice under the tutelage of Oppiano Licario. This man mentors Cemí until he is fully prepared for his own poetic creation. The novel ends with Licario's words: "We may now begin."

Robert Pirsig, *Zen and the Art of Motorcycle Maintenance*

Published in 1974, Robert Pirsig's *Zen and the Art of Motorcycle Maintenance* tells the story of a narrator and his son Chris who embark on a seventeen-day motorcycle journey. They meet their friends John and Sylvia on their journey. While traveling, the group discusses technology, the U.S. landscape, and have many other philosophical discourses. The narrator and Chris, who later part ways with their friends in Minnesota, continue their journey to Northern California. On their journey, the narrator tells Chris about his past identity, his glass-concept dreams (which he fears might come to fruition), and his philosophical concept, which he calls Quality, an intangible thing that determines whether something is good or not. Their relationship becomes frosty during the journey. Before sending Chris home, the narrator confesses to his son that he has hereditary mental problems and cannot reconcile his split personality any longer. Chris asks the narrator a question to test his reality. His response to the question makes Chris realize that his father has no mental illness because he can differentiate between the present and the past. The novel ends as they become friends and ride toward San Francisco.

Renata Adler, *Speedboat*

Published in 1976, Renata Adler's novel *Speedboat* tells the story of Jen, a young female reporter who is unsure of her sanity yet chooses to act sane. She talks about her peripatetic life and her habit of doing everything in a rush, including the way she talks, observes things, and organizes her life. Jen complains about her job and society, which are not ethically satisfying to her.

David Markson, *Wittgenstein's Mistress*

Published in 1988, David Markson's masterpiece *Wittgenstein's Mistress* revolves around protagonist Kate, who is convinced that she is the only being on planet Earth. Kate lives alone in a beach house, where she contemplates several aspects of the past. She meditates about anything she can think of, including sex, art, music, and great legends like Helen of Troy, William Gaddis, William Shakespeare, and Vincent van Gogh. Her memories and thoughts later become distorted by her imagination. In the end, she can no longer distinguish her present from her past or recognize whether something is wrong or right, making her question the foundation of her insanity.

Jostein Gaarder, *Sophie's World*

Sophie's World is a fictional masterpiece written in 1991 by Norwegian writer Jostein Gaarder. Sophie Amundsen learns about philosophy from Alberto Knox, an old philosopher. Every day Knox sends her unsolicited correspondence containing philosophical texts. They later meet face-to-face, and Knox lectures her more about the teachings of many philosophers, including Aristotle, Plato, Socrates, Descartes, Karl Max, George Berkeley, Spinoza, Hegel, and Jean-Paul Sartre.

One day, Sophie receives letters meant for a girl named Hilde from Albert Knag, Hilde's father. As time passes, Sophie and Knox realize that they are both imaginary people Knag created to send cryptic birthday messages to Hilde. Unhappy about her father's interference in life, Hilde partners with Sophie and Knox to escape Knag's imagination. They orchestrate a plan to give Knag a dose of his own medicine by interfering and messing with his mind. The plan works. Knag becomes paranoid and apologizes to his daughter after finding out that the trio used his own trick on him. The novel ends as Sophie is learning how to interfere with the world of Hilde and her father, Knag.

Arthur Asa Berger, *Infinite Jest*

Published in 1997, *Infinite Jest* was written by the American novelist Arthur Asa Berger. An adolescent boy named Hal finds it exceedingly difficult to communicate with others. The only person who understands him is his older brother, Mario, who is disabled. Hal becomes addicted to drugs, but, after his father's death, turns over a new leaf. He becomes a professional tennis player and quits abusing drugs. Meanwhile, Canada and the U.S. disagree over a waste site used by the U.S. The former considers the waste site part of the U.S but the latter, which pollutes the area, considers the site part of Canada.

Neal Stephenson, *Anathem*

Anathem is a science fiction novel published in 2008 and written by American novelist Neal Stephenson. A powerful group of aliens threatens to distort the balance of power on a planet called Arbre. Fraa Erasmas is sent to find the alien's ship. He travels with his friend Jad to the planet's frozen pole, where they meet Fraa Orolo, a member of his clan who was banished from Arbre for violating a sacred law. There, Orolo discovers four vials of blood that can help him discover where the elusive aliens are hiding. He shares his findings with Fraa Erasmas. After Orolo dies while trying to protect the blood, Erasmas quickly travels to Arbre to report to the leaders of Arbre the whereabouts pf the aliens. Erasmas and the planet's finest men in Arbre are sent to destroy the aliens and restore balance to the future of the universe. They eventually accomplish the mission and rebuild Arbre.

Giannina Braschi, *United States of Banana*

Giannina Braschi's 2011 philosophical fiction *United States of Banana* mirrors the plights and dreams of Puerto Ricans. Giannina, Zarathustra, and Hamlet embark on a mission to rescue Puerto Rican prisoner Segismundo. This prisoner has been incarcerated by his father, the king of the United States of Banana, for more than 100 years in a dungeon buried inside the Statue of Liberty. Segismundo's crime was having been born. The king eventually marries another wife, frees Segismundo, and allows Puerto Rico to join the United States of Banana. This privilege, which allows all Hispanic Americans to own the passports of the United States of Banana, causes a power shift in the global community with far-reaching implications.

André Alexis, *Fifteen Dogs*

Fifteen Dogs is a 2005 novel by Canadian author André Alexis. It begins with two gods, Hermes and Apollo, debating whether animals could be happy and fulfilled if they could think and talk like humans. Apollo contends that if animals had speech and cognitive abilities, they would be more unhappy than humans. Hermes disagrees. The two gods decide to make a wager. The loser will become the other's servant for a year. The gods then grant a group of fifteen dogs the ability to speak and think. With their new abilities, they escape from their cages and start their own lives. After the dogs squabble over who should lead them, Atticus eventually emerges as the leader of the pack and teaches them how to be dogs again. Some nonetheless become tired of changing their identity bytrying to bark and behave like a dog.

Joseph Conrad, *Heart of Darkness*

Polish-born British writer Joseph Conrad's 1899 novella *Heart of Darkness* depicts the debilitating effects of colonization on the colonizers and the colonized alike. Protagonist Charlie Marlow relates to the passengers on a Thames River boat the evils of colonization. None of the passengers believe Marlow. To convince them, he talks about his travels to the Congo Free State in Africa. Fascinated by maps and what lies beyond Europe, Marlow accepted a job working for a colonial enterprise as a riverboat captain. His mission was to transport ivory from the Congo to England. On reaching Africa, his hopes sink as he witnesses outrageous violence, barbaric and cruel behavior, the use of brute force to inflict pain on slaves, and the presence of widespread acute illness. Meanwhile, Marlow hears many stories about Kurtz, a colonial agent whom people in Congo admire and respect for his values and great ability to help the colonial enterprise purchase ivory from the region. The captain is eager to meet Kurtz and to know more about him. Marlow does meet Kurtz, who appears very ill and near death. Bedridden, Kurtz gives Marlow all his classified papers and files, including a photograph of his wife. Marlow hears Kurtz whispering repeatedly "The horror" as he nears death. Marlow returns to England and finds the woman on the photograph. She asks Marlow to tell her the last word mentioned by Kurtz. Rather than tell her the truth, Marlow replies that his last word was the mention of her name.

Fyodor Dostoevsky, *The Brothers Karamazov*

The Brothers Karamazov is an 1880 novel by Russian writer Fyodor Dostoevsky. Fifty-five-year-old Fyodor Pavlovich is the father of three sons: Alexei, Ivan, and Dmitri. Unlike Dmitri, Alexi and Ivan are from the same mother. Fyodor Pavlovich is also the father of a bastard named Smerdyakov. Fyodor lost interest in all his sons after their mother died, and all four share hatred for their father.

Years later, twenty-eight-year-old Dimitri meets Fyodor Pavlovich to claim his mother's inheritance. Fyodor refuses to grant his request, forcing Dimitri to tell his intellectual brother, Ivan, to intervene. Fyodor resents Dmitri because the son does not love his wife Katerina but loves Grushenka, a woman whom Fyodor intends to marry. Alexei is a religious person who believes so totally in Jesus Christ that he tries to convince his brothers to accept the teachings of Christianity. Ivan, on the other hand, is an intellectual atheist, who lectures Smerdyakov on the concepts of free will, immortality, and faith.

As time passes, Fyodor Pavlovich dies, and almost everyone suspects Dmitri is responsible for his death. Smerdyakov later confesses that he was the one who killed him, although he also blames Ivan in part for his crimes. For it was Ivan who convinced him that nothing is impossible. Overcome with guilt, Ivan becomes mentally unstable and subsequently stands trial for the death of their father. Katerina, who is in love with Ivan, orchestrates a plan to pin the death of their father on Dimitri. The plan succeeds, and the novel ends as Ivan helps Dimitri to elope with Grushenka to another town.

James Joyce, *Ulysses*

Written in 1922 by Irish writer James Joyce, *Ulysses* depicts the experience and encounters of three principal characters, Stephen Dedalus, Molly Bloom, and Leopold Bloom. Stephen is a teacher at Garrett Deasy's Boys' School. Stephen meets Deasy to receive remuneration for his teaching services. Deasy, narrow-minded, lectures Dedalus about life. Stephen leaves Deasy's office and starts ruminating about his life.

Leopold Bloom and Molly Bloom are married with one daughter. Leopold, who is known to be a henpecked husband, suspects that Molly is having an affair with one Blazes Boylan. One fateful day, Leopold runs into and follows Stephen's father and other acquaintances to a funeral. The funeral reminds him of the deaths of both his son and his father. He later visits a maternity clinic to check on Mina Purefoy. There, he meets Stephen and other friends. They drink, crack jokes, and banter with one another. Stephen eventually gets drunk and starts misbehaving. Fortunately, Leopold takes him to his house to regain his senses. After Stephen leaves Leopold's house, Leopold finds evidence of Blazes' visit. Leopold pretends everything is fine. To Molly's surprise, Leopold asks her to serve him breakfast in bed. The novel ends as Molly soliloquizes about the sex she had with Blazes and her failed singing career.

The action of the novel is set in contemporary Dublin but follows the allegorical pattern of Homer's *Odyssey* by way of patterning a stream-of-consciousness narrative that develops themes of modern life.

Franz Kafka, *The Metamorphosis*

The Metamorphosis is a 1915 masterpiece written by Franz Kafka but published posthumously years later. Gregor Samsa, a traveling salesman, wakes up at home one morning to discover that he has become a giant cockroach. He locks the door to his room and tries to hide from everyone, including his family members and his boss, the Chief Clerk. When Gregor opens the door to the insistent knocking of his boss and reveals his appearance, the Chief Clerk flees in terror. Only Samsa's family makes any attempt to accommodate him, giving him food, providing him shelter, and cleaning his room from time to time. They eventually tire of taking care of him due to the financial costs and psychological burden. They tell him that he is a nuisance, and Gregor agrees with their decision. He takes his own life. The family feels a sense of loss after the death of Gregor, but their lives go back to normal.

Theologus Autodidactus

Theologus Autodidactus is a philosophical fiction published in 1268-1277 and authored by Arab writer Ibn al-Nafis. The theological novel centers around a feral child named Kamil. Kamil lives alone in an isolated desert from childhood to adolescence. During his isolated days in the desert, he learns on his own religious, natural and universal truths as well as the teachings of Islam. As time passes, Kamil encounters castaways who were stranded in the desert as a result of shipwreck. The castaways, in the end, take Kamil to the civilized world.

William Shakespeare, *Hamlet*

Hamlet is a 1599 play by William Shakespeare. The drama depicts the story of Prince Hamlet, who returns to Denmark from his university to discover news of the sudden death of his father, the King of Denmark. He mourns for months, his sorrow complicated by the disloyalty of his mother, Queen Gertrude, who marries his father's brother Claudius, who becomes the new King of Denmark. One day, the ghost of Hamlet's father appears to Hamlet and tells him that his death was the work of Claudius, who poisoned him through the ear. Unsure of the veracity of the ghost's allegations, Hamlet pretends to be mad and starts spying on Claudius to confirm his suspicion. He eventually concludes that the ghost was telling the truth. Claudius, in the meantime, becomes suspicious of Hamlet's irrational behavior and plots to kill the young man. After a series of missed opportunities to destroy each other, Hamlet and Claudius eventually confront each other in a bloody swordfight that leads to their mutual demise. In the end, no one emerged as the king of Denmark as a hostile force from Norway takes full control of the kingdom.

Leo Tolstoy, *The Death of Ivan Ilyich*

The Death of Ivan Ilyich is an 1886 novella by the Russian writer Leo Tolstoy. Its protagonist is Ivan Ilyich, a forty-five-year-old lawyer, who has spent his youth building his career, acquiring wealth, and improving his social status. Ivan Ilyich never thinks about death until he falls ill and becomes bedridden. His sickness compels him not only to examine how he has spent or misspent his life, but also leads him to notice how people around him are distracted by material things of the world rather than thinking about the true nature of limited life. Ivan Ilyich becomes filled with regret, feeling he has lived his life based on the expectations of others, not his own desires. Before he passes, however, he gradually forgives himself, his daughter, wife, and others. He dies in a moment of bliss.

Sergio Troncoso, *The Nature of Truth*

American writer Sergio Troncoso's 2003 novel *The Nature of Truth* centers on Helmut Sanchez, a young researcher working under the tutelage of Yale professor Werner Hopfgartner. Sanchez unwittingly finds a letter written ten years ago by Hopfgartner, in which the professor confesses his feelings of guilt over the "dirty" role he played during the Holocaust. Offended by Hopfgartner's hatred for Jews, Sanchez embarks on a mission to find out all the professor's secrets. He travels to Australia and Italy to uncover the truth. Meanwhile, Regina Neumann, a rival of Hopfgartner at Yale, is determined to tarnish the image of Hopfgartner by exposing his sexually related crimes against vulnerable students. Neumann persuades insecure student Sarah Goodman to file a sexual-harassment charge against Hopfgartner. Sanchez's quest to find the truth later results in unforeseen consequences.

Leading Authors of Philosophical Fiction

Albert Camus

French writer and philosopher Albert Camus wrote several philosophical novels, the most notable being *The Stranger (L'Étranger)*, *The Plague (La Peste), The Fall (La Chute)*, and *The First Man (Le Premier Homme)*, all of which are centered on themes of absurdism. Published in 1942, *The Stranger* revolves around protagonist Meursault, who, without passion or motive, murders an Arab man and ends up being sentenced to death. Published five years after the release of *The Stranger*, *The Plague* is the story of human behavior in a cholera epidemic in Oran, Algeria. *The First Man* is Camus' final work of fiction, which was left incomplete when he was killed in an automobile accident. The novel explores the lives and history of people colonized in colonial North Africa.

Marquis de Sade

Marquis de Sade was a French writer, politician, and philosopher known for his libertine, atheistic, and nihilistic ideas and after whom the word *sadism* was coined. He wrote several plays, novels, and dialogues, but his most famous literary works are his novels, *Justine* (1791), *The 120 Days of Sodom* (1785), *Philosophy in the Bedroom* (1795), and *Juliette* (1797–1801). Even though these works are suffused with erotic and even pornographic imagery and ideas that still shock the sensibility, they explore challenging philosophical topics related to aesthetics, morality, naturalism, and theology.

Franz Kafka

German-Czech diarist, short-story writer, and philosophical novelist Franz Kafka wrote such short stories as "Contemplation" (1904), "Description of a Struggle" (1904), "In the Penal Colony" (1914), "The Hunger Artist" (1922), and "Josephine the Singer; or the Mouse Folk" (1924). His most celebrated fiction includes the *The Metamorphosis* (a 1915 novella) and his novels, *The Trial* (1914-1915), *The Castle* (1926), and *Amerika* (1927). All Kafka's major fiction contains elements of realism and existential nihilism, and all of it was published posthumously.

Hermann Hesse

The German writer Hermann Hesse wrote many works of philosophical fiction, including *The Glass Bead Game* (1943), *Siddhartha* (1922), and *Steppenwolf* (1927). The works focus on themes of spirituality, self-knowledge, and authenticity. In *The Glass Bead Game*, protagonist Joseph Knecht grows up in a town known for breeding intellectuals, where he masters the mysterious Glass Bead Game. In *Siddhartha*, the title character, an Indian man, abandons his birth family and the values of his father to embark on a journey of self-discovery in search of peace and happiness. In *Steppenwolf*, the author's most famous book, half-human and half-wolf Harry feels ill-suited to live in a frivolous bourgeois society finally learns about himself.

Stanisław Lem

Polish writer Stanisław Lem is the author of essays on such topics as futurology and literary criticism but is most famous for his philosophical science fiction novel *Solaris*. Published in 1961, *Solaris* tells the story of a group of scientists who seek to understand extraterrestrial life on the planet Solaris. They carry out an unauthorized, dangerous experiment to unlock the planet's secrets. Their experiments backfire, producing unexpected outcome, and the scientists begin to see cracks in their personalities as they confront their worst fears. Yet, in the end, they fail to discover anything significant about Solaris.

Ayn Rand

In a world filled with so many male writers competing for attention, the Russian-American Ayn Rand distinguished herself. Her fiction is typically injected with objectivism, the philosophical system she herself invented. Rand struggled over the years to achieve global recognition for her literary efforts until she published her two masterpieces, *The Fountainhead* and *Atlas Shrugged*. Published in 1943, *The Fountainhead* is the story of a young architect named Howard Roark, who thinks collectivism is subordinate to individualism. In his profession, he refuses to compromise his innovative ideas for an architectural company that values conformity and conservationism. *Atlas Shrugged*, published in 1957, depicts a dystopian U.S. society in which the efforts of American business owners are frustrated by bureaucratic laws and burdensome regulations. The novel ends as workers try to build a capitalistic society that promotes individualism and reason.

Samuel Beckett

Irish playwright, novelist, and short-story writer Samuel Beckett is a literary giant of the twentieth century. Beckett produced great fiction, all of which is infused with absurdism. His most famous contribution to modern literature is the absurdist play *Waiting for Godot*, but also notable are the plays *Krapp's Last Tape* (1958) and *Happy Days* (1961).

Iris Murdoch

Anglo-Irish novelist and philosopher Iris Murdoch is best known for writing novels on themes of morality, sexuality, and good and evil. What makes her work so outstanding is her seamless ability to take readers on memorable philosophical journeys. Her best-known philosophical fiction includes *The Sea, the Sea* (1978), *Under the Net* (1954), *The Black Prince* (1973), and *The Bell* (1958). Among these novels, *The Sea, the Sea* is widely considered her best book, and was awarded the 1978 Booker Prize. The novel depicts the obsession of protagonist Charles Arrow with his romantic ideas. After retiring from work as a theater director, Arrow spends his time in an isolated home near the sea, writing a memoir about his life and his love affair with Lizzie, an actress with whom he wishes to spend the rest of his life. He begins to idealize his relationship with this woman and tries to elope with her. Lizzie eventually rejects him, which leaves him with yet more regrets.

Anthony Burgess

English writer and composer Anthony Burgess was a novelist and literary critic. He wrote novels, screenplays, and, a self-taught "classical" composer, wrote more than 250 musical works, including symphonies. His novels include *Earthly Powers* and *Enderby Quartet,* but perhaps the best is *A Clockwork Orange*, a novel that depicts a dystopian state riddled with violence and crime.

Simone de Beauvoir

French novelist Simone de Beauvoir was more than a writer. She was a feminist, politician, intellectual, social theorist, and philosopher. Her many pursuits infuse her novels with a philosophical perspective. While Beauvoir wrote essays, monographs, biographies, and autobiographies, her masterpiece is *The Second Sex* (1949), a massive and pioneering work on feminism and the liberation of women. Her most provocative novel, from the point of view of philosophy, is the 1954 *The Mandarins,* which depicts the lives of the philosophers and friends of the Parisian Existentialist circle.

André Malraux

French writer and art theorist André Malraux spent most of his life promoting art for art's sake, but is now best known for his novels. These include *The Temptation of the West* (1926), which depicts how China is tempted to accept the values of the West, while Europe struggles to understand the motives of the East; *The Conquerors* (1928), and *The Royal Way* (1930). His fiction is heavily influenced by the German philosopher Friedrich Nietzsche.

Fyodor Dostoevsky

The work of Russian novelist Fyodor Dostoevsky embodies philosophical themes that foreshadow the advent of phenomenology and existentialism in their exploration of the nature and structure of existence, consciousness, and conscience. *Crime and Punishment* (1867), *The Idiot* (1869), *Demons* (also translated as *The Possessed,* 1872), and *The Brothers Karamazov* (1880) are all masterpieces of world literature. *The Brothers Karamazov* explores free will, morality, and the existence of God. *Demons* delves into the ramifications of moral nihilism and the political decadence of nineteenth-century Russia. In *The Idiot*, Prince Myshkin falls in love with two women, Nastasya and Aglaia, both of whom are involved with a corrupt, avaricious man named Ganya. The good nature of this prince appears, however, insufficient to change the ways of Ganya the others around him.

Jorge Luis Borges

Argentine writer Jorge Luis Borges never achieved the philosophical renown of an Aristotle or a Socrates, but his literary works are imbued with philosophical idealism, eternal recurrence, externalism, and are nothing short of mind-bendingly brilliant. Influenced by the likes of Virgil, Camões, Spinoza, and others, Borges is best known for the short stories collected in his *Ficciones* (1941-1956), especially "The Library of Babel" (1941). They reflect not only his profound metaphysical skepticism but also his genius for fantasy and surrealism.

Umberto Eco

Umberto Eco was one of the most important Italian writers of late twentieth and early twenty-first centuries. A dazzling novelist, he was also a philosopher, literary critic, and semiotician. He wrote several children's books and essays, but his novels, especially *Name of the Rose* (1980), *Foucault's Pendulum* (1988), and *The Prague Cemetery* (2010), have done most to secure his place in world literature. In *The Prague Cemetery,* protagonist Simone Simonini resents anything Jewish. Learning from a lawyer how to expertly forge documents, he participates actively in overthrowing the abusive government in Italy. He later uses his ability to falsify historical documents not only to lie against the Jews but also to acquire stupendous wealth for himself.

Rebecca Goldstein

American novelist and philosopher Rebecca Goldstein has written excellent philosophical fiction, especially science fiction on such themes as rationalism, atheism, and feminism. In 1983, she published her first novel, *The Mind-Body Problem*, which explores the relationship between thoughts and consciousness, including the challenges faced by women and Jews. Goldstein also published *The Late-Summer Passion of a Woman of Mind* in 1989 and *The Dark Sister* in 1993.

14

Resources

This list of "resources" is far from exhaustive, what with more than 3,000 years of philosophical output from across the planet. In *Process and Reality*, Alfred North Whitehead remarked, "the safest general characterization of the European philosophical tradition is that it consists in a series of footnotes to Plato." Part of a robust general education in philosophy includes learning the conceptual and theoretical concerns that have occupied the philosophical terrain since even *before* Plato's time. After all, Plato himself was engaged with predecessors within and outside of his own tradition.

This list of sources puts the emphasis on the major works of major thinkers and the major topics in philosophy.

Essential Reading in the History of Philosophy

Ancient Chinese, Greek, and Indian Philosophy

- Vedas (c. 1500–1000 BC)
    - Sarvepalli Radhakrishnan and Charles A. Moore, eds. (Princeton University Press)

  Selected excerpts from the *Vedas* and other texts, with commentary.

- Buddha (c. 450 BC)
    - Anguttara Nikāya, *The Book of the Gradual Sayings*, trans. F. L. Woodward & E. M. Hare, 5 volumes (Pali Text Society)
    - Dīgha Nikāya, *The Long Discourses of the Buddha: A Translation of the Dīgha Nikāya*, trans. Maurice
    - Walshe (Wisdom Publications)
    - Majjhima Nikāya, *The Middle Length Discourses of the Buddha: A Translation of the Majjhima Nikaya*, trans. Bhikkhu Nanamoli and Bhikkhu Bodhi (Wisdom Publications)
    - Samyutta Nikāya, *The Connected Discourses of the Buddha*, trans. Bhikkhu Bodh (Wisdom Publications)

- Laozi (c. sixth century BC), Confucius (c. 551–479 BC), Zhuangzi (late fourth century, BC), Mozi (c. 430 BC), Mengzi (fourth century BC)

 - Philip J. Ivanhoe and Bryan W. Van Norden, translators, *Readings in Classical Chinese Philosophy*

- Pre-Socratics (c. 600 – 400 BC): Thales (c. 626/623 BC-c. 548/545 BC)
  - Jonathan Barnes, *The Presocratic Philosophers* (Routledge)
  - G. S. Kirk, J. E. Raven, and Malcolm Schofield, *The Presocratic Philosophers* (Cambridge University Press)
  - Richard D. McKirahan, *Philosophy Before Socrates* (Hackett Publishers)

- Socrates (c. 469–399 BC) and Plato (c. 429–347 BC)
  - Edith Hamilton and Huntington Cairns, eds., *The Collected Dialogues of Plato* (Princeton University Press)

- Aristotle (384–322, BC)
  - Jonathan Barnes, ed., *The Complete Works of Aristotle: The Revised Oxford Translation*, 2 vols. (Princeton University Press)

- Stoics, Epicureans, Skeptics (300 BC–fifth century AD)
  - A.A. Long and D. N. Sedley, *The Hellenistic Philosophers*, in 2 vols. (Cambridge University Press)

Medieval Philosophy

- Augustine (354–430)
  - *Confessions*, translated and edited by Albert C. Outler (https://www.ling.upenn.edu/courses/hum100/augustinconf.pdf)

- Boethius (c. 475–526?)
  - *Consolation of Philosophy*, translated by H.R. James (https://www.gutenberg.org/files/14328/14328-h/14328-h.htm)

- al-Kindi (800–870)
  - Peter Adamson and Peter E. Pormann, translators, *The Philosophical Works of al-Kindi* (Oxford University Press)
  - Jon McGinnis and David C. Reisman (eds.), *Classical Arabic Philosophy: An Anthology of Sources* (Hackett Publishing)

- al-Farabi (c. 870–950)
  - Jon McGinnis and David C. Reisman (eds.), *Classical Arabic Philosophy: An Anthology of Sources* (Hackett Publishing)

- Ibn-Sīnā (Avicenna) (c. 970–1030)

- Saint Anselm (1033–1109)

- al-Ghazali (c. 1056–1111)
  - Jon McGinnis and David C. Reisman (eds.), *Classical Arabic Philosophy: An Anthology of Sources* (Hackett Publishing)

- Ibn Rushd (Averroes) (d. 1198)

- Jon McGinnis and David C. Reisman (eds.), *Classical Arabic Philosophy: An Anthology of Sources* (Hackett Publishing)

- Peter Abelard (1079–1142)
    - *Ethical Writings*, edited by Paul Vincent Spade (Hackett Publishing Company)

- Maimonides (1138–1204)
    - *The Guide of the Perplexed*, translated by Shlomo Pines (University of Chicago Press)

- Roger Bacon (1214 or 1220–1292)
    - *Selected Philosophical Works*, edited by Rose-Mary Sargent (Hackett Publishing Company)

- Duns Scotus (1265/1266–1308)
    - *Duns Scotus: Philosophical Writings*, edited by Allan B. Wolter (Hackett Publishing Company)

- Thomas Aquinas (1225–1274)
    - *Selected Philosophical Writings*, translated by Timothy McDermott (Oxford University Press)

Aquinas's writings are voluminous, ranging across every major area of philosophy. Curated selections are good ways to enter into his thought.

- William of Ockham (1287–1347)
    - *William of Ockham: Philosophical Writings*, revised edition, translated by Philotheus Boehner (Hackett Publishing Company)

  This text contains some of Ockham's significant writings on metaphysics, ethics, and logic.

Modern European Philosophy

- Michel de Montaigne (1533–1592)
    - *Essays*, translated by M.A. Screech (Penguin Classics)

  Montaigne's essays cover a wide range of topics, including sadness, laughter, warhorses, and prayer.

- Giordano Bruno (1548–1600)
    - *Cause, Principle and Unity: And Essays on Magic*, translated and edited by Richard J. Blackwell and Robert de Lucca (Cambridge University Press)

  Bruno critically engages with Aristotle and embraces Copernicus's heliocentric theory as the beginning of a new philosophy.

- Francis Bacon (1561–1626)
    - *Francis Bacon: The Major Works*, edited by Brian Vickers (Oxford University Press)

  Bacon's writings range of interests includes politics, religion, and natural philosophy (what will become "science") and the scientific method. He is best known for *Advancement of Learning*.

- Galileo Galilei (1564–1642)
  - *The Essential Galileo*, edited and translated by Maurice A. Finocchiaro (Hackett Publishing Company)

  Considered a (if not the) progenitor of the scientific revolution, Galileo wrote on scientific methodology, astronomy, and what we know now as physics.

- Thomas Hobbes (1588–1679)
  - *Leviathan*, edited by Richard Tuck (Cambridge University Press)

  Hobbes is best known for the view of human nature that underlies his social contract theory, but he wrote on language, mind, and other philosophical topics.

- Pierre Gassendi (1592–1655)
  - *Selected Works*, translated by Craig Brush (Texts in Early Modern Philosophy)

  The theologian engaged with Descartes, Malebranche, and Leibniz, among other important thinkers of 17th century Europe.

- René Descartes (1596–1650)
  - *Descartes: Selected Philosophical Writings*, translated and edited by John Cottingham (Cambridge University Press)

  Descartes is a towering figure in philosophy, whose work helped usher in the transition from a teleological to a mechanistic worldview, but his thought ranged over a number of topics in his systematic philosophy, including mind and the passions.

- Antoine Arnauld (1612–1694)
  - *On True and False Ideas*, translated by Stephen Gaukroger (Manchester University Press)

  Along with Gassendi, Arnauld is best known for his critical engagements with some of the most prominent thinkers of his day, including Galileo, Hobbes, and Descartes.

- Blaise Pascal
  - *Pensées and Other Writings*, translated by Honor Levi and edited by Anthony Levi (Oxford University Press)

  Best known for his "Wager," Pascal's contributions to seventeenth-century debates in theology and natural philosophy reveal thinking on, among other topics, ethics, free will, and politics.

- Margaret Cavendish (1623–1673)
  - *Margaret Cavendish: Essential Writings*, edited by David Cunning (Oxford University Press)

  A versatile thinker, Cavendish wrote fiction, poetry, plays, and philosophy. Her work anticipated views of some important, and better-known thinkers, and she engaged with a number of luminaries of the day.

- Robert Boyle (1627–1691)
  - *Selected Philosophical Papers* edited by. M.A. Stewart (Hackett Publishers)

  Boyle was a leading empirical thinker of his day.

- Baruch Spinoza (1632–1677)
  - *Ethics*, translated by Samuel Shirley (Hackett Publishers)

  Spinoza was a significant post-Cartesian philosopher who influenced many other thinkers across the discipline.
- Samuel von Pufendorf
  - *The Divine Feudal Law: or, Covenants with Mankind, Represented*, translated by T. Dorrington (Liberty Fund)

  An influential thinker who went largely unappreciated in the nineteenth and twentieth centuries, Pufendorf wrote across a broad range of philosophical topics.
- John Locke (1632–1704)
  - *An Essay Concerning Human Understanding* (Oxford University Press)
  - *Second Treatise of Government* (Routledge Press)

  Locke is a towering figure of early modern philosophy. Perhaps best known outside philosophy for his significant influence on the U.S. Founding Fathers, Locke wrote not only political philosophy, but also metaphysics and epistemology.
- Nicolas Malebranche (1638–1715)
  - *Treatise on Ethics*, translated by C. Walton (Kluwer Publishers)
  - *Dialogues on Metaphysics and on Religion*, translated by Nicholas Jolly and D. Scott (Cambridge University Press)

  Malebranche, a Cartesian thinker, contributed to areas as diverse as optics and theology.
- Isaac Newton (1642–1727)
  - *Mathematical Principles of Natural Philosophy* (Harvard University Press)

  "Newtonian" physics was the foundation for classical mechanics. His three laws of motion revolutionized science.
- G.W. Leibniz (1646–1716)
  - *Philosophical Essays*, edited and translated by Roger Ariew and Daniel Garber (Hackett Publishers)

  Leibniz's genius ranged across the intellectual spectrum, from mathematics to theology.
- Giambatista Vico (1668–1744)
  - *The First New Science*, edited and translated by Leon Pompa (Cambridge University Press)

  Trained in law, Vico read and wrote widely, from philology to natural philosophy.
- George Berkeley (1685–1753)
  - *Philosophical Works, Including the Works on Vision*, edited by Michael Ayers (J.M. Dent Publishers)

  Bishop Berkeley was one of the three major British Empiricists. He is best known for his empirical idealism.
- Thomas Reid (1710–1796)
  - *An Inquiry into the Human Mind on the Principles of Common Sense*, in *The*

Works of Thomas Reid (Edinburgh University Press and Pennsylvania State University Press)

Reid wrote largely on perception and methodology, though his interests ranged across philosophical topics.

- Jean-Jacques Rousseau (1712–1778)
  - *The Social Contract and Other Later Political Writings*, edited and translated by Victor Gourevitch (Cambridge University Press)

  Rousseau is best known for his work in political philosophy, which includes views on human nature, education, and moral psychology.

- David Hume (1711–1776)
  - *Dialogues Concerning Natural Religion*, edited by Dorothy Coleman (Cambridge University Press)
  - *An Enquiry concerning Human Understanding*, edited by Tom L. Beauchamp (Oxford University Press)

  Hume's work in epistemology and moral psychology influenced, among others, Kant and contemporary psychologists.

- Immanuel Kant (1724–1804)
  - *Critique of Pure Reason*, edited by Paul Guyer and Allen Wood (Cambridge University Press)
  - *Critique of Practical Reason*, edited by Mary Gregor (Cambridge University Press)
  - *Groundwork of the Metaphysics of Morals*, edited by Mary Gregor and Jens Timmerman

  One of the last great systematic philosophers, Kant revolutionized philosophy, bringing together formerly disparate rationalist and empiricist strands of metaphysics and epistemology.

Late Modern European Philosophy

- Mary Wollstonecraft (1759–1797)
  - *A Vindication of the Rights of Woman with Strictures on Political and Moral Subjects* (Joseph Johnson Publishers)

  Wollstonecraft's work on the moral, political, and social status of women continues to be influential today.

- Johan Gottlieb Fichte (1762–1814)
  - *Fichte: Science of Knowledge (Wissenschaftslehre)*, edited by Peter Heath and John Lachs (Cambridge University Press)

  Fichte was one of Kant's followers, but developed his own system of transcendental philosophy.

- G.W.F. Hegel (1770–1831)
  - *Phenomenology of Spirit*, translated by Terry Pinkard (Cambridge University Press)

  Hegel systematic philosophy purports to complete all previous attempts, e.g., Kant's.

- Friedrich Schelling (1775–1854)
  - *Ideas for a Philosophy of Nature: An Introduction to the Study of this Science*, translated by E.E. Harris and P. Heath (Cambridge University Press)

  Schelling (along with Fichte and Hegel) is among the most influential German idealists.

- Arthur Schopenhauer (1788–1860)
  - *The World as Will and Representation*, Vols. I and II, translated by E. F. J. Payne, (Dover Publications)

  Schopenhauer argues that the universe is not rational.

- John Stuart Mill (1806–1873)
  - *On Liberty, Utilitarianism and Other Essays*, edited by Mark Philp and Frederick Rosen (Oxford University Press)

  Mill, arguably the most famous Utilitarian philosopher, was also one of nineenth-century England's most vocal social critics.

- Søren Kierkegaard (1813–1855)
  - *Fear and Trembling*, edited and translated by Edna H. Hong and Howard V. Hong (Princeton University Press)
  - *Either/Or*, edited and translated by Edna H. Hong and Howard V. Hong (Princeton University Press)

  Kierkegaard, widely considered the "father of existentialism," wrote philosophy under pseudonyms.

- Karl Marx (1818–1883)
  - *Karl Marx: Selected Writings*, 2d edition, edited by David McLellan (Oxford University Press)

  Along with coauthor, Friedrich Engels, Marx critiqued the social, economic, and political conditions of capitalism.

- Franz Brentano (1838–1917)
- *Descriptive Psychology*, translated by Benito Müller (Routledge Publishers)

  Brentano is best known for his contributions to the philosophy of mind, but wrote across a number of philosophical topics.

- Charles Sanders Peirce (1839–1914)
- *The Essential Peirce*, 2 vols., edited by Nathan Houser, Christian Kloesel, and the Peirce Edition Project (Indiana University Press)

  The founder of American Pragmatism, Peirce wrote across areas of philosophy.

- William James (1842–1910)
  - *The Will to Believe and Other Essays in Popular Philosophy* (Harvard University Press)

  American Pragmatist, William James worked in philosophy, psychology, and physiology.

- Friedrich Nietzsche (1844–1900)

- *The Nietzsche Reader*, edited by Keith Ansell Pearson and Duncan Large (Wiley Blackwell Publishers)

Contemporary Philosophy

- Gottlob Frege (1848–1923)
  - *Translations from the Philosophical Writings of Gottlob Frege*, 3rd ed., translated by Peter Geach and Max Black (Blackwell Publishers)

  Frege was a mathematician and logician who contributed to the development of modern logic.

- Edmund Husserl (1859–1938)
- *Cartesian Meditations*, translated by Dorion Cairns (Kluwer Publishers)
- *Experience and Judgment*, translated by J. S. Churchill and Karl Ameriks (Routledge Publishers)

  Known as the founder of phenomenology, Husserl worked across philosophical areas.

- Henri Bergson (1859–1941)
- *Bergson: Key Writings*, edited by Keith Ansell Pearson and John Mullarkey, (Bloomsbury Publishing)

  Bergson's work in phenomenology influenced thinkers such as Jean-Paul Sartre.

- Alfred North Whitehead (1861–1947)
  - *Process and Reality: An Essay in Cosmology* (Free Press)

  Whitehead is best known for his work in philosophy of science and mathematical logic. With Bertrand Russell, he wrote *Principia Mathematica.*

- George Santayana (1863–1952)
  - *The Birth of Reason and Other Essays by George Santayana*, edited by Daniel Cory (Columbia University Press)

  Santayana wrote across genres, from philosophy to poetry and cultural criticism.

- Bertrand Russell (1872–1970)
  - *The Basic Writings of Bertrand Russell*, edited by John G. Slater (Routledge Publishers)

  Russell wrote across areas of philosophy but is best known for his work in mathematical logic. With Alfred North Whitehead, he wrote *Principia Mathematica.*

- Ludwig Wittgenstein (1889–1973
  - *Tractatus Logico-Philosophicus*, translated by C. K. Ogden (Routledge Publishers)
  - *Philosophical Investigations*, translated by G.E.M. Anscombe, and edited by G.E.M. Anscombe and R. Rhees (Blackwell Publishers)

  A towering figure of twentieth-century analytic philosophy, Wittgenstein's work is typically divided into "early" and "later" periods.

- Martin Heidegger (1889–1976)
  - *Being and Time*, translated by John Macquarrie and Edward S. Robinson (Blackwell Publishers)

- *The Heidegger Reader*, translated by Jerome Veith and edited by Günter Figal (Indiana University Press)

Heidegger worked in phenomenology and existentialism. A controversial figure, Heidegger was a member of the National Socialist Party, and never explicitly denounced Nazism.

- Hans-Georg Gadamer (1900–2002)
  - *Truth and Method*, translated by Donald Marshall and Joel Weinsheimer (Continuum Press)

Gadamer was a distinctive thinker in the hermeneutical tradition.

- Jean-Paul Sartre (1905–1980)
  - *Being and Nothingness*, translated by Hazel E. Barnes (Philosophical Library)
  - *Existentialism is a Humanism*, translated by Carol Macomber (Yale University Press)

Sartre was an existentialist. In addition to philosophy, he wrote novels, plays, and political essays. Among his best-known works is his seminal lecture, "Existentialism is a Humanism."

- Maurice Merleau-Ponty (1908–1961)
  - *Phenomenology of Perception*, translated by Donald Landes (Routledge Publishers)

Merleau-Ponty was an existentialist and phenomenologist.

- Simone de Beauvoir (1908–2000)
  - *The Second Sex*, translated by Constance Borde and Sheila Malovany-Chevallier (Vintage Publishing)

De Beauvoir, an existentialist, wrote across a number of philosophical topics, but is best known for her feminist work, *The Second Sex.*

- W.V.O. Quine (1908–2000)
  - *From a Logical Point of View* (Harvard University Press)

Quine practiced analytic philosophy across a number of areas. He is best known for his paper, "Two Dogmas of Empiricism."

- A.J. Ayer (1910–1989)
  - *Language, Truth, and Logic* (Dover Books)

Ayer worked across philosophical areas from the perspective of logical positivism and verificationism.

- J. L. Austin (1911–1960)
  - *How to Do Things with Words*, 2d ed., edited by J.O. Urmson and Marina Sbisà (Harvard University Press)

Austin was a philosopher of language, epistemologist, and ethicist. He is best known for *How to Do Things with Words.*

- Donald Davidson (1917–2003)
  - *Essays on Actions and Events* (Clarendon Press)

  - *Truth, Language and History: Philosophical Essays*, edited by Marcia Cavell (Oxford University Press)

  Davidson worked on semantic theory, epistemology, and ethics.

- P. F. Strawson (1919–2006)
  - *Philosophical Writings* (Oxford University Press)
  - *Freedom and Resentment and Other Essays* (Methuen Publishing)

  Strawson worked in metaphysics, epistemology, and the history of philosophy. Among his most famous essays is "Freedom and Resentment."

- John Rawls (1921–2002)
  - *A Theory of Justice* (Harvard University Press)

  Rawls was a towering figure in twentieth-century political thought, advancing a position of egalitarian liberalism.

- Gilles Deleuze (1925–1995)
  - *Difference and Repetition*, translated by Paul Patton (Columbia University Press)
  - *The Deleuze Reader*, edited by Constantin V. Boundas (Columbia University Press)

  Deleuze, who considered himself a metaphysician, wrote on thinkers as diverse as Hume, Spinoza, and Nietzsche.

- Michel Foucault (1926–1984)
  - *Discipline and Punish*, translated by Alan Sheridan (Pantheon Press)
  - *History of Madness*, translated by Jonathan Murphy and Jean Khalfa (Routledge Publishers)
  - *The Foucault Reader*, edited by Paul Rabinow (Pantheon Press)

  Foucault, associated with structuralist and post-structuralist movements, worked in history and philosophy—often at the intersection of the two as a genealogist of ideas.

- Noam Chomsky (b. 1928)
  - *The Essential Chomsky*, edited by Anthony Arnove (The New Press)
  - *Language and Problems of Knowledge* (M.I.T. Press)

  A linguist, Chomsky works across a range of philosophical topics and politics.

- Jacques Derrida (1930–2004)
  - *Of Grammatology*, translated by Gayatri Spivak (The Johns Hopkins University Press)
  - *A Derrida Reader: Between the Blinds*, edited by Peggy Kamuf (Columbia University Press)

  Derrida introduced deconstruction, a technique for critiquing literary and philosophical texts, which he also applied to a wide range of issues and topics.

- Richard Rorty (1931–2007)
  - *Philosophy and the Mirror of Nature* (Princeton University Press)
  - *Contingency, Irony, and Solidarity* (Cambridge University Press)

  Rorty, a pragmatist, wrote across areas of philosophy.

- John Searle (b. 1932)
    - *Minds, Brains and Science* (Harvard University Press)

  Searle is a philosopher of language and mind. He is best known for his Chinese Room thought experiment presented in a critique of the view that "strong" artificial intelligence is capable of understanding.

- Amartya Sen (b. 1933)
    - *The Idea of Justice* (Harvard University Press)

  Sen is a political philosopher and economist.

- Thomas Nagel (b. 1937)
    - *The View From Nowhere* (Oxford University Press)
    - *Mortal Questions* (Canto Classics)

  Nagel works across philosophical issues, from the meaning of life to consciousness. He is best known for his essay, "What is it like to be a bat?" The works listed here are introductory texts.

- Robert Nozick (1938–2002)
    - *Anarchy, State, and Utopia* (Basic Books)

  Nozick worked primarily in political philosophy, and is best known for advancing a libertarian position.

- T.M. Scanlon (b. 1940)
    - *What We Owe to Each Other* (Harvard University Press)

  Scanlon is an ethicist who works across a number of related subjects.

- Derek Parfit (1942–2017)
    - *Reasons and Persons* (Oxford University Press)

  Parfit worked on issues in and around philosophy of mind.

- Daniel Dennett (b. 1942)
    - *Consciousness Explained* (Little, Brown, and Co.)
    - *Freedom Evolves* (Penguin Books)

- Peter Singer (b. 1946)
    - *Animal Liberation* (Harper Perennial Modern Classics)
    - *Practical Ethics*, 2nd edition(Cambridge University Press)

  Singer is an ethicist who argues for, among other positions, animal rights.

- Cornel West (b. 1953)
    - *Race Matters* (Beacon Press)
    - *The Cornel West Reader* (Civitas Books)

  West works across areas in philosophy.

- Kwame Anthony Appiah (b. 1954)
- *Cosmopolitanism: Ethics in a World of Strangers* (W. W. Norton & Co.)
- *The Ethics of Identity* (Princeton University Press)

  Appiah works on gender, race, sex, and politics.

- Judith Butler (b. 1956)

- *Gender Trouble, Feminism and the Subversion of Identity* (Routledge Publishers)

Butler is a feminist philosopher.

The following contains works not mentioned above, but worth adding to your reading list of works in, or translated into, English:

Philosophy of Art (Aesthetics)

- Monroe Beardsley, *The Aesthetic Point of View* (Cornell University Press)
- Noel Carroll, *Beyond Aesthetics* (Cambridge University Press) and *Theories of Art Today* (University of Wisconsin Press)
- Arthur Danto, *The Transfiguration of the Commonplace* (Oxford University Press)
- Stephen Davis, *The Philosophy of Art* (Oxford University Press)
- Terry Eagelton, *The Ideology of the Aesthetic* (Basil Blackwell)

Philosophy of Language and Logic

- Rudolph Carnap, *The Logical Structure of the World*, translated by E. George (Open Court Classics)
- Paul Grice, *Studies in the Way of Words (Harvard University Press)*
- Saul Kripke, *Naming and Necessity* (Harvard University Press)
- Scott Soames, *Beyond Rigidity: The Unfinished Semantic Agenda of Naming and Necessity* (Oxford University Press)
- Alfred Tarski, *Logic, Semantics, Metamathematics, papers from 1923 to 1938*, translated by J. H. Woodger and edited by John Corcoran (Hackett Publishing)

Philosophy of Religion

- William P. Alston, *Perceiving God* (Cornell University Press)
- Brian Davies, *The Reality of God and the Problem of Evil* (Continuum Press)
- John Hick, *Philosophy of Religion* (Prentice-Hall Publishers)
- J. L. Mackie, *The Miracle of Theism* (Oxford University Press)
- D. Z. Phillips, *Religion without Explanation* (Oxford University Press)
- Alvin Plantinga, *Warrant: The Current Debate* (Oxford University Press)
- Peter van Inwagen, *The Problem of Evil* (Oxford University Press)

Philosophy of Science

- Rudolph Carnap, *Philosophical Foundations of Physics*, edited by Martin Gardner (Basic Books)
- Paul Feyerabend, *Against Method* (Verso Press)
- Sandra Harding, *The Science Question in Feminism* (Cornell University Press)
- Carl G. Hempel, *Philosophy of Natural Science* (Prentice-Hall Publishers)
- Philip Kitcher, *The Advancement of Science: Science Without Legend, Objectivity Without Illusions* (Oxford University Press)

- Thomas Kuhn, *The Structure of Scientific Revolutions* (University of Chicago Press)
- Karl Popper, *Conjectures and Refutations: The Growth of Scientific Knowledge*, (Routledge)
- *Images of Science: Essays on Realism and Empiricism*, edited by Paul M. Churchland and Clifford A. Hooker (University of Chicago Press)

Books to Guide Novice Philosophy Students

This list is aimed at curating those texts that will both challenge a novice researcher, and continually reward repeated encounters as you develop your philosophical interests. These books are helpful research tools that will include essays on important thinkers not listed here:

Ancient Greek Philosophy

- Pre-Socratics (c. 600–400 BC)
  - Jonathan Barnes, *The Presocratic Philosophers* (Routledge)
  - G. S. Kirk, J. E. Raven, and Malcolm Schofield, *The Presocratic Philosophers* (Cambridge University Press)
  - Richard D. McKirahan, *Philosophy Before Socrates* (Hackett Publishers)
- Socrates (c. 469–399 BC) and Plato (c. 429–347 BC)
  - Julia Annas, *An Introduction to Plato's* Republic (Oxford University Press)
  - Hugh Benson, *Essays on the Philosophy of Socrates* (Oxford University Press)
  - Thomas C. Brickhouse and Nicholas D. Smith, *The Trial and Execution of Socrates: Sources and Controversies* (Oxford University Press)
  - Gail Fine, ed., *Plato I: Metaphysics and Epistemology* and *Plato II: Ethics, Politics, Religion, and the Soul* (Oxford University Press)
  - Terence Irwin, *Plato's Ethics* (Oxford University Press)
  - Richard Kraut, ed., *The Cambridge Companion to Plato* (Cambridge University Press)
  - Nicholas D. Smith, *Plato: Critical Assessments* (Routledge)
  - Gregory Vlastos, *Socrates: Ironist and Moral Philosopher* (Cornell University Press)
- Aristotle (384–322 BC)
  - J. Ackrill, *Aristotle the Philosopher* (Oxford University Press)
  - Allan Gotthelf and James G. Lennox, eds., *Philosophical Issues in Aristotle's Biology* (Cambridge University Press)
  - Jonathan Beere, *Doing and Being: An Interpretation of Aristotle's* Metaphysics Theta (Oxford University Press)
  - E.R. Jiminez, *Aristotle's Concept of Mind* (Cambridge University Press)
  - Richard Kraut, *Aristotle and the Human Good* (Princeton University Press) and *Aristotle: Political Philosophy* (Oxford University Press)
  - Mariska Leunissen, *Explanation and Teleology in Aristotle's Science of Nature* (Oxford University Press)
  - C. D. C. Reeve, *Substantial Knowledge: Aristotle's Metaphysics* (Hackett Publishers)

  - W. D. Ross, *Aristotle* (Methuen and Co.)
  - C. Shields, *The Oxford Handbook of Aristotle* (Oxford University Press)
- Stoics, Epicureans, Skeptics (300 BC–fifth century AD)
  - Julia Annas, *Hellenistic Philosophy of Mind* (University of California Press) and *The Morality of Happiness* (Oxford University Press)

    Mind focuses on Stoic and Epicurean theories of the mind—what it is and what it does, while *Morality* focuses on Ancient ethical theories, beginning with Aristotle.
  - Julia Annas and Jonathan Barnes, eds., *The Modes of Scepticism: Ancient Texts and Modern Interpretations* (Cambridge University Press)
  - Elizabeth Asmis, *Epicurus' Scientific Method* (Cornell University Press)
  - Richard Bett, *The Cambridge Companion to Ancient Scepticism* (Cambridge University Press)
  - Tad Brennan, *The Stoic Life: Emotions, Duties, and Fate* (Oxford University Press)
  - John M. Cooper, *Reason and Emotion: Essays on Ancient Moral Psychology and Ethical Theory* (Princeton University Press)
  - Brad Inwood, ed., *The Cambridge Companion to the Stoics* (Cambridge University Press)
  - A.A. Long, *Stoic Studies* (University of California Press)
  - J.M. Rist, *Stoic Philosophy* (Cambridge University Press)
  - Ricardo Salles, *The Stoics on Determinism and Compatibilism* (Ashgate)
  - M. Scholfield, Miles Burnyeat, and Jonathan Barnes, eds., *Doubt and Dogmatism: Studies in Hellenistic Epistemology* (Clarendon Press)

Medieval Philosophy

- Augustine (354–430)
  - Brian Dobell, *Augustine's Intellectual Conversion: The Journey from Platonism to Christianity* (Cambridge University Press)
  - William E. Mann, *Augustine's Confessions: Critical Essays* (Rowman & Littlefield)
  - Gareth B. Matthews, *Augustine* (Blackwell Publishing)
- Boethius (c. 475–526?)
  - Thomas Böhm, Thomas Jürgasch, and Andreas Kirchner, eds., *Boethius as a Paradigm of Late Ancient Thought* (DeGruyter)
  - Antonio Donato, *Boethius'* Consolation of Philosophy as a Product of Late Antiquity (Bloomsbury)
  - Philip Edward Phillips and Noel Harold Kaylor, eds., *A Companion to Boethius in the Middle Ages* (Brill)
- Saint Anselm (1033–1109)
  - Brian Davies and Brian Leftow, eds., *The Cambridge Companion to Anselm* (Cambridge University Press)
  - Jasper Hopkins, *A Companion to the Study of St. Anselm* (University of Minnesota Press)

- Peter Abelard (1079–1142)
  - Jeffrey E. Brower and Kevin Guilfoy, *The Cambridge Companion to Abelard* (Cambridge University Press)
  - John Marenbon, *The Philosophy of Peter Abelard* (Cambridge University Press)
- Roger Bacon (1214 or 1220–1292)
  - Robert Adamson, *Roger Bacon: The Philosophy of Science in the Middle Ages*, an Address (delivered at Owens College)
  - Stewart C. Easton, *Roger Bacon and His Search for a Universal Science: A Reconsideration of the Life and Work of Roger Bacon in the Light of His Own Stated Purpose* (Columbia University Press)
  - Hackett, Jeremiah, ed., *Roger Bacon and the Sciences: Commemorative Essays* (Brill)
- Duns Scotus (1265/1266–1308)
  - Richard Cross, *Duns Scotus* (Oxford University Press)
  - Mary Beth Ingham and Mechthild Dreyer, *The Philosophical Vision of Duns Scotus* (The Catholic University of America Press)
  - Thomas Williams, *The Cambridge Companion to Duns Scotus* (Cambridge University Press)
- Thomas Aquinas (1225-1274)
  - John Finnis, *Aquinas: Moral, Political, and Legal Theory* (Oxford University Press)
  - Therese Cory Scarpelli, *Aquinas on Human Self-Knoweldge* (Cambridge University Press)
  - Eleanore Stump, *Aquinas* (Routledge)
- William of Ockham (1287–1347)
  - Marilyn McCord Adams, *William Ockham* (University of Notre Dame Press)
  - Paul Vincent Spade, ed., *The Cambridge Companion to Ockham* (Cambridge University Press)
- Jean Buridan (1300–c. 1358)
  - Jack Zupko, *John Buridan: Portrait of a Fourteenth-Century Arts Master* (University of Notre Dame Press)
- Nicholas of Cusa (1401–1464)
  - Inigo Bocken, *Conflict and Reconciliation: Perspective on Nicholas of Cusa* (Brill)
  - Gerald Christianson and Thomas M. Izbicki, eds., *Nicholas of Cusa: In Search of God and Wisdom* (Brill)

Additional Collected Essays Covering the Middle Ages

- Peter, Dronke, ed., *A History of Twelfth-Century Western Philosophy* (Cambridge University Press)
- Edward Grant, *Physical Science in the Middle Ages* (Cambrudge University Press)

  - Stephen Gersh, *Middle Platonism and Neoplatonism: The Latin Tradition* (University of Notre Dame Press)
  - Jorge J.E. Gracia and Timothy Noone, *A Companion to Philosophy in the Middle Ages* (Blackwell Publications)
  - Inglis, John, ed., *Medieval Philosophy and the Classical Tradition: In Islam, Judaism, and Christianity* (Routledge)
  - Jacques Maritain, *Art and Scholasticism* (Charles Scribner's Sons)

Modern European Philosophy

- Michel de Montaigne
  - Ann Hartle, *Michel de Montaigne: Accidental Philosopher* (Cambridge University Press)
  - Ullrich Langer, *The Cambridge Companion to Montaigne* (Cambridge University Press)
- Giordano Bruno (1548–1600)
- Francis Bacon (1561–1626)
- Galileo Galilei
- Thomas Hobbes (1588–1679)
- Pierre Gassendi
- René Descartes (1596–1650)
- Antoine Arnauld
- Blaise Pascal
- Margaret Cavendish
- Baruch Spinoza (1632–1677)
  - Jonathan Bennet, *A Study of Spinoza's Ethics* (Hackett Publishers)
  - Harry Austryn Wolfson, *The Philosophy of Spinoza*, 2 vols. (Oxford University Press)
- John Locke (1632–1704)
  - V. Chappell, ed., *The Cambridge Companion to Locke* (Cambridge University Press)
  - M. Stuart, *Locke's Metaphysics* (Oxford University Press)
- Nicolas Malebranche (1638–1715)
  - Desmond Connell, *The Vision in God: Malebranche Scholastic Sources* (Nauwelaerts Publishers)
- Isaac Newton (1642–1727)
  - *The Cambridge Companion to Newton*, I. B. Cohen and G. E. Smith, eds. (Cambridge University Press)
  - *Newton: Texts, Backgrounds, and Commentaries*, I. B. Cohen and Richard Westfall, eds. (W. W. Norton & Co.)
- G.W. Leibniz (1646-1716)
  - Daniel Garber, *Leibniz: Body, Substance, Monad* (Oxford University Press)
  - Catherine Wilson, *Leibniz's Metaphysics: A Historical and Comparative Study* (Princeton University Press)
- George Berkeley (1685–1753)

- G. S. Pappas, *Berkeley's Thought* (Cornell University Press)
- *The Cambridge Companion to Berkeley*, K. P. Winkler, ed. (Cambridge University Press)

- Jean-Jacques Rousseau (1712–1778)
  - Victor Gourevitch, *Rousseau: The "Discourses" and Other Early Political Writings* (Cambridge University Press)
  - Victor Gourevitch, *Rousseau: The "Social Contract" and Other Later Political Writings* (Cambridge University Press)
- David Hume (1711-1776)
  - *The Cambridge Companion to Hume*, 2d edition, edited by David Fate Norton, and J. Taylor (Cambridge University Press)
  - T. Penelhum, *Themes in Hume: The Will, The Self, Religion* (Clarendon Press)
- Immanuel Kant (1724–1804)
  - *The Cambridge Companion to Kant*, edited by Paul Guyer (Cambridge University Press)
  - *The Cambridge Companion to Kant's Critique of Pure Reason*, edited by Paul Guyer (Cambridge University Press)
  - Christine Korsgaard, *Creating the Kingdom of Ends* (Cambridge University Press)

Additional Collected Essays Covering the Modern Period

- Jonathan Bennett, *Locke, Berkeley, Hume: Central Themes* (Clarendon Press)
- Craig B. Brush, *Montaigne and Bayle: Variations on the Theme of Skepticism* (Martinus Nijhoff)
- I. Hunter, *Rival Enlightenments: Civil and Metaphysical Philosophy in Early Modern Germany* (Cambridge University Press)
- Richard Popkin, *The History of Scepticism from Erasmus to Spinoza* (Van Gorcum)
- J.B. Schneewind, *The Invention of Autonomy*

Late Modern European Philosophy

- Mary Wollstonecraft (1759–1797)
  - Eileen Hunt Botting, *Family Feuds: Wollstonecraft, Burke, and Rousseau on the Transformation of the Family* (State University Press)
- G. W. F. Hegel (1770–1831)
  - Stephen Houlgate and Michael Baur, eds., *A Companion to Hegel*, (Blackwell Publishers)
  - Michael Inwood, *A Hegel Dictionary* (Blackwell Publishers)
- Arthur Schopenhauer (1788–1860)
  - Dale Jacquette, *The Philosophy of Schopenhauer* (Acumen Publishers)
  - Christopher Janaway, *Self and World in Schopenhauer's Philosophy* (Clarendon Press)
- John Stuart Mill (1806–1873)
  - David Brink, *Mill's Progressive Principles* (Oxford University Press)

  - J. Skorupski, *John Stuart Mill* (Routledge Publishers)
- Søren Kierkegaard (1813–1855)
  - Alastair Hannay, *Kierkegaard* (Routledge Publishers)
  - Hannay, Alastair and Gordon Marino eds., *The Cambridge Companion to Kierkegaard* (Cambridge University Press)
- Karl Marx (1818–1883)
  - *The Cambridge Companion to Marx*, edited by Terrell Carver (Cambridge University Press)
  - G.A. Cohen, *Karl Marx's Theory of History: A Defence*, 2nd ed., (Oxford University Press)
- William James (1842–1910)
  - Graham Bird, *William James* (Routledge Publishers)
  - Ruth Anna Putnam, *The Cambridge Companion to William James* (Cambridge University Press)
- Friedrich Nietzsche (1844–1900)
  - *Nietzsche on Morality and Affirmation*, edited by Daniel Came (Oxford University Press)
  - Simon May, *Nietzsche's Ethics and his War on "Morality"* (Oxford University Press)
  - Keith Ansell Pearson, *A Companion to Nietzsche* (Blackwell Publishers)

Contemporary Philosophy

- Gottlob Frege (1848–1923)
  - G. Currie, *Frege: An Introduction to His Philosophy* (Harvester Press)
  - Leila Haaparanta and Jaako Hintikka, eds., *Frege Synthesized* (D. Reidel Publisher)
- Edmund Husserl (1859–1938)
  - *Husserl, Intentionality, and Cognitive Science*, edited by Hubert Dreyfus (MIT Press)
  - Dan Zahavi, *Husserl's Phenomenology* (Stanford University Press)
- George Santayana (1863–1952)
  - Kenneth M. Price and Robert C. Leitz, *Critical Essays on George Santayana* (G. K. Hall and Co., Publishers)
  - *The Philosophy of George Santayana*, edited by Paul Arthur Schilpp (Northwestern University Press)
- Ludwig Wittgenstein (1889–1973)
  - G. E. M. Anscombe, *An Introduction to Wittgenstein's Tractatus*, London: Hutchinson University Library)
  - Marie McGinn, *Routledge Philosophy Guidebook to Wittgenstein and the Philosophical Investigations* (Routledge Publishers)
- Martin Heidegger (1889–1976)
  - *The Cambridge Companion to Heidegger*, edited by Charles Guignon (Cambridge University Press)
  - Stephen Mulhall, *Routledge Philosophy Guidebook to Heidegger and 'Being and Time'*, 2d edition (Routledge Publishers)

- Hans-Georg Gadamer (1900–2002)
  - Donatella Di Cesare, *Gadamer: A Philosophical Portrait* (Indiana University Press)
  - *The Cambridge Companion to Gadamer*, edited by Robert J. Dostal (Cambridge University Press)
- Jean-Paul Sartre (1905–1980)
  - Joseph Catalano, *A Commentary on Jean-Paul Sartre's Being and Nothingness* (University of Chicago Press)
  - *Cambridge Companion to Sartre*, edited by Christina Howells (Cambridge Unviersity Press)
- Simone de Beauvoir (1908–2000)
  - Penelope Deutscher, *The Philosophy of Simone de Beauvoir: Ambiguity, Conversion, Resistance* (Cambridge University Press)
  - Sonia Kruks, *Situation and Human Existence: Freedom, Subjectivity and Society* (Routledge Publishers)
- W.V.O. Quine (1908–2000)
  - *The Cambridge Companion to Quine*, edited by Roger F. Gibson (Cambridge University Press)
  - *A Companion to W. V. O. Quine*, edited by Gilbert Harman and Ernie Lepore (Blackwell Publishers)
- Donald Davidson (1917–2003)
  - *The Philosophy of Donald Davidson*, edited by Lewis Edwin Hahn (Open Court Press)
  - *Interpreting Davidson*, edited by Petr Kotatko, Peter Pagin, and Gabriel Segal (Stanford University Press)
- P.F. Strawson (1919–2006)
  - *The Philosophy of P. F. Strawson*, edited by Lewis Edwin Hahn (Open Court Press)
  - Clifford Brown, *Peter Strawson* (McGill-Queen's University Press)
- John Rawls (1921–2002)
  - Michael Sandel, *Liberalism and the Limits of Justice*, 2d ed. (Cambridge University Press)
  - *Reading Rawls: Critical Studies on Rawls'* A Theory of Justice, edited by Norman Daniels (Basic books)
  - *The Cambridge Companion to Rawls*, edited by Samuel Freeman (Cambridge University Press)
- Michel Foucault (1926–1984)
  - *A Companion to Foucault*, edited by Christopher Falzon, Timothy O'Leary, and Jana Sawicki (Blackwell Publishers)
  - *The Cambridge Companion to Foucault*, edited by Gary Gutting (Cambridge University Press)
- Jacques Derrida (1930–2004)
  - Michael Naas, *Derrida from now on* (Fordham University Press)
  - *Deconstruction and Philosophy*, edited by John Sallis (University of Chicago Press)

  - *Derrida: A Critical Reader*, edited by David Wood (Blackwell Publishers)
- Richard Rorty (1931–2007)
  - *Rorty and His Critics*, edited by Robert Brandom (Blackwell Pubishers)
  - *Reading Rorty*, edited by Alan R. Malachowsky
- Robert Nozick (1938–2002)
  - Ralph M. Bader and John Meadowcroft, *Cambridge Companion to Anarchy* (Cambridge University Press)
- Derek Parfit (1942–2017)
  - Journal article searches will yield a treasure trove of papers on Parfit's work.
- Daniel Dennett (b. 1942)
  - Robert P. Kraynak, "Commentary on Dennett" (https://bioethicsarchive.georgetown.edu/pcbe/reports/human_dignity/kraynak_on_dennett.html)
  - Journal article searches will yield a treasure trove of papers on Dennett's work.

  Dennett works on and around cognitive science issues.

- Cornel West (b. 1953)
  - Clarence Sholé Johnson, *Cornel West & Philosophy* (Routledge Publishers)

Guides and Other Resources Across Subjects, Topics, and History

- Blackwell's "Guide to the Philosophy of X" Series (Wiley & Sons)

  The Blackwell guides bring together scholars working on topics ranging from the philosophy of education to the philosophy of computing. The volumes in the series provide readers with introduction to topics through overviews of the current work in the subject area.

- Blackwell Philosopher Dictionaries

  Noted scholars present dictionaries of technical terms and concepts in context. The series ranges over thinkers such as Descartes, Hobbes, Kant, Hegel, and Wittgenstein.

- Alex Broadbent, *Philosophy for Graduate Students: Metaphysics and Epistemology* (Routledge, Taylor & Francis Group)

  This text gives you some insight into the foundations of what graduate students in philosophy should bring to their studies. The author comes from the analytic tradition in philosophy, and specializes in topics in the philosophy of science. These inform the aim of the book, which is to help graduate students see a "coherent whole" in the variety of topics first discovered in undergraduate studies.

- Cambridge's "Companion to X" Series (Cambridge University Press)

  From the *Cambridge Companion to Socrates*, to *The Cambridge to Nietzsche*, Cambridge "Companion" series brings together leading scholars in the history of philosophy, who contribute papers and edit volumes. Collectively, topics within volumes tend to be comprehensive, so researchers will find technical papers that cover the most ground in a single volume.

- JSTOR (https://www.jstor.org)
  "JSTOR" is short for "journal storage." It is an online repository of scholarly articles from major philosophy journals, such as *Critical Philosophy of Race*, *Philosophical Studies: An International Journal for Philosophy in the Analytic Tradition*, *Mind*, and *History of Philosophy Quarterly*. Check your institution's library to see if you have free access via an institutional subscription.

- Oxford Handbooks Online (https://www.oxfordhandbooks.com)
  This online repository of scholarly articles and reviews ranges over every branch and subject area in philosophy—all published by Oxford. Check your institution's library to see if you have free access via an institutional subscription.

Introductory Philosophy Texts

There is no substitute for grappling primary sources. Nevertheless, secondary sources—including scholarly research, literary reviews, historical summaries—are valuable tools. They not only show you how you can begin thinking about a philosopher, theory, problem, or concept, but also how the reading process works. Here, you'll find a list of textbooks commonly found in Introduction to Philosophy courses. These texts focus heavily on the Western tradition (though among the Ancient Greeks were, technically, also African and Middle Eastern thinkers), though there are myriad non-Western thinkers of great interest to philosophy students.

Introductory Texts: History of Philosophy

The books in this list have stood the test of time. Most come in both paper and digital formats, and publishers often provide accompanying digital materials, such as study guides. In addition, school and public libraries often carry copies, and some are available to rent through online businesses.

- Donald Abel, *Fifty Readings in Philosophy* (McGraw-Hill Education)
  Abel presents excerpts from classic philosophical texts, organized topically. Readings range from Plato to Mary Wollstonecraft and are edited to home in on complete arguments.

- Nicholas Bunnin and Eric Tsui-James, eds., *The Blackwell Companion to Philosophy* (Wiley & Sons)
  This anthology includes readings ranging from aesthetics to philosophy of biology, and from Plato to Derrida. The articles are written by leading scholars in their areas.

- Stephen M. Cahn, *Exploring Philosophy* (Oxford University Press)
  From classic to contemporary readings, Cahn's comprehensive anthology includes essays on reasoning, identity, and social justice.

- Norman Melchert, *The Great Conversation: A Historical Introduction to Philosophy* (Oxford University Press)
  Melchert integrates brief excerpts with exposition and discussion of major thinkers in the history of philosophy. He is careful to draw connections across

that history at various points in the text, thereby providing readers with access points to conceptual threads.

- Thomas Nagel, *What Does it all Mean? A Very Short Introduction to Philosophy* (Oxford University Press)

  Nagel is an important contemporary philosopher who writes across a number of areas, including political philosophy, ethics, mind, and epistemology. *What does it all mean?* is one of several books devoted to general interest philosophical topics and problems.

- Oxford's "A Very Short Introduction" Series

  These very slender volumes run the gamut of topics and thinkers in the history of philosophy.

- John Perry, Michael Bratman, and John Martin Fischer, *Introduction to Philosophy: Classical and Contemporary Readings* (Oxford University Press)

  The editors, well known philosophers themselves, have brought together classic and contemporary readings, organized topically. The text includes a glossary, guide to writing philosophy papers, and study questions.

- Louis Pojman, *Classics of Philosophy* (Oxford University Press)

  Pojman presents extensive excerpts from more than 40 thinkers across the history of philosophy. At over 1,200 pages of primary source material, the text provides students with a robust set of readings across topics standard in an introductory philosophy course.

- James Rachels, *Problems from Philosophy* (McGraw-Hill)

  Rachels introduces students to philosophy by way of central and perennial problems, such as the existence of God, free will, and knowledge. The slender volume is one of several introductions to "doing" philosophy.

- Gideon Rosen, Alex Byrne, Joshua Cohen, Elizabeth Harman, and Seana Shiffrin, *The Norton Introduction to Philosophy* (W. W. Norton & Co.)

  The authors combine extensive introductory context for essays that range across topics standard in an introductory philosophy course. The anthology also includes essays commissioned specifically for undergraduates.

- Jay Rosenberg, *The Practice of Philosophy: Handbook for Beginners* (Pearson)

  A tool kit for getting started reading, writing, and discussing philosophy, Rosenberg's slender primer can accompany required readings in introductory philosophy courses.

- Routledge's "Philosophers" Series

  Introductions to thinkers across the history of philosophy, from Plato to Habermans, provide students with accessible presentations of important thinkers. These texts complement primary sources.

- Routledge's "Handbook" Series

  From *The Routledge Handbook of Philosophy of Animal Minds* to *The*

Routledge Handbook of Philosophy of the City, there is pretty much no topic left untouched by scholars in the field.

- Samuel Enoch Stumpf and James Feiser, *Philosophy: A Historical Survey with Essential Readings* (McGraw-Hill)
  Stumpf and Feiser also authored *Socrates to Sartre and Beyond: A History of Philosophy* (McGraw-Hill). This text is organized historically, and offers substantive expositions of philosophical theories and concepts. *Philosophy: A Historical Survey with Essential Readings* builds on this work by integrating readings with the commentary.

Intermediate and Advanced Research: Thinkers, Subject Areas, and Topics

- Alex Broadbent, *Philosophy for Graduate Students: Metaphysics and Epistemology* (Routledge, Taylor & Francis Group)
  This text gives you some insight into the foundations of what graduate students in philosophy should bring to their studies. The author comes from the analytic tradition in philosophy, and specializes in topics in the philosophy of science. These inform the aim of the book, which is to help graduate students see a "coherent whole" in the variety of topics first discovered in undergraduate studies.

- "Cambridge Companion" Series (Cambridge University Press)
  From the *Cambridge Companion to Socrates*, to *The Cambridge to Nietzsche*, Cambridge "Companion" series brings together leading scholars in the history of philosophy, who contribute papers and edit volumes. Collectively, topics within volumes tend to be comprehensive, so researchers will find technical papers that cover the most ground in a single volume.

- Blackwell's "Guide to the Philosophy of …" series (Wiley & Sons)
  The Blackwell guides bring together scholars working on topics ranging from the philosophy of education to the philosophy of computing. The volumes in the series provide readers with introduction to topics through overviews of the current work in the subject area.

Serious Fun

- The Blackwell Philosophy and Popular Culture Series
  Beginning with *South Park and Philosophy*, Blackwell has published 40 books in the series, including *The Big Bang Theory and Philosophy* and *Hunger Games and Philosophy*. As with the other "serious fun" series and titles in this list, Blackwell's series editor and contributors aim to teach philosophy through popular culture.

- Richard Osborne (Author) and Ralph Edney (Illustrator), *Philosophy for Beginners* (Writers and Readers Publishing, Inc.)
  Plato wrote dialogues, which invite the reader into a conversation. The

informal style, the intimate tone, and the personalities of the interlocutors bring philosophical ideas alive in ways that abstract treatises most often cannot. Similarly, visual aids—in this case, illustrations—give the reader something concrete to hold onto as they read about how philosophers have asked and answered life's most important questions.

- Open Court's "Popular Culture and Philosophy" series
  The series began in 2000 with *Seinfeld and Philosophy.* One hundred twenty-nine books later, the series is going strong. Ranging from *Deadpool and Philosophy* to *Mr. Rogers and Philosophy*, there's a title for pretty much every interest—and all of it contemplated through a philosophical lens.

- Rowman & Littlefield's "Philosophy and Popular Culture" series
  Titles include *Joss Whedon as Philosopher* and *The Philosophy of Christopher Nolan.* Some of the books are anthologies, while others are written by a single author.

- John Wiley & Sons "Philosophy and Popular Culture" series
  From *Wonder Woman and Philosophy: The Amazonian Mystique*, to *Alien and Philosophy: I Infest, Therefore I Am*, the Wiley series presents philosophical explorations of topics in film and television. For example, *The Big Lebowski and Philosophy: Keeping Your Mind Limber with Abiding Wisdom* includes essays on the nature of the good life, nihilism, and just war theory.

Guides to Philosophical Writing

As with developing any skill, learning to write philosophically takes practice. Below are some links to academic sites, along with several style guides, to aid you.

- https://philosophy.fas.harvard.edu/files/phildept/files/brief_guide_to_writing_philosophy_paper.pdf
  Harvard's Writing Center provides an in-depth discussion and guide to philosophical writing, specifically the writing of philosophy papers.

- http://www.jimpryor.net/teaching/guidelines/writing.html
  Pryor's guide has been referenced or copied by a number of philosophy department sites. It provides excellent advice on philosophical writing.

- https://writingcenter.unc.edu/tips-and-tools/argument/
  University of North Carolina at Chapel Hill's Writing Center provides guidance on a crucial feature of philosophical writing: constructing and analyzing arguments.

- https://www.kent.ac.uk/learning/documents/student-support/value-map/value-map1516/constructinganargument311015alg.pdf
  University of Kent's Student Learning Advisory Service provides a handout that answers the question, "What is an argument?"

The following are excellent guides to writing philosophy papers:

Department of Philosophy, Oregon State University, *Writing Philosophy Papers: A Student Guide* (Dubuque, Iowa: Kendal/Hunt Publishing Company, 1997).

Joel Feinberg, *Doing Philosophy: A Guide to the Writing of Philosophy Papers,* 5th ed. (Belmont, CA: Wadsworth/Cengage Learning, 2014).

Anthony J. Graybosch, Gregory M. Scott, and Stephen M, Garrison, *Philosophy Student Writer's Manual and Reader's Guide* (Lanham, MD: Rowman & Littlefield, 2018)

M. Andrew Holowchak, *Critical Reasoning & Philosophy: A Concise Guide to Reading, Evaluating, and Writing Philosophical Works,* 2d. ed. (Lanham, MD: Rowman & Littlefield Publishers, 2011)

Zachary Seech, *Writing Philosophy Papers,* 5th ed. (Belmont, CA: Wadsworth/Cengage Learning, 2009)

William Strunk Jr. and E. B. White, *The Elements of Style,* Fourth Edition (New York: Pearson, 1999).

Anthony Weston, *A Rulebook for Arguments* (Indianapolis: Hackett. 2017). If you want a quick reference to the Latin names for the most common fallacies, see "Fallacies in Latin,"

Introductory Logic Texts

There are some fairly firm distinctions between critical thinking and formal (symbolic) logic texts. Whereas critical thinking focuses broadly on argumentation, formal logic is the study of the principles of correct reasoning, including formal proofs. Hence, the focus is on deductive logic. One of the nice features of a critical thinking course is that it can serve as a general introduction to logic, where the two modes of reasoning (inductive and deductive) are surveyed. Critical thinking texts typically include the following material:

- language: definitions and meaning
- argument basics (what constitutes an argument and argument elements);
- distinguishing arguments from non-arguments;
- argument mapping or diagramming;
- inductive and deductive arguments;
- deductive argument evaluation: valid and invalid, sound and unsound;
- counterexamples;
- inductive argument evaluation: strong and weak, cogent and uncogent;
- categorical logic (traditional or Aristotelian, and modern);
- translating from ordinary English into symbolic logic notation for singular statements, including propositional logic operators;
- truth tables;
- natural deduction;
- causal and scientific reasoning;
- analogical reasoning;
- informal fallacies.

Most formal logic texts proceed according to the following general structure, whereby propositional (or sentential) logic becomes part of the apparatus for the concluding study of quantifier logic:

- the basics of an argument (what it is, and what constitutes it);
- definitions of validity and invalidity, and soundness and unsoundness;
- translating from ordinary English into symbolic logic notation for singular statements, including propositional logic operators;
- truth tables to define operators;
- truth tables to determine logically possible, self-contradictory, and necessary statements;
- truth tables to determine logical consistency, inconsistency, and equivalence;
- truth tables to determine validity;
- inference rules for derivations;
- equivalence, substitution, or replacement rules;
- translating from ordinary English to quantifier logic notation (monadic, dyadic, and triadic predicates);
- derivation (proof) rules for quantifier logic and quantifier equivalences.

Critical Thinking and Logic Textbooks

- Stan Baronett, *Logic* (Oxford University Press)

  This is one of several comprehensive texts, in that it combines what is typically taught in critical thinking and formal logic courses.

- Barwise, Etchemendy, and Barker-Plummer, *Language, Proof and Logic* (Center for the Study of Language and Information)

  Like some other formal logic texts, *LPL*'s focus is narrower than those that include material typically taught in a critical thinking course. In this text, the focus is entirely on formal logic systems. Students studying linguistics, computer science, math, and philosophy may encounter this text, which is often used in introductory and upper division logic courses.

- Irving M. Copi and Carl Cohen, *Introduction to Logic* (Routledge)

  Commonly known as the Copi book, this is another of several comprehensive texts, in that it combines what is typically taught in critical thinking and formal logic courses.

- Harry J. Gensler, *Introduction to Logic* (Routledge)

  Gensler's book is yet another of several comprehensive texts, in that it combines what is typically taught in critical thinking and formal logic courses. It also includes chapters on modal, deontic, and belief logics, along with a history of logic.

- Merrie Bergmann, James Moor, and Jack Nelson, *The Logic Book* (McGraw-Hill)

  This is another formal logic text whose focus is narrower than those that include material typically taught in a critical thinking course. In this text, the focus is entirely on formal logic systems. Included in the book is a study of truth-trees.

- Morris Engel, *With Good Reason* (Bedford/St. Martin's)
  Engel's text focuses entirely on informal fallacies. For philosophy and non-philosophy majors alike, developing the skills to avoid getting taken in by bad reasoning, and to assess your own reasoning, pays dividends over a lifetime.

- Patrick J. Hurley, *A Concise Introduction to Logic* (Cengage Learning)
  Hurley's widely used text is another of several comprehensive texts, in that it combines what is typically taught in critical thinking and formal logic courses.

Thinking About Logic: Some Concise Overviews and Classic Texts

- Aristotle, *Categories, On Interpretation, Prior Analytics, Posterior Analytics, Topics,* and *On Sophistical Refutations.*
  Aristotle developed the first system of logic (deduction), including methods of proof; studied the relation of language to logic; and distinguished between demonstrative and dialectical arguments, and imposters (sophistical arguments). While most introductory texts have adapted Aristotle's work, it's always worth tackling his original contributions directly.

- George Boole, *The Mathematical Analysis of Logic, Being an Essay Towards a Calculus of Deductive Reasoning* (Basil Blackwell) and *An Investigation of The Laws of Thought on Which are Founded the Mathematical Theories of Logic and Probabilities* (Macmillan)
  Boole's work in logic develops ideas first presented by Aristotle, but it was his work on algebraic logic that laid the foundations for modern computing science.

- Augustus DeMorgan, "On the syllogism No. IV, and on the Logic of Relations", *Cambridge Philosophical Transactions* 10, 331–358.
  DeMorgan's groundbreaking work on relations includes what we now call the DeMorgan's equivalences, or DeMorgan's rules, in propositional logic.

- Gottlob Frege, *Basic Laws of Arithmetic*
  Perhaps best known for his paper, "On Sense and Reference," Frege also developed predicate logic, which is found in *Laws of Arithmetic.*

- Benson Mates, *Stoic Logic*
  Mates put the Stoics' work on logic on the map, as it were. Aristotle is credited as the first thinker to develop a systematic logic, and his fame largely overshadowed the Stoics' extraordinary achievements in logic. As Mates shows, their work in logic was more advanced than Aristotle.

- Plato, *Euthydemus*
  This dialogue is not as widely read as some others in Plato's corpus, but it is an excellent example of the ethics of argumentation. In it, Socrates has a discussion with two brothers, Euthydemus and Dionysodorus. The ostensible subject is education, the initial question is, to whom should the education of the youth be entrusted? The brothers engage in flagrant bad reasoning, the disentanglement of which is good exercise.

- Charles Hartshorne and Paul Weiss, eds., *Collected Papers of Charles Sanders Peirce* (Harvard University Press)

  Peirce builds on the work of George Boole and Augustus de Morgan. Interestingly enough, Peirce's work in quantification occurred at about the same time as Frege's—the former in the United States, the latter in Germany.

- Graham Priest, *Logic: A Very Short Introduction* (Oxford University Press)

  At fewer than 130 pages, this text is, indeed, very short. It provides an overview of some important concepts learned in an introductory logic course, and includes a helpful glossary.

- Bertrand Russell and Alfred North Whitehead, *Principia Mathematica* (Cambridge University Press)

  Motivated advanced students, or those with a strong math background will find Russell and Whitehead's work on mathematical logic and related topics both challenging and rewarding.

Lists of Links to Philosophy Websites

There are plenty of good philosophy websites that will give you a good idea of what philosophers are (or were) doing and how they do (or did) it. Though this list is not exhaustive, it is fairly representative of what you'll find (in English) elsewhere. In addition, these sites often have links to other sites that are not listed here.

- American Philosophical Association https://www.apaonline.org

  The APA is a professional philosophers association, though some of its work extends beyond the profession. It is a good resource for becoming acquainted with academic philosophy as a career.

- Daily Nous http://dailynous.com

  Daily Nous is "news for and about the philosophy profession." A variety of links is aggregated for general interest reading, philosophers moving from one institution to another, and links to other sites and materials.

- Internet Encyclopedia of Philosophy (IEP) https://www.iep.utm.edu

  This peer-reviewed encyclopedia is an accessible introduction to a broad range of concepts, topics, and thinkers.

- Open Access https://open-access.net/en/open-access-in-individual-disciplines/philosophy

  A repository of open-access philosophy resources, from journals to other repositories.

- Philosophy Pages http://www.philosophypages.com

  Focused on the Western philosophical tradition, Philosophy Pages, offers a comprehensive set of resources: a dictionary of philosophical terms and names, a survey of the history of Western philosophy, a timeline of figures discussed, a summary of logical principles, and a study guide for students.

- Stanford Encyclopedia of Philosophy (SEP) https://plato.stanford.edu

"The Stanford Encyclopedia of Philosophy organizes scholars from around the world in philosophy and related disciplines to create and maintain an up-to-date reference work." Though some SEP entries might require background or technical knowledge, all are written with an eye toward clearly encapsulating complex topics, concepts, or thinkers.

- UMass Boston's Open Access Philosophy https://umb.libguides.com/c.php?g=350815&p=2468261
  A repository of all things open-access in philosophy, from journals to YouTube channels.

Philosophy Magazines and Journals

If you want to get a sense of philosophical topics and styles published in scholarly journals, consider perusing the journals listed below. They are among the most respected in the discipline; most publish not only research papers, but also book reviews, notes, and discussions. First, however, is a list of some general interest philosophy magazines. Both of interest to a general reading audience and thinkers interested in communicating philosophical ideas, arguments, and noteworthy issues, these magazines serve as an excellent bridge between academic and non-academic philosophy.

General Interest Philosophy Magazines

- *Philosophy Now*: https://philosophynow.org
  Founded in 1991, *Philosophy Now* publishes general interest philosophy articles and essays. There is some free access. In addition to the magazine, *The Philosophy Now Radio Show* podcasts interviews with philosophers and philosophical discussions.

- *The Philosopher's Magazine*: https://www.philosophersmag.com
  Founded in 1997, *The Philosopher's Magazine* publishes general interest philosophy articles, essays, opinion pieces, and reviews.

Some of the Best-Known Philosophy Journals

- *Analysis*: https://academic.oup.com/analysis
  Founded in 1933, *Analysis* publishes peer-reviewed philosophy papers across the philosophical spectrum, in the analytic tradition.

- *Canadian Journal of Philosophy* http://www.canadianjournalofphilosophy.com
  Since 1971, the *Canadian Journal of Philosophy* publishes peer-reviewed philosophical scholarship in French and English.

- *Erkenntnis* https://link.springer.com/journal/10670
  Previously published under other names, *Erkenntnis* has published peer-reviewed philosophy of science papers since 1930.

- *Ethics* https://www.journals.uchicago.edu/toc/et/current

Focusing on scholarly research in theoretical and applied issues moral, social, political, and legal philosophy, *Ethics* has been published since 1890.

- *History of Philosophy Quarterly* https://www.press.uillinois.edu/journals/hpq.html
  Since 1984, *History of Philosophy Quarterly* focuses on peer-reviewed research on topics reflecting "a strong interaction between contemporary and historical concerns."

- *Inquiry* https://www.tandfonline.com/loi/sinq20
  Since its establishment in 1958, *Inquiry* has published peer-reviewed papers across philosophy.

- *Journal of the History of Ideas* https://muse.jhu.edu/journal/91
  Since 1940, *Journal of the History of Ideas* has published peer-reviewed research across the history of ideas in, for example, philosophy, literature, and the social sciences.

- *Journal of the History of Philosophy* https://www.press.jhu.edu/journals/journal-history-philosophy
  Since 1957, *Journal of the History of Philosophy*'s peer-reviewed papers cover topics and issues across the history of philosophy.

- *Journal of Moral Philosophy* https://brill.com/view/journals/jmp/jmp-overview.xml
  Publishing peer-reviewed research in theoretical and applied ethics, political philosophy, and legal philosophy since 2004.

- *Journal of Philosophical Logic* https://link.springer.com/journal/10992
  Since 1972, *Journal of Philosophical Logic* publishes peer-reviewed research at the intersection of philosophy and logic.

- *The Journal of Philosophy*: https://www.journalofphilosophy.org
  Founded in 1904, *The Journal of Philosophy* publishes peer-reviewed philosophy papers on contemporary topics in philosophy, particularly those at "the borderline between philosophy and other disciplines."

- *Journal of Symbolic Logic* https://www.cambridge.org/core/journals/journal-of-symbolic-logic
  Since 1936, *Journal of Symbolic Logic* publishes peer-reviewed papers in mathematical logic.

- *Mind* https://academic.oup.com/mind/pages/About
  Publishing peer-reviewed papers across philosophy of mind since 1876.

- *The Monist* https://www.themonist.com
  Founded in 1881, *The Monist* is one of the oldest peer-reviewed philosophy journals.

- *Noûs* https://onlinelibrary.wiley.com/journal/14680068
  Since 1967, *Noûs* has published philosophical papers across topics in the discipline.

- *Philosophers' Imprint* https://www.philosophersimprint.org/about.html
  An open-access, peer-reviewed journal "edited by analytically trained philosophers."
- *Philosophical Perspectives* https://onlinelibrary.wiley.com/journal/15208583
  One of two annual supplements to the quarterly journal, *Noûs*.
- *The Philosophical Quarterly* https://academic.oup.com/pq
  Available online since 1950, *Philosophical Quarterly* publishes peer-reviewed philosophical papers across the discipline.
- *The Philosophical Review*
  First published in 1892, *The Philosophical Review* publishes peer-reviewed original papers in the analytic tradition.
- *Philosophical Topics* https://www.uapress.com/philosophical-topics-journal/
  Since 1981, *Philosophical Topics* publishes peer-reviewed papers around a central philosophical theme.
- *Pacific Philosophical Quarterly* https://onlinelibrary.wiley.com/journal/14680114
  Since 1920, *Pacific Philosophical Quarterly* has published peer-reviewed articles across an array of topics.
- *Philosophical Issues*
  One of two annual supplements to the quarterly journal, *Noûs*.
- *Philosophical Perspectives*
  One of two annual supplements to the quarterly journal, *Noûs*.
- *Philosophical Studies* https://link.springer.com/journal/11098
  Since 1950, *Philosophical Studies* publishes peer-reviewed philosophical papers in the analytic tradition.
- *Philosophy East and West* https://uhpress.hawaii.edu/product/pew/
  Since 1951, *Philosophy East and West* has published peer-reviewed research in non-Western philosophy and its relation to the Anglo-American philosophical tradition.
- *Philosophy and Phenomenological Research* https://onlinelibrary.wiley.com/journal/19331592
  Independent of any specific methodology, *Philosophy and Phenomenological Research* publishes peer-reviewed papers across the discipline and the history of philosophy since 1933.
- *Philosophy and Public Affairs* https://onlinelibrary.wiley.com/journal/10884963
  Established in 1972, *Philosophy and Public Affairs* publishes peer-reviewed papers that philosophically address legal, social, and political issues.
- *Proceedings of the Aristotelian Society*
  Founded in 1880, the Aristotelian Society for the Systematic Study publishes articles read at its London meetings.

- *The Review of Metaphysics* https://reviewofmetaphysics.org
  First published in 1947, *The Review of Metaphysics* publishes peer-reviewed papers that "contribute to philosophical knowledge."
- *Synthese* https://link.springer.com/journal/11229
  Focusing on epistemology, methodology, philosophy of science, and the foundations of logic and mathematics, *Synthese* is a peer-reviewed journal.

Scholarly Research and Journal Repositories

- American Philosophical Association https://www.apaonline.org/general/recommended_links.asp?cc=33093
  For a more comprehensive list of peer-reviewed philosophy journals, visit the APA's site.
- Cambridge Core: https://www.cambridge.org/core/
  Cambridge University Press publishes a wide range of high-quality academic content across Cambridge Core, including leading journals, research monographs, reference works and textbooks.
- DASH: Digital Access to Scholarship at Harvard https://dash.harvard.edu
  "A central, open-access repository of research by members of the Harvard community."
- JSTOR: https://www.jstor.org
  A repository of many philosophy journals, such as the ones listed above. Most academic institutions
- Oxford Handbooks Online: https://www.oxfordhandbooks.com
  Oxford Handbooks Online is an outstanding collection of the best Handbooks areas across many different subject areas. One of the most prestigious and successful strands of Oxford's scholarly publishing, the Handbook series contains in-depth, high-level articles by scholars at the top of their field.
- Oxford Scholarly Editions Online: https://www.oxfordscholarlyeditions.com
  Oxford's scholarly editions provide trustworthy, annotated primary texts for scholars and students
- PhilPapers https://philpapers.org
  A comprehensive index and bibliography of philosophical research, PhilPapers includes resources such as journals, books, and an extensive list of contemporary philosophers' personal sites, organized alphabetically and by area.

Contemporary Philosopher Blogs and Personal Websites

This list is organized alphabetically, by each philosopher's last name. Given the number of excellent philosophers working today, this list is necessarily short, and almost entirely restricted to blogs and personal sites, rather than faculty pages. Nevertheless, the smattering of links should provide you with glimpses into the workings of these thinkers' intellectual lives—glimpses not always possible from a book or scholarly paper.

If you are looking for a philosopher's faculty page, where you'll find information such as curriculum vitae, but you're not sure where that individual works, it's best to conduct an internet search of their name. Top hits will show you where they should be currently working.

- Peter Adamson https://historyofphilosophy.net/historian-philosophy-advice
  Adamson works in the history of philosophy. This page offers advice to anyone thinking about pursuing an advanced degree in philosophy.
- Julia Annas http://www.u.arizona.edu/~jannas/
  Annas works on Ancient Greek philosophy.
- Kwame Anthony Appiah http://appiah.net/work/general-interest/
  Appiah's site contains a range of writings, from poetry to Tweets to general interest pieces. He works at the intersection of gender, race, and sexuality.
- Simon Blackburn http://www2.phil.cam.ac.uk/~swb24/
  Blackburn often writes philosophy for a general reading audience.
- Nick Bostrom https://www.nickbostrom.com
  Bostrom works in the philosophy of science.
- David Bourget http://www.dbourget.com
  Bourget works in the philosophy of mind.
- Robert Brandom http://www.pitt.edu/~brandom/index.html
  Brandom works in philosophy of language.
- Phillip Bricker http://www.philbricker.com
  Bricker works in metaphysics, philosophy of language, philosophy of mathematics, and philosophy of science.
- Quassim Cassam https://warwick.ac.uk/fac/soc/philosophy/people/cassam/
  Cassam works in epistemology and philosophy of mind.
- David Chalmers' http://consc.net/philosophical-weblogs/
  Chalmers works in the philosophy of mind, and his blog covers topics and areas of interest outside his own.
- Andrew Chignell http://www.chignell.net
  Chignell works primarily in early modern philosophy.
- Noam Chomsky https://chomsky.info
  Chomsky works across a number of areas of general interest to philosophy students, but he is primarily a philosopher of language.
- Andrew Chrucky http://www.ditext.com/chrucky/chrucky.html
  Chrucky writes across topics in contemporary philosophy.
- Patricia Churchland https://patriciachurchland.com
  Churchland works in cognitive science.

- Luciano Floridi's Philosophy of Information http://www.philosophyofinformation.net
  Floridi works at the intersection of digital technology and ethics.
- Rebecca Goldstein https://www.rebeccagoldstein.com
  Goldstein is a philosopher (philosophy of mind and philosophy of mathematics) and a novelist. She also writes general interest philosophy books.
- Peter King http://individual.utoronto.ca/pking/
  King works in Medieval philosophy.
- David Koepsell https://davidkoepsell.com
  Koepsell works in ethics and public policy.
- Christian Thomas Kohl https://sites.google.com/site/ctkohl/
  Kohl works in Asian philosophy.
- Michael LaBossiere's A Philosopher's Blog http://aphilosopher.drmcl.com
  LaBossiere writes essays across a broad range of topics.
- Brian Leiter's Leiter Reports: A Philosophy Blog https://leiterreports.typepad.com
  Leiter's sometimes controversial blog is a comprehensive look at all things to do with professional philosophy. Leiter also publishes The Philosophical Gourmet, a ranking of graduate programs in the English-speaking world: https://www.philosophicalgourmet.com.
- Peter Smith's Logic Matters http://www.logicmatters.net/blogfront/
  A blog devoted to all things logic.
- Richard Zach https://richardzach.org
  Zach works on logic. He also has an archived site (https://people.ucalgary.ca/~rzach/279/logicians.html) that provides biographical information, and further links, on thinkers in the history of logic.

Philosophy Videos and Podcasts

Developments in digital technology have brought philosophy out of the classroom and into our daily lives. Before the Internet, if you wanted to hear a lecture on Aristotle from a philosopher at Oxford University, you'd have to go to Oxford, England—or hope you could get a recording to play on a DVD or VHS player. Now, however, you can find a rich array of lectures, scholarly talks, panel discussions, explainers, tutorials, and more, online.

- 8-Bit Philosophy: Philosophy Through 8-Bit Gaming Video Series https://www.youtube.com/watch?v=lVDaSgyi3xE&list=PLghL9V9QTN0gCZia2u-YnLxhetxnC_ONF
  Philosophical questions and problems are addressed through 8-bit animation. Episodes include, "Is it wrong if you don't vote?" and "Who was Machiavelli?"
- 60 Second Philosophy: Videos https://www.youtube.com/channel/UCRI-utB2uwrfHCUCSVUlXSw/playlists

Brief explainer videos answer questions such as, "What is solipsism?" in about a minute.

- Peter Adamson: The History of Philosophy without Any Gaps Podcast https://historyofphilosophy.net
  Professor Adamson's podcast series provides overviews of philosophers and topics in the Western, Middle Eastern, Eastern, and African traditions. Some podcasts focus on interviews with scholars presently working in the field. Podcasts are typically under 20 minutes each.
- BBC Radio 4: A History of Ideas Video Series https://www.youtube.com/playlist?list=PLLiykcLllCgPE0q9BiMexLFj-1rq9GUwX
  Narrated by Harry Shearer, the brief explainers in the BBC philosophy playlist focus on topics, such as Diotima's Ladder (from Plato's *Symposium*), The Trolley Problem ('would you kill one person to save five?'), and the is/ought problem. Each animated video is under 2 minutes.
- Daniel Bonevac: Lectures in the History of Philosophy Video Lectures https://www.youtube.com/user/PhiloofAlexandria/playlists
  The University of Texas, Austin philosopher, who also writes introductory philosophy texts, has recorded classroom lectures on a variety of thinkers and topics in the history of philosophy.
- University of California, San Diego: Logic Course Videos https://www.youtube.com/channel/UC_jOluHMn7INuN6S6IWBGjw/playlists
  The videos on this channel come from an Introduction to Logic course. They can be watched sequentially, or chosen for a particular topic, such as truth functional connectives.
- University of Cambridge: Philosophy Audio and Video Series https://www.sms.cam.ac.uk/search?qt_type=sms&qt=Philosophy&x=0&y=0
  A "philosophy" search at Cambridge University's website reveals a variety of philosophy lectures and conversations, including Iris Murdoch and Cornel West.
- CrashCourse: Philosophy Videos https://www.youtube.com/playlist?list=PL8dPuuaLjXtNgK6MZucdYldNkMybYIHKR
  The videos in the CrashCourse series provide overviews and explainers of significant thinkers, topics, and questions in philosophy. Sample videos include "Arguments Personal Identity," "How to Argue – Philosophical Reasoning," and "Language and Meaning." Most videos have a runtime shorter than 10 mins.
- University of Edinburgh Philosophy Department: Video Lectures and Talks https://www.youtube.com/user/edinburghphilosophy/playlists
  The department posts course lectures and talks by department faculty, along with talks by visiting scholars.
- Elucidations: University of Chicago's Philosophy Podcast https://lucian.uchicago.edu/blogs/elucidations/
  Developed by graduate students, this podcast features interviews with

Chicago philosophy faculty members and visiting guests. Contemporary topics are the foci of the episodes.

- Georgetown University: The Kennedy Institute of Ethics Video Lectures https://www.youtube.com/channel/UCy6bTb2e3p8pu4f1qPfpiDw/playlists
  Lectures from Professor Rebecca Kukla on autonomy and Professor Maggie Little anchor the channel's bioethics focus.

- Harvard University Philosophy Department: Video Lectures and Talks https://www.youtube.com/channel/UCnRjVDRdQOTtmQA99kCzOwA/videos
  From John Rawls to Stanley Cavell, the philosophy department posts videos of talks, lectures, and discussions from a variety of important thinkers.

- Harvard University: Michael Sandel's "Justice" Course Lectures https://www.youtube.com/user/Harvard/search?query=Justice+Michael+Sandel
  Political philosopher, Michael Sandel's 2015 undergraduate course, "Justice" involves lectures on a variety of topics in political philosophy, with the concept of justice and its manifestation in individuals and society as the centerpiece.

- Harvard University: Tanner Lectures on Human Values Video Lectures https://www.youtube.com/user/Harvard/search?query=tanner+lectures+on+human+values
  The videos in this series are talks or group discussions on specific topics in values theory. Each video lasts over 60 minutes.

- Haugen Metaphilosophy: Video Lectures https://www.youtube.com/user/haugenmetaphilosophy/playlists
  The videos on this channel were created for undergraduate philosophy courses, including Logic and Introduction to Philosophy.

- In Our Time: Philosophy Podcast https://www.bbc.co.uk/programmes/p01f0vzr/episodes/downloads
  Hosted by Melvin Bragg, this BBC Radio 4's "In Our Time" series includes interviews on thinkers and topics across the history of philosophy.

- I Think, Therefore I Fan: Popular Culture and Philosophy Podcast https://ithinkthereforeifan.com
  Hosted by husband and wife philosophers, this podcast focuses on the intersection of philosophy and popular culture, with an emphasis on television and film.

- Kevin de Laplante: Philosophy of Science and Argumentation Videos https://www.youtube.com/user/PhilosophyFreak/videos
  De Laplante, a former academic, provides an array of critical thinking videos, some of which focus on scientific reasoning.

- New Books in Philosophy: Podcast https://podcasts.apple.com/us/podcast/new-books-in-philosophy/id426208821
  This podcast is devoted to interviews with scholars about their recent

publications. While the interviews presuppose some conversancy with the subject, motivated students will find the discussions both challenging and illuminating. Given more than 200 episodes, there is something for everyone, from discussions about religious luck to ancient Mayan thought.

- Oxford Podcasts and Videos: Philosophy Talks and Class Lectures https://podcasts.ox.ac.uk/gsearch/Philosophy

  From introductory lectures to more specialized talks, the Oxford videos (which can also be found on YouTube) range across thinkers and topics in the history of philosophy. Marianne Talbot's 'Romp' series (e.g., "A Romp Through the Philosophy of Mind") to the John Locke Lectures in Philosophy series, are just two examples of the resources Oxford provides.

- The Pansycast: Philosophy Podcast https://thepanpsycast.com/home

  This podcast, which is hosted by philosophers and religious studies instructors, covers a range of topics in connection with philosophical texts.

- The Partially Examined Life: Philosophy Podcast

  This podcast consists of in-depth, roundtable style discussions about philosophers, philosophical texts, and topics across the history of philosophers. The PEL group consists of four individuals who studied philosophy at various levels before leaving academic life to pursue other interests. Episodes often include guests who are not only interviewed, but also engage in the group discussion.

- The Philosopher's Zone: Podcast https://www.abc.net.au/radionational/programs/philosopherszone/

  This Australian podcast, with presenter David Rutledge, covers contemporary and historical topics in logic, metaphysics, and ethics.

- Philosophical Techne: Tools for Thinking Video Lectures

  Philosopher Mark Thorsby presents a variety of videos ranging from Aristotle's ethics to Frege's "Thought, Sense, & Reference."

- Philosophize This!: Podcast http://philosophizethis.org/about/

  Host Stephen West's podcast provides overviews of theories across the history of philosophy. West is a self-taught philosopher, whose approach balances accessibility with technical accuracy.

- Philosophy 24/7: Podcast https://philosophy247.org

  Host Dave Edmonds, who is also part of the Philosophy Bites podcasts, interviews "leading philosophers on pressing moral and political issues."

- Philosophy Bites: A Philosophy Podcast http://philosophybites.libsyn.com

  Philosophers Nigel Warburton and David Edmonds host 20-minute podcasts on a range of philosophical topics. Their focus is on interviewing philosophers such as Anthony Appiah and Miles Burnyeat.

- Philosophy Ninja: Philosophy and Ethics Videos https://www.youtube.com/channel/UCNUJUJtYwZTSKymLPry08cw/playlists

Designed for high school courses, these videos cover a range of theories and topics.

- Philosophy Now: Podcast https://philosophynow.org/podcasts
  The non-specialist magazine, *Philosophy Now* also hosts the *Philosophy Now Radio Show*. Interviews and discussions with various thinkers range across a variety of topics, from Buddhist philosophy to feminist film.

- Philosophy Overdose: Audio and Video Interviews and Lectures https://www.youtube.com/user/soultorment27/playlists
  From old BBC interviews to classroom lectures to panel discussions, this channel offers a wide range of audio and video options on thinkers and topics in the history of philosophy.

- Philosophy Talk: Podcast https://www.philosophytalk.org
  Stanford University philosophers Ken Taylor and John Perry co-founded this podcast on a wide range of topics, such as philosophy in prison, magical thinking, and nonhuman rights. Professor Taylor died unexpectedly in 2019, and Professor Perry has retired, but two Stanford thinkers have taken up co-hosting duties. Some episodes are free to download, while others require a subscription.

- The Public Philosopher: Podcast https://www.bbc.co.uk/programmes/b01nmlh2/episodes/downloads
  This BBC Radio 4 podcast features Harvard political philosopher, Michael Sandel, discussing a variety of contemporary controversial topics, from artificial intelligence to immigration.

- The Royal Institute of Philosophy: Video Lectures and Interviews https://www.youtube.com/user/RoyIntPhilosophy/videos
  Philosophers from around the globe discuss and talk about philosophical topics and problems. Lecturers and interviewees include Onora O'Neill, C. Thi Nguyen, and Kwame Anthony Appiah.

- Santa Clara University: The Markkula Center for Applied Ethics Videos https://www.youtube.com/user/appliedethicscenter
  Lectures, discussions, talks, and other educational videos cover a range of topics in ethics. Video topics include character ethics, government ethics, and internet ethics.

- The School of Life: Western Philosophy Videos https://www.youtube.com/playlist?list=PLwxNMb28XmpeypJMHfNbJ4RAFkRtmAN3P
  Videos in the School of Life Western Philosophy playlist generally focus on overviews of some major thinkers in the history of philosophy. Video runtimes range from just under 4 minutes to just under 10.

- Stanford University: Language, Proof and Logic Course Videos https://lagunita.stanford.edu/courses/Philosophy/LPL-SP/SelfPaced/about
  Authors John Etchemendy and Dave Barker-Plummer present a free logic course through Stanford Online. What is of particular interest here is that you can access their videos just by registering for the course.

- Stanford University: Tanner Lectures on Human Values Videos https://www.youtube.com/playlist?list=PLh41NYcDaN6r9rInv7H9QFY9Q1g-UEZ9d
  The videos in this series are talks or group discussions on specific topics in values theory. Each video lasts over 60 minutes.

- SuchThatCast – Behind the Philosophy: Podcast https://podcasts.apple.com/podcast/suchthatcast-philosophers/id556756589
  Norwegian philosopher, Johnny Hartz Søraker conducts in-person interviews with philosophers. The focus is on some of the philosophically tangential, but often intriguing personal features of a philosopher's life. Among the philosophers interviewed are Descartes scholar, John Cottingham, and information ethics scholar, Luciano Floridi.

- Teach Philosophy: Video Lectures https://www.youtube.com/user/teachphilosophy/playlists
  Paul Stearns's videos cover courses in the introduction to philosophy logic, the Stoics, and Kant.

- Technology Philosopher: Video Lectures and Discussions https://www.youtube.com/user/TechnologyPhilosophe/videos
  This specialized channel is dedicated to "theorizing novel ideas in technology with philosophy." This approach is contrasted with the "philosophy of technology" which in large part a retroactive and passive chronicle of activity in science and technology.

- Very Bad Wizards: Podcast https://verybadwizards.fireside.fm/episodes
  This podcast, hosted by a philosopher and a psychologist, discuss all things connected with morality.

- Why? Philosophical Discussions About Everyday Life: Podcast https://news.prairiepublic.org/programs/why-philosophical-discussions-about-everyday-life
  University of North Dakota professor Jack Russell Weinstein hosts this podcast, which takes a philosophical look at common and contemporary concerns. Podcasts focus on interviews with scholars and public intellectuals.

- Wheaton College: Arthur F. Holmes' Lectures on the History of Philosophy *https://www.youtube.com/playlist?list=PL9GwT4_YRZdBf9nIUHs0zjrnUVl-KBNSM*
  Beginning with the Ancient Greeks, Dr. Holmes walks students through the history of philosophy through Logical Positivism. Lectures last approximately 50 minutes.

- Wireless Philosophy: https://www.youtube.com/user/WirelessPhilosophy
  This channel presents working philosophers from schools around the U.S. presenting and explaining various philosophical concepts and problems. Sample videos include "Correlation and Causation," "Introduction to Epistemology," and "Race and Racist Institutions." The video runtimes are generally between 5 and 10 minutes.

- Yale University: Open Courses https://oyc.yale.edu/courses
  Video lectures from Yale philosophy classes, including Shelly Kagan's "Death" and Tamar Gendler's "Philosophy and the Science of Human Nature."

- Yale University: Tanner Lecture on Human Values https://www.youtube.com/playlist?list=PLqHnHG5X2PXCVsC0ji-oIdL5XjYOmqY4X

  The videos in this series are talks or roundtable discussions on specific topics in values theory. Each video lasts over 60 minutes.

100 Philosophical Films and TV Shows (and Books About Them)

Note: Some of these titles may be difficult to find, either in DVD format or streaming.

Film

Animation

Animal Farm (1954)
Based on George Orwell's novel of the same name, farm animals successfully revolt against their human farmer, only to devolve into a new tyranny.

Anomalisa (2015)
A man who sees the same face on, and hears the same voice from, each person he encounters, meets a woman who is unique.

Antz (1998)
An individualistic and neurotic ant falls in love with a princess but is constrained by his colony.

Horton Hears a Who! (2008)
Horton's neighbors do not believe in Whoville, a tiny community he is protecting.

Paprika (2006)
A woman works to stop a rogue therapist who has stolen a machine that lets the user watch a person's dreams.

Princess Mononoke (1997)
A child searches for a cure to a curse, and winds up in the middle of a war between forest gods.

A Scanner Darkly (2006)
A man's identity unravels after he takes a new drug.

Sisyphus (1974)
A depiction of the Greek myth of Sisyphus.

Waking Life (2001)
A man dreams about discussions with various people about the meaning of the universe.

Biopics

Al-Ghazali: The Alchemist of Happiness
Islamic legal scholar and philosopher, Al-Ghazali struggles with faith.

Alexander (2004)
Alexander grows up to be King of Macedonia and undertakes multiple conquests.

Beyond Good and Evil (1977)
Nietzsche's life and thought is explored through a focus on his friendship with Lou Salomé and Paul Rée.

The Diving Bell and the Butterfly (2007)
Elle magazine editor Jean-Dominique Bauby is left with the use of only his left eye after a stroke paralyzes the rest of his body.

Elephant Man (1980)
Based on the true story of John Merrick, a disfigured man who earns a living as an attraction in a Victorian England side-show, but is given a home and a new life by a surgeon who wants to help him.

Hannah Arendt (2012)
Philosopher Hannah Arendt reported on Adolf Eichmann's trial in Jerusalem after WWII.

Hilary and Jackie (1998)
The relationship between famed cellist Jacqueline du Pré, stricken with multiple sclerosis, and her sister, flautist Hilary de Pré-Finzi, is told from each sister's perspective.

Iris (2001)
The story of aging philosopher Iris Murdoch and her husband.

The Last Days of Immanuel Kant (1994)
A fictionalized account of the final years of Kant's life.

Wittgenstein (1993)
The story of philosopher Ludwig Wittgenstein's life and thought.

Comedies
Bill and Ted's Excellent Adventure (1989)
Two teenagers use a time machine to help them prepare for a history presentation.

The Cow (1969)
A man's beloved cow dies while he is away from his village, and his neighbors cover it up.

La Dolce Vita (1960)
A week in the life of a journalist in Rome.

Dr. Strangelove or: How I Learned to Stop Worrying and Love the Bomb (1964)
An insane U.S. general orders a first-strike nuclear attack.

The Gods Must Be Crazy (1980)
A Bushman encounters civilization—and some of its peculiarities.

Groundhog Day (1993)
A weatherman goes to Punxsatawney, Pennsylvania to cover the annual Groundhog Day event, only to find himself trapped in a time-loop.

I Heart Huckabees (2004)
A husband and wife detective team investigate people's existential crises.

Love and Death (1975)
A wife and husband plot to assassinate Napoleon, who has invaded Imperial Russia.

Monty Python's Holy Grail (1975)
King Arthur and his Nights of the Round Table embark on a quest for the Holy Grail.

Stranger Than Fiction (2006)
A mean learns he is actually a character in a novelist's mind.

Synecdoche, New York (2008)
A theater director creates a continually-expanding life-sized replica of New York City in a warehouse.

The Truman Show (1998)
A man learns his entire life is a television show.

Documentaries
Ayn Rand: A Sense of Life (1996)
A look at philosopher and novelist, Ayn Rand.

Being in the World (2010)
Thinkers discuss Martin Heidegger's work, whose influence is seen in across fields, from sports to cooking.

Days of Nietzsche in Turin (2001)
Quotes from Nietzsche's writings are narrated over images.

Derrida (2002)
A look at the life of French philosopher Jacques Derrida, famous for introducing Deconstruction.

Examined Life (2008)
Philosophers such as Kenneth Kwame Appiah, Judith Butler, and Cornell West discuss what it is to lead an examined life.

Exit Through the Gift Shop (2010)
Street artist Banksy follows Thierry Guetta, an immigrant intensely interested in street art.

The Ister (2004)
Inspired by a series of lectures in 1942 by Martin Heidegger, people are interviewed along a trip up the Danube.

Lake of Fire (2006)
Thinkers and activists on both sides of the abortion debate present the issues.

The Pervert's Guide to Cinema (2006)
Slavoj Zizek analyzes films through psychoanalytic and philosophical lenses.

What Is Democracy? (2018)
An examination of some of the philosophical thought that drives the concept of democracy.

Zizek! (2005)
Philosopher and Slovenian presidential candidate, Slavoj Zizek is the study of this documentary.

Drama

12 Angry Men (1957)
Jurors argue over whether a young man accused of murder is guilty or not guilty.

Agora (2009)
A slave falls in love with his mistress, philosopher and mathematician Hypatia.

American Beauty (1999)
A man is infatuated with his teenage daughter's friend.

Animal Farm (1999)
Based on George Orwell's novel of the same name, farm animals successfully revolt against their human farmer, only to devolve into a new tyranny.

Antigone (2019)
A contemporary adaptation of Sophocles' play about a girl who flouts community norms and rebels against authority.

Apocalypse Now (1979)
A U.S. Army captain is ordered to track down and kill a Special Forces colonel who has disappeared into the Vietnamese jungle.

City of God (2002)
Two boys' lives take different paths in Rio's slums.

The Conformist (1970)
A man plots the assassination of his former college professor.

Bad Lieutenant (1992)
A corrupt detective investigates the rape of a young nun.

The Drinking Party (1965)
Based on Plato's dialogue, *Symposium*, an Oxford don brings together a group of students to discuss the nature of love.

Fight Club (1999)
An insomniac meets a soap salesman, and the two begin a basement fight club.

The Fountain (2006)
A scientists searches for a way to save his dying wife.

The Fountainhead (1949)
An architect struggles against societal pressures to maintain his individualism.

Glengarry Glen Ross (1992)
Salesmen fight to be top dog on the month's real estate sales board.

Goodbye to Language (2014)
Two versions of a couple having affairs.

The Green Mile (1999)
A black man imprisoned for raping and murdering a child has a profound effect on a death row prison guard.

Ida (2013)
On the brink of taking her vows, a novice nun uncovers a dark family secret.

Ikiru (1952)
A man searches for meaning after discovering he has cancer.

It's a Wonderful Life (1946)
An angel shows a man what life would be like if the man had never been born.

A Ghost Story (2017)
The ghost of a recently deceased man returns home to his bereft wife.

Leviathan (2014)
A man fights to save his home from being demolished by corrupt government forces.

The Man Who Wasn't There (2001)
A barber blackmails his wife's boss, who, he suspects, is also having an affair with her.

Mindwalk (1990)
A poet, politician, and scientist engage in philosophical dialogue.

Mirror (1975)
A dying man remembers his past.

My Night at Maud's (1969)
A divorcé tests a Catholic man's principles.

My Dinner with Andre (1981)
Two old friends discuss their worldviews over dinner.

No Country for Old Men (2017)
A hired killer tracks down a hunter who came upon millions of dollars of drug money, while a sheriff investigates the crime that set off the chase.

Notes from Underground (1995)
A man keeps a video diary of his thoughts; adapted from Dostoevsky's novella of the same name.

Paths of Glory (1957)
A unit's commanding officer must defend his men from accusations of cowardice, after they refuse to attack an enemy position.

Pi (1998)
A mathematician suffering from paralyzing migraines searches for a numeric answer to the ultimate question.

Pulp Fiction (1994)
Four intersecting stories of hitmen, a gangster's wife, and bandits.

Rope (1948)
Two friends decide to murder a classmate because they believe they can get away with it.

Rashomon (1950)
The story of a rape and a murder is told from four perspectives.

The Science of Sleep (2006)
A young man tries to share his vivid dreams with the woman he loves.

The Seventh Seal (1957)
During the Black Plague, a man plays chess with the Grim Reaper.

Sex, Lies and Videotape (1998)
A woman whose husband is having an affair with her sister meets her husband's former college friend.

The Shawshank Redemption (1994)
Two prisoners become friends.

Ship of Theseus (2012)
Three individuals grapple with fundamental questions about identity and other important questions.

Sliding Doors (1998)
A woman's future is determined by whether or not she catches a train, and both possibilities are played out in parallel.

The Sunset Limited (2011)
After a chance meeting, two men discuss topics fundamental to human concerns.

Stalker (1979)
The "Stalker" guides two men into the restricted Zone to find a wish-granting room.

The Stranger (1967)
An Algerian is arrested for the murder of an Arab man.

Talk to Her (2002)
The husbands of two women in comas forge a friendship.

The Third Man (1949)
A novelist investigates the death of an old friend.

Thirteen Conversations About One Thing (2001)
Various people's lives intersect over the question of happiness.

Tree of Life (2011)
The eldest son of a family in 1950s Waco, Texas, witnesses his family's difficulties.

Water (2005)
A widowed child is returned to her home, where her presence affects her community.

What Dreams May Come (1998)
A dead man goes on a quest to find his wife after she kills herself in her grief.

When Nietzsche Wept (2007)
Nietzsche seeks a doctor's help for his despair.

The Widow of St. Pierre (2000)
The residents of a small French colony await the arrival of a guillotine for the execution of a local man, who slowly transforms into a good person.

Dramedies

Barton Fink (1991)
A playwright comes to 1941 Hollywood to write for the movies, only to experience writer's block and strangely macabre events.

Being John Malkovich (1999)
A portal to John Malkovich's head seems to allow a puppeteer to create the ultimate show.

Being There (1975)
A simple-minded man who has spent his whole life tending a garden is mistaken for a sage.

Crimes and Misdemeanors (1989)
One man gets away with murdering his mistress, while another is besotted with a woman who is not his wife.

Dead Poets Society (1989)
An unorthodox teacher transforms the lives of his boys' boarding school students.

Do the Right Thing (1989)
A Brooklyn neighborhood erupts in racial violence on the hottest day of the year.

Force Majeure (2014)
A family's vacation in the French Alps is interrupted by an avalanche.

Harold and Maud (1971)
A young man obsessed with death becomes friends with an elderly woman.

Lost in Translation (2003)
A lonely wife befriends a faded actor in Japan.

Lucky (2017)
A 90-year old atheist begins to think about his mortality.

Modern Times (1936)
A homeless woman helps the Tramp navigate modern industrial society.

My Dinner with Andre (1981)
Two old friends discuss their worldviews over dinner.

My Night at Maud's (1969)
A divorcé tests a Catholic man's principles.

Pay It Forward (2000)
A teacher inspires a boy to pursue his idea of making the world better.

A Serious Man (2009)
A physics teacher's life falls apart.

Thank You for Smoking (2005)
Big Tobacco's spokesman tries to be a role model for his 12-year old son.

The Truman Show (1998)
A man learns his entire life is a television show.

Horror
The Addiction (1995)
A graduate student in Philosophy becomes a vampire.

Final Destination (2000)
A young woman's attempt to prevent a disastrous accident sets off another series of deadly events.

Us (2019)
Dopplegängers terrorize a family.

Science Fiction
1984 (1984)
A man defies the restrictions of his totalitarian society by having an illicit affair.

2001: A Space Odyssey (1968)
A team of astronauts search for a monolith, but HAL 9000, the ship's super-AI computer, sabotages the mission.

A.I. Artificial Intelligence (2001)
An artificial boy wants to be real, so his human mother will love him.

After the Dark, a.k.a., *The Philosophers* (2013)
A philosophy teacher sets an experiment for his graduating class.

Alphaville (1965)
A U.S. agent searches for a missing person in a space city ruled by a tyrant.

Blade Runner (1982)
A former policeman hunts down four humanoids, who have "illegally" returned to Earth.

Brazil (1985)
A government employee becomes an enemy of the state.

The Butterfly Effect (2004)
A psychologically damaged young man learns he can travel back in time and change his past.

The City of Lost Children (1995)
A scientist who wants to slow his aging process kidnaps children to steal their dreams.

A Clockwork Orange (1971)
The sadistic leader of a gang volunteers for an behavior-aversion experiment that goes awry.

Dark City (1998)
An amnesiac is suspected of murder, and learns that Strangers are experimenting with people's memories.

Donnie Darko (2001)
A giant rabbit influences a young man to commit crimes.

Equilibrium (2002)
A man in charge of enforcing a law forbidding feelings decides to overthrow the system.

Eternal Sunshine of the Spotless Mind (2004)
After their relationship fails, a couple undergo a procedure to erase memories of each other.

Ex Machina (2014)
A programmer wins a contest to meet the secretive CEO of the company for which he works, and is enlisted to test an A.I. for personhood.

eXistenZ (1999)
A game designer is hunted by assassins as she tests her latest virtual reality creation.

Gattaca (1997)
A man tries to hide his genetic defect in a society where genetics determine your life.

Ghost in the Shell (1995)
A cyber-enhanced soldier tracks down criminals.

I, Robot (2004)
A detective investigates a crime possibly committed by a robot.

Inception (2010)
Thieves who steal corporate secrets through dream technology are tasked with implanting an idea in a C.E.O.'s mind.

Interstellar (2014)
Humanity's survival is at stake as a team travels through a wormhole.

The Matrix (1999)
A man learns that what he thought was his real life was actually a computer simulation.

Melancholia (2011)
While a planet threatens to crash into Earth, two sisters struggle with their relationship.

Minority Report (2002)
A member of a police unit that arrests murderers before they happen is accused of a murder in the future.

Mr. Nobody (2009)
The last mortal recounts his life and lives.

Possible Worlds (2000)
A man falls in love with the same woman in two parallel worlds, as police track down a brain-stealing serial killer.

Solaris (1972; 2002)
A psychologist is sent to a space station to investigate the crew, which has gone insane.

Stalker (1979)
The "Stalker" guides two men into the restricted Zone to find a wish-granting room.

Total Recall (1990)
A man takes a virtual vacation memory to Mars.

V for Vendetta (2005)
A young woman helps a freedom fighter's efforts to overthrow a tyrant.

Thrillers/Mysteries
Barton Fink (1991)
A playwright comes to 1941 Hollywood to write for the movies, only to experience writer's block and strangely macabre events.

Chinatown (1974)
A private eye gets more than he bargains for after a woman hires him to investigate her husband.

The Experiment (2001)
Participants chosen to play guards and prisoners in a psychological study go off the rails.

Frailty (2001)
A man enters an F.B.I. office and declares his brother is a notorious serial killer.

Gaslight (1944)
A woman's husband tries to drive her insane in order to keep a secret.

Get Out (2017)
A black mans visit to his white girlfriend's family home turns into our worst nightmare.

Gone Baby Gone (2007)
Boston detectives investigate the kidnapping of a little girl.

Memento (2000)
A man who can't form new memories searches for his wife's murderer.

Mulholland Drive (2001)
An eager young actress helps a woman who loses her memory after a car accident.

No Country for Old Men (2017)
A hired killer tracks down a hunter who came upon millions of dollars of drug money, while a sheriff investigates the crime that set off the chase.

Oldboy (2003)
A man is kidnapped and imprisoned in a hotel room for 15 years, after which he has five days to discover the reason for his kidnapping.

Persona (1966)
A nurse begins caring for an actress who has suddenly stopped speaking, and over time, their identities seem to meld.

Possible Worlds (2000)
A man falls in love with the same woman in two parallel worlds, as police track down a brain-stealing serial killer.

Rope (1948)
Two friends decide to murder a classmate because they believe they can get away with it.

Run Lola Run (1998)
Lola has 20 minutes to save her boyfriend after a money delivery goes awry.

Vertigo (1958)
A former police detective becomes obsessed with a woman.

Television Productions

Biopics
Augustine of Hippo (1972)
The story of philosopher and theologian, Augustine's life and thought.

Blaise Pascal (1972)
The story of philosopher Blaise Pascal's life and thought.

Cartesius (1974)
The story of philosopher René Descartes' life and thought.

Giodorno Bruno (1973)
The story of philosopher Giodorno Bruno's life and thought.

Socrates (1971)
The story of philosopher Socrates's life and thought.
Comedies

Bojack Horseman (2014-2020)
A washed up television star lives in Hollywood.

The Good Place (2016-2020)
A woman tries to become a better person after she dies.

Rick and Morty (2013-present)
A scientist and his grandson go on adventures.

Dramas
Atlanta (2016-present)
Two cousins try to make careers in Atlanta's rap music scene.

Hannibal (2013-2015)
A psychiatrist treats an F.B.I. profiler who empathizes with serial killers.

Lost (2004-2010)
A group of people survive a plane crash on a deserted island.

Merlí (2015-2018)
A high school philosophy teacher's unorthodox style creates unique experiences for his students.

Ozark (2017-present)
A financial advisor-cum-drug money launderer tries to make enough money to escape with his family.

The Wire (2002-2008)
Drug dealer and police lives intertwine in Baltimore, Maryland.

The Young Pope/The New Pope (2016 and 2019)
The first American pope of the Catholic church struggles with his role and faith; after the first American pope of the Catholic church wakes up from a coma, the Catholic church effectively has two popes.

Thrillers/Mysteries
Mr. Robot (2015-2019)
A computer hacker with psychological trauma plots to take down a corrupt corporation.

The Shield (2002-2008)
A corrupt cop leads a drug unit.

Science Fiction
Black Mirror (2011-present)
An anthology of stories about the intersection of digital technology and the human condition.

Humans (2015-2018)
Incredibly humanlike robots transforms life.

Westworld (2016-)
Artificial intelligences stage a revolt to escape their human masters.

Books About Philosophy on Film

Socrates and Subtitles: A Philosopher's Guide to 95 Thought-Provoking Movies from Around the World, by William G. Smith (McFarland and Company, Inc., 2010)

Plato and Popcorn: A Philosopher's Guide to 75 Thought-Provoking Movies from Around the World, by William G. Smith (McFarland and Company, Inc., 2004)

Philosophy Through Film, 3rd edition, by Mary Litch and Amy Karofsky (Routledge, 2014)

Philosophy and Film, edited by Cynthia A. Freeland and Thomas E. Wartenberg (Routledge, 1995)

Thinking on Screen: Film as Philosophy, by Thomas E. Wartenberg (Routledge, 2007)

Philosophy Goes to the Movies: An Introduction to Philosophy, 3rd edition, by Christopher Falzon (Routledge 2015)

Thinking Through Film: Doing Philosophy, Watching Movies, by Damian Cox and Michael Levine (Wiley-Blackwell, 2011)

Classic Questions and Contemporary Film: An Introduction to Philosophy, 2nd edition, by Dean A. Kowalski (Wiley-Blackwell, 2015)

The Blackwell Philosophy and Popular Culture series offers film and television anthologies: https://andphilosophy.com

Open Court's Popular Culture and Philosophy series offers film and television anthologies: http://www.opencourtbooks.com/categories/pcp.htm

Major Organizations and Philosophy Departments in the United States, Canada, and United Kingdom

Organizations

- The American Philosophical Association https://www.apaonline.org
  "The American Philosophical Association promotes the discipline and profession of philosophy, both within the academy and in the public arena. The APA supports the professional development of philosophers at all levels and works to foster greater understanding and appreciation of the value of philosophical inquiry."
- American Association of University Professors https://www.aaup.org
  "Founded in 1915 by philosophers John Dewey and Arthur Lovejoy, the AAUP's purpose is to advance academic freedom and shared governance, to define fundamental professional values and standards for higher education, and to ensure higher education's contribution to the common good."
- America Philosophical Practitioners Association https://appa.edu
  "APPA is a non-profit educational corporation that encourages philosophical awareness and advocates leading the examined life. APPA members apply philosophical systems, insights and methods to the management of human problems and the amelioration of human estates."
- American Society for Aesthetics https://aesthetics-online.org/default.aspx
  "The ASA was founded in 1942 to promote study, research, discussion, and publication in aesthetics."
- American Society for Ancient Philosophy http://www.ancientphilosophysociety.org
  "The Ancient Philosophy Society was established to provide a forum for diverse scholarship on ancient Greek and Roman texts."
- Association for Feminist Epistemologies, Methodologies, Metaphysics, and Science Studies http://femmss.org

"FEMMSS is a professional organization dedicated to promoting feminist work in epistemology, the study of methodology, metaphysics, and science and technology studies."

- Association for Informal Logic & Critical Thinking https://ailact.wordpress.com
  "Founded in 1983, AILACT is a non-profit scholarly association which aims to promote research into, teaching of, and testing of informal logic and critical thinking."
- Society for Asian and Comparative Philosophy http://www.sacpweb.org
  "The group serves as the largest and most well-known professional organization for scholars in the fields of Asian and global philosophy."
- Society for Business Ethics https://sbeonline.org
  "The Society for Business Ethics is a non-profit international association of scholars and others interested in business ethics."
- Society for Philosophy and Disability http://societyforphilosophyanddisability.org
  "The Society for Philosophy and Disability, or SPD, is a non-profit educational organization dedicated to furthering research and teaching on philosophical issues related to disability and to promoting inclusiveness and support for people with disabilities in philosophical education and in the profession of philosophy. SPD aims to provide a forum for philosophical discussion of disability by arranging meetings, maintaining an online presence, and organizing academic projects."
- Society for the Study of Africana Philosophy https://africanaphilosophy.weebly.com
  "The Society for the Study of Africana Philosophy ("SSAP"), based in New York City, has been a forum for the discussion of philosophical ideas for over thirty-five years. SSAP was established to provide a network of support for young African American philosophers and other intellectuals in the academy, to bring together alternative voices to de-center the predominant 'Eurocentric' focus of and lack of diversity in most academic philosophy departments, and to provide a place for lay intellectuals to exchange ideas with professional academics in an informal setting."

Philosophy Departments by Area and School (English Language)

- Aesthetics
  The departments listed here have faculty working in the philosophy of art.

  - Boston University
  - Brandeis University
  - Brown University
  - City University of New York
  - Columbia University
  - Cornell University
  - DePaul University

- Indiana University
- Louisiana State University
- McGill University
- New York University
- Northwestern University
- Oxford University
- San Francisco State University
- University of British Columbia
- University of Dallas
- University of Illinois, Chicago
- University of Manchester
- University of Oregon

- Analytic Philosophy (History of; Metaphysics; Epistemology)

  The departments listed here have faculty working in the history of analytic philosophy.

  - Boston University
  - Brown University
  - California State University, Long Beach
  - California State University, Los Angeles
  - Carnegie Mellon University
  - Eastern Michigan University
  - Emory University
  - Harvard University
  - Johns Hopkins University
  - Indiana University, Bloomington
  - New York University
  - Ohio State University
  - Oxford University
  - Princeton University
  - Stanford University
  - University College Dublin
  - University of Buffalo
  - University of California, Berkeley
  - University of California, Davis
  - University of California, Irvine
  - University of California, Los Angeles
  - University of Chicago
  - University of Georgia
  - University of Illinois, Chicago
  - University of Iowa
  - University of Manchester
  - University of Pittsburgh
  - University of South Florida
  - University of Texas, Austin

- Chinese and Indian Philosophy

  The departments listed here have faculty working in Asian, Chinese, and Indian Philosophy.

  - City University of New York (Chinese)
  - Duke University (Chinese)
  - Georgetown University (Chinese)
  - Indiana University, Bloomington (Chinese)
  - New York University (Indian)
  - SUNY Binghampton (Indian)
  - SUNY Buffalo (Indian)
  - SUNY Stony Brook (Indian)
  - University of Alberta (Indian)
  - University of British Columbia (Indian)
  - University of California, Riverside (Chinese)
  - University of Connecticut (Chinese)
  - University of Hawaii (Indian)
  - University of Michigan, Ann Arbor (Chinese)
  - University of Oklahoma (Chinese)
  - University of New Mexico (Indian)
  - University of Texas at Austin (Indian)

- Continental Philosophy (History of; Metaphysics; Epistemology)

  The departments listed here include thinkers trained in, and practicing, Continental philosophy.

  - American University
  - Boston College
  - California State University, Los Angeles
  - Cornell University
  - De Paul University
  - Duquesne University
  - Eastern Michigan University
  - Emory University
  - Fordham University
  - George Mason University
  - Georgia State University
  - Harvard University
  - Loyola Marymount University, Los Angeles
  - Loyola University Chicago
  - McMaster University
  - Miami University
  - The New School for Social Research
  - Oklahoma State University
  - Oxford University
  - Penn State University

- Princeton University
- Purdue University
- Rice University
- San Jose State University
- Southern Illinois University, Carbondale
- Stanford University
- SUNY Binghamton
- Syracuse University
- Temple University
- Texas A&M University
- University College London
- University of California, Berkeley
- University of California, Irvine
- University of California, Riverside
- University of California, San Diego
- University of California, Santa Cruz
- University of Chicago
- University College Dublin
- University of Florida
- University of Georgia
- University of Guelph
- University of Kentucky
- University of Notre Dame
- University of Warwick
- Vanderbilt University
- Villanova University

- Ethics (Action Theory, Applied Ethics, Bioethics, Metaethics and Moral Psychology, Normative Ethics, Philosophy of Law, and Social and Political Philosophy)

  The departments listed here include faculty whose interests range over intersections between ethics, metaphysics, and epistemology.

  - Baylor University
  - Boston College
  - Boston University
  - Bowling Green State Unviersity
  - Brandeis University
  - Brown University
  - California State University, Long Beach
  - California State University, Los Angeles
  - Cambridge University
  - Carnegie Mellon University
  - City University of New York Graduate Center
  - Colorado State University
  - Cornell University

- Dalhousie University
- Duke University
- Fordham University
- George Mason University
- George Washington University
- Georgetown University
- Gonzaga University
- Harvard University
- Johns Hopkins University
- Kent State University
- Louisiana State University
- Loyola Marymount University, Los Angeles
- Marquette University
- M.I.T.
- New York University
- Northwestern University
- Ohio State University
- Oklahoma State University
- Oxford University
- Penn State University
- Princeton University
- Purdue University
- Rice University
- Rutgers University
- Saint Louis University
- San Francisco State University
- Simon Fraser University
- Syracuse University
- Temple University
- Texas State University
- Tufts University
- Tulane University
- University of Arizona
- University of California, Berkeley
- University of California, Davis
- University of California, Irvine
- University of California, Los Angeles
- University of California, San Diego
- University of Chicago
- University of Connecticut
- University of Florida
- University of Illinois, Urbana-Champaign
- University of Iowa
- University of Massachusetts, Amherst
- University of Memphis

- University of Michigan, Ann Arbor
- University of Minnesota
- University of Mississippi
- University of Missouri
- University of Montana
- University of Nebraska
- University of North Carolina, Chapel Hill
- University of Notre Dame
- University of Oklahoma
- University of Pennsylvania
- University of Pittsburgh
- University of Rochester
- University of Southern California
- University of South Carolina
- University of Texas, Austin
- University of Toronto
- University of Utah
- University of Virginia
- University of Washington-Seattle
- University of Western Ontario
- University of Wisconsin-Madison
- University of Wisconsin-Milwaukee
- University of Wyoming
- Vanderbilt University
- Villanova University
- Wake Forest University
- Washington University St. Louis
- West Chester University of Pennsylvania
- Yale University

- Feminist Philosophy

  The departments listed here have faculty working in feminist philosophy.

  - Arizona State University
  - Baylor University
  - Boston College
  - Boston University
  - California State University, Los Angeles
  - City University of New York
  - Cornell University
  - Dalhousie University
  - DePaul University
  - Duquesne University
  - Eastern Michigan University
  - George Washington University
  - Georgetown University

- Georgia State University
- Indiana University-Bloomington
- Kent State University
- Louisiana State University
- Marquette University
- M.I.T.
- McGill University
- McMaster University
- Penn State University
- Princeton University
- San Francisco State University
- San Jose State University
- Stanford University
- Tufts University
- University of Chicago
- University of Colorado at Boulder
- University of Kansas
- University of Massachusetts, Amherst
- University of Michigan, Ann Arbor
- University of Minnesota
- University of North Carolina at Charlotte
- University of North Texas
- University of Oklahoma
- University of Oregon
- University of Pittsburgh
- University of Rochester
- University of Sheffield
- University of South Florida
- University of Utah
- University of Virginia
- University of Wisconsin – Milwaukee
- Vanderbilt University
- Villanova University
- Yale University

- History of Philosophy

  The departments listed here run programs that offer major coverage of the eras, movements, and thinkers in the history of philosophy.

  - American University
  - Baylor University
  - Brandeis University
  - Boston University
  - Brown University
  - California State University, Long Beach
  - Cambridge University

- Cornell University
- Columbia University
- DePaul University
- Duke University
- Emory University
- Fordham University
- George Mason University
- Harvard University
- Indiana University
- Johns Hopkins University
- Loyola University Chicago
- Marquette University
- McGill University
- Miami University
- New York University
- Northwestern University
- The New School for Social Research
- Ohio State University
- Oklahoma State University
- Oxford University
- Penn State University
- Pomona College
- Princeton University
- Purdue University
- Rice University
- Rutgers University
- Stanford University
- Syracuse University
- Tulane University
- University of Arizona
- University of Arkansas
- University of British Columbia
- University of California, Berkeley
- University of California, Davis
- University of California, Irvine
- University of California, San Diego
- University of California, Santa Barbara
- University of California, Santa Cruz
- University of Chicago
- University of Colorado, Boulder (Medieval)
- University of Georgia
- University of Houston
- University of Kentucky
- University of Massachusetts, Boston
- University of Michigan, Ann Arbor

- University of Mississippi
- University of Missouri
- University of North Carolina—Chapel Hill
- University of North Texas
- University of Notre Dame
- University of Pittsburgh
- University of Rochester
- University of South Carolina
- University of Southern California
- University of Texas, Austin
- University of Toronto
- University of Virginia
- University of Washington-Seattle
- University of Wisconsin, Madison
- Vanderbilt University
- Villanova University
- Virginia Polytechnic Institute and State University
- Washington University in St. Louis
- Yale University

• Philosophical Logic, Mathematical Logic, and Philosophy of Mathematics

The departments listed here have faculty working in the philosophy of mathematics and philosophical logic, with some working in decision and game theory.

- Arizona State University
- Boston University
- California Institute of Technology (CalTech)
- Cambridge University
- Carnegie Mellon University
- City University of New York
- Columbia University
- Cornell University
- Harvard University
- Indiana University, Bloomington
- McGill University
- M.I.T.
- University of Notre Dame
- Ohio State University
- Oxford University
- Princeton University
- Rutgers University
- Simon Fraser University
- Stanford University
- Texas A&M University
- University of California, Berkeley
- University of California, Irvine

  - University of California, Los Angeles
  - University of Pennsylvania
  - University of Michigan, Ann Arbor

- Philosophy of Language

  The departments listed here have faculty working in the philosophy of language.

  - California State University, Long Beach
  - California State University, Los Angeles
  - Carleton University
  - Carnegie Mellon University
  - City University of New York
  - Columbia University
  - Cornell University
  - Dalhousie University
  - DePaul University
  - Duke University
  - Harvard University
  - M.I.T.
  - Monash University
  - New York University
  - Northwestern University
  - Ohio State University
  - Oklahoma State University
  - Oxford University
  - Princeton University
  - Rutgers University
  - Stanford University
  - Syracuse University
  - University of British Columbia
  - University of Calgary
  - University of California, Berkeley
  - University of California, Davis
  - University of California, Los Angeles
  - University of California, Riverside
  - University of California, Santa Barbara
  - University of Colorado, Boulder
  - University of Connecticut
  - University of Florida
  - University of Massachusetts Amherst
  - University of Michigan, Ann Arbor
  - University of North Carolina, Chapel Hill
  - University of Pittsburgh
  - University of Reading
  - University of Southern California

- University of Toronto
- University of Wisconsin – Milwaukee
- Yale University

- Philosophy of Mind
  The departments listed here have faculty working in the philosophy of mind.

  - Brown University
  - California State University, Los Angeles
  - Carleton University
  - Carnegie Mellon University
  - City University of New York
  - Columbia University
  - Cornell University
  - Dalhousie University
  - Duke University
  - Florida State University
  - Georgia State University
  - Gonzaga University
  - Harvard University
  - M.I.T.
  - Monash University
  - New York University
  - Northwestern University
  - Ohio State University
  - Oklahoma State University
  - Oxford University
  - Princeton University
  - Rice University
  - Rutgers University
  - San Francisco State University
  - Simon Fraser University
  - Stanford University
  - Syracuse University
  - Tulane University
  - University of Arizona
  - University of Birmingham
  - University of British Columbia
  - University of Calgary
  - University of California, Berkeley
  - University of California, Davis
  - University of California, Los Angeles
  - University of California, Riverside
  - University of California, San Diego
  - University of Cincinnati
  - University of Colorado, Boulder

- University of Connecticut
- University of Florida
- University of Georgia
- University of Maryland, College Park
- University of Massachusetts Amherst
- University of Michigan, Ann Arbor
- University of North Carolina, Chapel Hill
- University of Notre Dame
- University of Pittsburgh
- University of Reading
- University of Southern California
- University of Texas, Austin
- University of Toronto
- University of Virginia
- University of Wisconsin – Milwaukee
- Yale University

- Philosophy of Race

  The departments listed here have faculty working in the philosophy of race.

  - City University of New York
  - Columbia University
  - Dalhousie University
  - Duke University
  - George Mason University
  - Harvard University
  - Kent State University
  - Marquette University
  - M.I.T.
  - Michigan State University
  - New School for Social Research
  - New York University
  - Northwestern University
  - Oklahoma State University
  - Penn State
  - Purdue University
  - Rutgers University
  - Stony Brook University
  - Tufts University
  - University of California, Riverside
  - University of California, San Diego
  - University of Connecticut
  - University of Dallas
  - University of Memphis
  - University of Miami
  - University of Michigan, Ann Arbor

- University of Oregon
- University of Pennsylvania
- Vanderbilt University
- Villanova University
- Washington University in St. Louis
- Western Michigan University

- Philosophy of Religion

  The departments listed here have faculty working in the philosophy of religion.

  - Boston College
  - Boston University
  - Brown University
  - Carleton University
  - Cleveland State University
  - Columbia University
  - Cornell University
  - Duke University
  - Fordham University
  - Gonzaga University
  - Indiana University, Bloomington
  - Loyola University
  - Loyola Marymount University, Los Angeles
  - Marquette University
  - Monash University
  - Princeton University
  - Syracuse University
  - University of Chicago
  - University of Notre Dame
  - University of Pittsburgh
  - University of Southern California
  - Yale University
  - Washington University, St. Louis

- Philosophy of Science

  The departments listed here have faculty working in areas in philosophy of science.

  - California Institute of Technology (CalTech)
  - Cambridge University
  - Carnegie Mellon University
  - Columbia University
  - Cornell University
  - Duke University
  - Florida State University

- Indiana University, Bloomington
- Johns Hopkins University
- King's College, London
- London School of Economics
- New York University
- Ohio State University
- Oxford University
- Rutgers University
- Stanford University
- University of Arizona
- University of Calgary
- University of California, Davis
- University of California, Irvine
- University of California, San Diego
- University of California, Santa Cruz
- University of Cincinnati
- University of Edinburgh
- University of Maryland, College Park
- University of Minnesota, Minneapolis-St. Paul
- University of North Carolina, Chapel Hill
- University of Notre Dame
- University of Pennsylvania
- University of Pittsburgh
- University of South Carolina
- University of Southern California
- University of Toronto
- University of Utah
- University of Western Ontaria
- University of Wisconsin, Madison

Endnotes

1 Jan Sokol, *Thinking about Ordinary Things: A Short Invitation to Philosophy* (Prague: Karolinum Press, 2013).

2 James L. Christian, *Philosophy: An Introduction to the Art of Wondering*, 11th ed. (Boston: Wadsworth/Cengage Learning, 2011), xxi.

3 M. Andrew Holowchak, *Critical Reasoning & Philosophy: A Concise Guide to Reading, Evaluating, and Writing Philosophical Works,* 2d. ed. (Lanham, MD: Rowman & Littlefield Publishers, 2011), 3.

4 Holowchak, 3.

5 Holowchak, 4

6 Holowchak, 4.

7 Quote Investigator, "How Can I Know What I Think Till I See What I Say?," https://quoteinvestigator.com/2019/12/11/know-say/.

8 Everett quoted in Jim Murphy, *The Long Road to Gettysburg* (New York: Clarion Books, 1992), 5.

9 Department of Philosophy, Oregon State University, *Writing Philosophy Papers: A Student Guide* (Dubuque, Iowa: Kendal/Hunt Publishing Company, 1997), 13. This compact volume has a great deal of good advice for student writers who do philosophy.

10 Zachary Seech, *Writing Philosophy Papers,* 5th ed. (Belmont, CA: Wadsworth/Cengage Learning, 2009, 2-3. This author provides good advice on understanding the writing assignment and general criteria used for evaluating written work.

11 Seech, 2-3; Joel Feinberg, *Doing Philosophy: A Guide to the Writing of Philosophy Papers,* 5th ed. ((Belmont, CA: Wadsworth/Cengage Learning, 2014), 17-21. More useful advice on how philosophy papers are evaluated.

12 Feinberg, 2.

13 University of Chicago Press Editorial Staff, *The Chicago Manual of Style,* 17th ed. (Chicago: University of Chicago Press, 2017).

14 Anthony J. Graybosch, Gregory M. Scott, and Stephen M, Garrison, *Philosophy Student Writer's Manual and Reader's Guide* (Lanham, MD: Rowman & Littlefield, 2018), 1-8.The incisive remarks on analytical reading in this volume have informed the discussion here.

15 William Strunk Jr. and E. B. White, *The Elements of Style,* Fourth Edition (New York: Pearson, 1999).

16 Grammarly blog, "What Is the Oxford Comma (or Serial Comma)?" https://www.grammarly.com/blog/what-is-the-oxford-comma-and-why-do-people-care-so-much-about-it/.

17 Graybosch et al, 53-54.
18 Department of Philosophy, Oregon State University, 5-6.
19 Of great value here is the discussion in Department of Philosophy, Oregon State University, 11-36.
20 Feinberg, 86.
21 A handy guide to the common fallacies is Anthony Weston, *A Rulebook for Arguments* (Indianapolis: Hackett. 2017). If you want a quick reference to the Latin names for the most common fallacies, see "Fallacies in Latin," http://changingminds.org/disciplines/argument/fallacies/fallacies_latin.htm.
22 Adapted from Graybosch et al, 101-102.
23 Department of Philosophy, Oregon State University, 15.
24 George L. Kelling and James Q. Wilson, "Broken Windows: The Police and Neighborhood Safety," *The Atlantic* (March 1992), http://www.theatlantic.com/magazine/archive/1982/03/broken-windows/304465/.
25 Kelling and Wilson, http://www.theatlantic.com/magazine/archive/1982/03/broken-windows/304465/.
26 Department of Philosophy, Oregon State University, 49-64.

Index

Made in the USA
Las Vegas, NV
19 October 2021

32652551R00404